INCESTUOUS
FAMILIES

An Ecological Approach
to Understanding and Treatment

By the same authors

Families Before and After Perestroika: Russian and U.S. Perspectives
(edited by J. W. Maddock, M. J. Hogan,
A. I. Antonov, and M. S. Matskovsky)

Human Sexuality and the Family
(edited by J. W. Maddock, G. Neubeck, and M. B. Sussman)

A NORTON PROFESSIONAL BOOK

INCESTUOUS FAMILIES

An Ecological Approach to Understanding and Treatment

James W. Maddock, Ph.D.
Noel R. Larson, Ph.D.

W. W. NORTON & COMPANY • *NEW YORK* • *LONDON*

Portions of Chapter 3 previously appeared in somewhat different form in Maddock, J. W. (1990). Promoting healthy family sexuality: A guide for clinicians. *Journal of Family Psychotherapy 1*, 49–63. Copyright © 1990 by Haworth Press. Used by permission.

Portions of Chapter 4 previously appeared in somewhat different form in Larson, N. R. & Maddock, J. W. (1986). Structural and functional variables in incest family systems: Implications for assessment and treatment. In T. S. Trepper & M. J. Barrett (Eds.), *Treating incest: A multimodal systems perspective* (pp. 27–44). Copyright © 1986 by Haworth Press. Used by permission.

Portions of Chapter 5 previously appeared in somewhat different form in Maddock, J. W. (1988). Child reporting and testimony in incest cases: Comments on the construction and reconstruction of reality. *Behavioral Sciences & the Law 6*, 201–220. Copyright © 1988 by John Wiley & Sons, Ltd. Used by permission.

Portions of Chapter 12 previously appeared in Maddock, J. W., Larson, P. R., & Lally, C. F. (1991). An evaluation protocol for incest family functioning. In M. Q. Patton (Ed.), *Family sexual abuse: Frontline research and evaluation* (pp. 141–174). Copyright © 1991 by Sage Publications. Used by permission.

Table 6.1 is reprinted from Liddle, H. A. (1983). Diagnosis and assessment in family therapy: A comparative analysis of six schools of thought. In Keeney, B. (Ed.), *Diagnosis and assessment in family therapy* (pp. 25–28). Copyright © 1983 by Aspen Systems Corporation. Used by permission.

Table 6.2 is adapted from Spoentgen, P. A. (1992). *Goal-setting in family therapy with intrafamilial sexual abuse families.* Unpublished doctoral dissertation (pp. 87–88). Department of Family Social Science, University of Minnesota. Used by permission.

Table 7.2 is reprinted from Matthews, J. K., Raymaker, J., & Speltz, K. (1991). Effects of reunification on sexually abusive families. In M. Q. Patton (Ed.), *Family sexual abuse: Frontline research and evaluation* (p. 149). Copyright © 1991 by Sage Publications. Used by permission.

Table 7.3 is reprinted from Heiman, M. L. (1988). Untangling incestuous bonds: The treatment of sibling incest. In Kahn, M. D. & Lewis, K. G. (Eds.), *Siblings in therapy: Life span and clinical issues* (pp. 139–140). Copyright © 1988 by W. W. Norton. Adapted from original by Finkelhor, D. (1984). *Child sexual abuse: New theory and research.* New York: Free Press, a Division of Simon & Schuster. Copyright © 1984 by David Finkelhor. Used by permission.

Printed in the United States of America

First Edition

Manufacturing by Haddon Craftsmen, Inc.

Library of Congress Cataloging-in-Publication Data

Maddock, James W.
    Incestuous families : an ecological approach to understanding and treatment / James W. Maddock, Noel R. Larson.
        p.   cm.
    "A Norton professional book."
    Includes bibliographical references and index.
    ISBN 0-393-70193-X
    1. Incest victims — Rehabilitation.   2. Ecological family therapy.
3. Ecopsychiatry.   4. Incest.   I. Larson, Noel Ruth Weber.
II. Title.
RC560.I53M33   1995
616.85'8360651 — dc20   95-11870   CIP

W. W. Norton & Company, Inc., 500 Fifth Avenue, New York, NY 10110
W. W. Norton & Company, Ltd., 10 Coptic Street, London WC1A 1PU

1 2 3 4 5 6 7 8 9 0

To our parents,

Dorothy E. Maddock *Ruth W. Larson*
Robert P. Maddock *Gordon J. Larson*

who loved us well,

and to our children,

Beth Maddock Magistad *Brian Dale Maddock*

who help us continue to know the difference.

Contents

Acknowledgments

W<small>E WOULD LIKE TO THANK</small> our present and former colleagues at Meta Resources Institute in St. Paul and at the University of Minnesota—Twin Cities for their encouragement, support, and active assistance in developing and testing our ideas about incest treatment. We have appreciated the many opportunities for exploration and dialogue in the context of clinical work, teaching, training, and research. We are also grateful to our client families for sharing their lives and working together with us to make their family experiences meaningful and rewarding without sexual abuse. Students and participants in a variety of courses and workshops have helped us examine, critique, and refine both our theoretical principles and our therapeutic approaches. Some agencies, hospitals, and clinics across North America and in Europe (particularly Denmark) have taken our ideas, adapted them to particular settings, and given us valuable feedback about what did and did not work well with clients. We feel very fortunate to be part of this network of effort, and we value our personal and professional connections in these locations.

In preparing this book, we particularly appreciate the editorial feedback provided by Sally Maison, Ph.D., and Eva Hildebrand, M.S.W., who could be counted on to offer supportive but challenging comments on how we were expressing our ideas. A student research team in the Department of Family Social Science at the University of Minnesota, coordinated by Mary Seabloom, helped by reading early drafts and by creating the "Mother of All Bibliographies (MOAB)" on child sexual abuse and family violence, from which this book's references are drawn. Ann O'Grady-Schneider's ongoing support and eye for detail helped immeasurably in the final preparation of the manuscript. A special word of thanks to Kyoko Katayama, M.S.W., whose artistry produced the Meta Resources logo that appears on the cover of this book. Our editor, Susan Barrows Munro, and her associate, Regina Dahlgren Ardini, provided us with enthusiastic support and just the right balance of patience and push to bring the manuscript to completion amidst a profusion of competing priorities.

To these individuals, and to others too numerous to name, we offer our most sincere thanks. And to many friends and family members who have taken part in the journey on which we learned about, and now write about, incestuous families, we extend our deepest gratitude.

JWM & NRL

Introduction

THIS BOOK IS THE PRODUCT of twenty years of experience working with sexually troubled families. Prior to that time, we had worked individually and together with sexually dysfunctional couples and with individuals of all ages who were having various sexual adjustment difficulties. Our training as marriage and family therapists oriented us toward the interactional aspects of client problems, even when these appeared to be rooted in the developmental experiences of individuals. Several clinical phenomena converged to lead us toward an interest in family sexual abuse. The first was the recognition by one of the authors (NRL) that a large number of sexually dysfunctional women for whom accepted approaches to individual and group treatment were not effective revealed at some point in therapy that they had been sexually abused as children (usually by a family member or a close acquaintance in a caretaking role). Second, both authors noted that the majority of treatment failures in couple sex therapy involved partners who were sexually "dissatisfied" rather than, or in addition to, suffering from a sexual dysfunction. In many of these cases, complex family-of-origin dynamics, especially family sexual abuse, appeared to be a contributing factor to their difficulties. Third, because of our backgrounds in both family therapy and sex therapy, we often were referred "special cases" by professionals in primary care settings, particularly clients with multiple psychiatric disorders (many of whom—both male and female—had histories of sexual abuse and violence) as well as clients whose sexual behaviors created legal difficulties.

In addition to the clinical factors that motivated our attention to family sexual abuse, we were fortunate enough to work at the University of Minnesota Medical School's Program in Human Sexuality at a time when research and training opportunities were abundant, and both private and government funding were adequate to support them. One of the authors (JWM) has had an ongoing theoretical interest in combining the developmental frameworks underlying the study of human sexuality with the systemic frameworks underlying the study of the family. Taken together, this combination of investigation, dialogue, and concrete clinical experience has provided us with an opportunity to develop and test our theoretical ideas and applied principles. We believe that we can speak now with some confidence about various aspects of the intrapsychic, interpersonal, and societal components of incest. Further, our clinical approach to treating incestuous families and family members has been tested sufficiently to demonstrate its validity and effectiveness. Although not the only way or the "right" way, we believe our approach provides reasonable assurance against recidivism and generally positive outcomes for individual family members and for the family as a whole.

Originally, we planned to write a single book on treating all forms of child sexual abuse, using incestuous families as an illustration of how to deal with the dynamics of perpetration and victimization. However, by the time we had written most of the manuscript, the material was too complex and too lengthy; therefore, we decided to divide it into two smaller books with different but related emphases. Based upon our ecological perspective, we are convinced that working with the dynamics of family sexual abuse can equip clinicians to better understand the key systemic elements leading to child sexual abuse outside the family as well. Further, understanding family sexual abuse lends insight into the family patterns that can arise in response to nonincestuous sexual abuse, as well as into the marriages and relationships of adult survivors of sexual abuse.

We recognize that many therapists working with sexual abuse victims or perpetrators (including incest) have little or no training in family therapy, nor are they likely to have an opportunity for ongoing therapeutic contact with the families of their clients, given current approaches to intervention and treatment. In both books, we make a case for trying to arrange such contact on a regular basis. However, we have separated our discussion of incestuous families and family therapy from our more general consideration of treating victims and perpetrators of child sexual abuse. This book and our book *Child Sexual Abuse: An Ecological Approach to Treating Victims and Perpetrators* should be thought of as complementary, though each volume is independent and can be read on its own.

We have labeled our approach *ecological* because this term captures the complexity of working with sexual abuse, especially when it takes place within a family context. The interrelationships of many social systems must be considered during any kind of intervention into family sexual abuse, particularly in connection with clinical assessment and therapy. In our view, incestuous family dynamics can be fully understood only with reference to the relationships of family members to each other, to their families of origin, and to their societal context, as well as the psychological impact of these on each individual. This is the "ecology" of incest. In addition, one must recognize the complex influences of the social environment itself. Sexual abuse of children reflects problems of gender, social structure, cultural values, and even political issues. Therefore, an ecological approach to incest treatment does not focus on "curing" individuals of personality disorders that accompany sexual offending or result from sexual victimization. Rather, it works to creatively rebalance the relationships of family members to each other and of the family to the larger community, while at the same time restructuring the personal and sexual identities of family members.

These concepts and principles are elaborated theoretically in Chapter 2 and applied throughout the book. Some readers may be tempted to omit Chapter 2 or to skim it briefly. Such a cursory reading at least will familiarize the reader with the principles that are described and illustrated in the remainder of the book. Certainly, many effective therapists have minimal interest in formal theory. However, we encourage readers to examine and ponder the concepts and principles presented in that chapter. We urge this for at least two reasons.

The first reason is that theory is more than just an abstract set of ideas, far removed from the everyday practice of therapy. Theory is a summary of experience that has been examined and understood. We agree with Larry Constantine (1986) that theory is unavoidable; it is the way that therapists organize and make sense out of their personal lives and work, just as families organize and make sense out of their experiences together. At the beginning of some university classes and training workshops, we ask participants to indicate the theoretical approach to therapy with which they most closely identify. Invariably, the highest number raise their hands in response to the category "eclectic." When we discuss what they mean by this term, what gradually emerges is the fact that many of the students and therapists have little or no conscious sense of their own conceptual frameworks. They recall theories they learned during their formal education, and they remember certain techniques from training workshops they have attended. However, they recognize that formal frameworks do not seem to capture fully the experience of being a clinician; therefore, they choose to think of themselves as borrowing something from previously learned theory. We applaud them for the realization that an overly close identification with any one theory can be hazardous to effective practice. As Carl Whitaker (1976) has pointed out, too much devotion to a given school of therapy can turn therapy into a religion, making the practitioner into a "missionary" who is vulnerable to being eaten by cannibals. On the other hand, we caution our trainees against eclecticism as a cover-up for "sloppy thinking," since the lack of a coherent understanding of one's efforts as a therapist can seriously interfere with the efficiency, if not the effectiveness, of those efforts. Our orientation draws heavily upon psychodynamic and object relations theories, nested within a family systems framework. We also have been influenced by the work of Milton H. Erickson, M.D.—particularly his orientation toward working respectfully with both the conscious and the unconscious of the individual.

The second reason we urge readers to engage as fully as possible with the theoretical material in Chapter 2 is inherent in the nature of the approach represented by this book. More than anything, systems theory is a *way of thinking* about the world and about human experience. Initially, this may seem intimidating to some. To be asked to think about one's work in a new way can imply a threat to one's theoretical allegiances, cherished beliefs, and familiar ways of working. A therapist does not always welcome this sort of challenge. However, it also can be stimulating and exciting. We have enjoyed watching participants in workshops and consultations respond enthusiastically to systems concepts and to understanding some aspect of clinical experience in a new way. One of the reassuring things about systemic training is that learning can be thought of as an open-ended model-building process, as a reframing of existing principles and practices. We assure trainees that they can still make use of what they already know and do. However, they will understand therapist-client interactions in a new way and may be able to put a "new spin" on therapeutic techniques already familiar to them. At the same time, we must admit that working systemically can alter a therapist's sense of his/her work in a far-reaching fashion, which sometimes has a dramatic effect on clinical behavior. Further, it can lead to a new understanding of relationships with clients, and it can alter those relationships dramatically. Finally, working systemically can transform the therapist's view of the therapeutic endeavor within the complex, multilayered ecosystem of social intervention—a particularly important matter for treatment of family sexual abuse.

All in all, we believe that spending time with the theoretical material in this book will better acquaint the reader with our thinking about some complex issues, thereby better preparing her/him for the application and illustration of these ideas in the remainder of the book. It also may challenge the reader to reflect on his/her own notions about the therapeutic enterprise and to reorganize these to be more effective and/or efficient.

Our ecological model is intended to be appropriate for designing family-oriented incest treatment programs (as well as programs for families of those involved in nonincestuous child sexual abuse). In addition, the principles and techniques described here can be used by therapists in individual or group practice or in agencies without structured incest treatment programs, since one need not see the whole family to work from a family systems framework. Our approach does not require a large number of professional colleagues and numerous resources for intervention into family sexual abuse. Just as an individual who conscientiously recycles waste materials makes an important contribution to global ecology, so an individual therapist with the recognition and commitment to doing therapy ecologically makes a significant contribution to the well-being of a particular family and its members, as well as to the community.

Both this book and our book on treating victims and perpetrators are written from our perspective as therapists educated and working primarily in the United States. We also have had opportunities to conduct training workshops and consultations in Canada and in a number of European countries, particularly in Scandinavia, allowing us to compare and contrast the thinking and experiences of clinicians in other social contexts. We are grateful for the chance to learn through these cross-cultural experiences. Some of the approaches used in other countries have avoided certain pitfalls common to incest intervention in the United States, enabling us to think more broadly about what could work in our society. Overall, we have been struck by the *commonalities* among contemporary highly technologized, communications-oriented societies as they confront the problems associated with intervention into child sexual abuse. We have written a book that we hope has meaning and utility for therapists working in these societies.

A final note: For convenience in this book, we use the feminine pronoun to refer to incest victims and the masculine pronoun to refer to perpetrators. This reflects the most typical cases and is not intended to hamper recognition of the fact that a sizable minority of incest victims are males and some perpetrators are females. When referring to other family members or to therapists, we have acknowledged both genders.

INCESTUOUS
FAMILIES

**An Ecological Approach
to Understanding and Treatment**

CHAPTER 1

The Incest Phenomenon

*The significant problems we face cannot be solved at the
same level of thinking we were at when we created them.*

— Albert Einstein

IN RECENT YEARS, the terms "family" and "sexuality" have been publicly
linked in a particularly negative way, that is, in the emerging recognition
of the problem of family sexual abuse. Once thought to be extremely rare,
some recent estimates of incestuous experience run as high as 10–20% in
the general population (Briere & Runtz, 1989; Finkelhor, Hotaling, Lewis,
& Smith, 1990; Russell, 1983). At best, this figure is highly speculative.
However, it reflects the belief of some experts that the reported incidence
of child sexual abuse is merely the "tip of the iceberg." In one of the most
sophisticated studies of incest prevalence, Russell (1986) concluded that
as many as one in twenty female children have been abused by fathers or
stepfathers, and an additional number by siblings, uncles, grandfathers,
and even mothers. The estimated incidence of incest for males is less than
half the female incidence—partly because a higher proportion of males are
molested by adults outside the family (Finkelhor et al., 1990; Gonsiorek,
Bera, & LeTourneau, 1994; Vander Mey, 1988).

Recently, the high estimated incidence of all forms of child sexual
abuse, including incest, has been seriously challenged by some researchers
and clinicians (e.g., Fincham, Beach, Moore, & Diener, 1994a; Haugaard
& Emery, 1989; Kutchinsky, 1994; Wakefield & Underwager, 1988; Wyatt
& Peters, 1986). Some carefully controlled surveys and some analyses of
earlier studies estimate the actual incidence of child sexual abuse to be
less than 2% or even 1% of the *general* population (Kutchinsky, 1992a;
Sjoegren, 1994). Whatever the reporting difficulties or the definitional
problems involved, one thing is clear: A substantial portion of reported

This chapter was written in collaboration with Catherine Fourre Lally, Ph.D.

sexual abuse experiences takes place within the nuclear or extended family or in a related caretaking situation, thus qualifying them as "incestuous" in their relational dynamics. Further, even those skeptical of the prevalence of abuse agree that serious sexual exploitation often contributes to the development of later emotional and interpersonal problems.

DEFINITIONS

We presume that exploitation occurs in any sexual contact between two persons whose major purpose is the erotic gratification of one individual (though perhaps serving other purposes as well) without regard for the feelings and/or choices of the other individual, or of the impact of the behavior upon that other individual. Thus, the most relevant factors to assess in judging behavior as abusive (regardless of what may be perceived as the immediate outcome of such behavior) are:

- the motivation of each person participating in the encounter
- the stage of development of each individual (as well as their developmental stages relative to each other)
- the dynamics of power and control in their interaction[1]

Assessment of these factors can help to distinguish sexual abuse from the natural, erotically tinged touching that is a normal part of growing up—being bathed by a parent, being examined by a physician, individual masturbation or sex play with peers, even the hugging, kissing, and stroking that are (hopefully) part of the sensual fabric of everyday life in families. Of course, any of the behaviors just described could become difficult for a particular child, and might even have undesirable consequences; however, the experiences should not be thought of as "abusive" unless there are problems in *all* of the three areas outlined above.

Based upon these considerations (which are explored in more detail in later chapters), we define "child sexual abuse" as *body contact (including kissing, touching, fondling of genitals, penetration of mouth, vagina, or anus) or behavior (e.g., exposing, photographing, "talking dirty") intended to erotically arouse an adult without regard for the reactions, choices, or effects of the behavior upon a child.* Typically, such contact or behavior takes place between a child or adolescent and a person who is developmentally, and usually chronologically, older and/or is considered to be in a different generation from the victim.

---

[1]Finkelhor and Korbin (1988) suggest that "child abuse" can be defined most generally as "the portion of harm to children that results from human action that is proscribed, proximate, and preventable" (p. 4). Within this framework, they go on to specify various dimensions that can be analyzed in order to define more specifically what is abusive across cultures that have very different norms and expectations of behavior.

In our view, sexual abuse can be considered "incestuous" in its dynamics if it occurs between *two members of the same family (or stepfamily) or between a child and someone who is considered to be in an ongoing caretaking role with the child (e.g., foster parent, live-in babysitter, long-term child care worker)*. These latter situations would not always be considered incestuous within a legal framework, although they would be prosecutable as "child sexual abuse." Recently, the term "incestuous" has been used to designate a variety of transactional patterns that do not necessarily involve erotic contact in the explicit sense, including such things as references to "emotional incest" (Love, 1990) and "organizational incest" (White, 1986). In our view, these are ill-applied metaphors for various kinds of boundary breakdown, and they should not be confused with the more precise definitions that are required in order to specify the occurrence of intrafamilial sexual abuse. In both defining and intervening into family sexual abuse, we support a mid-range approach: Sexually abusive behavior should always be taken seriously; however, it should not be overgeneralized or responded to more extremely than will be helpful to all family members involved.

CURRENT STATUS OF THE FIELD

Earlier efforts to conceptualize incestuous behavior (e.g., Stoller, 1975; Weinberg, 1955) focused on incest as a subcategory of pedophilia, using dynamic models of individual psychopathology. More recently, incestuous behavior has been described in terms of interaction factors in the family context (e.g., Alexander, 1985; Bentovim, 1992; Gelinas, 1988; Justice & Justice, 1976, 1979; Kroth, 1979; Mayer, 1983; McCarthy & Byrne, 1988; Thorman, 1983; Trepper & Barrett, 1986). Nevertheless, substantial disagreement continues to exist regarding the degree to which incest is a form of *family* dysfunction rather than a direct result of *individual* psychopathology (Faller, 1981; Finkelhor, 1988; Friedrich, 1990; Garbarino, 1977; Mayer, 1983; Salter, 1988; Sgroi, 1988; Tierney & Corwin, 1983; Trepper & Barrett, 1986, 1989). The extent to which certain attitudes or behaviors characterize incest family members other than the perpetrator or the victim is unclear. Still unanswered are many questions about the family characteristics and dynamics that accompany either perpetration or victimization experiences: Are families in which incest occurs somehow different from other families — in addition to having an individual member who is a perpetrator? Do families create perpetrators through certain patterns of attitude and behavior? What role, if any, do families have in healing sexual abuse victims? Under what circumstances do child victims of sexual abuse become adult perpetrators? What role, if any, can their families play in the rehabilitation of child abusers? Do all family members somehow participate in the interaction patterns that characterize incestuous abuse, thereby setting the stage for its transmission to future generations? To what degree do incest dynamics reflect broader socialization and relational patterns in modern technological society, thereby providing social support for this particular form of family dysfunction?

Despite continuing controversies about the dynamics of intrafamilial sexual abuse (which have considerable implications for approaches to treatment, as we shall explore later), some aspects of the phenomenon are widely agreed upon. Trepper and Barrett (1989) discuss the scholarly and professional consensus about both the extent of the incest problem and the apparent effects on individuals and families. Their observations can be summarized as follows:

- While not always abusive, sibling contact may be the most common form of incestuous activity.
- Father-daughter and stepfather-stepdaughter incest accounts for 75% of all *reported* cases of incestuous contact.
- Sexual abuse is five times more likely to occur in stepfamilies than in families in which no remarriage has taken place.
- Reports of the less common forms of incest—father-son, mother-son and mother-daughter—are increasing.
- Although the increase in reports of intrafamilial sexual abuse is due, in part, to increased public attention, the research evidence available suggests that the actual incidence of incest may have increased through the twentieth century.
- Although adult survivors of incest regularly report negative effects on personal adjustment and relationships, the majority of incest victims do not remain severely impaired psychologically in adulthood.
- Most adults who experienced incestuous abuse characterize the experience negatively or even traumatically; only a tiny fraction consider such experiences to have been positive.
- The most common negative long-term effect of incestuous abuse is some form of sexual dysfunction. Other commonly reported complaints include low self-esteem, difficulty in relationships, and the use of denial as a defense mechanism.
- The more explicitly erotic the incestuous contact and the closer the relationship between victim and perpetrator, the more negative the long-term effects reported. However, negative effects can be mediated by situational factors at the time of the abuse, particularly by the presence of a supportive family member.
- Although comprehensive long-term research is lacking, evidence to date suggests that all members of an incest family are likely to experience some pain and suffering as a result of the incest and/ or its discovery. The family as a whole does seem to display certain negative systemic characteristics.

Even the concept of treatment "success" is disputed (Friedrich, 1990; Trepper & Barrett, 1989; Wyatt & Powell, 1988). Some view the goal of intervention into incest as separating family members and enhancing their self-differentiation; others advocate keeping family members together and improving interaction. Some believe that adult victims of child abuse need support and connection with their families of origin; others argue that these families are "toxic" and should be cut off from contact. Some consider that the best way to handle all child sex abusers is to remove them from society permanently; others contend that therapeutic treatment in the context of family support can overcome antisocial behavior and permit the perpetrator to become a safe and useful citizen. Data on which to base solid conclusions regarding these complex issues are sparse.

A MAJOR CONTROVERSY IN CHILD SEXUAL ABUSE: VICTIM ADVOCACY VERSUS FAMILY SYSTEMS

The phenomenal growth of incest treatment programs in recent years makes it apparent that professionals working with family sexual abuse can have very different underlying assumptions about the nature of the problem and the proper approach to intervention. Such differences often appear most dramatically between professions, for example, between attorneys, child protection workers, and therapists. These differences can impair coordination in the identification of sexual abuse and subsequent intervention. A tension between concern for victims and concern for families is reflected in the child protection system. On the one hand, societal regard for the sanctity of the family and its right to privacy may inhibit investigations that could lead to removing an endangered child from a household. Across North America, the failure or inability of child protection workers to act on suspected child abuse reports have led to notable instances of revictimization, permanent injury, and even death of children. On the other hand, accusations of child abuse followed by severe family disruption, foster care, and lengthy court battles have led some parents to form organizations such as Victims of Child Abuse Laws (VOCAL) and, more recently, the False Memory Syndrome Foundation, which attest to the abuse of parents by a system created to protect their children (Dziech & Schudson, 1991; Gardner, 1991; Wakefield & Underwager, 1988; Wexler, 1990). Bias in either direction cannot guarantee protection, and social service workers are all too familiar with tragic cases when the system fails.

Victim or family biases can strongly influence the process and outcome of therapy as well. These prejudices are most clearly differentiated in the theoretical literature on child sexual abuse. Practicing clinicians, searching for what works, are likely to be more eclectic. However, theoretical beliefs and personal values can have a profound impact upon the course of therapy, particularly in an area as controversial as family sexual abuse. Failure to recognize and acknowledge theoretical and personal biases about child sexual abuse can interfere with the effective practice of therapy and can harm rather than help clients.

Sometimes, even the professionals involved in family sexual abuse interventions polarize into opposing camps. Workers in child protective services and correctional institutions often emphasize advocacy for victims, external control of incestuous families, and an individual approach to treatment. Therapists who work with families often argue that incest is best understood from a systems perspective, that is, as a symptom of distorted elements in family process for which the entire family should be treated. The so-called "victim advocacy" approach grew out of the child advocacy and feminist (particularly anti-rape) movements of the 1970s (Berrick & Gilbert, 1991; Conte & Shore, 1982; Grauerholz & Koralewski, 1991; Hechler, 1988; Herman, 1992; Lebow, Raisen, & Caust, 1982; Rosenfeld, 1979). The approach predominates in the child protection, criminal justice, and correctional systems, as well as enjoying popularity among a variety of therapists, particularly those who are trained primarily in psychodynamic psychology and work mostly with individual clients. The so-called "family systems" approach is rooted in the origins of family therapy in the 1950s and 1960s; however, its most rapid growth through the mental health professions occurred in the 1980s (Becvar & Becvar, 1988; Broderick & Schrader, 1981; Montgomery & Fewer, 1988; Thomas & Wilcox, 1987; Whitchurch & Constantine, 1993). Few mental health professionals who want to be viable in today's competitive marketplace would omit "marriage and family problems" from their list of advertised specialties. Therefore, the popularity of family systems approaches to incest treatment has been increasing, though they are not yet widespread.

Definitions and Assumptions

A therapist's theoretical assumptions and beliefs regarding the definition of a clinical problem are the foundation for his/her therapeutic interventions. Here, we will briefly summarize the contrasting definitions and assumptions of victim advocacy and family systems approaches to family sexual abuse.

The victim advocacy approach emphasizes the rights and protection of the child victim and the nonoffending parent (usually the mother). The perpetrator is usually pathologized, identified as having individual abnormalities which culminate in sexually deviant behavior patterns. Etiology may be explained in psychodynamic, behavioral, physiological, or moral terms (Fish & Faynik, 1989). The victim is also targeted for treatment, in order to recover from the trauma associated with her victimization and to regain a stable sense of identity and self-esteem. In this approach, the impact of child sexual abuse is conceptualized in intrapsychic terms, resulting in recommendations for assessment and treatment that are largely individual in focus (e.g., Finkelhor & Browne, 1985).

By contrast, the family systems approach assumes circular causality and interdependence of family members' functioning so that behavioral problems such as incest "represent the cumulative interaction of all members of a system over one or more generations" (Friedrich, 1990, p. 168). Similarly, all family members are affected by the sexual abuse. In this view, the family structures itself around the dysfunction. Maintaining the distorted family structure perpetuates and is perpetuated by intrapsychic distortions, which seem to follow parallel patterns among family members. The family systems approach also emphasizes that each member can play a role in restructuring the family and preventing further abuse (Ribordy, 1990).

Although the actual application of each of these approaches can lead to some similar objectives and strategies, we can contrast their key assumptions in a theoretically pure form (Table 1.1).

Treatment Models

In its purest form, victim advocacy assumes a pathological individual in a neutral context abusing an innocent and less powerful individual. The task of helpers is to remove the perpetrating individual from that context in order to protect the victim(s). The victim advocacy model generally stresses separate treatment for the sexual abuse victim and the perpetrator. Separation of victim and perpetrator is deemed necessary for the majority of the treatment process; relatively few therapists actively make serious efforts to reunite the family in its predisclosure form. Programs with a victim advocacy orientation typically originate in a child protection agency (Bander, Fein, & Bishop, 1982) or as part of a court-ordered offender program (O'Connell, 1986; Taylor, 1984).

Some victim advocacy-oriented programs involve group treatment, particularly concurrent groups for victims, perpetrators, nonoffending spouses, and siblings. Some even include marital or family sessions at some point. However, the focus of therapy remains largely individual and intrapsychic. For example, Taylor (1984) lists ten "universal" treatment issues that must be dealt with in the successful treatment of an incest perpetrator, each addressing a psychological deficit such as fear of authority, sense of isolation, sexual insecurity, and the like. Most often, therapists taking this approach recommend that the offender have no contact in any form with the victim until substantial parts of the treatment are completed (e.g., O'Connell, 1986). The no-contact rule is designed to ensure that the victim has an opportunity to heal the emotional wounds resulting from her victimization. A prominent characteristic of the victim advocacy approach

TABLE 1.1
Underlying Assumptions of
Victim Advocacy and Family Systems Approaches

Victim Advocacy	Family Systems
Children are vulnerable; they need protecting.	Children are resilient; they need not absorb parent's pathology.
Incest is rape, a power-oriented crime that requires punishment.	Incest is a form of family pathology representing an imbalance in the system that requires treatment.
The pathology of the perpetrator is central, and should be labeled a "mental disorder."	The pathology of the family is central, and should be labeled "dysfunctional."
Punishment clarifies who is responsible, and alleviates the victim's guilt.	Punishment increases the shame of the perpetrator and exacerbates the family's problem; victim feels guilty.
Incest always traumatizes children, thus always indicating treatment.	Incest sometimes traumatizes children, necessitating an evaluation of child and family to evaluate treatment needs.
Because of their vulnerability, children should be treated individually or in peer groups but never with their parents, which could be traumatizing.	Treatment must include all family members, since all have learned victim/perpetrator interaction patterns that underlie the abuse.
Someone (preferably the perpetrator) should always leave home when the incest is discovered, to protect the victim from further abuse.	Leaving home is not always necessary, can upset family stability, and can be even more traumatic, placing undue emotional and economic hardship on mother and other members.
Prosecution is important to confront the perpetrator's denial and force ownership of the crime.	Prosecution is important as leverage to coerce treatment, but may also be damaging to the family.

8

Children should testify against their parents; it confirms their reality and alleviates their guilt and anxiety.	Children testifying against their parents is a replication of the intergenerational boundary violation, giving them inordinate amounts of power.
Children should confront their parents directly and be taught how to report the abuse if it happens again.	Professionals should do the confronting to avoid violating the family hierarchy and promoting grandiosity in the children.
Sexual gratification of the perpetrator is the main underlying dynamic, utilizing children to meet adult needs.	Maintenance of the family system is the main underlying dynamic, with incest serving a balancing function in the family.
Incest is *the* problem; thus treating the effects of the incest and preventing its recurrence is sufficient for the family to be healthy.	Incest is a symptom of family pathology, so treatment must include structural change in addition to symptom removal.
Court evaluations for both victim and perpetrator should be done separately, thus preventing contact that might further traumatize the victim.	Court evaluations that are family-interaction based are critical to evaluate strengths of the family as well as its weaknesses.
The mother is also a victim of the father's abuse, unless she aligns with the father, and becomes a co-perpetrator through active or passive collusion.	All family members are capable of both victim and perpetrator behaviors, since they are familiar with the underlying patterns of interaction.

9

is the assumption that resolving the impact of the abuse precedes rather than follows the restoration of the relationship between perpetrator and victim. Some programs are a hybrid, providing family therapy for part of the treatment process (usually later in the program), while emphasizing the advocacy position of the victim's individual therapist throughout the treatment (e.g., Ryan, 1986).

In its purest form, the family systems model assumes a set of pathological relationships to which all family members contribute in some measure. Therefore, the therapeutic task is to change their ways of relating. Family systems treatment programs include models that employ multiple modalities of individual, group, marital, and family therapy with concurrent group or individual sessions as the primary focus. Giarretto's (1982a, 1982b) program description is an often-cited example of the successful use of peer groups as part of the multimodal treatment program. Giarretto has stated clearly his belief that "conjoint family therapy was found to be inappropriate for a family in the early throes of the crisis" (p. 272). Family counseling is listed as fifth out of six treatment procedures, following individual, mother-daughter, marital, and father-daughter counseling. Peer group work is commonly therapist-led rather than self-help and may constitute the primary therapy mode (Phelan, 1987). Some family programs may employ conjoint sessions with various subsystems within the family in preparation for total family therapy (Fish & Faynik, 1989; Hoke, Sykes, & Winn, 1989). All these models characterize themselves as family treatment; yet, they are distinct from treatment of the nuclear or multigenerational family in the absence of peer groups.

In the family systems treatment model, dysfunctional family structure is considered the primary target for change (Alexander, 1985; Barrett, Sykes, & Byrnes, 1986; Trepper & Barrett, 1989). The basic therapeutic concept of "restructuring" is directed toward restoring appropriate intergenerational boundaries, changing dysfunctional power hierarchies, and eliminating problem-engendering interactional behavior patterns (Asen, George, Piper, & Stevens, 1989; Trepper, 1986). Because structural issues involve all family members, conjoint marital and family sessions are the treatment of choice. The basic premises of the family systems approach do not preclude the insistence that the abusing parent accept full responsibility for the sexual abuse, nor are the wishes of the child victim regarding contact with that parent disregarded.[2] In fact, individual and/or group

---

[2]The issue of "responsibility" is often a source of serious misunderstanding between advocacy-oriented and systems-oriented theorists and therapists. For example, a recent book cowritten by Christopher Bagley, a widely published Canadian expert on child sexual abuse, continues to reflect severe confusion about the family systems approach, including seriously misinterpreting one of our own previous publications. "Family systems therapy assumes participation of all members of the family in child sexual abuse, and so looks for motivation and sometimes for responsibility in each. The focus is on family dynamics rather than sexual behaviours, *with the intent to distribute responsibility* [italics added] and to place guilt in

sessions for various family members are often included at various stages of the treatment process. However, the key focus is on the integrity of the family and on the utilization of existing and potential family resources to restore the family as a unit and individual family members to functional status (Gelinas, 1986). Therefore, family sessions are typically preferred to other treatment modalities. Further, systems approaches often attempt to eliminate the therapist's role as agent of social control (a common role in victim advocacy programs), in order to avoid some of the more negative effects of intervention, such as more guilt, anxiety, social stigma, and victimization among family members (Asen et al., 1989; Bentovim, 1992; McCarthy & Byrne, 1988).

Advantages of Each Approach

Some advantages of each approach are worth noting; following are those of the victim advocacy model.

Ease of utilization. Since they rely on commonly existing therapy modalities, victim advocacy approaches to incest treatment are relatively easy to implement for both public and private community agencies. Individual and group therapy already exist in these agencies; therefore, appropriate groups for child or adolescent victims, spouses, and siblings can be developed rather quickly. Group treatment for perpetrators fits well in prison settings, while sessions with spouses and/or children are disruptive and call for special procedures not easily accomplished in secure facilities. Similarly, child guidance clinics are well-versed in therapy for children, but staff often become uneasy when asked to take responsibility for treating parents as well. Finally, the rapid expansion of peer-counseling and specialized women's treatment programs in the past two decades has made it rather easy for these programs to accommodate therapy for adult incest survivors and wives of perpetrators; however, they often have little interest and/or expertise in treating male perpetrators or entire families.

Clarity of assigned roles. In the multidisciplinary, multiprofessional world of child abuse work, a victim advocacy approach clearly designates the perpetrator's responsibility and the victim's trauma, making it easier for the various service agencies and individuals to carry out their respec-

---

perspective. . . . This alerts us to the fact that the family systems approach often embodies some of the worst faults of the older school of psychoanalysis in *seeing the adult male aggressor as only partially, or sometimes not at all, at fault; sometimes family systems theory attributes a major share of responsibility to mother and daughter in collusion* [italics added] (Larson & Maddock, 1985)" (Bagley & King, 1990, p. 150). We know of no serious family systems theorist or therapist who absolves the perpetrator of moral responsibility for his actions or who tries to blame other family members for the abuse.

tive tasks. Assessment and evaluation are simpler because criteria are rigorously, though rather rigidly, defined. Certain cause-and-effect relationships are assumed; therefore, protection workers, judges, prosecutors, correctional facilities, and even family members can clearly assign fault. The community can more easily provide support and treatment for the victim while punishing the perpetrator and/or coercing him into treatment. Even "uninvolved" family members are less likely to be troublesome, since the model focuses primarily upon the perpetrator and victim.

Pragmatic problem-solving. The primary emphases of victim advocacy approaches are (a) stopping the abuse and (b) restoring the victim to healthy and effective functioning. The practical step of removing perpetrators and/or victims from households is the fastest way to solve the first problem, and the possibility of recidivism is virtually eliminated if the perpetrator and victim have no contact through the treatment process. As pointed out above, whether the separation of perpetrator and victim is the most effective way to treat the victim is still a matter of debate. However, clinical data suggest that a sizable number of victims can function effectively in their lives without the necessity of long-term therapy, if the atmosphere in their households is one of support (Briere, 1988; Finkelhor, 1984; Kendall-Tackett, Williams, & Finkelhor, 1993).

Recognition of the social context. A feminist perspective is clearly represented in victim advocacy approaches; namely, the recognition of male/female power inequities inherent in a patriarchal culture and the resulting *reality* of abuse and violence within the family. Thus, incest can no longer be dismissed simply as the "fantasy" of seductive children sometimes described in the Freudian clinical literature (Conte, 1991; Masson, 1984; Rush, 1977, 1980). Further, attention is focused on the ways in which child socialization processes are distorted by the distance and dominance of the male family role and the vulnerability of women, particularly in the realm of sexuality.

Cost benefit. For a variety of reasons, victim advocacy treatment programs cost less than family systems programs—at least in the short run. Since fewer individuals are directly involved in treatment, and group therapy is common, treatment costs can be lower. Further, this approach fits more readily into the traditional framework of medical practice, utilizing well-established diagnostic codes. Consequently, third party reimbursement is more likely to be available to the victim, whereas fewer insurance companies will pay for marital and family therapy or for adjunctive treatment of other family members. In addition, payment for perpetrator treatment is more likely to be denied altogether (since the offense is judged a criminal action rather than a mental disorder) or to be available on the basis of a diagnosed psychiatric condition.

Similarly, family systems approaches have some advantages over those of victim advocacy.

Holistic focus on the family. Family systems treatment addresses the underlying structural problems of the family, thereby increasing the likelihood that the family will survive as a unit. Divorce is less likely to be considered a desirable outcome of intervention, and treatment is aimed more at stabilizing than at disrupting the family during a time of crisis following disclosure of the abuse. Although more complicated to organize initially, family systems treatment eventually is likely to offer helping professionals more points of contact with the dysfunctional family system and each of the individual family members.

A positive orientation. Given their focus on structural and functional issues in the family, family systems approaches are somewhat less likely to induce hostility and resistance to intervention efforts. Further, this orientation permits treatment to facilitate resolution of conflict via change rather than by cutting off members from the family. Hence, children experience less alienation and loss, including less guilt about having had a role in getting a relative into trouble with the law. Similarly, the nonoffending spouse is less likely to have to choose sides between a child victim and a perpetrating partner. Finally, family systems approaches can bypass some of the power struggles characteristic of victim advocacy, thereby improving the chances of working successfully with nonadmitting perpetrators, who are often considered "untreatable."

Reinforcement of intergenerational boundary. Family systems approaches are able to focus directly on the problematic intergenerational and interpersonal boundaries that characterize the incestuous family. In contrast to many victim advocacy programs, the children — particularly the victim(s) — are less likely to continue in their "parentified" role, and parents are helped to remain appropriately in charge of the family. Therefore, marital issues and parental issues are easier to distinguish and to resolve.

Utilization of family strengths. Family systems approaches can capitalize on any strengths that characterize individual family members and/or the family as a unit. This permits the family to act more directly as its own curb against further abuse. In addition, the therapist is able to work with family transactional patterns directly rather than indirectly, guiding toward positive forms of interaction and making corrective interventions to avoid new dysfunctional patterns that can result from the disruption of disclosure.

Long-range effectiveness. Although family systems treatment can be more time- and labor-intensive in the earlier stages, the total amount of intervention time can be less than that of victim advocacy programs. Some treatment can be conducted in conjoint marital and family sessions that would otherwise require individual or group sessions for each family member. The overall duration of intervention is sometimes longer in family systems treatment than in separate victim and perpetrator treatment programs; however, family sessions in the later stages of treatment can be held infrequently without losing either therapeutic effectiveness or the monitoring functions of intervention. Perhaps most important is the preventive aspect of family systems treatment. Efforts at family restructuring, or "second order change" in an incest family (Becvar & Becvar, 1988; Keeney, 1983; Watzlawick, Weakland, & Fisch, 1974), represent an investment in the long-term mental health of each family member (even those not directly involved in the abuse), thus helping to disrupt the potential intergenerational transmission of abuse.

Coordination of services. Family systems approaches can help prevent or overcome the triangulation mechanisms that characterize both the incestuous family and some of the elements of intervention. Therapy is thereby more likely to be a stabilizing influence, a kind of structural "glue" that can help to modulate the intense reactions among family members and helping professionals that often occur following disclosure. The systems approach can facilitate various professionals choosing roles to play vis-à-vis the family and various individual members rather than being thrust into certain positive or negative stances that typically occur as the perpetrator/victim interaction pattern spreads from the family into the helping environment.

Disadvantages of Each Approach

Victim advocacy treatment approaches, particularly mandatory programs related to criminal justice agencies, may not fully appreciate the complexities of coordinating the helping efforts of protection workers, police, the courts, and medical or psychiatric specialists. Particularly problematic is the negative impact of the dual role played by some helpers both as therapists and as agents of social control. Another weakness in the victim advocacy model is the failure to adequately address strained family relationships (particularly between child or adolescent victims and nonoffending spouses) and practical problems of father-absent families (including economic deprivation and the loss of a potentially caring figure for at least some family members) (Friedrich, 1990). Victims themselves often report ambivalent feelings regarding the loss of their fathers (Conte, 1985; Gelinas, 1986). Even temporary removal of the perpetrator from the home may contribute to the development of artificial or negative family coalitions that can interfere with treatment efforts. Already parentified children may gain even more inappropriate power, further violating the generational boundary. A recent study evaluating the effects on treatment of offender removal reports that "a sizable number of adults in our study felt offender removal had contributed to the breakup of their marriage and that their marriage could have been salvaged if the offenders had not been removed from the home" (Wright, 1991, p. 145).

Perhaps the greatest shortcoming of the victim advocacy model is its frequent failure to deal adequately with perpetrator/victim dynamics manifested by *all* members of an incestuous family—even those not directly involved in the abuse. Removing a perpetrator and treating a victim may end the identified abuse; however, other forms of physical, verbal, and emotional abuse often remain firmly embedded in the family's interaction patterns. Among other things, excluding the father from the home does not end his influence on the family system (Fish & Faynik, 1989). In addition, the abusive behavior of numerous mothers (sometimes including sexual abuse) may be overlooked by those taking a victim advocacy approach.

Family systems approaches also have their shortcomings. They have been criticized for failing to account for extrafamilial child sexual abuse (Conte, 1986; Finkelhor, 1986) and for neglecting the larger sociocultural context that permits men to perpetrate against children and women with impunity (Barrett, Trepper, & Fish, 1990). Feminists have argued that, rather than being a symptom of disorganization in a particular family, sexual exploitation is an organizing principle of family life that is supported by the larger oppressive, patriarchal social system (Carter, Papp, Silverstein, & Walters, 1986). Further, feminist criticisms of the "collusive mother" theory and of systems conceptualizations that blame victims for abuse are now common (Caplan & Hall-McCorquodale, 1985a, 1985b; Gilgun, 1984; Goldner, 1991; Myer, 1985; Wattenberg, 1985). These feminist critiques challenge the notion of circular causality that could allow the perpetrator to be relieved of responsibility for his abusive behavior (Taggart, 1985).

Family systems approaches may also lack a focus on individual psychopathology, often ignoring existing research data related to deviant arousal patterns, which suggest that incest perpetrators, like nonincestuous child abusers, are sexually aroused by children (Conte, 1986, 1990). While family systems therapists may address issues of sexuality and gender incidentally, they risk focusing so exclusively on family dynamics that the sexual pathol-

ogy of the perpetrator is largely ignored. Even highly skilled family therapists are typically unfamiliar with the specialized knowledge of sexual
psychophysiology.

At the same time, a whole family approach to treatment can fail to
provide enough support for the child victim, particularly if she does not
appear to be suffering overtly. More subtle or hidden forms of trauma
might be ignored, placing great pressure on an individual family member
to participate in family interaction in treatment for which that individual
is ill-equipped. Most problematic of all in the family systems approach is
the issue of further abuse. What is an acceptable level of risk that the
perpetrator might again abuse the victim or another family member? Victim advocates are clear in their response—*no* risk is acceptable—while
those taking a family systems approach might argue that the benefits
obtained might be worth some risk of recurrent incestuous contact.

The Status of the Debate

The debate over which treatment approach is most effective continues,
though on different terms than in the past. Currently, controversies about
"false memory syndrome" have again tended to polarize both the professional community and the public, overshadowing more reasoned discussions of ways to detect, respond to, and treat those involved in child
sexual abuse (Barden, 1994; Campbell, 1992; Fincham et al., 1994a, 1994b;
Hagons, 1991; Loftus & Ketcham, 1994; Myers, 1994; Ofshe & Watters,
1994). Another striking feature of recent literature is the relative lack of
meaningful discussion between those actually doing therapy with incest
victims, perpetrators, and families and those involved in policy formation,
detection, and investigation of child sexual abuse—another reflection of
the debate between legal advocates and systemically oriented therapists.
Unfortunately, highly competent professionals with differing theoretical
perspectives continue to engage in bitter disputes over definitions of sexual abuse and the welfare of child victims, in the process immobilizing
helping agencies and risking further damage to families. At the same time,
many frontline professionals struggle to combine elements of the two approaches in an effort to work effectively with a given victim or perpetrator
or family at a given point in time.

Some attempts have been made to respond to the criticisms of each
approach by blending critical features of both into new models. Finkelhor's
(1986) four factor model described earlier was an attempt to "expand
analysis of sexual abuse beyond the limitations of the family systems approach while maintaining its insights" (p. 58). However, the model emphasizes individual psychology; only one factor focuses on ecological influences such as poor supervision of children, family crowding, and the like.

Further, the model does not deal directly with family structure, which is the hallmark of the systemic understanding of family sexual abuse.

Trepper and Barrett (1989) have developed an approach called the multiple systems model, which assumes that incest has no single cause. Instead, "all families are endowed with a degree of vulnerability based upon environmental, family, individual, and family-of-origin factors, which may be expressed through incest if a precipitating event occurs and the family's coping skills are inadequate" (p. 22). At the theoretical level, the successful blending of the two orientations remains in question. Some concepts, such as "victim advocacy" and "therapeutic neutrality," would appear to be mutually exclusive. At the practical level, however, treatment programs rarely reflect either approach in its purest theoretical form. The everyday needs of clinicians working with the complexities of family sexual abuse requires pragmatic eclecticism.

At the same time, a lack of theoretical integration has left the practice of incest treatment without a solid foundation for assuring that *both* individuals and families in which children are sexually abused receive effective treatment whose positive outcomes can be documented. On the one hand, many therapists using "pure" family systems principles have been ill-equipped to deal with the complex intrapsychic processes of traumatized victims and characterological perpetrators. In addition, the cautiously non-judgmental attitudes of family systems approaches have been inadequate to handle the complex power/control distortions that lie at the heart of child sexual abuse. On the other hand, the naivete of many victim advocate therapists has led some well-intended interventions to devastate the lives of families in ways that might have been avoided by a more balanced approach. Some therapists who are themselves incest survivors have failed to distinguish their own motives for revenge or repair from the needs of their clients. In addition, the advocacy emphasis in child sexual abuse has contributed to a societal preoccupation with victimization as a core component of personal identity for women—an emphasis which we believe is misplaced and even dangerous.

CONCLUSION

In this book, we present an approach to incest treatment that is not so much an integration of these two contrasting approaches as it is a model arising from assumptions that permit—and even embrace—the co-existence of contrasting emphases. Our ecological perspective recognizes the extreme complexity of incestuous behavior, whose occurrence reflects intrapsychic dynamics of individuals, structural and functional patterns of family interaction, sociocultural influences on gender and erotic experience, and even situational circumstances. This perspective leads to an equal appreciation of the complexity and diversity of intervention into family sexual abuse.

Appropriately, a systems perspective deals with *systems*. However, concern for systems does not preclude concern for individuals. Indeed, individuals are systems, too, as well as primary subsystems in the complex ecology of larger social systems. At the same time, we must never forget that the systems we study as family researchers, the systems we probe as family interviewers, the systems we assist as family therapists—all are composed of human beings: living entities with bodies that can be bruised and broken, as well as psyches that can be damaged and brutalized.

Certainly, the language of systems and the descriptions offered by systems theorists can easily take on a kind of mechanistic and impersonal tone. Further, the idea of therapeutic neutrality that is so central to systems thinking (Selvini-Palazzoli, Boscolo, Cecchin, & Prata, 1980; Sluzki, 1983; Tomm, 1984a, 1984b) can be distorted to produce collusion with the status quo on issues of social importance, such as family violence. The growing attention to abuse and violence in families forces us to confront the relationship between what happens inside of particular households and what happens in society in general, as well as between what happens in the therapy hour and what happens in the everyday lives of clients. In focusing on these relationships, we are inevitably being systemic, or, more particularly, ecological.

To be ecological is not to ignore the sources of social violence or to look away from the ugly realities of bad behavior. Quite to the contrary, to be ecological is to appreciate each and every living thing and its relationship to every other thing; it is to consider the importance of *all* of the complex influences on human behavior and meaning and feelings. Further, to be ecological is to be inevitably and necessarily *ethical*. To be ecological is to examine the contributions of all parts of an ecosystem to the survival and well-being of all other parts. In short, to examine family violence and abuse ecologically is to pay careful attention to all of the factors in both foreground and background and to carry an attitude of personal ethical concern for the objects of our efforts, whomever they may be (even perpetrators).

Further, an ecological approach is necessarily *dialectical*. Rather than creating polarization between individual points of view, between approaches to intervention, between genders, between social institutions, between helping professionals, ecology facilitates synergy, that is, a synthesis without loss of individual uniqueness and autonomy. Ecology is multiperspectival, gaining depth of understanding by juxtaposing various points of view. Ecological efforts are intended to increase the likelihood that interventions will be effective and will contribute something positive to all parties involved in the transaction.

In short, an ecological framework invites creative dialogue to gain understanding and involves alignment of efforts to produce positive changes. In this book, we will focus primarily upon the work of the therapist treating family sexual abuse. However, because therapy takes place within the complex ecology of the incestuous family, the therapist inevitably must be involved with representatives of other social systems, such as child protection workers, attorneys, and physicians. Chapter 11 examines in more detail the coordination of efforts by those who intervene into child sexual abuse.

CHAPTER 2
An Ecological Perspective

The precise balance between the moral and the strategic elements of [therapy] cannot be prescribed in the abstract. But the beginning of wisdom consists of recognizing that a balance needs to be struck.

—Henry Kissinger[1]

THIS CHAPTER PRESENTS the theoretical framework within which we approach incest family treatment. Of course, our thinking has evolved gradually out of our work, aided by discussions with each other as well as with clinical colleagues and participants in training workshops. In what follows, we formalize some concepts and principles, fitting them into a coherent set of assumptions and connecting them with a variety of related theoretical frameworks.

THE STATUS OF THEORY
IN FAMILY THERAPY

Family therapy emerged after World War II from several strands of thought, as well as from the practical need to help couples and families reestablish stability following the disruptions of that war. Theories about human behavior in small groups, the influence of the child guidance movement, a growing interest in Freudian thought, and models for treating mental illness (particularly schizophrenia) all combined to give momentum to the idea of working with entire families on their common problems rather than, or in addition to, working with a single individual on intrapsychic issues. Especially influential as theoretical underpinnings for family

---

[1]We have substituted the word "therapy" for the term "American foreign policy" in this quote from *Diplomacy* by former U. S. Secretary of State Henry Kissinger (New York: Simon & Schuster, 1994).

therapy were various aspects of general systems theory, particularly the information theory known as "cybernetics" (also refined in the crucible of the World War II effort to develop sophisticated weapons guidance systems).

Although "family systems theory" is the general name most often given to the conceptual foundation of family therapy, the past few decades have witnessed the growth of many different family systems theories, some of which bear little resemblance to each other. While sharing a conviction that the family can be understood as a system, most of the theoretical formulations are, in fact, ad hoc models and explanations of the personal beliefs, ideas, and working styles of certain articulate and/or charismatic clinicians. Reflecting some of the social upheaval of the 1960s and 1970s in North America, the family therapy field grew fractious, dividing into competitive schools of thought explicated and debated at national conferences and in professional journals. At the same time, the majority of clinicians working with families on an everyday basis seemed to grow increasingly atheoretical, focusing instead on whatever practical techniques seemed best suited to their own ideas and working styles. By the early 1980s, a longing for integration was taking hold, not only among family therapy theorists but between family therapists and individual therapists. Also increasing were strident voices critiquing family therapy in both theory and practice for its lack of explicit attention to the issues of gender, race, and social class. They argue that by embracing the seemingly apolitical, "universal" principles of systems theories, family therapy reflects the values and views of white, middle-class males, ignoring the realities of family diversity and perpetuating important social injustices (Allen, 1978; Goldner, 1988; Hare-Mustin, 1986; Luepnitz, 1988; McGoldrick, Pearce, & Giordano, 1982; Saba, Karrer, & Hardy, 1989).

Over approximately the past decade, discussions of family therapy have focused on the philosophical assumptions and values underlying its practice. Competition among the various theoretical orientations has been overshadowed by a broader debate on the question of what is adequate as general theory for family therapy. One line of argument has it that theory is an impediment to clinical practice and limiting to a clinician (e.g., Haley, 1978; Whitaker, 1976). Another contends that every therapist utilizes some sort of working theory, whether or not it is formally labeled as such (Constantine, 1986; Keeney & Sprenkle, 1982; Lebow, 1984). A few writers in the family field (e.g., Doherty, 1986; Falzer, 1984; Rabkin, 1986; Shields, 1986) have explicitly acknowledged that the issues are not new, nor are they limited to the field of family therapy. Rather, they have emerged from a longstanding tradition of philosophical debate, and they reflect the same paradigmatic reorganization that characterizes the natural and social sciences. These and similar discussions are important. They are an indication of the field's struggles to transcend the partisanship of therapeutic schools, to integrate the principles of work with families and with individuals, and to take adequate account of the diverse influences of gender, culture, and historical context on the practice of therapy.

The past decade has also seen the emergence of promising work on family ecology, which analyzes the transactions between individuals, families, and the larger environment (see Bubolz & Sontag, 1993, and Herrin & Wright, 1988, for historical reviews). Until recently, the focus of these ecological models has been largely on the utilization of material and financial resources in home management and family decision-making. Fewer theorists have undertaken the complex task of explicating the ecological aspects of family relationships (Auerswald, 1968, 1971; Bronfenbrenner, 1979, 1986; Burr, Day, & Bahr, 1993; Garbarino, 1977, 1982; Henley-Walters & Devall, 1989; Pence, 1988; Rettig, 1993; Wright & Herrin, 1988). Further clarification of concepts is needed, along with better integration into the more detailed conceptualizations of general systems theory (Whitchurch & Constantine, 1993). Research and practical applications are still problematic due to the high level of abstraction that typically characterizes systemic and ecosystemic models (Sprey, 1988).

DIALECTICS AND ECOLOGY

The term "dialectics" has many meanings and applications, all of which somehow convey the idea of *a relationship of tension between form and movement* (Rychlak, 1976). Everything is both one thing and another, both what it is and something different. Dialectics reflects the conviction that a phenomenon can be understood only through its *relationship* with other phenomena, not as something in and of itself. However, the *constitutive* aspect of dialectics is equally important. As Baseeches (1980) notes, "Although a relationship is often thought of as a connection between things, where the things are taken to exist prior to the relationship [between them], the phrase 'constitutive relationship' is meant to indicate the opposite—that the relationship has a role in making the parties to the relationship what they are" (p. 406). Dialectically, all relationships can be thought of as transformative, giving rise to new forms of experience for individuals that, in turn, alter other relationships (Gendlin, 1962; Welwood, 1985).

The term "ecology" also means many different things. It is reflected in the idea of humans living in simple harmony with nature, in the Darwinian notion of evolutionary biology, in the concepts of family management and decision-making in home economics, in the study of patterns of human or animal population changes around the globe, in the principles of sociobiology that examine the interrelationships of species and specific environments (Bateson, 1972; Bubolz & Sontag, 1993; Hargrove, 1989; Knoetig,

1993; Micklin & Choldin, 1984; Naess, 1989). The ecological approach is characterized by its prominent emphasis on the interaction *between* systems rather than on the properties and processes of any one system. In our view, ecological theory has particular potential as a comprehensive framework for organizing knowledge of human behavior as well as highlighting convergence among disciplines that seek to understand human experience in its varied contexts (Fox, 1990; Herrin & Wright, 1988; Lovelock, 1988; Naess, 1989; Wright & Herrin, 1988).

Human ecology theory focuses on human transactions[2] with both physical and social environments, thereby including transformational dynamics of matter, energy, and information—all of which are important to a truly comprehensive understanding of human experience. The concept of "ecosystem" itself is premised on dialectics: the *relationship* between a system and its environment, through which each is *constituted* as a subsystem and an ecosystem. A system's boundary separates the system from other systems and also connects the system to its ecosystem.

Within an ecological framework, dialectics is more than a holding together of oppositional elements in creative tension (Hegel's classic notion of thesis/antithesis/synthesis), although it includes this. Dialectics refers also to the relationships between various systems that, together, produce an ecosystem. Any given system is composed of parts—which are themselves systems. Thus, every system is an ecosystem to the systems that compose it. At the same time, every system is a subsystem within other systems that make up its environment; therefore each system has an ecosystem. *Any given system both has and is an ecosystem* (Odum, 1983). For example, a family is an important ecosystem to its individual members (subsystems); at the same time, a family is a subsystem within a larger social ecosystem.

Dialectics and Human Systems

Over the past several decades, dialectical thinking has had an impact on conceptual and methodological efforts in contemporary social science, perhaps most notably in developmental psychology (e.g., Baseeches, 1980; Erikson, 1959; Kegan, 1982; Piaget, 1970; Riegel, 1979; Rychlak, 1976). A dialectical approach to family transactions, particularly the relationship of

[2]Since dialectical transformation is a dynamic process occurring simultaneously among many subsystems, the term "transactional" is more descriptive of ecosystemic relationships than the term "interactional." Interactional models tend to be two-dimensional when used to explain and/or predict the behavior of systems, in that they presuppose constancy in the related variables. In contrast, all parts of a transactional field are characterized by mutual influences in which all related systems ultimately change. Even different levels of organization in an ecosystem interact in reciprocal ways; therefore, subsystems can be functionally and meaningfully related to each other (complementary) without having to possess particular characteristics (Spiegel, 1971; Weinberg, 1975; Wynne, 1988a).

stability and change, has been explored by some writers in the field of family therapy (e.g., Keeney, 1983; Liddle, 1984; Melito, 1985). Examinations of paradoxical phenomena, both in family interaction and in family intervention, necessarily have been concerned with dialectics (e.g., Cronen, Johnson, & Lannamann, 1982; Haley, 1984; Selvini-Palazzoli, Boscolo, Cecchin, & Prata, 1980; Watzlawick, Beavin, & Jackson, 1967a, 1967b; Watzlawick, Weakland, & Fisch, 1974; Weeks & L'Abate, 1982). Family process descriptions reflecting dialectics are to be found most explicitly in the work of Boszormenyi-Nagy (1985, 1987), Charny, (1972, 1986, 1992), Constantine (1986, 1988), Stanton (1981, 1984), Stierlin, (1969, 1987), and Wynne (1988a)—all of whom have been interested in synthesizing various aspects of theory as a basis for family therapy. In addition, historical dialectics characterize the work of certain critical family theorists (e.g., Chodorow, 1978; Poster, 1978; Thorne & Yalom, 1982).

Bopp and Weeks (1984) have concluded that conceptualizing change as *transformation* has a great deal of relevance to family therapy. Weeks (1986) believes that systems approaches to date have perpetuated the same subject-object polarities found in previous schools of psychology and psychotherapy. Calling for an "intersystems approach" that bridges between personality theory and family theory, he suggests that what is needed is "a metatheory that guides us in transcending the alienating dichotomies of subject and object, individual and system, system and system" (p. 6). In our view, the dialectical approach to ecology outlined here can provide such a metatheoretical framework.

Dialectics conceptualizes being as a continuous process of *becoming* (Bergson, 1944; Prigogine, 1980; Teilhard de Chardin, 1965, 1966; Whitehead, 1929). From this notion of the dialectical relationship of potentiality and actuality is derived the concept of life as the actualization of being, and the goal of human life as survival with meaning (Heidegger, 1962; Tillich, 1951). In everyday experience, both the self and the world are constructed through social participation and language (Anderson & Goolishian, 1988; Epstein & Loos, 1989; Gergen & Davis, 1985). Developmental psychology clearly demonstrates that transactions between the organism and environment begin very early, prior to birth (Ford & Lerner, 1992; Lerner, 1978). Humans are dynamically interactive from the moment of conception—even the prenatal relationship between mother and fetus has a role in constituting the participants to be who they are. Human communication is a reflexive process in which participants in a relationship dialectically co-create meanings, thereby defining the relationship in particular ways and, in turn, being defined by it (Cronen, Johnson & Lannamann, 1982; Pearce & Cronen, 1980; Tomm, 1987a, 1987b). The description of systems, scientific or otherwise, reflects the parallelism between the structures of physical reality and the human cognitive capacity (Maturana & Varela, 1980).

Ecological Balancing

Taken together, the dialectical and ecosystemic processes described above make it possible to creatively juxtapose structural, functional, process, and critical models of human behavior in a variety of contexts, including family interaction patterns and the therapeutic process. At the heart of the theoretical metamodel underlying the ecological approach to therapy is a recognition that, in order to be dealt with effectively, any given system — such as an individual person or a family — must be recognized as *both* a subsystem and an ecosystem, that is, its ecology must be understood. Therefore, the fundamental task of the therapist intervening into a family problem such as incest is *ecological balancing* — the process of transforming subsystem/ecosystem relationships.

Balance is the fundamental organizing principle of dialectics, central to the process of becoming (Hegel, 1910/1807; Heidegger, 1962). The relationships between systems in an ecosystem require continuous balancing in order to assure the survival of both the systems themselves and their ecosystem. As Bateson (1972) pointed out, systems that destroy their environment destroy themselves. *Ecologically, balance is a process of transforming the relationships between subsystems in an ecosystem without either losing the interdependence between them or destroying the overall integrity of the ecosystem of which they are a part.* For example, throughout its life cycle a family is preserved as an ecosystem to the individuals that compose it only by permitting and encouraging continuous transformation in the relationships between the members, without destroying their interdependence as family subsystems. This ecological balance is expressed through *patterns of reciprocal interaction* between systems, transactions that have been referred to by such terms as "cogwheeling" (Erikson, 1959), "coevolution" (Keeney, 1983) and "structural coupling" (Maturana, 1985). Ecologically, balance is "the pattern that connects" (Bateson, 1972). It reflects the total interdependence of all systems and ecosystems on a continuous basis. This view of the universe as a living, self-renewing ecosystem has been given the label "Gaia" (Lovelock, 1979). The dialectical process of ecological balancing is one of continuous recalibration, relating subsystem to subsystem in structural transactions, thereby also constituting larger ecosystems.

In complex systems, such as families or social groups, transformative processes can take many different forms; practically speaking, specific events and outcomes are unpredictable. To the degree that a designated system endures as a subsystem interacting transformatively with other subsystems in a manner useful for their shared ecosystem, it can be said to be "successful," or "healthy." However, the viability of any given system does not prevent dysfunctional transactions between its subsystems. Neither does it preclude the disintegration of some of the subsystems that constitute it as an ecosystem. Within families, these transformations are directed at creating dynamic balances that maintain the autonomous identities of individual members, relate members to one another in mutually helpful and meaningful ways, maintain the family as a functional system, and contribute to the integrity of the larger community and physical environment.

DOING THERAPY ECOLOGICALLY

Here, we define and outline an approach to therapeutic intervention that we are calling "ecological." Our use of this term does not imply a new school of therapy or even a connection with any particular contemporary theoretical approach to family therapy. Our work reflects a variety of established principles of therapy, and it has been influenced by different sources in the course of our own training. We use the term "ecological," in part, because related terms (such as "systemic" and "ecosystemic") already have particular connotations in the family therapy field—the former with the Milan groups and the latter with a number of family therapy theorists (Constantine, 1986; Gray, Duhl, & Rizzo, 1969; Keeney, 1983; Selvini-Palazzoli et al., 1980; Whitchurch & Constantine, 1993). Our ideas about therapy have much in common with these systemic and ecosystemic approaches; however, our concerns are broader. Since the term "ecological" has gained international recognition as an important general concept, we believe that it can serve as a broad framework within which a variety of more particular models of therapy can be fitted.

In our view, an "ecological therapist" is one who thinks about human systems and how they operate in the ways we have outlined above. Further, this way of thinking influences the actions taken by the therapist based upon his/her understanding of the therapeutic process. In a sense, all therapists already *are* systems thinkers in that they encounter systems and ecosystems in their everyday experience. However, the ecological paradigm previously described is intended to organize thinking in a more formal way. This paradigm has met with some resistance in the United States, probably due to the society's traditional emphasis on individualism, pragmatism, and technological mastery. Little wonder that behavioristic principles are perhaps the most uniquely American contribution to the history of psychology and psychotherapy (Bandura, 1969; Crosbie-Burnett & Lewis, 1993; Skinner, 1953; Wolman, 1960). European therapists appear to have an easier time understanding and applying the principles of ecological thought. Indeed, some of the most interesting and useful ecosystemic concepts and techniques have originated in countries outside the United States, such as Italy, Germany, Norway, and Australia (Andersen, 1990a, 1990b; Boscolo, Checchin, Hoffman, & Penn, 1987; Stierlin, 1969; White & Epston, 1990). These countries seem to live with more everyday awareness of both dialectics and ecosystems. Western dialectical philosophies have been influential in the cultures and educational systems of many European countries for centuries. Perhaps more important, however, is the fact that Europeans live in closer proximity to each other's countries and cultures. Necessity often requires that they learn each other's languages. Further, the cycles of history have repeated themselves more often (in both positive and negative ways) over the longer course of European civilization. Similarly, dialectics is so central to many Eastern philosophies that it is taken for granted in the life experience of many Asian societies. Finally, we should note that ecological awareness is a fundamental part of the thinking and experience of most of the long-existing, nontechnological cultures of the world. Highly technologized societies are just beginning to recognize that they have something important to learn from these primary cultures about both human and environmental systems.[3]

Once internalized, an ecological perspective cannot be ignored. When one has stepped inside the ecosystemic paradigm and become aware of the systemic processes involved in all human and environmental dynamics, one cannot be made *un*aware. Like putting on a pair of glasses and seeing the world more clearly, one comes to depend upon the view that is built into the lenses. The mind now "knows" how the world can be perceived, and things viewed through the glasses become very difficult to disregard. Thus, taking an ecological approach is largely a matter of adding layers of recognition and making use of these in particular ways. An ecological perspective enriches — and admittedly complicates — one's experience of the world, including the practice of therapy.[4]

A METAMODEL FOR THERAPY

Technically, what is presented here is a metamodel of the therapy process; that is, a framework into which can be fitted the theoretical model and working style of a particular therapist. Alternately, what follows might be thought of as a "generic" model of systemic therapy — a way of under-

---

[3]The medical and mental health professions are beginning to pay attention to insights and principles of healing from native peoples around the world. These have proved useful in conceptualizing the general processes of therapy as well as in providing treatment to individuals within these cultural traditions (e.g., Dilworth-Anderson, Burton, & Johnson, 1993; Epston, 1989; Spiegel, 1982; Tafoya, 1994).

[4]Worth noting is the fact that some family therapy theorists emphasize "giving up" linear thinking when adopting an ecosystemic perspective. Typically, this occurs in discussions of "cause and effect" versus "circularity" in understanding environmental influences on human behavior. Dell (1986) and others have noted that models of human behavior, including therapy models, can make use of *both* ways of understanding behavioral dynamics. We agree. In addition, we find it more useful to emphasize what the ecological approach can *add* to a therapist's knowledge and behavior rather than asking the therapist to give up something already acquired and internalized.

standing *in general* what therapists think and do when working systemically. The reader should remember that models are not considered "true"
or "false" in any absolute sense. Rather, they are judged by whether they
are understandable within one's existing view of the world and practically
useful in reaching one's desired goals.

Modes of Intervention

Broadly speaking, there are four major modes of intervention in which
mental health practitioners can be involved. The first is *assessment,* the
process of gathering information and applying expert knowledge in order
to judge the status of a client's problem and to understand the context
within which the problem is occurring. Inevitably, assessment has an element of evaluation in it; that is, some criteria are applied and some judgments formed about the individual(s) and the situation being assessed.
Some of the most typical assessment criteria include: health (normal-
pathological), legality (legal-illegal), morality (right-wrong), and utility
(helpful-harmful). Usually, a clinician will make a multidimensional assessment using a combination of the above criteria, plus others. Some aspects
of assessment are so specialized that they require the efforts of more than
one professional. For example, various professionals may be involved in
assessing the legal status of a particular form of behavior discovered in
connection with reported incestuous abuse, the medical status of genital
injuries or diseases acquired in connection with sexual abuse, or the psychological status of a child following an incident of forcible rape.

A second mode of professional involvement is *counseling,* a process of
helping clients achieve certain self-defined goals by operating effectively
within the existing structures of their experience. Counseling involves the
utilization of resources that are already available to clients. The goal is to
make a particular decision or to solve a particular problem. Typically,
counseling capitalizes on the strengths of the individual or family, provides
emotional support and information to overcome deficits, acts as a reflector
and clarifier regarding steps in problem-solving, and reinforces positive
accomplishments. The counseling may be crisis-oriented. For example, a
child protection worker may do some counseling with parents regarding
what steps to take to support their child who has been sexually abused by
a babysitter.

A third form of intervention is *therapy.* This involves assisting clients in
restructuring their intrapsychic subsystems and/or the relational ecosystems of which they are a part. Overall, the goal of therapy is to equip
clients to accomplish tasks they have not managed successfully in the
past. Some of these restructurings are necessitated by developmentally
predictable experiences, for example, adjusting the marriage relationship

following the birth of a baby or launching an adolescent from home into independent adulthood. Others result from circumstantial events, such as anxiety attacks following a rape or depression connected with a serious medical diagnosis. In either case, therapy creates conditions whereby clients (whether individuals, couples, or families) develop new resources for solving a particular problem as well as other problems that might be encountered in the future.

The fourth mode of intervention is *management,* the external manipulation of the parts of a system and/or an ecosystem in order to produce certain conditions judged to be necessary for the ultimate benefit of a client and/or the welfare of others or of society. Some management actions are rather routine, for example, a psychiatrist manages the medication regimen of a patient. Other management interventions are more vigorous and comprehensive, necessitated when a client's autonomy is seriously compromised or completely absent, for example, in instances of sexual or physical abuse of young children. Sometimes, management activities undertaken from outside a particular client system have the eventual goal of restoring autonomous functioning to that system, such as removing an abused child from a home temporarily until one or both parents can function more appropriately. Clearly, management behavior sometimes overrides the autonomy of a client system in an authoritarian way, for example, when arresting an abusive parent or legally terminating parental rights. Most often, management interventions should be thought of as short-term and intermittent—although an ongoing management function might be required in some situations, such as child abuse.

At the level of everyday professional practice, these four modes of intervention sometimes overlap. For example, a professional doing therapy with an adult incest survivor may have to hospitalize a client who becomes acutely suicidal (management); a child protection worker (case manager) may offer some supportive counseling to a single mother whose husband has been arrested for incestuous abuse; a therapist working with a group of sex offenders may be required to report a recurrence of abuse (management). From an ecological perspective, however, each incident of stepping outside one's designated role in dealing with child sexual abuse runs a risk of compromising one's effectiveness in that role. Therefore, we shall argue in later sections of this book that such deviation from one's major role ought to be done only when absolutely necessary and in the most limited way possible.

The major focus of this book is on methods of therapy, although the complex ecology of intervention into the incestuous family system inevitably requires consideration of the other modes as well. Practical issues related to choosing a professional role and selecting a client unit are discussed in detail in Chapter 6.

Guiding Principles

Within the conceptual framework described earlier in this chapter, several major principles characterize the ecological therapist's way of thinking about the therapeutic endeavor:

- First and foremost, the ecological therapist is *holistic* in his orientation, recognizing that the ecosystemic context is the foundation for every meaningful intervention into a troubled client system. No matter how many people are in the room, the ecological therapist structures his work with the client's social and physical environments in mind.
- In addition, the ecological therapist places primary emphasis on *relationships*, recognizing that every client unit (even an individual) is both part of a social environment for other individuals and a participant with others in a variety of larger social contexts.
- Further, the ecological therapist recognizes that the client unit is a system-in-transformation; therefore, the therapeutic effort represents only a contribution to an ongoing transformational process rather than a final "cure." Therapy is a *co-evolutionary process*.
- Finally, the ecological therapist pays attention to his/her own place in the total ecology of the client's problematic situation, choosing an appropriate *ecological niche* from which to make some useful contributions.

THE THERAPEUTIC PROCESS

Any actual steps in the therapeutic process must be preceded by a critical decision: Who is the client? On the surface, the need to specify the client unit would appear to be self-evident. However, in our experience as family therapy trainers and supervisors, the lack of clear-cut client identification—or the loss of clarity after initial identification—is a common occurrence in working with family sexual abuse. The therapist's eventual efforts at ecological balancing will be decided in large measure by the system that is chosen as the client unit, which will determine, in turn, the more specific selection of "relevant survival units" in the complex, everchanging ecology of therapy. Aiding the individual victim's post-abuse recovery, assisting the perpetrator and spouse to maintain or dissolve their marriage, helping the entire family stay together—each represents a therapeutic decision with ecological implications.

In addition to selecting a client unit, the therapist must decide what role she or he will take in the ecology of intervention, particularly when some or all of the clients may be participating involuntarily. Some therapists may be assigned a role by virtue of their employment, for example, a child psychologist working for county court services may be expected to do individual or family assessments on all clients referred in connection with incestuous abuse. However, many therapists have some choices to make regarding the aspects of intervention in which they will participate.

In principle, the ecological therapist can work with many different client units, ranging from a single person to a family to an entire institutional system, such as a school district. The choice of role and the selection of a client unit together constitute the establishment of a new ecosystem called "therapy," with its own unique identity. From the ecological perspective, a new set of transformational processes has been initiated, inevitably requiring the recalibration of balances in related subsystems and ecosystems.

When the therapist has identified the components and overall organization of the therapeutic system, four aspects of the therapy process can be conceptualized: (a) data gathering, (b) hypothesizing-strategizing, (c) positioning, and (d) intervening. Although these can be distinguished as "steps" in therapy for purposes of discussion, in actuality they are successive transactional processes which are the elements of a continuously woven fabric. These patterns are repeated in large and small ways to form the tapestry of treatment (Figure 2.1).

Data Gathering

Data gathering is the first step in any clinical intervention. In connection with assessment, data gathering consists of obtaining as much information as possible from the client system. However, we are using the term in a somewhat broader sense; in ongoing therapy, *data gathering is a continuous process of using the senses to observe patterns of relationship between parts of the client system.* "Observe" here means using all of the therapist's senses to gather "bits" of data that might be relevant to under-

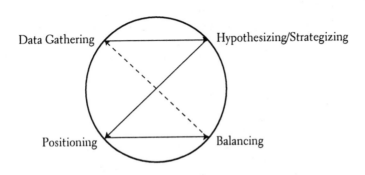

FIGURE 2.1 Ecological Therapy: A "Generic" Model

standing and helping the client(s). The therapist is most likely to use hearing (spoken language) and seeing (nonverbal behaviors) to gather data. Body therapists include kinesthetic data gathering as a regular part of the therapeutic process, using touch to sense tensions in the body that are believed to accompany states of stress and unresolved psychological issues.

What any therapist observes are *patterns*. Because systems are constantly in transformation—that is, the relationships of subsystems in an ecosystem are constantly changing—patterns are the raw material of observation. In fact, a pattern is best defined as *a process of relating that can be observed*. In a book on general systems theory, Weinberg (1975) defined a pattern as anything that can be recognized if observed again. In a training workshop for therapists, one of the originators of neurolinguistic programming (Bandler, 1978) once offered this guideline for therapists concerning pattern recognition: If something happens once, it's a random event; if something happens twice, it could be a coincidence; if something happens three times, it's a *pattern*.

Data gathering occurs at both macro- and microlevels. On the one hand, when a client talks about a difficult or problematic situation, the therapist listens to the general story in order to understand what is occurring. On the other hand, data gathering also takes place when the therapist notices a client's small nonverbal gesture, a slight change in voice inflection, or the recurrence of a certain phrase over several sessions. Literally, data exist everywhere during a therapy session and should be used as a basis for other steps in the therapeutic process.

Data gathering efforts depend primarily upon two things. The first is the client's model of the world, which will determine how the problem is experienced in life and how it is presented in therapy. The second is the therapist's model of the world, including his/her professional theoretical persuasion as well as personal sensory system and accompanying style of data processing (Bandler & Grinder, 1975). On the basis of these factors and of ideas gained from previous clinical experience, the therapist can create possibilities for helping the client.

Hypothesizing-Strategizing

The second element of the therapeutic process has two closely related components: making a series of educated guesses about the client problem situation and devising some ideas about how to respond. The term "hypothesis" has been used by ecosystemic theorists (e.g., Keeney, 1983; Selvini-Palazzoli et al., 1980; Tomm, 1984a, 1984b) to help therapists recognize that their interpretations and ideas about client problems are neither true nor false; they are only more or less useful in helping clients. We often remind our students and supervisees that there is no such thing as the "right" intervention with a client at a given moment in time—this would imply that all other interventions which might be tried would be "wrong." Instead, there are a variety of potential interventions; having an hypothesis provides the therapist with a guideline for organizing his behavior and judging its effect on the therapeutic process.

More technically, *hypotheses are organized ideas about the patterns of relationship between two or more parts (subsystems) of a client system.* Hypotheses connect together various parts of an ecosystem in an effort to gain understanding and/or to produce a particular effect in that ecosystem. Included in these connections should always be a relationship between the client's problem (or whatever part of it is in focus at that particular time) and the ecosystem of which it is a part. Some hypotheses are made at the macrolevel (about general client characteristics or the overall problem being presented by a client).

EXAMPLE

The incestuous behavior in the Elwin family seems to be related to attempts by Mr. Elwin to substitute affectionate and erotic attention from his daughter, Jessica, for that which he lost when his wife returned to her night-time nursing job. Further, the father's close alliance with Jessica, with whom he is very jealous and controlling, may help substitute for his loss of influence with his wife, who returned to work for financial reasons despite his protests.

Hypotheses are also important at the microlevel (about specific incidents or behaviors in the therapy context).

EXAMPLE

Each time Debbie mentions a particular kind of incident, her face contorts in a particular way and her voice changes before she starts to cry. This could mean that Debbie is beginning to connect with her anger or rage with the victimization in addition to the sadness that she's already been feeling; therefore, it might be useful to raise the issue of anger at her sexually abusive grandfather now, even though she has denied it before.

Hypotheses are made on an ongoing basis. The challenge for the therapist is to devise hypotheses that are *useful* in the therapeutic process. This requires a balance between pursuing a given hypothesis long enough to prove fruitful and discarding the hypothesis soon enough to avoid wasted effort or, worse, "getting stuck" in a problem with the client.

Closely related to hypothesizing—the other side of the same coin—is strategizing,[5] a plan for what sort of intervention to use to check out and/or act on an hypothesis. A strategy can be an idea for a particular line of questioning, a particular helpful suggestion, a particular behavioral style, or a general approach to dealing with the client's problem. Hypothesizing and strategizing go hand-in-hand. Implied in a rich hypothesis that connects various parts of a client ecosystem in a meaningful way are some ideas about how to do something useful with the patterns that have been perceived. Like the hypothesis, the strategy must bridge various client subsystems, assisting in restructuring these relationships while still maintaining the overall organizational identity of the client ecosystem.

EXAMPLE

If the therapist hypothesizes that an incest father is erotically involved with his daughter both to regain affection lost from his working wife and to compensate for lack of influence on his wife's decision to return to work, the therapist might select such general strategies as dealing in individual sessions with the offender's anxiety and sadness at losing his wife's attention or scheduling conjoint sessions to work on power/control issues in the marriage.

EXAMPLE

If the therapist hypothesizes that certain nonverbal behaviors signal an adult survivor's readiness to deal with anger at the perpetrator, the therapist might say something like: "I wonder if, along with demonstrating your sadness at having some of your childhood innocence and trust destroyed by your grandfather's abuse of you, at least some of your tears are tears of rage that haven't yet found another way to come out?"

Like hypotheses, strategies can reflect either macrolevel or microlevel processes. Some general strategies inevitably guide the direction of therapy for a considerable period of time, and they may manifest themselves

---

[5]In the field of family therapy, the term "strategic" has come to be associated with a particular therapy approach, associated with the work of Jay Haley (1973, 1976, 1984) and Cloe Madanes (1981, 1984). In the mid-1980s, we came to a conclusion about the necessity of combining hypothesizing and strategizing while we were experimenting with Milan-style work with incest families using a one-way mirror and a consultation team. At about the same time, Karl Tomm (1984a, 1984b, 1985) published a series of articles explicating the work of the Milan family therapists and arriving at a similar conclusion. Tomm (1987a, 1987b) argued that even circular questioning is a form of active intervention which requires choosing a particular question at a particular time (a strategy) based upon a particular hypothesis. While our use of the term "strategizing" (and Tomm's) is compatible with many of the concepts and principles of strategic therapy, we are using the term in a less doctrinaire, more generic fashion to refer to the therapist's overall process of thinking and deciding what to do in connection with her/his idea about what is going on with a client system in general or at a given moment in therapy.

in many different interventions using many different techniques at various points. Some specific strategies will be applied only at a given moment in therapy and may be implemented so rapidly as to seem almost automatic — indeed, some are spontaneous. A nod of the head, a smile, or a simple declaration of "Good!" when an abuse victim appears to be experiencing some feelings of anger reflects a strategy of reinforcement for the victim's hypothesized early attempts to cope with feelings and motivations that she tends to attribute only to perpetrators.

Naturally, this connection between hypothesizing and strategizing occurs more readily as a therapist gains clinical experience. Responses that are largely automatic or semiconscious are drawn from an internalized map of understandings of clients ("successful" hypotheses) and a repertoire of plans ("successful" strategies) which have been proven useful in the past with this client or others. Therefore, the clinician's skill at this component of the therapeutic process is continuously enhanced, serving as an ever more accurate compass guiding the direction of treatment. At the same time, however, a trap exists for the therapist. Relying too heavily upon internalized experience — whether general theories or specific automatic responses — can interfere with the therapist's capacity to appropriately gather data and to interpret *this particular* client's behavior on *this particular* occasion, thereby causing the therapist to falter in assisting the client.

Positioning

We label the third element of the therapeutic process "positioning." This term refers to the stance, perspective, and/or attitude of the therapist vis-à-vis the client at a given moment in time. More technically within a cybernetic systems framework, *positioning refers to where and how to insert information (feedback) into a client ecosystem.* The location of the therapist's chair in the room; his style of dress, nonverbal gestures, and tone of voice; to whom in a family a remark is addressed; the therapist's expressed attitude toward the problem or toward particular family members; use of language, symbols, and metaphors — all of these are aspects of the positioning process as therapy proceeds. Positioning helps create the context in which therapeutic interventions will occur.

One of the hallmarks of the well-known school of structural family therapy (Minuchin, 1974; Minuchin & Fishman, 1981) is a technique known as "joining the system." In our view, this is a misleading term for an important step in the therapeutic process. Making contact with clients is certainly a critical part of therapy and should begin in the very first session. From the ecological perspective, however, the therapist's existence *outside* of the individual or family system is precisely what makes her or him valuable to the client(s). Rather than becoming part of the client system per se, the therapist is part of the client's ecosystem that "connects" with elements of the client system. Together, therapist and client(s) co-evolve a new (eco)system known as "therapy."

Family therapist Steve de Shazer (1982) has referred to a "binocular model" of therapy to describe the process of co-evolving a therapeutic system. He notes that depth perception is possible for humans only because we have two eyes several inches apart located in the front of our heads. Each eye sees a slightly different image of an object, and these objects are blended by the brain into a perception of depth. Metaphorically, the same process occurs in therapy. Client (C) and therapist (T) each have a view of the client's problem, reflecting a unique set of meanings. As they interact in therapy, each must blend the other's view with his/her own in order to come to some sort of understanding. The client can only have his/her own meaning of the problem (C) to which has been added the therapist's meaning (T), creating a shared meaning (C + T); similarly, the therapist can only have his/her own meaning in combination with the client's meaning (T + C). Neither can have the other's view in a pure form. Only by co-evolving their views into a new, shared reality can something useful happen in therapy (de Shazer, 1982, 1985; Friedman, 1993; Hoffman, 1981; Keeney, 1983). The implications of this will become clearer when we discuss the nature of interventions in the next section.

The concept of positioning also helps clarify the often-misunderstood notion of therapeutic "neutrality" (Selvini-Palazzoli et al., 1980; Sluzki, 1983; Tomm, 1984a, 1984b), which has created controversy among therapists in the field of child abuse. Ecologically, neutrality refers to *equidistance from all parts of the client system* rather than to suspension of the therapist's personal values. Therapists can never be "neutral" with regard to issues of family violence and abuse; further, interventions into abusive situations represent broader societal values in an active way. Therefore, neutrality is best understood in the context of ecological balancing principles, since it refers to the overall stance of the therapist rather than to specific positions that the therapist may take during the course of therapy.

An important aspect of a therapist's potential effectiveness is the ability to position herself flexibly during the course of therapy. According to a well-established cybernetic principle, the part of a system with the greatest flexibility has the greatest power to influence the system (Bandler & Grinder, 1975; Weinberg, 1975). An effective therapist needs to be able to reposition him- or herself rather freely within the therapeutic ecosystem, developing alliances with different family members at different points in time; sometimes acting as a buffer and other times as a bridge between members; on some occasions being very active and controlling, on other occasions being rather passive and distant. Gelinas (1988) refers to this as "multilaterality" and considers it a key component of incest work. Based upon the deep and continuing loyalty of incest family members to each other before, during, and after disclosure of the abuse, the therapist is challenged to take into account "every family member's needs and interests, lifting up people's sides if they themselves are unable to do so" (p. 36).

Therapeutic positioning should be done as thoughtfully as possible, reflecting the hypothesizing-strategizing upon which a particular intervention is based. The place in a system from which an intervention originates and the place(s) toward which it is directed are enormously important in determining its effect. Equally important is the task of directing an intervention at a specific space/time point in the ongoing transformational process of the client system while also keeping in mind the ecology of the larger ecosystem (how the intervention will *fit* into the overall scheme of things). This challenge is somewhat like an engineer making an adjustment in the operation of a space satellite without interfering with the satellite's overall operation and course trajectory. Readers already experienced in working with abusive families will recognize the particular difficulty of finding an appropriate "ecological niche" in the therapeutic ecosystem with clients who are participating in treatment on an involuntary basis.

EXAMPLE

In a joint session between an adolescent incest victim, Phyllis, and her father, Mr. Stevens, the family therapist chooses to sit at an equal distance between the two family members to conduct the session. By previous agreement, Phyllis is accompanied to the session by her individual or group therapist, who sits near her serving as a quiet advocate.

The therapist begins by addressing the perpetrator, Mr. Stevens, expressing sympathy and appreciation for the challenge and emotional difficulty he faces in hearing the critically important message of the victim (thereby providing support and reinforcement to Phyllis even while appearing to address the father). The therapist then emphasizes the importance of listening carefully and silently to what the daughter has to say until Mr. Stevens is certain that he has fully understood her point of view (thereby conveying the expectation that the perpetrator will be largely a receiver rather than sender of messages during the session).

Orchestrating a session in this manner reflects careful thought given to appropriate positioning as well as to the hypothesizing-strategizing that underlies the decision to hold such a session.

Balancing

The final element in the therapeutic process is *balancing*, the label we have given to any form of change-oriented intervention into a client ecosystem. In the cybernetic theory of Bateson (1972, 1979), it is "news of a difference" to the client(s). In the collaborative co-evolution of therapy, the relationship between therapist and client needs to "make a difference" that is useful to the client (Keeney, 1983). Typically, a balancing intervention is helpful in resolving a problem or set of problems brought to therapy by the client(s). Sometimes, however, what a client needs more than a solution to a problem is the experience of mutuality in a relationship.

Each balancing step in therapy should *fit* within the therapeutic ecosystem. In this sense, each balancing maneuver is an instance of the broader principle of the ecological balancing that underlies the entire therapeutic endeavor. An intervention that is ecologically sound reflects attention both to the specific problem or issue brought by the client and to the larger client ecosystem. The parameters of any therapeutic intervention are, on the one hand, that it be sufficiently noticeable to the client to have an effect on restructuring the relationship between some client subsystems, and, on the other hand, that it not damage or destroy the integrity of the client ecosystem toward which it is directed. Within these limits, a great many variations are possible so that the therapist need not worry about trying to find the "perfect" intervention.

In certain ways, the balancing process in ecological therapy is parallel to the process of *interpretation* to produce insight in traditional psychodynamic approaches (Freud, 1900; Langs, 1978; Levy, 1984; Mahrer, 1985; Raney, 1984; Scharff & Scharff, 1987). Both are generic principles rather than techniques unique to any single theoretical school or therapeutic style. Both are carried out in the therapeutic process to bring about certain objectives; exactly how and when they are done varies according to the therapist's theoretical stance and personal style. Every psychodynamic therapist knows that the art of interpretation is a cornerstone of therapy practice and is based upon skills learned in training and refined in the course of ongoing clinical practice. Similarly, we believe that the art of *balancing* is a fundamental aspect of clinical work within the systemic paradigm. Like interpretive skills, balancing skills can be learned and practiced. In fact, they are so basic to working with clients that virtually every therapist has already learned some important components of this process, by whatever names they may be known. In the remainder of this section, we will discuss and illustrate some concrete steps to be taken in balancing interventions. The remainder of this book will describe a variety of applications of balancing in the realm of incest family treatment.

Based upon the broader principle of ecological balancing discussed earlier in this chapter, each therapeutic intervention should reflect the attempt to increase the *autonomy* and/or *coherence* and/or *adaptability* and/or *flexibility* of the client system toward which it is directed.[6] More specifi-

---

[6]These terms refer to "success criteria" for ecological balancing in order to simultaneously preserve the identity of subsystems and the integrity of an ecosystem: *organizational autonomy* measures a system's capacity for self-regulation; *coherence* measures congruent interdependence of the parts of a system; *adaptability* measures the relative degree of change

cally, the therapist will emphasize different aspects of ecosystemic structure and function at different times in therapy. Some interventions will
be directed at balancing power/control dynamics; others at structure/
organization, change/stability, or chaos/order; sometimes, the therapist
will work to balance among these various dialectical elements themselves.
Choices about where and how to direct balancing interventions are made
on the basis of the data gathering, hypothesizing-strategizing, and positioning processes previously discussed.

Further elaboration of balancing techniques requires that we introduce
an additional dialectical construct: *pacing/leading*. This term is borrowed
from the literature on Ericksonian hypnosis and neurolinguistic programming (Bandler & Grinder, 1975; Grinder, DeLozier, & Bandler, 1977;
Lankton, 1985).[7] The pace/lead dialectic is itself a balancing process. It
refers to *actions of the therapist* while intervening; that is, pace/lead is the
"how to" of balancing.

Pacing. Pacing is matching one or more elements of a client's experience. It can occur verbally or nonverbally, generally or specifically, with or
without conscious acknowledgment. The ability to pace requires that a
therapist pay exquisitely careful attention to client behavior through ob-
servational skills. The therapist then matches the client's behavior in one
or more ways as that behavior is occurring. Pacing can be very general; for
example, a male therapist who normally wears a suit, dress shirt, and tie in
a hospital clinic might remove his coat, loosen or remove his tie, and roll
up his shirtsleeves when meeting with a client whose standard mode of
dress is bluejeans and flannel shirts. Pacing can be very straightforward; for
example, the well-known Rogerian technique (Rogers, 1961) that mirrors
emotions back to clients: "It sounds as if that bothers you very much."
Pacing can be highly focused; for example, using the same word or phrase
that a client has used to describe his experience: "In addition to your wife,
who else in your life do you feel is 'always on your back'?" Pacing can be
extremely subtle, designed to connect with the client's unconscious; for
example, the therapist might adopt the same posture in the chair as the
client, or talk in a similar tone of voice, or even match the client's rate of
breathing.

Many pacing techniques are very familiar and natural to therapists,
acquired through years of clinical experience. Some pacing seems to hap-

---

occurring in the internal structures of a system within its ecosystem; and *flexibility* measures
the range of ecosystemic conditions over which a given system can function. For more
detailed discussion of these concepts, see the theoretical article on "Ecological Dialectics"
by Maddock (1993).

[7]Milton H. Erickson is world-renowned as a practitioner of hypnotherapy. However, his
influence has spread far beyond his use of formal trance inductions. Through the writings
of Jay Haley (1973) and others (e.g., Lankton & Lankton, 1986; Ritterman, 1983), Erickson's
ideas and techniques have had a profound impact upon the field of family therapy.

pen spontaneously in the course of therapy, for example, when similar metaphorical language is used by both therapist and client. Sometimes, it is the client who is pacing (and leading) the therapist. This is a natural occurrence; however, it can trap the therapist into losing control of the session or getting stuck "inside" the problem along with the client.

Sufficient pacing can be a significant problem when working with incest families. Not only is there the difficulty of adequately pacing all family members — itself a significant challenge in family therapy — but in addition, the particular characteristics of incestuous families and the circumstances of treatment can create obstacles to pacing family members other than the victim. Perpetrators may be particularly challenging to pace; we are convinced that some of what makes sex offenders seem resistant and difficult to treat are, in fact, contextual issues in the therapeutic ecosystem that interfere with pacing.

Leading. Leading is introducing something "different" into a client's experience. Like pacing, it can occur verbally or nonverbally, generally or specifically, with or without conscious acknowledgment. Leading can be thought of as building upon, or extending, pacing. Theoretical and clinical work with hypnosis has established an important principle for change which may seem to run counter to common sense: Many people in many situations will make changes in their perceptions, attitudes, or actions only when sufficient pacing of their experience has occurred. For example, contrary to the popular image of stage hypnosis (where it appears to naive observers that subjects are "talked into" a state of trance), genuine trance actually depends upon the hypnotist spending enough time matching (pacing) the current experience of the subject so that a special kind of rapport is established which allows the hypnotist to suggest a change in experience to the subject (leading) and which the subject, in turn, agrees to accept (Bandler & Grinder, 1975, 1979; Lankton, 1980, 1985; Matthew, 1985).

The suggested lead by the therapist can consist of a verbal insight, an emotionally supportive comment, a nonverbal reinforcement such as a nod or smile, a confrontive remark, a challenging question, a directive for action. For example, a question such as, "How do you think your parents would respond if you were to talk directly with them about how angry you are?" can lead a client toward considering direct communication in a family that acts out their negative feelings in indirect ways. Like some pacing, some leading is very subtle, designed to have its greatest impact on the client at a subliminal, or unconscious, level. Faced with a hyperreactive client who is emotionally agitated, the therapist might first pace the client's breathing rate and then gradually slow his own rate so that the client can follow into a more relaxed state. Similar changes can be accomplished through changes in voice intonation or rate of speaking (Bandler & Grinder, 1975; Lankton, 1980).

Leading techniques are part of the everyday behavior of therapists, in whatever form is most familiar based upon theoretical orientation and personal style. More challenging is the art of *balancing* based upon the pace/lead dialectic. In our experience as trainers and supervisors, the most common therapist error is to depend too heavily upon leading without sufficient pacing. As we have indicated, this misbalance occurs most readily with clients whose behaviors, meanings, and models of the world are significantly different from those of the therapist — often, this includes sex offenders. However, working with abuse victims who seem helpless and overdependent can also frustrate therapists and create a tendency to overbalance by leading. Conversely, working with adult survivors can become overbalanced in the direction of pacing as therapists attempt to be emotionally supportive, thereby inadvertently reinforcing self-defeating, victim-like behaviors in their clients.

Pacing/Leading. Pacing and leading together constitute a balancing intervention. An effective lead must be well-connected to the pacing that precedes it in order to be appropriately grounded in the client's experience. Sometimes the pace/lead balance hinges on a nuance of language or a slight modification of a previous statement from the client. For example: "So you warn yourself you could get into trouble each time you go into her room at night [therapist paces perpetrator client's previous statement] . . . and then you ignore your own warning!" [therapist leads client to recognize internal parts of himself that are in conflict]. Further, a pace/lead intervention needs to reflect accurately the therapist's hypothesizing-strategizing and positioning in order to make a difference that makes a difference to the client (Bateson, 1972; Keeney, 1983). That is, effective interventions are in line with the overall objectives of treatment, and they also fit within the therapeutic ecosystem at a given point in time.

Effective balancing interventions are *ratified* in the client's experience (another term borrowed from hypnosis). Ratification involves "making true" the changes introduced by the pace/lead balancing. In other words, if the balancing intervention fits within the therapeutic ecosystem in such a way as to make a difference to the client, then the client's model of the world will now include the change so that subsequent experience (even a moment later) will reflect this restructuring of subsystems. Thus, an individual client who is an abuser may actually feel remorseful for the first time following the therapist's successful intervention in promoting the offender's cognitive understanding of the victim's terror without shaming the offender in the process. Or members of a family in which incestuous contact has occurred may quite suddenly come to recognize the rather

pathetic nature of the offender's misguided attempts to wreak revenge on
his abusive parents by abusing his nephews and nieces, whereas before
they could only experience his behavior as perverted and frightening.
Ratification of client experience can be assisted by the therapist. Sometimes, this occurs quite naturally as a result of checking out the client's
current understanding verbally or by observing interaction between family
members. At other times, the therapist may wish to test the client's altered
experience via a directive such as a homework assignment.

Of course, not everything that is said or done in therapy fits the specific
definition of a balancing intervention like those we have described here.
Some of the questions or statements of therapists serve other purposes,
such as data gathering. Other communication in therapy can be thought
of as relationship maintenance, the sort of incidental interaction that occurs between persons involved in a common endeavor. Eric Berne (1964),
the founder of transactional analysis, labeled this type of exchange "passing the time." However, establishing and maintaining a relationship of
mutuality over time is sometimes at the heart of therapy with sexual abuse
victims or perpetrators; therefore, seemingly innocuous conversations between therapist and client can be directly relevant to treatment objectives.

Finally, we should acknowledge that numerous balancing interventions
in therapy occur somewhat automatically. Put another way, experienced
clinicians—and probably many individuals who are just starting out as
therapists—react *intuitively* to clients' communication and behavior in
ecologically balanced ways. Perhaps this has to do with their overall personality traits and social skills, something that would help explain research
findings on therapeutic process that suggest that the general interpersonal
skills of the therapist may have more to do with therapeutic effectiveness
than any particular theoretical or technical training (Gurman, Kniskern, &
Pinsof, 1986).

Summary of the Therapeutic Process

The ecological treatment process should be understood as a genuine
collaboration. Just as hypnotic trance is not one person being controlled by
another, therapy is not one person being changed by another. Rather,
*therapy is a complex reciprocal process of co-evolving a desired altered state
for the client system*, a process that will also have an effect on the therapist.
This is true even when a client's participation is not entirely voluntary. At
the very least, a child molester who has been reported or a family that has
been investigated for sexual abuse wants to be "out of trouble." Even this
can serve as a starting point for therapy.

The components of this metamodel are applicable at both the macro-
and microlevel. Based upon the data gathered during initial assessment,

some hypotheses and strategies will become part of overall treatment planning. Others will emerge spontaneously out of a particular transaction between client and therapist. Similarly, the therapist will utilize both broad balancing interventions (such as deciding when to see the entire family together or particular members individually) and very focused interventions (such as mirroring the rationalizations of an incest offender and then pointing out the value of denial as a defense mechanism). Although they can be conceptualized as discrete steps, the elements of the process become "seamless" as they are operationalized. The successive feedback loops from the client stimulate the therapist so that she/he is continuously engaging in one or another of these processes, even if not fully aware of which of the steps is occurring—gathering data, hypothesizing the meaning and significance of the client's behavior and devising an appropriate response, selecting a particular stance or posture for that response, and responding by balancing the ecology perceived at the moment.

PROFESSIONAL ETHICS
IN INCEST TREATMENT

Therapy ethics need to be recognized as both ecological and moral phenomena in order to better understand the nature of individual responsibility within a complex social ecosystem. Here, the term "therapy ethics" refers to more than legal requirements or codes of professional conduct, though these are included. Ethics involves reasoning and decision-making about good or right actions based upon one's personal values and moral character (Corey, Corey, & Callahan, 1993; Doherty & Boss, 1991; Drane, 1982). Some feminists have argued that a systemic perspective on interpersonal violence omits the concept of responsibility and leads to blaming the victim—usually a female—for the crime (Bograd, 1984; Hare-Mustin, 1980, 1986; Imber-Black, 1988; Lebow, 1986). Indeed, this view of human behavior does alter traditional ideas of causality; just as linear notions of cause and effect are challenged by the systemic paradigm, so are oversimplified notions of fault and blame (Dell, 1985, 1986, 1989; Fish, 1990; Wendorf & Wendorf, 1985). However, contrary to the arguments of some critics of systems therapy (e.g., Hare-Mustin, 1980; Imber-Black, 1986), ecological analysis can actually strengthen the concept of individual responsibility by highlighting the *ethical* aspects of the problem rather than simplistic causal explanations (Dell, 1989; Lundberg, 1990). At the same time, the concepts of co-evolution and co-responsibility help us recognize the network of complex interconnections between all aspects of treatment and many events outside of treatment, with implications of responsibility for influencing in unseen and unanticipated ways the lives of clients and the systems of which they are a part.

Every human culture and religious system has prohibitions against threatening or harming an innocent individual. Unfortunately, humans appear to be infinitely creative at rationalizing their efforts to overpower one another, particularly for a "just cause." Nevertheless, victimization represents a clearcut violation of the basic moral imperative to enhance humanity by allowing individuals to develop and maintain their personhood within a community of other persons (Tillich, 1963). Systemic thinking does not remove this moral imperative, but intensifies our awareness of it. Every individual is related to other individuals; therefore, every person is part of the social context of other persons. Therefore, the autonomy and identity of any particular person is determined, in part, by the characteristics and actions of the persons in his/her social environment. A kind of interpersonal tension is inevitably created between individuals insofar as they are all part of a larger social system and are all striving toward survival and self-fulfillment within the confines of their physical and social environments. Thus, the fundamental requirement for survival of any individual is ecological balance because the very interaction of two or more individuals always produces something *new*—thereby changing the environment and requiring adaptation to these changes. From the systemic perspective, then, morality can be thought of as a function of the relationship of various systems to one another as part of a larger ecosystem (Taggart, 1985). This moral imperative might be called "responsible flexibility" whose ultimate goal is ecological balance, or, in more personal terms, "integrity."

Ethical Challenges in Family Therapy

Working with incestuous families raises complicated issues regarding the role of the therapist vis-à-vis each individual in treatment in light of the focus on the family system. As we have seen, aspects of therapy as routine as emotional support become more difficult to provide when several clients are in the room. Acting as a gatekeeper for information flow between family members, particularly when dealing with family secrets, can be burdensome. Power inequities between the genders and the generations are highlighted, thereby politicizing some therapeutic decisions. Complex legal and moral issues are part and parcel of therapy. Therefore, the concept of *therapeutic responsibility* broadens and deepens (Green & Hanson, 1989; Hare-Mustin, 1980; Smith, 1991; Wendorf & Wendorf, 1985).

The ethical responsibility for interventions with sexually abusive families may seem overwhelming. Therapists have consulted attorneys to define their legal limits of liability, hoping to reassure themselves that such work need not be as risky as it presently appears. Little comfort is to be found. Legislation governing the practice of mental health care continues to be enacted, and attorneys continue to warn of future increases in malpractice litigation. In short, the willingness to bring social systems into the domain of mental health care has created added layers of ethical and legal complexity never envisioned by the original architects of the psychotherapeutic process, just as the physicians of a century ago could not have imagined the moral and legal dilemmas to be faced as a result of recent advances in biotechnology. In addition to the ethical complexities arising from working with the internal dynamics of incestuous family systems, broader social trends related to child abuse and family violence have contributed significantly to the ethical challenges faced by contemporary family therapists (Doherty, Boss, LaRossa, Schumm, & Steinmetz, 1993; Liddle, 1991; Stokols, 1992).

Because mental health care interfaces with so many of these basic aspects of human existence, quite naturally it is an arena in which social, ethical, and legal controversies are played out. Recent public debates over family values have sharpened these issues even further, reminding therapists of the nature of the helping professions as both *moral* and *political* endeavors. Nowhere is this more apparent than in treatment of abusive or violent families.

ECOLOGICAL CONSIDERATIONS FOR FAMILY THERAPY ETHICS

Family therapists working with family sexual abuse are challenged to operationalize personal values, professional principles, and societal mandates without falling prey to the extremes of rigid ethical legalism or total ethical relativism. Some kind of framework is needed to bridge the requirements of personal accountability (both the therapist's and the client's) and the reality of the transactional complexity of the therapeutic relationship. As Doherty and Boss (1991) have observed, the field of family therapy in the 1990s must confront "the development of an ethical stance that is informed by systemic thinking yet does not vitiate centuries of tradition upholding individual rights and responsibilities" (p. 634).

Health—particularly mental health—is a *value,* reflecting societal consensus regarding personal behavior, social transactions, and even internal states of mind as well as physiological conditions (Maddock, 1973). Judgments of mental health or family dysfunction are not completely verifiable on objective grounds, nor are they based totally upon individual self-appraisal. Rather, mental health is best viewed as a meaningful way of organizing an individual's or couple's or family's experience within the context of a physical and social environment—an outgrowth of dialogue between family members and their social context. Admittedly, social consensus regarding mental health or positive family functioning is more difficult to achieve amidst the complex ecology of a diverse culture. Therefore, we must be prepared to accept the criteria of health as *emerging* from the historical process rather than as fixed at any given point by any given individual or group (Beahrs, 1986; Bursztajn, Feinbloom, Hamm, & Brodsky, 1981). What is needed is to persuade the public that science itself is a form of "extended conversation" (Tomm, 1986), conducted for the purpose of arriving at a consensus about how to effectively manage transactions with the environment.

Viewing therapy as a co-evolutionary process erases the false distinction between the person of the therapist and his use of techniques, or, similarly, between a therapist considered humanistic and one considered behavioristic or strategic. Systemically, the helping process embraces *both* personhood and technique in a dialectical fashion, creating a synthesis without removing the inevitable tension of the balance that has to be struck between them in each and every clinical encounter. Simply put, the humanity of the therapist is the connecting link with the client, without which change cannot occur—a truth sometimes lost in the mechanistic language of family systems therapies (Taggart, 1982).

From an ecological perspective, therapeutic *mutuality* is recognized as a dialectical process involving balances between a variety of interpersonal and contextual variables (Dell, 1984; Matthew, 1985; Tomm, 1986). A clinician can behave in new and useful ways in a therapeutic relationship only to the degree that clients cooperate by allowing such behavior. Further, the behavior of the clinician will facilitate change only to the degree that it represents a difference in the clinical situation that, in turn, makes a difference to the clients, who can then make changes useful in their lives outside of the clinical encounter. Ecologically speaking, therapy is a process of consensual coordination between therapist and clients in a mutual effort to maximize balanced transformations within and between all members of the therapeutic system (Breunlin & Schwartz, 1986; Hoffman, 1981; Keeney, 1983). This is true even when clients are participating in treatment on an involuntary basis.

The Ethics of Co-responsibility

Inevitably, the notion of co-evolution requires an equally systemic concept of ethical *co-responsibility* (Wendorf & Wendorf, 1985). As we indicated above, systemically based ethics has been subjected to some harsh criticism by a number of feminist authors (e.g., Hare-Mustin, 1980, 1986; Imber-Black, 1986; James & McIntyre, 1983), premised upon the recognition of unequal distribution of power between males and females, both inside and outside of families. However, we believe that personal responsibility should not be understood in causal relationship to interpersonal or social power (Dell, 1989). Proportionality is a legal justice concept rather than a personal moral concept; ethically, one cannot be partly responsible any more than one can be partly moral. Therapists, clients, participating agencies are *equally responsible* for the outcomes of treatment. This is true because value does not exist or have meaning in itself, but emerges out of the interaction between the parties in their mutual process of becoming something different, while at the very same time actualizing what they essentially are (Buber, 1937; Tillich, 1963). Something genuinely new is created in the clinical encounter, and all involved parties are influential in determining what emerges from the encounter.

It is this concept of co-responsibility that must guide the structuring of therapy. The therapist is required to select a particular system (individual/ dyad/family/organization) to designate as the client, the unit for which some good is to be attained, some right action is to be taken. Since the client system is inevitably interacting with other systems, both near to it and distant from it (for which some kind of good or right must also be judged)—and all these systems are within the context of a larger ecosystem striving to maintain its overall organization—the entire network of inter-acting units must be recognized by the therapist as part of the ecology of therapy. As a result, the potential client unit for helping can be as specific as an individual or as general as an extended family, an organization, or even a community. Further, the systems relevant to the therapeutic pro-cess may vary at different points, challenging the therapist to decide which client systems should "survive" in an everchanging configuration of treat-ment. If ecological treatment of sexually abusive families is to be con-ducted effectively and ethically in the future, this fluid structure of the therapeutic process must be recognized and legitimated by both the men-tal health care system and the legal system.

The Ethical Therapist

To be effective, the family therapist needs to be successful at ecological balancing. To be ethical, the family therapist needs to possess certain virtues that facilitate co-responsibility in the therapeutic process.

- The ethical therapist is one whose rationale for professional work is fundamentally ethical, distinguishing the moral concept of re-sponsibility from the scientific notion of causality. Much of a ther-apist's effectiveness is based upon his moral authority, conveyed to clients as communication worthy of acceptance and as account-ability for words and actions (Doherty, 1995; Maddock, 1973).
- The ethical therapist understands change as a constant, thereby viewing life as a process of *becoming,* renewing itself in uniquely individual and creative ways. From this perspective arises a basic sense of hope and optimism. Those who do not have a feeling of contributing positively to the life process should not be therapists; they would be hypocritical.

- The ethical therapist views the client unit within its social and physical context. Therefore, she or he is prepared to identify a client system with which to work and equally prepared to expand, contract, or modify the identified unit as the clinical situation requires.
- The ethical therapist recognizes that any action taken by a helping professional alters the *environment* of the client system rather than the client system itself. The client system may respond to this environmental influence with change; however, the power for change always remains with the client(s).
- The ethical therapist has excellent boundaries and a strong sense of professional and personal identity. This characteristic is crucial for permitting a therapist working with family sexual abuse to take appropriate responsibility for the structure of treatment by freely and flexibly connecting and disconnecting with a changing client system in a sensitive and effective manner. The ethical clinician is also good at distinguishing client goals and outcomes from his own professional and personal goals. A major aspect of effective boundaries is self-awareness in the realm of values, a critical attribute for clinicians.[8]
- The ethical therapist has a well-developed sense of professional obligation. In addition to a solid set of personal values, this includes a willingness to bear the burden of the highest standards of professional integrity (including both moral character and a commitment to maintaining a positive image of ethical integrity in the public eye) as well as a strong identification with his/her profession and its code of ethics. Working policies save the wear and tear of continuously reopening basic stances on professional behavior, and allow one to focus more effectively on applications to particular situations.
- The ethical therapist recognizes that there is no single, right way to do therapy; one can only do what is useful at a given time for a given client system. A correct intervention can never be known in advance, though educated guesses can be made. Further, the principle of escalating sameness in systems (Watzlawick et al., 1974) reminds us that anything which produces a particular result, if done long enough or in enough different situations, will eventually reach the point of being ineffective or even harmful rather than helpful to the client system.
- The ethical therapist is flexibly responsive, thereby creating a wide range of behaviors that are "good" for clients. The most powerful

[8]Personal therapy is often an important contributor to good boundaries. We believe that ethical therapists should be willing to be consumers of helping processes as well as practitioners of the art of helping.

element of any system is that element with the greatest range of choices for action; the ethical clinician works across a broad range of behavioral patterns. This quality is much easier to talk about than to implement, for all human beings are finite, with particular characteristics, limitations, and idiosyncrasies.

- The ethical therapist balances confidence and humility. Having established a solid sense of personal and professional identity, he can do whatever works to promote change, within the limits of personal and professional integrity. At the same time, appropriate humility is recognizing that one cannot work equally well with everyone. In addition, professionalism requires acknowledging that many things technically possible to do in therapy ought *not* to be done for ethical reasons.

- The ethical therapist is motivated primarily by a genuine concern for clients rather than by a personal need to be helpful. Fantasizing other careers may even be a sign of professional maturity. Hopefully, the therapist has worked through the family of origin and developmental issues that contributed to an earlier choice of the profession, and now he or she is able to be more appropriately altruistic.

CONCLUSION

The theoretical material presented in this chapter provides a broad perspective for understanding the nature of reality and human existence. Although we believe that a systemic paradigm characterizes all technologized societies at the end of the twentieth century, we have argued that it would be useful for therapists to self-consciously adopt a certain way of understanding human experience, human problems, and the nature of change. Therefore, we have presented a metamodel which can serve as a framework for therapeutic process. This framework is *generic* in two senses: First, it is a way of describing what, in fact, does happen in therapy from an ecological perspective (regardless of a therapist's theories or beliefs or even acceptance of systemic principles); second, it is a framework to which a particular therapist's own theoretical principles, acquired techniques, and personal style can be rather easily adapted if the therapist chooses to work systemically.[9] Finally, we have explored some of the ethical implications of adopting this framework in the conduct of family therapy; these will be explored further in the remaining chapters.

[9]As we were editing this manuscript, we came across an excellent book with some similar ideas about the use of multiple flexible frameworks in the practice of family therapy. The authors' thinking about the complex multilevel structure of therapy and the basic concepts of therapy process bear a striking resemblance to ours, reinforcing our notion that these principles are somehow "generic" in the therapeutic endeavor; see Breunlin, Schwartz, & MacKune-Karrer (1992).

CHAPTER 3

Family Sexuality in Ecological Perspective

> *So far society has not helped us find a comfortable place for sex in our lives. It remains for parents to foster healthy sexuality in their children by creating a family atmosphere where sexual feelings are respected as a vital aspect of life through which one enhances caring relationships.*
>
> —Miriam & Otto Ehrenberg (1988)

IN THE LAST CHAPTER, we referred to some ideas about family ecology that have developed during this century, most of them in connection with issues in family economics and home management. Although ecological theory has not yet been applied extensively to the study of family relationships or family therapy, some of the concepts and principles are potentially useful for understanding family sexual abuse and its treatment. From the ecological perspective, a "family" can be defined as *the primary transformational unit in the self/world relationship*, regardless of its size or formal structure or the nature of the ties between its members. A family is the basic context in which human beings are transformed into persons—participants in complex social systems who retain autonomous identities as individuals; conversely, the family transforms elements of the social and material environment into meaningful components of experience for its members. Ecologically, then, a family can be thought of as a *process*, a way of relating humans to their near and distant environments via both concrete (behavioral) and abstract (symbolic) transactions (Chubb, 1990).

As we have already indicated, transformational patterns are the basic units of observation in an ecological approach; therefore, subsystem/ecosystem relationships are the primary "building blocks" of any descriptive or explanatory model of family phenomena (Gottman, 1982). While this complicates theory development, it also permits a more precise designation of complex phenomena within the systemic paradigm. In addition, concepts and principles that are ecological help specify the family's role as an interface between material resources of the environment, the personalities of its members, and the social processes of its cultural context (Beutler, Burr, Bahr, & Herrin, 1989; Bubholz & Sontag, 1993; Buckley, 1967; Rettig, 1993).

Perhaps most important, viewing the family from an ecological perspective highlights the fact that families function in extremely diverse ways. Those families identified as having a specific problem such as incestuous abuse cannot be characterized in a particular way—there is no single "type" of incest family, or of any other "kind" of family. Rather, families can be healthy or unhealthy in many different ways. They can function effectively based upon diverse characteristics and a variety of relationships among members as well as upon a variety of factors in their immediate life situations and in the larger environment. As we shall see, this awareness is extremely important for establishing treatment goals for incestuous families—indeed, for all clients in therapy.

SEXUALITY IN THE FAMILY SYSTEM

Our approach is grounded in the assumption that sexuality is a fundamental aspect of human existence. It is one of four basic dimensions of human experience, and thus of family life. The others are: the *systemic* dimension, which is the unifying, organizing principle of human interaction, including family relationships; the *developmental* dimension, which reflects the reality of movement in life from birth to death (the human life cycle) and, similarly, the stages of family life (the family life cycle); and the *cultural-historical* dimension, which provides a meaningful context for human experience reflecting the intersection of space and time.[1]

Sexuality can be thought of as having three major components. These can be conceptually distinguished, though they are not actually separate in human experience: biological femaleness and maleness and accompanying reproductive capacities, i.e., *sex*; behavioral self-expression and social role construction linked to sex, i.e., *gender*; and the pleasurable expression of embodiment, i.e., *eroticism*. Although sexuality is rooted in biology and

---

[1]When dealing with social context issues in this book, we frequently use the phrase "technologized societies" to refer to both North America (the United States and Canada) and other societies around the world (e.g., Western European countries and Japan). These societies have taken the "next step" in urbanization and industrialization in their reliance on technology, particularly rapid communication, as the basis for their economic and social stability. As indicated in the Introduction, we believe that our descriptions of family dynamics and family problems are generally applicable to these societies, despite their differences in geographic location, economic organization—even cultural and religious traditions.

expressed in individual personality, it must be understood within particular sociocultural contexts. Despite some evolutionary variables that are common to all human societies, sexuality as a whole is a social and historical phenomenon. It is mixed with broader cultural patterns, and it changes along with these. The sexual attitudes, ideas, and behaviors of different social classes, groups, and strata within a society are also very different; therefore, there exist specific sexual subcultures according to gender, age, ethnicity, socioeconomic status, religion, and sexual orientation.[2]

Several important generalizations regarding the nature of family sexuality are important as groundwork for our discussion of the dynamics of family sexual abuse:

Sex is a basic dimension of family life, an important motivator of marriage as well as the vehicle for transmitting life from one generation to the next. Therefore, sexuality is inevitably reflected in the actions of family members.

Gender is a key aspect of family organization. Gender-linked factors powerfully affect patterns of interaction and communication among all family members, reflecting differences in individual experience and social expectation.

Physical embodiment is expressed in family life as well as individual life. The family shapes and gives meaning to the bodies and physical attributes of its members. There is an erotic (pleasure-oriented) component to many aspects of family life, ranging from curious self-stimulation to interpersonal affection. The task of finding appropriate physical and psychological distance between members is a necessary part of family development.

Family development patterns and the psychosexual development of individual family members are mutually influential. On the one hand, stages of family development are strongly influenced by the sequence of significant events in the psychosexual development of individual family members; on the other hand, patterns of individual psychosexual development are powerfully affected by changing patterns of family interaction at various stages of the family life cycle.

Sexual meanings and behaviors in the family intersect with a variety of elements in the family's historical and cultural environment in mutually influential ways. How a family deals with sexuality affects its relationship to its surrounding community; likewise, what happens in the larger society

---

[2]For further discussion of these issues, see Foucault (1977); Gagnon & Simon (1973); Kon (1988).

has an impact on family sexuality. Family members' experiences outside of the family, as well as circumstantial factors in the broader social and physical environment, inevitably affect their sex-related behavior.

Unfortunately, the fact that the terms "family" and "sex" are most likely to appear together in discussions of incestuous abuse reinforces the prevailing attitude that sexuality is a family *problem* rather than a natural part of family *process*. This perspective is probably rooted in a deep cultural ambivalence regarding sex, influenced by a heritage of mind/body dualism and a male-dominated social structure that conflicts with abstract ideals about the rights and freedoms of all individuals. To these can be added the impact of recent technology on reproductive processes, a period of rapid social change, and increasing cultural pluralism. Even if uniformity of opinion about basic values and codes of sexual conduct once existed in America — and very likely it did not — such a consensus is no longer present (Bullough & Bullough, 1977; Gagnon & Simon, 1973; Reiss & Reiss, 1990). Today, North Americans have to choose from among a variety of competing value systems, cultural norms, and lifestyle options upon which to base their personal sexual decision-making.

The social boundaries of families in today's technologized societies have generally become more open to cultural influences regarding sex. Various reasons have been offered for this: increased media impact within the home (especially television); loosening of traditional religious values (though more traditional values have been reflected in the United States in the past several decades); earlier onset of adolescence and accompanying peer group influence; heightened awareness of cultural and ethnic pluralism; and a variety of other cultural and technological factors. Undoubtedly, each of these has had some influence. Their overall effect is to confront the American family with the necessity of more frequent and substantial changes in sexual meanings and behavior patterns than in the past.

Shifts in cultural expectations of gender-linked behaviors have occurred rapidly but unevenly in our society, meeting with considerable resistance in some quarters. The result is conflict between competing values, for example, between those wishing to preserve the traditional traits associated with feminine or masculine images and behavior and those wishing to minimize gender differences. The changes to date, and the controversies accompanying them, have produced considerable confusion about gender roles for many individuals.[3] In technologized societies, lines of interdependence between the sexes have shifted rather dramatically within the family. The traditional family system was based upon gender alliances; males

---

[3]Extensive discussions of these issues can be found in Bernard (1972); Dinnerstein (1976); Farrell (1986); Hite (1987); Scanzoni, Polonko, Teachman, & Thompson (1989); Thorne & Yalom (1982).

did "men's work," and females did "women's work" (although the nature of the work designated to each gender varies widely from culture to culture). In contrast, many of today's families depend less upon gender-differentiated role functions. Instead, generational role alliances have become more prominent—that is, parents on one side, children of either gender on the other.

Contemporary family life is characterized more by diversity than by similarity. The reality of family life is far different from the idealized images traditionally portrayed in the media. Generalizations about "the family" mask the wide variety of family forms, family lifestyles, and family experiences that actually comprise life in North America. Such generalizations can also conceal an assortment of sexual values, attitudes, and behaviors found within families. Each distinct cultural, socioeconomic, and religious subgroup in any society exhibits some unique sexual attitudes and behavior patterns. Even geographic location and the resulting particularities of individual and family lifestyle influence sexual behavior, such as the impact of climate upon styles of apparel or the significance of geographic isolation upon the incidence of close intermarriage among rural clans. A nation's history is actually composed of many histories; similarly, the sexual histories of individuals and families are complex and varied. The significance of these differences for understanding sexuality has increased as sex has moved from the private into the public sphere of life (Bullough & Bullough, 1977; D'Emilio & Freedman, 1988; Reiss & Reiss, 1990).

Within this framework of cultural ambiguity, conflicts abound, both between and within individuals. In the 1990s, North American society appears to be sharply divided on major sex-related issues. Extremism characterizes much of the debate. There is strong support for both conservative and liberal orientations—with each viewpoint claiming to reflect the majority—while a sizable number of citizens cling to middle ground, either out of apathy or out of preference for moderation. Certain of these divergent views are based upon religious beliefs, for example, the opposition to free choice about abortion. Other issues are characterized more by subjective opinion and practical arguments, for example, the debate over the connection between pornography and sexual violence. It is within this complex and diverse cultural context that the phenomenon of child sexual abuse, particularly incest, must be understood.

POWER AND CONTROL
IN THE FAMILY SYSTEM

Both power and control are necessary and legitimate components of human experience, particularly in the context of close, ongoing relationships. If not kept in balance, however, they can become distorted and create negative interaction patterns, including within the family (Cartwright, 1959; Cromwell & Olson, 1975; Gray-Little & Burks, 1983; Haley, 1976; Stock, 1985).

In its simplest dictionary definition, power is *the capacity to influence.* Power is the energy of life, literally and figuratively moving out and taking up space in the world. Control can be defined most simply as a reciprocal to power, that is, as *the capacity to restrain or regulate influence.* Control is the boundedness of life, recognized in the inevitable limitations on everything that exists. In our view, power and control are interactive concepts that can be understood best in relation to each other. Defined in this way, a deeper meaning arises out of the tension between them, and the terms can be combined into a single dialectical construct: *power/control* (Figure 3.1).

The human experience of power/control is the experience of living as a self interacting with a world. Selfhood develops through interaction with social and material environments. The infant's recognition of having an influence on the environment gradually evolves into a broader sense of competence which undergirds identity (Hartmann, 1958). However, in achieving self-identity through social interchange, the developing individual also learns to know the sense of "otherness" that is basic to the experience of control. The power of personhood expressed in any form by any particular individual is always limited by the personhood of other individu-

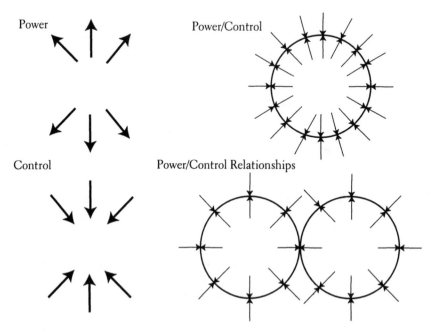

FIGURE 3.1 Power/Control Dynamics

als (e.g., Buber, 1958; Mead, 1934). Thus power/control interaction patterns — and accompanying tensions — inevitably characterize all human relationships.

If control becomes excessive in a relationship, the opportunity for individual self-expression or self-actualization is reduced; when power dominates, the stage is set for competition and conflict. In human interactions that are positive and effective, a balance of power/control is achieved. The result is an experience of *mutuality*, in which the characteristics of each party to the interaction are influential in the outcome, and regulation is a shared endeavor (Erikson, 1959, 1968; Wynne, 1988a). In the experience of mutuality, each individual can retain a sense of self-identity and worth while simultaneously feeling connected and even intimate with others as part of a larger relationship system (Stierlin, 1969; Wynne, 1988a). Put another way, in a relationship characterized by balanced power/control, or mutuality, participants are both *a part of* the relationship and *apart from* the relationship as individuals. Although there are numerous family dynamics influencing the evolution of violence or abuse, probably most important are the distortions in power/control which arise within the family's two major dyadic structures — male-female and parent-child relationships.[4]

Power/Control in Male-Female Relationships

The two aspects of the power/control dialectic are divided somewhat along gender lines. Traditionally, males have expressed their personal and social power outside the home (in competition with other males) while their power within the family was largely unchallenged. At the same time, females have been permitted virtually no expression of power in the public realm; however, they have been charged with controlling families and households in a variety of ways, such as restraining children, providing moral influence, and limiting male sexual access. Strict segregation in roles and spheres of influence has provided a context in which these gender-linked expressions of power/control created a kind of stability, despite the increasingly recognized disadvantages of this arrangement for females. One of the major problems for women in these strongly gender-differentiated families has been their vulnerability to violence and victimization.

Recent changes in social expectations and gender-linked role behaviors have produced a different context for power/control expressions both inside and outside the family. Connections between the workplace and family life are now more apparent (though still problematic), and the

---

[4]Power/control and its dynamics in abusive relationships are discussed in greater detail in our book *Child Sexual Abuse: An Ecological Approach to Treating Victims and Perpetrators*.

boundaries between them are more diffuse. Motives for marrying have shifted, and companionate rather than functional aspects of marital interaction are emphasized. At the same time, demographic and economic shifts have created a variety of social pressures on the family. The net result of all these changes is an increase in interpersonal ambiguity and family stress which appears to have added to the propensity for conflict and even violence between the genders (Boss, 1988; McGoldrick, Anderson, & Walsh, 1989).

Some have responded to these difficulties by calling for a return to "traditional family values" and to the strict segregation of gender roles which, they contend, will reestablish harmony between family members. These arguments ignore the accumulated evidence that such "harmony" often has existed at considerable personal risk to women and children (Chapman & Gates, 1978; Finkelhor, Gelles, Hotaling, & Straus, 1983; Goldner, 1985; Taggart, 1985; Walker, 1989). On the other side are those who call for even more radical and sweeping changes in family and social structures in order to essentially eliminate gender linkages to social roles and to fundamentally reconstitute interaction patterns between the genders (Boss & Thorne, 1989; Thorne & Yalom, 1982; Walker, 1989).

Although the personal and social costs of this dilemma are now recognized, no immediate solution is likely. The problem will be solved, we believe, only by fundamental changes in the socialization of *both* males and females, as well as structural changes both inside and outside the family. The complex systemic nature of male-female interactions throughout society must be fully appreciated in order to comprehend the paradox that is embedded in it in order to make possible genuine, lasting changes. Otherwise, families will continue to transmit the preconditions for victimization from one generation to another. As Virginia Goldner (1985) has put it:

> Without a complex model of the dialectics of power between men and women in families, feminist thinking could be critiqued for its linearity, leading to a simplistic politics of "women-as-victims" of men, of society, of envious mothers, patriarchal fathers, and so on. Insofar as feminists are tackling the more difficult questions, such as how and why women collude in their own domination, family therapists can offer a conceptualization that incorporates [the] insight that symptoms are strategies for control in human relationships. Without confronting the shadow side of power, the power of weakness, the paradoxical ambiguity of women's oppression will remain obscure. (p. 44)

Men cannot "give" women power; women have to exert themselves and take it. However, in the process they will find themselves giving up certain kinds of control, assuming the same kinds of risks that men have assumed by going out into the world to find arenas in which to utilize their power in both competitive and cooperative ways. Similarly, women cannot "allow" men to have control, for then they would still be in control of the allowing. Men must gain better control of themselves so that they can enter more fully into relationships with women, with children, and with each other. They must learn to express themselves persuasively without intimidating; they must learn to cooperate more fully and to compete less often. Such changes will inevitably cost them a certain amount of social power as they realize control over themselves, their time, and their lives in new and different ways. These are subtle but enormous changes to make within human systems; yet, what better arena for achieving them than within the family?

Power/Control in Parent-Child Relationships

Helpless at birth and facing a long period of relative dependency, infants are nonetheless enormously influential in their interpersonal worlds, initiating patterns of interaction that result in new interpersonal systems and help constitute significant adults as "parents." While uncontrolled in many aspects of their physical functioning and behavior, infants and young children exert substantial control over those with whom they are dependently connected due to the power of their helplessness, that is, their need for care. Human development occurs via a series of crises and stages through which individuals are transformed on their way to maturity (Erikson, 1959). The positive reciprocal interactions composing parent-child relationships help maintain flexible boundaries between the generations, which allow for the identity and autonomy of both children and parents while facilitating the periodic transformations required by the maturational process.

The pitfalls in this process are readily apparent. If parents abuse the power granted by their size and status—exploiting their children physically, emotionally, or sexually—they teach a pattern of interaction that leaves children vulnerable to the development of adult victim or perpetrator identities (Ryan, 1989). As the primary context in which children constitute their identities through relationships, the family is the most powerful shaper of the self-world structure that lies at the heart of a child's evolving sense of humanity and individuality. At the other extreme lies another trap: Parents can be intimidated by the significant burden of responsibility placed upon them by their children's vulnerabilities, resulting in their being tyrannized by the needs and desires of their children. American culture has contributed to this intimidation by considering children to be "products" of families—their behavior supposedly a direct result of particular actions or inactions, personal characteristics, or even random mistakes of parents. Some children react to this intimidation dynamic by grandiosely behaving as if they were "parents" of their own parents, thereby facilitating a breakdown of their families' intergenerational boundaries (which the parents unconsciously permit). Among other things, both of these extremes represent distortions in the power/control balance between the generations. In the context of industrialized, technologically-oriented societies, increased attention to parenting behaviors often conveys the impression that children come off a household assembly line like automobiles or fast food. Over the past several decades, many "how-to-raise-your-child" books have stated or implied that there are recipe-like steps to the parenting process, as if parents only need to master a series of techniques to rear perfect children.

Not surprisingly, important aspects of these parenting dynamics are gender-linked, related to the power/control differentials discussed above. Traditionally, primarily mothers have been expected to *control* their children—using the authority and/or physical prowess of fathers as a disciplinary tool to coerce conformity ("Just wait until your father gets home"). On the other hand, fathers have been expected to model power and competence while remaining largely absent from the home, using mothers as agents of control ("I'm busy now; go ask your mother"). Under these restrictive conditions, mothers who try to exercise power in direct ways in their families are often treated as inept or hostile, while those who exercise power outside of the home—that is, like males—may be considered neglectful. Similarly, males who try to control their children directly using the power mechanisms learned from their own families and their culture become vulnerable to charges of child abuse. On the other hand, if males take on more typically feminine modes of control they risk ego-damaging labels of incompetence, such as "wimp."

These patterns are beginning to change, but slowly. The current period of transition in gender role socialization is particularly unsettling for both parents and children, characterized as it is by ambivalence and ambiguity. Based upon changes in demographics, economic conditions, and social organization, future families are likely to require greater sharing of child-rearing functions by males and females (Rossi, 1977). As long as society coerces females to be tied tightly to childrearing as an extension of their childbearing, they will be forced to concentrate more heavily on control mechanisms and will lose opportunities for direct expressions of power, both within the family and the larger society. Similarly, males who are prevented from major investments of time and energy in the direct aspects of childrearing will continue to lack skills in the dynamics of control and are likely to persevere in seeking direct expressions of power for ego gratification. In the world outside the family, this can mean achievement and social status; inside the family, it can lead to perpetration and abuse.

Intergenerational relationships need a balance in power/control expression, in everchanging configurations through the life cycle. Parents must come to understand that there can be only *guidelines* for childrearing rather than specific steps, thereby increasing their tolerance for ambiguity and improving their capacity for flexibility of responses to their children's behavior. Balance and flexibility have been found to be lacking in parents who exploit and abuse their children (Alexander, 1985; Daro, 1988; Trepper & Barrett, 1986). Helping parents facilitate their children's development through flexibility is not an easy task. Ambiguities and the tensions of either/or choices with unknown outcomes will continue to be unsettling. Further, the adults involved in childrearing need to have a sufficiently solid sense of autonomous identity to endure the continuous relationship realignments required by the developmental process. In short, parents must be capable of mutuality and must avoid interaction patterns of perpetration/victimization.

FAMILY SEXUAL HEALTH

Our ecological perspective understands family sexuality as a complex phenomenon involving individual family members, the family as a system, and the larger social context (Maddock, 1989). On the basis of our experiences as sex educators and as clinicians working with sexually dysfunctional couples and families, combined with deductive and critical analyses of the literature on family systems and on sexual development, we have identified several primary components of family sexuality that can serve as criteria for *family sexual health.* The sexual dimension of family life intersects with all of the other existential dimensions, resulting in a wide variety of mutually influential variables. Several sex-related aspects of family interaction seem particularly important in determining the capacity of the family to function in a healthy manner. Within shifting historical and cultural contexts, patterns of balance emerge from everchanging configurations of interaction in these realms throughout the family life cycle. Among the most important:

Status and influence of females and males. Within a family, male and female influences may be valued differently. Gender differences may be accentuated or minimized. Certain ways of perceiving, thinking, communicating, and behaving may come to dominate life in a particular family. Some of these may represent genuine differences in gender-linked modes of experience (Gilligan, 1983; Rossi, 1985). Others may be attributed to one gender or the other as a social stereotype and then be praised or derogated by family members (Thorne & Henley, 1975; Thorne & Yalom, 1982).

Regulation of erotic distance. One family may be characterized by rigid boundaries around all body-related matters, emphasizing privacy, lack of interpersonal closeness, and denial of pleasure in physical existence. Another family may oversexualize many of the interactions between members, attempt to break down all personal boundaries of privacy, and make eroticism and its consequences a major emphasis in members' experience.

Orientation toward power/control. The balances of power and control are easily distorted. Power and control may be differentially distributed among family members largely along gender lines and/or between the generations. Interactions characterized by power/control struggles set the set the stage for abuse and even violence between family members.

Flexibility in sexual expression. A particular family may emphasize so extremely a single "right way" to behave that members are unable to adjust to the changing requirements of individual or family life cycles, nor can they respond well to alterations in their social context. Another family may be characterized by such randomness and extreme individualism in patterns of sexual behavior that the family lacks any common core of values or standards by which to hold members accountable, resulting in extreme unpredictability and disorganization. Assessment of flexibility is relevant to both gender and erotic aspects of family sexuality.

Patterns of sexual communication. A family may lack motivation, comfort, and even the vocabulary to transact sex-related business among members, and thus they are seriously limited in their capacity for honesty, intimacy, and change in this aspect of experience. Another family may overdepend upon sexual channels of communication to handle unrelated issues. Sexual innuendoes or insults may interfere with the capacity of members to be emotionally intimate or mask underlying relationship problems. Either underdeveloped or overburdened sexual communication processes can seriously jeopordize the transformative balances required to maintain sexual health.

Nature and compatibility of sexual meaning systems. Sexuality has meaning and significance in the relational context in which it occurs. That is, patterns of interaction among family members create a network of shared meanings, which, in turn, serve as a basis for further behavioral sequences between members, creating new meanings upon which additional behavior is based, and so on (Barton & Alexander, 1981). This is not an explanation for the causes of behavior; rather, it identifies how interactional behavior is maintained by a circular and reciprocal process of "meaning-making" shared by members of a family system. Sex does not have the same meaning to every family member; in addition, the forms that behavior can take in a family are limited by the structure of that particular system (Maturana & Varela, 1987). Some forms of family interaction (for example, talking openly about sexual matters) are more conducive than others to the creation of shared sexual meanings.

Ecological fit of the family in its historical and cultural contexts. Every family must establish its boundaries in such a way that, on the one hand, members have a sense of their own unique identity as a unit and, on the other hand, the family carries on the traditions and values of its origins while interfacing effectively with the larger community of which it is a part. A family is challenged to avoid overly rigid boundaries which prevent appropriate information exchange with its social environment; at the same time, it should not be so permeable to social input that its identity is lost and it becomes simply a mirror of transient trends in popular culture.

The Concept of "Sexual Health"

In its 1965 charter statement, the Sex Information and Education Council of the United States (SIECUS) declared as its central purpose the establishment of human sexuality as a "health entity" (Fulton, 1965). Nearly a decade later, a task force of the World Health Organization (WHO) issued the first comprehensive definition: "Sexual health is the integration of somatic, emotional, intellectual and social aspects of sexual being, in ways that are positively enriching and that enhance personality, communication and love" (WHO, 1975).

Most clinicians are aware that identifying criteria of "health" is more complex than specifying the conditions of disease. Even WHO's generic definition involves value-laden terms that are subject to many different interpretations. Further, notions of health depend, in part, upon changing cultural conditions and are influenced by a wide variety of factors. Ultimately, health is a complex biopsychosocial concept, integrating objective data with the values of particular individuals within particular sociohistorical contexts.

The challenge is to develop meaningful criteria of health that can be applied to specific situations by helping professionals. Some years ago, one of the authors (JWM) utilized the WHO definition to devise the following criteria for assessing the sexual health of individuals seeking clinical services:

- the conviction that one's personal and social behaviors are congruent with one's gender identity, and a sense of comfort with a range of sex role behaviors
- the ability to carry on effective interpersonal relationships with members of both sexes, including the potential for love and long-term commitment
- the capacity to respond to erotic stimulation in such a way as to make

sexual activity — including any activity that is not harmful or exploitive — a positive, pleasurable aspect of one's experience
- the maturity of judgment to make rewarding decisions about one's sexual behavior that do not conflict with one's overall value system and beliefs about life (Maddock, 1975, p. 53)

The overall emphasis of these criteria is on processes rather than on outcomes. Nevertheless, these are principles whose contents can be specified and even measured in human experience; included are such things as amount of cognitive knowledge about sex; degree of self-awareness; extent of emotional comfort with sexual activities; utility of value system in making sexual decisions. Of course, the conclusions drawn about these processes in relation to overall health will reflect prevailing cultural norms and personal values.

Sexually Healthy Families

To the degree that a family endures as an interacting system while successfully accomplishing transformations in its members' relationships in ways acceptable to its social environment, it can be said to be "healthy." However, since these transformations take many different forms, specific outcomes are impossible to predict. Therefore, family members and family professionals must rely on guidelines for transactions within the family system as well as between the family and its environment.

The intersection of the sexual dimension of family life with the other existential dimensions produces a complex structure of mutually influential subsystems, both concrete (e.g., individual styles of dress and grooming habits) and abstract (e.g., individual attitudes toward nudity and privacy). Failure to maintain transformative balances between these subsystems can threaten the health, and even survival, of individual family members as well as the effective functioning of the family as a coherent unit.

Healthy sexual functioning within the family reflects the ecological balancing of various elements of family experience. Within the ecological framework, healthy family sexuality can be defined most broadly as *the balanced expression of sexuality in the life of the family, in ways that enhance the personal identities and sexual health of individual family members and the organization of the family as a system, functioning effectively within its social and material environment.* More specific guidelines arise from juxtaposing the components of individual sexual health with the sex-related aspects of family interaction listed above. In addition, the framework of values that guide the family and its social ecosystem must be considered in assessing the sexual health of a specific family in a specific situation (Edel, 1961; Laney, 1968). From all of these elements, we have derived five general criteria which can be said to characterize family sexual health:

- *a balanced interdependence among all family members based upon respect for both genders as legitimate and valued,* including their physical embodiment and their ways of experiencing and conceptualizing reality—regardless of perceived similarities and differences between males and females
- *a balance between boundaries that defines individual family members* and that maintains suitable physical, psychological, and social boundaries relevant to their respective ages and stages of the life cycle—while supporting appropriate gender socialization and personal erotic development
- *balanced (verbal and nonverbal) communication among family members* that distinguishes between nurturing, affection, and erotic contact while helping all of these to occur between appropriate persons in developmentally suitable ways
- *shared sexual values, meanings, and attitudes among family members,* permitting a balance between shared family goals and activities, on the one hand, and individual decisions and actions, on the other
- *balanced transactions between the family and its social and historical environments,* reflected in reciprocity between family members' sexual attitudes, meanings, and behaviors and those of their families of origin and their community

Within the context of contemporary technologized cultures, these criteria suggest a profile of the sexually healthy family that distinguishes it from the extremes of sexually neglectful or sexually abusive families. Both gender-linked and erotic aspects of sexuality are recognized and respected as part of the family's ongoing experience together and in the lives of each family member. The family supports congruence between each member's biologically given sex and his/her gender identity. However, categorical gender roles are minimized, and flexibility in gender-linked behaviors is encouraged, consistent with effective social functioning in a given cultural and historical context. At the same time, gender-linked differences in ways of experiencing and representing the world are acknowledged. Efforts are made to blend these modalities where possible and, where not possible, to allocate decision-making and action in complementary rather than conflictual ways.

Power/control modalities are balanced between the genders and the generations, recognizing appropriate developmental stages and individual characteristics. Both male and female family members have the opportunity to initiate activities, to influence decision-making, and to establish appropriate personal boundaries. Both genders can exercise self-control (erotically and otherwise), as well as give up control temporarily for periods of spontaneity, play, and emotional expressiveness. Children in the family are not viewed simply as products of the family, but as individuals whose unique characteristics are reflected, in part, in their sexuality. There is a generational structure through which appropriate guidance, protection, and support are supplied by parents to permit the unfolding of child and adolescent sexuality in age-appropriate ways. The sexuality of younger members is respectfully nurtured rather than exploited to meet the needs of the older generation. The family supports the sexual differentiation of its members, allowing them as much freedom as possible in line with personal integrity and family values. Transactions in the family are designed to foster the development of a solid sense of gendered self-identity, erotic capacity, and a rewarding sexual life style.

To promote positive body awareness and self-image in all members, the sexually healthy family utilizes positive forms of touch and physical interaction. The unique physical attributes of each family member and his/her potential for erotic expression are viewed positively. Sexual boundaries are clear and functional, though also flexible to allow for appropriate adaptations to changing developmental requirements of members. There is respect for the physical and emotional privacy of each member while allowing for positive energy and information exchange between various family members.

Wife and husband are secure in their personal sexual identities and exhibit an appropriate degree of flexibility in sexual role-taking and role-making. They convey to each other (and to their children) respect and appreciation for the erotic aspects of their marriage relationship and engage in erotic and affectional interaction that is regarded as mutually rewarding. Their patterns of sexual exchange reflect freedom of choice and the capacity for negotiation, along with warmth, caring, and concern for each other's welfare. Their erotic interaction is based upon a sufficient degree of shared sexual meaning and interest to be considered satisfying to each. Included in their relationship is an agreed-upon means of taking responsibility for the reproductive potential and possible consequences of their sexual expression. The sexually healthy family communicates effectively about sex, using language that can accurately convey sexual information, reflect feelings and attitudes of members, and facilitate decision-making and problem-solving regarding sexual issues.

In the sexually healthy family, parents provide positive sex education for their children, combining accurate information with a specific context of family values, guided by developmental principles. Sexual attitudes and values are transmitted from one generation to the next primarily through positive interaction patterns in everyday life. However, the family also has at its disposal a body of accurate information about sexuality that can be shared, with appropriate consideration for the developmental stage of each family member. Developmentally oriented sex education is premised upon a principle of gradualism which neither artifically inhibits the age-appropriate erotic interests and expressions of family members nor prematurely exposes individuals to situations that they are not equipped to handle.

Members of the sexually healthy family share an overall value system that facilitates effective and rewarding sexual decision-making, encouraging autonomy consistent with respect for individuality but balanced by concern for the integrity of the family unit. The social boundary of the sexually healthy family permits information exchange between the family and its environment so that it can remain meaningfully related to its social context. The family's value system reflects the uniqueness of the family while also sufficiently reflecting its community context; conversely, the family accepts the capacity of its individual members to appropriately represent its collective sexual integrity to the outside world.

There can be no single version of family sexual health, nor is there any one means to promote it. Because sexuality is a fundamental dimension of family experience, events of sexual significance often accompany transitions between developmental stages of individuals and of the family. In addition, shared sexual meanings and values sometimes fluctuate significantly and rapidly in a family's life cycle. For these reasons, it is a hallmark of sexual health that a family can master and adapt to new sexual circumstances both inside and outside the system and can also transform its sexual structures and functions to accommodate more fundamental alterations in its life circumstances.

FAMILY SEXUAL DYSFUNCTION

In our view, gender-linked distortions in power/control dynamics and ambivalence regarding eroticism are the two most significant cultural factors that set the stage for negative expressions of sexuality, both in individual experience and in family life. Of course, their influence varies greatly from one individual or family to another. The majority of people in our society are *not* involved in forms of sexual abuse, either as perpetrators or as victims. Yet, it has become clear that the dynamics of sexually linked conflict, abuse, and violence touch the lives of many more people than was previously recognized. In fact, we contend that the emergence of these two interconnected phenomena in technologized societies—power/control imbalances and erotic ambivalence—contributes to the creation of a rape-prone culture, that is, a culture in which the dynamics of sexuality are regularly distorted in ways that permit sexual violence and abuse to occur in the context of ongoing close relationships (such as in the family) as well as in chance encounters between strangers. We believe that understanding the dynamics of sexuality within a systemic framework can facilitate our understanding in ways that we believe can permit more effective remedial intervention as well as prevention of child sexual abuse.

The issues of gender imbalance and erotic ambivalence touch the lives of virtually everyone in contemporary technologized societies. For some, the issues may seem mostly abstract topics for lively debate at social gatherings. But for large numbers, the issues are more concrete, experienced as the fear of repelling an unwelcome sexual advance on a date, the anxiety about losing custody of one's children in a divorce due simply to gender, the stress of trying to balance career requirements with home and family life, the terror arising from the sudden eruption of violence in the midst of a marital disagreement. Conflicts abound, both between and within individuals; underlying them are questions still unanswered and controversies still unresolved. Should women and men be considered equal in all respects? Are the genders the "same"? What differences, if any, are important? Should erotic behavior be considered a natural expression of humanity, or is it a relatively uncontrollable passion against which careful precautions should be taken? Does exposure to nudity or information about sex promote bodily comfort, or does it break down natural inhibitions and threaten social order? Do men and women have similar views of the world, or are they specific to each gender? Is homosexual behavior a manifestation of genetic abnormality or simply a life style choice? Should growing children learn a wide range of possible behavior patterns, or should parents seek the security of familiar life styles that reflect gender differentiation? Does exposure to explicit sexual depictions promote socially offensive sexual behavior or provide necessary information? The issues are endless, and virtually all of them have implications for family life. Sexual ambivalence has contributed to anxiety and symptom formation on a widespread basis, making sexual problems among those most commonly brought to therapists by individuals, couples, and entire families.

In the past three decades, family interaction patterns have been studied widely, and some progress has been made in understanding the social and interpersonal sources of family problems. Until recently, however, very little attention was given to the sex-related dynamics of family interaction, other than sexual relations in marriage and sex education of children. Now, feminist critiques of family roles and the exploding literature on family sexual abuse have helped to create a broader awareness of the complex manifestations of sexuality in the lives of family members.

Sexually dysfunctional families are characterized by various kinds and degrees of distortion in their handling of gender and erotic issues. Of course, every family has some difficulty dealing with some of these issues at various times. This need not signal serious disturbance. However, in view of the cultural context of ambivalence described above and its impact upon individuals in modern technologized societies, a surprising number of families experience a noticeable amount of sexual dysfunction. In the remainder of this chapter, we examine some of the characteristics of families that fail to deal successfully with the dynamics of gender and eroticism.

Sexually Neglectful Families

Perhaps the most common way of dealing with the issues outlined above is an attempt to supress altogether the sexual dimension of family life. In such families, the lack of acknowledgment of gender issues and eroticism is one of the outstanding features of family experience. This has been powerfully highlighted in our clinical work over the past 25 years. Family-oriented sexual histories are an important component of assessment, in routine cases of couple sexual dysfunction as well as family sexual abuse. A question with which we commonly begin a history-taking interview is, "What kind of general atmosphere regarding sex existed in your home as you were growing up?" By far the most frequent response to such a question is that sexuality somehow wasn't dealt with; sex was most notable by its absence from family life. Most clients were left to "figure out things" for themselves, and their subsequent sex histories are narratives of their often confusing and painful struggles to do just that. Rarely do clients claim appreciation for their parents' ability to acknowledge and deal creatively with gender and eroticism in family life. Far more common is the experience of having sexuality be, in a word, *neglected.* The following paragraphs provide a general profile of some of the characteristics of severely sexually neglectful families. [5]

In their most extreme form, sexually neglectful families virtually ignore their members' sexuality, except perhaps in the marital relationship. Spousal roles and tasks are assigned on a rigidly gender-differentiated basis, and emphasis is on the functional, particularly procreational, aspects of erotic expression. Parent-child relationships often receive more attention and energy than marriages. However, positive physical contact is reserved largely for infants, primarily for practical caretaking reasons. Anxiety and disgust are often associated with bodies and their functions. Family members evidencing overt interest in the body or erotic matters may even be punished. The internal atmosphere of sexually neglectful families is often cool and distant; there is little genuine emotional warmth or intimacy. Family members are unconsciously oriented toward the regulatory functions of the family, particularly with regard to body matters and to pleasurable activities such as play. Even erotic encounters between spouses — which are likely to be infrequent and/or conflictual — are characterized by

---

[5]We do not want to create the impression that there is a particular "type" of family that is sexually neglectful. Here, we are highlighting only some of the patterns from this dimension of family experience. Families in which sexual neglect occurs, like families in which sexual abuse occurs, have many different qualities and characteristics, including some strengths.

minimal communication, limited repertoire, and stylized activities lacking creativity.

Family interaction patterns are organized primarily around control. In the context of a society that ascribes greater status power to males, females are socialized to be controlled and controlling. Power in such families is typically expressed indirectly; overt conflict and confrontation are discouraged. Control is exercised primarily through shaming and guilting mechanisms. This can result in aggresssively manipulative behavior by females in an effort to compensate for males' tendencies to be passive and withdrawn in interpersonal relationships. Overall, the ethic of sexually neglectful families emphasizes separateness and individuality, particularly for males.

Sex is discussed little within such families. If necessary at all, sex-related communication occurs in an abstract fashion so that no connection is made between the topic and the personal experiences of family members. Parents may become obsessed with eliminating ideas or behaviors thought to have sexual significance for their children. As a result, children may develop an overbearing conscience which may become generalized enough to create a sense of shame about any form of erotic interest or expression. Members of sexually neglectful families often adopt an extreme pattern of attitude and behavior: either vigorously denying sexual interest and avoiding all overt activity *or* manifesting a fascination with eroticism and "acting out" certain issues in a compulsive fashion.

Some sexually neglectful families may espouse abstractly a seemingly positive view of sex, perhaps even commenting with religious fervor on its "beauty" and "sanctity." In these families, such an attitude may be illusory, reflecting a denial of the reality of embodiment and perhaps a desire to ignore genuine gender conflicts or erotic difficulties that could threaten the overall stability of the marriage or family structure. When family members are isolated from one another, there is little opportunity for reality testing and dialogue that might promote growth and change.

Though extreme, the families described above reflect characteristics of large numbers of contemporary North American families. Despite the evident public fascination with sexual matters, there is ample evidence of a generalized kind of "sexual neglect" characterizing technologized societies. Perhaps efforts to overcome these neglectful patterns has had something to do with the apparent rise of the other unhealthy extreme of family sexuality.

Sexually Abusive Families

At the other extreme of misbalance from sexually neglectful families are sexually abusive families. However, what appear to be polar opposites at first glance actually are dialectically related. Sexually neglectful and sexually abusive families bear some striking resemblance to each other, as well as having certain distinctly different characteristics.

Our ecological perspective on family sexual abuse concerns itself not only with the possible psychopathology of a perpetrator or the effects of abuse on a victim. We are also interested in disturbances in parent-child relationships, malfunctions among various family dyads (particularly the spouses), family role performance difficulties, interactions of the family with the community, and even the overall societal context that shapes family members' attitudes and behaviors related to sexuality, intimacy, and child socialization (Alexander, 1985; Bronfenbrenner, 1979; Garbarino, 1977; Gelles, 1987; Trepper & Barrett, 1986, 1989). What follows is a general overview that can be compared and contrasted with the description of sexually neglectful families. More specific dynamics of family sexual abuse are examined in detail in the following chapter.

Sexually abusive families are typically closed, undifferentiated, and inflexible, characterized by sexualized dependency. The boundary between such a family and its community is likely to be rigid, isolating the family as a unit and preventing important social feedback. Implicitly, a rule evolves that all significant needs can be met only by other family members. Within these enmeshed families, the boundaries between generations and individual members usually become diffuse and ambiguous, resulting in generalized role confusion. The children often perform tasks more appropriate for adults, while the parents abdicate certain important responsibilities in order to compete with their children for scarce emotional resources. Genuine nurturance is largely unavailable to the children, forcing them into premature developmental patterns, including inappropriate erotic behavior. In one family, a father and oldest daughter may be involved in sexual contact over a period of years. In another, one of the younger children — male or female — may be coerced into sexual activity by a grandparent, uncle, or older cousin.

Male influence predominates in sexually abusive families, supported by members of *both* genders. Role expectations are extremely rigid, grounded in traditional social stereotypes. Direct expressions of power by older males are frequent, and coercion — sometimes direct and sometimes covert — is likely to be the family's primary regulatory mechanism. Females are viewed by both genders as relatively helpless victims of male prerogative. Intrapsychic boundary diffusion characterizes individual family members' sense of reality; fact and fantasy are often intermingled. Due to enmeshment and limited emotional resources, family members must yield their autonomy in order to belong. Difference is experienced as distance, and individuality is equated with disloyalty. These families are shame-based. Low self-esteem is likely to be particularly acute in relation to personal body image and sexual expression.

To counter shame, manage emotional pain, and minimize cognitive dissonance, these families rely primarily on psychic defense mechanisms. The most common and powerful of these is *denial*, enabling members to engage in distorted thought patterns which lead, in turn, to intricate rationalizations for the incestuous contact and for other problematic behaviors within the family. For example, a perpetrating father may be genuinely convinced that his sexual contact with one of his daughters is useful preparation for her to be more open than her mother to sexual variety as an adult. Sexual abuse has various meanings and functions within different incestuous families. In some, the incest can be primarily a misguided attempt to show affection. That is, the involved individuals can feel temporarily connected to each other emotionally, thereby maintaining the fiction that they are a "close-knit" family. In other families, anger is sexualized in order to deal with frustration and disappointment engendered by family interaction. Regardless of the individual circumstances or understandings of the sexual contact in a particular family, a framework of distorted sexual meaning encompasses the family system in such a way that vulnerability for sexual abuse is created.

CONCLUSION

We have now introduced some basic concepts of family sexuality from an ecological perspective. In the following chapter, we examine in more detail some processes that characterize intrafamilial sexual abuse and some social context variables that influence its occurrence. Understanding the ecosystemic dynamics of incestuous families can assist therapists in formulating and implementing effective principles for assessment and treatment.

CHAPTER 4

Sexual Abuse in the Family System

> *Few family problems cause as much disruption and nega-*
> *tive consequences for all as intrafamily child sexual*
> *abuse. While sex can be one of the closest ways people*
> *bond with one another, within a family it can result in*
> *chaos.*
>
> — Terry Trepper & Mary Jo Barrett (1989)

EVEN AMONG FAMILY PROFESSIONALS, simplistic generalizations about in-cest families are common—for example, all incest families are "en-meshed," and all mothers somehow "collude" in the abuse. In reality, incest family dynamics are varied and complex. At the same time, clinical experi-ence and subjective reports by victims suggest that some patterns of sexual abuse may be predictable and that incest may reflect more general disturb-ances in family interaction patterns (Alexander, 1985; Finkelhor, 1986; Gelinas, 1988; Mrazek & Kempe, 1981; Ray, Jackson, & Twonsley, 1991; Russell, 1986; Tierney & Corwin, 1983). However, it is unclear which family dynamics contribute most substantially to the occurrence of incest. Certain family characteristics, such as "boundary problems," are frequently cited (Bass & Davis, 1988; Gelinas, 1988; MacFarlane & Waterman, 1986). Yet nonincestuous families demonstrate many of these same characteris-tics without evidence of social dysfunction.

The stance taken in this book is that incest is primarily a distortion of the sexual dimension of family experience, arising out of a complex combination of mutually influencing variables in each of four categories:

- *Intrapsychic influences* are the internalized conflicts of family members regarding sexuality, perhaps reflecting organic problems, mental disorders, or disturbances in early life. In incest families, the most significant intrapsychic issues are deficits in self-esteem and the accompanying feelings of shame and rage, along with unresolved sexualized dependency needs.

- *Relational variables* involve disruptions in interpersonal transactions between family members. Most prominent are misbalances in power/control between the genders, interpersonal boundary violations, distortions in sexual meaning, and poor communication (particularly in regard to sexuality).
- *Developmental variables* are those that arise from the inability of individuals and/or the family system to cope effectively with various kinds of change. The primary developmental influences in sexually abusive families are intergenerational boundary disturbances and role confusion.
- *Situational factors* may be events occurring inside or outside the family on a circumstantial basis, or they may be environmental influences. The single most prominent situational variable affecting the occurrence of family sexual abuse is opportunity (Finkelhor, 1984), such as child care by the perpetrator or loss of inhibition through alcohol or drug abuse by perpetrator and/or victim.

Along with other clinicians and researchers (e.g., Daro, 1988; Finkelhor, 1986; Friedrich, 1990; Trepper & Barrett, 1989), we believe that child sexual abuse does not have a single cause; rather it arises out of a complex combination of influences in these four areas. Therefore, understanding incest requires a consideration of the interrelationships of these issues, and effective intervention must find some way to address each of them. The remainder of this chapter describes the distortions in family sexuality that appear to structure and give meaning to incestuous behavior.

BOUNDARIES AND FAMILY STRUCTURES

A boundary distinguishes a system from its environment, delineating the organizational wholeness, or autonomy, of the system (Keeney, 1983; Maturana & Varela, 1987). Ultimately, a boundary is the key factor in determining what a given system is, how it is organized, what processes will occur inside it, how it will interact with its environment—and also in predicting how the system is likely to behave in the future (Dell, 1985).

As described in Chapter 2, structures are patterns of action and meaning in family systems, recurrent sequences which give shape to the relationships between family members (Breunlin, Schwartz, & MacKune-Karrer, 1992; Keeney, 1983). Within the boundaries of the family, members conduct patterned transactions, reciprocally influencing each other in ways that are characteristic and somewhat predictable. This does not mean simply that each member's actions "cause" reactions in others in a linear way; rather, family members' actions periodically converge in ways that create systems of shared meaning which will guide members' future behavior together. This is the sense in which all family members participate in dysfunctional behavior such as sexual abuse.

In the view taken here, incest is a reflection of a family system that is organized in a relatively closed, undifferentiated, and rigid fashion, a product of substantial boundary disturbances in four areas: (a) the boundary between the family and its social environment; (b) the boundary between adult and child generations in the family; (c) interpersonal/role boundaries between family members; and (d) intrapsychic boundaries within family members.

Family-Society Boundary

In a variety of ways, incest families protect their sexual secret by constructing barriers between the family system and its social environment. By insulating themselves from critical social feedback, family members can draw only upon each other for emotional support, self-esteem maintenance, and reality-testing. An implicit rule evolves that all important emotional needs are to be met within the family system. Others to whom family members might turn for sharing and intimacy are regarded as hostile intruders who in some way threaten the survival of the family unit. This closed, highly autonomous family system limits opportunities for growth and renewal, producing a scarcity of resources while fostering inappropriate overdependence among family members and producing "enmeshment," that is, limitations on self-differentiation (Bowen, 1978; Minuchin, 1974; Schnarch, 1991).

When these families come into contact with outside social and/or legal systems, their boundaries rigidify even more as they attempt to maintain stability and keep the family intact. The harder that therapists or others try to penetrate this protective shell, the more the family as a whole is likely to resist any kind of change and may take on the veneer of a "united front." Indirect approaches to assessment and treatment rather than heavy confrontation appear to be the most successful means of promoting positive change. At the same time, systems outside the incest family must appear powerful enough for family members to respect, since concentrations of power reflect a structural fit between the family and its environment. Simply put, power (even abusive power) is a language the incest family understands. A recognition of this orientation toward power is a critical element in successful therapy.

EXAMPLE

The Lipske family is referred for treatment following the confirmation of allegations of sexual abuse of 15-year-old Jennifer by her father. Included in the session are Jennifer, her parents, and her 12-year-old brother,

Randall. Jennifer, who is adopted, is currently residing in a foster home. She wants to return home, but the protective services worker has decided that can happen only when the therapists working with the case indicate that it is safe for her to return. The father is in a sex offender treatment group at another agency.

Therapist: The county social worker told me over the phone last week that your family can be reunited at home when the two therapists agree that it is okay. Did she talk with you about what would constitute "safety?"

Father: No, she didn't. But it seems to me that it should be soon. Jennifer wants to come home right now, and I know I'm ready to have her home with us. We're all ready. After all, it's been five months already since the county took her out.

Therapist: Five months is a long time to have your daughter living away from home. [*To the father*] I'm really pleased that you feel you have made enough progress to be able to parent your daughter differently than you did before. However, your therapist and I agree that you have a ways to go before you will be ready. If you wish, I can tell you what we think you need to accomplish before we can support Jennifer's coming home.

Father: I don't know why you guys can't trust us when we say we're ready. We've done everything you've asked us to do and then some. Look at Jennifer. She wants to come home. She's not afraid. Just ask her.

Therapist: [*Looking at the daughter*] Jennifer, do you feel safe coming home at this point?

Jennifer: Of course I do. My dad is telling you the truth. Why don't you trust him?

Therapist: As you know, your dad has broken the law by sexually abusing you, and both he and you have lied about it, so we have good reason not to trust his or your judgment about your readiness to move back home.

This family is presenting a united front in an attempt to return all family members to the household—a rather typical stance. Father and daughter are aligned; if other family members had been asked about safety, they also would have said they were ready for Jennifer to move back home. The therapist has aligned herself with the father's therapist and the child protection worker rather than with the family, increasing the family's insecurity and resultant defensiveness. A different scenario might have emerged if the therapist chose to ally with all or part of the family. Further, while the therapist is accurate about the clients having lied earlier, inadvertently she has shamed them by pushing them directly on their reality-testing, something that appears to be interpreted by the father as a power move. Alternatively, the therapist might have succeeded in reality-testing without shaming them by choosing another frame of reference for her words:

Father: I don't know why you guys can't trust us when we say we are ready. We've done everything you've asked us to do and then some. Look at Jennifer. She wants to come home. She's not afraid. Just ask her.

Therapist: I'm really pleased to hear how invested you are in parenting your daughter, and how confident you are about your progress. I, too, believe you all have made considerable progress during the past several months. It must be extremely frustrating to feel so ready, and not have the green light yet to go ahead.

Father: You bet it's frustrating. How can we prove to you that we're ready?

Therapist: Frankly, Mr. Lipske, I think your focus for proof is misdirected. Instead of proving something to me, I think your family and the two therapists need to be able to convince the county that you're ready. They are legally responsible for monitoring Jennifer's safety at home, not I. How would each of you feel about inviting the social worker to meet with your family and the two therapists to talk about what the county needs to be convinced that Jennifer will be safe at home? [*To the father*] I suspect that one of the things we will need to address with the protection worker is your having been dishonest with the authorities during the initial stages of the investigation.

Father: I know. It's probably hopeless.

Therapist: Well, I don't think it's hopeless. I can understand how you believed that lying would protect your family. All of you were terrified and desperate. However, from the county's perspective—and mine—you were hurting the family rather than helping it.

Father: Okay, so it was a mistake to lie, and I probably shouldn't have told Jennifer to lie either. I don't think we can ever convince them that we will be truthful now.

Therapist: I'm really impressed that you can admit your mistake in lying to the authorities, and in convincing Jennifer to protect you by lying as well. I think that indicates some progress. I suspect that a lot more of the kind of honesty you've just conveyed to me could, in fact, convince the county that you have made important changes.

In this latter instance, the therapist aligns with the family and with the father's therapist, clearly identifying the child protection worker as the agent of social control. She seeks a stronger connection with the family by empathically framing their dishonesty as a misguided attempt to protect the family. The father provides the therapist with an opening to make a critical shift in the family's view of therapy. Instead of focusing on "looking good" by hiding vulnerabilities, the therapist clearly frames progress as exposing vulnerabilities in an attempt to develop a more fruitful basis for their continuing work together.

Intergenerational Boundary

Dependency problems and enmeshment produced by the emotional isolation of incest family members promotes the blurring of boundaries between adult and child generations (Burkett, 1991). Family members are pressed into service to meet each other's needs regardless of age or developmental stage. While some literature on incest (e.g., Thorman, 1983) has identified a reversal of roles between mothers and daughters, we believe that the phenomenon can be described more accurately as "role-confusion" and "role-exchange" among all incest family members. Contrary to healthy family functioning, children in incest families perform developmental tasks appropriate to adults, while parents abdicate certain important responsibilities and compete with their children for limited emotional resources. As a result, the nurturance necessary to healthy development (Erikson, 1963) may not be available, in turn creating deficits in important areas of psychosocial development and exposing children prematurely to adult tasks — including incestuous contact. This dilemma is further complicated by the tendency of these "parentified" children to respond with pseudomature behavior, which is adaptive in the short-run but in the long-run promotes a grandiose belief that they are capable of meeting any and all emotional needs of other people. Thus, the stage is set for incest victims of one generation to later select spouses who may again victimize them and/or their children.

EXAMPLE

The Petras family is referred for therapy following disclosure of the father's anal intercourse with his 5-year-old son, Mark. During one session, which includes the parents, the victim, and his 3-year-old sister, Mrs. Petras begins sobbing when she describes how painful it had been to find out about what was happening in the family. Mark gets up from his seat beside his mother, walks across the room, and brings back a box of tissues, offering one to her as he sits down again. She takes the box of tissues and continues talking about her agonized feelings.

Therapist: I can see how painful it is for you to be in this family right now. [*Looking around at each family member*] I wonder if it is just as painful for Mark?

Mother: Well, he's pretty young to understand all this. I don't think it affects him as much as it does his father and me. Of course, you could ask him.

Therapist: Yes, we could ask him, but I think it would be asking a lot of a 5-year-old to expect him to be articulate about what must be extremely complex feelings.

Mother: Mark is pretty advanced. He really understands more than most kids his age.

Therapist: You might be right. I wonder if it is possible that Mark understands *too much* for his age?

Mother: Do you really think it's possible to understand too much? Mark has always has been ahead of other children in his development. Why, when his sister was born, he would hold her and talk to her and comfort her just like a parent. It was absolutely amazing!

Therapist: [*To the father*] What is it like to be in competition with a preschooler for your place in the family?

Father: What do you mean? I'm not competing with my son, for heaven's sake.

Therapist: I'm not so sure. When your wife was crying just a bit ago, who took care of her?

Mother: No one. That's the problem!

Therapist: Oh, I disagree. I very clearly saw someone take care of you [*Nodding toward the boy*]. I was both impressed and sad when I watched Mark give you a tissue when you were crying. I was impressed, because it reminded me of what a kind and generous child he is. But I also was sad, because he seemed to be the one burdened by the responsibility for being helpful to you.

Father: I know Mark's a good kid. But his mother has him so tied into her that no one else can be important.

In this exchange, the therapist makes an opening for himself to address inappropriate intergenerational boundaries without shaming the son. He positively reframes the boy's helpfulness, but sets the stage for removing the burden of caring for his mother, a role which has made him into both a partner for the mother and a rival for the father. At the end of the session, the therapist schedules a conjoint marital session to work with the couple on their disappointment with each other.

Interpersonal Boundaries

Since human beings are autonomous living systems who can relate to each other in larger social systems, it is also possible to speak of a family's "interpersonal boundaries," which delineate individuals as subsystems within the family ecosystem. These are demarcations of psychosocial influence and meaning that extend beyond the skin of the individual into the interpersonal environment (Kantor & Lehr, 1975). Incest families are often characterized by substantial boundary diffusion between members, inhibiting their powers of self-differentiation (Bowen, 1978). In order to be supported and nurtured in a system characterized by enmeshment and scarce resources, members must yield their autonomy. Personal boundaries are sacrificed in order to belong. Interaction produces symbiotic relationship patterns in which each member believes that his or her survival is dependent upon the psychological and emotional status of the other members. This goes beyond—though it also includes—a symbiotic bond between incest perpetrator and victim; it permeates the entire family and is more accurately conveyed in Bowen's concept of an "undifferentiated family ego mass" (Kerr, 1981). Differentiation of self—involving independent thought, feeling, desire, and behavior by each family member—is threatening to the organization of the incestuous family system. Since differentness is experienced as distance, and individuality as disloyalty, control issues become prominent. Members who threaten the system through autonomous behavior may become the targets of scapegoating and escalating abuse. Despite their attempts to feel connected to each other, incest family members often describe themselves as "lonely" or "empty."

These factors trigger a variety of dysfunctional reactions among family members, including pervasive fear of abandonment, compensatory defense mechanisms, increased shame, and low self-esteem. Further, a variety of "double bind" interaction patterns develop (Bateson, Jackson, Haley, & Weakland, 1956; Watzlawick et al., 1967a, 1967b), and members may evolve a range of instrumental behaviors—particularly sex-related behaviors—as a means of coping with stress (Straus, 1980). Gradually, these patterns are incorporated into the intrapsychic experiences of family members and expressed in their interpersonal transactions.

EXAMPLE

The Winter family is referred for treatment following the father's prosecution for sexually abusing his 16-year-old daughter. He was in jail when therapy began, but he is able to attend evening sessions as part of a release program. In the session are the parents, Frank and Betty, the daughter, Kristin, and her two brothers, David, age 17, and Paul, age 14. Early in the session, the boys complain that they are spending most of their time on weekends and after school taking care of the horses (the family breeds show horses as a hobby) because "Kris had to open up her big fat mouth and send Dad to jail." The mother joins in the complaining, talking about how hard it is to manage all the chores and parent the children, while working part-time. As they talk, Kristin looks uncomfortable, and the therapist interprets this as shame.

Therapist: Hold on a minute. I'm confused. I'm not sure who all of you are upset with — Frank or Kristin.

Paul: Why would we be mad at Dad? He can't do anything; he's in jail. He wouldn't be there if Kris had kept her mouth shut. Now we all have to suffer because of her.

Therapist: Well, that may be true. [*Addressing the brothers*] But knowing how good the two of you are at speaking up, I suspect that it would have been only a matter of time before one or both of you talked about the incest.

David: Not a chance. We're smart enough to know better. We would never have done to Dad what Kris did. And look what has happened to Mom. She can hardly function now!

Therapist: It must be difficult for all of you to be without your Dad for now. [*To the parents*] You two have been pretty quiet about your sons' belief that Kristin has destroyed the family. Does Kristin really have that much power in the family that she can either hold it together or destroy it simply by telling the truth?

Father: Well, in a way the boys are right. All Kris needed to do was tell me to stop and I would have. She didn't need to blab it to everyone under the sun. We could have handled it in the family. And it has been harder for everyone, even Kris, to have me wasting my time in jail when I could be helping at home.

Therapist: [*To the father*] Then, it sounds as if you agree with David and Paul that it's Kristin's fault you are in jail. [*To the mother*] Betty, I wonder if, as the only other female in the family, you agree with the men? Your husband and your sons see you as overburdened and collapsing, although you strike me as stronger than that. What's your take on the question of who's at fault for your husband being in jail?

Mother: I can't believe what I'm hearing. [*To her sons*] It's not your sister's opening her mouth but your father's opening his fly that got him where he is! He hurt us then and he's hurting us now by letting his daughter take the blame for what he did!

Therapist: So there is a difference between the genders on the question of who's responsible for Dad's being in jail. I am extremely relieved, because I was beginning to think that this family has a rule against disagreement. At least the women can disagree with the men, and vice versa. I wonder if the males can disagree with each other?

The therapist makes a structural shift away from the daughter as scapegoat to divided coalitions between males and females. For the moment, the daughter is no longer alone in the family, her mother having made a firm parental move in the direction of protecting her by holding the father accountable for the abuse. At this point, it might be tempting for the therapist to push the accountability issue; however, the therapist elects to work on the interpersonal boundaries so that more complete differentiation can take place. This, in turn, increases the possibility that the father can begin to take some responsibility for his actions. Further shifts in coalitions can be anticipated in this case.

Intrapsychic Boundaries

The term "boundary" has been a useful metaphor for analyzing individual psychodynamics since the time of Freud (1938), who was actually a rather creative systems thinker with his ideas about the relationships between id, ego, and superego as structures of personality. Intrapsychic boundaries reflect the subsystems, or parts, of personality structure, whose significance is in their relationship to each other and to the overall organization of personality. In the psychologically healthy individual, various psychic structures are integrated in such a way as to support autonomy and to permit functioning of the personality in a coherent, coordinated way (Slipp, 1984). When so-called "psychopathology" occurs, the intrapsychic ecology is structured in a maladaptive way that does not fit well with the structure of the environment, resulting in distortions of meaning and behavior.

To minimize the cognitive dissonance and emotional pain created by the familial abuse while maintaining their emotional dependency and interpersonal enmeshment, incest family members rely heavily on defense mechanisms. Often the most powerful defense is *denial*—the inability to consciously recognize certain feelings and/or experiences. Denial is common in abusing families of all kinds (Hoke, Sykes, & Winn, 1989; Sgroi, 1982). It is adaptive in coping with pain and trauma, and it serves to reduce the threat of exposure to the world outside the family. Denial occurs not only about the incest; it is also likely to be pervasive in each member's personal experience and is expressed in various ways in family interaction. Denial enables family members to engage in distorted thought patterns that, in turn, lead to intricate rationalizations of symptomatic and problematic behaviors.

Used consistently, denial and related defense mechanisms impair feedback processes within the family and distort members' perceptions of reality. Thinking that they must behave in certain ways to survive, family members remain stuck in their distorted power/control patterns, repeating sequences of perpetration/victimization. Participation in these sequences increases their feelings of shame and powerlessness, in turn promoting further emotional isolation and perceptual distortion. Due to the protective nature of denial, family members typically are thrown into crisis when the incest secret is revealed to the outside world or comes to light within the family. Frequently, this crisis fosters further denial as the family coalesces to resist change. Emotional regression is common at this time, and accounts of the incestuous behavior may change as resistance is mobilized in an effort to ensure individual and collective survival.

EXAMPLE

The Forest family is referred by the county social service agency following disclosure of the sexual abuse of two girls, ages 12 and 14, by their stepfather. The stepfather has admitted abusing each girl in turn, from about age 10 to age 12. He appears to be highly motivated for treatment.

Therapist: I am impressed with the willingness of all of you to be here today. I know it may be somewhat scary, and perhaps painful, for you to talk with a stranger about what has happened in your family. We have time to talk about what actually happened at some later time; right now, I'd like to ask if you are willing to talk about what it has meant for each of you to know that sexual abuse has occurred in your family. I'd like to start with you, Mr. Forest. What do you think it meant that you became sexually involved with your children?

Father: I don't understand what you mean by "what it meant." Are you asking why I did it?

Therapist: Not exactly. I don't know about you, but I can always come up with reasons for why I did something after I've done it. Usually, that's not terribly helpful to me because most often I am simply justifying to myself why I did what I did. What I think would be more helpful is if you could look inside yourself and ask yourself the question, "What was I attempting to accomplish for me, my wife, my stepchildren, and/or the family by becoming sexually involved with my stepdaughters?"

Father: Well, I can tell you what I told myself. You see, the girls' father walked out on them when they were kids. And when I came on the scene, they were greatly in need of a father. So I did everything I could to become a father like they never really had. And the closer we got — well, it just happened. You know what I mean?

Therapist: I think I do, but let me say back to you what I understand you to be saying. In order for you to feel really connected to the children, and to make up for what they had missed with their biological father, you decided to really work at loving them. But somewhere along the way, the line between loving them and "falling in love" with them became blurred. Is that what you're saying?

Father: Well, I hadn't ever really thought about it quite like that, but now that you put it that way, I guess that could be true.

Initially, the therapist frames the father's behavior in a manner that connects with some part of his internal experience, while giving him an "explanation" for his behavior that does not convey shaming. Then, she begins to connect his experience of the incest with that of his stepdaughters.

Therapist: [*Speaking to the girls*] From what he has said, it sounds as if your stepfather was trying to do something positive for you — to love you — when he began being sexual with each of you. But I suspect that your experience might have been different from his. I wonder if you could talk a bit about what the sexual contact meant to each of you? Of course, it might have had a very different meaning for each of you.

Older daughter: At first, I guess it seemed okay until he started doing it to her [*pointing at her younger sister*]. Then I felt hurt. He told me I was "special." But he lied. That's why I told my counselor at school.

Therapist: So your father being sexual with you started out to be something you felt okay about, but then it made you feel bad. How do you feel about it now?

Older daughter: How do you think I'd feel? I'm mad! [*Begins to cry softly*] And look at him — he doesn't even feel bad about it.

Therapist: Perhaps you feel sad, too, because it's turned out this way. [*To the younger daughter*] Can you talk about what all this has meant to you?

Younger daughter: I don't know ... I get confused. It seemed like he didn't care about my feelings ... that he hated me or something. I don't want him to love me if it's going to make me feel so bad.

Therapist: [*To the father*] It seems as if each of your daughters has had a different experience of your sexual involvement with them than you had. Instead of feeling loved, they've ended up angry, or scared and confused. What started out as well-intended on your part became hurtful to your daughters. I wonder how it happened that you were able to fool yourself so completely about its effects?

The therapist begins gently testing the father's denial by addressing the daughters' experience of the sexual abuse. However, in an effort to sidestep his defenses, she does not continue to focus on the discrepancy between the family members; instead, she builds on the discrepancy and frames the challenge to his denial as an internal issue — how does he manage to fool himself about the consequences of his actions? — implying that different parts of himself are in conflict with one another.

Taken together, these four boundary disturbances in incestuous families reveal a distorted family structure in which sexuality has become a vehicle for exploitive interaction. Just as they have contributed to family sexual "dis-ease," these boundary problems create obstacles to effective intervention into incestuous family systems. Careful positioning is required to assure that the sexual abuse can be stopped without producing even greater disturbances within or among family members.

MEANINGS/FUNCTIONS
OF SEXUAL ABUSE

The psychological motivations of incest perpetrators have been explored by a variety of clinicians and researchers, and varied findings have been reported (Barnard, Fuller, Robbins, & Shaw, 1989; Conte, 1991; Groth, Hobson, & Gary, 1982; Langevin, 1983; Maletzky, 1991; Mayer, 1988). Similarly, family theoreticians have speculated on the possible functions of incest within a family system, some reporting that it seems to be a way for certain families to stay together, others believing that it may be an attempt on the part of someone in the family to break free from an enmeshed structure (e.g., Alexander, 1985; Justice & Justice, 1976; McCarthy & Byrne, 1988; Sholevar, 1975). In our view, incest does not serve the same specific functions in every family in which it occurs; however, like all human behavior, incest is somehow meaningful within its context.

Meaning evolves from the particular patterns of interaction that characterize a given family, and it serves as a basis for further sequences of behavior between family members (Barton & Alexander, 1981; Breunlin et al., 1992). However, understanding the meaning of behavior in terms of its context does not imply direct causality; rather, it demonstrates how behavior can be created and maintained by a circular and reciprocal process of "meaning-making" that is central to shared family experience (Lally & Maddock, 1994; LaRossa & Reitzes, 1993; Reiss, 1981). Of course, the forms that actions can take in a given family are limited by its structures, and we have already noted that the structures of the incestuous family permit—perhaps even encourage—the sexual abuse. However, the function that the incest serves in a given family system arises out of the network of meanings that ties together those particular family members and influences their patterns of interaction in a recursive fashion.

Particular motivations and purposes for incestuous behavior in a given family are unique to the individuals involved. However, we believe that incest can be understood as serving one of four broad functions in the interpersonal transactions of involved family members: *affectional* functions, *erotic* functions, *aggression* functions, or *rage* functions. When placed on a continuum and integrated with other family characteristics, a typology of meaning is created that can be useful for assessment and treatment planning for incestuous families (Table 4.1).

Affection-Based Incest

A significant amount of incestuous behavior appears to serve as a means of expressing affection between two or more family members of different generations. Contrary to a popular stereotype, the perpetrator's motivation is only occasionally based upon not having enough sexual contact with his

TABLE 4.1
Incest Family Typology

Affection-Based	Erotic-Based	Aggression-Based	Rage-Based
Positive intent	Positive intent	Negative intent	Negative intent
Object connection	Object connection	No object connection	Object displacement
Nonviolent	Nonviolent	Often violent	May be life-threatening
Power motive minimal	Power motive possible	Power motive present	Power motive primary
Individual psychopathology not critical	Individual psychopathology usually not critical	Individual psychopathology may be critical	Individual psychopathology critical and primary

wife, although chronic sexual *dissatisfaction* typically plagues the marriages of incest perpetrators (see Chapter 10). Some incest fathers engage in a quasi-courtship process with their daughters in a misguided attempt to show affection and feel emotionally close. This objective can increase the likelihood that the abuse will continue on a longer term basis and that sexual intercourse will eventually take place between father and daughter as a result of the perpetrator's efforts to consummate the relationship between them as "lovers."

Important to the development of this type of incestuous behavior is the significant lack of more common forms of physical nurturing and affection available to family members. This increases the likelihood that the child will accept sexual contact — perhaps even seek it out — in an attempt to meet normal needs for touch, physical closeness, affection, and emotional support. Physical force and other forms of coercion are largely unnecessary in affection-based incest, since the child may appear cooperative and compliant. Consistent with the theme of a parent-child "love affair," the sexual activity is usually conducted in a highly clandestine manner, and elaborate steps may be taken to deceive other family members — some of whom, like the spouses in many extramarital affairs, may somehow recognize that they are part of an emotional triangle without knowing the identity of the other party. The incest victim herself may be quite reluctant to expose the sexual secret and thereby be forced to give up her privileged status with her father. She may develop a hostile, competitive relationship with her mother and her siblings, and she may align with her father in intrafamilial conflicts. Unless unwittingly revealed by the participants or accidentally discovered by others, this type of incest may continue until one of several developmental factors intervenes to produce significant conflict between parent and child; for example, the daughter becoming interested in a dating relationship with a boyfriend or the father turning his attention to a younger sibling.

Interviewing or testing members of an affection-based incest family may reveal anxiety, depression, and above-average dependency needs. However, individual psychopathology is usually not sufficient to inhibit relatively effective functioning in most areas of life. This is particularly true for the perpetrator. Eventually, the child may begin to suffer some stress-related symptoms or social maladjustment based upon isolation from peers and conflict with other family members.

EXAMPLE

The Grimm family is referred for treatment following the father's admission that he had sexual intercourse with his 17-year-old daughter, Tiffany. Tiffany was adopted as an infant, as were her three younger siblings. She is described by everyone in the family as "the light of her father's life." As a young child, she followed him everywhere. Mrs. Grimm admits she was relieved that her husband was so invested in the girl, since it freed her of major responsibility for one of the four children and seemed to make Tiffany "more responsible" in caring for the three younger ones. Mrs. Grimm has her own bookkeeping business, which requires long hours of uninterrupted concentration. She often feels conflicted about her roles as a businesswoman and mother; however, she is aware of feeling best about herself when she is working. Mr. Grimm, an architectural engineer, has always been physically affectionate with her, as he is with the other children. However, as Tiffany grew older, he became aware of occasional sexual feelings toward her, but thought them to be natural.

One night when Tiffany was 12, they were lying on the floor watching television, and he fondled her breasts. This became a regular late night ritual during that summer; gradually, his sexual behavior with her expanded to include touching her genitals. Over the next two years, they added oral genital contact to their repertoire of activities. At age 14, Tiffany and her father had sexual intercourse while on a camping trip together with the other children (Tiffany and her father slept in the same tent).

For nearly three years, Mr. Grimm and his daughter had weekly sexual contact, until she developed a relationship with a boy her own age and began to pull away from her father. Jealous of her affection for her boyfriend, the father became more controlling. Following a major verbal conflict with her father, Tiffany told her boyfriend about the incest, and he eventually convinced her to tell her school counselor.

Erotic-Based Incest

An incestuous family that eroticizes many of the interactions among its members can be labeled "pansexual." Sexual meaning is attached to everyday interaction patterns among family members, sometimes including the extended kinship network as well. The incestuous behavior in this type of family may involve both parents and most or all of the children. Sometimes, the sexual contact takes the form of a "game." The family's primary bond appears to be its projections of eroticism into everyday life — into language (especially humor), physical appearance, family rituals, and recreation. Lack of privacy may be equated with trust. Family members may be shamed or made to feel guilty by one another when they try to exercise control over access to their own bodies, personal spaces, and possessions, or to claim privacy in the bathroom or bedroom. Family photograph albums or home movies may include sexual depictions; some families even make child pornography for home use or commercial sale. Variety in sexual behavior is common, including voyeurism, exhibitionism, group sex among family members. Family members may be encouraged to use sex as a medium of exchange with their social environment, for example, by becoming prostitutes. Unlike the other types of incest families, the pansexual family often may allow significant individuals outside the family to participate in its erotic activities — a hired farm hand, a favorite in-law, a live-in babysitter, a trusted family friend.

In erotic-based incest, the sexual contact may or may not include sexual intercourse, since much of the focus is on teasing and titillation that does not require consummation to have meaning and reinforcement value. Violence is seldom used to insure compliance, since family members are socialized into a pervasive erotic atmosphere. However, power/control struggles may exist just under the surface; subtle but strong pressure on individual family members makes participation difficult to resist.

A pansexual family may be able to maintain its secretive sexual behavior for a long time, partly because the incestuous pattern may not fit traditional criminal definitions or public stereotypes of sexual abuse (though this has begun to change as a result of some widely publicized cases in recent years). When the behavior becomes known to others, persuasive evidence may be lacking and family members may collude to prevent further exposure. Erotically based incest families may come to light in a variety of ways: inappropriate sexual behavior by younger family members at school, noticeable sexual acting-out in the community, extrafamilial sexual abuse by one of the family members, even by tracing neighborhood stories about the family.

As in affection-based incest, individual psychopathology is relatively rare among pansexual family members. However, there may be subclinical levels of certain personality traits typically designated as "characterological" or "antisocial." Sometimes, the integration of eroticism into family interaction patterns is so pervasive — and denial of it so well-established — that family members stop noticing the distinctly erotic character of their interactions and lose most of the anxiety that would normally accompany such socially deviant behavior. Nevertheless, the pansexual family often includes one or more members (particularly children) who are symptomatic—suicidal, anorectic, self-mutilating, even overtly psychotic.

Cynthia, an obese 27-year-old, is referred for therapy following hospitalization precipitated by a suicide attempt after a long history of depression. She describes her family as "sleazy," indicating that she grew up thinking of herself as "dirty." During an assessment interview, it becomes clear that virtually all aspects of Cynthia's childhood were sexualized. She remembers watching television with her parents and siblings, with everyone remarking frequently on women's "tits" and "asses." The dinner table was a regular time for the latest sexual joke from her father's office or her older brother's peer group. Throughout childhood, Cynthia was constantly criticized by both her parents for being too skinny or too fat (depending upon her age), always because "the boys won't like you if you look like that." Cynthia remembers her father frequently grabbing her mother's breasts and genitals through her clothes, often while commenting negatively on her small breasts. Cynthia's father regularly sat on the toilet in the family bathroom with the door open, reading his newspaper and talking to other family members. Cynthia's parents or her older brother always seemed to find an excuse to use the bathroom when she or her sister were in the shower. The children's pubertal development was a regular subject of conversation by family members. At times, it seemed to Cynthia as if everything had a sexual meaning.

Worst of all for the girls were their father's frequent visits to their bedroom at night, at which time he would often kiss each of them on the mouth and then touch their genitals with his fingers to "check for evidence" that they were "doing what you're not supposed to be doing." Cynthia relates that she and her sister once complained to their mother about this behavior, but she assured them that their father was "only teasing."

Aggression-Based Incest

Unable to express hostility in more appropriate ways, aggression-based incest families use sexualized anger to deal with their frustration and disappointment over various aspects of their lives. In this type of family, the perpetrator may deal angrily—even violently—with the victim, who may be only a scapegoat for the perpetrator's masked hostility toward another family member or toward someone in the outside world. For example, father-daughter incestuous contact may occur in connection with the perpetrator's wish to punish his wife for her lack of attention or erotic interest. Or an adolescent male may sexually exploit a younger sister in retaliation for what he perceives as rejection by his father, whom he believes shows intense favoritism toward the girls in the family while physically abusing the boys.

Although free-floating hostility is prevalent in this type of incestuous family, members typically feel powerless to have any kind of direct impact upon each other. Nevertheless, because he is part of a system character-ized by diffuse interpersonal boundaries, the perpetrator is often con-vinced that his victimizing actions will negatively affect the person(s) about whom he actually feels hostile. As a self-protective maneuver, the perpetrator usually chooses a very vulnerable member of the family as his victim; thus, his real intentions and motives are less likely to become known. This pattern helps to maintain the family rule that direct confron-tation and negotiation between conflicting members cannot occur. The intent to hurt someone via incestuous activity contrasts with the dynamics of affection-based and erotic-based incest, in which the behavior serves as a misguided effort at positive communication. The aggression-based incest dynamic creates an atmosphere that fosters individual psychopathology as well as serious distortions in family structure. Physical abuse may accom-pany the sexual abuse. Suicidal depression and various forms of self-destructive behavior often result, based upon the underlying lack of im-pulse control combined with a generalized fear of direct interpersonal conflict.

EXAMPLE

The oldest of four children, 17-year-old Karl is referred for treatment for sexually abusing two of his sisters, ages 14 and 16. He is a heavy user of marijuana and a poor student in school. Karl's father is a salesclerk who is a chronic alcoholic, verbally abusive to his wife, and hostile to and distant from his children. Karl and his father have had several fist fights since Karl became a teenager, usually when both have been drinking. Karl suspects that his father might have had sexual contact with his sisters because of the way he looks at them; however, he has no proof of such activity. Karl also reports that his parents have a great deal of conflict about their sexual relationship; he has often heard them fighting about it when his father is drunk.

When Karl was 14, he was anally raped by an older cousin and his friends. At the time, Karl didn't think of it as rape—it was just "horsing around." However, in therapy he can identify feelings of fear and pain. When asked what he was thinking about when having intercourse with his sisters, Karl indicates that his thoughts usually have been on his father. He has thought about how much he hates his father, and how pleased he is that he is taking his sisters away from his father, who seems to believe he "owns" all of the children. As therapy progresses, Karl recognizes he has learned from a variety of sources that sex and anger are linked; positive attachments with anyone have been impossible for him.

Rage-Based Incest

The final functional category of incestuous behavior is rooted in conspicuous individual psychopathology. Here, the perpetrator acts out his existential rage with one or more family members. Rather than conscious, focused anger, the behavior is a primitive expression of the shame/rage cycle arising out of longstanding frustration. Typically, the perpetrator's rage is rooted in his own long history as a victim of abuse, violence, or developmental crisis, producing an internal psychic structure characterized by continuous vigilance against threats to survival. In some instances, the rageful incest perpetrator is fueled by full-blown psychotic processes. As a result, some perpetrators directly manifest out-of-control rage, while others seem oddly detached from any affect at all. Sometimes, the abuse is impulsively explosive; other times, it is meticulously planned, carried out in a cold and calculating manner, and accompanied by earnest rationalizations. Occasionally, the explanations for the abuse are bizarre, as in the case of a father who physically beat and anally raped his young adolescent son, explaining that he needed to teach the boy "what he has to watch out for from those damn faggots." In rage-based incest, the sexual abuse and accompanying violence may be life-threatening.

If rage-based incestuous contact erupts suddenly, other family members — or the victim — may respond by reporting the event so that outsiders can intervene. In these instances, fear overrides family loyalty. If the abuse is planned and episodic, family members may conclude they have to "live with it," although defensive measures may be taken by at least some individuals, for example, a child who frequently stays overnight at the house of a friend. Sometimes, however, the rage of the perpetrator serves as a kind of organizing principle for the family; the system may structure itself around this rage as a source of power. Members' routine defenses may become part of the family's overall social script. Some family members may learn to take a generalized victim stance toward life; others may pride themselves on learning how to "con" the perpetrator in order to avoid victimization — a maneuver that can be utilized outside the family as well.

In summary, the rage-based incest family can contain an extremely pathological individual and may be one of the most dysfunctional of family systems. This type of incestuous family is most likely to both reflect and contribute to the individual psychopathology of its members. The functional adaptations that permit survival in such a family are usually at odds with the requirements of effective interpersonal relationships and healthy behavior patterns in the outside world.

EXAMPLE

Maria, age 16, is referred for therapy from the hospital that treated her severely lacerated arms and legs, wounds which were self-inflicted. Maria reports that she was not trying to kill herself when she cut her limbs with a razor blade, carefully missing major veins and arteries. Instead, she reveals that she could not tolerate her emotional turmoil any longer and needed to distract herself with physical pain. In the past, she only needed to cut herself once or twice, and she would feel less emotionally distraught. This time, things were different. This episode occurred after she regained consciousness, having been beaten and raped by her father. Maria reveals that she has been beaten and sexually molested by her father on a number of occasions; however, never before has she thought that he wanted to kill her. Maria reveals that, when she was younger, she was also beaten regularly by her mother for "allowing" her father to have sex with her.

THE PERPETRATOR/VICTIM
INTERACTION PATTERN

Public concern about various forms of violence and abuse in American homes has increased in the past decade. Numerous researchers (e.g., Figley, 1985; Finkelhor, 1984; Straus, Gelles, & Steinmetz, 1981) have been investigating what general family structures and/or what characteristics of particular families and/or what qualities of certain family members set the stage for domestic victimization and abuse. As the major social context for close interaction and the primary vehicle for child socialization, the family is a prominent influence in transmitting the social predispositions and psychological vulnerabilities that underlie victimization, as well as an arena in which violence and abuse can occur.

Power/Control Distortions

Both power and control are legitimate and important aspects of human experience. Neither of them should be seen as "bad," nor should they be thought of as opposites. Rather, they can be considered two sides of the same coin, meaningful because they are *different but related*. Their meaning arises, in part, out of the dialectical tension between them. A problem with power will always involve a problem with control; conversely, a problem with control will always involve a problem with power.

Excessive control in a relationship system leads to deprivation, that is, to limits on self-expression and/or meeting of personal needs. The reaction of a severely deprived individual (or group) is one of desperation. Therefore, situations characterized by control lacking sufficient power for balance are likely to create patterns of *deprivation/desperation*—loss of influence or access to resources for influence, in turn producing feelings of gloom, a sense of hopelessness, and, ultimately, despair. Excessive reliance on control can be one significant result of being victimized. Numerous abuse victims develop psychic defenses to guard against further intrusion into the self. However, without sufficient power of selfhood, these defenses often become self-defeating. The victim's attempt to consolidate all behavior around control produces an identity characterized by feelings of isolation accompanied by a sense of extreme vulnerability. In therapy, this "victim stance" is distinguished by what it can prevent rather than by what it can create. Self-efficacy is missing, an essential ingredient of healthy relationships.

EXAMPLE

Pamela is a 29-year-old woman referred after hospitalization for a psychotic episode. The precipitant for her hospitalization seems to have been her mother's death from cancer two months ago. Pamela was living and working a considerable distance from her parents when she got a call from her father asking her to come home and care for her mother. Pamela came home and took care of her mother for five months prior to her death. After the funeral, Pamela's defenses collapsed and she was unable to return to work. Brief hospitalization seems to have reinstated her coping mechanisms; however, Pamela believes she is still "too weak" to return to work.

Pamela presents for outpatient therapy appearing somewhat depressed but well-defended. Clearly, her self-esteem has been damaged, but for several months she rebuffs any attempts on the part of the therapist to help her value herself and act in her own interest. She dismisses all of her positive traits and accomplishments, arguing with the therapist that they are "worth nothing" and could be done "by anyone."

Eventually, Pamela reveals to the therapist a long history of physical abuse by her father and sexual abuse by her mother. She has never had any feelings about these events and claims they have not affected her in any adverse way because she is "determined not to let them." The therapist confronts Pamela about her noticeable weight loss, and the client admits to cycles of binging and purging since her mother's death.

When power dominates a relationship system, the stage is set for exploitation. In more extreme cases, one party may "overpower" another, violating boundaries in ways that can produce physical and/or psychological damage. Situations characterized by power without an appropriate balance of control often lead to patterns of *exploitation/violation*—the capacity and willingness to use coercion or force to achieve one individual's (or group's) goals at the expense of another. Some children who grow up in sexually abusive families may rapidly develop a power-oriented, exploitive behavior pattern in response to their own victimization. Instead of attempting compensatory overcontrol, they give up (self) control and begin to abuse others; that is, they begin to be perpetrators. Though this response is most often found among abused males, it occurs among females as well, including those who continue to be victimized in their families.

EXAMPLE

Fifteen-year-old Sarah is referred for therapy following a complaint that was filed against her by the parents of a child she fondled while babysitting. The parents and the child protection agency have agreed to defer prosecution if Sarah will go to therapy and to drop charges altogether if she successfully completes treatment. After talking with Sarah's mother about the situation, the therapist decides to ask Sarah's entire family to attend the initial session.

In taking a family history with all members present, the therapist learns that Sarah has an older half-brother from her mother's first marriage. This boy is described as a severe behavior problem throughout his childhood and adolescence, and Sarah's parents state that he "psychologically tortured" Sarah for a number of years before he left to move in with his father. Sarah's mother embarrassedly comments that she think that Sarah is sometimes verbally and physically abusive with her brother, three years younger.

In an individual interview following the family assessment, Sarah acknowledges that she was also sexually molested by her older brother but has never told her parents. Further, she admits that sometimes she intentionally hits or kicks her younger brother in the genitals.

Since power/control is a single construct reflecting reciprocal systemic dynamics, the distortions of deprivation/desperation and exploitation/violation often merge into a complex and dangerous scenario: *the perpetrator/ victim interaction pattern.* This term refers to a negative transactional process that tends to be self-perpetuating in the context of an ongoing close relationship. Most simply stated, individuals are victimized when they are in control of something that is desired by other individuals who are willing and able to overpower the victims to obtain what they want. Insofar as the perpetrators fail to obtain what they desire from others, they are likely to escalate their use of power and to have less and less self-control. Similarly, insofar as victims are overpowered and forced to give up what they control, they are likely to try harder to regain control, thereby triggering further efforts to overpower them. The longer it continues, the more skewed the perpetrator/victim interaction pattern becomes. When the perpetrator/ victim interaction sequence occurs repetitively over time, it is commonly referred to as a "cycle of abuse" (Bentovim, 1992; Gelles, 1987; Hunter & Kilstrom, 1979; James & Nasjleti, 1983).

Maintaining the Cycle of Abuse

Behaviors and consequences associated with the abuse cycle have come to public attention in a variety of ways, most dramatically in connection with battered wives and children (Gibbs, 1993; Greenspon, 1993; Kaminer, 1994; Mason, 1991; Quindlen, 1993; Thomas, 1994). There appear to be strong similarities in the perpetrator/victim interaction patterns of physical and sexual abuse. However, we believe that the mechanisms of power/control imbalance that work to *maintain* the cycle of abuse between individuals in ongoing relationships are still not well understood. When perpetrator/victim patterns operate in ongoing relationships, the behaviors of those involved appear to reflect a kind of "higher order" equilibrium, despite the obvious power/control misbalances. The capacity of a perpetrator to intimidate through power becomes very controlling, while the overcontrolled helplessness of a victim can be extremely powerful. Perhaps the well-documented resistance to change of *both* perpetrators and victims is rooted in the relative stability of this internalized interaction pattern. Similarly, the characteristics of larger social systems that support perpetrator/victim interaction patterns are reflected in the persistence of abuse in certain kinds of relationships and in certain kinds of settings (Bentovim, 1991, 1992; Finkelhor et al., 1983; Grauerholz & Koralewski, 1991; Jenkins, 1990; McCarthy & Byrne, 1988; Straus, 1980; Walters, 1975).

Clinical evidence has shown that individuals, and even entire families, can organize their identities around victimization experiences so thoroughly that they carry with them a propensity for replicating perpetrator/victim interaction patterns in many aspects of their lives and relationships. The pattern becomes familiar enough to provide a certain kind of security in coping with the contingencies of life. Evidence of this can be found among physically abused children who want to remain in close proximity to their violent parent(s) as well as among battered wives who return to their husbands following a beating. In addition, an individual trapped in the abuse cycle may now be able to play the role of *either* victim *or* perpetrator. Therein lies a potential trap for those who wish to intervene into the perpetrator/victim interaction sequence without sufficient awareness of the ambivalence felt by all participants in the system regarding being "rescued."

DOUBLE BINDS IN THE
INCESTUOUS FAMILY

Together, significant boundary disturbances and perpetrator/victim interaction patterns produce "double bind" transactional structures in the sexually abusive family system. These are most prominent in the area of distance regulation, reflecting damage both to family members' ability to separate and to their ability to connect (Flaherty, 1991). The result is a deep-seated ambivalence with regard to proximity and distance that characterizes all family members to some degree and is a major structural contributor to incestuous contact (McCarthy & Byrne, 1988). This may

explain some of the disagreements that can occur among various professionals working with the same incest family; in addition to their own
subjective biases, they may be seeing different qualities of the family or of
individual members. One worker might believe that family members are
being open and cooperative, while another concludes that they are secretive and resistant. Just as action and meaning are recursively related in all
family systems, the beliefs, attitudes, and emotions of incest family members are enacted in transactional sequences that are often confusing and
dysfunctional. By definition, family members cannot resolve the double
binds without restructuring the fundamental beliefs upon which they are
premised, and the incestuous behavior is a continuous reinforcement of
these beliefs at the same time that it is an expression of the family's
dysfunction.

Damage in the Ability to Separate

Both clinicians and researchers have frequently noted that incestuous
families are characterized by "enmeshment" (Alexander, 1985; Fredrich,
1990; Larson, 1980; MacFarlane & Waterman, 1986; Trepper & Barrett,
1989). Operationally defined as a lack of interpersonal boundaries and
resulting emotional overinvolvement, enmeshment makes erotic contact
between family members a possibility; therefore, it is one of the vulnerability factors to be evaluated when assessing family dynamics. Within enmeshed family structures, appropriate sequences of self-differentiation
and development are all but impossible. As a result, some family members
may begin to distinguish themselves as individuals through psychological
and/or physical symptoms (such as bulimia, psychotic episodes, or suicidal
depression) in an attempt to escape their suffocating circumstances. Following are some of the double binds reflecting enmeshment.

1. *Independent identity and action are experienced as disloyal.* No individual in an incestuous family can become too autonomous without risk of
the abuse coming to light, within or outside of the family. Thinking or
feeling differently than other family members is discouraged through ridicule or active censure. Often, there are sanctions against trying to behave
independently. Efforts to develop significant relationships outside of the
immediate or extended family are often suspect. For example, an adolescent may be forced to have sexual contact with her father as if she were an
adult while being prevented by him from engaging in certain social or
extracurricular school activities with her peers because she is "too young."

EXAMPLE

Seven-year-old Maya is "her father's pride and joy," receiving much
more attention from him than do either of her younger brothers. She
appears enthusiastic and engaging, with a quick wit and a challenging

personality. Maya is also unconventional; she loves to wear unmatched socks and shoes and to dress in outrageous costumes. Her father reports that he and his wife engage in endless battles over Maya's eccentric tastes and behavior. Sometime in the past, they arrived at an agreement that he would take responsibility for Maya if he wanted her to dress and behave in a manner befitting his image of the family of a successful corporate attorney. Thereafter, he began to groom and dress Maya each day, choosing her clothes, styling her hair, giving her a bath each evening before bedtime. During these times in the bathroom each evening, Maya's father began sexually molesting her. Maya then resisted his attempts to groom her, both sexually and in appearance. She became more disheveled and more rebellious than ever, eventually complaining enough to her mother about the bathing routine that the incest came to light.

2. *Setting boundaries is seen as an act of defiance.* One of the most fundamental boundaries in human experience is the capacity to refuse. Saying "no" is considered a hallmark of development in young children, as they gain an increased sense of control over themselves and their world when they first acquire language as toddlers. Gradually, young children learn to limit the influence of their previously all-powerful parents, becoming more independent in the process. In incestuous families, however, setting boundaries is equivalent to rejection, for it is perceived as a significant threat to any family member's need for nurturance and support. In addition, refusing to participate in a particular activity may be an attempt by weaker members to gain more control, or it may be a form of punishment used by those who are more powerful.

EXAMPLE

Kimberly, the youngest of five children from a rural farm family, has always resented her father's intrusiveness into her privacy. For years, he would come into the bathroom when she and her two sisters were using the toilet and into their bedroom when they were dressing for school or getting ready for bed. At 15, Kimberly could no longer tolerate her father's behavior. With support from her sisters (who were no longer living at home), Kimberly decided to set a limit the next time her father appeared in the bathroom or bedroom at an inappropriate time. One evening he entered her bedroom while she was undressing, and she told him to leave. Immediately, her father flew into a rage, tearing off Kimberly's nightgown and beating her nearly unconscious. Kimberly is the first of his daughters to actively defend her boundaries with her father, and her defiance was met with escalating abuse.

3. *Individual identity requires compliance with others.* The struggle for autonomy is usually associated with identity development (Erikson, 1959,

1964). In incestuous families, boundary disturbances require that personal identity coalesce around the expectations of other family members, particularly the most powerful male(s). While typical adolescent attempts to be distinctive in appearance, dress, and behavior are not always welcomed by parents, they are tolerated in families that function effectively, and respectful dialogue between the generations is possible. Intergenerational and interpersonal boundary diffusion in abusive families make it difficult to be unique, resulting in a loss of individual strengths and resources. As a consequence of the frequent repetition of perpetrator/victim interaction sequences, children in an incestuous family may fail to develop the necessary inner core of selfhood required for effective functioning in the world. In extreme cases, a "pseudo-identity" may develop, ranging from trauma-based narcissism to dissociative personality to obsessive workaholism.

EXAMPLE

Patrice is the oldest child in a family of three girls. Her mother was pregnant with Patrice when she married, and Patrice believes that her mother is ashamed of her and has always favored her younger sisters, who were both planned children. Patrice's strategy for dealing with this perceived rejection has been to struggle to gain her mother's approval by being a good student, helpful at home, and dutiful in every way—but to no avail. When Patrice was 10, her parents divorced, and Patrice increased her efforts to be hard-working and supportive even though she felt depressed at the loss of contact with her father.

Patrice reports that her mother has always taken great interest in Patrice's personal hygiene and elimination behavior. Patrice had twice-weekly enemas administered by her mother from age 2 to age 12 (when she began her menstrual periods). When Patrice was 10, her mother forcibly inserted a tampon into her vagina; thereafter, Patrice was required to painfully "practice" inserting tampons, with her mother's assistance, until she began menstruating, at which point her mother introduced her to douching. Now 13, Patrice has been hospitalized following a suicide attempt by overdosing on her mother's antidepressant medications. Her explanation is that she can no longer pretend to be happy, which is contributing to her mother's depression; therefore, Patrice believes that things would be better for her mother and sisters if she did not exist.

4. *Survival is threatened both inside and outside the family.* Central to surviving within many abusive families is the paradoxical belief that an individual member cannot survive without the family. While life inside the family may be difficult, even traumatic, life outside the family is portrayed as even more dangerous. Given family members' lack of internalized identities and the family's emotional deficits, the message of threat in the outer world is easy to perpetuate. Sometimes, this social isolation can take the

form of serious psychophysiological disorders which prevent children from attending school or adults from working. Members of some incest families have been known to become suicidal when they move away from home or when another family member falls ill or dies.

Bruce, age 9, is the second child from his mother's second marriage. Intelligent, musically talented, and obedient, he appears to be the favorite of his mother's three children. Upon entering the third grade, Bruce began developing stomach pains of such severity that he could not go to school. Medical tests found nothing wrong. However, a school counselor discovered that Bruce's digestive disturbances and school absences coincided with the separation of his mother and father. The children spend every other weekend with their father. Paradoxically, Bruce often worries aloud about how his father is doing living alone, while at the same time often misses the visits due to his severe stomach pains. A family history obtained by the therapist seeing Bruce and his mother reveals that Bruce's grandmother had committed suicide shortly after she divorced her husband for sexually abusing their daughter (Bruce's mother). The therapist begins to wonder about the possibility of Bruce being sexually abused by his father.

5. *Self-sacrifice may be the only effective way to gain love.* Members of sexually abusive families are typically starved for love, but are also prohibited from giving or receiving it. Any family member—victim or perpetrator or even someone uninvolved in actual incestuous contact—may come to rely upon victim-like behaviors to gain recognition and acceptance. Simultaneously, members may exploit each other in efforts to sabotage support that they cannot get for themselves. Some incestuous families have been compared by their therapists to groups of toddler-age children whose operating principle seems to be that "negative attention is better than no attention at all." These underlying dynamics may help explain the high suicide risk among members of incestuous families, as well as the incidence of self-mutilating behaviors among young incest victims and adult survivors.

Norma is a 23-year-old single woman suffering from severe anorexia/bulimia who currently weighs only 89 pounds. She has been hospitalized in half a dozen different eating-disorder treatment programs, often for months at a time. Approaches to treatment have ranged from supportive group therapy to behavior modification to art therapy; at times she has had to be put in restraints and force-fed. Currently, Norma is not in a treatment program, and contends she will never, ever go back into the hospital, although she is willing to come to outpatient therapy.

In giving her history, Norma reports growing up in a family in which she and her four siblings essentially raised themselves, with almost no attention from either of their parents for any reason. Norma also reports being physically tortured and sexually molested by her older brother, but her complaints to her parents brought no response. Two of Norma's three siblings have committed suicide, and Norma believes that she will be next. She continually tries to get her parents involved somehow in her life, including inviting them to attend therapy with her; however, they have refused to do anything more than to pay for her hospitalizations. Norma seems willing to die in her attempts to be loved by her parents.

Damage in the Ability to Connect

The characteristics that impede incest family members' interpersonal connections are less widely discussed than those involved in enmeshment. However, the damage to connection is equally problematic and creates its own array of double binds.

1. *People who love and trust each other are expected to hurt one another.* Most incest family members come to believe that abusive patterns of interaction (though not necessarily sexual abuse) are "normal." The family develops an increased tolerance for various forms of hurtful behavior, including shaming, destructive criticism, disrespect, judgmental blaming, and even violence. Both active and passive forms of aggression are common. When these behaviors take place within a contradictory framework that contends, "We are a close family, and we love each other," a powerful double bind results.

EXAMPLE

Lila is the mother of three children, ages 7 to 14. Her husband, Eugene, was a successful local politician, considered charming and charismatic. Recently, Lila's oldest son told a school counselor that he was being sexually molested by his father. Protection authorities were notified, an investigation confirmed the charges, and Eugene was prosecuted. He is currently in a half-way house for treatment some distance from home. Lila has been horrified by the entire series of events; however, she is determined to keep the family going and to make an effort to deal with the problems in their marriage.

In the course of their couple therapy, Lila has confronted Eugene about the sexual abuse and his responsibility for avoiding their sexual problems and exploiting their son. Eugene's response is to get angry and verbally abusive; however, when the therapist points out what is happening, both

Lila and Eugene explain these are just signs of his "normal temper," and that his references to her as a "bitch" and a "cunt" are not really intended to hurt her. Both husband and wife maintain that his expressions are indications of how comfortable they are with each other, and the verbal explosions give Eugene a chance to "vent his emotions" in a way he can't afford to do in his highly visible political position.

2. *Setting boundaries with each other is an act of rejection.* Depriving family members of the right to set boundaries equates every "no" with personal rejection. Limiting access to oneself or one's property is experienced as withholding because the pervasive boundary diffusion translates most attempts at privacy and self-assertive behavior into negative messages to other family members, which are then interpreted as "You don't love me." Thus, the fundamental ethic of closeness and love among family members is continuously contradicted by feelings of isolation and loneliness.

EXAMPLE

Eartha has come for counseling to a local family service agency. She is a young mother of two preadolescent girls, both of whom she suspects have been sexually molested by her current live-in partner, Al. However, she does not want him reported, because she is "not really sure." In telling her story, Eartha discloses that Al consumes a significant amount of alcohol on a daily basis. She also reports that he wants her to be with him every moment when she is at home; often, she feels bored, and sometimes even suffocated, by his attention to her. Eartha complains that Al is no longer a good lover; she has lost interest in sex with him, and they do a lot of fighting as a result. Their poor sexual relationship is one reason why she thinks he has been molesting the children. Eartha also believes that Al is stealing money from her purse to buy drugs. Further, he often arrives unexpectedly at the discount store where Eartha works and pesters her for money to take the children to a movie or amusement park or to eat out. Eartha admits she is stressed and unhappy with her relationship, but is afraid to put limits on Al out of fear that he will leave her.

3. *Honesty and openness create pain, and empathy is to be exploited.* Within a framework of expectations that all personal thoughts, feelings, and experiences of every family member should be continuously available to others in the family, honesty and openness become dangerous. In the context of insufficient emotional resources, actual empathy is seen as a sign of weakness and vulnerability. More typical feelings of attachment and love become increasingly distorted by perpetrator/victim interaction patterns, resulting in more pain and compensatory attempts at pseudo-

openness. As family members lose or fail to develop a sense of personal identity over time, the futility of expressions of empathy and support becomes a self-fulfilling prophecy.

Twelve-year-old Sonja has been sleeping in her father's bed for four years. She reports that her mother has always had a problem with insomnia, complaining that she is unable to sleep when anyone else is in the room and becoming "frantic" and "crazy" over sleep loss. Sonja's father, on the other hand, claims that he cannot and will not sleep alone. When she was just a young child, Sonja often heard her parents fighting about this, with her father threatening to leave the marriage if his wife would not sleep with him.

One night when Sonja was 8, her mother asked if she would sleep next to her father so the mother could get a good night's sleep. Fearing another fight between them, Sonja agreed, and she has continued to sleep with her father ever since without complaining. This established pattern was interrupted by a suicide attempt on Sonja's part and her subsequent hospitalization, during which she revealed that during the night her father has been fondling her breasts and genitals.

4. *Being dependent is dangerous.* As previously described, weakness in the sexually abusive family is often an invitation to exploitation. The ethic of family closeness is accompanied by a growing recognition that to be needy is to risk being manipulated and abused. Together, these create one of the most powerful of double binds for all incest family members. Directly asking for help, either inside or outside the family, becomes so risky that symptomatic or self-destructive behaviors may develop as an indirect expression of unmet dependency needs.

Francis is a single mother of five children, one of whom has been accused of sexually abusing his younger sister. In a family therapy session, Francis is asked by the therapist if she had noticed any changes in her 13-year-old daughter's behavior that might have been a clue to the molestation by her 17-year-old brother. After several moments of thought, Francis replies that her daughter occasionally jumps to the ground from her second-story bedroom window, once injuring herself sufficiently that she was hospitalized with some broken bones in her feet. Another time, she sprained her ankle and was sent to live with her grandmother while she recuperated. Questioned further, Francis recalls that, on four different occasions, the same daughter has admitted using a combination of liquor and medications to make herself ill so that she did not have to go to school.

However, Francis has interpreted all of these instances simply as rebellious attempts to gain more freedom as the girl neared adolescence.

5. *Sexual feelings are associated with fear, hurt, anger, and power/control conflicts.* When developmentally inappropriate sexual activities are introduced into the lives of children, they learn to associate negative or conflicting emotions with sexual expression. Under the guise of intimacy, closeness, and love, perpetrators and victims are involved in transactions that reflect confusion, fear, pain, and anger. Unable to escape these powerful conflicting emotions, victims may be traumatized or may retreat into symptomatic behavior. The contradictions of loving words with physical pain or of physical pleasure with feelings of fear and anger create internalized double binds that can impair personal functioning and relationships for a lifetime. Simultaneously, these same internalized paradoxes help explain why a number of incest survivors may replicate abusive patterns in their adult relationships or may derive pleasure from physical and emotional pain during sexual encounters, even when their actions result in powerful feelings of shame.

EXAMPLE

Kathy, a 28-year-old secretary, seeks sex therapy to deal with what she calls her "sexual shame." During the initial interview, Kathy reveals that she can become sexually aroused only when her partner pinches her labia and nipples quite hard, or spanks her until her buttocks feel hot. With great embarrassment, Kathy explains that she has found these activities pleasurable for as long as she can remember; recently, however, the pressure required for her to feel pleasure is so great that her nipples and labia are bruised, and both she and her partner are becoming concerned.

When a sexual history is taken, Kathy reluctantly admits that she was sexually molested by her older brother from age 11 to age 14. Her brother would squeeze her developing breasts or massage her buttocks while he masturbated by rubbing against her until he ejaculated. He threatened to "beat her bloody" if she ever told anyone about the abuse, and she has kept silent until now.

Taken together, these double bind patterns in the connecting and differentiating capacities of incest families contribute to self-perpetuating intrapsychic structures which can maintain the potential for abuse in the lives of individual family members and even transmit this potential down through succeeding generations in the family. This has important implications for intervention into the sexually abusive family system, since it is through the filters of these double bind patterns that all interventions into the family—*including therapy*—are experienced. At best, every family member, including a child victim, will be somewhat ambivalent about being "helped" by outsiders. Similarly, family members in treatment will continue to experience a variety of double binds with each other and with outsiders and will frequently behave in ways that create parallel double binds for those who intervene.

OVERVIEW: THE GOALS
OF FAMILY TREATMENT

Professionals who work with incestuous families should be able to help family members work toward positive expressions of sexuality as well as to avoid sexual abuse. Too often, negative issues occupy full attention, and the articulation of positive objectives for sexual expression is avoided because of the anticipated complications of value conflicts. The ecological perspective described in Chapter 3 represents an attempt to generate process-oriented principles that can guide family members toward sexually healthy forms of interaction. These principles can be used as a basis for devising effective intervention strategies.

The temptation for clinicians dealing with their own ambivalence about sexuality is to become either laissez-faire with regard to sexual behavior — do whatever feels good, everyone is free to do his/her own thing — or moralistic in dictating to clients how they should behave sexually. The former may occur unnoticed in treatment due to the implicit ethic of neutrality that has come to characterize the professional identity of many therapists. The latter can happen in a direct and open fashion, or unwittingly, by continuing to find things for the individual or family to work on in therapy, without ever recognizing it as an attempt to shape clients into a particular value-laden image of the "ideal" family.

The overall goal of treatment should reflect ecological balancing, which is more comprehensive than preventing a recurrence of abuse but more modest than curing all of the ills of a perpetrator or victim. Within the ecological framework we have presented, balancing is understood as an ongoing transformational process directed toward ecosystemic survival. From this perspective, judgments of family viability ultimately can be made only by comprehensively investigating the family's ecology: (a) the individual identities of family members, (b) their transactional patterns, (c) the organization of the family as a unit, and (d) the place of the family in its cultural and historical context.

CONCLUSION

In this chapter, we have discussed difficulties in the sexual dimension of family life — particularly the results of power/control imbalances between the genders and erotic meaning-distortions among all family members—that can set the stage for intrafamilial sexual abuse. Further, we have examined ways in which these difficulties can result in the development of a perpetrator/victim interaction pattern, which is expressed outwardly in family transactions and is internalized by family members such that it comes to influence their overall experience of the world. Fostering positive family interaction, which will counteract abuse, requires balancing power/control dynamics among family members and facilitating appropriate boundary-setting so that members can experience their individual and collective sexuality in positive ways.

CHAPTER 5

The Revelation of Incest

*When pain has been intertwined with love and closeness,
it's very difficult to believe that love and closeness can be
experienced without pain.*

— Gloria Steinem (1992)

A S EVENTS OF THE PAST DECADE have amply demonstrated, merely identifying victims of sexual abuse often requires monumental effort and
leads to unanticipated or controversial outcomes. On the one hand, inves-
tigators of child sexual abuse must overcome the inertia of a society unwilling and ill-equipped to acknowledge the extent of sexual exploitation of its
children. On the other hand, the dynamics of a highly technologized,
communications-oriented culture have "popularized" child sexual abuse to
such an extent that a public backlash has begun to challenge its nature
and extent. This chapter examines the experience of revealing incestuous
abuse and suggests guidelines for responding to the revelation.

THE ISSUE OF TRUTH
IN INCEST REPORTING

Questions about accuracy in reporting childhood sexual abuse have
come to public attention once again, this time in the dramatic controversy
over "false memory syndrome" now being debated by mental health and
legal professionals throughout North America and abroad (e.g., Ceci &
Bruck, 1993, 1994; Doris, 1991; Feldman-Summers & Pope, 1994; Gardner, 1992; Hagons, 1991; Howitt, 1992; Kutchinsky, 1992b, 1994; Loftus,
1993; Vizard & Tranter, 1988; Wexler, 1990; Yapko, 1994). One professional (Barden, 1994) working at the interface between the mental health
and legal professions has labeled the debate over recovered memory therapy "the psychotherapy-legal issue of the century." However, a number of

writers (e.g., Hedges, 1994; Masson, 1984; Yapko, 1994) have pointed out
that these issues are not new; they date back to the time of Freud and to
ideas and controversies that shaped the earliest history of psychotherapy.
They were not resolved definitively then, and, in light of new knowledge
about human cognition and memory, they appear even more complicated
now (Ceci & Bruck, 1994; Fincham et al., 1994a, 1994b; Goodman &
Bottoms, 1993; Goodman, Rudy, Bottoms, & Aman, 1990; Loftus, 1993;
Pezdek, 1994). The complexity of the connections between childhood
experience and adult behavior, as well as questions about the influence of
traumatic childhood events on various forms of adult psychopathology,
have profound implications for the work of professionals in a variety of
fields. Further, dealing with the aftermath of various forms of child abuse
from both legal and mental health perspectives has begun to force realignments of professionals in these fields and may very well alter the nature of
their interaction in the future—something we believe would be positive
for both professions.[1]

   In this chapter, we are concerned with the experiences of children
within their families; therefore, we shall discuss briefly questions about
the reliability of children as reporters of abuse and circumstances that
might lead them to be untruthful about abuse or to be susceptible to
suggestions from others that abuse has taken place when it has not. A
variety of recent books have examined these issues in great detail (e.g.,
Doris, 1991; Gardner, 1992; Gelles & Loseke, 1993; Goodman & Bottoms,
1993; Howitt, 1992; Nicholson, 1988; Zaragoza, Graham, Hall, Hirschman,
& Ben-Porath, 1995). In this chapter, we highlight only the principles
that are most important to understanding and treating families in which
incestuous contact appears to have occurred.

   Identifying the issue of accuracy of children's reports of incestuous
contact primarily as "telling the truth" versus "lying" about sexual abuse is
a vast oversimplification. Similarly, debating adult or childhood memories
of sexual abuse as either "true" or "false" misleadingly suggests that human
memory operates like a video camera that either is working properly or is
broken. These artificial dichotomies place an unnecessary burden upon
everyone concerned, particularly upon a child who reports abuse. More
important, the reality of human experience is ignored: Truth is never
totally "objective," but always comes in versions. No individual—adult or
child—imparts complete truth when recounting an experience. Rendering
an experience to others is always and necessarily an *interpretation* of that
experience, based upon both the circumstances of the experience being
recalled and the current circumstances under which it is being reported to
others. Therefore, it seems more useful to frame the issue as follows: *What*

---

[1]We examine these issues in greater detail in Chapter 11 and in our book *Child Sexual Abuse:
An Ecological Approach to Treating Victims and Perpetrators*, where the focus is on working
with adults who were sexually abused as children.

are the factors that influence the ways in which sexual abuse is described by children, and how are such descriptions to be understood when they are reported to others?

Sexual abuse reporting by children has begun to be explored from this phenomenological perspective. Some writers have focused on matters of children's cognitive development, language ability, and suggestibility (e.g., Ceci & Bruck, 1994; de Young, 1986; Loftus, 1993; Loftus & Davies, 1984; Siegel, 1991; Zaragoza et al., 1995). Others have emphasized the practical problems of interviewing children in emotionally stressful circumstances such as court hearings (e.g., Friedrich, 1990; Goodman, 1984; Vizard & Tranter, 1988). Still others have examined the dynamics of psychosexual development and resultant influences on children's representations of their sexual experiences (e.g., Constantine & Martinson, 1981; Finkelhor, 1984). To date, only a few writers have explored the impact of abuse experiences on children's reporting and testifying behavior (cf. Burgess, Holmstrom & Sgroi, 1978; Feldman-Summers & Pope, 1994; Finkelhor & Browne, 1985; Kendall-Tackett, Williams & Finkelhor, 1993). Best known in this regard are probably Summit's (1983) elaboration of a "child sexual abuse accommodation syndrome" and Gardner's (1987, 1992) discussions of a "parental alienation syndrome."

Experiencing and Constructing Reality

Life consists of experiences — an ongoing flow of transactions between a living organism and the environment. Two physiological mechanisms — a complex sensory system and an organizing brain — permit humans to construct "maps," or models, of their world. Therefore, *humans simultaneously perceive and create their experiences*. Experiences are "registered" through the senses, organized into some sort of meaningful, recognizable units, and somehow incorporated into what has come to be called "memory." This process of constructing reality apparently begins prenatally. Internalized meanings from past experience serve as a basis for present behavior. What is retained in an individual's memory is not the totality of a particular experience — one cannot go back and "have" one's tenth birthday over again — but some sort of organized neurochemical structure that reflects the impact of the experience upon the individual. Considerable progress has been made in recent research on brain function (e.g., Brown, 1991; Gazzaniga, 1985; Kinsbourne, 1982; Maturana & Varela, 1987; Popper & Eccles, 1977). While many details are not fully understood, it is clear that human thought processes are heavily influenced by the structure of the central nervous system itself, by the accumulated impact of life experiences, and by the current context of the acts of thinking and languaging. Every life event influences one's model of the world, transforming it into something new while building upon what is already present (Edwards, 1979; Kolb, 1984). However, memory is selective, influenced by a variety of factors, such as one's motivation to notice and remember, one's expectations in a particular situation, one's personality and style of dealing with life experiences, as well as various components of the situation in which one remembers and relates these memories to others (Loftus, 1993; Yapko, 1994).

Further complicating the process is the fact that an individual who is having a particular experience is involved in mapping it from the "inside," that is, constructing a personal theory to explain the experience (Gazzaniga, 1985). The experience this individual represents will be subjective in that it will never correspond exactly to a rendering of the same event by another individual—or even by the same individual on a subsequent occasion. Thus, two or more individuals involved in the same situation are actually having two *different* experiences in which each is outside the experience of the other to some degree, and neither is totally objective. However, these individuals can compare their experiences verbally—they are actually comparing their internal models of experience—in order to arrive at some kind of agreement about what has transpired. Of course, human language itself is an imperfect vehicle for rendering one's experience. Language is already at least two steps removed from the immediacy of lived experience itself; it is a verbal rendering of an internally coded representation of a sensory perception.

Further, language and cognitive representation may be more independent of each other than previously recognized. Information influencing the interpretation of experience may exist in the brain without being accessible to language; therefore, the information is unable to be shared in a direct way (Brown, 1991; Gazzaniga, 1985; Maturana & Varela, 1987). Nearly everyone at some time has difficulty finding the right words to express the essence of a particular experience. Yet communication, both verbal and nonverbal, is the only way that humans have of sharing their experiences with each other, thereby achieving some degree of mutual understanding. Through communication about their experience, humans construct a meaningful social world. Sharing experience leads to overlapping models of the world, or shared meanings, which are the basis for interactions (Gendlin, 1962; Kolb, 1984; LaRossa & Reitzes, 1993; Nelson, 1985; Osborne, 1981). That is, a certain group of individuals agree to behave as if a particular shared map of reality were objectively true. Some such maps of the world may be widely shared, for example, certain scientific principles. Other human representations are shared by particular groups of individuals, such as religious beliefs. Still other representations are highly idiosyncratic, for example, the conviction of two individuals that they are in love. Idiosyncratic maps of the world that vary too greatly from social consensus or that violate agreed upon versions of reality can result in some persons being socially isolated, censured, or considered "crazy."

A representational map is continuously transformed by shared social experiences. Every individual's model of the world is in dialogue with the models of others, challenging and being challenged, in an effort to achieve consensus. Everyone's map of the world has a taken-for-granted quality until it is challenged. The individual simply assumes that things *are* the way she/he experiences them based upon the internal organization of the brain's representations. In the everyday world, these are referred to as "biases" and "habits" — automatic ways of thinking and behaving. The only way that humans come to know anything at all is when some kind of a difference is introduced into their experience from the world outside, thus transforming their representations of the world and leading them to change their behavior in some fashion (Bateson, 1972, 1979; Kolb, 1984). This *continuous* reconstruction of a working reality is "learning," a process that takes place outside of awareness as well as through conscious effort. Clearly, the reconstruction process is open to input from a variety of sources, including factors in the present context that influence the recall of experiences that supposedly occurred in the past (Brown, 1991; Ceci & Bruck, 1993; Gardner, 1992; Yapko, 1994). Even under the most ideal conditions, individuals reach adulthood with cognitive and emotional "baggage" which is not well-suited to certain life experiences and must be relearned in laborious and sometimes painful ways.

The Motivation to Lie

Probably all children sometimes lie to adults (just as adults sometimes lie to each other). For a variety of reasons, children may consciously omit, distort, or add to their descriptions of their experience when recounting them to their parents or others. Children may tell lies to make themselves look good, to avoid getting into trouble, to express anger, or inflict revenge, or for a wide variety of other reasons in particular situations. Honesty as a moral trait has been found to be associated with a variety of developmental and situational variables (Kohlberg, 1976; Rest, 1986).

At the same time, it is important to recognize that the majority of children are *not* lying when they report or describe being sexually abused by an adult. Believability should be the basic stance adopted by professionals to whom children report sexual abuse. The therapist's primary working hypothesis in response to a description of incestuous sexual contact should not be "This child is probably lying." Nevertheless, an investigation of reported sexual abuse ought to proceed from the standpoint of obtaining a comprehensive assessment of the child's report within the context of the family and larger community (Fincham et al., 1994a, 1994b; Robins, 1992). Similarly, a therapist ought to place a child's report of sexual abuse into a context of meaning that includes the possibility that the child may be motivated to lie or distort his/her experiences based upon particular family dynamics or situational circumstances.

Conscious lying about the occurrence of incestuous abuse has been found to be associated most often with some aspect of "parental alienation syndrome" (Gardner, 1992), particularly in connection with separated or divorced parents of younger children or with power/control struggles between parents and teenagers. In each of these situations, a child or adolescent may have discovered that she can accomplish certain objectives by charging a parent, sibling, or other relative with sexual abuse, even if such a charge is later refuted. In the case of divorce, the actual reporting of abuse is frequently done by a parent following descriptions of certain situations with the other parent by their child. In these instances, the charges — if they are untrue — may be more a matter of the child's suggestibility to parental concerns than of lying per se, although children have been known to "go along" with charges of sexual abuse by one parent against the other when they were quite aware that the behavior being reported had not actually occurred.

For reasons that will discussed in the remainder of this chapter, we believe that a child's report of incestuous sexual contact inevitably will contain elements of ambiguity and distortion based upon the internalized conflicts of the child in relation to the family. In other words, we are convinced that *all* children who describe or report sexual abuse within the family may be tempted to lie, or at least to shade the truth in some fashion. This might involve covering up abuse that has actually occurred in order to protect their families, distorting some of their descriptions of the sexual activity in order to protect themselves, or embellishing a story about supposed abuse in order to accomplish particular objectives of their own. The therapist dealing with a reported incest situation ought to anticipate this dynamic and be prepared to deal with it. We believe that effective intervention and treatment of incest must strike a balance by creating an atmosphere of safety for the alleged victim and her family (which will encourage her to be truthful) along with an aura of appropriate openness and uncertainty (in which the child's report can be thoroughly explored and even challenged). Whole family assessments help make this possible (see Chapters 6 and 7).

The Question of Suggestibility

All human beings are "suggestible" if by the term we mean that they are capable of being led — or misled — toward certain ideas or beliefs (Doris, 1991; Yapko, 1994). Based upon their level of cognitive development as well as their life circumstances of dependence upon adult authority figures, children may be particularly susceptible to suggestions or pressures to believe certain things, and even to doubt the validity of their own experiences. Indeed, this sort of suggestibility is precisely what may make possible the sexual seduction of a child without the presence of direct coercion or force. As we have indicated, much of the affectionally based and erotically based sexual abuse of children relies upon subtle cognitive distortions and persuasive explanations that betray a child's trust by altering the nature of her experience and understanding of sexual contact with a perpetrator.

These same psychological processes can operate to lead children gradually to an understanding that they have been sexually abused. If children can be persuaded to understand and take action to prevent abuse or to report abuse if it occurs, then these processes have been utilized in a positive way for preventive education. However, if these processes occur when sexual contact has not taken place, then children may "falsely" report abuse, or, in the presence of certain adults, be persuaded to agree that something has transpired in their experience that cannot be corroborated by more objective facts. Ample evidence exists both in clinical reports and in research studies that children can be persuaded to recall, believe, elaborate upon, and even vigorously defend certain "memories" of their experience that can be shown not to have occurred (Ceci & Bruck, 1994; Doris, 1991; Loftus, 1993). Further, it is perfectly possible to condense a number of aspects of past experience into a "memory" of a single event or to construct a current "memory" in order to help explain a number of different phenomena (Hedges, 1994; Kantor, 1986; Loftus, 1991; Ofshe & Watters, 1994; Yapko, 1994). Professionals trained in clinical hypnosis are well-aware of the process of "confabulation" which helps all individuals make sense out of their experience. Further, hypnotically trained clinicians depend upon the use of "embedded suggestions"—indirect suggestions that bypass critical thinking—to assist clients with a variety of positive changes in the context of therapy. These same processes make it possible for children (and adults) to "construct" memories of sexual abuse that did not occur or to "explain" various aspects of their experience by connecting them to the idea of sexual abuse, particularly if those intervening into suspected instances of incest inadvertently "suggest" sexual contact to the children.

Such suggestions can occur in the context of therapy because the therapist is well-intentioned but naive about the nature of remembering (Yapko, 1994), has his/her own motivations for believing that sexual abuse is so widespread that each report is almost certainly true (Kutchinsky, 1992b, 1994), or is underinformed about the complex dynamics of therapeutic transference (Hedges, 1994). The power differential in the therapeutic relationship can make even adult clients highly suggestible, just as children are more suggestible in relation to powerful adults upon whom they are dependent (including therapists). Research shows that several factors are powerfully influential in leading a child—in a family or in therapy—to construct false realities or to elaborate on nonfactual suggestions provided by an adult:

- the need to have a memory be complete and meaningful (that is, to "make sense"), as well as to eliminate ambiguity (that is, to "be certain")
- a tendency to comply with authority
- an effort to gain acceptance from another person (Doris, 1991; Loftus, 1993; Yapko, 1994)

For their part, therapists and others intervening into suspected sexual abuse are likely to offer directly or embed indirectly suggestions of abuse for a variety of reasons (Yapko, 1994, p. 117):

- pressure from the legal system (to avoid a lawsuit)
- a backlash against the previous societal tendency to minimize or suppress reports of sexual abuse
- pressure from other therapists to recognize abuse rather than being accused of denying or minimizing it
- the security of having a ready explanation for a number of client symptoms (i.e., the PTSD diagnosis)

We agree with Yapko's (1994) conclusion, based upon the findings of numerous researchers, that *memories of past experiences cannot be assumed to be totally reliable without outside corroborating evidence to support them.* Therefore, therapists involved with suspected cases of incestuous abuse should maintain an open-minded, appropriate attitude of skepticism while proceeding on the conviction that the accusations alone signal that the family needs help. Further, therapists should avoid premature closure on the "facts" of alleged abuse, conveying instead an attitude of openness to all family members. Not only will this approach be useful as an aspect of family treatment, it is also likely to elicit more accurate reports of events by family members. When recall is permitted to flow freely in an unstructured fashion, it tends to be more accurate than when information is gathered by direct questioning (Ceci, 1991; Ceci & Bruck, 1994; Gardner, 1992; Yapko, 1994).

The remainder of our discussion in this chapter (and in the rest of the book) presumes that incestuous contact *has*, in fact, taken place in the family referred for therapy. However, the various ecological guidelines suggested for assessment and treatment of incestuous families are also relevant to therapeutic work with families in which the reality of family sexual abuse is uncertain. Except in the relatively few cases in which frivolous accusations of incestuous abuse are made by individual family members for reasons having little to do with actual family dynamics, even false accusations or misleading reports made by children are likely to reflect dysfunctional transactional patterns amenable to the interventions we will describe.

DILEMMAS IN DISCLOSING
FAMILY SEXUAL ABUSE

In this section, we explore factors that influence a victim's disclosure of incestuous experiences and the resultant problems in interpreting this account. Since human behavior is best understood by examining the transactions between individuals and their physical and social contexts, the primary basis for interpreting a child's experience is the nature of the interaction between the child and her family, as well as between the child and the larger community. However, the nature of the abused child's relationship to each of these contexts, as well as their relationship to each other, inevitably create major obstacles to presenting an objective and reliable description of incest. The nature of the account, in turn, affects the handling of the allegations of abuse by the legal and criminal justice systems, as well as by health and helping professionals called upon to intervene.

The Family as a Primary Learning Context

Often described as a network of kinship ties or as a social unit supporting physical and economic survival, a family can also be defined ecologically as *the primary social context that organizes the ongoing experiences of its members into meaningful and purposeful patterns* (Constantine, 1986; Garbarino, 1992; LaRossa & Reitzes, 1993; Reiss, 1981). The family is the major social mechanism for transforming its members' models of the world via shared experience. Since some sort of family unit is the principal socialization vehicle for virtually all children, it can be thought of not only as the major setting for mapping the world, but also as the chief architect of the mapmaking process. In his or her family, the child learns not only a great deal about *what* meanings to construct out of his or her experience, but also *how* to construct a version of reality. The younger the child, the more pervasive is the family as the context of his or her lived experience. Thus, the family is more powerful in influencing the representations of reality held by the young child than will be the case when he or she is older.

Even as adults, family members tend to take for granted their shared representations of reality. These shared meanings become implicit family *rules* which significantly affect how the family functions (Breunlin et al., 1992; Ford, 1983; Watzlawick et al., 1967a, 1976b). The intensity of closely shared experiences and the pervasive influence of family interactions on the individual mapping processes make family-related psychic representations particularly resistant to self-awareness and even less amenable to challenge or change. Children and adults alike feel most comfortable in social contexts that support rather than challenge their existing models of reality. Much is at stake in family members' maintenance of consensual reality, including such things as security, self-esteem, and a sense of closeness. The younger the child, the more prominent are these family representations in her personal map of reality.

Therefore, the child is particularly vulnerable when contexts outside of the family challenge the family's representations and rules as meaningful ways to organize experience. Typically, such challenges occur gradually in the context of normal development. A growing child's ways of understanding reality are altered to meet changing circumstances. Even under the most ideal conditions, individuals reach adulthood with cognitive and emotional response tendencies that are not well-suited to certain life experiences and must be relearned in laborious and sometimes painful ways. Childhood victims of incest are particularly disadvantaged in two important ways: First, some of the family's rules are at considerable variance with socially acceptable models of family life; second, the broader social context may challenge the incest family's model of the world in abrupt, unexpected, and intrusive ways—thereby occasioning considerable cognitive dissonance and emotional upset.

Factors Influencing the Representation of Incest

Data about the experience of incest are based largely upon the recall of adult victims and upon interpretations of childhood experiences by professionals who work with abused children. The data are inevitably influenced by the broader social context, that is, by the shared social representations of incest that have emerged in our society. Some of these are controversial, for example, debates over freedom of parents to raise their children as they see fit without governmental interference in family life (Davis, 1991; Doxiadis, 1989; Gordon, 1988; Sommers-Flanagan & Walters, 1987). Some of the representations are influenced by particular circumstances out of which they emerge, such as divorce and custody battles (Gardner, 1992; Thoennes & Tjaden, 1990). Uncovering the "real" experience of incest is impossible. Even arriving at a single standard of interpretation is unlikely, given the complexity and everchanging nature of the influencing variables. At best, there may emerge some consensus about certain interpretive principles useful for examining and organizing the data on incestuous experiences described by children and reflected in the reminiscences of adults.

From the ecological perspective, the structures and functions of the incestuous family system have a primary influence on a child's mapping of incestuous experience. These dynamics have already been discussed. Here, we simply note a number of ways in which they impact upon the child in connection with reporting abuse.

- The experience of the family unit both as the primary guarantor of physical and emotional survival and as a source of pain and confusion (therefore, a threat to survival) creates the victim's fundamental double bind regarding separation and connection.
- The victim may be affected more by a fear of harm and the associated lack of interpersonal trust that becomes part of her map of reality than by the sexual contact itself. What results is an internalized sense of vulnerability and, often, feelings of "craziness."
- The social isolation of the incest family often deprives the victim of broader socialization experiences (particularly in the sexual realm) that could otherwise mitigate some of the effects of the abuse or provide an occasion for reality testing that might lead to earlier reporting. Thus, the victim's representations of reality outside the family are typically constricted, and she is likely to lack a well-developed sense of reality testing.
- The blurring of boundaries and resulting role confusion in the incestuous family often lead the victim to develop pseudo-mature behavior which may be adaptive initially, but is likely to lead in the long run to a grandiose belief that she can meet any and all emotional needs of other people, even at the cost of her own well-being. This "parentification" phenomenon creates substantial ambivalence in victims regarding their role in the family.
- Since power/control distortions are embedded in the organization of the incestuous family, members who threaten the system through autonomous behavior often can become the targets of scapegoating and escalating abuse. These dynamics are likely to create in the victim a pervasive fear of abandonment, increased shame, and low self-esteem that make it difficult to maintain her individual sense of reality.
- The denial and related defense mechanisms that characterize the abusive family distort not only the representations of reality by the victim, but the reality construction process itself. One common result is a pattern of misrepresentations and rationalizations concerning family interaction, including the incestuous contact.
- The incest victim typically experiences males and females in the family as continuously in conflict. Her internalized model of gender relationships is likely to be perceived in terms of the perpetrator/victim interaction pattern, premised on powerful, uncontrolled males exploiting vulnerable, powerless females who are dependent upon them. Out of this map of reality can evolve an adult role as either a victim or a perpetrator, thereby setting the stage for the intergenerational transmission of abuse.
- Since significant distortions in sexuality characterize the incestu-

ous family, the erotic representations of the victim are likely to
include misinformation, attitudinal conflicts, and a curiously paradoxical mixture of naivete and pseudo-sophistication stemming
from her premature exposure to sexual contact with an older
person.

- From the confused intermingling of nurturance and eroticism, as
well as the emotional deprivation that typically characterizes her
family system, the incest victim often learns to distrust her own
sensory system. She has discovered that she cannot rely on feelings
of pleasure or pain to guide her in judging the meaning of an
experience, or, if she does, the meaning of her experience will not
align with its meaning to others inside or outside the family.

- The emotional atmosphere of the incestuous family is usually
characterized by ambivalence and insecurity. As a result, the victim may internalize a paradoxical attitude regarding her relationship to the perpetrator, her family, and even to the outside world:
"Nothing I do makes any difference" juxtaposed with "I am responsible for the feelings and well-being of (the perpetrator) (the family) (everyone I know)." As a result, the victim may appear to
others as brittle and cynical, even at a very young age.

INTERPRETING THE IMPACT OF
INCEST ON CHILDREN

We do not make a blanket assumption that all children who are sexually
abused are traumatized by the experience. While most sexually abused
children are negatively impacted by the abuse and may require help to
minimize the effects of their victimization experiences, a careful trauma
assessment is critical to evaluating the overall impact of the abuse on each
child. If the child has been traumatized in connection with incestuous
contact, the sexual violation indeed may be central in the assessment
process. However, other factors may be equally or more critical to explore:
threatened or actual physical abuse by the perpetrator or other family
member; forced isolation from other family members or from peers as a
result of the incestuous liaison; the victim's perception of abandonment
by one or both parents; even the crisis occasioned by reporting the abuse.

Incest as Trauma

The meaning of sex changes throughout life. During childhood and
adolescence, a changing body image helps to mold personality, erotic interests are shaped and channeled by social influences, and decisions about
sexual behavior are placed into the context of an emerging value system

(Fisher, 1989). As the child develops, new sexual experiences are fitted into her existing map of sexuality. The degree to which an incest victim can integrate her sexual abuse experiences into her model of the world — that is, can construct a meaningful personal theory to explain the behavior — will determine the immediate impact of the experiences upon her. In the incestuous family, the meanings and functions of sex and love, of pleasure and pain, and of nurturance and exploitation are often intermingled. For some victims, the nature of the incest family's meaning framework may make it *easier* to assimilate the abuse. In these instances, the inappropriate sexual contact "fits" part of her map of reality. The degree to which incestuous experiences are integrated into a victim's existing meaning framework varies from individual to individual and is dependent upon a great variety of influencing factors, including the broader sexual context.

Janoff-Bulman (1992) has described trauma as "the abrupt disintegration of one's inner world," shattering fundamental assumptions and filling the mind with frightening thoughts and images of malevolence, meaninglessness, and self-abasement. Traumatized victims come "face to face with a dangerous universe, made all the more frightening by their total lack of psychological preparation" (p. 63). Similarly, we believe that the greater the discrepancy between the meaning of the incestuous contact and the overall map of reality held by the child, the greater the likelihood that the sexual contact will be experienced as traumatic at the time it occurs.

In our view, "trauma" can best be defined as *an emotionally intense experience that occurs without a suitable framework of meaning within which it can be placed for understanding and mastery* (cf. Sandler, 1960). In other words, the experience has highly charged emotional impact without an adequate internal explanation, thereby interrupting the child's ongoing flow of "felt meaning" (Gazzaniga, 1985; Gendlin, 1962). The result is severe, perhaps overwhelming, anxiety out of which symptomatic behavior can arise. Of course, at the time the incestuous contact is first initiated, a mental search is undertaken to find a fitting explanation for the experience and a suitable way to represent it in her map of reality. Given the limitations of her childhood experience and the distortions in her family's framework of meanings, the child may find it easy to settle upon representations that serve to manage the trauma but may be socially inappropriate or personally maladaptive. She may conclude that she has behaved badly in some way she does not fully understand, but nevertheless requires punishment. She may surmise that she has been singled out in a particular way for special love and attention by the perpetrating family member. Perhaps she gradually accommodates herself to the idea that she should sacrifice her own desires and happiness to meet the needs of her father who is sexually deprived. Regardless of content, the victim's need to resolve the cognitive dissonance will necessarily motivate her to construct some sort of theory about the abuse which permits her to feel more comfortable and act more effectively within her context (Adams-Tucker, 1982; Finkelhor & Browne, 1985; Janoff-Bulman, 1992; Janoff-Bulman & Frieze, 1983; Summit, 1983). If she remains isolated within the meaning-distorting context of her family system, the victim's representations of the incestuous experiences are likely to be characterized by denial and to contain elements detrimental to her development as an autonomous, effectively functioning individual. As a result, these representations may "work" within the family system but create dissonance in her interactions with the broader social context outside the family.

The complexity of these processes makes it clear that drawing simplistic conclusions about incest as trauma can be misleading. Further, this understanding helps explain why some individuals seem to have little difficulty with incestuous behavior at the time it occurs, but may develop emotional reactions and symptoms later. If incestuous contact is meaningful to the child at the time it takes place—that is, coherently integrated into her existing map of reality—then it is unlikely to produce immediate psychological trauma. However, if other experiences and their representations upset the coherence or change the meaning of the incestuous activity for the victim, then problems, even trauma, can develop at some time *after* a particular experience has occurred. Therefore, it is quite possible for an individual to "discover" that she is an incest victim in connection with a subsequent cognitive reorientation—for example, by reading a published account of victimization, comparing experiences with school friends, or even working on family issues in therapy—*and to be traumatized in the process* (cf. Pfohl, 1984).[2]

These cautions regarding the judgment of psychological trauma in no way minimize the significance of either short-term or long-term damage that can result from incest experiences. Clearly, incestuous contact during childhood often creates a variety of negative emotional effects, establishes a particular vulnerability to stress, and sets the stage for certain maladaptive patterns in interpersonal relationships (Beitchman, Zucker, Hood, DaCosta, & Ackman, 1991; Beitchman et al., 1992; Browne & Finkelhor, 1986). An experience that does not qualify as "traumatic" in the sense defined above is by no means necessarily positive, either at the time or later in the individual's life. Trauma and benefit are not two ends of a single continuum. Reactions to the experience of incest can range from fear to disgust to ambivalence. The young victim may well understand clearly what is happening and be able to fit the experience into her map of reality rather easily—and still feel very negative about it. However, she

---

[2]Unfortunately, it is also possible for an individual to "discover" abuse and develop symptoms in relation to an unsubstantiated belief that she has been sexually abused some time in the past (cf. Doris, 1991; Hedges, 1994; Loftus & Ketcham, 1994; Ofshe & Watters, 1994; Terr, 1990; Yapko, 1994).

may not manifest the reactions that health care or legal professionals — and the public — usually associate with trauma, thus casting doubt upon her credibility if she reports the abuse (Summit, 1983).

If a child's map of reality is organized around continuous patterns of abuse and/or neglect, then a given incident of incestuous contact is less likely to be experienced as traumatic because it is anticipated and because it has become "meaningful" within the context of the child's experience. Indeed, it is further confirmation of the child's map of the world as an exploitive place in which relationships are characterized by perpetrator/ victim interaction patterns. This meaningful familiarity probably accounts for the tendency of some victims of domestic violence to remain in proximity to their perpetrators, even though such a choice lacks common sense. On a more positive note, some evidence suggests that victims who are not necessarily traumatized by the incestuous contact but experience very negative emotions in connection with it are more likely to come forward to report the abuse (Finkelhor, 1984). These individuals may actually experience less long-range damage as a result of their assertiveness in bringing the abuse to a halt, or even by making an effort to do so.

The Meanings of Incest to the Child

As we indicated earlier, uncovering the "real" experience of incest is impossible. Over the years, however, we have encountered a significant number of different meanings that incestuous sexual encounters can have for children. This awareness has been enormously helpful to us in our attempts to understand seemingly illogical responses by child victims, such as wanting to return home to the perpetrator immediately, protecting the perpetrator from the system, and vigorous recantations. While the following list certainly is not exhaustive, it is indicative of the wide range of potential responses of children, both positive and negative. Some children hold contradictory meanings, while others move through a sequence of various meanings in the course of reporting, intervention, and treatment. Every incest victim constructs a meaning that fits within the context of her experience; when reporting the incest, the child's most immediate need is to be understood and to have her experience validated in some way. Recognizing how the incestuous contact fits into the larger context of the child's experience is a significant contributor to effective therapy. Some examples:

- *I like this, but it is not right.*
- *I like this, and it is alright.*
- *I don't like this, and it is not alright.*
- *I don't like this, but it is necessary.*

- *I know it's wrong, but it makes me special.*
- *I love my father, but I hate him for doing this.*
- *I'm proud to be treated as an adult.*
- *I like this, but my mother is really angry at me.*
- *I don't like this, but my mother wants me to do it.*
- *I like this, and it makes my sisters/brothers jealous.*
- *I don't like this, but I'm protecting my sisters/brothers.*
- *I am terrible for leading my parent(s) astray.*
- *I must be bad for God to punish me this way.*
- *Now I've got something to use against my father/mother.*
- *My mother will go away if I don't do this with my father.*
- *The only way I can survive is to do this.*
- *Why does my body feel good when my brother does bad things?*
- *My father must really love me to take such a big risk.*

In any particular family, each child who has been abused may have a different—perhaps diametrically opposed—meaning for the sexual contact. Within an individual victim, several contradictory meanings might coexist, confusing the child and contributing to her hesitation to disclose the abuse. Ironically, sexual abusers who are overtly threatening and/or violent confuse children less, since their fearful reactions are appropriate and consistent with their experience. Seductive perpetrators who appear affectionate and loving during sexual encounters, or who are positively involved and nurturing at times other than when abusing, tend to generate the most confusing responses in their victims, because they cannot easily accommodate the contradictions in their experiences.

The Intrapsychic Effects of Childhood Incest

Though each child reacts uniquely, the responses of victims to incestuous abuse appear to have certain characteristics in common. From our perspective as therapists, the issues of primary significance to incest victims are those related to *power/control distortions* and to *loss and abandonment*. Certain themes seem to pervade the lives of incest victims, and these themes may follow them into adulthood. Following are some of the core losses that may impact upon the psychosocial development of incest victims.

Loss of childhood "innocence." According to Janoff-Bulman (1992), three fundamental assumptions need to underlie all humans' experience of the world: (a) the world is benevolent; (b) the world is meaningful; and (c) the self is worthy (pp. 5–6). These core assumptions help structure an individual's internal world, serving as a foundation for basic trust (Erikson, 1950, 1963). Overwhelming life experiences shatter these assumptions, leaving the individual vulnerable; their innocent belief in a just world has been destroyed (Janoff-Bulman, 1992; Lerner, 1980; Silver & Wortman, 1980). As we have indicated previously, victims of incestuous abuse are particularly likely to experience this shattering of fundamental assumptions since the source of their pain or trauma lies within the system from which they derive greatest security and meaning.

Loss of parental care and support. Sexual abuse itself constitutes a form of abandonment by a perpetrating parent, particularly when the perpetrator exploits the child's needs for nurturing, love, and physical affection by converting it into his own sexual gratification. The victimized child begins to experience ambivalence about closeness; being cared for means experiencing pain. If intervention into the incestuous family leads to physical separation from one or both parents, anxiety over abandonment is likely to become even more acute, particularly for younger children. In some cases, separation from the perpetrating parent and/or other family members may be more traumatic than the abuse itself. One child with whom we worked clearly articulated the reality of her experience: To be safe, she had to give up the one she loved the most.

Loss of child role in the family. Related to a victim's loss of parental support is a loss of childhood status in the family. Becoming a parental "peer" via her sexualization, she loses some of the freedom and spontaneity that characterize childhood. Her behavior begins to be based upon its perceived impact upon her parent(s). Over time, a consistent focus on the needs of the parental generation can damage her judgment, rendering her less and less capable of meeting her own needs and thereby deepening her victimization.

Loss of self-esteem. Having been exploited for the gratification of an adult, the incest victim loses her sense of basic worth, a loss that has been described as "the damaged goods syndrome" (Porter, Blick, & Sgroi, 1982). Friedrich (1990) has pointed out that there may be an inverse relationship between stigmatization and age: Naivete about sex may protect younger children, but sexual shame increases as the victims grow older. The sense of being damaged may deepen when victims are removed from their homes against their will or if they are further exploited by professionals who intervene in an effort to punish the perpetrator.

Loss of control over survival and well-being. This loss has been characterized as an incest victim's experience of "powerlessness," which is considered by Finkelhor and Browne (1985) to be one of the traumagenic factors in abuse. However, we believe that this phenomenon is more accurately referred to as a loss of *control*, since numerous victims continue to have a certain power within the family—such as attractiveness to the perpetrator, special status vis-à-vis their siblings, peer status with their parents, and the like. What the incest victim lacks is the capacity to stop the abuse; she cannot control access to her own body on her own terms. In some way, her well-being is subject to the will of the perpetrator. Sometimes, the victim is able to do some bargaining related to the abuse, for example, how often she will permit sexual contact or what she will receive in return, for example, spending money. Frequently, symptoms exhibited by an incest victim arise from the need to develop some sense of control over her physical and/or psychological processes, even if it be only a useful delusion, for example, pretending to be asleep during the sexual contact, leaving her body via dissociation, self-mutilation, or self-starvation.

Loss of capacity to trust adults. The victim of incestuous abuse has been betrayed by one or more persons upon whom she has depended for caring and nurturance. Abusive parenting results in the loss of a relationship and impairs children's attachment capacity, often precipitating symptoms of depression, unresolved grief, and increased dependency (Friedrich, 1990). Sexually victimized children deal with their damaged ability to trust in a number of different ways. Some internalize the meaning of the betrayal in such a way that they equate it with "love" and develop a kind of comfort from the familiarity of the experience. Others accurately perceive the betrayal and come to feel a sense of hopelessness. Still others externalize their feelings of loss and become impulsively sociopathic, convinced that "I can't trust anyone to give me what I want, so I will do whatever I please." These are children who begin to demonstrate perpetrator behavior at an early age.

Loss of normal coping mechanisms. A combination of boundary disturbances in the family and the intrusiveness of sexual abuse are likely to overwhelm the incest victim's normal ways of coping with anxiety, forcing her to devise more extreme mechanisms to deal with stress. Serious symptoms—dissociation, obsessive-compulsive behavior, self-injury, suicidality—can emerge as desperate attempts to avoid anxiety. Unable to turn to parents for support, the child is forced to look inward to find ways to insure survival. The therapist is challenged to recognize serious symptoms as positive coping mechanisms rather than simply negative outcomes of abuse that have no meaning to the victim.

Loss of normal sexual development sequences. The uniqueness of sexual abuse experiences, particularly at the hands of close relatives, almost invariably disrupts the developmental sequences that characterize normal psychosexual maturation. Once these experiences occur, they are retained as "body memories," even if (in some cases) details of the abuse are unavailable to the victim's conscious memory. Johnson and Feldmeth (1993) have developed a sexual behavior continuum for nonpsychotic children (age 12 and under) to assess the relative level of sexual disturbance. They identify four behavioral clusters, which allow for overlap (pp. 41–48):

- normal sexual exploration—children who voluntarily and mutually examine each other's bodies visually and tactilely (e.g., playing "doctor") or who experiment with various gender role behaviors (e.g., playing "house")
- sexually reactive behavior—children whose focus on sexuality is out of balance in relation to their peers
- extensive mutual sexual behaviors—children who participate in a variety of adult sexual behaviors with other children of their own age and conspire to keep the behaviors secret
- molestation—children whose thoughts and actions are pervaded by sexuality and who are likely to use force or coercion to engage in sexually explicit behaviors with other children

Friedrich (1990) highlights two other sexually reactive behaviors among child victims: children who experience disruption in sexual identity, and children who become severely inhibited and even aversive to any sex-related experiences. Our own clinical experience has revealed a strong association between the nature, frequency, duration, and relationship status of the incest and the degree of developmental damage to the victim. In addition, we have encountered some degree of correlation between the meaning/function of the sexual abuse within a particular family and the degree of damage to the victim's sexual development. In our experience, children from erotic-based and anger-based families typically demonstrate more sexual pathology than those from affection-based or rage-based families.

THE EXPERIENCE OF REVEALING INCESTUOUS ABUSE

The experience of disclosing incest as an adult contrasts with childhood reporting in a number of significant ways. In childhood, the abuse is usually current. Further, the child lacks the physical and emotional distance from her family that an adult survivor usually has gained in the course of her cognitive, social, and emotional development. The child is dependent upon her family for her physical and economic survival. Prior to dealing with her incest history, the adult survivor is likely to have broadened her map of reality, entering into shared social meanings with others in a society that has now defined child sexual abuse as a social problem. Thus, some momentum is created for further altering her representations of the incest experience. Only in unusual circumstances has such momentum been gained by the child victim. Perhaps the most significant contrast between adult and child reporting of incest is the issue of compulsion. The adult survivor seldom faces the *necessity* of interfacing with the legal and criminal justice systems in connection with her decision to deal openly with the abuse (except when there are other family members currently being abused or at risk for abuse). Rather, she may plan a course of action that includes decisions about how much to involve her family-of-origin in her life and what changes, if any, to seek in her relationships with the perpetrator and other family members. Even under these circumstances, the reports of adult survivors and their therapists make it clear that the reconstruction of incestuous experiences is enormously complex, emotionally taxing, and filled with difficult and often painful decisions that have important psychological and relational implications (cf. Bass & Thornton, 1983; Janoff-Bulman, 1992; Meiselman, 1978; Russell, 1986).

The Challenge of Reconstruction in Childhood

Overall, the child who is involved in the reconstruction of incest faces a major challenge to her map of reality — indeed, to her very sense of survival and selfhood. On the basis of her victimization, she is compelled to juxtapose her experience as an incest family member with her experience as a reporter within the social service and legal systems. She is then to render the "truth" about her experience in a consistent and convincing manner, despite the fact that this is likely to result in substantial disruption of her family life and possible confinement of the perpetrating family member. Her position at the interface of these conflicting social contexts makes dealing openly with the incest a rather formidable task.

When she reports the incest, the victim's primary context for the construction of meaning begins to change amidst substantial conflict, producing further disruption in her life. In choosing to talk about the abuse outside the family, the incest victim breaks some of the most important rules of her family system. On the one hand, when incest is reported and subsequent intervention measures are taken, the rigid boundary around the enmeshed family is breached and the victim experiences the possibility of escape from her dilemma. At the same time, she is placed in yet another double bind. The child is now told by outsiders that "telling the truth" will *help* her and her family. However, members of her family may very well respond to her disclosure by resisting outside intervention and even scapegoating her. Having been raised in a family system that emphasizes paternal authority, the child is now caught between conflicting authority figures; once again, she can be victimized by events over which she has little or no control. Further, her sense of vulnerability is likely to increase in relation to her fear of abandonment by her parents. If the family indeed does break up, she may feel that her very survival is threatened. In addition, she may view the representatives of the outside social systems as having been dishonest with her because their efforts to "help" have created more family disruption.

Investigation and treatment of sexual abuse provoke a major challenge to the map of family reality that the victim has heretofore constructed. At best, this challenge is disorienting to the child; at worst, it is traumatic, producing deep-seated ambivalence. Outsiders question her closely about her experiences, and one or both parents may dispute her recollections; now she must struggle with the discrepancies between her representations of experience and the representations of the same persons who have been most influential in teaching her how to map reality—an enormously stressful situation that she cannot avoid except by altering or recanting her story (Summit, 1983).

In addition, reporting the incest usually triggers significant changes in the family, that is, in the victim's primary social context. Sometimes the child experiences herself as choosing a change; at other times, it may seem to her that things are shifting spontaneously despite her wishes. The cessation of abuse is only one of the changes taking place in connection with reporting. Unforseen consequences may also occur, such as parents divorcing, the perpetrator leaving home, or the victim being placed in foster care. These are repercussions over which the victim has little or no control, although she may feel very responsible for them. Thereby, the family's incestuous pattern is replicated—the victim's relationship with the perpetrator once again has special implications for the entire family.

Paradoxically, the reporting of incest and its aftermath typically perpetuates one of the basic boundary violations in the incestuous family: intergenerational boundary diffusion. The victim's parentified role continues, or even increases, for now she holds some aspects of her family's future in her hands. What she reports, and how, may seriously affect her parents' (or grandparents' or uncle's or brother's) marriage, the perpetrator's freedom, and the subsequent composition of her family. She has traded one form of involvement in the world of adulthood for another form that may be even more burdensome and frightening to her.

The previously confused meanings and functions of sex in the incest family may become even more complex in the aftermath of reporting. Additional family members who are let in on the secret now intermingle their own representations of sex and their own perceptions of the relationship between the perpetrator and the victim. In some families, the incest is experienced as a kind of competition between mother and daughter for the attention of the father. In others, revelation of the incest becomes ammunition in an intergenerational conflict between overcontrolling parents and a rebellious daughter. In still others, new agendas emerge in which the *recounting* of sexual incidents as well as the sexual incidents themselves fuel power struggles between family members over who is to be believed. Clearly, these issues are involved in many of the disputed cases of reported incest and contribute to the growing public controversy over "false memory syndrome" and the accuracy of incest reporting.

A Clash of Contexts

The reporting of incest by a minor virtually always forces the family to interact with a variety of outside social institutions. These institutions — child protection services, law enforcement agencies, the courts, treatment resources — create a variety of different contexts, each with a representational system of its own, within which the incest victim must render her experiences. Certain practical problems are created in dealing with young victims of sexual abuse, including language barriers, unfamiliarity with legal and courtroom procedures, short attention span, difficulty in understanding certain concepts, repetition in reporting or testifying, and the like (deYoung, 1986; Faller, 1984; Gardner, 1992; Goodman et al., 1990). However, in the view taken here, *the outcome of an incest report by a child is primarily determined by the interaction between the victim's existing map of reality (which includes the incest experiences) and the representations of incest held (individually and collectively) by the larger community and its agents.*

Predictably, this has a number of implications for the management of intervention subsequent to the revelation of the abuse. The first matter at issue is that incidents which have taken place *within* the child's family context have to be rendered to persons who are *outside* of that context — persons who may act against the family. This creates a conflict that is internalized by the child, leading to adaptational behavior in the form of restructuring her version of events to meet the perceived requirements of each context. This tendency to develop a plausible and consistent version of reality, which can be rendered in a variety of different contexts, appears to be a rather universal mapping characteristic of humans (Bandler & Grinder, 1975, 1976; Festinger, 1957; Kolb, 1984). Motivation to align the versions of reality appears to be even stronger when an individual perceives that discrepancies will lead to conflict or threaten her security.

In the likely event of legal action, the dilemma of the incest victim is further heightened. An adversarial legal proceeding presumes that only one person's reporting of events is "true," or at least is more accurate than any other account. There is a built-in contradiction in such proceedings, presumably recognized by the professionals involved. On the one hand, legal proceedings purport to disclose "facts" on the basis of which decisions are made intended to reflect the principle of justice. At the same time, most attorneys and criminal justice personnel recognize that a hearing or trial involves a process of constructing a version of reality persuasive enough to convince a judge or jury to decide something in a particular way. This confrontation with the subjective/objective dilemma is difficult for a child, particularly for an incest victim whose intrapsychic boundaries have been extensively violated and whose representations of reality are already constructed around double binds, discrepancies, and deceit. The incest victim often has constructed a fragile and vulnerable version of reality. Her ability to maintain her intrapsychic and interpersonal boundaries in the face of intrusiveness and exploitation is tenuous, particularly in relation to changing contexts outside of her family. Therefore, the primary objective of a legal proceeding—to establish guilt or innocence "beyond a reasonable doubt"—constitutes a *major* challenge to the incest victim. Heretofore her reality has been forced to be fluid and accommodating to others in a unique way. The insistence upon a firm and indisputable account of her experience places her in an often unappreciated dilemma. This dilemma might even exceed the boundaries of her map of reality. For these victims, courtroom experiences can be equally or more traumatic than participation in the incestuous experiences themselves.

The incest victim's internalized understanding of cause and effect relationships is also severely challenged by certain investigative and legal procedures whose very outcome depends upon the establishment of such connections between events. An incest victim is simultaneously powerless and powerful within her family. The constant boundary violations and intrusiveness of the sexual abuse leave her anxious and vulnerable, yet, over time she may come to feel important to the perpetrator for her sexual availability. Further, she may occupy an influential position among her siblings or in relation to her parents' marriage because she is able to promote family harmony by satisfying the perpetrator's sexual demands. In short, the incest victim is both helpless and grandiose, feeling herself to be vulnerable but also convinced that her behavior is a matter of considerable consequence to other family members. The result is cognitive confusion and emotional ambivalence. Her map of reality may be more ambiguous and internally inconsistent than those of other children her age. When asked to describe linear sequences of behavior and to link them causally, she may be unable to do so convincingly. This same phenomenon underlies the vagueness that frequently characterizes the incest victim's account of her consent to the sexual contact. She may believe that her body and behavior are "owned" by the perpetrator; however, she is likely to feel burdened by a sense of personal responsibility for a variety of events and their consequences within the family system.

The rigid boundary between the incest family and the outside world probably has produced an exaggerated sense of loyalty to the family and may have trapped the victim in a web of secrecy. Against the social backdrop of generalized ambivalence about sex, the sexual secret is a source of anxiety and shame for the victim; understandably, she is self-protective in her revelations. With the discovery or reporting of the incest, the blanket of secrecy is pulled away. Private and personal information becomes a matter for open discussion, even of public record. Her need for self-protection is increased, influencing her rendering of the experience to others. No matter how often she is reassured by outsiders of the importance and appropriateness of "telling the truth about everything," the victim will continue to experience significant ambivalence at breaking the rule of secrecy. Inevitably she will feel vulnerable and ashamed of the revelations because of what they may reveal about *herself*. If required, testifying in court is likely to be one of the most difficult experiences of her life—a profound challenge to her map of reality and her self-concept, no matter how angry she is at the offender or how relieved that the incestuous contact has ceased.

Finally, it is worth noting that the reporting and substantiation of incest often is regressive for the child. It requires her to return mentally to circumstances in which she was not adequately in control of her life, that is, to her map of victimization. Under these circumstances, she is very likely to orient herself in familiar ways that affect her rendering of her experience and her behavior. The result is a structural parallel between her interaction patterns with her family and her interaction patterns with representatives of social service and legal systems. In short, no matter how appropriately and carefully she is treated in the aftermath of reporting, the incest victim is certain to behave in some ways that will hamper the process of investigation, prosecution, and treatment. Unfortunately, these behavior patterns, which have been so extensively described and analyzed in the literature on incest, still tend to surprise many well-intentioned helping professionals when they appear in the context of intervention— for example, in ambiguous courtroom testimony, loss of motivation for legal action, or resistance to therapy. Unless dealt with adequately, these behaviors can trigger interaction patterns between the victim and the professional community that lead to further victimization, to failure of prosecution, and perhaps even to collapse of the entire intervention effort.

CONCLUSION

The foregoing represents a descriptive analysis of the experience of childhood incest, first in the context of the family system and then in the context of other social systems involved in interventions subsequent to reported abuse. We have argued that both similarities and differences in intrafamilial and extrafamilial contexts make it impossible to render a completely objective and totally reliable account of incest. In some situations, this can seriously hamper efforts at investigation, prosecution, and treatment. Reporting the experience of incest in the context of social intervention involves a complex process of reconstructing a reality that has very different meanings inside and outside of the family context. A victim of childhood incest is required to describe experiences whose meaning and significance for her may change radically as she reports them. Therefore, representatives of the social service and legal systems—and therapists, in particular—should base their efforts not only upon the information contained in the child's account, but also upon the particular dynamics of the family and the specific circumstances surrounding the reporting and subsequent evolution of the case. To be most helpful, interventions into incestuous family systems should involve compassion for all members, clarity of role, specific objectives, careful coordination among professionals, and considerable flexibility—all combined with large measures of tolerance and patience.

CHAPTER 6

Systemic Assessment of Incest

When a family member asks for help, the professional must exhibit the skill of a tightrope walker in taking the necessary steps to protect the minors while simultaneously avoiding any confirmation of the splitting of the family into "bad guys" and "good guys."

—Stefano Cirillo & Paola DiBlasio (1992)

S OME INCEST TREATMENT PROGRAMS have elaborate protocols for gathering data and conducting psychological evaluations, particularly on victims and perpetrators. This is especially true in hospital-based and prison-based programs, where the data are more likely to be used in legal proceedings and where case files are maintained more meticulously for legal protection of the institutions. Rigorous assessment procedures help ensure that data will be collected in a uniform manner, despite the tense and chaotic conditions that typically accompany initial intervention into the incestuous family. In addition, carefully assembled information on the status of family members at the beginning of treatment can serve as a basis for later evaluations, including pre- and posttreatment comparisons and overall evaluation of treatment programs (see Chapter 12).

THE CHALLENGE OF ASSESSMENT

Problems in assessment and diagnosis have plagued the field of family therapy from its earliest days (Broderick & Schrader, 1981; Fisher, 1977; Glenn, 1984; Keeney, 1983). One major issue is whether a family can be labeled "pathological" or whether the term should be reserved for use only with an individual, who can then be said to be suffering from a "mental disorder" (Dell, 1983; Denton, 1989, 1990; Glenn, 1984; Wynne, Shields, & Sirkin, 1992). A related issue involves debate over whether any such thing as "pathology" or "dysfunction" even exists—or are these merely terms for judgments made about individuals who do not conform to social expectations (Glenn, 1984; Szasz, 1961)? These issues come into sharp focus in the matter of assessing incestuous families. Are incest *families* dysfunctional—perhaps "incestogenic" (Kutchinsky, 1994)—or are they merely unfortunate in having a dysfunctional *member*? Are incest perpetrators sick or criminal or sinful or all three? Or are they none of these, merely reacting shortsightedly to certain stressful circumstances?

The dilemma is further complicated by the fact that intervention into child sexual abuse juxtaposes three different social institutions—the legal system, the mental health care system, and the social service system—with their differing sets of assumptions, methods of inquiry, terminologies, and even differing goals for intervention. The results can be significant confusion and conflict, making assessment extremely difficult. Within this complicated context, the therapist is challenged to find a way to implement the crucial steps in an assessment process: making a connection with each family member, understanding each member's version of the problem, becoming familiar with each member's model of the world, and understanding the context within which the family has evolved a situation that requires treatment for one or more members. Assessment of all of these factors is important as a basis for determining what therapeutic steps are most likely to be helpful to various family members and to the family as a unit.

Should assessment of family sexual abuse be considered a form of crisis intervention? The answer is both yes and no. Certainly, incest is sometimes uncovered in the midst of a family crisis for which one or more family members have sought professional help. Equally as certain, the uncovering of incest always should be taken seriously, and plans should be made for some sort of intervention. However, the revealing of incest to uninvolved family members and to others outside the family is what most often precipitates a family crisis; rather than intervention into crisis, intervention *is* the crisis. This has substantial, but often unrecognized, implications for professionals who intervene and for therapists who work with family members. Perhaps the medical terms "emergent" and "acute" can be helpful in orienting the professional involved in sexual abuse assessment. These terms imply that the situation has an immediacy requiring significant attention; things are on the edge of crisis, and some kind of action should be taken. The challenge of intervention into incest is to manage things well from the outset.

Diagnosis in Family Therapy

Assessment of a family prior to treatment can be a very lengthy and complicated affair. Within the field of family therapy, formal psychiatric diagnoses used to identify individual psychopathology are regarded with mixed feelings. Therefore, many family therapists approach assessment ambivalently, particularly when they are referred families from the courts or social service agencies amidst controversy over whether the presenting problem is "family dysfunction" or "individual psychopathology," as in incest cases. Nevertheless, considerable attention has begun to be paid to the matter of assessment in family therapy (e.g., Beavers, 1976; Denton, 1989, 1990; Glenn, 1984; Keeney, 1983; Kinston, Loader, & Miller, 1987; Olson, Russell, & Sprenkle, 1989), from which have emerged at least a few points of consensus despite considerable diversity:

- Most family therapists consider assessment to be an ongoing process, something which cannot be definitively completed in one or even several sessions with the family. New data will emerge as the therapy proceeds, perhaps leading to new understandings about the "real" problem that needs to be treated.
- Most family therapists tend to view diagnoses as working hypotheses rather than as definitive descriptions of either individuals or family units.
- Family therapists are likely to understand the problems of family members primarily in transactional terms. Even if they recognize and accept a standard DSM-IV diagnostic categorization, such as an affective disorder or a personality disorder (American Psychiatric Association, 1994), they will focus primarily upon how the characteristics of such a disorder may impact upon the identified patient's relationships with others, including family members.
- Family therapists typically view the "causes" or supporting influences of problematic behavior as at least partly contextual. No matter how "disturbed" an individual may appear to be, her pathology is understood as arising from, or triggered by, influences in a particular situation. Typically, the external circumstances will receive as much attention from the family therapist as the intrapsychic dynamics of the client.
- Family therapists often tolerate, even promote, complexity in diagnosis to a greater degree than most individual therapists. Their attention to interpersonal transactions and environmental contexts makes family therapists resist the reductionistic classifications often favored by legal and social service agencies (and insurance companies).
- Many family therapists understand assessment, like other aspects of intervention into family systems, as a "co-evolutionary process;" that is, a clinical diagnosis is a construction arising from the mutual efforts of therapist and client(s) in treatment rather than an objectively verifiable characteristic of an individual or a family per se (de Shazer, 1983; Hoffman, 1981; Tomm, 1984a, 1984b).

Taken together, these characteristics of diagnosis in family therapy may help explain why many therapists treating incest believe that working with entire families is a formidable undertaking, particularly in light of the tension created between the fluid, co-evolving process of therapy and the tight, often demanding requirements of the legal system (see Chapter 11). An additional issue complicating diagnosis and assessment is the wide range of specific principles and differing styles to be found among family therapists—which is characteristic of individual therapy approaches as well. A comparative summary of diagnostic approaches in the major models of family therapy is presented in Table 6.1.

Models for Structuring Incest Assessment

Currently, several systemically oriented models exist for assessing incestuous families. Trepper and Barrett (1989) consider *vulnerability* the key variable, and they recommend examining it in relation to four areas:

- socio-environmental factors (for example, gender issues, chronic family stress, social isolation, tolerance of incest in the family's surrounding community)
- family-of-origin factors (for example, family themes regarding male/female roles and relationships, incidence of sexual abuse in previous generations, perception of emotional neglect or deprivation)
- family systems factors (for example, family structure, communication between members, abusive style, function of the incest)
- individual psychological factors (for example, cognitive distortions, personality disorders, sexual fantasies, capacity for nurturance)

Developed specifically to assess incest families, Trepper and Barrett's model is particularly useful in that it considers positive family coping mechanisms and also provides the therapist with a balance between individual and family variables in assessment.

Kinston, Loader, and Miller (1987) have constructed a protocol that evaluates six elements of individual and family functioning:

- affective status (family atmosphere, nature of relationships, emotional involvement, affective expression, individual moods)
- communication (continuity, involvement, expression of messages, reception of messages)
- boundaries (individual autonomy, family cohesion, intergenerational boundary, family-environment relationship)
- alliances (spousal relationship patterns, parent/child relationship patterns, sibling relationship patterns)

TABLE 6.1
Comparative Outline of Diagnosis/Assessment
in Six Models of Family Therapy

Relevant Concepts	Methods/Role of Therapist	D/A Within the Therapy Model
BOWEN THEORY		
Family's anxiety level and emotional reactivity Degree of differentiation of self of each family member General level of functioning across the generations Family projection process Emphasis on triadic vs. dyadic relationships Flexibility—rigidity Family's responsiveness to stress Family's operating principles	Is objective, detached from family emotional system Collects data from parents on: history of symptoms development, functioning of nuclear family and its interaction with family of origin, and the extended family of each spouse Uses genogram to organize data	Differentiation of self from family of origin as a goal is only possible after a careful assessment of the historical context of the family
SYSTEMIC THERAPY: MILAN ASSOCIATES		
Systemic understanding—how the historical and current pieces of the family puzzle fit Circular causality—interdependent and complementary nature of symptoms Information is a "difference" in relationship Referral process and contextual factors	Uses circular questioning—asking one person about two others: emphasis on difference Generates family members' reactions to and perceptions of symptoms Hypothesizing organizes therapist's behavior, sensitivity to feedback from family regarding hypotheses Neutrality prescribes a stance at an objective, nonaligned metalevel	Data-gathering, neutral stance of the therapist permits useful interactional data (feedback) and self-report information to emerge Systemic hypothesis is based on circular causality Therapist prescribes rituals, tasks, and paradoxical prescriptions

TABLE 6.1
Continued

Relevant Concepts	Methods/Role of Therapist	D/A Within the Therapy Model
SYMBOLIC-EXPERIENTIAL: WHITAKER		
Complementarity of symptoms Focus on analogic, meta-phoric, symbolic Degree of separateness-connectedness Intergenerational themes Growthful, creative aspects of symptoms Scapegoats anxiety-relieving function Desperateness as a readiness factor in change Therapeutic relationship	Therapeutic use of self: reading awareness of own responses, self-disclosure Assesses family's ability to tolerate natural inter-personal stress of family life; degree of family nationalism (esprit de corps); ability to play; role flexibility; toleration of deviance (creativity)	D/A process is seen as potentially stultifying and impinging on therapeutic spontaneity and relationship Battle for structure and for initiative phases highly diagnostic/prognostic Therapist pushes for expansion of self, flexibility of roles
STRUCTURAL: MINUCHIN		
Focuses on structure, organization of the family, subsystems, boundaries, hierarchy, alliances, coalitions, family life cycle, enmeshed-disengaged continuum as a guide D/A an active, experiential process; diagnosis seen as a result of therapist's interventions Isomorphs and partial constructs of reality Wider social unit Search for strengths	Uses self as an instrument/a therapeutic probe Seeks interactional data from self-report and in-session sequences (enactment) Identifies the presenting problem within the structures, sequences, and surrounding context D/A and intervention are arbitrarily divided D/A is ongoing, based on continual feedback	Through a continual, experiential reading of the family structure (made up of repeating patterns), therapist uses self to challenge and realign/restructure relationships Therapist accesses aspects of family members that are available but unused New relational realities become self-reinforcing

Continued

TABLE 6.1
Continued

Relevant Concepts	Methods/Role of Therapist	D/A Within the Therapy Model
STRATEGIC: HALEY		
Focus on presenting problem; ahistoric, symptoms as relationship metaphors, as adaptive in relationships	Conducts a structured initial interview	Therapist solves presenting problems in the social contexts in which they exist through directives (straightforward and paradoxical) designed to interrupt the patterned sequences and realign the hierarchic incongruities of the malfunctioning organization
Symptoms conceptualized analogically, worked with digitally	Promotes data generated from self-report and in-session sequences	
	Observational skills important	
Family life cycle, transition points	Use of feedback	
	Language of the family has assessment value	
Sequences of behavior, hierarchical organization	Flexibility vs. standardization of methods	Creation of greater complexity in the family system
Wider social unit		
Traditional diagnoses crystallize problems		
BRIEF THERAPY: MRI		
Ahistoric, symptom-focused	Closely tracks self-reports about sequences of attempted solutions in context	Unit of therapy can be one person
Emphasizes sequences of observable interactions, seen as mutually causative and reinforcing (circular causality)	Definition of the "more of the same" sequences	Therapist determines the "customer" goals and works to interdict the vicious cycles of mishandled attempted solutions through strategic directives (often symptom prescription)
Symptoms seen as the result of mishandling of problems—the attempted solution is the problem (over- and underemphasis)	Determines "who is the customer": the most motivated	
	Understands the idiosyncratic language or world view of the "customer"	
Symptoms at life's transitional points		
Communication theory: levels, rules, congruence		

- adaptability and stability (family organization and relationship to environment)
- family competence (conflict resolution, decision-making, problem-solving, parental management of children)

A similar family assessment model has been devised by Fisher (1977):

- structural descriptors (roles, splits, boundaries, communication and interaction patterns, conflict resolution, family views of the external world)
- controls and sanctions (power and leadership, flexibility, control, dependence/independence, differentiation/fusion)
- emotions and needs (affective expression, need satisfaction, emotions versus instrumental needs, affective family themes)
- cultural factors (social position, cultural heritage, environmental stressors, socio-cultural attitudes)

However, Fisher adds a fifth area of assessment:

- developmental factors (the relationship of the other four to the developmental stage of each family member)

Hindman's (1989) "Sexual Victim Trauma Assessment" is one of the most detailed of the structured assessments in the field of child sexual abuse. It has been formalized into a multipage data collection form, which includes seven general categories:

- assessment of referral
- assessment of environment
- background information
- symptom perspective
- relationship perspective
- developmental perspective
- situational perspective

Hindman's assessment system was designed specifically for sex abuse *victims* of all ages; however, utilized as a guide for assessing each member of an incest family, it can provide the therapist with a great deal of information about individual family members and, less directly, the overall family system.

ECOLOGICAL ASSESSMENT

Each of the models summarized above, or a combination of them, can be helpful to the therapist in structuring assessments of incest families.

However, therapeutic intervention with these families, or even with individual family members, requires some special considerations in the assessment phase that reflect the unique nature of incest as a clinical phenomenon. From our ecological perspective, the general goal of the therapist should be to help all family members. Therefore, two broad principles are central to effective clinical assessment:

1. The data gathered by any method should include information about meanings and patterns of ecosystemic relationships that are relevant to the overall goals of ecological balancing for healthy individual and family sexuality.

2. Assessment should supply information that can be used as helpful feedback to family members in their efforts to meet their individual and collective goals as these evolve from the treatment process.

Guidelines for Structuring
an Ecological Assessment

Several more specific guidelines for structuring assessment are also important in the ecological approach to therapy (see Chapter 2):

1. Assessment should begin with the first phone contact and continue through several sessions until the transactional patterns of each particular family are thoroughly familiar to the therapist. When clients enter therapy involuntarily, early-stage observations may be particularly critical for assessing such things as family coalitions or patterns of resistance, on the basis of which useful hypotheses can be generated (Cirillo & DiBlasio, 1992; Madanes, 1990; Trepper & Barrett, 1986).

2. Data should be gathered directly from as many family members as possible; ideally, the entire family should be seen together at an *early* date. Further, the therapist should be prepared to encounter disparate, and usually conflictual, versions of the presenting problem as well as differing motivations for treatment. No single family member can convey the reality of life within the family; therefore, the therapist should be cautious in order to avoid generalizing the important principle of "believing the victim" into an uncritical view of the family as experienced by one member.

3. The involuntary nature of most incest family therapy has a powerful role in shaping the behavior of family members; the process of intervention into family sexual abuse changes the family. Therefore, the therapist should recognize that the family she or he is assessing is already different from the family that existed before the revelation of the incest. An extension of this principle is the reminder that the therapist's own ideas, attitudes, and values (like those of other key professionals involved with the family) will influence clinical assessment just as they influence the outcome of treatment.

4. Assessment should focus on individual and family strengths as well as on problems and limitations. Some helping professionals see only the pathology of the incest family and fail to notice the family's resources (Gelinas, 1986). In our experience, most incest family members share certain characteristics that can be utilized effectively in treatment. Further, there may be useful support systems for change in the extended family or in the community.

5. Standardized psychometric tests should be used with caution in clinical assessment of incest families since they are still of questionable value in capturing the complexity of transactional processes among family members. While considerable progress has been made in the last decade in constructing tests that measure aspects of health and pathology in families (Akister & Stevenson-Hinde, 1991; Epstein, Baldwin & Bishop, 1983; Grotevant & Carlson, 1989; Kinston et al., 1987; Olson et al., 1982, 1985), important questions still remain regarding interpretation of relational data (Gottman, 1982; Larsen & Olson, 1990; Shields, 1986). In addition, the network of intrapersonal and interpersonal processes that set the stage for incestuous behavior are only beginning to be understood.

The extreme complexity of the incest phenomenon makes ecologically oriented assessment of the entire family both necessary and difficult. Intrafamilial sexual contact can arise from various family configurations under differing social conditions; as we have pointed out, families have a variety of ways of structuring themselves in relation to the behavior. Further, families react to intervention in different ways, challenging the therapist to find a position vis-à-vis the family from which both helpfulness and leverage for change can be generated when these are likely to seem antithetical to family members. Once family members (including the perpetrator) feel understood and respected by those who intervene, they can begin to cooperate in the process of ending the abuse by rebalancing some of their transactional patterns with each other and with their surrounding community.

Choosing a Role

Of critical importance when treating family sexual abuse is the therapist's decision about what role to take in the complex ecology of intervention. This decision is not as straightforward as it initially may appear, as many clinicians with extensive experience in family sexual abuse treatment will attest. However, an ecological framework also provides a critical principle that clarifies the role of the therapist: *Data gathered in the process of clinically assessing the incestuous family should NOT be used in a formal, court-ordered evaluation of either a victim or a perpetrator* — except in certain highly unusual circumstances in which *all* involved family members decide together that it would be in their collective best interest to convey specific information to outside authorities. To provide balance in the social ecology of intervention, the roles of formal evaluator and family therapist ought to remain distinctly separated.

Some incest cases can turn into nightmares for therapists, involving verbal attacks by family members and their attorneys, formal charges of malpractice made to state regulating agencies, even criminal or civil suits by accused parents. Many years ago, following an assessment report that resulted in a family refusing to continue treatment with one of the authors and petitioning the court for a new therapist at another clinic, we learned an important lesson: Being a family therapist in a sexual abuse case precludes acting in other capacities — particularly, conducting a formal evaluation. Most of the complaints or suits against therapists working with incest families are based at least in part upon the clinician having a primary role in the formal (legal) evaluation of one or more family members, as well as in treatment. Similarly, there have been problems in a number of rural communities when social workers or psychologists who conduct child protection investigations are assigned as therapists to the same families against whom they have filed petitions for protective court orders.

This dilemma is particularly acute in the early stages of intervention, when formal evaluations concentrate on ascertaining whether sexual abuse, in fact, has occurred and what measures need to be taken to assure that it does not continue. Further, the results of such evaluations often become part of a court record that will influence the criminal conviction and sentencing of the perpetrator as well as family members' living arrangements. Having had a major role in determining these matters via an initial evaluation, is it any wonder that the therapist's subsequent efforts to "help" may be met with resistance by the perpetrator and often by other family members as well? Such duality of roles can create virtually insurmountable obstacles to effective family therapy, and we strongly recommend against it.[1] Rather, the therapist ought not to conduct formal evaluations on victims, perpetrators, or other family members if he or she anticipates participating in the subsequent treatment of any or all of these individuals. Requests for treatment summaries or status reports that arise

---

[1]The relationship between psychological evaluations and treatment of *individuals* is somewhat more equivocal. However, caution is advisable here as well, particularly for a therapist working within the systemic paradigm. Essentially, formal evaluations that are submitted to courts represent a form of client advocacy that is inevitably based upon the therapist's stake in the outcome, whether it be assessment of damage to the victim by the offender or assessment of the current status of the offender based upon "successful" treatment by the therapist. As indicated in Chapter 1, we are not condemning advocacy in the course of treatment. Rather, we are cautioning that it needs to be recognized for what it is, and considered for its effects upon the family system and the larger social ecosystem involved in treatment. Further discussion of this issue can be found in Chapter 11, as well as in Bera (1990), Scheinberg (1992), Trepper & Barrett (1989).

in the course of therapy also can create problems; however, there are clinical strategies that can effectively bypass these difficulties. These are discussed in our consideration of the social ecology of incest treatment in Chapter 11.

Selecting a Client Unit

Implied in the choice of a role for the helping professional is the selection of a corresponding client system for treatment (one or more family members). The identification and maintenance of the client system in a sexually abusive family is more complicated than it might seem at first, both for theoretical and practical reasons. The focus on "relevant survival units" within a complex ecology challenges those who intervene. Presumably, a therapist who wants to help a troubled individual or family is not anxious to preside over the demise of the client unit identified as the recipient of the proffered help. Further, the potential recipients of therapeutic assistance are members of the same family who may be at odds with each other and who may see efforts to help one member as a form of interference with their own interests. As a result, the therapist may be put into the awkward position of choosing sides. Finally, the entire context of therapy often is pervaded by a coercive atmosphere created by intervention decisions made by the broader social ecosystem. Therefore, the therapist is faced with a significant dilemma: *What constitutes the client unit?* From the answer to this question flow other decisions about the continuing survival of other ecological (sub)systems: Shall the family continue to survive as a family? Shall one or both parents continue to raise their children? Shall the marriage continue? What ideas, attitudes, and behavior patterns need to be altered, or perhaps eliminated, because they promote socially unacceptable activities? How shall the therapist deal with the victim's ambivalent fear of—and attachment to—the perpetrator?

Maintaining Confidentiality

An important component of therapy with incestuous families is the issue of confidentiality, both between the therapist and the family and between family members themselves. Because abuse must be reported, the therapist is ethically responsible for informing family members about the limits of confidentiality. And because the issue of secrecy is likely to be one of the powerful dynamics of the incestuous family system, the manner in which the therapist does this is important.

Approaches to confidentiality in family therapy vary according to the theoretical orientation and personal style of an individual therapist (Gumper & Sprenkle, 1981; Imber-Black, 1993). This is particularly true when dealing with family secrets. Although most therapists agree that secrets between members often have a detrimental effect on family life — and that the secretive aspects of incest are among its most destructive influences — their manner of dealing with secrets in general and with the incest secret in particular varies widely. Some family therapists prefer direct, no-nonsense warnings to family members: "I don't keep secrets, so don't tell me anything that you don't want everyone to know" or "I am required to keep records of all our sessions and to report any instances of abuse or inappropriate contact, or of anything else that could indicate a threat to the children. You need to know that this kind of observation of you as a family is part of my job." Others feel more comfortable promising complete confidentiality to family members — except for the required reporting of additional instances of abuse. Still others apply the principles of confidentiality more selectively, without necessarily making it clear to the family that they are doing so. Typically, this involves keeping private some of the revelations of the victim (and perhaps other children) while discussing and/or reporting certain disclosures of the perpetrator. We believe that such covert selectivity should be discouraged.

Predictably, our approach to confidentiality reflects our efforts at ecological balancing. Of course, we inform the family of our reporting responsibility — emphasizing it as a *requirement* in an effort to pace the victim-like orientation that we believe characterizes all family members to some degree. Regarding confidentiality among family members, we are more equivocal but still overt, balancing our power to organize the therapeutic ecosystem with our concern for the nature of our relationship with *each* of the family members. Basically, the message to the clients is twofold, and somewhat paradoxical: "I will respect the confidence of each family member as long as you will trust me to use that information for the benefit of the entire family. When you tell me something privately, I will let you know if I believe that keeping it private will interfere with my relationship with anyone in the family or with my efforts to help all of you. I don't want anyone in the family to be at a disadvantage because some information has to be kept secret. But I also believe that it is important for each member of the family to have some privacy." This approach immediately suggests the opportunity for dialogue regarding personal issues. Further, it conveys recognition of boundaries and of inevitable tensions in the ecology of family life — thereby beginning the effort to work on the ambiguity of individuality and relationship that lies at the heart of the incestuous family's predicament.

Confidentiality with regard to the social system also poses dilemmas for the therapist. If she or he is hired by a court to conduct a formal evaluation and report the results, the limits of confidentiality are clear: Everyone agrees that any data gathered verbally or through formal testing will be returned to the court, along with the therapist's professional opinions. If one is functioning as an individual's or family's therapist, however, the process of communicating with the court is more complex and could become a stumbling block to both assessment and treatment. One method that has been useful in some cases is to develop an agreement with family members that they will be afforded an opportunity to review any assessment or progress reports before submission to the court, with the right to add their views to the therapist's material. Writing the reports from a "positive perspective"—one that most family members will tolerate without too much resistance—becomes a skill well worth developing when working with these highly vulnerable families.

"Juggling Things into Place"

Overall, the ecological approach to clinical assessment is characterized by an informality and fluidity that must be balanced with appropriate professional responsibility and personal integrity. Our goal is a comprehensive understanding of the individual family members as they interact to form a family unit that, in turn, interacts with a social community and a historical tradition (family-of-origin and cultural influences). This makes each assessment unique in terms of how interviews are scheduled and structured, as well as what clinical instruments are used. In addition, clinical assessment is a rather drawn out process, intermingling with therapeutic efforts from the first moment of contact with family members. Even when asking questions that are designed to serve our treatment planning, we are simultaneously attempting to make things better for the family. In our own clinical work and in our training, this first stage of therapy during which assessment is a primary focus has been given the very appropriate but not very scientific label of "juggling things into place."

Since therapy is segregated from formal evaluation, we work most often with families who are referred from other professionals or agencies. However, comprehensive evaluations often have not been completed, particularly with the entire family. Therefore, an assessment of the family as an ecosystem in which sexual abuse of one or more children has occurred is usually warranted. At the same time, formal evaluations of the victim(s), and perhaps the perpetrator, may have taken place already. In these instances, family assessment must be fit into an even more complex ecology of existing descriptive reports, psychological diagnoses, and legal orders. In addition, family members arrive for treatment with a wide variety of personal agendas, some related to their life together as a family and others to individual purposes. Sometimes these agendas are coordinated among family members and are designed to oppose the therapist. Other times, the agendas involve mixed antagonisms among family members, for example, a mother who supports the victim and siblings who are angry at the victim for reporting the abuse and disrupting family life. Still other times, the agendas are largely unconscious; the family is looking for help, but the defense mechanisms of denial and resistance prevent some or all members from recognizing their own investments in returning things to "the way we were."

Referring professionals outside the family also are likely to have a variety of agendas for treatment. Some who are sympathetic to family systems notions may want the therapist to be the Rescuer who cures the family of its collective ills. Others whose roles involve primarily victim advocacy may want the therapist to be a Surrogate Parent so that the effects of abuse on the children are minimized or reversed. Some referring professionals really want the therapeutic process to prove the guilt or innocence of the perpetrator, particularly in situations where the extent of abuse is unclear. A significant number of attorneys who refer men accused of sexual abuse want the treatment to help their clients "look good" to the courts, thereby hoping to reduce legal sentences or even to bolster the case for innocence. But there are also attorneys who believe that the therapist will facilitate the admission of abuse by the perpetrator, thereby substantiating the legal charges and increasing the likelihood of conviction. We know of some situations in which referring professionals, particularly attorneys, have been duplicitous with therapists, for example, supposedly referring for treatment with the promise of honoring a client's privacy, then issuing subpoenas for therapy records in order to bolster the case for innocence or guilt related to legal charges. Small wonder that the family therapist needs to be adept at juggling. Many different individuals, some with opposing agendas, have a stake in the outcome of treatment. Therefore, the task of establishing a clear set of treatment objectives at the outset of therapy is a major challenge.

Identifying the Problem Helpfully

An important part of the assessment process is to transform the statements of family members regarding the situation into an "ecological problem." Recognizing that truth always comes in versions, the therapist should absorb the individual perceptions of the situation and interrelate them so that (a) the family can understand the problems as interconnected, (b) the interconnected problems are framed in a *solvable* fashion (Haley, 1976), and (c) the family members begin to view the therapist as a helpful resource in solving the problems. Unfortunately, this solution-focused approach is often overlooked in incest treatment. Instead of starting with a problem that is meaningful to the client system or to individual family members—particularly the perpetrator (who is often the most powerful person in the system, at least until the moment of public disclosure, when the victim typically assumes this role)—the therapist begins somewhere else. Frequently, this involves accepting the problem as defined by "outsiders" in the legal or social service systems. As a result, the perpetrator and/or the spouse and/or the entire family begin to have a power struggle with the therapist over the definition of the *real* problem. We believe that this wastes a lot of valuable time and can often get treatment off to a bad start. Instead, we accept the problem(s) as defined by the family members (even if these definitions are very different for different members), and we work to find a general definition of a dilemma upon which everyone in the family can agree, for example, "It seems that members of this family are very upset right now" or "People in this family seem to be unhappy with each other, and there's a lot of confusion over what's been happening, who knows what, and whom to believe."

Problem definition also can be framed in a way that reflects the reality of the legal and social circumstances outside of the family, such as, "You were referred here after several of the girls verified Dad's sexual contact with them. Now that formal charges have been filed, things seem really up in the air. You might not even be able to live together as a family anymore, and the future is very uncertain for all of you." Even the acknowledgment "Mostly, it appears that you would like all of the agencies and legal authorities out of the picture, so that you could get on with your lives" is a way of conveying a generic sense of understanding to family members, while at the same time positioning the therapist in a more neutral role of observer and potential helper.

Sometimes the coercive motivation for therapy can be acknowledged and used by the therapist to align himself with the family system without choosing any particular "side" within the family, for example, "To sum things up, then, you're here primarily because the court requires it so that the kids can come back home, and you'd rather be left alone. . . . Well, I'm in pretty much the same position; someone has to work with you because the court requires it. So, I guess we're stuck in this together, and we need to find a way to make the best of it." This kind of problem definition also has the advantage of pacing the patterns of victimization familiar to family members. While seldom is it possible to get complete agreement from every family member on all aspects of the situation, the resourceful therapist should be able to find a way to phrase some kind of problem that encompasses the family as a system: "It seems that some of you are very clear about what you want—you want Dad out of the house. Others—including you, Mom—aren't at all sure about what to do at this point." Or even, "So various family members are going in different directions, that's very clear."

In all systemic therapy, framing the client's problem as something solvable is an important early step (de Shazer, 1985; Haley, 1976; O'Hanlon, 1987; Watzlawick et al., 1974). Simply being in therapy, even involuntarily, implies that something needs to be done that the clients have not been able to do themselves. In the case of an incest family, the very act of social intervention can give a message of failure to all family members—to the perpetrator, for being a "sexual pervert"; to the nonoffending adult, for being an inadequate parent; to the child victim, for failing to stop the abuse or not reporting it sooner; to the siblings, for either not recognizing or not reporting the abuse. This makes it particularly difficult to define a shared problem with a common solution. However, this challenge must be met by the therapist in order to establish the rapport required for genuine therapeutic change to occur in the family as a system.

The solution-focused problem definition also acknowledges that there are resources in the family system (Gelinas, 1986). Sometimes, therapists treating incest families overlook this, particularly in the earliest stage of treatment. Family strengths can be uncovered in a variety of ways. One way is to ask each family member: "What is it that you think I should know in order to be helpful to you?" From the answers to this question, the therapist will get information about what various family members think is "wrong" and about what they believe needs to happen in order to make things "right." In addition, the question contains an embedded message from the therapist that is crucial to the family: "*I would like to be helpful to each of you.*"

Framing the problem ecologically not only is useful for establishing rapport with family members, it also provides the therapist with some guidelines for assessing the scope and severity of the factors underlying the presenting situation. That is, understanding how the incestuous behavior is embedded in various layers of the ecosystem orients the therapist to pay some attention to each of them. Further, it is the basis upon which a treatment plan will be devised—a plan for the order and manner in which issues within and between various subsystems will be addressed (Breunlin et al., 1992). Within an ecological framework, family assessment focuses primarily upon boundaries between family members (and between the family and its social context), the meanings and functions of the abuse within the family system, and disturbances in relationships between particular family members (most often, between the offender and his spouse and between the victim and her parents). In addition, investigating the "intrapsychic ecology" of at least some family members may be important to a comprehensive understanding of the family system that can make therapy both effective and efficient.

ASSESSING BOUNDARIES

When working with a sexual abuse victim or perpetrator or an entire incest family, the therapist will need to address all four areas of potential boundary dysfunction: family-society, intergenerational, interpersonal, and intrapsychic. However, the degree of dysfunction in each boundary area will vary among families and even between members of the same family.

Family-Society Boundary Assessment

The degree to which family members permit the therapist to make a personal connection is one good indicator of the status of the family-society boundary. During initial interviews and as therapy proceeds, the therapist should keep track of her/his own feelings about individual family members and about the family as a unit. Additional feedback can be obtained by observing the family's interaction with other helping professionals and agencies that might be involved in the case. The nature of the family's social boundary also can be evaluated by gathering some information from family members during the early sessions. For example: How socially active in the community are various family members, and in what groups or organizations? How much contact do family members have with their extended family network, and on what occasions? What kinds of contacts do family members have with friends or neighbors, with peers at school or work? How are in-laws treated? Who is each family member's "best friend"? What are the major recreational activities of the family? Under what circumstances are children permitted to attend social or recreational events at school or in the community (and, if applicable, what are the dating rules for adolescents)? When, if at all, do family members seek advice or support from persons outside the family? Along with the therapist's internal sense of connectedness to the family, the answers to these and similar questions will help provide an initial assessment of the nature of the boundary relating the family to its social context.

Intergenerational Boundary Assessment

Boundary dysfunction between the generations is recognized most easily in the incestuous contact itself. However, other generational boundary violations are also common in incest families. These include "spouse-ifying" or "parent-ifying" children in a variety of ways, by involving them in tasks and decisions inappropriate to their ages as well as burdening them with meeting the emotional needs of adults. Conversely, adult family members may seem somewhat child-like themselves, primitive in their expressions of emotion or inappropriate in their behavior directed at meeting personal needs. Sometimes, a palpable sense of competition for scarce resources — including attention from the therapist — exists among family members. Some parents may be unable to think developmentally, that is, unable to distinguish between behaviors appropriate to children and those appropriate to adults. The following observations by the therapist can be useful in assessing intergenerational boundary dysfunction: What age-inappropriate behaviors are demonstrated by the children in the family (in such things as household tasks, family decision-making, or even personal manner and style of dress)? To what extent are rules and limits applied to various family members without regard for age or stage of development? To what degree are children overinvolved (through knowledge or direct experience) in adults' personal lives, marriage relationship, or sexual relationship? Who has major responsibility for the care of younger children in the household, and under what circumstances?

Interpersonal Boundary Assessment

Lack of support for self-definition is a striking characteristic of many incestuous families. However, some families will violate personal boundaries directly in threatening or coercive ways, while others will hamper individuality more subtly. Family members themselves are unlikely to be good sources of information about interpersonal boundary-setting and self-differentiation (although there are occasional exceptions to this, particularly among victims); therefore, direct questions typically yield few insights. Instead, careful observation by the therapist is important: Who speaks for the family as a unit, and which members speak for other members, who may not have a voice? How easily do family members (particularly the parents) tolerate differences of opinion? How comparable are family members' perceptions and feelings about the same events or issues? How often do family members challenge each others' opinions, and what are the responses to such challenges? How is the uniqueness of each family member recognized? How are expressions of individuality rewarded? How much pressure is exerted on the therapist to view issues in the same way that the family collectively views them? How does the family respond to challenges by the therapist? Forming an impression of *each* member of the incestuous family as an individual is a challenging but critical task at the beginning of treatment. By the time the initial assessment is completed, the therapist ought to have identified a key element of uniqueness in the identity of *every* family member, an element that can be called upon when interpersonal boundary issues are being addressed as treatment proceeds.

Intrapsychic Boundary Assessment

Reality distortions occur in a variety of ways in incestuous families. Although certain themes are typical of these families, members of a given family do not necessarily manifest the same degree or kind of psychological distortion. Intrapsychic boundary problems among various family members can be varied and even contradictory; some individuals may block awareness of abusive behaviors of any sort, while others are emotionally reactive to all forms of disagreement or conflict within the family. Assessing intrapsychic boundary problems is a complex process, requiring constant vigilance on the part of the therapist with regard to his or her own reality-testing. A therapist trying to assess intrapsychic boundaries may find him- or herself feeling confused about factual information, over-anxious about helping family members relieve their emotional pain, or intimidated by the expressions of hostility or rage directed at him or her by some family members. In addition, the therapist's theoretical orientation and personal values will affect the assessment outcome. Some therapists trained in family systems theories may be insufficiently prepared to recognize and cope with certain expressions of individual psychopathology to be found in a particular family. Conversely, some therapists trained psychodynamically may categorize too quickly certain behaviors in terms of an individual theoretical model without sufficient regard for the adaptive nature of these intrapsychic processes within a particular family system. In addition, some patterns of intrapsychic distortion may provoke strong countertransference reactions in one particular therapist and not another. For these reasons, working with a cotherapist or a consultation team can be useful during the assessment period (see Chapter 9).

The therapist can gather useful data regarding intrapsychic boundary disturbances through both individual interviews with each family member and sessions with the entire family together. Comparison of the stories of individual members and careful observation of family transactions can provide considerable insight into intrapsychic distortions. Do certain family members appear to have unique understandings of specific historical events in the family? Does one individual—particularly the perpetrator or the victim—set an inappropriate affective tone for other family members? The therapist can also compare his or her own analysis of actual events in treatment sessions with the individual reactions of each family member. Sometimes open-ended questions or tasks can be given to the family as aids to assessing the relationship between intrapsychic distortions of individual family members and interpersonal or intergenerational boundary problems. For example, a family whose members (including the reported victim) all are denying the existence of incest can be asked to discuss with each other their ideas about why the social service or legal system has labeled the family "sexually abusive." Alternately, the therapist may wish to give the family a semistructured task such as those utilized in standardized family assessments. For example, in a family assessment protocol developed at the Mental Research Institute (Watzlawick, 1966), parents are privately instructed to take 15 minutes to cooperatively teach their children the meaning of a proverb ("A rolling stone gathers no moss"). Open-ended experiences such as these can provide the therapist with insights simultaneously into several areas of boundary disturbance in the family.

As the therapist assesses boundary disturbances in all four areas of family experience, the task is to avoid being drawn into the family's distorted realities—a considerable challenge in some families. Accurate assessment of boundary issues provides an important foundation upon which to base effective family treatment. Not only does it point toward particular treatment objectives, it also serves as a basis for constructing useful hypotheses and determining the most helpful therapeutic stances (positioning). Addressing boundary issues in the incestuous family during the assessment process can be therapeutic in and of itself.

ASSESSING MEANING/FUNCTIONS
OF THE ABUSE

In the broadest ecological sense, incestuous activity in a family is directed at *survival*. The abusive behaviors of perpetrators are premised upon the need to cope with life in the family and the broader social ecosystem—survival patterns learned in their families-of-origin and triggered by precipitating factors in their current lives (Barrett & Schwartz, 1993; Gelinas, 1988; Trepper & Barrett, 1989; Vasington, 1989). However, if the premise of the typology we presented in Chapter 4 is correct—that incestuous behavior has different meanings and serves different purposes in various families—then planning for effective treatment requires that the therapist accurately assess the systemic function of the incest as quickly as possible. Too often, the therapeutic approach reflects the particular structure of the organized treatment program to which the incest family is referred rather than the specific characteristics and needs of a particular family. For example, a highly confrontive program that directly challenges family members to deal with anger and shame issues may be very useful to an aggression-based incest family, while the same approach to an affection-based incest family may generate high anxiety, magnify shame, and promote passive resistance. Any incest treatment program will be randomly successful with a certain number of client families; however, it risks being ineffective with a particular family if it fails to address the family's internal experience of incest in a meaningful way. Informal discussions among workers in the incest treatment field suggest to us that families who leave treatment (voluntarily or involuntarily) because they do not seem to fit a program model are at highest risk for recidivism.

Of course, the investigation of meaning in the incestuous family system inevitably brings the therapist face-to-face with the family's defense mechanisms and resistance to intervention. Most extreme are the offenders— and perhaps other family members, including the victim—who have actually blocked any memory of the abusive sexual contact. Often, these adults were sexually abused as children, and they may have suppressed those memories as well. Some of the most blatant intrapsychic distortions can occur in connection with how the family explains incest to itself. For example, an offender might indicate that he has been providing his own method of sex education for his children. Some couples might explain away the allegations on the grounds that their children are simply rebellious and have concocted the stories of sexual abuse to challenge the family rules (and sometimes they are correct). Occasionally, offenders may contend that they are acting on wisdom not yet acquired by the rest of the population, for example, a command from God that has been revealed to them during prayer. Since these distortions of reality may be perceived as necessary for survival, some rationalizations for incestuous behavior are remarkably subtle. We have encountered such things as: a mother who encouraged her adolescent daughter to exchange beds with her because she could not tolerate her husband's snoring; an offender who justified his sexual contact with his daughter because he could not get an erection since his wife had gained so much weight; daughters in a large family who, without complaint, permitted their father to examine and compare their breasts as part of a "teasing game;" a father who regularly masturbated his preadolescent son to erection and then measured the boy's penis with a ruler in order to reassure himself that his son was developing normally. These same defense mechanisms sometimes carry over into interactions with the therapist, for example, when an entire family fails to complete a particular assessment questionnaire because they "don't understand it," when an offender and his spouse explain their presence in treatment as concerned parents of a daughter with "an overactive imagination," or when a perpetrator fails to pay his therapy bills with the explanation that his attorney told him "not to do anything that would make me appear guilty of something I didn't do."

Questions addressed to all members during a family session can be useful in elucidating the nature and extent of these defensive distortions, along with generating data on the family's overall sexual meaning system. Generic questions that do not appear to focus directly upon the sexual abuse also can be useful, for example, asking family members to come to a consensus on the five "best" and five "worst" things about their family, or using exploratory circular questions such as "Who is closest to whom in this family?" and "Who is most upset/least upset about the involvement of the family with the legal system?" (Cecchin, 1987; Selvini-Palazzoli et al., 1980; Tomm, 1987a, 1987b). Keeping the focus on *meaning* rather than facts permits the therapist to explore the family's experience in detail from the earliest interviews while minimizing the family's tendency to cast her in the role of investigator and resist her.

The four types of incestuous family process described in Chapter 4 can serve as guidelines for developing treatment approaches that are compatible with both the functional meanings and the structural characteristics of various incest families. To distinguish between transactional processes that are affection-based, erotic-based, aggression-based, or rage-based (or some combination of these), the therapist can ask questions and make observations based upon several principles:

- *The emotional ambiance surrounding the sexual relationship.* What emotions were associated with the sexual contact by the perpetrator, the victim, and any other family members who knew about the incest?
- *The degree to which the perpetrator wishes to make and maintain a connection with the child as an individual.* Did the perpetrator use knowledge of the child's personality or build upon the nature of their relationship in order to seduce the child, or was the child simply an object whose body was de-personalized for exploitation by the perpetrator?
- *The degree of overt or covert coercion involved in the sexual contact.* Did the perpetrator use or threaten violence, or did the victim perceive the threat of violence for noncompliance?
- *The role of power/control in the relationship of perpetrator and victim, as well as its pattern in the family as a system.* How do the perpetrator and the victim characterize the influence that each had upon the other, and what kinds of limitations, if any, did the perpetrator or the victim place upon the nature or frequency of the sexual contact?
- *The overall psychopathology of the perpetrator.* What other evidence of emotional disturbance, pathological interaction, or personality disorder is demonstrated by the perpetrator?

While no formal diagnostic instrument exists to assess the meaning of sexual abuse in a given family, often it can be inferred from a combination of answers to interview questions and responses to clinical assessment measures. We have devised several specific questions to glean such information and have used these to construct hypotheses regarding the function of the sexual contact within a particular family system. A key question to ask the perpetrator is: "What were you thinking and feeling when you were involved in sexual contact with your daughter/son/sister/etc?" Affection-focused incest is reflected in responses such as "I wanted her to feel loved" or "I was helping her feel like she was part of the family" (about an adopted child) or "I was teaching her about sex" or "I was thinking about how important she is to me"—even though such statements also reflect defensive rationalizations for the sexual contact. Perpetrators from erotic-based families are more likely to respond with statements such as "I enjoyed watching her feel good when I touched her" or "I was thinking about how much fun we were having" or "I wanted her to be sexually responsive with her future husband" or "We were just doing what came naturally, so I wasn't thinking about anything except what we were doing." Aggression-focused perpetrators might respond with comments such as "I was thinking about my father—how I could finally do something to hurt him" or "I was thinking about how fat and disgusting my wife's body is compared to my daughter's" or "I was thinking about taking him away from his mother" (with reference to a former wife). This question is less likely to elicit an informative response from a rage-based perpetrator. Answers may come in the form of challenges to the interviewer ("You people think that everything has to be about sex!"), violent expressions directed at the victim ("I did it because she's a bitch, and she needed to be taught a lesson!"), or even apparently unrelated autistic comments that can be startlingly revealing of psychopathology ("I was thinking about those sluts who want a ride but won't get in the car with me").

Questioning the victim (usually in an individual interview) also can be useful in assessing the meaning and function of sexual abuse in the family. Questions such as the following can provide important information on the victim's experience of sexual abuse and yield insights into her overall role in the family: "Who do you think is more important to your father—your mother or you?" "How were you feeling when your brother came to you wanting sex?" "What do you miss most now that your uncle is not being sexual with you?" "How was your body feeling during the sexual touching?"

If the victim's replies to such exploratory questions include mostly positive content, affection is likely to be the primary meaning/function of the sexual abuse: "I know that I'm my stepfather's best friend" or "My father likes me more than the others" or "I feel especially loved when he is touching me." Victims from pansexual families often respond to such questions less positively, but more matter-of-factly: "My father likes to tease us, and it's supposed to be all in fun" or "When we grab each other, that's because our parents told us that brothers and sisters are supposed to love each other" or "Dad took all the doors off our bedrooms and the bathroom so we wouldn't misbehave." Victims from anger-based families in which sex is a form of aggression frequently discuss the sexual abuse with a mixture of fear and confusion, or even dissociation: "I knew he was going to hurt me, and I just wanted to get away" or "I was scared and I cried, but he wouldn't stop" or "When I heard him coming down the hall, I would lie in my bed and go away in my mind" or "My heart was pounding and he kept saying this was good for me, but I couldn't understand why he didn't stop because he was hurting me." Rage-based incest calls forth the most extreme replies from victims, who frequently are harmed physically and may even fear for their lives: "I thought he was going to kill me if I didn't do it with him—he looked so angry" or "It felt like he was tearing me apart and all I wanted to do was scream, but then I was afraid he would beat me worse" or "I was wanting my mother to save me, but she couldn't because she's afraid of him too."

Questions about sexual meaning also can be addressed to the entire family, or to siblings and other family members who were not involved in the incest. For example: "What comes to mind for you when you think about sex?" or "Who in the family is closest to your father (the perpetrator)?" or "Who is most distant from your father?" or "How do people in this family show that they are angry with each other?" Similar questions can be asked of the nonoffending spouse, in either an individual or couple session: "Who is the greatest competitor for your husband's affection?" "What role has sex played in your marriage?" "What do you think it means that your husband decided to be sexually involved with your daughters (instead of) (in addition to) having sex with you?" Any of these queries may provide a new piece of information or serve as the basis for a new hypothesis potentially useful in working with a particular family. Most important is the recognition that a general hypothesis regarding sexual meaning and the function of the incestuous contact should not be based upon the responses of any single family member. Rather, the therapist should look for *patterns in the combined responses of family members*, and then attempt to confirm or disconfirm an hypothesis in ongoing work with the family.

ASSESSING PERPETRATOR/VICTIM INTERACTION PATTERNS

In addition to appraising boundaries and meanings in incestuous families, assessing perpetrator/victim interaction patterns is crucial to the therapist's understanding of individual and family dynamics. To date, most incest literature focuses on issues between the perpetrator and victim(s), often labeling other family members in terms of their lack of involvement, for example, the "nonoffending spouse" (Blick & Berg, 1989; Horton, Johnson, Roundy, & Williams, 1990; Ingersoll & Patton, 1990; Kroth, 1979; Salter, 1988). Previously, we argued that virtually everyone in incest families internalizes perpetration/victimization patterns. Therefore, there are *no* uninvolved family members — which, we repeat, is *not* to say that everyone is somehow responsible for the abusive behavior. However, the therapist should recognize that the stances taken by particular family members within the complex ecology of the incestuous family are not necessarily identical to those of formally designated perpetrators or victims.

Although females are more likely to be victims and males to be perpetrators of sexual abuse, these gender-linked generalizations clearly are insufficient as a basis for effective clinical work. Since both victim and perpetrator stances are rooted in early victimization or trauma experiences, a variety of developmental and situational factors influence when and how individuals will function more as victims or as perpetrators later in their lives (Finkelhor, 1986; Gelles & Cornell, 1985; Gilgun 1988, 1990, 1991b; Horton et al., 1990; Janoff-Bulman, 1992; Russell, 1986; Ryan, 1989; Shapiro & Dominiak, 1992). Over years of work with incestuous families as well as with nonincestuous sex abuse victims and offenders, we have come to recognize that involvement in perpetrator/victim interaction patterns teaches the participants something about both roles. While this should not blur the issue of individual responsibility for abusive behavior, it acknowledges what many therapists have recognized for years: *Abuse victims are capable of perpetrating behaviors, and perpetrators often act in victim-like ways.* The therapist should assess the orientations of each family member as well as the transactional patterns between members in order to identify the sometimes subtle manifestations of perpetrator/victim interaction.

The victim stance is evidenced in disruption of self-expression. The modal response of the victim is to feel unstable, anxious, and confused; problems and difficulties are experienced in self-blaming ways: "I'm at fault." The victim feels tremendously responsible for everything that happens in her life; yet she simultaneously feels helpless to bring about good results or to eliminate bad ones. A defective sense of self is reflected in the victim, often expressed in symptoms such as depression and suicidal ideation, dissociative disorders, psychosomatic problems (especially eating disorders, unexplained pain, and sexual dysfunction), drug and alcohol abuse, and even self-injuring behaviors.

By contrast, the perpetrator stance is revealed in negativity and blame, which are directed toward the world as defective. While victims turn inward and disrupt their own functioning under stress, perpetrators act out, disrupting the lives of others and justifying their behavior based upon the failure of others. The perpetrator holds himself blameless for problems and difficulties, including abuse; his relationships assume that others are at fault when things go wrong. As a result, many of his behaviors are antisocial while his explanations for them are self-justifying.

To escape the tension of the power/control distortions they have internalized, both perpetrators and victims can manifest maladaptive extremes of behavior. These can be assessed by examining distortions in balance that are revealed in several areas of individual and family experience.

Responsibility. Paradoxically, both perpetrators and victims typically vacillate between underresponsibility and overresponsibility in their behavior, sometimes expressing impotence and other times omnipotence. Seldom can either strike a balance; seldom do they act responsibly toward themselves while remaining responsive to the needs and feelings of others. For example, an anorectic victim of child sexual abuse may feel completely helpless to protect herself from her abuser (even as an adult who has left home) while exhibiting a steely determination for self-starvation. Another

victim may assume no responsibility for leading a marginal life as an emotionally crippled person on public welfare while investing immense energy
in meeting every need and whim of her well-to-do parents. Similarly, a
perpetrator may confidently rationalize his antisocial behavior while simultaneously expressing his inability to act on improving an unsatisfactory
sexual relationship with his wife. Another may contend that he was unable
to resist the physical charms of his adolescent daughter while proudly
proclaiming his role as the responsible head of the household to whom all
other family members are answerable. Assessing the particular ways in
which family members express their distortions in power/control, and
with whom, is a useful base upon which to generate hypotheses and strategies for treatment.

Resistance. Both perpetrators and victims demonstrate resistance to
therapy, even though victims initially may seem more cooperative. At
certain times, any member of an incestuous family may deny feelings,
motivations, intentions, or even the reality of objectively observed behaviors. The opposite also occurs; one or more members may obsessively
rework every detail of a given event or ruminate endlessly about a particular issue. Of course, either of these patterns can disrupt intervention efforts. Assessing family members' forms of resistance—including pseudo-
cooperation—can be extremely important in formulating treatment
strategies, particularly in deciding whether direct or indirect approaches
will be most helpful.

Perception. Distinguishing between subjective distortions of reality and
more objective accounts of experience among incest family members can
be a substantial challenge. In their strategies for survival in a climate of
abuse, both victims and perpetrators create "fluid" realities. Frequently,
this underlying fluidity is frequently revealed in their responses to inqui-
ries in the course of assessment. The message is: "Whatever I need to
believe to get through this is what is real." Such reconstruction of reality
can serve to protect others as well as themselves. For example, victims
sometimes block memory of certain details of abusive episodes, both to
ease their own pain and to protect other family members from being hurt.
Similarly, perpetrators may construct elaborate rationalizations for their
abusive behavior, both to avoid detection and to minimize difficulty for
the child victim.

Defenses. A hallmark of incest therapy is working with rigid defense
structures designed to keep outsiders from effecting change, which is perceived by family members as a threat to their individual or collective
survival. Many professionals in the sexual abuse field seem to believe that
perpetrators' defenses are rigid and impervious, while victims tend to be

underdefended and vulnerable. In our experience, *both* perpetrators and victims are able to mobilize defenses against therapeutic intervention. While the perpetrator's defenses may look like attempts to maintain invulnerability, those of many victims manifest themselves as attempts to maintain vulnerability. Both patterns reflect a brittle rigidity, making it challenging to devise therapeutic interventions that are not experienced as threatening.

Involvement. Perpetrators of abuse usually appear to others as isolated, while victims seem to be unboundaried, even symbiotic, in their relationships with others. Because merger is never truly possible, victims, too, often experience themselves as isolated and alienated. On the other hand, some incest perpetrators use the sexual contact as a way to ward off their loneliness and isolation through physical merger; of course, they are not successful in filling their inner emptiness, thereby adding to their loneliness. The underlying structure of enmeshment that characterizes incestuous families maintains this paradox of isolation amidst emotional and sometimes physical fusion.

The perpetrator/victim interaction pattern is a dialectic that is internalized within each family member and enacted in the transactions among members, as well as in the sexual abuse. Those who intervene into the family system should anticipate the reciprocal expression of both perpetration and victimization in one or more of the ways we have described above. Formal identification of perpetrator(s) and victim(s) during assessment is insufficient as a foundation upon which to develop an effective treatment plan. Rather, effective treatment requires that the therapist identify patterns and adopt a flexible stance toward each family member based, in part, upon the expectation that both perpetration and victimization will be expressed in reaction to the stresses of intervention. Admittedly, this complicates treatment, though we believe that dealing with it effectively improves the long-range results of intervention for both victims and perpetrators as well as for the family system.

ASSESSING INDIVIDUAL
PSYCHOPATHOLOGY

Just as considerable debate exists over legal, social, and mental health definitions of "incest," so also considerable debate exists over judging and labeling the psychopathology of individual incest offenders. A variety of descriptive typologies have been offered, some of which are helpful in conveying a sense of the underlying dynamics of incestuous behavior. However, we are wary of typologies of persons, including sex offenders, because of how pejorative they can become, reifying an individual's entire identity around the nature of specific inappropriate or socially offensive behaviors. This is particularly true of individuals involved in incestuous activities, for their motivations, perceptions, and behaviors are extremely varied, which serves to make individual clinical assessment especially challenging.

One of the most controversial issues is the question of how many incest perpetrators are *pedophiles,* that is, oriented specifically toward children as objects of sexual interest. Some clinicians and researchers believe that the vast majority of incest offenders are pedophiles, while others estimate the figure at less than 5% (Barbaree & Marshall, 1989; deYoung, 1982; Finkelhor & Lewis, 1988; Langevin, 1983). For a time, incest offenders as a category were distinguished from pedophiles largely based upon their choice of a family member rather than engaging in more typical pedophilic molestation with a broader range of children, including strangers. However, this distinction is questionable in view of the fact that a clear majority of *all* adult-child erotic contacts occur between individuals who are known to each other, even if the adult is not involved directly in caretaking activities with the child. Further, it has now been recognized that a significant number of incestuous abusers (again, the exact percentage is not known) also have molested children outside of their families (Abel, Becker, Cunningham-Rathner, Mittleman, & Rouleau, 1988; Conte, 1990; Finkelhor, 1984; Mayer, 1988; NRC, 1993; Rouleau, 1988). Most important to appreciate is that a simple division between "pedophile" and "nonpedophile" is insufficient for understanding child sex abusers. Much more complex discriminations need to be made as a basis for both research and clinical intervention.[2]

From an ecological perspective, labeling incest offenders as pedophiles ought to be done very cautiously because of its pejorative implications. In our clinical experience, very few incest perpetrators consistently report sexual interests, fantasies, and interactions with children as their primary sex object preference or as their primary sexual outlet over an extended period of time. However, a sizable number of these clients have at least incidental involvement with children or adolescents other than the identified victim. We prefer not to think of these individuals as pedophiles in the sense in which the term is used in traditional psychiatric nomenclature. Nevertheless, included in treatment ought to be some efforts to reduce or eliminate the dynamics that motivate abusers' potential responses to young partners, particularly under conditions of increased stress.

The boundary between clinical assessment of perpetrators and the gathering of forensic evidence is sometimes blurred by therapists and others

---

[2]For a more thorough discussion of the issues involved in developing theoretical frameworks and diagnostic categories for child sexual abusers, see Hall (1989), Johnson & Feldmuth (1993), Knight (1988), McGovern (1991).

intervening into incestuous families. Instruments designed to collect data on psychological and social characteristics of perpetrators or to evaluate treatment efforts may be applied mistakenly in an effort to validate whether abuse did, in fact, occur—typically, in a legal context. Along with the growing controversy over false accusations of incest has come increasing preoccupation with foolproof methods of detection and evaluation. Even existing technology—such as using anatomically correct dolls with victims or polygraphs with perpetrators—has come under fire (Goodman & Aman, 1990; Howitt, 1992; Realmuto, Jensen, & Wescoe, 1990; Zaragoza et al., 1995).

The primary methods for assessing adult perpetrators often include such standardized instruments as the Minnesota Multiphasic Personality Inventory (MMPI), the Millon Clinical Multiaxial Inventory, and the Rorschach Ink Blot Test. Verbal interviews using polygraphs or exposure to erotic stimuli using penile plethysmography are also rather common. Detailed discussion of these is beyond the scope of this book. Instead, we will comment briefly on some of the issues involved in using these standardized approaches to perpetrator assessment. Though the information gathered by such means can be interesting and potentially useful for treatment, more research is needed before we can conclude that these various methods adequately assess the intrapsychic ecology that underlies child sexual abuse.

Paper and Pencil Inventories

Standardized testing has been used for decades to evaluate individuals with a broad range of mental health problems, including those involved in incest and other sex offenses (Barnard et al., 1989; Hollin & Howels, 1991; Ingersoll & Patton, 1990; Murphy & Peters, 1992; Prentky & Quinsey, 1988). Some of the more sophisticated tests, such as the MMPI, use special scales designed to judge the validity of response patterns, helping to identify individuals who might be consciously lying or unconsciously biasing their responses in certain directions. Other instruments, particularly projective tests such as the Rorschach, rely on the expertise of seasoned interpreters who can detect seriously biased or invalid responses. No matter what the response patterns to these kinds of measures, we strongly advise therapists *not* to rely on test results alone to establish the validity of incestuous abuse or to determine which perpetrators should be incarcerated and which treated. The average therapist should make use of specialists when interpreting the personality profile of an incest perpetrator or victim and should place these judgments into the broader context of her clinical assessment in order to develop a viable treatment plan. Lest this seem too obvious for mention, we note that we are aware of numerous cases in which test results have been introduced as evidence to support the guilt or innocence of an incest perpetrator. In addition, extraordinary claims sometimes have been made regarding the meaning of various scales and profiles. Finally, we warn the reader of the danger of administering tests for purposes of formal evaluation and then basing therapy on the results of these tests, particularly if some legal rulings against the perpetrator have been predicated in part upon the test results. This boundary-confusing mixture of evaluation and therapy is discussed further in Chapter 11.

Since perpetrators are capable of substantial intrapsychic boundary distortion, a sizable number demonstrate little psychological distress on personality inventories such as the MMPI. In our experience, incest offenders who begin therapy without admitting the abuse can have more normal-looking personality profiles on MMPIs or Millons than those who have admitted the abuse, even though the nonadmitters may eventually acknowledge their behavior in the course of treatment. It may be that those perpetrators who admit their abuse are experiencing internal conflicts which produce measurable emotional and psychological stress, while a significant number of nonadmitters have successfully dissociated these experiences (and perhaps also their experiences as victims). We detected this phenomenon even among imprisoned *female* sex offenders when one of the authors (NRL) devised an experimental treatment program at the Minnesota Women's Prison.

To our dismay, the use of tests with incest offenders and other sex abusers is sometimes reflected in legal disputes that pit one assessment instrument or test interpretation against another. We believe that a "battle of the experts" over test results of incest perpetrators is detrimental to the credibility of mental health professionals in relation to the legal issues involved in child sexual abuse. Partly, this is a matter of modesty on the part of the mental health professional and of recognizing the boundary between the objectives of treatment and those of the criminal justice system.

Polygraph Tests

Our concerns about polygraph testing are similar to those about written instruments. Over the past 20 years, we have worked with some accused sex offenders — including incest perpetrators — who passed polygraph tests and later admitted guilt. False positives — the appearance of guilt when an individual has not committed an offense — can also be a problem (British Psychological Society, 1986; Gardner, 1992; Meyer, 1984). Of course, polygraph results and other data often are consistent as well; we only urge caution and the use of multiple data gathering methods when assessing child sexual abuse situations, particularly incest. Since polygraphs measure physiological correlates of distress when lying, it is important to remember that occasional incest perpetrators, like victims, appear to dissociate from their molestation experiences. Although polygraph tests, or the threat of them, are sometimes used by clinicians to extract confessions from perpetrators in early stage assessments, we have had success beginning family therapy and permitting these revelations to occur gradually. Clarifying the perceptions, motivations, and behavior patterns of the perpetrator in therapy sessions can alert the therapist to the possibility of other victims, identify potential safety risks, and even indicate what modalities and methods of treatment might be most effective. Although some issues cannot be addressed directly—particularly in the initial stages of intervention when the defensiveness and resistance of the perpetrator is likely to be highest—there are a variety of ways in which individual and family assessment interviews can be conducted to permit the therapist to draw some conclusions about the nature of the abuse (see Chapter 7).

Again we are advocating clear boundaries between the agenda of the therapist and those of legal and social service personnel. Certainly, the therapist ought to promote *honesty* with self and others in his or her work with perpetrators. However, truthfulness is not synonymous with having the perpetrator admit to a crime—the latter is a legal objective. Confession and forgiveness can be enormously useful as rituals during therapy, but they should emerge out of changes within the client rather than being extracted by external pressure, since maintaining an external locus of control replicates the dynamics of the perpetrator/victim interaction pattern. For this reason, we are skeptical of the use of polygraphs to evaluate "progress" at various points in treatment. Given the complexities and distortions of meaning in the incestuous family system, well-intentioned efforts to verify the abuse may result only in conscious or unconscious alignment of the versions of reality reconstructed by the perpetrator and that of the victim.

Plethysmography

For similar reasons, the use of a penile plethysmograph in child sex abuse investigations and treatment is problematic, particularly in incest cases. Originally designed as a research instrument to document sexual arousal by measuring increased penile blood flow in response to erotic stimuli, now it is utilized frequently to identify arousal in response to deviant stimuli, to evaluate change in arousal patterns over the course of treatment, or as a biofeedback device to assist in voluntary self-control of arousal (Barnard et al., 1989; Gardner, 1992; Langevin, 1991; Laws, 1989; Murphy & Peters, 1992). In some cases, plethysmography has been used to prompt confessions from denying perpetrators, although a major developer of the device clearly states that the penile tumescence plethysmograph is neither a "sexual lie detector" nor a predictor of future sexual offenses. Rather, "properly obtained and interpreted, the penile evaluation can generally make it possible to determine the gender preference, age preference, and in many cases the type of sexual activity of interest to both an offender and a non-offender" (Farrall & Card, 1988, p. 262).

The use of penile plethysmography in child sexual abuse cases raises some issues not yet adequately addressed, though they are potentially surmountable. The first is lack of standardization of the sexual stimulus materials (either auditory or visual) used, making it difficult to draw conclusions about discriminatory deviant responses among those measured. A second problem is lack of research on response patterns of nonoffenders to the same materials assumed to measure deviant responses in offenders. If a substantial population of nonoffending men can get erections while listening to or watching sexually provocative materials that include children (and we suspect this might be the case), are deviant arousal patterns an appropriate focus or are some other variables more significant in the sexual abuse process? A third problem is the relationship of deviant arousal to more normal sexual response patterns in a particular individual; deviant responses may fail to be elicited by the artificial stimuli used in plethysmography. Finally, there is an issue of appropriate controls over the use of plethysmography. For example, it has been used in conjunction with electric shock in aversive conditioning procedures — including with adolescents — to extinguish arousal to certain stimuli; the long-term effects of this kind of treatment are not yet known. We are concerned about its possible impact upon the perpetrator/victim dynamics that are embedded in the intrapsychic ecology of some, or perhaps all, sex offenders. Until these issues have been addressed satisfactorily, it would seem prudent to consider plethysmography an experimental technique rather than a definitive measure of sexual deviance or of clinical change.

CONSIDERATIONS IN THE ASSESSMENT OF CHILDREN

A detailed discussion of assessing children who report sexual abuse is beyond the scope of this book. This process has been thoroughly explored by a number of other authors.[3] Some authors focus forensically, with assessment defined primarily as documenting the truth or falsehood of the allegations. Others concentrate more on the psychological aftereffects of the perceived trauma, from a developmental or child psychology perspective. Most assume that the child has been traumatized by the sexual abuse,

[3]For example: Boat & Everson, 1986; Donovan & McIntyre, 1990; Everstine & Everstine, 1989; Friedrich, 1990; Friedrich et al., 1992; Gil, 1991; Gil & Johnson, 1993; Gomes-Schwartz, Horowitz, & Cardarelli, 1990; Haugaard & Reppucci, 1988; James, 1989; MacFarlane & Waterman, 1986; Schetky & Green, 1988; Sgroi, 1988, 1989; Walker, 1988; Walker, Bonner, & Kaufman, 1988; S. White, 1986.

and they structure the evaluation process accordingly. Consistent with our ecological orientation to family sexual abuse, we focus upon the assessment of children within the abusive family context.

As we have mentioned previously, not all sexually abused children are traumatized by the experience. While most children involved in incest are negatively affected by the experience and should be offered help to minimize its impact on their lives, a careful trauma assessment is critical to evaluating the overall influence of the abuse on a particular child. If the child has been traumatized, the sexual violation may be central. Often, however, other factors may be equally or more critical to deal with in therapy, for example, actual or threatened physical violence among family members, isolation from family and peers connected with maintaining the incest secret (and perhaps subsequent alienation for revealing it), perceived or actual abandonment by parents.

If an incest case is referred from the legal system, psychological assessments may have been completed previously (perhaps including reports from school or day care, community agencies, and other professionals involved in intervention).[4] However, a family evaluation is much less likely to have occurred; therefore, important data from the child's experience may be missing from the interview write-up and testing results.

Perpetrator/Victim Interplay

Assessing the perpetrator/victim interaction dynamic *within* a child victim can be a difficult task to undertake. While a therapist may recognize, in principle, that all family members in an abusive system learn the pattern, assessing its manifestations in a naive, sometimes traumatized, young child may seem unnecessary or even counterproductive (it may appear to be "blaming the victim"). Therefore, we want to emphasize again that the perpetrator/victim interaction pattern is an ecological term to describe the intrapsychic and interpersonal templates that guide behavior based upon past experience—it is *not* a term of moral judgment or of concrete behavioral description. As we have repeated often throughout this book, the perpetrator/victim interaction pattern can, and usually does, persist long past the time that the actual abuse has ceased. Quite probably, it is the vehicle for the transmission of abuse from one generation to the next via *both* victim and perpetrator.

Usually, it is easy to recognize victim-like behavior in children, even at a very young age. Lack of eye contact in communication, cowering body posture, verbal self-recriminations, expressions of fear and anxiety in relation to the parent(s), parroting parental comments, and the like point to

[4]Friedrich (1990) offers an excellent overview of psychological tests that are useful for evaluating child sexual abuse victims.

an individual with little sense of self-efficacy and an external locus of control. Sometimes, these children may even appear to be "asking" for abuse in their manner of communicating and behaving — the role of victim has become familiar and automatic. The victim orientation also may be more subtle, or at least indirect, manifesting itself in poor school performance, recurrent physical illness, unexplained depression, precocious sexual behavior, or repetitive instances of being emotionally or physically abused by peers.

Should a very young child ever be considered a "perpetrator"? From our standpoint, the question is academic and clinically irrelevant. The issue is to recognize evidence of the perpetrator/victim *pattern* in the intrapsychic dynamics and interpersonal behaviors of even the youngest child who has been victimized on any consistent basis by other family members. Sometimes, the acting out is blatant, as in physical aggression, destroying property, stealing, and the like. Other times, it is more subtle, such as compulsive lying, crass manipulation of peers or family members (including parents), or inappropriate expressions of sexual interest and behavior. We are convinced that the pattern can be detected in children as young as toddler age without having to be as flamboyant as those depicted in science fiction thrillers — although some behavioral symptoms can be dramatic.

EXAMPLE

A three-year-old child who was sexually abused by both her mother and stepfather consistently urinates and defecates on the floors throughout her foster home, smearing her feces into the carpet, onto walls, furniture, draperies, and even the family pets while she screams and yells angrily. There is no evidence of organic problems or pain associated with the wetting and soiling. Other than this behavior, she engages in age-appropriate verbal and nonverbal interactions with her foster parents and siblings, is affectionate, bright, and engaging. Everyone involved in the case agrees that she is reacting to the stresses of her victimization and separation from her parents by "acting out" rather than "acting in." That is, this particular child is behaving intermittently in an aggressive way toward the world rather than collapsing into dysfunctional internal symptoms. This "perpetrator-like" behavior may or may not continue into the future, based upon a variety of factors, including the responses of others to her current aggressive behavior.

EXAMPLE

Five-year-old twin boys have been anally raped by their 12-year-old brother. At every unsupervised opportunity, both boys persistently light fires at home and at school. During one visit to the family therapist, they even light a fire in the hallway outside of the office. Verbally and nonverbally, they express genuine delight at the opportunity to watch the fires, though neither can adequately describe his motivation. Up to the present, all forms of punishment or negative consequences for the fire-setting have been completely ineffective in changing the behavior.

EXAMPLE

An 8-year-old girl was physically abused by her mother and sexually molested by several of her mother's various live-in lovers. She was removed from her mother's care, and neglect charges were filed. When referred for therapy in addition to her residential treatment, she is aggressively seeking out younger children, luring them to out-of-the-way places, and then molesting them by sucking on their genitals and inserting various objects into their vaginas and rectums.

EXAMPLE

A 10-year-old boy has been sexually abused by his father, a man revered by his community for his gentleness and dedication to children, especially in the context of his church. At the time of referral to therapy, the boy has a several-year history of torturing, mutilating, and killing domestic pets and other small animals he is able to capture. Besides mutilating the animals in various ways, he also sets fire to them to kill them. He reportedly has no emotional reaction to the animals' pain and suffering and shows no remorse for his behavior. However, in the presence of family members, peers, and adults in his environment, he is exceptionally polite and well-mannered, obedient, responsible, and even solicitous. He is frequently compared favorably with his father.

Similar to symptoms traditionally associated with victimization—depression, self-injury, elective mutism, and the like—the behaviors described above clearly indicate serious psychological disturbance. Characterizing them as "perpetrating" behaviors is intended to alert the reader to the presence of the perpetrator/victim interaction pattern even in very young children who have been identified as sexual abuse victims. With this awareness, the therapist can decide what stance to adopt in working with the child as well as what position to assume in the ecology of family treatment. The perpetrator/victim interaction patterns that are deeply embedded in many incestuous family systems operate in multiple directions and may involve some or all family members, including the children. Further, the victim and other children often will behave in ways associated with any or all of the three roles in the perpetrator/victim/rescuer triangle (see Chapters 7 and 9).

Psychological Symptoms

Assessing the psychological impact of abuse upon child victims requires some specialized skills (Friedrich et al., 1992). If not specifically trained in

child therapy, the family therapist should be prepared to work cooperatively with a child therapist if the victim(s) or siblings appear to manifest
emotional or behavioral symptoms as a result of the abuse or of intervention. In our experience, some symptoms associated with sexual abuse
abate rather rapidly as the efforts of the family therapist begin to gain
momentum. However, some symptoms actually escalate during the initial
stages of treatment; as therapy progresses, particular symptoms may sub-
side and others may surface. All of these changes reflect the child's attempt to recalibrate feelings and behaviors in response to changes occurring within the family system. As such, the meaning and function of the
symptoms should be recognized and accommodated in the therapeutic
process (de Shazer, 1982; Haley, 1967, 1976; Keeney, 1983; Watzlawick et
al., 1974). Moving too quickly or extremely toward symptom removal in
the victim can precipitate a "backlash" of symptoms in the child or in other
family members, resulting from the boundary distortions and enmeshment
dynamics that characterize the incestuous family system.

Of course, some symptoms in a child require sustained individual attention. Certainly, severe depression, eating disorders, self-mutilation, dissociative experiences, alcohol or drug abuse, and the like should be treated
with individual therapy, medication, or even hospitalization as required.
Ideally, the family therapist has cooperative working relationships with
child and adolescent psychiatrists who are knowledgeable about perpetra-
tor/victim dynamics and can provide appropriate medical care without
underreacting or overreacting to the manifestation of these dynamics in
the behavior of the child.

Evidence of a narcissistic wound to the sexually abused child is common. The victim often believes that she has been singled out by the
abuser, leaving her feeling "defective" and "different" from her peers and
even her siblings. Intervention into the family may do little to alleviate
this experience; in fact, the events following the revelation of incest may
exacerbate the child's feelings of shame and alienation. Therefore, the
therapist(s) working with the child should pay close attention to her reactions to *intervention* as well as to the abuse. Some of the child's difficulties
may not be apparent in treatment, or even in the context of family life.
Therefore, gathering information about peer relationships and adjustment
in school and neighborhood activities can be useful in treatment planning.
Even adolescent victims who can verbalize their thoughts and feelings
about the abuse may find themselves alienated from their peers and unable to integrate their experiences in the family with the routines of school
and friendships. Thus, a variety of symptoms may develop secondary to
the revelation of incest and the family's subsequent status, including treatment efforts.

The therapist should avoid the temptation to work too directly in family
sessions with the emotional or behavioral problems of the children. Such

actions can undermine the legitimate authority of the parents and may simply increase the family's boundary difficulties. Instead, the family therapist should work with the parents to support the children and to accept responsibility for gathering any necessary resources for special assistance (see Chapter 10 for a discussion of strengthening the parental coalition).

Assessing Special Needs

Incestuous families typically are multiproblem families; therefore, children in these families—even if they are not the actual victims of sexual abuse—often manifest a variety of special needs. As a result of the perpetrator/victim dynamics in their families, these special needs may not be adequately addressed, leaving them particularly vulnerable to exploitation, and complicating the symptoms that result when abuse does occur. For example, a sizable number of incest victims are children with developmental disabilities, physical handicaps, or chronic illnesses. They may be easier for the perpetrator to seduce or coerce into sexual activity; further, they may be given little credibility by others when they attempt to report the abuse. Hearing-impaired children may be selected for sexual abuse (both inside and outside of families) because they are less able to communicate effectively with others, thereby providing the perpetrator with greater protection. Some young incest victims, particularly those who have been adopted, may already suffer from a failure-to-bond that leaves them emotionally needy and vulnerable to abuse. This combination of alienation from parents and exploitation by a family member raises obvious questions about motivation for adoption.

EXAMPLE

A wealthy couple with two biological children adopted three infant girls from war-torn Vietnam in the early 1970s. The father began having oral sex and intercourse with all three adopted children when they reached adolescence. History-taking in therapy revealed that the father had been a virgin prior to being drafted into the U.S. Army for the Korean War. While on active duty, he regularly had sex with young Korean prostitutes. Upon returning home, he married his high school girlfriend, and their sexual relationship in marriage was marked by conflict and intermittent sexual dysfunction in both spouses.

Finally, some incest victims already may suffer from school performance problems related to learning disabilities or from social adjustment problems linked to a variety of temperamental and/or developmental factors. These issues can increase their vulnerability to sexual abuse by lowering self-esteem, alienating them from supportive social environments, and predisposing them toward atypical behavior patterns. Once victimized, the discrepancies are reinforced. For example, a socially insecure child may be more content to concentrate her attention on maintaining the incestuous liaison with her favorite uncle; a child performing poorly in school may find excuses to remain at home engaging in regular sex play with his siblings; and the young teenager who is having intercourse with her father may feel "too old" to have things in common with her junior high school peers.

Therapists involved with incestuous families may find some of these special circumstances beyond the scope of their expertise and should be prepared to refer young clients for adjunctive services. At the same time, the family therapist has a unique opportunity to observe the "ecological fit" of these behaviors within the family system (useful for diagnostic purposes) and to mobilize parental efforts and family resources to address these issues from within the system. Referral outside of family therapy should not occur precipitously; focusing family energy on meeting special needs of young incest victims or siblings can be an excellent way to realign family boundaries, reduce perpetrator/victim interaction patterns, and facilitate cooperative efforts toward common goals among family members. All of these are important contributors to healing the family from the effects of sexual abuse and its revelation to outsiders.

GOAL-SETTING WITH
INCEST FAMILIES

As stated above, families involved in incest treatment are often multiproblem families. Physical abuse, alcohol and drug addiction, high marital conflict (including battering), child behavior problems, medical problems, and individual emotional disorders have all been found in greater than average amounts among families in which incest has occurred (Cirillo & DiBlasio, 1992; Kroth, 1979; MacFarlane & Waterman, 1986; Renshaw, 1982; Spoentgen, 1992; Trepper & Barrett, 1989; Waterman, 1986). Further, working with incestuous families often involves working with trauma, characterized by sometimes extreme forms of psychopathology in individual adults or children as well as by the complex network of individual and systemic defenses discussed earlier. Finally, these families often present for assessment in a conflicted and chaotic condition soon after the discovery or reporting of the abuse, requiring that treatment begin in the midst of crisis.

Together, these factors can seriously hamper the efforts of the therapist to devise goals for therapy other than the explicit objective of preventing further sexual abuse. As a result, treatment sometimes is driven by forces outside of the therapy process itself. Resistant, multiproblem incest families whose referral to treatment is involuntary challenge the therapist to organize and remain in charge of the treatment process. The importance of clearly defined treatment goals in therapy has been emphasized by many writers (Blythe, 1988; Cirillo & DiBlasio, 1992; Friedrich, 1990; Justice & Justice, 1976; Watzlawick et al., 1974). Specific goals serve as a guide for organizing therapy as well as a way of assessing progress. Much specialized incest treatment is in the form of fixed programs with standardized objectives and treatment techniques. At the other extreme, therapists in general mental health settings are often without any programmatic structure to guide them in determining useful directions to take with these difficult families. Thus, specialized treatment programs may pay too little attention to the heterogeneity in presenting problems and may be so focused on dealing with the incest that other elements of abuse, neglect, or family conflict may go unaddressed. By contrast, general therapy approaches may provide so little structure and direction that the therapist may be unable to budge the family in any clearcut direction of change. Both of these problems can seriously impede treatment effectiveness and may even encourage therapist burn-out (Walsh & Olson, 1989).

A Goal-Setting Framework

A goal-setting framework for incestuous families has been devised and tested by Spoentgen (1992). It is explicitly ecological and utilizes compatible principles from family management theory and family systems theory (Deacon & Firebaugh, 1988; Paolucci, Hall, & Axinn, 1977; Rettig, 1993; Rice & Tucker, 1986). The framework organizes the process of purposeful family change toward established goals without specifying content, thereby enabling a therapist to use it to devise goals specific to each family that can be interrelated with other social systems. The framework is summarized in Table 6.2.

This type of ecologically oriented framework can serve as a vehicle for the convergence of goals among family members as well as between the family, the therapist, and outside agencies. Directions can be taken that simultaneously (a) meet the needs of society for the family to conform with cultural norms, (b) meet the needs of the family to satisfy the requirements of outside agents of social control and thereby rid themselves of external pressure, (c) meet the needs of individual family members to reduce conflict and restructure their relationships for mutual comfort and security, and (d) meet the needs of the therapist to contribute effectively to positive family change.

By emphasizing the goal-setting, planning, and implementing aspects of family management, the therapist demonstrates respect for the resources of the family, recognizes the potential contribution of individual family members, and establishes a positive tone of expectation for change—particularly for the family to rebalance the power/control dynamics that un-

TABLE 6.2
Steps in Goal-Setting

---

1. *Perceive needed or wanted change.*
   The needed or wanted change has been perceived by at least one family member or suggested by outside input such as the therapist.
2. *Problem-solving.*
   The objective is to clarify each person's perception of the current situation and determine if others are uncomfortable with this situation.
3. *Agree to solve the problem.*
   If several family members agree that a problem exists, then a definite commitment is made to work on the problem.
4. *Discuss problem definition/meaning.*
   Each family member states her/his personal needs, feelings, values, and desires about the perceived problem. Each person describes how the current situation is different from what is wanted or needed.
   Guidelines for family members that may help Steps 4, 5, and 6 flow more smoothly:

   • Exclude personal reactions to allow freedom to express ideas.
   • Focus on the issue, not on personalities.
   • Listen with empathy and without interruption.
   • Speak with clarity and directness.
   • Respect different points of view.
   • Bring feelings out in the open rather than suppress them.

5. *Resolve issues of different perceptions/definitions/meanings.*
   Differing perceptions, needs, and values expressed in Step 4 are negotiated to develop a summary of the problem definition/meaning for the overall family. Strong feelings may arise during discussion.
6. *Create alternatives.*
   The objective in this step is to generate alternative solutions and goals. The alternatives are developed, expanded, and combined so that the needs of several family members can be met.
7. *Decide on a goal.*
   The objective of this step is twofold:

   • Analyze goal and value issues of family members.
   • Analyze how preferred solutions protect these values as well as allow for individual needs.

   Pros and cons of significant alternatives are discussed and a preferred alternative is chosen. If no alternative can be chosen, a return to Step 1 may be needed to reclarify the problem.

---

derlie the perpetrator/victim interaction pattern. Simply put, the framework invites the family to work with the therapist to answer the question, "How did this happen to us?" and then to execute a plan to prevent a recurrence of the problem (Trepper & Barrett, 1989). Because of the dysfunctional nature and negative social status of family sexual abuse, dealing with these issues requires that a dialogue take place between family members and representatives of the larger community. In addition, this ecological framework conveys an expectation that the family will take an active part in determining and implementing needed changes. Overall, then, a goal-setting framework can permit the therapist to approach the family with an attitude of *respect* while not condoning the abusive behavior that precipitated the need for treatment.

Use of a Treatment Contract

In our work, the term "treatment contract" is used in a general sense to refer to the *mutual understanding between therapist and client(s) regarding the goals of treatment and how they are to be accomplished.* Such contracts change with the varying conditions of treatment. Most important from an ecological perspective is that the therapeutic system be formed with a clear understanding by all parties of what constitutes its relevant survival units, of what ecological niche the therapeutic system occupies in the larger ecosystem of intervention, and of what rules guide the ecological balancing operations of therapy. We have some reservations about formal contracts, due to the risks of expanding the legalistic frame of reference that already surrounds treatment. Since the primary needs of incest family members (especially the perpetrator) center on relationship issues, the formalities of therapy can actually interfere with the process of bonding that needs to take place between therapist and family during assessment. In addition, formal contracts can create an atmosphere of surveillance within the therapy setting that is more appropriately left to child protection workers and the legal system.[5] In our experience, family members may have all the wrong motives for agreeing to such terms initially. Nevertheless, the element of accountability is an important component of the therapeutic relationship that eventually can become a bond of trust between therapist and family, as well as between family members. For this reason, a context of legal and social coercion can be an enormously helpful form of leverage for family treatment.

CONCLUSION

The role of the family therapist as treatment coordinator often requires the skills of a variety of circus performers: tightrope walker, juggler, lion

[5]One exception to this is our regular use of formal contracts when doing assessment and mediation with divorcing couples, particularly when there have been allegations of sexual abuse against one parent by the other. In these instances, we use contracts to ensure agreement by both parties that neither the therapist nor the records will be used in a legal custody battle. This agreement maximizes the possibility that the issues can be resolved therapeutically rather than through power maneuvers by either spouse.

tamer, and ringmaster. Yet all of these activities should be carried out with a firm sense of the proper role of the therapist and a clear eye on the goals of treatment (as opposed to other objectives of intervention). Genuine ecological assessment further demands that the therapist delicately balance between being an objective outsider who can consider the overall social situation and an understanding insider who potentially can be helpful to each family member and to the family as a whole. In this chapter, we have summarized several models of family sexual abuse assessment, and we have presented some ecological principles that can guide such an assessment in order to set the stage for treatment that benefits all family members and the family as a system.

CHAPTER 7

Structuring Family Treatment

> *Unless effective family treatment is provided for cases of intrafamily child sexual abuse, it can be predicted that every family member is at risk to act out subsequent scenarios of sexual abuse.*

—Suzanne Sgroi (1982)

I N OUR VIEW, the hallmark of a systemic/ecological approach to incest treatment is a focus on the *family* as the primary unit of intervention. That is, sessions with the family are considered the principal mode of treatment, and individual or group therapy with victims, perpetrators, and others are adjunctive. Many of the agencies that claim to have "family therapy" programs for incest seldom or never work with family members together, at least until a stage called "reunification" occurs near the end of treatment (Everstine & Everstine, 1989; Hollin & Howells, 1991; Kroth, 1979; Matthews, Matthews, & Speltz, 1991; Plyer, Woolley, & Anderson, 1990).[1]

THE CASE FOR FAMILY TREATMENT

For reasons that should be clear to the reader by now, we believe that programs working with family members separately often sacrifice some important resources for change as well as create confusion among family members regarding the role of the therapist as helper, advocate, or agent

---

[1] We do not wish to convey the impression that gathering together members of a family in the same room automatically constitutes "family systems therapy." For some years, the family therapy field has labored to counteract this impression among both professionals and the public. As we have pointed out numerous times throughout this book, a systemic approach to therapy is both a way of thinking about human problems and a way of working that pays attention to relationships and context—regardless of how many individuals meet together during the session.

of social control. For similar reasons, we believe that family therapy also ought to be used as a major modality of treatment for perpetrators or victims of *nonfamilial* sexual abuse. In addition to its role in the physical and emotional care of its members, the family is the primary social context for their life experiences and the major template for the creation of their social meanings. Of course, some might argue that the dynamics of abuse and neglect make a family system more harmful than helpful in the treatment of a traumatized individual. Sometimes this is true. However, the legitimate desire to eliminate incest and other forms of child abuse may tempt social agencies to interrupt too quickly the patterns of family life that are familiar to members, including abuse victims. It is our contention that, *in any event*, family dynamics will have a significant impact upon any changes made by individual family members. Further, a family may have useful resources hidden beneath a surface of family pathology (Gelinas, 1986). In other words, positive changes are limited by the contexts of both meaning and behavior that exist inside of individuals ("intrapsychic ecology") as well as in the relationships between members ("interpersonal ecology"). Once having intervened, social agencies are challenged to maximize the utility of their efforts for individual clients — *who are also part of a family*. Working with family members together helps retain a network of relationships that can be restructured during treatment, supporting the changes made by individuals. Finally, family therapy facilitates a sense of ethical co-responsibility for change among family members.

Support for family involvement in treatment has come from a number of different experts in the field. Henry Giarretto, one of the pioneers in incest treatment, found that the degree of parental involvement and responsibility in treatment was highly correlated with a positive outcome for child victims (Kroth, 1979). His treatment follow-up, which studied dozens of variables, indicated significantly lower rates of alcohol and chemical use, running away from home, school absence, sexual promiscuity, and delinquent behavior. In addition, the victims showed improved grades, better relationships with peers, and fewer conflicts with siblings. Kroth concludes:

> [I]f one supposes that children who experienced incest have an increasing tendency toward social maladjustment and are, as a consequence of the molestation, more prone toward delinquency, sexual acting-out, substance abuse, et cetera, [then] receiving family therapy entirely contradicts such a prognosis. (p. 100)

These data point to changes in underlying family dynamics rather than simply the cessation of abusive behavior. The children also experienced fewer abandonment fears, since over 90% of them were reunited with their families within the first month of treatment. In a follow-up study of

594 child sexual abuse cases treated in the program (of which 79%, or 475, were incest offenders), the recidivism rate was only 0.6%.

Other studies also have demonstrated that the degree of parental concern for their children and the extent to which victims are supported by their families are highly correlated with positive treatment outcomes for child victims (Fromuth, 1986; Leaman, 1980; Peters, 1985). In her quest to understand the transformation process from sexual abuse victim to perpetrator, Gilgun (1988) identified the following as major contributors: poor relationships between perpetrators and parents, poor male-female relationships modeling by parents, and social isolation of the perpetrator and, often, the family. These results support family systems treatment, suggesting that further isolation from parents subsequent to intervention might even *promote* future sexual perpetration.

The case for family treatment can be argued from the standpoint of therapeutic process as well. Collective resistance to change in incest families has sometimes been cited as a rationale for separating family members during much of treatment (Bentovim, 1991). However, working with family process can bypass a great deal of resistance by eliminating many of the power struggles between family members around differing versions of reality. Further, the therapist working with the entire family can deal more directly with the negative forms of triangulation that inevitably characterize the incestuous family system. Conjoint family therapy also combats the shame and secrecy surrounding the sexual abuse, dynamics that were very likely exacerbated during the processes of reporting and intervention leading to treatment. Finally, therapy with all family members provides the therapist with increased points of contact with a dysfunctional family system, increasing the likelihood of triggering useful change.

In systemic terms, family therapy can work to modify the context within which the intrapsychic and interpersonal dynamics of abuse are enacted, at the same time addressing family members' needs to improve their functioning as a unit in the aftermath of reporting and intervention. Advocating for family therapy in treating child and adolescent victims, Gelinas (1988) argues:

> [F]amily therapists have the most direct impact on the actual relational structures in which the incest occurs. The impact on those relational structures can be more direct than the one-step-removed work necessarily implied by individual or group work with a child. . . . It is important to work with familial relational imbalances as directly and powerfully as possible because the family is currently constituting the child's relational developmental context and will continue to do so. Even if the child and family are separated, the relationships are maintained psychologically and remain in the child's head. Most interventions, including actual physical separation from the family, do not change that. The child will continue to function as before in the old relational patterns and will tend to re-create her familial relational patterns in future relationships. (pp. 33–34)

Of course, there are some limitations on working with entire families in incestuous situations. Some of these are practical. Offending fathers may be in jail; victims may be hospitalized; some family members may have separated or been sent away to live with others subsequent to discovery of the abuse. Other limitations are psychological. The stress reactions of certain victims or the rage of certain offenders may make their presence in the same room too emotionally volatile or even physically dangerous. Rage-based family systems, in particular, may contain a blatantly out-of-control offender or seriously traumatized family members. However, these are exceptions to more common patterns of incest family interaction. We believe that treatment should not be predicated on this type of control and protection by those outside the family. Rather, therapy should be based on the expectation that family members can work together to solve problems and bring about positive change. Family members should be separated in treatment only when direct evidence of harm or the threat of harm is present. In our experience, *some small risk of reabuse needs to be tolerated* for family therapy to be conducted most effectively and efficiently; with appropriate safeguards inside the treatment process itself, the danger of further abuse is quite minimal.

SPECIFYING TREATMENT OBJECTIVES

In her provocative book on working with violent couples and families, Cloe Madanes (1990) observes that therapists often are uncomfortable discussing the moral values that are inextricably tied to treatment goals. Contending that effective therapy requires "moral reference points," she explicates eight goals common to all therapies (pp. 9–14):

1. *To control action.* Therapy can help clients control their own behavior deliberately, rather than being controlled by others or being overwhelmed by uncontrollable impulses.

2. *To control mind.* Therapy can contribute to changing the context of a person so that unpleasant or unhelpful thoughts and feelings will change.

3. *To control violence and anger.* Therapy can transform anger into positive actions and encourage the patience and tolerance necessary to exist in a family and in society.

4. *To encourage empathy.* Therapy can encourage empathy toward others and a sense of justice as part of a well-adjusted and emotionally satisfying life.

5. *To encourage hope.* When a therapist is hopeful, clients can be hopeful about their own lives. An important task of therapy is to create a framework within which hope is possible and certain client goals can be attained.

6. *To promote tolerance and compassion.* Therapy can foster tolerance as a basis for good relationships between people, along with the compas-

sion necessary for an appropriately protective environment in which the young can grow and develop.

7. *To encourage forgiveness and kindness.* Therapy can introduce the idea of forgiveness into situations in which there is alienation and can encourage in clients the kindness that is so important in all ongoing relationships.

8. *To promote harmony and balance.* Therapy can help clients avoid both excess and deprivation in their lives, encouraging them instead to seek harmony and balance in their thoughts, feelings, and behaviors within their physical and social environments.

Most sexual abuse treatment programs are predicated upon eliminating the abuse, a socially desirable goal that may or may not be welcomed by various members of the family. Often lacking are carefully crafted *positive objectives* agreed upon by therapist and client(s). While stopping the sexual abuse certainly ought to be a primary goal of incest treatment, it should never be the sole objective. Despite differences in approach and technique, most systemically-oriented therapists agree that, in addition to dealing with the intrapsychic conflicts of the perpetrator, victim, and other family members, therapy ought to address structural issues in the family system, interpersonal patterns of transaction among family members, and contextual issues between the family and society.[2]

Of course, treatment emphasis varies according to the theoretical framework, specific client population, and professional practice context of each therapist. For example, consistent with their belief that sexual or physical abuse is a symptom of family pathology, Cirillo and DiBlasio (1992) state that their central goal is to "modify the dysfunctional patterns in which the violence is rooted. Thus, our ultimate objective is to enable the family to recover its own child-raising functions" (p. 10). The premises of the Santa Clara County Child Sexual Abuse Treatment Program developed by Giarretto include: "(a) the child-victim is best served if she can be returned to her own family; (b) to accomplish this aim, the family system must be changed from an abusive to a nurturing one; and (c) to expedite the return of the child to a healthy familial environment, systematic collaboration is required among police, legal-judicial personnel, social workers, therapists, and the family members themselves" (Giarretto & Einfeld-Giarretto, 1990, p. 219). The program's overall goals are to "resolve anger, hostility, shame, fear, and jealousy so that the people can communicate and function as a family again without incest" and to "aim at healing the

---

[2]These emphases are reflected in the historical progression of incest treatment. For example, compare the following accounts of treatment over the past thirty years: Lustig, Dressler, Spellman, & Murray (1966); Justice & Justice (1976); Gutheil & Avery (1977); Giarretto (1982a, 1982b); Mrazek & Bentovim (1981); deYoung (1982); James & Nasjleti (1983); Mayer (1983); Lutz & Medway (1984); Taylor (1984); Alexander (1985); Bentovim, Elton, Hildebrand, Tranter, & Vizard (1988); Gelinas (1988); Sgroi (1988); Trepper & Barrett (1989); Friedrich (1990); Ingersoll & Patton (1990); Cirillo & DiBlasio (1992).

family, ridding involved persons of stigma, and maintain the family unit through re-educating the members and teaching them their various roles" (Vander Mey & Neff, 1982, pp. 727–728). The Centre for Child and Adolescent Development in Edmonton, Alberta — which attempts to combine systemic, feminist, and victim-advocacy frameworks — has as its main goals "to identify and help family members change all forms of both perpetrator and victim behaviors and to assist and motivate the family to make those structural and/or interactional changes that will allow all members to relate openly and congruently and to live, together or apart, in safety and security" (CCAD, n.d., p. 10).

Some programs list differing treatment goals for individual family members, most of which are directly connected with the abuse. For example, goals for child victims may include: to validate the expression of their various feelings surrounding the abuse; to help them think about the sexual abuse in ways that are less destructive to their self-image; and to help them integrate their conflicted feelings toward the perpetrators. Goals for other family members also are primarily abuse-oriented. For example, goals for nonperpetrating mothers may include: to help denying mothers to accept that the sexual abuse really did happen; to assist them in protecting their children from reabuse; to help them become more nurturing, less guilt-inducing, and more positive with their children (Damon & Waterman, 1986, p. 247).

More than others, Friedrich (1990) emphasizes goal-setting *with* clients, utilizing Goal Attainment Scaling (GAS) which can enable family members to measure their progress in concrete terms. Viewing goal-setting as part of both evaluation and treatment, Friedrich stresses the importance of being able to show what changes actually have occurred when interfacing with the legal and social service systems. Specific goal-setting also concretizes what family members are trying to accomplish in therapy, providing family members with a greater sense of involvement as well as increasing their internal locus of control over the changes they are experiencing. By agreeing on goals, family members, including the children, take joint responsibility for working actively to improve family relationships. Finally, GAS can make change seem manageable to family members rather than negative and overwhelming. Goals represent hope.

Our ecological approach to treatment involves ten general objectives brought by the therapist to the therapeutic encounter. Within each of these, more specific objectives are devised with various family members and with the family as a unit, on the basis of which treatment proceeds and is evaluated.

1. *Realign structural boundaries.* Based upon an understanding of the boundary distortions that typically characterize families in which sexual abuse has occurred, the therapist seeks to restructure the relationships of

intrapsychic and familial subsystems, as well as the relationship of the family to its social context (Figure 7.1). These efforts focus primarily on fostering self-differentiation of individuals, increasing reciprocity in relationships among family members, facilitating clarity and appropriateness of generational roles and responsibilities, and improving connections between the family and its community (including families of origin).

EXAMPLE

The Johnson family seeks therapy in connection with the mother's suspicion that her husband sexually abused his stepdaughter (now 19) when she was a child. Although no legal action has been taken, Mrs. Johnson has made it clear that she will not stay in the marriage unless the family enters therapy. She has recently completed chemical dependency treatment, after seriously abusing alcohol and prescription medications for most of her adult life. Mrs. Johnson can now acknowledge that, in many ways, she has acted like an "irresponsible child" in her family for years. Married very young following a pregnancy, she and her first husband divorced after two years. She married Mr. Johnson when her daughter, Vicky, was 3 years old, and subsequently had three more children, two boys and a girl.

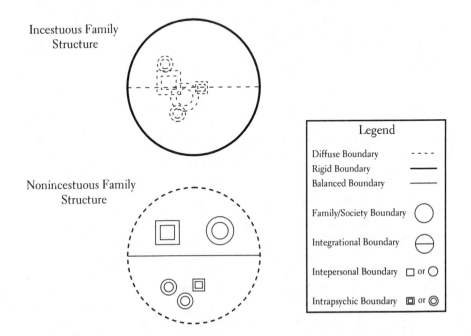

FIGURE 7.1 Boundaries in Incestuous and Nonincestuous Families

As a child, Vicky was both compliant and extremely competent; she grew up as the major parental figure for her three younger half brothers, as a companion to her stepfather, and as a supportive, sympathetic confidante to her own mother. In contrast, the three boys have always been difficult and rebellious, rude, and even physically abusive to their mother. Mrs. Johnson believes they learned this behavior from their father, who often shamed and humiliated her in front of the children, frequently threatened her, and physically slapped her on a number of occasions when she had been drinking.

When she was 13, Vicky's positive behavior abruptly changed. She began staying out all night, drinking, and stealing from her parents. Several times, she ran away. Finally, she was sent to a juvenile home, where she continued to be difficult; eventually she reported that she had been raped by a male staff member. At age 16, Vicky was sent to a foster home, where she also was sexually abused. Subsequently, Vicky began group therapy in a program for adolescent victims of rape and sexual abuse. She married at 19, about the same time her mother went through chemical dependency treatment.

In the context of several family sessions, Vicky revealed her current and past sexual problems, including her history of abuse, and she revealed having been sexually molested by her stepfather from age 10 to age 13, at which time she left home. It is clear that the women in the family are now grasping the tragic reality of their family life, while the men seem to believe that everything in the family is perfectly fine except for the "overly sensitive, neurotic, angry women" who are trying to blame others for their problems.

2. *Enhance family communication.* Incest families are characterized by indirect communication, necessitating "mind reading" among members which, in turn, produces further interpersonal boundary diffusion. The therapist can be helpful by modeling and eliciting clear, direct, emotionally congruent communication regarding all aspects of individual and family behavior, including the sexual abuse itself.

EXAMPLE (CONTINUED)

Communication in the Johnson family reflects both overeroticized and hostile interchanges. Vicky and her mother talk about their anger toward the males in the family (including some pejorative comments about men in general). During therapy sessions, Mr. Johnson and his sons often wink, make hand gestures, and allude to private humor between them (much of it sex-related), clearly engaging in a language that excludes the females. Father and sons appear to be adept at manipulating arguments in the name of "rationality," often leaving the women confused and unable to justify their positions. As a result, they usually acquiesce to the more powerful males. It appears that the lower status females often end up pitted against each other, so that neither mother nor daughter have an ally in the family power structure.

3. *Improve family conflict-resolution processes.* Disagreement and conflict in sexually abusive families are often opportunities for exploitation and violation; sometimes, the sexual abuse itself is an expression of unresolved conflict. Creating an environment in which it is safe to express differing thoughts and feelings is crucial to family healing.

EXAMPLE (CONTINUED)

The need for males in the Johnson family to maintain their power means they must continually compete among themselves — unless the conflict involves females, in which case, they must succeed as a group in "winning." In therapy, the males appear to stick together, minimizing any differences between them and seeking ways to pit the females against each other. When these tactics succeed in eliciting either tears or aggression, Mr. Johnson and one or both boys verbally condemn or physically threaten the mother and daughter. The females vacillate between arguing overtly with each other and joining together to verbally attack the males as a group. This climate does not permit any possibility of negotiation.

4. *Improve family problem-solving processes.* Families in which incest occurs are typically poor at problem-solving. Since members are easily threatened and perpetrator/victim interactions patterns are readily triggered, high anxiety and low trust tend to recycle problems through the family. As a result, most incest families are characterized clinically as "multiproblem families." Teaching problem-solving skills such as negotiation and compromise contributes to reducing abusive interaction patterns, both by improving the self-confidence of individuals and by uniting family members in coordinated efforts toward common goals despite differences.

EXAMPLE (CONTINUED)

For many years, Mr. Johnson's incestuous relationship with Vicky was an ongoing threat to his power in the family. In his attempts to be seen as faultless in all areas of his career and family life, he found it necessary to challenge the credibility of his daughter. During the period when he was abusing her, he often accused her of being a "slut" when she showed even the slightest interest in boys, or he accused her of abusing chemicals and lying about it — accusations that precipitated major battles in the household.

For her part, Vicky was a paradox. On the one hand, she was highly competent, raising her younger siblings by fixing their meals, washing their clothes, and overseeing their schoolwork. On the other hand, she had occasional periods of dissociation and intermittent temper tantrums. As an adolescent, she acquired labels such as "delinquent" and "schizo-affective disorder." When problems in the Johnson family could not be resolved, Vicky *became* the problem. When she was finally removed from the home, the remaining family members believed that they had "gotten rid" of the family problem, despite Mrs. Johnson's active chemical addiction, serious ongoing marital conflicts, and the verbal and physical violence that characterized the family.

5. *Decrease shame and increase self-esteem.* Members of an abusive family often share an internalized sense of defect, fostered and maintained by repetitive perpetrator/victim interaction patterns. Transformation of the shame-based family identity is difficult, but critical to successful treatment. It requires identifying the pain of the perpetrator's own victimization experiences, along with encouraging the victim(s) to give up a negative identity in favor of a more self-responsible, but less familiar sense of self. While individual therapy may be useful for some members, family therapy permits members to express feelings, seek support, and practice nonexploitive ways of relating under the guidance of the therapist (provided the therapist can resist the urge to play Rescuer).

EXAMPLE (CONTINUED)

Despite the complex, conflictual dynamics of the family, the Johnsons make every effort to appear "normal" and "successful" to others outside the family. In fact, "looking good" has been one of the primary objectives of the family for years. An overcompensating need to be "perfect" particularly characterizes the males. The boys are all good students and heavily involved in extracurricular activities at school. Mr. Johnson and his sons were embarrassed by the mother's decision to enter chemical dependency treatment, and they have been humiliated by Vicky's acting out behavior as an adolescent. To cope with this shame, family members "explain" Vicky's problems by attributing them to her birth father, who abandoned her following her parents' divorce. The rationale for condemning and demoralizing the females for their problems becomes more apparent as therapy progresses. Mrs. Johnson reveals her struggle to keep from abusing chemicals again as the perpetrator/victim interaction dynamics within the family become more overt. Mrs. Johnson soon reveals that she, too, was sexually molested as a child by her alcoholic grandfather.

6. *Rebalance power/control issues.* Almost always, incest family members require assistance in developing better power/control balances, within themselves and in relation to each other. By utilizing both power and control in appropriately balanced ways (and by protecting family

members from further victimization by each other or by outside agencies), the family therapist models new patterns of behavior within a safe environment in which survival need not depend upon the dynamics of abuse.

EXAMPLE (CONTINUED)

Clearly, the males in the Johnson family operate as perpetrators a good deal of the time. Undercontrolled and overrelying on power, they are verbally and physically aggressive in their interactions with each other and with Mrs. Johnson, Vicky, and her younger sister. Periodically, however, Mr. Johnson and the boys become extremely controlling; via shaming, withholding, or refusal, one or more of them invite the females to strike out aggressively. When they are successful in eliciting loss of control by one or more of the females, the males can then maintain their illusion of "perfection" and "innocence" while continuing to behave as perpetrators for another period of time.

7. *Create appropriate empathy.* Characterized by poor boundaries, victims of sexual abuse may be mistakenly thought of as empathic. However, genuine empathy requires boundaries clear enough to distinguish one's own pain from that of others, uncharacteristic of abuse victims. Similarly, perpetrators usually have dissociated from the pain of their own childhood victimization with the same result — an inability to be genuinely empathic. Family therapy provides an excellent opportunity to foster *interdependence* (a balance of dependence and independence) among family members — understanding, support, and cooperation between individuals who are connected yet separate.

EXAMPLE (CONTINUED)

Mr. Johnson describes his childhood as idyllic, with wonderful, loving parents and strong, positive ties to his siblings (all boys). However, he admits that, as an adult, he has only rare contact with his parents, who live in another state. He rationalizes this by explaining that he has been "too busy working and raising a family." The situation is the same with his brothers and sisters, all of whom "have their lives to live and are busy people too." Similarly, the Johnson boys describe their lives as "great," except for the embarrassment of their mother's and sister's problems. Each boy seems to believe that the sexual abuse of Vicky did not occur or was so minimal as to be nothing more than a "misunderstanding." None of the males is interested in therapy; they are attending only because Mrs. Johnson is "blackmailing" them.

When mother and daughter describe their lives as filled with hurt and anguish, the males dismiss the accounts or ridicule the females. Even Mrs. Johnson's account of a childhood filled with the pain of parental alcoholism, family financial disasters, her own sexual victimization, and the violence that characterized her first marriage brings only silence or dismissing remarks from her husband and sons.

8. *Desexualize/resexualize relationships.* Defining generational boundaries and developmental needs helps family members in desexualizing expressions of affection and nurturance. In the context of family therapy, privacy needs of individuals can be emphasized and members can be helped to devise appropriate means of expressing affection. In addition, distinctions can be made between the legitimate erotic expression of the marital partners and the age-appropriate behaviors of the younger generation. Helping the adult partners create a satisfying sexual relationship begins in family therapy when the therapist legitimizes the alliance and emphasizes its uniqueness in family experience.

EXAMPLE (CONTINUED)

Mr. and Mrs. Johnson report an extremely unsatisfactory sexual relationship since before they were married. Despite a high frequency of sexual contact in the early years, neither partner found it satisfying. Mrs. Johnson has never been orgasmic (except on several occasions in the incestuous relationship with her grandfather). Mr. Johnson is described by both as a life-long "ladies man," whose self-esteem is primarily based upon his sexual prowess along with his career success. All of the children are aware of his history of sexual involvements, and he has frequently boasted to his adolescent sons about his escapades, conveying his disappointment with his marital sex life and encouraging them to "get as much experience as possible" before marriage.

After pretending to be interested and responsive for a number of years, Mrs. Johnson finally gave up. She recognized her husband's flirtatious behavior with other women and (correctly) suspected him of a number of extramarital involvements. Mr. Johnson justified these as attempts to make his wife jealous and, therefore, more interested in sex. As a result, however, her disinterest deepened and her chemical abuse worsened. For a time, she put greater energy into their sexual relationship when he began to act provocatively with Vicky (though she never suspected the actual abuse). Soon, however, her interest diminished again, at which time Mr. Johnson began thinking of his wife's disinterest as a justification for turning to his stepdaughter for sexual gratification. This way, he rationalized, his wife couldn't really be angry with him for chasing other women outside the family.

9. *Develop family rituals.* Positive rituals are frequently absent in incest families, resulting from high anxiety, mutual distrust, unresolved conflict, and problematic communication. Family therapy can be a vehicle to pro-

mote positive rituals that enhance family stability and cooperation (Imber-Black, Roberts, & Whiting, 1988). In fact, family treatment itself can serve as an initial ritual making a positive impact upon the family as a unit.

EXAMPLE (CONTINUED)

The few rituals in the Johnson family are largely segregated by gender. Although they formally celebrate national holidays and Christian events such as Christmas and Easter, none of the family members has much emotional investment in any family activities associated with these times. Mrs. Johnson has tried for years to involve her family in activities with either of their families of origin; however, Mr. Johnson, and one-by-one the children, are "too busy."

Until she was 10, Vicky always had a birthday party; at that age, the parties stopped, and the only current acknowledgement of her birthday is a card signed by her mother in the name of both parents. Her sister, the youngest, has always been treated similarly. By contrast, Mr. Johnson takes his sons for a "boys' night out" on their respective birthdays. On his birthday, mother and daughter cook him a dinner of his favorite foods. The Johnsons have never had any regular rituals such as bedtime stories, game nights, or family outings. No family member is able to identify a favorite story, movie, television show, or activity of another member.

10. "Trouble-shoot" other symptoms. While some incestuous families appear to be relatively free from serious symptoms beyond the sexual abuse, most are characterized by other family problems, such as financial difficulties, chemical dependency, psychiatric symptoms, academic/work problems, or various "acting out" behaviors (Cirillo & DiBlasio, 1992; MacFarlane & Waterman, 1986; Renshaw, 1982; Spoentgen, 1992; Trepper & Barrett, 1989; Waterman, 1986). Intervening into the sexual abuse can bring to light other family difficulties; family therapy can mobilize family resources to deal with these problems. The timing of intervention into issues other than the abuse is important; the potential for assistance in resolving them can identify the therapist as a helper to the family rather than simply an intruder.

EXAMPLE (CONTINUED)

With great difficulty, Mrs. Johnson has managed to stay sober, although there is some concern about her continuing need for high doses of medically prescribed antidepressants. It has become clear that the oldest son, now 17, needs professional help to deal with his increasing physical aggressiveness; the therapist has referred him to a domestic violence program to work on anger management. During marital therapy, Mrs. Johnson has acknowledged going on occasional spending sprees, charging thousands of dollars on the family credit cards. Mr. Johnson has been upset, but has refused to admit that he is incapable of providing whatever income the family needs. As a result, the family is now in moderate financial difficulty and owes some back taxes. To everyone's shock, Mrs. Johnson also has admitted doing some shoplifting in department stores after her husband canceled one of their credit accounts which he labeled "frivolous." She is quite aware that this behavior was a way of striking back at her supposedly "perfect husband." The youngest son, age 13, has been evaluated as "abusing" alcohol and is being considered for an outpatient treatment program. The therapist is recommending some sessions of sex therapy for Mr. and Mrs. Johnson, although neither of them indicates much interest, and they have begun to talk about the possibility of separation.

MODALITIES OF TREATMENT:
AN OVERVIEW

Until now, treatment for family sexual abuse has consisted primarily of therapy for victims and therapy for offenders. As we indicated in Chapter 1, family-centered incest treatment is still relatively rare. Young victims often are treated by child psychologists on an individual basis; frequently, the nonoffending mother is the only other family member participating in treatment. Psychodynamically oriented play therapy is a primary treatment modality for young children, focusing on overcoming the emotions and symptoms that are often secondary to abuse: traumatic stress, inappropriate guilt, chronic anxiety, depression, low self-esteem and poor social skills, repressed anger and hostility, inability to trust, blurred role boundaries and role confusion, self-mastery and control, and pseudo-maturity and acting out (Long, 1986). Most adolescent treatment is talk therapy, often in groups, focusing on the issues listed above.

Perpetrators are treated most often in groups, while incarcerated, in halfway house residential programs, or on a follow-up outpatient basis (Marshall, Laws, & Barbaree, 1990). Individual therapy also occurs in many cases. Typically, little or no contact takes place between the perpetrator's therapist and the victim's therapist (Bera, Hindman, Hutchens, McGuire, & Yokley, 1990). This is a logical extension of the assumption that no contact should occur between the victim and the perpetrator. Sometimes, mothers who refuse to ensure the termination of parental involvement by the offender are viewed with suspicion by helping professionals (Gomes-Schwartz et al., 1990; McCarthy, 1990; McCarthy & Byrne, 1988). Often confrontational in tone, the primary emphases of perpetrator treatment include acknowledging responsibility for the crime (eliminating denial), developing an understanding of the impact of abuse on the victims (empathy training) (Bera, 1990; Hildebran & Pithers, 1989), reworking cognitive distortions (McCarthy, 1990), and relapse prevention (impulse control training) (Maletzky, 1991). Agendas for therapy and social control are often mixed in perpetrator treatment. For example, Mayer (1988) suggests three purposes for group therapy with sex offenders: (a) to provide adjunctive, ongoing support in a safe, secure, and consistent setting; (b) to monitor abusive behaviors in conjunction with primary therapists, adult probation, parole personnel, and child protective services specialists; and (c) to therapeutically intervene into abusive behaviors. Barnard et al. (1989) state that "the primary goal of the treatment of the child molester is to control the deviant behavior patterns, impulses, and preoccupations that impel the sexual orientation toward children. These characteristics must either be internally or externally inhibited to reduce the risk of repeated offenses" (p. 71).

Given the volume of reported child sexual abuse, many treatment agencies and institutions have developed group programs to treat family members. Usually, there is a program for each specific category — separate groups for perpetrators, spouses, victims, and siblings of victims. Often, groups are structured around topics such as revealing the secret, guilt and responsibility, self-esteem, sexuality, expressing feelings, and even practical matters such as preparing for a courtroom appearance (Blick & Porter, 1982; Mandell & Damon, 1989).

Many incest treatment programs allow for the possibility of some family work, usually toward the conclusion of the primary treatment effort with individuals. Often utilized as a means to structure the reunification process, in these programs family therapy is an arena in which all family members can express their feelings about past events and future fears. In addition, these family sessions can provide an opportunity for family members to make a decision about staying together or separating (Blick & Berg, 1989). Some programs include only a single family session to accomplish "forgiveness" or "reunification," although ongoing group therapy for entire families is becoming more widespread (Dovenberg, 1985; Friedman, 1988). Treatment programs organized around family therapy as the major mode of intervention are still in the minority, but are increasing.

INDIVIDUALIZED VERSUS PROGRAMMATIC TREATMENT

The majority of sexual abuse treatment occurs within a programmatic framework (Giarretto, 1982a, 1982b; Knopp, 1984; Mayer, 1984; Trepper & Barrett, 1989). Along with the obvious benefits of simplicity and efficiency, Trepper and Barrett note that a therapy *program* is likely to be taken more seriously by a severely dysfunctional family, since it connotes experience, continuity, and professionalism. However, there has been little consensus on programmatic treatment approaches to incest families (Bulkley, 1981; Carnes, 1983; Kroth, 1979; MacFarlane & Bulkley, 1982; Renshaw, 1982). Even today, there are few "pure" programs based upon a single theoretical approach, although underlying conceptual frameworks usually are discernible in a given program. Few long-term outcome studies are available, though most programs report that incest perpetrators and their families are "helped" by involvement in therapy, and recidivism is the most widely used outcome measure (see Chapter 12).

Although we agree with Trepper and Barrett's emphasis upon the importance of having family members take the problem — and the treatment — seriously, we have concluded that many incestuous families are best dealt with outside the context of formal sexual abuse treatment programs. In our experience, the heavy-handedness of many intervention efforts through social services and legal agencies can promote resistance and defensiveness in family members. Entering an identified treatment program requires public acknowledgment, which may greatly increase the shame that underlies resistance. In addition, formal programs may highlight the severity of consequences occasioned by reporting the abuse, thereby heightening the anxiety and guilt of all family members, even the victim whom the program purports to help. Finally, programs have an organization and a sequence that may suit an agency staff, but might not match the particular structures, meanings, and styles of a given family. This lack of fit can greatly hamper effective therapy. Certainly, sequencing and integrating various therapeutic modalities requires some judgment on the part of the therapist. However, understanding the structures, meanings, and dynamics of a particular family always is crucial to effective therapy. On this basis, we organize therapy to interlock with these variables from the beginning.

If incestuous behavior indeed does serve different functions in different families, then it would appear important to assess the meaning/function of the incest in a given family when planning for its treatment. Too often a family is treated in a certain way because of the particular characteristics of a treatment program rather than the specific characteristics of that family. For example, a highly confrontive program that focuses on identifying and dealing with anger between family members may be very useful to an aggression-based incest family, while the same treatment approach to an affection-based incest family may generate confusion and resistance. Any given treatment program will be randomly successful with a certain number of client families. Informal discussion by professionals in the field suggests that incest perpetrators or families who drop out of treatment programs because they do not seem to "fit" are high risk for recidivism. The four categories of incestuous behavior described in Chapter 4 can serve as guidelines for utilizing treatment approaches that are well-matched with both the functional meanings and the structural characteristics of various incest families (Table 7.1).

TABLE 7.1
Incest Family Typology: Treatment Considerations

Affection-Based	Erotic-Based	Aggression-Based	Rage-Based
Outpatient treatment	Outpatient treatment	Outpatient/inpatient treatment	Inpatient treatment
Family therapy primary	Group therapy for family members primary	Group therapy for family members primary	Individual therapy primary
Separation not necessary	Separation sometimes necessary	Separation usually necessary	Separation always necessary and important
Perhaps group therapy	Family therapy	Family therapy	Group therapy
Marital therapy	Marital therapy	Marital therapy	Perhaps family therapy
		Perhaps individual therapy	Perhaps marital therapy
Structural/strategic family approaches, supportive group therapy, collaborative and narrative approaches also useful	Small group approaches, addiction approaches, structural/strategic family and marital therapy, narrative approaches sometimes useful	Directive group approaches, structural/strategic family and marital therapy, empathic and narrative approaches useful	Psychodynamic (object-relations) individual therapy, supportive group therapy, possible structural/strategic family and marital therapy if appropriate

Treatment of Affection-Based Incest

The family for whom incest is an affection-based process has a number of strengths upon which to build during treatment, since its underlying theme is the desire for positive contact. Family members should be encouraged to function as individuals, while coordinating with each other in order to accomplish tasks in a mutually beneficial way. Boundary issues can be worked on rather explicitly. The disruption produced by revealing the incest often provides sufficient motivation to forestall its recurrence. Therefore outpatient treatment with an emphasis on the entire family can be both effective and efficient. The family often has other resources and strengths useful for treatment (Gelinas, 1986). For example, the affiliative needs of family members can be directed at forming supportive networks with others outside the family, thereby helping break down the rigidity of the boundary between the family and its social environment. Focusing on self-differentiation within the family system (techniques characteristic of structural and Bowenian family therapy approaches) appears to be effective with this type of family. Usually, it is helpful if the perpetrator can remain in the home with other family members for the duration of the treatment process. Affection-oriented incest perpetrators can be aided by individual therapy focusing on repairing early victimization experiences and self-differentiation, as well as by participation in a group, where the emphasis should be on building self-esteem, improving cognitive judgment, and enhancing social skills.

Treatment of Erotic-Based Incest

Because misguided eroticism has permeated nearly all aspects of life in the pansexual family, a rather directive approach to therapy is typically helpful. However, because the underlying motivations are still positive (in most cases), outpatient treatment programs can be effective. Living arrangements for family members should be dealt with carefully and thoroughly. Distorted erotic interaction patterns are so well-established that they may be difficult to reorganize, and recurrent boundary violations may call for the physical separation of certain family members. Open group homes, halfway-houses, and other living arrangements that deemphasize sex as a basis for social interaction can be useful adjuncts to treatment.

The combination of rigid sexual stereotypes and role-related power/ control struggles that characterize pansexual families requires education, attitude change, and reality-testing skills for promoting positive change in the family system. Thus, cognitive-behavioral techniques or rational-emotive therapy can be especially valuable. Group therapy with peers may also be useful, particularly in the earlier stages of treatment. Perpetrators' and victims' groups, peer support programs such as Parents United, sexual addiction treatment models — any of these may be helpful in facilitating alternative ways of experiencing sexuality in interpersonal relationships. Relationship therapy with a sexual focus is likely to be very important for the perpetrator and his partner. Family sessions are important again in the later stages of treatment when intrapsychic and interpersonal issues have been resolved sufficiently to permit positive forms of intimacy between family members.

Treatment of Aggression-Based Incest

Depending upon the assessed degree of impulse control and the potential for power/control struggles to result in further abuse or violence, various members of an aggression-based incest family may require controlled living situations. Perpetrators can benefit from inpatient treatment, and victims may need the protection of a sheltered residence or foster care home. While it can be helpful for family members to be separated from each other during the earlier phases of therapy, some treatment programs maintain this separation far past the time when it is necessary or useful. Highly confrontive group treatment approaches can facilitate family members learning to deal creatively with anger and conflict in relationships, without linking these to sex. Marital therapy with an emphasis on conflict resolution is usually necessary. Similarly, family therapy focusing on intergenerational power struggles and developmental issues can serve to open up channels for negotiation and problem-solving. Treatment for all family members should attend to underlying issues of shame and low self-esteem. Some members may require a period of intense individual therapy to repair self-deficits and build ego strength to enable them to maintain their identities in the context of close interpersonal relationships.

A variety of structural and strategic family therapy techniques used throughout the course of treatment can aid in therapy for aggression-based incest. As therapy progresses, an approach such as Nagy's contextual family therapy can be helpful in rebuilding a coherent family identity. Here, the focus is typically on trust, loyalty, justice, forgiveness, repair of previously ruptured relationships, creative handling of conflicts, and formulating a plan for a common future. Of course, some families remain permanently split, their negative history too powerful and their members' vulnerability too great to permit even the rudiments of mutuality.

Treatment of Rage-Based Incest

The propensity for violence and the pathological behavior of the perpetrator (and sometimes other family members) should be the overriding factors determining the structure and process of therapy for rage-based incest. Inpatient treatment in a locked hospital or prison program often is necessary for the perpetrator, who usually is unable to control his episodes of sexual and/or physical abuse. Sometimes, legal restrictions make family-oriented treatment impossible. When it is undertaken, a combination of individual and group therapy is likely to be most helpful to the perpetrator in uncovering and restructuring deep-seated emotional conflicts. In our view, empathic, supportive group therapy is substantially more effective than high confrontation groups, since the latter tend to evoke shame and trigger rage, which lie at the core of the self.[3] At some point in group or individual treatment, the perpetrator's own role as a victim is likely to surface, accompanied by shame and anxiety that threaten to overwhelm

---

[3]We are firmly convinced that it is *never* useful to intentionally trigger shame reactions in clients, although shame will occur inevitably in the course of treatment, and it can be worked with therapeutically. Shame/rage reactions and their treatment are discussed in greater detail in our book *Child Sexual Abuse: An Ecological Approach to Treating Victims and Perpetrators.*

him. Without support and other appropriate responses by the therapist and others, the reexperiencing of victimization can again trigger massive defense mechanisms and render the perpetrator impermeable to outside influence. Until this therapeutic crisis has been successfully surmounted, the perpetrator is unlikely to be amenable to interactive therapy with other family members.

Other members of the rage-based incest family also may require individual therapy to prepare them for more interactive treatment. Depending upon type and degree of symptoms, some individuals can benefit from long-term therapy or even residential treatment. The issues of rage-based victimization are typically structured into the personality systems of some or all family members insofar as they have been part of a family ecology that has sustained the sexual violence over a lengthy period of time (in contrast to situations in which only one or several episodes of abuse occur before they are reported and the perpetrator is removed from the home). Many victims of rage-based sexual abuse will manifest their own patterns of perpetrating behavior, keeping the family in crisis if they remain in the home or creating abusive situations if they are placed outside the home.

Rage-based incest families often dissolve permanently; termination of parental rights — sometimes voluntarily, sometimes involuntarily — is a frequent sequel to uncovering the abuse. Both parents may lack the interpersonal capacity to provide support and nurturance for any or all of the children, and protection authorities may have to intervene quite actively to curtail the generalized abuse and neglect. Even under these circumstances, some amount of family-focused therapy is recommended in order to contribute to the positive long-range functioning of the children. The very crisis created by intervention into the sexual abuse requires that these children restructure their own intrapsychic boundaries in order to accommodate a new family ecology. Foster parents or adoptive families can be included in treatment on an as-needed basis to assist in this restructuring process. Children raised in chaotic, rage-dominated families are likely to enter surrogate families with inappropriate behaviors which will necessitate extra efforts to integrate them into new, more secure social environments not characterized by perpetrator/victim interaction patterns.

All in all, we prefer the flexibility offered the therapist by a more individualized approach to therapy rather than the familiarity and security of a programmatic approach to incest treatment. At the same time, an organized program, particularly if group-oriented, may be both effective and economical within the context of certain communities that have limited resources for intervention and treatment of child sexual abuse — as well as within the emerging context of managed care (see Chapter 11). Even here, an experienced family therapist inside or outside of an agency can serve both as primary therapist and as coordinator of treatment efforts by moving certain families or family members in and out of particular treatment components as appropriate to their individual needs.

TIMING THE COMPONENTS
OF TREATMENT

Little professional agreement exists regarding the timing of various incest treatment components. Most therapists who work mainly with child victims believe that individual or group treatment of family members should be well underway before family sessions begin (Blick & Berg, 1989; Friedrich, 1990; Sgroi, 1982). Some family therapists concur (e.g., Bentovim, 1991; Ingersoll & Patton, 1990). Matthews, Raymaker, and Speltz (1991) surveyed a number of social service, criminal justice, and treatment agencies regarding the desirable preconditions for family reunification. Their results are summarized in Table 7.2.

Some family-oriented therapists also prefer to delay family sessions until individual and/or group therapy have led the offender to admit the abuse and be able to apologize convincingly to his victim(s). For example, a family apology session can be used as a transition into family therapy (Trepper, 1986; Trepper & Barrett, 1989). Organizing treatment around family sessions and viewing other therapy modalities as adjunctive is still rare (Gelinas, 1988). Some programs concentrate on marital therapy following therapy with the entire family (e.g., Cirillo & DiBlasio, 1992). Trepper and Barrett utilize marital therapy at strategic points to accomplish certain treatment objectives. Giarretto (1976) has spelled out what he believes to be an optimal sequence of treatment for father-child incest: (a) individual counseling for child, mother, and father; (b) mother-daughter counseling; (c) marital counseling; (d) father-child counseling; (e) family counseling; and (f) group counseling (including Parents United and Daughters and Sons United self-help groups).

Since our ecological approach to treatment is *process*-oriented rather than program-oriented, a single order for utilizing the various modalities of therapy cannot be specified. In our experience, families with children of comparable ages and even similar abuse histories may require very different sequences of therapy. The following issues should figure into decision-making regarding the progression of therapy:

- the degree of trauma demonstrated by the victim(s)
- the meaning of the sexual abuse to the victim, the perpetrator, and to the family system as a whole
- the orientation and style of the perpetrator in relation to the perpetrator/victim interaction pattern
- the orientation and style of the nonoffending adult(s) in relation to the perpetrator/victim interaction pattern

TABLE 7.2
Desirable Preconditions for Family Reunification

Victim
   Able to acknowledge and discuss the sexual abuse
   Does not blame self for the abuse
   Willing to be reunited with entire family
   Confident about ability to report any further abuse
   Feels safe and protected in the home if the perpetrator is to be returned

Perpetrator
   Accepts full responsbility for the sexual abuse
   Shows empathy for the victim
   Shows remorse for the offense
   Willing to talk with the victim about the abuse, making appropriate apologies
   Demonstrates understanding about the motivation for the abuse
   Resolves family-of-origin issues

Spouse
   Able to put victim's need for protection first
   Able to confront the offender and express anger
   Able to discuss the abuse openly
   Holds offender responsible for the abuse
   Does not blame the victim

Family
   Desires to reunify
   Completed treatment
   Openly discussed the sexual abuse together
   Identified potentially risky situations and formulated a protection plan
   Involved in a family support system; not isolated
   Demonstrates healthy ways of interacting
   Makes concrete changes in the home

- the orientation and style of the children in relation to the perpetrator/victim interaction pattern
- structural family patterns following revelation of the abuse
- reactions of the family to social intervention
- the overall stability of the marital unit
- the parental competence of the adults
- the nature and severity of individual and/or family problems other than the sexual abuse

   Together with these factors, the therapist must decide which aspects of individual and family functioning are most amenable to intervention from the outside, as well as which individuals are most likely to make a solid connection with the therapist, and under what circumstances. Assessment is an ongoing aspect of therapy, helping to determine how to make contact with various parts of the client system, what stances to adopt, and how to formulate and implement useful interventions (Keeney, 1983; Tomm, 1984a, 1984b). Despite the need to deal with each family uniquely, some general guidelines can be helpful in sequencing various therapy components:

- The sooner family therapy can be instituted, the more quickly the family can stabilize sufficiently to make effective use of therapeutic intervention.
- The first stage of therapy inevitably will focus on "crisis," and the therapist should assess the reaction of each individual family member to this crisis of revelation as well as the impact of the crisis on the family's overall functioning. This requires meeting with each family member individually as well as with the entire family.
- Early in treatment, one or more sessions should be scheduled with the marital partners (even if neither of them is the perpetrator) in order to examine the marital interaction as well as to convey an expectation that they will collaborate toward certain goals.
- Confrontation sessions between family members (if necessary) are best scheduled when the individuals involved appear sufficiently stabilized to prevent unnecessary psychological diffusion and possible revictimization.
- Dyadic sessions with family members other than the marital partners should be utilized sparingly to avoid blurring the intergenerational boundary. However, as treatment progresses, meeting with various parent-child combinations can be useful in restructuring family coalitions.
- Marital therapy with a sexual focus is typically most useful in the later stages of therapy, when the spouses are sufficiently differentiated to withstand the stresses of altering established behavior patterns and to be intimate without fear of boundary diffusion.
- While family sessions are critical at the beginning of therapy and should be utilized intermittently throughout treatment, they become particularly important again late in treatment in order to facilitate the integration of therapeutic changes into the overall family system.

Sample Timelines

Tailoring treatment to the characteristics of the client unit requires considerable flexibility on the part of the therapist or treatment team, who simultaneously must juggle numerous assessment variables while developing, implementing, refining, and maintaining a treatment format. Numerous other variables also modify therapy's sequencing and timing, for example: legal proceedings alter family living arrangements; the perpetrator completes a prison term; new symptoms develop in a victim; financial problems affect the family's style of life; children return to the home from foster care; a spouse files for divorce from the perpetrator; previously unreported abuse comes to light; a new child protection worker or guardian ad litem is assigned to the case. Any of these factors may impact the family or their situation in ways that require the therapist to revise hypotheses or strategies, reposition herself in the therapeutic system, or refocus on particular issues. Once again, the therapist is challenged to be adaptable and flexible without losing her power/control balance.

Figure 7.2 depicts sample timelines that illustrate some of the treatment patterns that might be devised for differing client situations.

Each of these treatment recommendations represents a judgment by the therapist regarding useful ways to creatively align with each family member and to gain leverage within the family structure for positive therapeutic change. Again we emphasize that the therapist should be prepared to alter any treatment plan on short notice if circumstances warrant. At the same time, the coordinating therapist should be able to maintain a steady course in the face of potential reactivity by various family members to events in their lives and in the treatment process. Sometimes family therapy can even be used to facilitate participation by family members in decision-making about their own treatment.

EXAMPLE

The Martinez family is referred for therapy subsequent to the revelation by the 14-year-old daughter that she has been involved in oral-genital sexual contact with her father for nearly five years. Assessment reveals an affection-based process in which the father seduced his daughter into an "affair" to replace his sexually disinterested wife, who has been ailing (with lower back problems) and unavailable (a part-time day job and night shift factory work). Immigrants from Puerto Rico, the family is hard-working, upwardly mobile, and educationally oriented — all five children are high achievers in school. Supported by his cultural background, the father is clearly the leader of the family. He strongly advocates for the value of intellect and "rationality" in order to succeed at life, although he appears to be a very intuitive and impulsive person. In the rule system of the family, emotions are considered problematic, and all decision-making requires clear, rational criteria that are vigorously stated (and enforced) by the father. Other than the immediate rationalizations about his sexual cravings, the perpetrator is at a loss to explain his sexual contact with his daughter. He simply labels it "stupid" and expresses genuine remorse.

FATHER-ADOLESCENT DAUGHTER
AGGRESSION-BASED INCEST

Treatment Plan

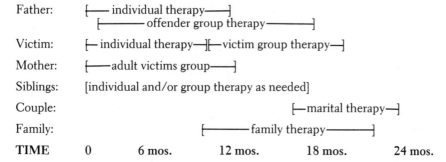

Father: [—— individual therapy——]
           [———— offender group therapy————]
Victim: [— individual therapy—][—victim group therapy—]
Mother: [——adult victims group——]
Siblings: [individual and/or group therapy as needed]
Couple: [—marital therapy—]
Family: [————family therapy————]
TIME   0   6 mos.   12 mos.   18 mos.   24 mos.

FATHER-PREPUBESCENT DAUGHTER
AFFECTION-BASED INCEST

Treatment Plan

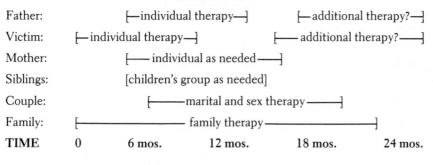

Father: [—individual therapy—]   [—additional therapy?—]
Victim: [—individual therapy—]   [—— additional therapy?——]
Mother: [—— individual as needed ——]
Siblings: [children's group as needed]
Couple: [——marital and sex therapy ——]
Family: [———————— family therapy ————————]
TIME   0   6 mos.   12 mos.   18 mos.   24 mos.

FIGURE 7.2   Sample Timelines

The family works well together in a number of joint sessions while the daughter attends an adolescent victim's group and the father is seen individually on an intermittent basis. Following some assistance in obtaining medical treatment for the wife's back problems, marital therapy is initiated. After careful planning and coordination, the perpetrator is referred to a sex offender treatment group with a therapist whose style is highly confrontive. In his occasional individual sessions with the family therapist, the father complains about the group therapist and comments frequently on how bad it must make the other group members feel to be pushed so mercilessly by the group leader. This opens the way for the individual therapist to explore the feelings of the perpetrator more di-

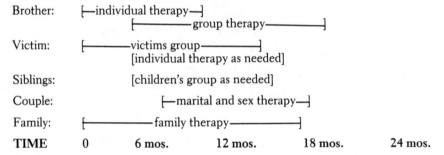

FIGURE 7.2   Sample Timelines (continued)

rectly, first about his observations of other group members and eventually about his own role in the group. The group therapist reports that this man gradually has become a mediator between the leader and group members by talking about his own feelings and exploring the feelings of other clients as they enter or prepare to leave the group. The perpetrator spends about six months in weekly group therapy, followed by a peer-led support group and occasional marital sessions to do problem-solving in the greatly improved marital relationship. There is no recurrence of the incest.

SIBLING INCEST

While not the most commonly reported type of inappropriate sexual contact within families, sibling incest is perhaps the most frequently occuring, perhaps as much as five times more frequent than father-daughter incest (Finkelhor, 1979; Gebhard, Gagnon, Pomeroy, & Christenson, 1965; Johnson & Feldmuth, 1993; Russell, 1983; Wyatt, 1985). In an early study of New England college students by Finkelhor (1979), 15% of the young women reported sexual contact with a sibling, while only 1% were abused by fathers or step-fathers. Ten percent of the young men surveyed indicated sibling sexual contact, while none reported parental incest. Predictably, generating accurate estimates of sibling incest is complicated by the difficulty of distinguishing between exploitive sexual behavior and more acceptable childhood sex play within the family. In addition, siblings may be less likely to report their sexual involvement to parents or other adults, despite the presence of exploitation and even violence. Another barrier to developing accurate frequency estimates is the fact that some sibling contact is hidden within multigenerational incest families (such as the pansexual family), but it is not reported even after the adult-child sexual abuse has been exposed—perhaps because the children fear even greater family disruption.

Meanings of Sibling Incest

Views of "normal" childhood sex play vary greatly across cultures and even between groups in the same society. Some cultures treat sexual activity among young siblings very casually, while others impose strict sanctions against such contact. Despite the uncertainty involved in distinguishing incidental sex play from sexual abuse among siblings, some generally accepted guidelines have emerged in the United States. The major criteria (Finkelhor, 1980) are:

- the difference in age and development of participants (three or more years commonly is considered abusive, as is contact between a child and a sibling who is developmentally delayed)
- the types of sexual behavior involved (vaginal or anal insertion, oral-genital contact, and intercourse tend to be thought of as abusive)
- the presence of coercion or force

Duration of the contact, motivation of the participants, and corollary negative behavior can also be indicative of abuse (Wiehe, 1990). Therapists assessing sibling incest should explore such questions as: What are the relative power positions of the participants? If not forced, did either participant feel coerced or intimidated? Was secrecy involved? How developmentally appropriate were the specific sexual activities? (Sgroi, 1988). Friedrich's Child Sexual Behavior Inventory (Friedrich, 1991; Friedrich et al., 1992) can be useful in evaluating the impact of sibling sexual contact. In addition, analysis of family structures and consideration of sexual meanings within a given family can help the therapist determine when sibling sexual involvement is problematic and may require follow-up treatment. For example, a situation might call for intervention if the siblings are of similar ages but highly discrepant in power and are anger-based in their patterns of interaction, even if the type of sexual contact appears innocuous at first. Left untreated, the sexual interaction could progress into more intrusive behavior and coercive dynamics, particularly if accompanied by family boundary distortions.

There is some evidence that sibling incest is more likely than adult-child contact to be acceptable to both participants. Bank and Kahn (1982) describe two dominant patterns of sibling incest: "power-oriented, phallic, aggressive incest and nurturing, erotic, loving incest" (p. 178). Power-oriented incest parallels the typical descriptions of adult-child incest—an older sibling (usually a male) exploits a younger, more vulnerable sister or brother. This dynamic reflects what we have labeled aggression-exchange incest. "Loving incest" is similar to the sexual contact we have described as affection-based.[4] Bank and Kahn agree with our view that this type of incest represents compensation for unmet emotional needs due to inadequate parenting. Siblings who have formed their own marriage-like partnership often develop intense romantic feelings for each other, lessening the chances that either will consider their involvement to be abusive. We have encountered cases in which siblings continued their sexual activities over a number of years until one left home. A young adult woman once sought therapy with one of the authors to deal with her sense of abandonment by her older brother, with whom she was sexually involved until the night before his wedding. Adult males or females sometimes enter treatment for sexual dysfunction with no conscious recognition that their difficulties are related to unresolved issues and maladaptive response patterns associated with long histories of sibling incest.

Heiman (1988) has adapted Finkelhor's (1984) four preconditions for sexual abuse to a model of sibling incest (Table 7.3). The factors she cites are clearly related to the structural boundary difficulties and meaning distortions characterizing the incestuous family system we have described. From our perspective, sexual involvement between siblings in these families is a small step rather than a large one. The most significant question is not why sibling incest takes place, but why it occurs when parent-child

---

[4]We are convinced that both erotic-based and rage-based incest also occurs among siblings. By definition, the pansexual family is likely to include sexual activities among siblings, often coerced or encouraged by one or both parents. Rage-based sibling incest most often involves a character-disordered adolescent who is both sexually and physically violent with younger sisters and/or brothers.

TABLE 7.3
Preconditions for Sibling Incest

Preconditions	Factors Related to Each Precondition
1. *Motivations to sexually abuse*	
Emotional congruence	Arrested emotional development
	Need to feel powerful and controlling
	Need to fulfill dependency needs
	Need to bind anxiety
	Revenge toward absent parental figure(s)
	Need to prevent disintegration of ego or family
	Re-enactment of childhood trauma
	Provides nurturance and object constancy
Sexual arousal	Modeling of sexual behavior present in the home
	Normal, exploratory sexual behavior arouses further desires
	Awakening and awareness of sexuality
Blockage	Inadequate social skills
	Inadequate understanding of sexuality
	Unresolved oedipal conflict
	Mixed messages within environment, such as repressive norms and permissive attitudes
	Inability to relate to opposite sex peers similar in age
2. *Overcoming internal inhibitions*	Drug/alcohol abuse
	Psychosis
	Inadequate impulse control
	Failure of incest inhibition mechanism in family
	Inability to take another's perspective
	Sexuality between siblings is minimized as child's play
	Lack of defined boundaries placed on sexual behavior
	Modeling
3. *Overcoming external inhibitors*	Absent parents
	Lack of supervision of siblings
	High access of siblings to one another
	Unusual sleeping or rooming conditions
4. *Overcoming victim's resistance*	Victim is emotionally insecure or deprived
	Victim is dependent on offending sibling
	Reports of sexual contact have been dismissed
	Victim lacks knowledge about sexual abuse
	Victim enters relationship as a way of maintaining family integrity
	Coercion

incest does *not*. At the same time, sibling incest frequently is discovered in the course of treating parent-child sexual abuse. In his sample of 50 adolescent male incest offenders, O'Brien (1989) found that 22% came from families in which additional incestuous behavior was present. Further, he found that 36% of the mothers and 10% of the fathers of these adolescents themselves were childhood victims of sexual abuse, compared to only 9% of the mothers and 5.5% of the fathers of nonincestuous adolescent child molesters. When both parent-child and sibling incest are occurring in a particular family, incestuous contacts also are likely to exist within the extended family system — perhaps including grandparents, aunts, uncles, and cousins, as well as in-laws. In these families, we have yet to encounter a "first generation" incest situation; instances of abuse in previous generations always have surfaced at some point in therapy.

Violence in Sibling Incest

Wasserman and Kappel (1985) identified verbal coercion in 57% of the cases in their study of 161 adolescent sex offenders (both incestuous and nonincestuous), with physical force threatened or actually used 35% of the time. In O'Brien's (1989) study of adolescent male sibling incest offenders (N = 50), 41% of the perpetrators used physical force, 7% of which involved weapons (usually knives). Siblings sometimes force their victims to submit to sexual abuse by their friends as well.

Sibling rivalry may account for some of the violence accompanying incest between children in the same family, particularly when appropriate nurturing from parents is missing. Sometimes, parents obviously favor one child, who then is scapegoated by her siblings. Siblings may cling together for support, which can include sexual involvement, when they are severely neglected and/or physically abused by parents. Another possible explanation for the violence might be compensation for lack of authority accorded adults; that is, similar to his victims in age, size, and social status, the sibling perpetrator may escalate his use of force to assure compliance. This increase in aggression may serve also to reduce the likelihood that the incest will be reported, due to the victim's fear of retaliation. Still another explanation for the substantial violence that often accompanies sibling incest may be simply the fact that the participants are children or adolescents who are less able than adults to control their aggressive as well as their sexual impulses.

EXAMPLE

Jeannette, age 19, seeks therapy for problems of self-esteem and difficulties in dating relationships. In the course of her history, she describes severely neglectful parents and several years of sexual and physical abuse by her brother Jack, three years older than she. From the time she was 11, Jack verbally shamed and humiliated her in front of her peers. Privately, he forced her to perform oral sex on him, sometimes demanding that she fellate his friends as well. When Jeanette complied, he would be "nice" to her. When she did not comply, he would kick her and burn her with cigarettes.

Approaches to Treatment

Our approach to treatment of family members involved in sibling incest does not differ significantly from that of families affected by adult-child sexual abuse. This is to be expected given our belief that the intrapsychic and social ecologies of all forms of incestuous activity are largely the same. The structural origins and meaning distortions giving rise to perpetrator/ victim interactions patterns can result in various forms of abuse or violence.[5] The recent growth in treatment programs for young sex offenders has been substantial; in 1982, 22 such programs were identified (Johnson, 1988). In a more recent national survey conducted by the Safer Society program, Knopp and Stevenson (1989) identified a total of 573 public and private treatment programs and service providers for juvenile sex offenders, located in every state except Alabama, Arkansas, and Mississippi. The report did not differentiate services focusing specifically on juvenile *incest* perpetrators. However, an analysis of the treatment models indicated that 43% of the programs and providers utilizing multiple treatment modalities described themselves as family systems-oriented, compared to only 8% of those using a single treatment modality. Considering that most juvenile sexual perpetrators and most victims of abuse by juvenile offenders are still living with their families of origin, we find the lack of focus on family-oriented treatment rather disturbing. Also unsettling is the frequency with which a variety of methods of treatment whose long-range results are not yet fully understoood (such as aversive conditioning and libido-altering drugs) are employed with juvenile offenders.

Of course, some families react to sibling incest as if it were not a serious problem, viewing intervention as an overreaction by outsiders. Even parents who genuinely are concerned about such activity may believe that a minimum amount of individual counseling for their children will resolve the problem rather quickly—and occasionally it does. Just as with families

---

[5]Still unanswered are many questions about the overlapping and distinct characteristics influencing sexual abuse as opposed to physical abuse within family systems. Certainly, families involved in *any* sort of abuse or violence—what Bentovim (1992) has termed "trauma-organized" family systems—have some elements in common; however, it is not yet clear why some families manifest incestuous behavior while others engage in marital battering and/or physical abuse of children.

involved in adult-child incest, resistance to treatment may be substantial on the part of some or all family members. Pacing such families may require initially accepting the orientation toward the sibling participants as identified patients, and enlisting the parents as resources to the therapist in the children's treatment. Exploring instances of prior victimization and the underlying perpetrator/victim interaction patterns in the family requires a bond of trust between therapist and all family members as well as considerable patience and persistence. Addressing these issues is important for successful treatment, because limiting therapy to the incest victim and sibling perpetrator who are still living with their family increases the risk of recidivism.

Some sibling incest families manifest notable parental psychopathology. In a study of 25 such families, Smith and Israel (1987) characterized the parents as emotionally and physically unavailable, sexually overstimulating, and involved in an atypically large number of extramarital liaisons. This combination of factors suggests that children in these families may learn to equate all forms of nurturing and intimacy with erotic activity. Further, the findings of Smith and Israel support the notion that children involved in sibling incest are seeking from each other something they are missing from their parents. Finally, some sibling incest family pathology lies within the adolescent experience itself. In their search for a coherent personal identity, adolescents often seek to merge psychologically with others in a premature bid for intimacy (Erikson, 1963). Ego strength that is insufficient for interpersonal empathy and for impulse control frequently produces a variety of "experimental" behaviors among adolescents; sometimes, such explorations can include incest. Therefore, successful therapy requires attention to ego development and identity consolidation, even if the young client's familial and social context do not fully support such maturation.

In summary, we echo O'Brien's (1989) conclusion regarding treatment of sibling incest:

> The implications for treatment are clear. Family involvement in the treatment of the sibling offender is critical since family system dynamics probably played a significant role in the development and maintenance of the sibling abuse. Specific structural interventions to correct dysfunctional family patterns need to be employed. (p. 30)

CONCLUSION

Family therapy often is the most critical subsystem in the ecology of intervention into incest because it can create a powerfully influential environment for all family members simultaneously. In addition, working with the entire family improves coordination of family goals and treatment objectives. Organized appropriately and coordinated with other elements of treatment, family sessions can make use of existing family resources and family transactional patterns to facilitate positive restructuring with far-reaching consequences. In the following chapter, we describe and illustrate principles that should guide the processes of therapy with incestuous families.

CHAPTER 8

Boundaries and Structural Issues in Family Treatment

[Family] patterns, which until recently have been seen as the major obstacles and problems encountered in working with incest families, are potentially the most powerful resources available for effective treatment.

—Denise Gelinas (1986)

THROUGHOUT THIS BOOK, we have argued that family therapy should be the cornerstone of treatment for family sexual abuse and even for most nonincestuous sexual abuse victims and perpetrators. The family therapist's ecosystemic perspective, as well as her position in the overall ecology of social intervention into sexual abuse, equips her particularly well for the role of treatment coordinator. Previously we described common structural characteristics of families in which incest has occurred. Boundary difficulties create a variety of distortions in transactional patterns between individuals which, in turn, impact upon the feelings, attitudes, and meanings—both personal and shared—of family members. Responding to these distortions, family members begin to relate in a variety of dysfunctional ways, sexually and more generally. The incestuous abuse usually is only one of a variety of maladaptive patterns characterizing these families. Effective family therapy requires that the therapist understand and utilize these patterns to restructure the family system.

THE STANCE OF THE THERAPIST
WORKING WITH INCEST FAMILIES

The therapist's theoretical orientation and individual style naturally influence his or her approach to treating family sexual abuse. They also determine just how a therapeutic alliance with the family system is established. Friedrich (1990) aptly observes that the presence of a therapist is rarely viewed by an incestuous family as a positive opportunity for growth and change, at least initially. Most often, family members are in treatment because they are required or coerced rather than because they are voluntarily seeking to restructure the family system. Incestuous families who enter therapy enthusiastically should be regarded skeptically; they may be manifesting a subtle form of resistance that can be termed "pseudo-compliance."

The relationship between the therapist and the family most likely reflects the same sort of ambivalence that distinguishes the relations between the family members themselves (McCarthy & Byrne, 1988). Even though the family is working effectively on important issues, the connection between the therapist and individual members is seldom secure until well into the treatment process (Friedrich, 1990). The more typical expressions of connection and transference are likely to be absent from therapy, or to be feigned rather than genuine. Therefore, the therapist must be content with little or nothing in the form of direct feedback and must endure considerable ambiguity regarding the impact of treatment on family members.

Exploring trust and loyalty issues in the incestuous family often is an excellent way to address the boundary diffusion and lack of individual differentiation (Bowen, 1978; Schnarch, 1991). The use of positive connotation (de Shazer, 1982; Selvini-Palazzoli, Cecchin, Prata, & Boscolo, 1978) is one excellent way to creatively meet their active or passive resistance to intervention. Some family members may explicitly voice their mistrust of the therapist. The therapist can respond by observing, quite accurately, that the lack of trust is understandable under the circumstances and is evidence of a willingness to take care of themselves in the face of intrusion by outsiders—a sign of family loyalty. This observation can become, in turn, the basis for dealing with trust and betrayal within the family or for exploring differences in meaning and behavior around loyalty among various family members. More subtle forms of resistance to the therapist sometimes can be addressed by following up on the positive connotation of loyalty with observations about differences and conflicts between individual family members. Framing these issues, particularly in relation to the therapist, can produce "creative triangulation" within the family that is useful in restructuring boundaries. For example, the therapist might highlight differences between family members by commenting to someone: "You apparently agree with my observation on how your family avoids conflict, but that seems to contradict what your sister said earlier about how sick and tired she is of family members picking at each other all the time." Alternately, the therapist can ask circular questions requiring family members to distinguish themselves in some way: "Who in this family would be most likely to trust me, if that were to happen?" or

"Who do you think can hold out the longest when it comes to being suspicious of an outsider?"

Paradoxical strategies can be useful in working with overt opposition to treatment. However, heavy-handed or simplistic paradoxes used with abusive families can be unproductive or even dangerous. Cirillo and DiBlasio (1992) label paradoxical injuctions "impossible" to use with abusive families. We agree with their caution, but disagree with their conclusion. Paradox is inherent in therapy as in life; a "therapeutic paradox" simply is something that is problematic or appears contradictory in one ecological subsystem, while being helpful or true in another part of the ecosystem (Keeney, 1983). Working skillfully with the inherent paradoxes (Schnarch, 1989) in incestuous family systems can be among the most powerful and helpful techniques to be offered by the therapist, while imposing artifically constructed paradoxical injunctions on families mandated to treatment can be very damaging. In our ecological approach, inherent paradoxes are elicited and elaborated carefully via the use of balanced pacing and leading questions and statements.

EXAMPLE

Therapy has begun with the Kowalskys, a large incest family in which several of the daughters have been sexually molested and the sons have been physically abused. In an early session, the father argues that nothing sexually inappropriate has taken place and that he only "spanks" his sons when they need it to insure that they will be "good citizens" as adults. He contends that all family members are mentally healthy and that no one "needs therapy."

Therapist: Mr. Kowalsky, I want to compliment you on your dedication to parenting and on the confidence you apparently have in your family. Over the years, I've worked with a lot of families in which the parents don't really trust their children and want to control what they say in therapy. [*Turning to the children*] I'm impressed by your father's pride in you for standing on your own and saying directly and honestly what you think and feel, because this, indeed, *is* a mark of mental health [**pace**]. Of course, sometimes speaking out will lead to disagreement, even conflict, between family members — and this can be helpful, too [**lead**].

By juxtaposing these comments with Mr. Kowalsky's dogmatic assertions, the therapist has set the stage for family members to wrestle with the inherent paradox they have brought to treatment. In order to fulfill the father's mandate to be "mentally healthy," the children are invited to speak up and even to disagree with other family members (including the father). If they do not, the therapist has opened the door to challenging the father's evaluation of his family's mental health.

Family members whose behavior is socially unacceptable — and probably personally offensive to the therapist — present a considerable challenge to developing therapeutic alliances. The common admonition to "find something to like about a client" may not be enough. All therapists occasionally encounter clients whom they dislike; sometimes, if the feelings are strong enough, a referral is necessary. Working in the field of child abuse, a therapist often may feel some ambivalence about a relationship with certain family members. Under these circumstances, two things can be helpful in making a therapeutic connection with each member of an incestuous family. First is the recognition that the perpetrator/victim interaction pattern underlying the family system signals that *each* individual is struggling with victimization issues that threaten his or her survival. This can assist the therapist in developing empathy for all family members, including the perpetrator. The second aid to connecting is the notion of rising to a *challenge*. That is, the therapist's internal motivation can be somewhat like that of a participant in a game of cards or a chess match. Figuring out a "successful strategy" can create a bond between two or more persons engaged in a common endeavor. Perpetrators in particular appreciate a well-played game; a surprising number admire a therapist who can "see through" them or "outwit" them elegantly — paradoxically, this can be helpful in establishing rapport.

EXAMPLE

The Bretini family is referred for treatment following the revelation of sexual contact between the father and his 15-year-old daughter. There are two other children in the family, a 13-year-old son and another daughter, age 11. During the first several therapy sessions, Mr. and Mrs. Bretini appear to be exceptionally open and cooperative, while the children resist involvement in every possible way. They are defiant, hostile, and noncommunicative — except for complaining continuously about the absurdity of their presence in therapy. They openly abuse the therapist as she attempts to develop a treatment contract with the family. The parents do not directly acknowledge their children's hostility, nor do they intervene in any way. They act as if all family members are equally invested in therapy and are working together on problematic issues. Given the circumstances under which the abuse was reported, the therapist hypothesizes that the children are acting out their parents' resistance to therapy as well as reflecting the hostility underlying the marriage relationship. The therapist assigns the parents 2 tasks: Work together to figure out how to help their children feel more positive about therapy, and devise a specific set of goals for treatment that all family members could agree to.

At the next session, the children's resistance appears to have melted away, although they manifest the kind of age-appropriate anxiety and defensiveness that is to be expected in family treatment. By contrast, both parents are surly toward the therapist and openly antagonistic toward each other. Now the therapist can begin to work with the family dynamics as they really are rather than as they have been manipulatively constructed by the parents. Attention can now be given to strengthening the generational boundary and addressing the parentification of the children.

Therapeutic hypotheses and strategies with incestuous families can be as varied as the families themselves, limited only by the creativity of the therapist (and professional ethics). However, structural guidelines are also important to assure that interventions are effectively positioned for maximum impact on the incestuous family system.

WORKING WITH FAMILY COALITIONS

Much of the treatment literature assigns incest family members specific roles: *offender, victim, nonoffending spouse, uninvolved sibling.* Legally, these terms have meaning and validity; however, from a therapeutic perspective, such labels can be misleading. Relationships among family members represent a variety of transactions, since perpetrator/victim patterns typically underlie the entire family system. Effective therapy with incestuous families requires separating legal definitions from the transactional patterns of family life. Arising from boundary dysfunctions, some structural elements are generally characteristic of incestuous families while others are more idiosyncratic. Most apparent during therapy are the structural *coalitions* among family members that represent a particular family's way of responding to contextual challenges to its survival. Although these coalitions may be displayed most dramatically in the period immediately following discovery or disclosure of the abuse, they typically reflect persistent underlying transactional patterns now brought to the surface by crisis.

In their ground-breaking work with father-daughter incest families in Ireland, McCarthy & Byrne (1988) challenged therapists to recognize the complex transactional patterns of life in these families. They view incest in part as "a particular family's somatic expression of its struggle to be child-centered, to shift its gender roles, and to value emotionality, proximity, and nonhierarchical social relations" (p. 183). In their view, disclosure of the incest by a child typically occurs in connection with a shift in the marital relationship, a shift that allows the previously existing coalitional pattern to collapse and a new one to emerge. McCarthy and Byrne identified two different coalitional patterns in father-daughter incest: (a) the mother aligns with the father and the social system aligns with the daughter, or (b) the mother aligns with the daughter and cooperates with the social system against the father. To avoid being trapped and depowered by the intrafamilial conflict, they advise the therapist to position him- or herself in the center of the system, imagining "that giving voice to the 'heart' of the problem might bring forth the cybernetic balance for a system in pursuit of linear control" (1988, p. 189). The similarity of our "search for patterns" with that of McCarthy and Byrne has inspired us to elaborate our experiences with incestuous family structures in terms of the coalitions formed by family members that permit incest to occur and their relationship to coalitions that emerge as a consequence of the revelation of incest and subsequent intervention.

To date we have identified nine recognizable coalitions among members of incestuous families, some of which are more common than others. Certain of these may be rather transitory, influenced by the particular conditions of abuse disclosure events during intervention. However, these configurations are important in helping the therapist determine how to position herself for greatest effectiveness during various stages of treatment.

Parents Against Children

In these families, the parents and children may be pitted against each other, sometimes in dramatic ways following the disclosure of abuse (Figure 8.1). Often it becomes evident to outsiders that the "nonoffending spouse" was in some way aware of the sexual abuse, but ignored it to avoid dealing with the threat to the marriage and to her own role as a wife and mother. A sizable number of nonoffending spouses were childhood victims of abuse themselves. Since there is no supportive parent who can assure protection of the children from further abuse in these families, the victim(s) and perhaps other children are often removed from the home. In the aftermath of intervention, some of these parents do not even fight for the return of their children. Sometimes, both parents are accused of sexual perpetration, although the spouse is rarely involved in a direct way. When the perpetrator rather than the child is removed from the family, the remaining parent may embark on a campaign to enlist siblings in blaming the victim (or another child who revealed the secret) and urging her to recant. Based upon their mutual dependency and deficits of self, the spouses sometimes grow even closer following disclosure of the abuse. To avoid prosecution, they may even terminate parental rights. Alternately, the children may be kept out of the home by protection workers certain that further abuse and neglect are inevitable.

Despite the apparent obstacles, this family coalition has some positive characteristics upon which the therapist can draw. For one thing, the generational boundary can be recognized more clearly here than in other

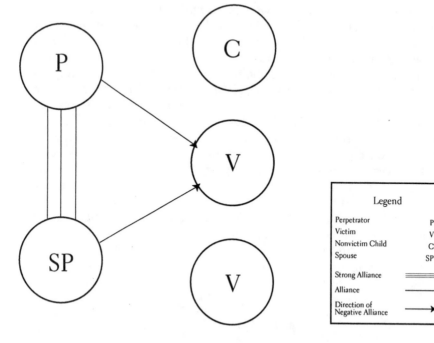

FIGURE 8.1 Parents Against Children

coalitional patterns. For another, there is a spousal bond—albeit a dysfunctional one—with some loyalty, dependency, and attachment focused upon one another rather than solely upon the children. The therapist can move back and forth across the generational boundary, allying him- or herself sometimes with the parents and other times with the children. This movement itself metaphorically conveys the message that the therapist can respect and make connections with both generations despite their alienation. More specifically, the therapist can work to convert the parents' negative stance "against the children" into a more functional sense of parental identity "in relation to" the children. Conversely, the therapist can help the children feel more secure in being children because their parents are working cooperatively to look after them in more positive ways.

The primary trap for therapists intervening into this coalitional pattern is to be seduced into rescuing the children from emotional abandonment by their parents—in effect, competing to be a better parent than the parents themselves. This temptation is very understandable since, in a sense, the children have been abandoned by the parents' misguided loyalty to each other. However, this stance may blind the therapist to his or her responsibility for helping the spouses utilize their own resources as parents. Of course, careful assessment at the beginning of treatment sometimes determines that both spouses are simply too immature to function as adults and will require considerable individual therapy before they are capable of providing the nurturing behavior needed by children. This judgment should not be made too quickly; formal evaluation and outside consultation can help the therapist avoid this negative countertransference trap. At the same time, we acknowledge that there are occasional situations in which children in incestuous families should be permanently removed from the care of their parents.

One effective way to deal with this coalition is to assign one therapist to work with the couple and another to work with the children. The parents' therapist can focus on marital, sexual, and parental issues (see Chapter 10), while the other therapist utilizes the sibling coalition to deal with individual issues of the children. Coordinating carefully to avoid taking sides in the struggle between parents and children, the two therapists can occasionally meet together with the entire family. Their shared challenge is to empower individual family members in age-appropriate ways. Children from these families are sometimes seduced by the power they gain in reporting the perpetrator, and they are reluctant to give it up. One or more of the children may become troublesome to foster parents or protection personnel because they want to maintain their adult-like status. In effect, the children have become grandiose as a way of countering parental rejection. These challenges may be daunting to some professionals, leading them to avoid family therapy with this type of family coalition when, in fact, direct intervention into the family system could be extremely helpful.

Nonoffending Spouse and Victim Against Perpetrator

The second family coalition is rather common and is considered by many to be the ideal configuration for treatment. The nonoffending spouse and the victim are aligned against the perpetrator, often with the victim's siblings and other relatives included in the alliance (Figure 8.2). If separation is deemed necessary, the perpetrator is removed from the home and may be imprisoned. This pattern fits well with the the goals of social service and legal systems, since the children appear to have an ally and protector who will continue to provide competent parenting in the absence of the perpetrator. When this is actually the case, therapy with the family unit may proceed quite efficiently, and treatment of the victim(s) is facilitated by a solid support system. However, appearance may not be reality in this coalition, and therapy may become more complicated. In our experience, dependency relationships in this configuration may be confused and confusing. The victim and other children in the family may

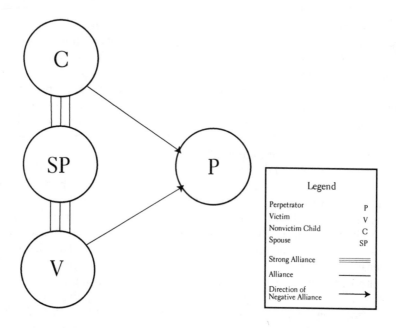

FIGURE 8.2 Nonoffending Spouse and Victim Against Perpetrator

be functioning in a parental capacity. One possibility is that the victim is sufficiently parentified that she shifts easily from being quasi-spousal with the perpetrator to being quasi-spousal with the nonoffending parent. In other instances, closer analysis reveals that *all* of the children in the family have assumed responsibility for meeting the emotional needs of their parents. In both of these situations, the children's alliance with one spouse against the other reflects a continuation of their participation in unresolved marital conflict — an extension of the intergenerational and interpersonal boundary diffusion that gave rise to the incest. Occasionally, this pattern involves a (legally) nonoffending parent who nevertheless engages in abusive behavior with the children. Though the destructive behavior might not be recognized by outside agents of social control, it may surface in the context of therapy and need to be addressed. Sometimes the absence of the identified perpetrator from the home triggers episodes of punitive behavior by the spouse directed at the victim and/or her siblings. Yet the children may continue to be loyal to this parent because she is now their sole source of support and security. As a result, the perpetrator/victim interaction pattern may continue to be part of life in this family.

Divorce is a common outcome of this family configuration, sometimes encouraged by social and legal agencies in order to ensure future protection of the children. In most cases, we recommend that a decision regarding divorce be deferred until later in treatment. This permits the therapist to focus on intrapsychic dynamics of the spouses as well as marital and sexual issues before turning attention to problems in parent-child relationships. In our experience, it is difficult to modify the nonoffending parent's overinvolvement with the children until some of her own emotional needs are addressed and power/control issues are appropriately framed within the context of the marital relationship. Some individual or group therapy might be indicated for the nonoffending parent (as well as for other family members). However, in our opinion family therapy with this configuration should not wait until the end of treatment. This reinforces the perpetrator's position as an outsider and weakens the marital bond, thereby encouraging the children to remain grandiosely parentified in order to insure their own survival. Instead, effort should be directed at correcting the distorted boundary structures of the incestuous family in order to reduce the risk of continuing perpetrator/victim interaction patterns, now aimed at the identified offender by other family members.

The primary trap for therapists working with this pattern is to align automatically with the spouse/victim/sibling coalition against the perpetrator. Such a position increases the chance of divorce and might even set the stage for additional expressions of perpetration/victimization by other family members—some of which are likely to be directed at the therapist. The therapist may find it difficult to create an alliance with such an alienated couple, fearing that he or she might be viewed by the nonoffending parent as unsupportive of her and her children. The neutrality of this position may be questioned by those who espouse feminist or victim advocacy arguments that women should not be seen conjointly in therapy with abusive men. If the therapist's flexibility in working with this coalition is limited for any reason, we suggest that both parents have their own therapist and that the therapists coordinate their efforts, occasionally meeting together for couple and family sessions. We are convinced that this option is well worth considering, in order to avoid the family fragmentation so likely to result from intervention into this coalitional pattern. Although there are cases in which incest perpetrators should be kept isolated from other family members (particularly in rage-based cases), we believe that premature disruption or termination of family relationships can create unintended stresses and negative outcomes for family members.

Family Against Victim

The third family coalition is one of the most common patterns encountered by therapists. It reflects the family's emotional extrusion of the victim who has violated the family/society boundary by revealing the incest secret (Figure 8.3). Whether or not they have been sexually abused, all

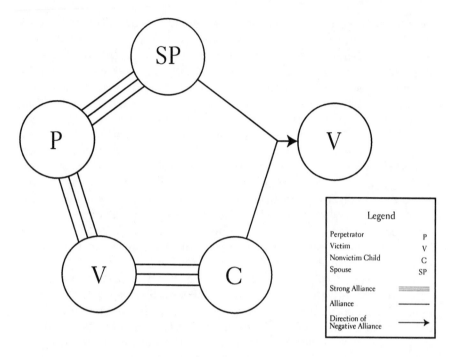

FIGURE 8.3 Family Against Victim

family members tend to align themselves with the perpetrator against outsiders who appear to threaten the family's survival. When this occurs, the abuse victim is typically removed from the home; if she does not recant, she may remain permanently alienated from the family system. Hidden victims are quite common in this family pattern, since siblings may be hesitant to report their own abuse after seeing what happens to the child who did. Protective and legal agencies may settle for prosecution based upon the testimony of a single identified victim, hoping that she does not give in to the pressure to rejoin her family by recanting. As a result, the victim may be prohibited from seeing her parents for an extended period of time in order to reduce the possibility of changing her story under pressure from the family. This extended separation impedes family therapy and may also pose a dilemma for those who conduct a formal evaluation with the child—her symptoms and psychological status may be due as much to the stress of family separation as to trauma from the sexual abuse itself. Further, the victim may be labeled "crazy" by other members of her family, either as an immediate reaction to her disclosure or as an ongoing effort to challenge her credibility since she has refused to be constrained by family loyalty. Sometimes, the identified victim in this family coalition also has been emotionally abused by other siblings who are trying desperately to maintain the approval of their parents and to avoid abandonment.

Family therapy can play a particularly important role in the treatment of this family coalition. The family therapist is challenged to transform a "traitor" into someone who has made a positive contribution to the family's eventual well-being. Violating the code of secrecy can be reframed as an act of courage, an attempt to help the family by bringing anxiety and pain to the attention of those who can offer assistance. To accomplish this, the therapist can position him- or herself in such a way as to encourage an alliance between the identified victim and the nonoffending spouse. As an alternative, efforts can be made to find a "soft spot" in the family's boundary that can allow the child to reenter the family by relating to certain members in a different way.

Two major traps face the therapist. The first is a temptation to align too fully with the identified victim, respond to her vulnerability, and lose sight of the fact that the entire family system is the client. The second trap is to set the stage inadvertently for family members to experience a mutually exclusive challenge to their loyalties—to force them to choose between the perpetrator and the victim. To avoid these pitfalls, the therapist should identify the entire family as the client (the victim also may have her own individual or group therapist) and should direct his efforts almost exclusively to family restructuring. At the same time, individual family members may require some therapy on a one-to-one basis. However, therapists working with individual family members ordinarily should *not* participate in family sessions, in order to reduce the threat of declaring loyalties or defending points of view. Rather, family therapy should be paced to accommodate the readiness of various family members to contribute to common goals without sacrificing their individual boundaries and objectives in the process. This approach may prove challenging to the therapist who has difficulty tolerating ambiguity in his treatment efforts. However, individual intrapsychic repairs and family structural realignments must proceed sensitively and in synchrony so that family members can renegotiate their relationships without divisive challenges to their loyalty or threats to their survival—no small endeavor given the premises of this family configuration!

Family Against Social System

This family coalition may appear after a child has revealed the secret of incest and subsequently recanted her story in order to reenter the family system (Figure 8.4). Families with this configuration may also be referred based upon outsiders' suspicions of abuse or circumstantial evidence of abuse such as medical or behavioral symptoms in one or more children.

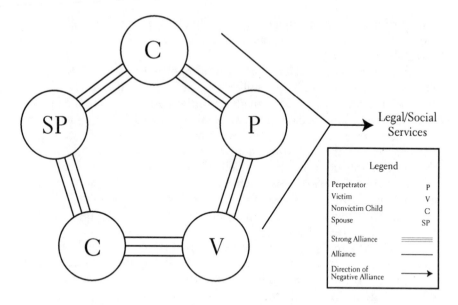

FIGURE 8.4 Family Against Social System

These families can be extremely frustrating to legal and social service personnel. If the victim identifies abuse and an investigation begins, she is likely to recant, and further follow-up may be blocked because accurate information is difficult to obtain. Without prosecution, these families tend to retreat into isolation or even relocate geographically in order to avoid further surveillance by authorities. Paradoxically, we believe that this coalition is best treated primarily in family therapy, in order to capitalize on the strong loyalty bond that exists. Attempts at therapy with individual family members often meet with particularly strong resistance, since individuals feel unable to survive outside the boundaries of the family system.

Unfortunately, family therapists rarely get to work on an ongoing basis with this family configuration, unless sufficient leverage is gained by legal authorities to coerce these families into treatment. Sometimes an identified victim may be seeing a child therapist, though without much success due to the child's enduring loyalty to the family system. If circumstances do permit family treatment, then the therapist is challenged to position him- or herself as an ally to the entire family unit. In the early stages of treatment, the therapist may be required to adopt a strategy of aligning him- or herself with the family *against the social system* that has intervened into their lives. This approach should be coordinated carefully with legal and social service professionals, so that they can be cast by design into negative roles as agents of social control rather than being negatively triangled by the therapist without their consent (see Chapter 11). Of course, one objective of therapy with this type of family coalition is to help members recognize that they need not view society as an enemy. However, until this objective has been met, legal and social service personnel must tolerate negative responses and behavioral inconsistencies on the part of some or all family members.

A major trap for the therapist working with this family coalition is to be seduced into *actual* antagonism toward social service or legal representatives working on the case, thereby creating a structure of intervention that is isomorphic and reinforcing to the family's defensive structural rigidity. We have had considerable success treating these families when child protection workers, attorneys, judges, guardians ad litem, or probation officers were willing to take a hard line as agents of social control in order to provide us with greater flexibility in organizing family therapy. Partly, the challenge is to keep families in therapy long enough to accomplish boundary restructuring against considerable resistance.

The use of a consultation team working behind a one-way mirror can be very helpful in treating this family coalition (see Chapter 9). The team can serve as a vehicle for monitoring the relationships between various subsystems in the therapeutic ecosystem, as well as the relationships between the therapy system and other systems in the social environment such as the child protection agency. Further, a team can help family members become accustomed to surveillance by outsiders, permitting the therapist to assume a variety of positive and negative stances without jeopardizing his or her inevitably fragile connection with the family system. Finally, a team can assist the therapist by participating in the creation of various therapeutically useful triangles that allow family members to have allies outside the family system.

Antagonistic Male and Female "Camps"

Alignments along gender lines are rather characteristic of incestuous families in general. In some families, this is expressed vividly as gender-linked coalitions antagonistic to each other (Figure 8.5). Males and females may engage in overt or covert battles for power and/or control, with sexual abuse serving an expression of hostility or as a manuever to subjugate members of the other sex. If the victims are females, the mother identifies with them; removing the male perpetrator from the home represents a victory for their gender. In some families with this configuration, both the father and the sons may be sexually abusing the female children. In addition, the boys may express sexualized hostility toward their mother by name-calling, inappropriate nudity, or even intrusive voyeurism. If separation or divorce follows disclosure and intervention into the abuse, the male children (even if they have also been sexually abused) often elect to live

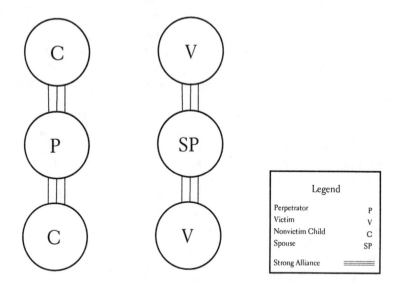

FIGURE 8.5 Antagonistic Male and Female Camps

with their father if he is not incarcerated. If they remain in the family home when their father is removed, they may continue to represent his presence by assuming grandiose and disrespectful stances toward female family members. Depending upon their ages, they may leave home prematurely in an effort to avoid control by the mother.

This family configuration challenges the family therapist in several ways. Clearly, the gender of the therapist may be an issue itself; male and female cotherapists are likely to be most effective. A marital/parental alliance is virtually absent, making it difficult to deal with generational boundary issues. Conflict levels often are high and may include physical abuse and violence. Any attempt to provide support for one member may be viewed by others as hostility and betrayal. Dysfunctional allegiances should be addressed gradually in order to minimize resistance and avoid fragmenting the family system, whose connections are strong but negative and brittle. Initially, the therapist should make an effort to loosen the overly intense emotional bonds between each parent and his/her same sex children. Clearly, marital therapy should be emphasized in treating this family coalition. Since generational role reversals are likely to be strong, family members need help giving up caretaking by children and accepting parenting from the adults.

Victim advocacy approaches to intervention can work well with this family configuration, at least initially. However, a major trap can be the therapist's own conscious or unconscious gender biases. A belief that one gender is good and the other evil, or that men are inevitably perpetrators and women are inevitably victims, undermines the therapist's capacity to contribute effectively to power/control balances in the family. Further, such beliefs increase the therapist's risk of falling into the Rescuer trap. Inevitably, perpetrator/victim interactions will take place, with both genders displaying *both* kinds of behavior. By helping all family members learn to utilize both power and control—without becoming either a perpetrator or a victim him- or herself—the therapist can build a foundation of trust with family members and can assist them in developing relationships premised on acceptance and mutuality rather than antagonism. Key among the goals of successful treatment should be a strong marital/parental coalition and positive, age-appropriate relationships among the siblings.

Victim and Social System Against Family

This coalitional pattern evolves in a significant number of incestuous families when the predominant framework of intervention is victim advocacy. When a victim reveals family sexual abuse and the social system responds with a massive intervention effort, the process of moving *toward* the victim(s) for protective purposes can lead to moving *against* the family (Figure 8.6), producing a defensive coalition that excludes the victim. This configuration can generate antagonism and confrontation, both within the family and between the family and outside professionals. Some of these

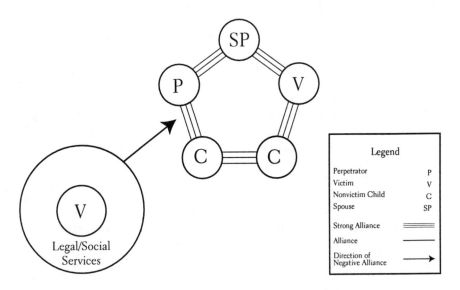

FIGURE 8.6 Victim and Social System Against Family

situations erupt into intrafamilial disputes involving lawsuits against accused perpetrators, countercharges of "false allegations," legal claims
against therapists and other professionals working with family members. If
young victims are removed from their homes and placed in foster care,
some families may take extreme measures and launch a counteroffensive
against social service agencies, therapists, and even foster parents. In turn,
the social system may respond with even greater displays of power or
control in an effort to punish or contain the family — including termination
of parental rights. As in some other family configurations, additional hidden victims in the family are unlikely to reveal their abuse and risk amputa-
tion from the family system. Because of spouses' perception that independence is a threat to survival, divorce is uncommon in this coalition.

Having both a family therapist and a child therapist can be very useful
in dealing with this family configuration. The child therapist's role is to
work directly on intrapsychic damage to the victim(s) created by distorted
family patterns and resulting sexual abuse. The family therapist helps
create a safe environment to which the victim can return, focusing on
boundary issues with other family members and on the perpetrator/victim
interaction patterns that are prevalent in family transactions. Simultaneously, the family therapist must pay attention to the relationship between
the family and its social environment. This requires identifying the client
unit as including the social service and legal representatives involved in
intervention. From an ecological perspective, two rigidly protective systems with parallel structures are recognizable. In effect, two "families" are
fighting over physical (and perhaps legal) custody of a child.

The therapist's major trap is to lose ecosystemic perspective and join
either of these systems against the other. The therapist's position can be
lonely and uncomfortable, particularly if members of both systems are
angry because they have been unable to secure his exclusive allegiance.
He or she is challenged to be particularly creative and flexible in an effort
to create therapeutically useful balances between these systems as well as
within them. At some stages, therapy is likely to include family sessions
without the child victim. However, the therapist should also persuade the
legal system of the importance of having the victim available to participate
in family therapy as deemed appropriate. At times ecological therapy can
include foster parents, attorneys, guardians ad litem, protection workers,
and school personnel. A consultation team can be a helpful resource for
the family therapist. The team can serve to increase the therapist's flexibility in addressing the protective rigidity of both the incestuous family and
the intervention system. If steps are not taken to counteract it, this coalition naturally tends to create negative triangles and escalating power/
control struggles with the potential to further victimize everyone concerned — including the therapist! Framing treatment objectives on which

all parties can agree is especially difficult but critically important to a successful treatment outcome.

"Couples"

Within this family configuration, each parent has formed a strong coalition with a particular child (Figure 8.7). On the one hand, a perpetrating parent and child victim are emotionally and sexually close. At the same time, the nonabusing parent is also emotionally enmeshed with another of the children. Sometimes, two siblings (usually of different genders) have also paired up in an intense relationship that can include incest. Occasionally, both parents are sexually involved with different children, although the secondary incestuous relationship may be mostly symbolic, for example, sharing a bed or eroticized nongenital touching. If the incest is reported and the perpetrator is removed from the home, the victim also may wish to leave, since she is now without emotional support to cope with antagonistic relationships with other family members, particularly the remaining parent and allied sibling.

Intervention that fails to address the secondary incestuous relationships as well as the abandonment issues of nonaligned children will have limited impact upon this dysfunctional family system. The family therapist's major challenge is to facilitate a "divorce" of the parent-child couples, something

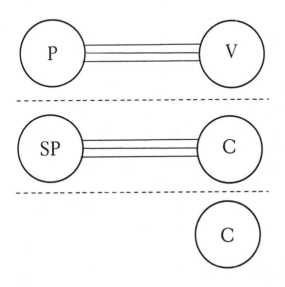

Legend	
Perpetrator	P
Victim	V
Nonvictim Child	C
Spouse	SP
Strong Alliance	≡≡
Diffuse Boundary	- - - - -

FIGURE 8.7 Couples

that the dyads are likely to resist. If successful in this effort, the therapist can focus on rebuilding the marriage partnership and assisting the spouses in developing appropriate parenting skills. However, the children (including the victim) may also be resistant, since successful therapy has the effect of "demoting" them from inapproporiate adult-like status. This resistance can be reduced if attention is given to developing stronger relationships among the siblings so that an age-appropriate support network is formed as an alternative to the intergenerational alliances.

There are two major traps for therapists working with this family configuration. The first is to separate the parent-child coalitions too quickly, ignoring the intrapsychic fragility and dependency of the individual partners. The capacity for independence occurs gradually; these are separations that must be mutual, lest they result in lingering dysfunctional attachments which will undermine therapeutic progress. The second trap is to inadvertently replace one dysfunctional configuration with another. For example, some therapists may consider treatment successful when they have aligned the nonoffending spouse with the children against the perpetrator. As we have indicated above, however, this coalitional pattern has difficulties of its own, including an increase in the likelihood of divorce if insufficient attention is given to the developmental status of the nonperpetrating spouse and the loyalties of the children (including the victim) to the perpetrator.

Parent Against Parent

This family coalition appears to be growing in frequency, perhaps in relation to an increase in no-fault divorce and joint-custody arrangements sanctioned by family courts throughout North America. Amidst divorce proceedings that pit spouses against each other in a battle for legal and/or physical custody of their children, allegations of sexual abuse have been escalating (Figure 8.8). Accusations are most likely to be leveled by a mother against a father or stepfather, although counteraccusations by fathers of physical, emotional, or sexual abuse by mothers also are increasing. The emotionally charged adversarial context of divorce makes allegations of sexual abuse extremely difficult to verify, particularly when the children are very young. More than in most other circumstances, parents may embed ideas, memories, and fears of sexual abuse in the minds of their children. Sometimes, these efforts by parents are conscious and malicious. More often, they are unconscious, reflecting well-intentioned attempts to provide effective support and control over the lives of children during an emotionally difficult time. Parents may be unaware of how deeply some children are affected by spousal hostility and by fears of abandonment, or how suggestible children can be when their loyalty to one parent or the other is challenged. Caught up in the turmoil of hos-

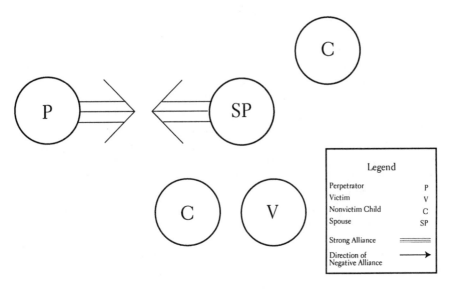

FIGURE 8.8 Parent Against Parent

tile parents ending a marriage, a young child may elaborate a chance remark like "Father touched my bottom in the bathtub" or "I slept in Daddy's bed in his apartment" into a full-blown account of sexual abuse under pressure of repeated or intrusive forms of questioning by her anxious mother.

A family therapist can be extremely helpful in dealing with this configuration, particularly if he or she is skilled in working with separation, divorce, and remarriage. Clear personal and professional boundaries are also required, as is a high tolerance for ambiguity. The therapist's role as the *family's* therapist must be clear to everyone concerned, even though the family is in the midst of restructuring. Overall, the therapist's goal should be to assist the child(ren) in maintaining a meaningful attachment to both parents during and after the divorce, along with helping the (ex)spouses to parent effectively and to *coordinate* their parenting efforts to the greatest degree possible. Boundary work has particular importance, for the restructuring of divorce requires boundary flexibility at the same time that the therapist may be working to help strengthen diffuse generational, interpersonal, and intrapsychic boundaries. Indeed, some adept ecological balancing is required in order to assist parents in creating a safe and nurturing environment for their children while attending appropriately to their own needs for security and support at a difficult time. This therapy can be long and tedious since even competent parents can be developmentally regressed and emotionally needy during the divorcing process; even many nonincestuous parents turn inappropriately to their children for support. If, in fact, sexual abuse has occurred in the context of divorce, then adequacy of self-structure and resultant parental effectiveness have been compromised already. Dealing with incest uncovered during the divorcing process is an exceptionally complex therapeutic challenge.

The major trap with this family coalitional pattern should be apparent: *The therapist must refuse an investigatory or confirmatory role regarding the abuse.* In some sense, the therapist is required simultaneously to believe everyone and no one. Further, the therapist is challenged to pay careful attention to something that the legal and social service systems may fail to recognize; namely, that the child caught in the middle of a vicious divorce may be much more traumatized by the potential loss of a parent than by sexually inappropriate behavior — even behavior that could be judged to be abusive. Particularly traumatic could be the loss of both parents, even temporarily, when an accusation of abuse leads to a countercharge, and a child protection agency takes rapid action to place the child in a foster home while investigation proceeds. The family therapist should leave the investigation of sexual abuse allegations to the appropriate agency. At the same time, it is important to report any abuse uncovered in the course of treatment. Because of the inherent conflict between social control and therapeutic neutrality, we often require that divorcing parents sign a written contract agreeing not to use our records and our testimony in connection with any subsequent legal proceedings (Gardner, 1986). However, even a written agreement of this nature does *not* absolve the therapist of legal responsibility for reporting abuse or guarantee that she will not become involved in legal action regarding abuse which might be taken against either parent.

Orphans

In this final family configuration (Figure 8.9), all family members — including the parents — appear to function at low levels of psychosexual development (early childhood to mid-adolescence). The majority of adults in these families are of normal intelligence, although some may have been previously diagnosed as learning impaired or socially immature. In our experience, some of the seeming developmental delays are secondary to severe sexual and/or physical abuse in their own families of origin — though the clients may be in therapy for some time before this is revealed. This family configuration frequently is associated with co-perpetration, that is, both parents have become sexually involved with the children without regard to age or gender. If both parents should be removed from the home or incarcerated, divorce may occur simply because the parents cannot maintain any relational intensity during the period without con-

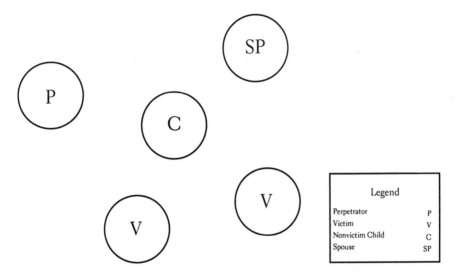

FIGURE 8.9 Orphans

tact. Symptoms among the children in this coalition are varied; their etiology may be a lack of structure and nurturing as much as sexual abuse. The family context is marked by overwhelming neglect and deprivation, along with boundary intrusion and resultant stress, leaving the children unsocialized and perhaps developmentally disabled. In our experience with this type of family coalition (particularly when both parents have been incestuously involved), parental rights often have been terminated either voluntarily (for example, as a plea bargain) or forcibly. We have noted a peculiar lack of emotion connected with the termination process, perhaps an unsettling indication of the inability of these family members to bond with each other.

Therapy with this family is a significant challenge. It requires assisting the parents with "growing up," while simultaneously helping them become cognizant of the needs of their children and their resulting parental responsibilities. Marital therapy is unlikely to be effective until some individual identity consolidation has occurred in each of the partners. Parts of treatment may have the quality of play therapy, for all family members may appear regressed, unmotivated for change, and unable to utilize insight or analyze behavior. Individual therapy may be indicated for some or all family members. Participation in groups does not appear to be particularly useful, although some of these families may benefit from family group therapy in which they can observe models of family connectedness.

MANAGING INTERGENERATIONAL
BOUNDARIES

Most researchers and clinicians agree that incest families are characterized by inappropriate intergenerational boundaries and that this is a problem to be addressed in therapy. Earlier incest literature noted primarily
mother-daughter "role-reversal," while current authors discuss more generalized patterns of role confusion among all family members (Horton et al.,
1990; Mayer, 1983; Thorman, 1983). Few therapy objectives are as critical
as boundary repair for relapse prevention and long-term treatment success.
Unfortunately, boundary problems often are aggravated by the very processes of reporting and intervention. Some aspects of investigation and
prosecution are particularly likely to reinforce boundary difficulties. Foremost are the investigative interviews, during which children may experience feelings of disloyalty to one or both parents when they are asked to
reveal family secrets. More subtle but equally as troublesome is the process
by which children may be convinced to sit in judgment of the perpetrating
parent or older sibling. Though necessary for legal prosecution, this represents a clear instance of role reversal that is difficult for some children to
handle. It may even be structurally parallel to the seductive processes by
which the victim and others in the family were first persuaded to keep the
incest secret. The child now is asked to join forces with powerful outsiders
against the perpetrator and perhaps other family members. Testifying
against the perpetrator in court further exacerbates the problem. No matter how much support and preparation are provided her, the child incest
victim is asked to be, in some sense, "bigger" than her parents by taking
direct responsibility for stopping the abuse. There is a fine but critical line
to be drawn between helping the victim in the family be appropriately
self-assertive to avert further abuse and making her responsible for relapse
prevention.

As things progress in intervention and treatment, further boundary
violations may occur. For example, the children may be asked to choose
where they want to live, whether they wish to be visited by either parent,
or whether they are ready to return home from foster care. While a child's
feelings and desires certainly should be seriously considered in such matters, we firmly believe that *adults* should make these decisions (perhaps
the nonoffending parent in cooperation with a protection representative,
guardian ad litem, or therapist) and that they should convey their responsibility for such decisions clearly to the child(ren).

Occasionally we have encountered another structural problem—well-
meaning foster parents are invested with official "authority" over the children's biological parents (including the perpetrator) rather than only over
the children. If foster parents have direct authority to decide how often
the children see their parent(s), the circumstances surrounding the con-

tact, how long visits will last, and the like, then the biological parents are being treated as children and intergenerational boundary confusion is prolonged. Here, too, we believe that such decisions should be made, when possible, by one or both parents or, when necessary, by an appropriate outside authority such as a protection worker. Consultation with all parties involved—parents, foster parents, children, and therapist(s)—usually is helpful.

Strategies to Realign Intergenerational Boundaries

As in other aspects of therapy, there are a wide variety of possible strategies to address intergenerational boundary realignment. Most prominent is to *support the executive function of the parental dyad*. Insofar as it is possible given the particular circumstances of each case, the therapist should act to support and empower the parents (including the perpetrator) to assume appropriate parental functions and decision-making regarding their children (see Chapter 10). Of course, this can be complicated when community agents of social control have assumed technical, although temporary, responsibility for the abused child(ren). Nevertheless, it is important that the therapist carefully evaluate which decisions have been removed from the parents by the authorities and which still can be supported in the therapeutic setting. Even simple decisions in therapy can be used to reflect support for appropriate intergenerational boundaries—or will reveal the absence of such boundaries. For example, the parent(s) attending a session can be responsible for where children sit and how they behave, who responds to particular questions, and when to deal with certain matters involving the children. As therapy progresses, the parents can be helped to manage more complex issues with their children: dealing with disruptive behavior, deciding which family members will attend a given session and who might be excused for a conflicting commitment, deciding on the focus of a given family session, and so on. Of course, a parent sometimes may exercise these responsibilities manipulatively; however, the therapist still can gain valuable insight into intergenerational family dynamics. Most important is that the therapist at all times acknowledges appropriate generational boundaries and promotes internal locus-of-control by the adults in the family.

EXAMPLE

An incestuous family, the MacGregors, enters the therapy room for an initial session, and the parents direct the identified 9-year-old victim, Allison, to sit between them, while the four other children choose their own chairs elsewhere. When all family members are seated, the therapist asks Allison: "Does it feel good to sit where you can be protected, or do you feel a bit cut off from your sister and brothers?" Then, he questions each sibling: "If Allison could sit anyplace in the room she wished to sit, where do you think she would choose to sit?" Each child is asked to elaborate on the advantages and disadvantages of each location for the victim. Next, Mr. and Mrs. MacGregor are politely asked to provide their rationale for requesting that their daughter sit between them. If their answers indicate that they are thinking of Allison's comfort, they are complimented for their thoughtfulness. If they respond by observing that she needs to sit with them in order to be controlled, they are complimented for their good judgment. The therapist then comments in an off-hand manner, "It's always so fascinating to see where family members sit when they come to therapy," and immediately changes the subject.

In this interchange, the therapist has gathered information about family structure, has learned something about the role of the victim in the family, and has reinforced the leadership of the adults. Despite a possible attempt by the parents to isolate the victim from her siblings, the therapist has created a bridge between them by involving them in the intervention.

Another therapeutic strategy to realign intergenerational boundaries is to *structure and maintain appropriate adult and child roles.* Children in incest families usually can be characterized as "parentified." The parents frequently can be observed relying on their children for things that they should be managing themselves. While the perpetrator's dependence on one or more children for sexual gratification is the most obvious example, other role confusion is also common. For example, a daughter (often the victim) may have major responsibility for managing the household or parenting the younger children, a son may be relied upon to help support the family financially while the father gambles away his salary, or the children collectively may be expected to spend most of their free time meeting their parents' social, recreational, and companionship needs. The therapist should act to disrupt boundary-crossing interaction whenever possible and should firmly designate behavior as appropriate for one generation or the other (recognizing, of course, that many behaviors are not necessarily generation-specific).

EXAMPLE

During a family therapy session, Sheila, one of the children who has been sexually abused by her stepfather, leaves her chair to comfort him when he begins to cry as he voices his remorse. The therapist must now facilitate a shift in caretaking responsibility without shaming either the parent or the child. First, the therapist compliments Mr. Clarke on having helped raise such a sensitive stepdaughter; then, he compliments Sheila for her courage in being willing to forgive and reach out to her stepfather even though he has acted inappropriately.

These remarks set the stage for the therapist to begin exploring in circular fashion the caretaking patterns within the family: "Which of the children is most likely to comfort Mom when she's upset?" "Which of the children are most likely to comfort each other?" "Who is best at making Mom feel better when she is feeling bad, and who is best at making Dad feel better?" Answers to these and related questions give the therapist a better understanding of the emotional caretaking patterns of this family.

At some point, the therapist observes that there is another normal and predictable, but more difficult, aspect of comforting when it is done by children who are caring and sensitive; namely, sometimes feeling angry, burdened, and even guilty. Permission is thereby given for the children to express their negative feelings about their caretaking of their parents. Several options can be pursued. The therapist might inquire, "What do you think would happen if you didn't try to comfort your (stepfather) (mother)?" or "What are you afraid will happen if you don't try to take care of your parents when they are upset?" Additionally, the children can be asked to distinguish between situations in which they think they can be comforting and/or helpful to their parents, and when they believe that their parents have needs that can only be met by another adult. Further, the parents can be asked to consider the differences in their needs at different times, and they can be encouraged to distinguish between these situations for the sake of their children. This strategy serves to increase family members' awareness of the distinctions between adult and child roles; it even can be elaborated into a discussion of the sexual needs and interests of adults, and how these often differ from the sexual and emotional needs of children.

A third strategy to support appropriate intergenerational boundaries is to *establish and maintain the "generational boundary" of the therapist.* This can be difficult when working with incest families, because perpetrators often experience power as competition while victims experience it as exploitation and abuse. In order to adequately pace both victim and perpetrator stances in the family, the therapist may need to vacillate intentionally between low-key reassuring nurturance and explicit demonstrations of personal authority. This has to be done without falling into the trap of rescuing the victim, in order to avoid competing with the parents or undermining the victim's own efforts at assertiveness. Similarly, the therapist should avoid unnecessary power struggles with the perpetrator, since overpowering him also will undermine the parental role and reinforce boundary diffusion.

EXAMPLE

Mr. Carson, who sexually abused his 14-year-old stepson, Norman, has returned home recently after one year in a residential treatment program for sex offenders. In his stepfather's absence, Norman has been a "surrogate spouse" to his mother (a relationship they began to develop years ago after she divorced the boy's biological father). Norman's role in the household has been that of companion, sometime decision-maker, and coparent of two younger stepbrothers, David and Rodney. Open conflict has broken out since Mr. Carson's return to the home, and the family solicits help from the therapist. For a year, Norman has had no curfew, no requirements for study or chores, no set bedtimes. For the most part, he has been helpful and responsible without such requirements. However, his stepfather now expects him to study three hours each evening, to be in bed by 10:30 on weeknights and by midnight on weekends, and to do his chores according to a prearranged schedule.

Norman appeals to the therapist for help, contending that he has no need for such rules and documenting how successfully he has functioned in his stepfather's absence. To bolster his case, he states his belief that he has been more successful than his stepfather in not abusing privileges. Mr. Carson counters by pointing out the boy's insolence, as well as his unrealistic expectations that he can set all his own rules even though he is only 15 years old. The stepfather also remarks that he wonders whether women can really be effective in controlling males' natural tendency to be aggressive and unruly.

Though the therapist may be tempted to take sides on some of the issues or to challenge the perpetrator's remark about women being unable to control men, she knows that she must avoid anything that will undermine the generational boundary and perhaps even damage her own credibility with any family members. Instead, the therapist observes that it is the responsibility of parents to cooperatively establish policies and procedures for the family. She instructs them to discuss with each other the son's request while he listens silently. They proceed to do so.

During this conversation, Mrs. Carson reveals that she has been less structured with her children than she would like to have been while her husband has been away from home. She admits that she has given Norman more freedom in part because she wanted him to keep her company and to help her around the house. She wishes that she could have been stricter about the rules; however, her loneliness and insecurity made it difficult for her. Understandably, Norman is upset upon hearing these disclosures from his mother, and he begins to berate both his parents for being "dishonest" and "uptight." The therapist intervenes, addressing Mrs. Carson, "I can certainly understand your loneliness and your need to have some help from your son. I wonder if you can understand how confusing it is to him to believe he has earned some freedom and then to have it taken away from him." The mother nods her assent. Then the therapist asks Mr. Carson, "Can you understand how difficult it is for your sons to go through so many adjustments in connection with your being gone and then returning home?" He replies affirmatively. Addressing Norman, the therapist points out that teenagers virtually never like the rules their parents establish, "You wouldn't be 'normal' if you did."

The therapist then asks all family members to do some individual thinking about specific rules regarding homework, chores, hours, and the like for each of the children, based upon their ages. Assigning them a family conference to exchange information about their respective ideas, she instructs the parents not to arrive at any decisions regarding the rules, "Instead, I would like the two of you to listen carefully to the wishes of each of the boys, then do some thinking on your own. Then I would like to meet with you next week to help you as parents come to an agreement about the rules you want to have for your family — after which you should have a conference with each of the boys individually to announce and discuss your decisions." In this sequence, the therapist remains accessible to family members as a resource without breeching the family's boundary by entering into the conflict or expressing opinions on the merits of various arguments. Further, she role-models a balance of power/control in her own behavior while facilitating the family's efforts to recalibrate power/control issues related to the perpetrator's post-treatment return to the home.

MANAGING INTERPERSONAL BOUNDARIES

Therapeutic interventions designed to facilitate clear interpersonal boundaries in an enmeshed family system are especially challenging because separation and individuation are likely to be experienced as threats to individual members' survival. These fears are activated in the process of incest reporting and intervention; in response, substantial resistance may be generated. Since the enmeshed family structure is rooted in attempts to compensate for deficits in the selfhood of family members, any sort of separation triggers primitive abandonment fears and feelings of extreme vulnerability. As we have indicated, the sexualized dependency that characterizes enmeshed incest families is actually an attempt to master the bonding process. However, without a well-developed sense of self, each family member is unable to balance dependence and independence, that is, incapable of genuine *interdependence*. Adults and children alike manifest this difficulty, thereby contributing to the intergenerational boundary problems discussed above.

In light of this interpersonal boundary diffusion, it is easy to understand why interventions that remove individuals from the home are likely to trigger abandonment panic among all family members — often leading to feelings of being victimized by the social and legal services. Early in treatment, family members are less likely to directly express their feelings of

vulnerability and more likely to act them out via hostility toward the therapist, passive-aggressive resistance to treatment, defensive rationalizations
about the incest, and a variety of manipulative behaviors. Recognizing
these as protective mechanisms can help the therapist develop some empathy for all family members and build trust that will allow eventually for
more direct expression of the underlying vulnerability.

Strategies to Realign Interpersonal Boundaries

Despite a genuine wish to be helpful to family members, the therapist
inevitably is experienced as a threatening presence as well as a potential
source of assistance. In his or her interactions with particular members or
with the family as a unit, the therapist's individuality creates anxiety in the
clients as they struggle with the desire to fuse dependently and the urge to
repel defensively. Recognizing and utilizing this ambivalence is the key
to effectively restructuring the clients' interpersonal boundaries in order
to facilitate self-differentiation.[1]

One of the least threatening ways to work with the interpersonal boundary problems of an incest family is by *supporting differences among family
members.* Highlighting differences that emerge in a therapy session can be
useful: commenting on differences in hair style or clothing; underscoring
differences in language patterns or facial expressions; exploring unique
characteristics such as likes and dislikes or personal habits. Sometimes a
simple comment in passing is adequate; other times an observation can be
elaborated into a dialogue. Such interventions can be useful when family
members are having difficulty dealing with conflict, when the therapist
senses unspoken disagreement between two or more individuals, or when
one family member is struggling with strong emotions. Circular questioning is an excellent tool both for gathering information and for drawing
distinctions between family members (Boscolo et al., 1987; Penn, 1982;
Selvini-Palazzoli et al., 1980; Tomm, 1985). At some point, the therapist
may even wish to make explicit the family's rule about the dangers of
difference, and to ask such challenging questions as "What is dangerous
about thinking or feeling or acting different in this family?" "What happens
if someone disagrees with (mother) (father) (child)?" "If someone were to
disagree with others in the family, who would it most likely be?" "Who is
most different from everyone else in this family?"

An additional strategy for interpersonal boundary realignment is to *help
family members take responsibility for themselves in age-appropriate ways.*
Previously, we observed that "rescuing" is a common activity in families

---

[1]Working with clients' relational ambivalence and its impact upon interpersonal and intrapsychic boundaries is discussed in greater detail in our book *Child Sexual Abuse: An Ecological
Approach to Treating Victims and Perpetrators.*

dominated by perpetrator/victim interaction patterns. In incestuous families, rescuing often is an attempt on the part of one family member to absorb another family member's anxiety (an additional reflection of the enmeshment). If successful, both individuals—and perhaps other family members—will feel less anxious temporarily. Rescuing can take many forms, such as completing a task (for example, homework) for another family member, serving as the interface between a family member and an outsider, performing parental functions for adult family members, and the like. Some rescuing processes are more subtle, such as expressing another family member's feelings, precipitating a conflict with a highly anxious member in order to discharge his or her energy as anger (often causing the rescuer to be victimized and feel worse), developing somatic symptoms as an expression of family stress, doing "mind-reading" to anticipate the needs of another family member, and so on. The incestuous activity itself may be a child's attempt to rescue one of the parents or their marriage. The therapist can interrupt the rescuing process in a number of ways, by commenting on it when it occurs (or is about to), by asking family members to identify the rescuer in a particular interaction, or by devising more elaborate strategies in the form of homework assignments. Enabling family members to take responsibility for themselves is a challenging but important aspect of family restructuring. Along with such restructuring, the therapist will need to support and coach family members as they learn to tolerate the anxiety that will inevitably result from *not* rescuing each other. They can be assured that this anxiety will be reduced as each family member gains confidence in his own and others' ability to take appropriate responsibility for personal feelings, intentions and actions.

EXAMPLE

During a family therapy session, Mr. and Mrs. Rosen are dealing with a conflictual aspect of their fragile relationship when, Nancy, their 15-year-old daughter who was sexually abused by her father, begins to cry quietly. Asked by the therapist to give voice to her tears, Nancy describes feeling badly about reporting the abuse and causing such a rift between her parents and wondering aloud if she should be the one to leave the family. In response, her parents turn their attention toward Nancy, each reassuring her that she is loved. At this point, the therapist compliments the daughter on her concern for her parents, noting that she has rescued them from an obviously difficult and painful interaction. Then, he asks her what she believes might happen if her parents were to continue their discussion? Nancy replies with her fears about a divorce, a sentiment immediately echoed by her two younger siblings. Mr. and Mrs. Rosen quickly assert that they would never consider divorce, at which point the therapist observes that the spouses need more time in therapy before making a decision about the marriage and suggests that the future of the fragile marriage is something about which they *should* be worrying. Finally, the therapist cautions the children that worrying is a difficult habit to break all at once, and he advises them to continuing worrying about whether their parents are worrying about the marriage.

Another strategy for realigning interpersonal boundaries is to *help family members experience their own feelings as separate and distinct from those of others.* Since shared meanings and behavioral patterns underlie the relationships of all family members, it is predictable that certain emotional themes will emerge in family life. Because the incestuous family stresses sameness as a guarantee of survival, most members express similar feelings about ideas and events (often including the incest). Those who do not may be criticized, rejected and even victimized by other family members. These difficulties are further complicated by the common tendency toward dissociation that characterizes sexual abuse victims, perpetrators, and sometimes other family members, thereby increasing the fluidity and diffusion of emotions within the family. Dealing with emotions in genuine, open, and useful ways represents one of the greatest challenges in therapy with incestuous families. By definition, the therapist is seen as "different" and therefore as suspect by most family members. As a result, expressions of empathy and support for clients' painful feelings often are dismissed or disputed. Further, the therapist should avoid exposing negative emotions too quickly or too fully to prevent family members from reacting with tremendous shame and vulnerability. Similarly, highlighting emotional differences between family members must be timed carefully in order to keep one family member from being victimized by others.

EXAMPLE

Well into treatment for sibling incest, the Phillips family is currently attending family therapy sessions focusing on family restructuring now that both the perpetrator and the victims have completed group therapy programs. The therapist has been involved intermittently with this family for more than a year, and she has a solid relationship of trust with each family member.

Following an interaction between two early adolescent family members during which one begins to cry, the therapist observes, "Helen, I notice that you have some feelings expressing themselves in your tears, while, Bonnie, you don't seem to be having any emotional reaction at all. I wonder if the two of you are feeling very different about the sexual contact with your brother, or if you actually feel similarly but express your emotions in different ways [note that difference is presumed]. Of course, your experiences with your brother were quite different. Would you two be willing to talk with other family members now about what you see as the similarities and the differences in your incest experience and its effects on you?"

Finally, interpersonal boundary realignment can be aided by *helping family members speak for themselves*, both with each other and with those outside the family. The widely known "speaking for self" guideline in therapy (e.g., Guerney, 1977; Lederer & Jackson, 1968; Miller, Nunnally, & Wackman, 1975, 1976) is frequently violated in incestuous families. The emphasis on family loyalty and the emotional enmeshment of family members typically seduce individuals into believing that the family speaks with "one voice" and that each member can represent the experience of any other. Uniformity of opinion may be extolled as a significant virtue in incestuous families, further quashing conflict. The therapist should expect to serve as a gatekeeper and communications coach when interacting with incestuous families. He or she is likely to find him- or herself interrupting when one family member begins to answer for another, checking out with each individual when a family consensus is assumed, questioning how one member is able to make a significant decision for another, challenging the assumption that everyone believes the same thing about a particular subject, and especially supporting family members when they dare to speak out against the group. Circular questions exploring communication and conflict can also be very useful, as can self-reflexive exploration of the experience of a particular family member.

EXAMPLE

Faced with an overbearing stepfather, Martin (who is an incest perpetrator with his stepsons), and four remaining family members who seem intimidated into complete passivity during the early sessions of family therapy, the therapist decides to utilize "family sculpture" techniques to assist in assessment and to facilitate interaction (Satir, 1967). Each family member in turn is requested to create a sculpted scene using all of the family members to illustrate (a) how she or he views current family relationships, and (b) how she or he personally would like things to be. The second child, Lorraine, shyly volunteers to begin. With verbal support and coaching from the therapist, she assigns places to various family members, seating her mother in a distant corner of the room and assembling her siblings on their knees in a circle around their stepfather, who is told to stand with his armed folded. Themes of power and abandonment have now begun to be revealed. The therapist continues coaching each family member to do the sculpting, emphasizing the uniqueness of each scene and the insights of each individual.

MANAGING INTRAPSYCHIC BOUNDARIES

The intrapsychic ecology of humans is typically referred to as an individual's "personality." Most incest family members suffer some degree of intrapsychic boundary confusion that leads to significant psychological defenses and even may result in substantial psychopathology (usually, but not always, seen most dramatically in the victim and the perpetrator). There is general agreement on the potential for incestuous abuse to create recognizable psychological problems for a sizable portion of victims; however, the exact relationship between short-term and long-term effects of abuse still is not well understood.[2] As we have noted previously, the nature and extent of psychopathology of incest perpetrators is still controversial; indeed, there are still many unanswered questions about the personality structures of all child sexual abusers.[3]

At its most extreme, intrapsychic boundary diffusion produces individual psychopathology that is best addressed in intensive individual therapy. Sometimes—in the case of many rage-oriented incest perpetrators and a few severely disturbed victims—this pathology is so severe that the individual is unable to participate in family therapy. Denial may be so dramatic or symptoms so bizarre that communication about the sexual abuse or even about the dynamics of family life is impossible. Sometimes, the risk of violence is so great that an individual must be locked up or forcibly prevented from having any contact with family members. More often, intrapsychic difficulties are expressed in moderate individual symptoms such as anxiety, depression, or tolerable behavioral problems, which can be partially controlled by medication and aided by participating in therapy. The disturbed intrapsychic ecology of individuals also is displayed in incest family transactional patterns, where it is both cause and effect of problems in behavior and meaning between family members as described above. In addition to her own diagnostic procedures and skills, the family therapist may be aided by formal evaluations conducted by other professionals, by testing, and by specialized assessments to determine whether an individual family member is a good candidate for family therapy—most are.

The therapist works to balance intrapsychic subsystems in much the same way that he or she contributes to interpersonal balances within the family system. Each strategy and intervention is unique, based upon the particular hypothesis emerging out of the flow of family and therapeutic processes at a particular moment in time. Nevertheless, several guidelines can be offered for therapeutically balancing intrapsychic dynamics within the context of family therapy.[4]

[2]Cf. Beitchman et al. (1991); Berliner (1991); Briere (1992); Conte (1988); Conte & Schuerman (1987); Finkelhor (1990); Friedrich & Reams (1987); Gomes-Schwartz, Horowitz, & Cardarelli (1990); Starr & Wolfe (1991); Wyatt & Powell (1988).
[3]See for example Araji & Finkelhor (1986); Barnard et al. (1989); Burgess, Hartman, & McCormick (1987); Groth & Birnbaum (1979); Groth et al. (1982); Johnson (1985); Knight (1985); Knight & Prentky (1990); Langevin (1983); Lanyon (1991); McGovern (1991); Meloy (1988). We discuss in detail the subject of intrapsychic disturbances of sex abuse perpetrators and victim/survivors, and approaches to treatment of both, in our book *Child Sexual Abuse: An Ecological Approach to Treating Victims and Perpetrators.*
[4]For further discussion of the role of individual work in relation to family therapy, see Pearce & Friedman (1980); Sander (1979); Slipp (1984); Sugarman (1986); Whitaker (1986).

Strategies to Realign Intrapsychic Boundaries

First and foremost, it is important to *facilitate a balance of power and control within each individual* as well as between family members. Chapter 9 contains a detailed discussion of therapeutic strategies for interrupting and rebalancing the perpetrator/victim interaction pattern.

Similarly, each client should be helped to *strike a balance between stability and change*. Some family members, particularly the perpetrator(s), mobilize strong defenses against what they view as the therapist's attempts to create a "personality change." Other family members, particularly the victim(s), may be so uncentered and vulnerable that their personalities are fluid and lack stability. Often, it is helpful for the therapist to reassure clients that changes in their lives don't require "new personalities" and that each individual has personal strengths and positive resources that can serve as a basis for new behaviors.

EXAMPLE

During a family session, Bill, a 16-year-old boy who sexually molested his 12-year-old sister, becomes angry about being the focus of so much attention from the therapist and other family members. Sarcastically, he inquires about the possibility of being referred to a surgeon to undergo "brain surgery" so that he can be exactly the way everyone else in the world wants him to be. Recognizing the client's resistance as a need for security and a defense against shame, the therapist responds empathically and suggests that perhaps the emphasis has been too much on how he can be different and not enough on how he should stay the same. She then asks each family member to tell Bill what characteristic of his they most admire and would not want him to change under any circumstances. When this has been done, the therapist apologizes to Bill for taking these positive things for granted, and she expresses her appreciation to him for pointing out this oversight to her.

A third guiding principle for working on the intrapsychic ecology of each family member is to help *create a balance between internal reality and external actuality*. Tension at the interface between inner and outer worlds is inevitable in human experience (Erikson, 1963; Kohut, 1971, 1977). Self-deficits in both victims and perpetrators of sexual abuse make it difficult to manage this tension, resulting in a variety of symptoms. If a particular client is experiencing internal symptoms, such as a mood disorder or somatic complaints, then the efforts of the therapist ought to be directed toward helping the client "externalize" the underlying dynamics. This can be done by focusing on transactional patterns among family members (such as marital conflicts that create panic attacks in a child), certain life experiences and their practical consequences (such as sexual abuse that caused an emotional shutdown leading to depression or even dissociation), and the like. For individuals who are experiencing overwhelming internal reactions, an *external* focus can help relieve symptoms and create more adaptive patterns of behavior. Conversely, if a particular client is experiencing external symptoms, such as a conduct or eating disorder, the therapist should assist the client in focusing on *internal* processes. Individuals who "act out" typically are missing some internal cues to their feelings and reactions to life experiences. They may need help drawing appropriate inferences in social situations (such as whether or not the abuse victim really was interested in having sexual contact), inserting rational thoughts between their emotions and their reactive behaviors (such as controlling aggressive impulses), and paying more attention to their impact on others.

EXAMPLE

During a marital therapy session, Mr. Arturo, who molested his 9-year-old daughter, expresses anger at his wife about the amount of time she spends with her family-of-origin. He believes that she has been neglecting her duties as a wife and mother, accusing her of being more invested in her family than in him or the children. Immediately, Mrs. Arturo begins to cry, gazing at the floor without speaking. After several moments, Mr. Arturo turns helplessly to the therapist, explaining that he has brought up this subject repeatedly, and his wife is unwilling to discuss it.

The therapist proposes an experiment, and the husband agrees. He instructs the client to focus for a few moments on his own internal thoughts and feelings and see if he can identify any feelings other than anger that are connected with this situation. After several minutes of silence, Mr. Arturo looks up with misty eyes and reports that he has remembered how scared he was as a young child when he was left alone by his mother. At the urging of the therapist, he talks to his wife about these feelings, expressing concern about their children as well as about his own struggles with loneliness. Mrs. Arturo listens to her husband, but remains silent. The therapist then asks her if she is willing to go inside herself for a moment to identify the meaning of her tears when her husband raises concerns about her time with her family. Very quickly, she identifies that she, too, often is lonely and scared by the demands of the family and the everyday world. This, she admits, is a major reason for her frequent return to her parents' home. At this point, the therapist has succeeded in revealing the reality of each client's isolation, provided each with some insight into the other, and set the stage for the couple to work together toward a common goal.

Finally, the therapist should *help clients understand and organize their behavior in ways that are fitting within their social context.* Unfortunately, the social context for individual members of an incestuous family includes the incest family itself. Therefore, therapeutic interventions with any individual will be experienced through the more or less distorted family structures and meanings that we have described in this chapter and elsewhere. It is for this reason that we stress the importance of family therapy as the cornerstone of incest treatment. However, working on intrapsychic issues of family members confronts both therapist and client with a paradox. Every client is an individual who must successfully manage the dialectical tension of his or her internal and external worlds; however, elements of the client's external ecology are in conflict—the family is undergoing restructuring in response to coercive pressure from representatives of the larger social community. Therefore, the client's internal ecology must adapt to the context that the family is *becoming* as well as what it has been. The result for virtually all incest family members is confusion, anxiety, and divided loyalties; at its worse, this can produce dissociative responses or sociopathic behavior. Any therapist working with one or more members of an incestuous family must confront this fluid reality, and it is one of the primary reasons for the necessity of an ecological approach to incest treatment.

EXAMPLE

In an early family therapy session, Rhonda, an 8-year-old girl who was molested by her paternal grandfather, is visibly upset. She is struggling with a conflict between her own view of the fondling by her "Grampa," whom she loves, and the view presented to her by professionals in the social service and legal systems. With great emotion, Rhonda protests, "My Grampa *wasn't* trying to hurt me like the social worker said. I know he wouldn't hurt me on purpose. He loves me." She looks to her parents to make sense of her confusion, but they seem to be paralyzed. On the one hand, they want to agree with her; on the other hand, neither wants to appear to be minimizing the seriousness of the abuse.

The parents appeal to the therapist for assistance in explaining the situation to their daughter. Much to their relief, the therapist responds, "It's true. Your grandfather wouldn't want to hurt you. In fact, after talking with him I believe he was trying to be affectionate with you just as you thought he was. He does love you. However, the way that he chose to be affectionate with you wasn't good for you, and he knows that—and now he's sorry about it. Grandparents and grandchildren aren't supposed to touch each other in those ways; those ways are saved for adults who are married or are being romantic. And you knew something wasn't quite right about it, didn't you? So you can be glad that your grandfather loves you and wants to be with you, but you can also be unhappy that he did things that were not right and made you feel confused. So he won't be able to be alone around you for awhile, until you and he and everybody else are sure that he won't make that same mistake again—because he's made your parents and other people angry, and he's caused the family a lot of trouble."

In addition to these general principles for dealing with intrapsychic boundary issues among incest family members, a number of specific techniques should guide the process. These can assist the therapist in dealing with the meaning distortions and power/control misbalances that produce such rigid defenses in incestuous families. They may be thought of as ways to "package" the therapist's rebalancing interventions. They include:

- Avoid direct power/control struggles, particularly those related to perceptual differences (for example, taking sides on whether something did or did not occur).
- Find areas of agreement between therapist and client, and build change-oriented interventions from these areas (for example, using pace/lead techniques).
- Frame observations and suggestions positively whenever possible; even the most problematic or negative behavior has some utility which can be used as a basis for understanding and changing it.
- Clarify the meanings of various behaviors (particularly the incest) among family members, while emphasizing that understanding the meaning of the behavior for others is not the same as condoning it. Reinforce differences in perspective among family members without derogating the experience of any individual.
- When facing distorted perceptions or flawed cognitions, work to alter them incrementally over a number of sessions rather than through direct confrontation in a single session (which can cause breakdown in victims and increase resistance in perpetrators).
- Be prepared for, and respond supportively — even positively — to, regressions in cognitions, emotions, or behavior. Coach the client to find something "instructive" in the "slip."
- Focus on small, concrete changes rather than grand schemes for "curing" individual family members.
- Remember that truth always comes in versions; sometimes, a useful reality is far more important than objective "fact" in promoting therapeutic progress (although lying and other direct forms of dishonesty should be challenged).

Taken together, these principles and guidelines facilitate the boundary realignment and intrapsychic rebalancing required for family members to reduce the chances that the incest will recur and to interact more constructively in all areas of family life. This approach can be used effectively in family therapy sessions or on a one-to-one basis with individual family members. A variety of strategies and techniques can be utilized in each session. For example, positively connoting family members' communications and behavior (even when they appear to demonstrate "resistance") can be useful in gaining rapport and confronting denial. Heightening family members' awareness of discrepancies in viewpoints can be beneficial, particularly when the therapist does not advocate for any perspective as the "right one"—although temporarily aligning with one member's perception to add credibility to that individual can be important. All of these techniques can be extremely useful when applied within the context of "multilaterality" (Gelinas, 1988), which is so critical to effective therapy with enmeshed families.

EXAMPLE

Joanne Nola is a single parent with a 12-year-old son, Frankie, and a 5-year-old daughter, Rebecca, from her two previous marriages. Frankie and some of his friends have been accused of sexually molesting Rebecca. Although his friends acknowledge inappropriate behavior, Frankie denies the incest. Nevertheless, he has been placed in a group home, based upon the allegation along with his history of theft and of physical violence with his mother and stepsister. Frankie's biological father is in prison for aggravated rape of his current girlfriend, and he is known to have physically abused Frankie. Mrs. Nola has vacillated in her response to her daughter's allegations of sexual abuse by her son. Frankie has been her primary companion since her last divorce; she misses him, and she is angry at her daughter for "sending him away." Ironically, Mrs. Nola was molested by her own father when she was a young adolescent, but her mother never believed her story.

Following several assessment interviews with various combinations of family members during which Frankie continuously and angrily proclaimed his innocence, the therapist begins a family therapy session by acknowledging how difficult things must be for everyone in the family at this point in time.

Therapist: Joanne, you've lost your primary companion, someone you've come to depend on, despite the conflicts between you. In addition, you are in the awkward situation of having to believe one of your children and not the other. Frankie, you've lost the privilege of living at home, and you've been accused of something you believe you didn't do. And Rebecca, you're in the uncomfortable position of having both your mother and your stepbrother angry at you because you told the truth about something that happened to you. I assume that all of you love and care about each other; however, at the moment, you can't express or receive that love because of all the tension surrounding this sexual abuse situation.

The family members sit silently, both children staring at the floor, as the therapist continues.

Therapist: [*Addressing the mother*] Joanne, have you ever loved and been
    angry with someone at the same time?

Mother: Of course. I love my children even when they do bad things. But
    sometimes all the love gets driven out of me, like with my first hus-
    band, Frank—Frankie's father—because he's such a violent person.
    He proved that by raping his girlfriend, just like he used to force me
    to have sex when we were married. I couldn't trust him, and I can't
    forgive him for all that.

The therapist now pursues her hypothesis that Frankie probably is
getting a double message from his mother regarding his acceptability to
her when he does "bad things."

Therapist: Joanne, do you still love your mother even though she never
    has believed that your father molested you when you were a teen-
    ager?

Mother: Sure, I love her. But I've always been angry with her about that.

Therapist: [*Continuing to look directly at the mother*] Do you think
    Frankie could be as generous as you are—still continue to love you
    even if you were to decide not to believe him about the abuse?

Mother: I'm not sure. I . . . hope so.

Frankie: [*Visibly agitated*] You can't believe that lying little shit!

Therapist: [*Ignoring Frankie's outburst and continuing to look at the
    mother*] Joanne, was it scary for you to tell your mother about your
    father molesting you?

Mother: Yes.

Therapist: Then, I wonder if it was just as scary for Rebecca to tell you
    about what happened to her, especially since she knows how close
    you and Frankie have been since the divorce.

Mother: Yes, I suppose it was. But I love Rebecca too. That's what makes
    all this so difficult. I know she needs me to believe her, just like I
    needed my mother to believe me. But Frankie gets so upset when I
    give any indication of believing Rebecca. And I'm afraid he'll get
    violent again.

Therapist: [*Venturing a more direct interpretation*] I'm wondering if what
    you see as Frankie's anger—I agree that he *does* appear angry—but I
    wonder if he's really just worried that you'll "divorce" him and never
    forgive him just like you did his father if he were to admit what his
    sister and his friends say he did. In a way, it just proves how much he
    loves you and how important it is for him to maintain a good relation-
    ship with you despite whatever behavior has occured in the past. Do
    you think you can find a way to reassure Frankie that you would not
    get rid of him or hate him, no matter what?

Mother: [*Turning to her son and responding immediately*] Frankie, I wouldn't abandon you or hate you, even if you did do what Rebecca says. And I don't believe she would lie to me about it, because she loves you too.

Rebecca is now crying quietly, and Frankie is silently looking at the floor. Gently, the therapist takes another step.

Therapist: Joanne, think about it for a moment, and then tell Frankie if there is anything he could ever do that would make you stop loving him.
Mother: [*After a long silence*] No, nothing.
Therapist: I admire the depth of your love and devotion to your children. [*Turning to the boy*] Frankie, I believe what your mother says, and I think you should too—but it's important that you make your own decision about that. [*Then to the mother*] Joanne, do you think you're ready to let Rebecca know you believe her about the sexual contact, even if Frankie gets very angry.
Mother: [*Firmly*] Yes, I do believe her. [*Begins to cry*] Rebecca, I'm sorry it's taken me so long to let you know I believe you. I didn't know how to let you know that without making it seem like I didn't love Frankie. But I love you both, and I want you both to know it.

Frankie continues to stare at the floor with an angry, sullen expression.

Therapist: [*Still addressing the mother*] Joanne, I think you may have to repeat to Frankie what you said about loving him anyway.
Mother: Frankie, I *do* still love you, even though I believe what Rebecca says you and the boys did to her.
Therapist: Frankie, you appear to me to be mad at both your mother and your sister. I want to encourage you to stay angry at both of them—at least until the next time we meet—since it can help you learn that you can survive even if your mother doesn't agree with you. You're about the right age to learn that lesson. Actually, I think you're rather brave to risk being angry with your mother even though you know now that it won't get her to change her mind. However, I'm curious about why you need to be angry at your little sister, who is only five years old. That seems just a bit cowardly to me, because she's small and vulnerable, and your mother has been counting on you to protect her.

Frankie glares at the therapist, but says nothing.

The dialogue above reflects the therapist's effort to restructure boundaries and meanings among family members whose connections reflect classic enmeshment; they are strong, but distorted and brittle. The crisis of reporting the abuse has threatened the very core of the family's coherence as a unit. On the one hand, the therapist respects the nature of the bonds between family members and capitalizes on these as she can. On the other hand, she encourages new realities to emerge within the family in order to reinforce a paradox inherent in incestuous systems—one can be criminally hurtful and yet be loved. Of course, this structure of meanings and transactions still contains dysfunctional elements. For example, the intergenerational boundary issue remains to be confronted. For the time being, the therapist accepts the inappropriate metaphor of mother and son "divorcing" in order to avoid shaming them while they are trying to re-establish a bond based upon commitment, stability, and forgiveness rather than upon fear and anger.

MANAGING THE FAMILY-SOCIETY BOUNDARY

Therapeutic efforts to normalize the boundary between the family and society often are missing from incest treatment programs. To the contrary, some highly confrontive, coercive treatment approaches have the effect of thickening the family-society boundary and increasing the family's resistance to social interchange in the future. In our view, the therapist has a responsibility to assist the family as a system to achieve an appropriate "ecological fit" within its social context, over and above eliminating the illegal incestuous behavior. Family members need to recognize that a variety of needs can be met outside the family. The social isolation that permitted family members to ignore critical social feedback must be disrupted sufficiently to permit reality-testing of ideas, attitudes, and behavior in the larger community. Perhaps most important of all, family members must be helped to feel that they have the support of their community and, in return, that they owe some allegiance to the mores and standards of that community.

Disclosure of sexual abuse and subsequent social intervention often represent family members' worst fears about exposure to the outside world. It is rather common to hear adults in incestuous families contend that the family was doing "just fine" until child protection workers or the police began interfering with their lives. While such comments reflect the family's pattern of denial, they also convey an experiential reality: Life inside the family probably *was* easier for most members (with the possible exception of the victim) prior to the crisis of discovery.

Frequently, incest family members maintain significant relationships only within their extended family network, particularly with grandparents on one or both sides of the family. As we have indicated, the enmeshed dynamics and the incest itself probably originated in previous generations, further isolating the family from its surrounding community. We have found it extremely beneficial to involve members of the extended family in incest treatment, and we have gathered as many as thirty family members for special therapy sessions to discuss themes and issues extending back several generations. Boundary difficulties can be addressed more directly and efficiently when multiple family members work on them cooperatively. Of course, the level of resistance and collusion also can increase. Working with large incestuous families usually requires cooperative efforts by two or more therapists. In our experience, however, the time and energy required to interact with numerous members of incestuous families are more than offset by the benefits of greater leverage for change and greater good for the community.

An important component of boundary work with the incestuous family is members' experience of interaction with "peers." The absence of such relationships for either generation increases the potential for relapse. Group family therapy and peer support groups such as "Parents Anonymous" offer clients an opportunity to experiment with altering social boundaries and increasing boundary flexibility. The therapist also should encourage the children to invest in peer friendships and to become involved in activities outside the family. This requires clear permission and support from the parents, since the family's own boundary problems and the incest secret itself may have acted to inhibit and isolate the children, particularly the victim. Similarly, the therapist should work explicitly with the perpetrator and other adults to assist them in developing close friendships, collegial work relationships and social networks with individuals of *both* genders. Some nonfamily associations can arise from common interests in leisure time or recreational activities. Church-related events and service activities can be beneficial as well. Key to improvement of the family-society boundary is the ability of family members to develop relationships of trust and sharing outside the family system, so that intimacy and nurturance can be explored in nonfamilial, nonsexualized contexts. The therapist should be prepared for the fact that some incest family members may not be sufficiently secure or socially competent to handle extrafamilial peer relationships until well into treatment.

Certain ritualized activities can be useful in fostering trust and improving social skills. Folk dancing, square dancing, and the currently popular country line dancing can address a variety of boundary issues. They involve couples (appropriate generational boundary), socially acceptable touching (appropriate interpersonal and intrapsychic boundaries), appropriate gender interaction (appropriate interpersonal boundary), and opportunity for general socializing (appropriate family-society boundary). Athletic teams such as softball and bowling, as well as civic activities ranging from bake sales to neighborhood clean-up can provide similar benefits. The same kinds of age-appropriate activities for children should be encouraged. Team-focused athletics and group activities are to be emphasized over pastimes that are more isolating (such as computer games). Music and sports have near universal appeal to children and youth, and they are increasingly available to both genders.

Finally, incestuous families with adolescents will require particular attention to issues associated with dating and social life. To an even greater degree than in nonincestuous families, these parents are likely to need help making appropriate judgments about age-appropriate guidelines and rules for dating. Intergenerational and interpersonal boundary confusion related to the incest may have left their mark on all family members to such an extent that they may fall prey to behavioral extremes. Some victims are terrified of any kind of social contact that may lead to the necessity for decision-making about sexual behavior. Others are so relieved by the cessation of incestuous contact that they grandiosely believe their social behavior now will be totally unrestricted. Correspondingly, some parents (particularly perpetrators) may self-righteously protect their children from exposure to sexual dilemmas while others have no awareness of developmental guidelines or are sufficiently intimidated to adopt a laissez-faire attitude toward adolescent relationships. Without fail, issues of adolescent social and sexual behavior should be addressed in the context of therapy. This is best done in a series of sessions with varying configurations of family members, including only the parents, all adolescent siblings, the entire family, mother and daughter(s), father and son(s), and perhaps the perpetrator and victim(s).

Even if the therapist makes an excellent connection with the family system for the duration of treatment, the family's barriers against outsiders may remain in place after treatment has been completed. Unfortunately, some incestuous families simply redraw their boundaries but maintain their social rigidity by including only other incestuous families in their circle of friends after treatment. Like reformed alcoholics turned teetotaling preachers, some incest family members acquire an evangelical zeal that permits them to remain intolerant of anyone they perceive to be different from themselves — and therefore to be ignored or resisted.

EXAMPLE

The Blanck family is beginning family therapy now that Renee Blanck has completed a female sex offender treatment program. Renee admitted sexually fondling her 11-year-old son, Ricky, and having him stimulate her genitals on a regular basis. The abuse was revealed after Ricky told a school friend about the activity, and the friend later told his parents, who reported it to the local child protection agency. Afraid of losing her son, Renee did not immediately admit to the abuse; she is a single parent whose husband abandoned the family and moved to a neighboring state with another woman almost two years earlier. Prosecuted for the incestuous abuse, Renee was advised by her attorney to plead guilty, after which she was sentenced to 5 years in prison and another 5 on probation. The prison sentence was suspended pending successful completion of a residential sex offender treatment program for women; it will be invoked only if she reoffends or drops out of therapy prematurely.

The treatment program staff report that Renee did excellent work in her therapy; however, she has remained socially isolated and withdrawn since returning home. The family has been reunited following Ricky's completion of individual therapy and the return of the children from foster care. Ricky, too, has been depressed and socially withdrawn; he is currently on antidepressant medication.

Therapist: Well, it seems that individuals in the family have been working very hard to resolve the issues that were raised by the sexual abuse. Renee, I know you've really struggled to make certain that you could return to taking care of your kids, and I think you can be proud of yourself.

Mother: Thanks. Ricky means everything to me.

Therapist: Ricky, you've been very courageous in working to understand your own feelings and also being understanding of what went on with your mother that led to her making some inappropriate decisions about how to show you that she loves you. [*The boy says nothing, but smiles in a somewhat embarrassed way.*] I think that you both may be ready to take an important step in your therapy; however, it may be a scary step to take, even though it's very important.

Mother: [*Glancing nervously at Ricky and then addressing the therapist*] What do you mean?

Therapist: When Richard left two years ago, it apparently felt to both of you as if your world were collapsing. In different ways, each of you had made him the most important thing in your life. Renee, you've come to recognize how you turned to your son to fill the gap created when your husband left you. Ricky, you now recognize how desperately you needed to have your mother reassure you that she wouldn't leave too. Renee, you can see how your depending on Ricky to give life meaning and provide affection led to your sleeping together and eventually becoming sexual with him. Now that you both have come to recognize what went wrong and are working on rebuilding a new and trusting relationship, it would be easy to miss something critically important, and I'm worried about it.

Mother: What do you mean?

Therapist: [*Looking back and forth between mother and son*] I'm worried about how little else you have in your lives besides each other.

Mother: [*Protesting*] I think we have a lot of things in our lives. Ricky has school, and I have my job. Both of us are happy with those things. Between homework and paperwork, I don't think we have time for much else.

Son: Yeah. I like school pretty well, but I always have lots of homework to do.

Therapist: And I believe that both of you *should* be proud of your work. You are both conscientuous, hard-working people. You have your work or school, and you have each other—that's important, but it's not enough. There are no other people in your lives who are important to you, and you have no other interests except each other. That's not good.

Mother: When Richard was here, we ate out once in awhile, went to the movies, and even took some trips together. We also did some projects around the house. Those were fun to do, but they cost money, and now we can hardly make ends meet.

Therapist: I understand that your financial situation isn't good right now. But I want to point out what you just said. Do either of you see any common theme in your activities when Richard was still living at home? [Mother and son look at each other and then shake their heads negatively.] All of the activities involved only the three of you. Based upon what you've each told me in the past, it appears that your family has had very little involvement with anyone else, even when Richard was around. As important as family activities are, I believe that everyone needs other people in their lives as well. I worry that you're expecting all of your needs to be met only by each other.

Mother: [*Defensively*] As you well know, everyone dumped me when they found out what I did to Ricky. I mean, I wasn't really close to anyone anyway, but now I'm really alone!

Therapist: Then now is the time to work on making some new friends. Of course, getting close to other people always means that we could get hurt—that's inevitable in any relationship. But by not risking getting hurt, you're depriving yourself of an opportunity to get some of the rewards of a relationship. [*Turning to the son*] Ricky, what happened to your friendship with the boy you told about the incest?

Son: I got really mad at him, and we had a big fight. I guess I know now that he wasn't trying to hurt me or anything, but I still don't feel like being around him.

Therapist: So are you hanging around with anyone at school? Do you have any really good friends you can talk to?

Son: No, I guess not.

Therapist: Then it must be lonely, and that's no fun. [*Pauses for a long moment*] I would like to ask both of you to do a "homework" assignment. Are you willing to do that? [*The mother nods in agreement.*]

Son: Tell us what it is first!

Therapist: No, first you tell me if you're willing to trust that I won't make you do anything that isn't good for you or that you would find too unpleasant.

Son: Okay.

Therapist: Ricky, I'd like you to sit down by yourself and make a list of interesting things that you would like to do—outside of your home—and include the names of at least a few kids your age with whom you might do them. Renee, I would like you to do the same. After you've both made your lists, then I would like you to sit down together and share them with each other. Each of you just listen to what the other one has on the list. Don't make any other suggestions about activities, but if either of you thinks of someone else you know who might be available to do a particular activity, then give the other person that suggestion. Do these things before our next session, and bring in your lists, so that we can talk about them together. Agreed? [*Both mother and son nod.*]

Over the course of the next several months, the therapist acted as a "coach," helping Renee and Ricky pick out an activity every week that each could do without the other. This steady encouragement was critical in helping loosen the emotional enmeshment of mother and son, as well as providing support for each to take the risks of interpersonal connection despite self-esteem problems (which continued to be a focus in individual therapy).

CONCLUSION

Dealing effectively in therapy with the structural and functional distortions of incestuous families can be difficult; however, it is crucial in promoting genuine changes that can benefit all family members. Recognizing problematic configurations and restructuring boundaries in the family system can have powerful effects on both the interpersonal and intrapsychic ecologies of incest family members. Altering sexual meaning patterns within the family can create a milieu that is restorative for both victims and perpetrators of abuse. The issues and approaches discussed in this chapter are crucial to successful family-focused intervention into incest. However, they are not enough. The family therapist also must find effective ways to address the perpetrator/victim interaction patterns that have arisen from family members' distorted ecologies. It is to this task that we direct our attention in the following chapter.

CHAPTER 9

Resolving Perpetrator/Victim Interaction Patterns in Family Treatment

Incestuous sexual abuse of a child cannot develop in a family unless there are pervasive relational imbalances.

—Denise Gelinas (1988)

THOUGH FAMILY THERAPY can proceed in many different directions and be conducted in many different ways (reflecting theoretical orientation and personal style), certain issues are critical to address with incestuous families, and particular principles have been found to be helpful in working with these issues effectively and efficiently. In this chapter, we focus on approaches that are most helpful in disrupting dysfunctional patterns and replacing them with more positive forms of interaction among family members. We also describe the use of a consultation team to assist the therapist in working with the complex ecology of the incestuous family.

INTERVENING IN THE PERPETRATOR/VICTIM INTERACTION PATTERN[1]

Most interventions into family sexual abuse depend upon exerting additional power on behalf of the victim(s) and/or control in relation to the

[1]The intrapsychic and transactional processes of the perpetrator/victim interaction pattern, along with specific therapy strategies for working with individual perpetrators and adult victim/survivors, are discussed further in our book *Child Sexual Abuse: An Ecological Approach to Treating Victims and Perpetrators.*

perpetrator. Typical problem-solving approaches to individual or family therapy are usually insufficient. On the one hand, victims may suffer severe psychological reactions, requiring intensive ongoing therapy. This can include such things as: emotional support and reassurance, opportunities for telling their stories to believing listeners, boundary-building efforts, dealing with shame, mobilizing justified anger, reestablishing body integrity and appropriate sexuality, fostering nonexploitive attachments, building self-esteem, and providing help with practical problems of everyday life and relationships (Figley, 1986; Friedrich, 1990; James, 1989; James & Nasjleti, 1983; Kaufman, 1980; Trepper & Barrett, 1989). Positive social support, protective services—even legal redress and financial compensation—all may contribute to rebalancing power/control and to healing the wounds of victimization.

Perpetrators, too, are usually difficult to treat. Therefore, many are incarcerated rather than treated, and those who are treated have traditionally received only minimal therapy. Gradually this is changing. The success of group therapies in particular has been documented, and family-of-origin work is becoming more common during the treatment process (Bera et al., 1990; Hollin & Howells, 1991; Lockhart, Saunders, & Cleveland, 1989; Salter, 1988; Trepper & Barrett, 1989). Confronting shame, improving self-concept, learning to manage feelings without acting out, increasing communication and social skills, educating about more flexible gender roles, overcoming sexual problems—all are cited as worthwhile emphases in offender treatment (Hollin & Howells, 1991; Horton et al., 1990; Maletzky, 1991; Marshall et al., 1990). Like victims, offenders often need practical help as well as therapy. Steady employment, a stable family situation, and involvement in the community are all important to their ability to apply therapeutic learning in their personal lives.

All too often, however, social intervention and subsequent treatment of incestuous family members are not adequate to permanently disrupt perpetrator/victim interaction patterns and facilitate the power/control balances necessary to achieve mutuality in relationships. Interventions must be fitted to the requirements of a complex ecosystem, that is, they must foster a new ecological balance. What may appear to be balanced in one subsystem may actually contribute to substantial imbalance in another subsystem. The complexity of this ecosystemic phenomenon is dramatically illustrated by the frequent resistance to social intervention by some or all members of families in which sexual abuse has occurred. Attempts to help these families with their power/control problems can be experienced by family members as a destabilizing intrusion that threatens their survival as a family unit and, therefore, as individuals (Armsworth, 1989). In the remainder of this chapter, we provide some guidelines for therapeutic interventions into the perpetrator/victim interaction patterns encountered in incestuous families.

Accepting Multiple Realities

Just as in therapy with other kinds of clients, *each incest family member's reality should be accepted as meaningful and important,* even though it may differ from others and may not square with some established facts. A frequent mistake made by therapists working with sexual abuse is to challenge immediately a client's account of experience when it differs from police reports or from the stories of other family members. The common advice to avoid reinforcing cognitive distortions of a perpetrator (Barnard et al., 1989; Jenkins-Hall, 1989; Maletzky, 1991; Salter, 1988) is well-intended, but misleading. Continuous challenges on matters for which the perpetrator takes no responsibility simply intensifies the existing power/control struggle between the therapist and client (which is always present in some form). Further, such challenges often are experienced as a threat to the client's surival and therefore deepen resistance. We have found it much more effective to pace the client's reality for a period of time until the client can be led rather than pushed toward a more realistic appraisal of his experience or until the accounts of various family members begin to converge in a way that has an impact upon him. We remind the reader that pacing a client is not the same as agreeing with him. Rather, the therapist remains equidistant from each client's individual version of events, embracing each while avoiding deadlocks and opening up space for "new" realities to emerge through dialogue. Sometimes, this is done in individual sessions with family members. Such meetings may permit the therapist to individually emphasize his or her support for a victim, while also gently challenging the self-understanding of a perpetrator. Yet some flexibility is also possible in the context of a session with the entire family.

EXAMPLE

Addressing the entire family, the therapist might say: "I am keenly aware that the information shared by each of you has similarities, but it is also dramatically different in some important ways [**pace**]. I know that each of you is telling the truth as you understand it [**pace**]. It seems that the court was more inclined to believe (daughter) than (father) [**pace**]. I am wondering how the courts' support of (daughter) and lack of support of (father) has affected relationships in your family [**lead**]?"

The perpetrator—and others—sometimes complain about all of the problems that the victim's reporting has created for the family. Such a stance is particularly likely early in treatment with a perpetrator who is denying the occurrence of the abuse or its impact on the victim.

EXAMPLE

To this sort of defensive posturing, the therapist might respond: "It's clear that your family's involvement with protection services and the legal system has been stressful for all of you [**pace**]. A social agency is now actively involved in monitoring your family life [**pace**], and this is going to continue until sometime in the future when things can be different [**lead**]. The court is telling you that you have sexually abused your daughter [**pace**], while you believe you have done nothing wrong [**pace**]. [*Addressing the mother*] This must put you in a difficult position [**pace**]. You might be feeling that you have to take sides on the issue, and abandon either your husband or your daughter [**pace**]. I suspect that your ideas have changed over the past several months [**pace/lead**]. Knowing both your husband and your daughter as you do [**pace**], I wonder if it might be possible for you to have your own idea about what the truth is [**lead**]? And I even wonder if you could keep your own ideas private for the time being, so that you can avoid the trap of having to take sides [**lead**]."

This approach sidesteps a power/control struggle with the family while at the same time reducing the tendency of family members to form negative coalitions such as parents against daughter or mother and daughter against father. At the same time, the therapist reinforces interpersonal and intrapsychic boundaries (distinguishing the wife's ideas from those of her husband, explicitly identifying the triangle already existing between the husband, wife, and daughter while giving the mother permission not to act on the dynamic). At first glance, it may appear that the child victim is unsupported by this strategy; however, this is not true. The therapist has subtly, but powerfully, aligned all of society with the daughter by saying to the perpetrator in front of her, "The court is telling you that you have sexually abused your child." In this way, the victim can be supported while also reassuring her that the family will not necessarily be destroyed by either her reporting or by the therapeutic interventions that will follow.

Similar approaches can be taken to other family members and other issues in the context of family therapy. For example, when a victim clings stubbornly to the belief that she is totally helpless or she expresses grandiosity about her role in the family, her reality should be accepted by the therapist before it is challenged.

EXAMPLE

Addressing the victim, the therapist might say: "So even though he and the family have been in therapy for over a year now, you're still not certain that you can trust your stepfather not to be sexual with you again [**pace**]. . . . It's probably true that you can't ever trust him in the same way that you did in the past [**pace/lead**], because a lot has happened that has been very difficult for both of you [**pace**]. He probably has some different feelings about you as well [**pace/lead**]. From what each of you has said, I'm guessing that you would both like to find a way to be comfortable around each other [**pace**]. I'm wondering what you would like from him that will help reassure you that he won't be sexually inappropriate any more [**pace/**

lead], and I also wonder what you yourself may need to do in order to be confident that you could protect yourself from him — or from anyone else — who tried to do something to you sexually that you didn't want to happen [lead]. Perhaps the two of you can discuss this for a bit while the rest of the family and I listen in [lead]."

The therapist has avoided triggering blame, has framed trust as a two-way issue, and has reinforced interpersonal boundaries by placing appropriate responsibility on each individual while suggesting that they can work together to solve a problem in which they have a common investment.

All members of an incestuous family will require some challenging of their realities as therapy proceeds. However, a variety of stances and strategies can be devised which accomplish this in small incremental steps without engendering undue resistance. In our view, permitting family members to develop their own helpful truths and shared meanings rather than imposing these coercively from the outside is a form of personal empowerment, as well as a sign of respect for boundaries — both of which are important objectives in the treatment of incestuous families.

Interpreting Cautiously

Within a framework of understanding and acceptance, *use caution in making interpretations; do not share insights too quickly*. Both victims and perpetrators readily feel victimized, and both may become suspicious. While not always overtly traumatic, victimization always involves an ego wound, an injury to the self. This wound is sometimes reopened by well-intended interventions that are experienced by clients as shaming or threatening. The therapist's interpretations of client thoughts or behavior can trigger a feeling of exposure beyond the client's control (an operational definition for *shame*). Victims can feel that the therapist is being intrusive and judgmental; perpetrators can feel depowered and controlled, making them even more guarded. This difficulty has little to do with the accuracy or inaccuracy of an interpretation; in fact, the more accurately penetrating the insight, the more likely it is to trigger shame and resistance. The therapist should be in charge enough of his own ego that he does not need to "perform" at the family's expense. Interventions packaged empathically and implemented gradually are far more likely to slip through the defensive mechanisms of both victims and perpetrators.

EXAMPLE

To the mother who has a victim-like orientation and is now being blamed by her daughter for not protecting her from the abuse, the therapist can say, "I can see how difficult it is for you to listen to your daughter's anger about your not recognizing that the abuse was occurring and, therefore, not helping her stop it [**pace/lead**]. It might be even more difficult for you to understand why you weren't aware of what was happening [**pace**]. Knowing how perceptive you are in general, and how careful you've been as a mother in many different ways [**pace**], can you understand how confusing it is for your daughter to have you be so unaware of this? [**lead**] Perhaps some part of you didn't want to know [**pace/lead**], and that's what is so confusing and, perhaps, difficult to accept, for your daughter and even for you" [**pace/lead**].

Many interventions with incest family members (as well as with other clients who have severe self-deficit problems) might be labeled *inferential* rather than interpretive. Individuals with intrapsychic and interpersonal boundary problems cannot easily find a way to "position" insights within the self or to assimilate the information in useful ways. In our training workshops, we sometimes use the analogy of a kitchen sieve or strainer with a live electrical wire placed into it. Interpretations for the most part will simply "run through" the individual like a sieve, without any significant impact or usefulness for change. However, if a particular interpretation strikes the live wire like a drop of water, "sparks will fly" and the result might be a short-circuit of the entire electrical system. That is, the client (particularly the victim or perpetrator) may shut down verbally and emotionally in an effort to survive the shame and humiliation produced within him or her by the insight. We are convinced that this dynamic is responsible for a significant number of the drop-outs from treatment programs for either victims or perpetrators. Perhaps it also accounts for some of the recidivism among offenders who are treated in high confrontation group programs or even in analytically oriented individual therapy. The family therapist is well-advised to delay major psychodynamic interpretations or family of origin analyses of either victims or perpetrators until therapy is well underway and a solid transference relationship has been established. Even then, "deep" interpretations should be offered with a good deal of caution.

EXAMPLE

Early in therapy, even if a victim solicits a "reason" for her apparent lack of resistance to the perpetrator's sexual seduction, the therapist should recognize the potential for severe shame and should reply with a simple inference rather than pushing the client too soon toward significant insight. He or she might reply: "You indicated that you had a strong connection with your father when you were young [**pace**]. That motivation, and the fact that a number of things in your family have combined to set the stage for sexual boundaries to be violated, seem to have made it easier for you to accept something you weren't really sure of [**pace/lead**]."

Pacing Established Power/Control Patterns

Begin therapy by pacing what is familiar in clients' experience: Victims understand and find security in control; perpetrators understand and find security in power. Helping a victim feel in control of as many (age-appropriate) parts of her life as possible is a good starting point, even though an eventual therapeutic objective is to empower her. Given that therapy itself is a form of influence for change, it has some elements of threat for victims of all ages, since *limiting influence*—including that of the therapist—is their primary mechanism for survival. Stabilizing the environment of children in an incest family—particularly if intervention has resulted in their removal from the home—is an important early objective. Since internal locus of control is central to healing, this may include honoring the victim's desire for no contact with one or both parents for some period of time. For other child victims, stabilizing the environment may involve immediate contact (perhaps supervised) with the perpetrating parent in order to relieve fears of abandonment.

EXAMPLE

Pacing power/control elements, the therapist might use remarks such as the following to set the stage for family therapy: "It's important that we slow things down now [**lead**]. Things are so confusing—I mean, it's so hard to know why this all happened, everything is so up in the air, and it may be difficult to know what to do next [**pace**]. . . . But I've been through this with lots of families before, and I know we can come up with a plan [**lead**]. I can arrange it so that we can get the whole family together here in my office—if you're willing [**pace** (of family loyalty)/**lead**]. . . . And I can take on some of the worrying for the family that you've been doing [**lead/pace**]."

Once a stable and secure context has been established in treatment, the therapist should shift the focus to empowerment in order to successfully resolve the victimization issues.

EXAMPLE

To successfully accomplish such a shift in focus, the therapist might say: "Now that you've made some decisions about taking care of yourself in certain ways, and you've seen how useful that has been for you [**pace/lead**], I'm wondering whether it might be helpful to you to consider what you want to do about contact with your family on Thanksgiving [**lead**]. When you first came to see me, you thought you needed to keep going home on the holidays, but you knew it made you very anxious and upset [**pace**]. So we figured out it would be best to keep your distance for awhile, until you were more sure of your own boundaries [**pace**]. Now that you're more secure about them, you might ask yourself what kind of relationship you want to have with your parents [**pace/lead**]."

While fostering the self-control of the perpetrator is a major treatment goal, it is best to begin his therapy with a focus on *power*. To be effective, the therapist must balance between conveying some respect for the power of the perpetrator (without sanctioning the abuse) and communicating a clear sense of her own power to influence the perpetrator. The perpetrator must be helped to recognize and respect the personal power of the therapist if the therapist hopes to be taken seriously. Almost inevitably, perpetrators will attempt to engage in power struggles with the therapist — even if they expect to be defeated, that is, victimized in some way. The trap is in the nature of the struggle itself. On the one hand, if the perpetrator client is successful at winning these power struggles, he learns that he cannot rely on the therapist as a source of strength. On the other hand, if he is overpowered by the therapist in a victimizing fashion, he experiences therapy as an unsafe environment. Again, the challenge is one of *balance*; the therapist must avoid being either "too little" or "too big" with the client.

EXAMPLE

If challenged regarding his or her willingness or ability to help a perpetrator, the therapist might say: "I have a very good track record with clients who have been in trouble with the law because I know how to deal with the system and I know how to help families work these things through [**lead**]; of course, I don't know yet whether you'll be able to take advantage of this, or even if you'll want to figure out what I know [**pace/lead**]."

If doubts or disputes regarding the value of therapy should escalate, the therapist can state: "You alone decide what kind of impact to let therapy have on you [**pace**], but if you want to work with me, you'll need to trust that I know things about this process that you don't and you'll have to agree to let me work with you in the ways that I think are most likely to get you where you want to go [**lead**]."

Gender can be a significant factor in determining the forms that therapeutic power struggles will take. For example, one of the authors [NRL] once consulted on a case in which a male perpetrator ended an initial interview with his female therapist by saying that he would like her to come home with him and "fuck my brains out." Understandably, the therapist's internal reaction was a mixture of anxiety and anger; however, she did not respond verbally to the comment. Her silence might have been read as fear, in which case the client could believe he had intimated her. Had the therapist responded with anger or punitive actions, the client most likely would have felt empowered (at least momentarily) by his ability to have an impact on her. However, either reaction ultimately would have impeded therapy by replicating the perpetrator/victim interaction pattern. A more useful response that could have empowered the therapist without being punitive toward the client would have been: "I certainly appreciate it when people compliment me, but I'm wondering what kind of things I've been saying or doing that would lead you to believe that I would be interested in sex with you?" Thereby, the therapist directly confronts the perpetrator, while positively reframing the client's crude and intrusive comment to her own advantage as a contribution to more data gathering in the context of their therapeutic relationship.

Setting Boundaries

Help victims and perpetrators set boundaries, using both supportive reassurance and firm insistence. The need for boundary definition and maintenance is recognized widely as an important treatment principle for victims. However, victims tend to set boundaries reactively rather than proactively. Ultimately, their attempts at overcontrol do not protect them from boundary intrusion; further, their reactivity may cause them to rebuff the empathy and support offered by others in response to their victimization. Some victims are very resistant to taking responsibility for setting boundaries, preferring to be extremely passive or excessively caretaking. Within the incestuous family, a victim is likely to use the perpetrator as a reference point for her reactive responses and organize her behavior around what she perceives as his needs and desires. However, when others in the family are also victim-like in their stances, the abuse victim may also try to take care of them through secrecy, self-sacrifice, and overresponsibility.

A major challenge in therapy with victims is to facilitate boundary development without triggering their abandonment fears (when they are not rescued by the therapist) or their shame (when they fail to live up to the therapist's expectations for boundary-setting). Modeling appropriate boundaries during therapy is an important ingredient of successful treatment.

EXAMPLE

The therapist might comment on boundary issues in the following way: "I'm pleased that members of the family feel safe enough in here to talk about their feelings, even when it's scary [**pace/lead**]. I'm also flattered that you're willing to share some family problems with an outsider [**pace/ lead**]. But it seems that everyone may be expecting me to figure out how you can be sure that Robert won't give the girls any trouble ever again [**pace**]. I can't do that [**lead**]. Everyone has to be responsible for setting her own limits, although you can get some help from each other and from outsiders [**lead**]. [*Addressing the perpetrator*] Robert, even after you've reached the point where your own boundaries are secure and appropriate, you'll still have to pay careful attention to the messages about boundaries that your sisters and others give you [**lead**]. [*Addressing the victims*] Your brother can't decide for you what kinds of touching or talking feels appropriate for you—all he can do is to be sensitive to hearing what the limits are and be willing to respect them [**pace/lead**]. You've all asked for some assistance from me [**pace**], and I'm happy to help, but you'll each have to figure out for yourself just how I can be most helpful to you [**pace/lead**]."

Also important is the attitude of the therapist, which should convey the expectation that the victim client will be able to successfully manage her own boundaries rather than requiring rescuing from others when these boundaries are challenged. This stance is particularly important but more complex when the client is a child. On the one hand, the intergenerational boundary requires that children should anticipate care and nurturing from their parents and should behave in line with this expectation. At the same time, an important part of self-development involves learning how to establish and maintain appropriate physical, psychological, and social boundaries in a variety of interpersonal contexts, including within the family. With child victims, the therapist should be alert for opportunities to encourage the balances required by appropriate boundaries.

EXAMPLE

Addressing an adolescent incest victim, the therapist might say: "It seems that you aren't yet able to set limits with your sister when she borrows your clothes without asking [**pace**]. That's understandable, because she has been doing it for a long time, and you didn't think you had any choice about it, just like you didn't think you had any choice when your father approached you for sex [**pace**]. But now you've learned that you DO have choices about these kinds of things [**pace**], even though not everything is a choice. For example, you can't choose to drive a car like an adult yet because you're not old enough to have a license [**pace/lead**]. When you arrive at the point where you decide you CAN set boundaries with your sister just like you have with your father, what kinds of things do you imagine yourself doing so that she won't just take your clothes without asking [**lead**]?"

This sort of intervention frames the child's inability to set a boundary as understandable and related to her sexual victimization by her father. At the same time, it offers her the opportunity for rehearsal, embedding the expectation that at some time she will establish an appropriate boundary with her sister, just as she has with her father.

Much of the literature on treatment of perpetrators portrays them as well-defended and in need of more boundary flexibility. In our experience, perpetrators require just as much boundary work as victims, both because their boundaries are actually quite porous and because their aggressive acting out intrudes on the boundaries of others. Like victims (because they *are* victims), perpetrators are highly reactive around boundary issues. However, unlike victims, perpetrators do not depend overtly upon others to rescue them. Instead, they protect themselves by abusing others, a kind of "preemptive first strike." Ironically, much of their perpetrating behavior is actually a boundary-setting mechanism, designed for self-protection. Recognizing this makes it easier to understand why offenders can be so righteously indignant when challenged about their abusive behavior.

These paradoxes inherent in perpetrator behavior highlight the complexity of treatment. The therapist needs to be able to accommodate multiple realities in order to make a connection with the perpetrator; just as with the victim, boundary issues are reflected in nearly every transaction.

EXAMPLE

Confronting an anger-oriented incest perpetrator about his continuing aggressive behavior, the therapist might say: "It seems to me that your name-calling and verbal threats of violence have accomplished exactly what you hoped they would [pace]; your wife became afraid of you and stopped challenging you, at least directly [pace/lead]. Recall that you and I had to deal with that when you first came to see me [pace]; I wouldn't let you try to intimidate me that way [pace], partly because I know that then I wouldn't be able to be of any help to you and partly because you shared with me that you have always wanted to be close to somebody—someone who could understand how painful your loneliness has been [lead/pace]. Can you see how your threats keep you from getting what, perhaps, you want most in your life—someone you can trust [lead]? I am wondering if you would be willing to consider some other ways of protecting yourself when you feel vulnerable [lead]. Clearly, you aren't yet ready to ask your wife for comfort when you feel vulnerable [pace]; that would probably be too scary [lead]. However, when you get really worked up, why not just tell your wife that you're too upset to talk, and call one of your group members to discuss things or try things out with me before being more honest and open with your wife [lead]?

This approach to intervention assumes that the client's anger is an attempt to protect his own vulnerability; therefore, changing his behavior is framed as setting a boundary both for himself and for his wife. The therapist invokes the utility of boundary-setting in the context of therapy, suggesting that the opportunity to control his emotions and to reflect on an issue outside of the primary relationship can result in a better outcome for the client. Thus, therapy serves as a temporary bridge between the client and the world, as well as a demarcation between the client's old way of responding and a potential new way with less anger, more openness and honesty that can result in closeness with his partner.

Minimizing Confrontation

Do not push victims too soon or too directly about what they want. Do not confront perpetrators too soon or too directly about what they have done. "What do you want?" is one of the most common questions asked in therapy, particularly during initial assessment interviews. In the context of the perpetrator/victim interaction pattern, however, this inquiry is often useless or even detrimental. The underlying dynamics of the pattern make the question a likely trigger for either shame (particularly on the part of a victim) or blame (particularly on the part of a perpetrator). Again we are emphasizing that high confrontation approaches to either perpetrators or victims can engender unnecessary resistance or produce secondary effects that interfere with achieving the long-range goals of treatment, particularly outcomes that are beneficial for the family as a whole.

Wounds to the self-system involve feelings of not *deserving* anything. If a victim does not believe she deserves positive things in her life, she will lack internal referents to determine what she wants or needs for herself. Therefore, she may literally be unable to respond to such a query by the therapist. Further, sexually abusive households are often structured to distort the developmental needs of children, making it difficult for the younger generation to recognize and express their needs and desires in age-appropriate ways. Often, the needs and wants of adults and children are intermingled so thoroughly that the needs of any individual are subjugated to the survival of the overall system. This explains, in part, the fierce loyalty some children have for their abusive parents (Gelinas, 1988).

An adaptive response to these dynamics is to suppress—perhaps even dissociate from—the experience of wanting anything in particular. A former client of one of the authors put it this way: "Why bother wanting something when you know you can't have it?" In our experience, perpetrators are apt to elaborate the converse of this principle: "If I want something, I won't get it from anyone else, so I just have to take it."

In a general way, victims want to feel better. Thus, the victim stance tends to invite rescuing to relieve them from their pain. The social service system or the therapist often comes to be seen as the vehicle for such rescue. Ironically, victims frequently feel worse after having been rescued from their abusers; now they may feel even more isolated and abandoned than before. This kind of profound disappointment creates a therapeutic crisis, to which the therapist must respond creatively in order to avoid having the client leave therapy or become mired down in helpless passivity.

EXAMPLE

Working with a child victim who is feeling anxious and depressed about having reported the incest, the therapist might say: "I know that you're feeling upset right now about having told your friend about the sexual stuff with your stepfather [pace]. It may be difficult for you to believe that you did the right thing [pace], even though I believe it and a lot of other people do too [lead]. You have told me that you would like things to be the way they were before you reported the abuse [pace], but we both know that's not going to happen [pace/lead]. Even though things are upset in your family right now [pace], I believe that you deserve to have things be better than they were before the sexual abuse was reported [lead]. Can you think of even one way that something is better for you now than it was before [lead]?

Similarly, with an adult victim: "You have been talking for several weeks about how painful it is for you to be around your family, since they refuse to take seriously the sexual abuse by your brother [pace]. It appears that they're not going to deal with it for the time being [pace]—and perhaps they never will [lead]. We've talked about how you have a tendency to do "all or nothing" when it comes to your family, which often leaves you feeling hopeless about your life when they can't give you what you want [pace]. . . . Knowing that you're not going to get the acknowledgement from them at this point [pace], is there something else that you could ask for just so you can test out the possibility of your having an impact on them to get SOMETHING for yourself? What about asking for that special cake your mother used to make for birthdays? Or maybe you could ask your father to take you and your husband out for a special dinner? Or perhaps your sister would be willing to help you make that prom dress for your daughter [pace/lead]?

With the child, the therapist maintains a realistic orientation while providing supportive understanding for the victim's difficulties in the aftermath of reporting. Helping the child think of even one kind of positive change in her life gently leads the victim toward an awareness that her life can improve. With the adult victim, the therapist attempts to find a way for her to be taken seriously by at least one member of her family of origin—anyone whom she believes is likely to respond in some way, giving the victim the experience of "rescuing herself" in relation to her family.

Although confrontation has been considered a hallmark of perpetrator treatment, we believe that shame-based individuals are extremely vulnerable. Confronting them too soon and too directly about their abusive behavior is experienced as a threat to their survival. Therefore, the confrontation either will be dismissed or will trigger well-established defense mechanisms, including denial. As children, perpetrators found ways to disconnect from the pain of their own victimization. As adults, they organize much of their lives around the avoidance of pain. Pushing them to deal with their abusive behavior is likely to trigger their avoidance reactions with a variety of results. Many offenders are adept enough to interpret what the therapist wants from them, and they will engage in a form of manipulative pseudo-cooperation to avoid their real issues and feelings. To confront others is to fuel their rage and righteous indignation at being misunderstood—feelings that are more familiar and comfortable than pain. Still others have deep-seated denial mechanisms which will not allow them to deal directly with feelings and relational issues at all. These perpetrators remain passively disengaged from any interactions designed to help them, thus frustrating their therapists and others involved in social intervention.

In place of high confrontation, we believe that carefully constructed strategies can sidestep resistance by working at the level of structure rather than directly processing feelings and psychological dynamics (although working directly with feelings or cognitive insights sometimes can be useful). The circular questioning format of therapeutic conversation defined by the Milan team (Boscolo et al., 1987) can be particularly useful during a family session.

EXAMPLE

The therapist can address each family member in turn, beginning with the perpetrator: "What is going on in this family that people seem to misunderstand each other so much?" or "Who is the most confused about why your family is here in therapy? What is he/she confused about?" or "I'd like to ask each of you to tell me what you would like most to be different in this family; pick out one thing that you yourself think is the most important thing that should be different."

Addressing the perpetrator more directly, the therapist might inquire: "Your wife and your son have told you that they were uncomfortable with the way you talked to and touched (daughter), and society is telling you that it's sexual abuse. What do you think is the greatest obstacle to your accepting the sexual contact as a big deal like others seem to?"

Or the therapist can creatively use triangulation to highlight the issues and to draw out the elements of resistance in the perpetrator: "You have said you just wanted to show (stepdaughter) how much you cared about her, and you wanted her to care about you—but somehow she became scared of you. What do you think could have led her to misinterpret you like that?"

If the conflict among the family members is more overt, the therapist can utilize it: "So you often think that (wife) is siding with (stepdaughter) against you—possibly because you're not the girl's biological father. Like now, when she's mad at you because she believes (stepdaughter) about the abuse. Which part of what (stepdaughter) says you did to her do you think that she misunderstood the most? And which part of the story your wife believes are you most upset about?"

Even if the perpetrator's resistance becomes more direct, the therapist can maintain a low-key, indirect stance and style, as in the following dialogue:

Therapist: I'm interested in hearing more about your experience of the situation that led to your being here.

Perpetrator: There's nothing more to it. I tuck my son in bed at night, and maybe fool around a little bit—you know, just playing—and the next thing I know there's a legal charge against me.

Therapist: So you can't understand how all this could result from just "playing around" [**pace**]?

Perpetrator: Yeah. It's ridiculous—the government people believe they can just come in and tell you how to raise your kids. Every kid has to find out about sex eventually, and he might as well know what to expect. This abuse stuff is crap [**opposition**]!

Therapist: But you told me that a bunch of kids used to grab you at camp and play around with you and it scared you because you didn't know about sex [**oppositional pace**].

Perpetrator: But that's different; I didn't know them at first. It's different when you find out from someone you know, from your own family [**opposition via rationalization**].

Therapist: Right; it's different [**pace**]. But your son said he told you he got scared, but you didn't listen to him [**oppositional pace/lead**]. And now you're not willing to listen to anyone else either [**oppositional pace**].

Perpetrator: I'm listening. I just don't see why everyone has to get so worked up about it [**mild opposition to oppositional pace**]. We could have straightened this out in the family, maybe just by coming to see you [**opposition to social control emerging as cooperation with therapist**].

Therapist: Right. You're here now [**pace**]. Now let's see if we can do something about getting rid of some of this crap [**lead/pace**].

In terms of power/control dynamics, the therapist is using his own power to control the client's opposition to external control, redirecting it in such a way that it can be more *internalized* by the client, which is, of course, a major therapeutic objective.

Ecologically Balancing the Perpetrator/Victim Interaction Pattern

Several additional principles guiding intervention into perpetrator/victim interaction patterns deserve mention here in the context of family therapy:[2]

Provide a structured context when working with victims or perpetrators— especially in the early stages of treatment. Both victims and perpetrators feel safer within treatment contexts that are relatively predictable. This is particularly true for individual and group therapies, where the clients are without the "protection" of an enmeshed family system. Their lack of internal and external boundaries creates continuous survival-based anxiety, which can be partially offset by a well-defined treatment regimen.

Within a structured context, maximize choice when working with victims or perpetrators. Neither victims nor perpetrators have much sense of an internal locus of control. Devising ways to develop their ability to make choices is an ongoing challenge in therapy, particularly in rule-bound systems such as prisons or certain victim treatment programs. Making choices for oneself is a reflection of power/control balance; that is, a joining of the capacity to influence with the capacity to direct that influence toward a particular purpose. Structuring therapy so that clients can choose whether or not to take time during group therapy sessions, whether or not to attempt a particular homework assignment at a particular time, whether or not to answer questions posed by anyone (including the therapist)—all help to foster internal locus of control. The major trap with victims is to overwhelm them by giving them too many choices too soon. The major trap with perpetrators is to give them too few choices, thereby replicating the patterns of overcontrol that tend to trigger perpetrating behavior.

Maintain a focus on the long-range goal of establishing a power/control balance in the lives of both victims and perpetrators. In addition to power/control balances inside themselves, victims and perpetrators must learn to balance power/control in their interpersonal transactions. Therapy can help them find ways to balance the need to influence others *appropriately* (power) with the need to limit the influence of others *effectively* (control). This balance in turn facilitates the development of personal autonomy and integrity along with the capacity to connect emotionally with others (Heatherington, 1990).

---

[2]Each of these principles is discussed in greater detail in the more general context of treating nonincestuous child sexual abuse in our book *Child Sexual Abuse: An Ecological Approach to Treating Victims and Perpetrators.*

Avoid enacting the Victim/Perpetrator/Rescuer triangle in therapy. Family therapy with abused children can easily entice a therapist to play Rescuer. Occupying this role is useless, even counterproductive, for all concerned. When management-type control is needed, help should be sought from others. The therapist should rescue one family member from another only as a last resort and only in the event that some kind of clearly demonstrable physical or psychological harm is imminent. The therapist who fails to heed this principle may find herself being victimized by her clients or being viewed as a perpetrator. In our training workshops, we have illustrated this principle using a tissue box metaphor. When a therapist has an abuse victim — or a perpetrator whose victim-structure has been uncovered — sobbing uncontrollably in his office, he may be tempted to reach over and hand a tissue to the client. This temptation should be avoided. It conveys to the client two messages: The first, a positive message, is that the therapist would like to be helpful; the second, a subtle negative message, is that the therapist perceives the client as incapable of obtaining something she needs. Instead, the therapist should wait until the client either asks for a tissue or takes one herself.

Avoid replicating perpetrator/victim interaction patterns among helping professionals and agencies. As we have already indicated (Chapter 4), incest family members manipulatively or unwittingly create triangles among themselves as well as among those outside the family with whom they interact. Often, these triangles are predicated upon victim/perpetrator/ rescuer dynamics. Despite good intentions, the therapist who fails to detect and disrupt these patterns may hamper treatment by inadvertently reinforcing the intrapsychic perpetrator/victim ecology upon which these clients' previous survival has been based. The therapist's ability to position herself firmly, but flexibly, and to implement multilaterality (Gelinas, 1988) on a consistent basis is continuously tested by managing the complex ecology of intervention into family sexual abuse.

THE CONSULTATION TEAM
AS AN ECOSYSTEM

Consultation has a rich history in the medical tradition; however it has only recently achieved some prominence among nonmedical professionals (e.g., Wynne, McDaniel, & Weber, 1986). The use of a consultation team is partly an outgrowth of supervision and training activities. In the past 10 years, however, live consultation has been extensively used in therapy itself, particularly by certain groups of family therapists (e.g., Andersen, 1990b; Berstein, Brown, & Ferrier, 1984; Campbell & Draper, 1985; de Shazer, 1982; Hoffman, 1981; Keeney & Ross, 1985; Madanes, 1984; Selvini-Palazzoli et al., 1980; Tomm, 1984a, 1984b).

The focus of consultation is on the transactions between two or more systems. It always includes a strong emphasis on the "fit" between the activities of the therapist and those of the clients, that is, on the nature of the evolving therapeutic ecosystem. Key to conceptualizing the operations of a team is the recognition that therapeutic interventions create a new context for the clients by working at a different systemic level and thus providing additional "depth" in the therapeutic endeavor (de Shazer, 1982; Keeney, 1983). In Maturana's terms, we can say that using a consultation team increases the richness of opportunity for structural couplings to occur and adds new possibilities for creative transformations in the therapeutic ecosystem (Maturana, 1985; Tomm, 1986). In the remainder of this chapter, we describe a process for making use of team consultation in connection with family therapy with incestuous families.

Purposes of Consultation

Three basic circumstances are particularly appropriate for utilizing team consultation. The first is a situation in which the therapist feels somehow "stuck" in working with a family. The therapist's sense of progress in treatment—and perhaps the family's as well—has been lost. Under these conditions, the purpose of the consultation is primarily to resolve an impasse in therapy.

A second rationale for a consultation team relates to an acute crisis in the therapeutic situation or in the life of the family. Here, using consultants sends a clear message to the family that the therapist is taking these events seriously. Sometimes, the authority of a team is needed to provide the family with a sense of hope that significant help can be obtained quickly, implying "[Even more than] two heads are better than one."

The third use for a consultation team is to provide a powerful and flexible ecosystemic context around a multiproblem family and some of their helping professionals who may have lost focus and coordination, and who may even be in conflict with each other—a rather common occurrence when working with incestuous families. The family therapist may need help keeping track of multiple family problems, or may require assistance in sorting out role confusion among the professionals involved and in coordinating the helping efforts. Sometimes, the therapist will face a situation in which the management efforts of various helpers have begun to interfere with the therapeutic changes attempted by family members. Or there may be evidence that a particular professional or agency is trying to manipulate the therapist to create a certain predetermined outcome. In these situations, certain professionals working with the family are invited to join the session, and the consultation team is challenged to adopt the broadest possible ecosystemic perspective in an effort to create opportunities for structural transformations that do not threaten the survival of the clients individually or as a family. Occasionally, the outside perspective of the consultation team may be useful in evaluating the relative merits of continuing therapy.

Team Design

The consultation process can involve a team of four to eight members. Originally designed for our clinical training program, the arrangement proved so successful that we began to employ team consultation in our regular clinical practice, particularly for multiproblem families such as those involved in incest. Commonly, we utilize two subteams, or consultation tiers. The first tier is the "microphone team," sitting behind a one-way window and using a microphone to transmit messages to the primary therapist via an earpiece. This team is responsible for observing the interactions of the systems in the interview room and making occasional interventions.

Most of the interventions occur through input to the primary therapist, although the earpiece is sometimes passed to someone else in the interview room such as a family member or another helping professional. One team member is assigned to be the team leader for a given session, and only that individual is permitted to use the microphone. Interventions are almost always a result of team consensus, although there are occasional spontaneous remarks offered by the team leader. Sometimes, the team is divided on the merits of a particular intervention and an informal vote must be taken. Practice is required to be able to offer suggestions that are both concise and effective.

Two kinds of intervention are possible. The first are those offered directly to the primary therapist, without any explicit acknowledgement by that individual. These interventions are typically "invisible" to the family and others in the interview room and may influence the direction of the session without their specific awareness. Other interventions are offered from the team explicitly to the family, to another professional, or to everyone collectively in the interview room. To make it clear to the therapist that these latter interventions are intended to be passed on overtly to the clients, the team leader always begins with the words, "The team would like the family (or whomever) to know . . . " The direct and indirect interventions by the consultation team typically have very different effects on the therapeutic situation.

The second tier, or "process team," usually observes the therapy session via videotape from an adjoining office. This team has no direct method of input into the interview room during the session. Its task is to observe the interactions of the entire therapeutic ecosystem, including the impact that the microphone team is having on the course of the session. In addition, members of this team are delegated to discuss various concluding comments, special interventions, or homework assignments that might be given to the family or to other participants in the interview. On rare occasions, a member of the process team may leave the office, move to the adjoining room, and confer with members of the microphone team. This usually is done when members of the second tier believe that the microphone team is missing some important information available in the therapy room or when it seems that the microphone team has inadvertently replicated some dysfunctional aspects of the family system and/or therapeutic system. These contacts are unusual, for they run a risk of creating competition between the teams for control of the session.

On some occasions, one member of the consultation team may spend part of a session in the interview room with the primary therapist. Rather than considering this cotherapy, the individual functions as a "team representative" in the interview, wearing the earpiece so that he or she serves as a channel of communication from the microphone team. Again, our early rationale was training. However, it soon became apparent that the decision to send in a team member is best made on the basis of judging the nature of the ecological balancing that the team can provide. For example, it may be easier to have an unpopular or oppositional stand taken by the team through a representative in the room in order to avoid "tainting" the primary therapist in the eyes of the family. Or a decision may be made to supply a gender balance if the helping professionals involved with a given family are either all male or all female. The choice to place a team member in the interview room typically is made in advance of a session, although it occasionally occurs spontaneously (with agreement by the primary therapist).

Session Structure

In our clinical work, therapy utilizing a consultation team typically involves a two-hour session divided into five parts.

Presession Briefing (20–30 Minutes); Team Focus: Data Gathering and Hypothesizing. The primary therapist meets with the consultation team to orient members to the family and the clinical situation. Early in our work, we invited other helping professionals and/or agency representatives involved with the family to attend this presession meeting. However, we discovered that this altered the ecosystem, creating feelings of competition among helping professionals and alignments between the team and various helpers which often worked to the disadvantage of the therapist or the family.

During this preparation period, specific decisions are made regarding the exact nature and method of information transmittal between team and primary therapist, based upon a joint evaluation of the family's needs. Over time, we have learned that this negotiation process is very important. Usually the therapist is left in charge of his or her own therapeutic interventions and will organize any input provided by the team. On a moment-to-moment basis, the primary therapist has a certain "feel" of the therapeutic process and how to implement it. It is as if the one-way window, while offering a broader "view" of the therapeutic system, also filters out elements that may be important to the actual implementation of balancing interventions provided by the team. To appropriately balance therapist input within the context of the therapeutic ecosystem, however, the team must have complete freedom to send messages directly to particular individuals in the interview room or to the group as a whole. Key to the success of the consultation process is the relationship of trust that emerges between therapist and team—and, hopefully, between family members and the therapeutic ecosystem—as this coordination occurs.

Clinical Interview (50–60 Minutes); Team Focus: Strategizing, Intervening, Hypothesizing/Strategizing (Circularity). Interviews with incestuous families (and any professionals who may be invited to the session) typically begin with all participants in the therapy room introducing themselves for the benefit of the observing team behind the one-way window. As the interview progresses, most individuals begin to participate. However, some family members or professionals may remain in the background, assuming more of an observer role in a conscious or unconscious attempt to avoid scrutiny by the team. Often, circular questions connecting the withdrawn individual to the family will initiate some useful interaction sequences. Occasionally, a helping professional will succeed in remaining aloof and uncommitted to the process. When this occurs, the team must make a judgment about the influence of this stance and decide whether to include or ignore the individual in any interventions.

Therapist-Team Consultation (10–20 Minutes); Team Focus: Rehypothesizing/Strategizing. When the primary therapist excuses him- or herself to join the consultation team for a meeting, family members and others are told that they will not be observed. During this period, they are free to talk privately or take a break for coffee or use the washrooms. The consultation meeting itself is carefully structured. It begins with a few moments of personal reaction from the primary therapist regarding the "feel" of the clinical interview. This provides the therapist with an opportunity for some "ventilation" to relieve the stress of dealing with the complexities of both the family and the consultation process. Members of the first tier microphone team may ask questions or make clarifications regarding the interview. However, they are not permitted to analyze, offer further suggestions, or otherwise continue the input process. After a few minutes, the second tier process team members have an opportunity to comment on the overall transactional patterns of the interview, including their views on the impact of the consultation on the family, the therapist, and other participants. This is followed immediately by suggestions for follow-up interventions, homework assignments, or other case management procedures which might be helpful. Then all members of the consultation team are permitted to engage in dialogue with the therapist. Various hypotheses and ideas begin to be organized into an overall strategy for intervening. Typically, a "macrostrategy" plus several "microstrategies" emerge from the discussion. These are refined and clarified until the therapist and team members have reached a consensus on their utility and on a method of implementation. If a particular intervention is to be made in the session, such as a homework assignment or a summary of the team's opinions, then the therapist carefully rehearses the intervention to be certain that each suggested element has been included.

Special Intervention Session (5–15 Minutes); Team Focus: Implementation of Strategy, Data Gathering for New Hypotheses. The therapist returns to the interview room to present the intervention to the family and other session participants. We have found it important for the therapist to avoid spending any length of time discussing or commenting on the consultation process, other than in the manner previously decided while meeting with the teams. When conveyed to the family and to any participating professionals, the origin of each aspect of the intervention is carefully labeled. This is part of the balancing process. It permits the therapist to disengage from selected elements of the intervention in order to maintain rapport with the family or with various adjunctive treatment resources. The therapist then terminates the interview, even though family members may leave puzzled or in some consternation. Enough time is spent only to be certain that the intervention is understood—most often, it is written down—and to schedule a future therapy session.

Postsession Debriefing (30–45 Minutes); Team Focus: Hypothesizing (New Circular Sequence). After the family (and any nonteam helping professionals) have left the office, the primary therapist and the consultation team have an opportunity for a more leisurely analysis of the therapeutic process. The focus is usually on broad ecosystemic patterns, although specific features of an interview may occupy some attention. Sometimes, additional hypotheses are generated, and possible strategies are entertained. If a follow-up consultation meeting has been scheduled—in our experience, two or three sessions at intervals of two to four weeks is typical—then these hypotheses set the stage for future efforts by the team. However, feedback on the actual results of the consultation must be awaited.

Occasionally, some conflict occurs in postsession meetings. This conflict is most often between various team members rather than between the team and the primary therapist. If necessary, the debriefing is redirected to focus on these issues. Given our ecosystemic perspective and convictions about structural isomorphism (de Shazer, 1982; Minuchin & Fishman, 1981), we typically find that the pattern of conflict within the team mirrors some patterns within the family, in the therapeutic situation, or between various individuals or agencies involved in the treatment process. An attempt is made to convert the conflict into data for further hypothesizing and analyzing in the consultative process.

Effects and Outcomes of Consultation

The initial impact of the consultation team on families and their helpers often is a combination of curiosity and agitation. Sometimes this reaction represents genuine confusion. On one occasion, the father of a suicidal 16-year-old girl whom he had abused lingered behind other family members as they left the interview room after a team assignment. He whispered urgently to the therapist, "Is this for real, or are you just trying to 'set up' my daughter?" The primary therapist responded by looking directly at the father and replying in an equally earnest manner, "This situation is very serious, and I know the team is very serious in its efforts to help us with their suggestions." Sometimes, confusion is accompanied by hostility. Some participants have been heard to mutter in disgust at a particular directive from the team or to respond with anger to a particular line of questioning. A very small number of participants have expressed a feeling of being "cheated" by the team experience, apparently believing that the team has misunderstood them or thinking that the team's efforts have failed to provide an immediate and complete solution to their problems. In either case, the team always takes full responsibility for the dissatisfaction of any clients. This stance further empowers the work of the primary therapist.

Viewed from the perspective of ecological balancing, the consultation team's impact represents an interesting paradox. Although directed toward balancing the family and its therapeutic ecosystem, the team's interventions sometimes seem extreme to family members. Because the team's interventions usually are directed at a different level of the ecosystem, they may seem more dramatic to the family—even though this same family may fail to recognize the extremity of behaviors occurring among its own members, such as suicidal ideation, abusive conflicts, or dissociative episodes. In a sense, change begins to occur as soon as the team forms a powerful yet flexible ecosystem around the therapeutic system and the family system. As a result, the family's behavior can be reframed in a variety of meaningful ways (de Shazer, 1982; Keeney, 1983; Selvini-Palazzoli et al., 1978; Watzlawick et al., 1974; Weeks & L'Abate, 1982). In effect, the family is forced to *adapt* to the balancing interventions of the team as an ecosystem.

Dramatic and immediate changes in family transactional patterns can occur following a consultation team session. For example, spouses may return home and begin to talk meaningfully about issues never before discussed, or a rebellious adolescent may become docile and cooperative. Occasionally, the consultation session triggers a family crisis in a therapeutically useful direction (virtually never have we had a distinctly negative outcome to a consultation team experience). More often, the changes are noticeable but gradual. Most of the effects appear within the context of the family's ongoing work with the therapist. This is particularly true with incestuous families, for whom family therapy is only one system within a larger ecosystem of intervention and management. Following team consultation, family therapy may gain new respect among associated professionals such as attorneys, protection workers, or parole officers.

In our experience, a small number of families get "hooked" on the consultation team process in such a way that it works to the disadvantage of the primary therapist. This is particularly true when certain kinds of changes occur rapidly following a session. Family members may begin to believe too much in the "magic" of the consultation effort, fostering passivity on their parts and perhaps creating maladaptive performance anxiety in the team. For this reason we do not use consultation teams on a routine basis. "Team-addicted" clients can be rewarding to work with initially; they seem to enjoy performing for the consultants. For a time, a new and powerful ecosystem can be formed. If the consultation team members and the primary therapist know how to use this dynamic fruitfully and recognize when to "uncouple" from the family and the helping ecosystem, then important therapeutic gains can be made via consultation. However, there is a genuine risk of the consultation team being co-opted into the incestuous family's ecosystem via structural isomorphism and ultimately rendered powerless in the therapeutic process. For example, this can occur if the team becomes merely one more competing element in the helping environment, thereby increasing extremes of opposition and hindering ecological balancing efforts.

A CONSULTATION TEAM
CASE ILLUSTRATION

The Gray family is brought in for consultation by a staff therapist. Originally, the case was referred to her because of allegations of incestuous contact between the children. However, sexual abuse per se is not the current focus of therapy, although Mrs. Gray has joined the therapist's adult survivor group to deal with her own history of incestuous abuse as a child. The mother is 32 years old, recently divorced from a physically abusive alcoholic husband and now living alone. Mr. Gray has no current contact with the family, since he is in prison for assault in a neighboring state. Physical abuse occurred throughout the marriage, and the partners separated intermittently. The couple began living together after Mrs. Gray's pregnancy and miscarriage when she was seventeen. They married when she became pregnant a second time two years later. Other than the mother's description of his violent nature, the only direct mention of the father by family members occurs when the two sons, ages 8 and 10, invoke his name either nostalgically ("We had more fun when we were living with just Dad alone.") or aggressively ("My dad would beat the shit out of those guys!"). Both boys, Allen Jr. and Andrew, have been diagnosed with hyperactive attention deficit disorder. Their school adjustment is poor, including truancy and destructive behavior. Both boys are a grade behind in school and attend special learning classes. Allen and Andrew are alleged to have been sexually abused by their 13-year-old sister, Allison, a quiet and withdrawn girl who is a marginal student, is not troublesome in school but has become increasingly oppositional with her mother. The mother reports discovering the children in "some kind" of inappropriate sexual activity. Mrs. Gray also believes that Allison was sexually molested by her father during one of the periods when he was living at home. Being a multiproblem family, the Grays have had contact with a large number of different clinical, social service, and legal agencies.

Mrs. Gray is currently unemployed and living on public assistance, though she has worked episodically doing housecleaning or cashiering. She appears very bright and articulate, though unmotivated. None of the children is currently living at home. The daughter has been placed in a foster family on a temporary basis, and the boys are together in a second foster home. Until recently, the mother had the younger boy, Andrew, living at home with her, having previously announced that he is her "favorite." However, when Andrew reported another incident of sexual contact with his sister while she was visiting home, he was removed and placed with his brother's foster family.

The family was referred to the primary therapist by the child protection worker for a "final try" at treatment prior to permanently removing the boys from Mrs. Gray's custody. Despite the complexity of the case and the high-pressure nature of the referral, the therapist reports some very fruitful sessions with the entire family. She describes a noticeable improvement in the mother's parenting competencies with the boys and some evidence that Mrs. Gray and Allison are beginning to develop a relationship appropriate for a mother and teenage daughter. However, progress has been slow, and representatives of the Department of Human Services are pressuring to conclude therapy (after approximately four months) and terminate parental rights. According to the therapist, part of the motivation for this appears to be the interest of the foster family in adopting Allen, the older boy. Understandably, this has put the mother into an adversarial position with the foster families, as well as with the child protection worker and the school social worker, all of whom wish to remove the children from her care permanently. The case is further complicated by the fact that the protection worker's immediate supervisor earlier served as Mrs. Gray's personal therapist at another community agency during the Grays' divorce—when the children were also temporarily removed from the home because Mrs. Gray was not trusted to protect them from their father's physical abuse. The therapist reports that Mrs. Gray is determined to fight for her children, even though her behavior gives evidence of ambivalence about a continuing parental role. The Gray family is brought to the consultation team at a point when the therapist believes that the other professionals involved are managing the case in such a way as to impede positive changes in family interaction via therapy.

Presession Meeting

The team's first major hypothesis concerns the family itself, which appears to be a fragmented system, with a paradoxical (though predictable) overlay of emotional enmeshment. While they previously may have demonstrated some capacity for adaptation to difficult circumstances, the involvement of multiple professionals and agencies attempting to help them now threatens their survival as a family. Almost on a daily basis, family members are relating to systems with greater autonomy and coherence than the biological family. Even Mr. Gray's incarceration is symbolic of the coercive pressures on family members to remain apart. Simply put, "centrifugal forces" (Beavers & Voeller, 1983) have rendered the family functionally powerless as a system. Whatever the family's adaptive capacity in the past is not in evidence now—except in the context of the family therapy sessions. Passivity, lack of leadership, role reversals, and externally imposed rules have created chaos. Family members spend most of their time reacting to influences from outside the family. For example, Allison's adolescent struggles with a rigid foster mother and Mrs. Gray's battles with the child protection worker and school social worker are siphoning off their energy for each other. Effective communication between family members is nearly absent, partly as a result of externally imposed conditions. For example, Mrs. Gray often is prevented from talking to her sons on the telephone because the foster parents believe it will upset the already difficult-to-handle boys. Other communication deficits are inherent in the family. Appropriate communication between the generations is virtually absent; mostly, verbal abuse and mild physical confrontations mirror the violence that previously characterized the marriage.

Ironically, the professional ecosystem surrounding the Gray family has become more cohesive in its interface with family members. However, aid to individuals has been supplied at the expense of the family as a system. Various workers increasingly are joining forces in opposition to the parenting efforts of the mother. Shortly before the consultation session, the primary therapist learned indirectly and accidentally that the protection supervisor is coordinating efforts by the foster family and other child workers to develop a plan for formal adoption of the boys. This is based on her conviction that therapy can be of no further benefit to this family. Implementation of her plan has begun without prior knowledge by either the mother or the family therapist. Various advocacy programs and helping services have adapted themselves individually and collectively to the Gray family system, assuring the survival of their respective roles and plans. Substantially more communication now occurs between family workers (except the family therapist) than between members of the family.

The team's second general hypothesis is that therapy is "stuck" because the primary therapist's efforts to work with the family as a cohesive system are being countered by the efforts of the surrounding helping systems to dismantle the family. The family as a "relevant survival unit" has been jeopardized, even though the family therapist was enlisted specifically to work toward its improvement. Clearly, the foster families and some of the involved professionals have determined already that disengaging members from the family unit is necessary to assure their individual survival.

On the basis of these two hypotheses, the team begins to strategize a variety of balancing influences which might, on the one hand, serve the interests of the therapeutic contract while simultaneously testing the Gray family's capacity to operate in more effective ways. The primary therapist requests specific help from the team in assessing the capacities of the mother to parent appropriately. She also expresses a desire for assistance in interacting creatively rather than negatively with the various other service professionals—since oppositional interaction would only mirror the behavior of family members and perhaps magnify the standoff between the family and the helping system. Finally, the therapist asks the team to observe closely the behavior of the various other professionals and foster family members. She is seeking to confirm whether her impressions of their stances and hidden agendas are valid or might instead result from her own unconscious feelings of competition and performance pressure related to being designated "the last resort" prior to dissolution of the family.

Team Clinical Interview

Eleven people attend the session. In addition to the four members of the Gray family are the daughter's (group) therapist, a school social worker, the child protection worker and her supervisor, both of the boys' foster parents, and the daughter's foster mother. Mrs. Gray also requested that her attorney be permitted to attend. However, the primary therapist refused this request in the belief that it might increase the antagonistic atmosphere of the session. Team members have expressed concern about the lack of a specific advocate for the mother and about the gender imbalance of the session, since all of the agency representatives are female. Therefore, it has been decided that the primary therapist would be joined in the interview by a male consultation team member, who is wearing the earpiece linking him to the microphone team. This decision is based upon an underlying strategy in which the team intends to focus any in-session interventions on heightening family cohesion and to make them in a clear and assertive style. This can provide the primary therapist with an opportunity to assume a middle-ground position in the event of conflict between the helpers and the family or between the helpers and the team.

When everyone has gathered, the therapist solicits impressions of the family's current functioning as a way of helping her assess the impact of the therapy thus far. As anticipated, those outside the family focus most of their remarks upon the individual family member with whom they are involved and take the position that family interactions are only negative and disruptive. Several explicitly state that the children would be better off without "interference" from their mother. Naturally Mrs. Gray is defensive. With occasional assistance from the therapist, she is able to state that she is not being given ample opportunity to interact with her children in an appropriate parental fashion without encountering obstacles from either the foster parents or the child protection workers. The therapist encourages her to document specific concerns, and she does so persuasively (in the team's opinion). In the context of the interview, the mother is able to be articulate and reasonable, only once becoming argumentative. During the session, considerable hostility surfaces between Allison and her foster mother, particularly in response to the woman's disparaging remarks about Mrs. Gray as a parent. Both boys are atypically quiet, apparently as a result of previous orders given them by the foster father.

Based upon observations during the session, the consultation team hypothesizes that the boys' foster family represents a rather rigidly enmeshed system at the opposite extreme from the Gray family's current chaotic fragmentation. The foster parents obviously pride themselves on their ability to keep Allen and Andrew "under control" more successfully than the boys' biological mother. The behavior of other participants varies during the session, though there is a consistent underlying theme of skepticism and disapproval. The foster mother in Allison's household is quietly dogmatic about how "things have to be." The school social worker is overtly critical and patronizing of Mrs. Gray. The child protection workers are primarily suspicious and defensive. Only the daughter's therapist is noncommittal regarding the family' future structure, occasionally asking clarifying questions.

Several major balancing strategies are utilized by the microphone team during the interview. Its spokesman in the session is directed to concentrate on helping Mrs. Gray evaluate the help she has been receiving from the foster families and social agencies, while aiding her in ignoring or deflecting (without hostility) the critical judgments of her by the others. This tactic is based on the team's conviction that this type of interaction pattern will be familiar to those assembled in the room. However, it will be refocused in a different direction — toward evaluating the adequacy of the helping ecosystem rather than judging Mrs. Gray's competence as a parent. In addition, the team is seeking to model cohesiveness by framing virtually all of its interventions in terms of "the team" rather than reflecting divisions within the team or oppositional stances (both of which can sometimes be useful when working with enmeshed incest families). Finally, the team is attempting to empower Mrs. Gray as a parent as well as to reinforce intergenerational boundaries. This is done by finding ways to support the validity of her perceptions, when appropriate, and by directing that the children "take a break" and leave the interview room when certain details of their mother's past life and current personality characteristics begin to be discussed.

Most of the team's directives are offered in an authoritative but reasonable manner by its spokesman. Occasionally, the team explicitly takes issue with observations of the foster parents or helping professionals that appear to be at Mrs. Gray's expense. This allows the primary therapist to be moderate on a number of matters and even to mediate between opposing points of view so that her neutrality in the ecosystem is reinforced and her flexibility is increased.

Additional specifically focused interventions also are made in an attempt to aid the family's efforts to behave less extremely and also to frame therapy as an important balancing variable in this conflictual ecosystem. For example, in response to Allison's complaint that she has been having serious conflicts with her foster mother just as she had formerly with her mother, the team compliments her for sacrificing some of her own happiness by living away from home and for helping the family by having some of her normal adolescent conflicts with someone other than her mother. Carefully worded in advance, the compliment is offered in order to (a) diffuse some of the conflict between the biological and foster mothers by putting them on the same side of the "generation gap"; (b) "normalize" the daughter's perception of her conflictual interactions with adults by reframing both their uniqueness and their purpose; (c) suggest the notion of a coalition rather than a conflict between Allison and her biological mother; and (d) subtly embed in all participants the idea that current events are leading to an eventual reunification of the family. This sort of intervention has been found useful by other therapists as a paradoxical means of dealing with disruptive behavior of adolescents (e.g., de Shazer, 1982; Haley, 1976, 1980; Madanes, 1981; Papp, 1983; Selvini-Palazzoli et al., 1978; Weeks & L'Abate, 1982). Our consultation team conceptualizes such interventions in terms of balance—reducing the artificially inflated importance of the behavior in the system, building meaning-systems between detached family members, restoring appropriate control previously lost by the parental generation, and the like.

Therapist-Team Consultation

Immediately following the interview with the family and others, consultation team members share their reactions to the session, largely confirming the primary therapist's impression that most of the helpers have given up on Mrs. Gray and are working, consciously or unconsciously, against the effort at family therapy. In their attempts to counter the family's original enmeshment, the helping group has unwittingly formed an even more tightly enmeshed ecosystem. This extreme stance is influencing the family in such a way that they are moving from chaotic enmeshment to equally chaotic disengagement. The homework team believes that the structure of the session has enabled the mother to be more adult-like in her behavior and has helped minimize the intrafamilial role reversals that generally characterize this family. Further, it is thought that the direct competition between the primary therapist and the child protection workers perhaps has been somewhat eased. The tension of opposition has been redirected away from the conflicts between the mother and the helpers toward the interaction between the helpers and the consultation team. Feelings of anger and frustration are voiced by members of the microphone team, who acknowledge that it was difficult to maintain a sense of balance in their interventions. Team members also acknowledge ambivalence about whether Mrs. Gray can adequately handle the responsibility of parenting all three children. Though presented as a "united front" during the interview, opinions are actually divided about the best course of action for this family. It is noted that the team's experience of uncertainty is probably isomorphic to the divisions among the various helpers at the start of their work with the Gray family. However, the overall conclusion is positive: During the interview itself, both the family and the helping ecosystem operated in more moderate and flexible ways; more extreme interactive patterns were avoided.

The following directives are offered by the homework team for the session participants:

1. Mrs. Gray is to be instructed to arrange weekend home visits for both of the boys together, rather than continuing to invite only her younger son. Plainly a balancing move directed at family cohesiveness, this action is predicated on the hypothesis that both boys have untapped resources for relationship-building with each other as well as with their mother.

2. The boys' foster parents are to be instructed to arrange for the visitations between Mrs. Johnson and her sons to take place in the home's upstairs living room rather than in the family room in the presence of other foster family members and the television set. This is proposed as a way to lessen the fragmenting forces that the foster parents are able to mount against the mother.

3. Mrs. Gray and her daughter's foster mother are to be directed to meet and agree on the rules that will govern Allison's behavior. It is to be specified that neither of them can change these rules without consulting the other, and a weekly phone call is recommended as a means to check progress on the application of the rules at each household.

4. Mrs. Gray and the child protection worker are to be requested to individually assemble lists of their expectations of each other. As a balancing variable, this intervention is designed to give the mother the legitimate power to have certain expectations about the nature of her interaction with the child protection system just as they have expectations of her. It is also an attempt to concretize both the level and kind of expectations held by the worker so that she and her supervisor cannot maintain impossible standards for the family. The previous lack of specificity has provoked in Mrs. Gray a kind of "crazy" reaction which has led to a sense of hopelessness about her capacity to parent.

5. The child protection worker is to be requested to make a second list, this one of her expectations for family therapy. This balancing action is designed to further empower the therapist within the helping system since she, like the mother, has been constrained by a diffuse form of accountability under the label of therapy as "a last resort."

6. The daughter is to be directed to continue to rebel and be difficult so that both her mother and foster mother have the opportunity to test the effectiveness of their agreed-upon rules and enforcement procedures. This paradoxical injunction makes the daughter a party to the cooperative efforts between the two women, as well as a contributor to the appropriate parenting endeavors of the adult generation.

It is suggested that the primary therapist return to the interview room with an attitude of slight confusion and disorientation in response to the prescriptions so that she can dissociate herself more easily from the team. Hopefully, this will permit the helping ecosystem to reduce oppositional reactions and to adapt in a more coherent fashion to the implications of the directives.

Intervention Session

The team's comments and assignments are presented to the participants by the team representative rather than by the primary therapist. The therapist says little other than to clarify or express support for the family members. Reactions of the participants are as follows: quiet but obvious satisfaction on the mother's part, confusion on the part of her daughter, boisterous expressions of pleasure by the boys that they will get to visit their mother together, silence on the part of the foster parents, and evident consternation by the child protection worker, her supervisor, and the social worker. It is obvious that some helpers want to protest. However, the comments and directives are so reasonable and are couched in such common-sense professional language that opposition is difficult without risk of appearing foolish or obstructive. The most negative comment is that "There's no evidence that this will help," a sentiment with which the primary therapist immediately agrees, followed quickly by an expression of her own willingness to "give it a try." The primary therapist then moves to end the session. Immediately the protection workers request a private meeting with the therapist, who pleads tardiness for her next therapy session and agrees to a later phone conversation instead. Such an attempt was anticipated by the consultation team, who advised the therapist that, for the time being, helpers meet only when Mrs. Gray can be present, in order to reduce her distrust of the helping system and to counteract the indirect communication that characterizes both the family and its ecosystem. Prior to the participants' leaving, arrangements are made for another session in which Mrs. Gray, the child protection workers, and the primary therapist will meet to review the results of the assignments, utilizing the consultation team at their own discretion.

Postsession Debriefing

At the ensuing meeting (which is, in fact, brief due to time constraints), the primary therapist expresses relief at not having to carry individually the burden of responsibility she has felt for "keeping the family together." In addition, she reports that she found the session helpful in gaining a greater understanding of the viewpoints and frustrations of the foster parents and the various professional helpers. She thinks she might now be able to interact more reasonably with them. In contrast, the team representative who sat in the therapy room reports feeling like the "bad guy" during the intervention session. At the same time, he expresses satisfaction at observing the obvious impact of the team's interventions on the overall ecosystem. Everyone present agrees that the mother's behavior in the interview was quite exemplary considering her history of dysfunctional interactions with her children and with various helping agencies.

It is hypothesized that some countering efforts might be made by one or more of the professional helpers—most likely the child protection workers—if they recognize any signs of "success" in the therapeutic effort. The family's attempts to be more cohesive now might threaten the enmeshment of the helping system. The consultation team briefly discusses possible responses by the primary therapist to avoid the polarization that has characterized so much of the work with the Gray family. Finally, emphasis is placed on maintaining the mother's orientation toward concrete behavioral change in line with her own wishes and expectations rather than permitting her to fall back on emotional complaints and victim-like responses to the overall situation.

Case Follow-up and Evaluation

The Gray family and their professional helpers respond in several ways to a total of three sessions with the consultation team. The team's prediction that the child protection workers would attempt to mitigate the effects of the consultation proves to be accurate. However, their attempt does not appear to be successful, thanks to skillful handling by the primary therapist. She manages to avoid lengthy phone discussions over the two weeks prior to a subsequent consultation session. Therefore the protection worker is forced to devise her lists of expectations for Mrs. Gray and for the family therapy. This marks the first time that the therapeutic effort has been organized around possible outcomes of treatment rather than being simply a time period whose implied passage would lead to termination of Mrs. Gray's parental rights.

Not surprisingly, Mrs. Gray appears to particularly benefit from the consultation team sessions. The therapist observes that the mother has "grown bigger" in the system as she no longer engages in continuous childish battles with the professionals. The developing crisis with protective services is averted, and the overall helping effort gradually shifts in the direction of again supporting and working with the family as a unit. Allison's oppositional behavior also moderates in response to greater cooperation between her mother and the foster parents. Visits between Mrs. Gray and her sons generally proceed more smoothly, although both boys continue to manifest some behavior problems. For the first time, discussions begin among the various helpers about the meaning and significance of Mr. Gray's role in the family. His previous behavior is discussed openly, and his current status and possible future contacts with his sons are considered, since all of these variables appear to play a role in their behavioral outbursts. Some plans actually begin to be made for his anticipated return to the city (it has been learned that he has been through chemical dependency treatment and will soon be released on parole).

Following the second consultation session, one important change occurs whose effects cannot be assessed immediately: The two boys are moved to a new foster home at the request of the foster parents. Difficult behavior is cited as the reason, although the consensus of others is that the boys have seemed easier to manage than in the past. The primary therapist and consultation team speculate that perhaps changes in rules, combined with greater competition from the mother and the recognition that possibilities for adopting Allen have been reduced, contributed to discouraging the foster family from further efforts with these children.

CONCLUSION

Creatively confronting the perpetrator/victim interaction pattern is at the heart of effective therapy with incestuous families. The principles outlined in this chapter can guide therapists in the process of developing hypotheses and devising strategies for productive intervention which can benefit *all* family members. Nevertheless, the process is often long and arduous. The ecology of social intervention into incest is so complex that it sometimes can impede therapeutic efforts. Since power/control distortions lie at the heart of the perpetrator/victim interaction pattern, considerable leverage may be needed to mobilize the efforts of all concerned toward positive outcomes for the family rather than only punishment and disintegration. A key variable in the success of treatment is to be found in therapeutic effort with the marital unit, which is described in the following chapter.

CHAPTER 10

Marital Therapy in Incestuous Families

Sexual animosity between men and women lies at the root of family discord; it also forms the basis for much of our social pathology.

—Gerald Schoenwolf (1989)

This task of becoming persons, therefore, is not something we have to do by ourselves. It is done for us, by the power of relationship to create us as persons.

—Jean Lanier (1970)

U NLIKE SOME HELPING PROFESSIONALS who work with family sexual abuse, we do not automatically assume that the marriage will, or should, be terminated when the husband (or wife) has been implicated in incest. Neither do we assume that the couple should stay together at all costs. Our approach is basically similar to therapy with nonincestuous couples who have serious marital problems: Time and attention should be focused first on resolving the immediate crisis that precipitated treatment, and then consideration can be given to the longer range issues of marital commitment and stability. We believe that professionals who communicate to the spouse that "You married a terrible person, and you need to get away from him" fail to recognize the strong ties of loyalty to the perpetrator that typically underlie the relationship, particularly when the spouse herself has been a victim of abuse (Gelinas, 1988). Instead, we focus on restructuring the relationships within the family system (as well as the intrapsychic ecology of each family member) and let the decision about marriage maintenance or divorce emerge from these changing ecologies.

Simply put, divorce should be one of the possible outcomes of *therapy* rather than an automatic result of the discovery of incest.

MARITAL DYNAMICS

The perpetrator/victim interaction pattern tends to be carried forward as an intrapsychic template by adult survivors of child sexual abuse, influencing their choice of partners and their transactions in marriage. Since incest perpetrators are likely to have been abused in some way as children, they also bring the perpetrator/victim interaction template into the marriage. The pattern pervasively affects either or both partners' expectations of marriage, their styles of conflict, the nature of their intimacy, their approach to parenting, and, not surprisingly, their sexual relationship. These problematic dynamics tend to characterize the marriage even in families in which neither spouse is involved directly in the incestuous activity, for example, in sibling incest situations.

The overall ecology of the incestuous family is reflected in the marital relationship in a particularly striking way. At its core are *unresolved dependency needs and resultant developmental deficits of self* in each partner. These, in turn, create a relationship structured around ambivalence with regard to proximity and distance (McCarthy & Byrne, 1988), giving rise to boundary problems. The partners experience difficulty both with separation and with connection; therefore, genuine intimacy is virtually impossible.

Power/control distortions also are prominent, leading to maladaptive patterns of conflict — typified by continuous or alternating sequences of passive/aggressive withdrawal or overtly abusive behavior. As we have noted previously, these distortions are linked to gender socialization. Therefore, both partners are likely to experience a sense of anxiety and anger in relation to the other sex. Even in the realm of intimacy, couple transactions reflect elements of the perpetrator/victim interaction pattern.

Couple communication is deficient and distorted, particularly with regard to genuine personal feelings or information about the self; therefore, conflicts are seldom resolved. Interactive tensions are marked by stress, manipulation, and deception, since the partners tend to project their own thoughts and feelings onto each other and to engage frequently in "mind reading" behavior. Communication about sexual issues is particularly likely to be difficult. Typically, language for direct and effective sexual communication is lacking; less often, the sexual channel of communication is overloaded and distorted.

A *lack of adaptive flexibility characterizes the marriage relationship.* Both partners are likely to be actively or passively rigid in relation to each other and to the outside world. The marital system has a brittleness that increases the likelihood of its self-destructing under shifting conditions (e.g., following the revelation of incest). The spouses do not respond well to changes in each other or in their children; alterations in their social environment also are poorly tolerated. As a result, the partners are ill-equipped to deal with developmental issues that arise inevitably in families. Unskilled at both relationship maintenance and at parenting, the spouses unwittingly set the stage for the incestuous behavior.

Sexual issues between the adult partners are inevitable in the incestuous family, even if they are not immediately evident. Somehow, one or (usually) both partners are sexually *dissatisfied*, in relation to frequency of contact, level of physical gratification, feelings of intimacy, or behavioral repertoire. Erotic transactions between the partners may be overemphasized in some fashion, creating an impression that the entire relationship rests on the condition of their sex life. With this burden, disillusionment and conflict are inevitable, thereby contributing to the perpetrator's motivation to seek contact with another sexual partner.

Lest the description above seem pejorative, we remind the reader that all individuals (including therapists) have developmental issues of selfhood which reflect shortcomings and maladjustments that can lead to problems in close relationships. What is significant about these issues in the marital relationships of many abuse perpetrators and victims is that (a) the self deficits are both primitive and pervasive, resulting in threats to survival, (b) the negative intrapsychic and interpersonal structures of the two individuals are a particularly good "ecological fit" with each other, and (c) the gender-linked distortions in power/control are especially influential in the partners' behavior. Taken together, these produce a marriage characterized by narcissism, hostile dependency, extreme vulnerability, and the potential for some kind of abuse. In addition, it sets the stage for one or both parents to turn to the children to meet needs that fail to be handled adequately between the adults.

TREATMENT OBJECTIVES

As in other aspects of incest family treatment, marital therapy should be directed toward positive relationship goals as well as resolving problems associated with the revelation of abuse. Here, too, feelings of not "deserving" anything so characteristic of victims may play themselves out in the marriage relationship, stalling efforts of either partner to improve their situation. As a result, the nonoffending spouse is vulnerable to moving toward divorce in the days following her discovery of the incestuous contact — unless she follows an equally tempting path of remaining loyal to her husband and disbelieving the victim's story. Providing hope for the marriage, while working to help family members accept and deal with the reality of the abuse, can be an important therapeutic contribution in the early stages of intervention.

Among other things, incest signals a troubled marital relationship. Working toward ecological balance with the incestuous family should include the potential for the marriage to be a "unit of survival." Even under the unpredictable conditions of intervention into a situation of suspected abuse, the therapist can adopt a stance similar to that used with other marital problems:

- Obtain a statement about the problem(s) from both partners.
- Gain an understanding of both clients' models of the world.
- Devise some general hypotheses and overall strategies for intervention.
- Frame a "solvable problem" requiring mutual effort by the spouses.

Presuming both spouses have a commitment to the marriage, the overall goal of this therapeutic endeavor should be clear to the therapist and clients: *to establish a healthy, effective marital relationship and parental coalition that can serve as a strong basis for family life and community participation.* When achieved, this outcome makes incestuous behavior intolerable and unnecessary in the eyes of both partners. Within this ecological framework, several more specific treatment objectives emerge from the marital issues outlined above:

Develop a solid foundation of interdependence between the partners. Satisfying participation in close relationships requires overcoming the self-deficits that characterize victims and victims-turned-perpetrators. For effective marital work, the therapist must have a strong relationship with both partners (another argument for the centrality of a family therapist who can work flexibly with various parts of the incestuous family system). Achieving a balance of independence and dependence between the spouses is no easy task; it is likely to be a focus of the therapeutic process throughout treatment. Some perpetrators have a conscious wish to be totally independent, with partners who are totally dependent upon them; their nonoffending spouses may hold a complementary view. Other couples may overemphasize mutual dependency, reflecting the inadequacy of self and fear of abandonment that characterize their internal ecologies. Very few couples in incestuous families consider independence a laudable goal for both partners; convincing manifestations of strong independence are seldom encountered in working with these family members.

Establish a functional balance of power/control between the partners. The specific expressions of this balance will differ from couple to couple; however, particular attention should be paid to gender linkages since distortions will continue to find support in the social environment, both inside and outside the family. Finding balances is a gradual process, though it should begin immediately in order to confront the perpetrator/victim interaction pattern that is structured into the relationship.

Enhance the capacity of the partners to balance separation and connection. The spouses can be helped to maintain appropriate boundaries (even in the face of inevitable ambiguities in life and in relationships) by learning methods to regulate distance that do not provoke fears of abandonment. In a parallel way, each partner's progress on self-development will assist *both* to better tolerate distance in the marriage. As a result, the amount of pseudo-intimacy that typifies these marriages can be reduced significantly.

Facilitate direct and effective communication between the partners. Emphasis on improving communication should occur secondary to work on power/control, since indirect or absent communication can be a tactic to avoid overt power/control struggles without resolving the issues. Positive changes in communication methods and styles should be directed at improving decision-making and problem-solving, including within the sexual relationship.

Increase behavioral flexibility and recognition of choices in the relationship. With an improved sense of self, better boundaries, and greater internal locus of control, each spouse has more options for action and less need to maintain a rigid stance in the relationship. Once convinced that they deserve to have choices, those with backgrounds of victimization can begin to experiment with new forms of freedom. However, a close relationship such as marriage makes such experimentation risky. The therapist can help the spouses recognize new possibilities, facilitate each partner in making choices and in communicating about those choices, and positively reinforce choices when they are made.

Increase sexual satisfaction in the marriage. The therapist's challenge is to help the partners strike a balance between their expectations for their sex life and the reality of the effort necessary to improve and maintain a mutually rewarding erotic relationship. Both behavior and meaning should be explored. Sometimes, treatment of a specific sexual dysfunction may be necessary. Frequently, the impact of the incest on the marriage will need to be approached in the same manner that the therapist might help a couple deal with a typical extramarital affair.

Improve parental competence. Bolstering the intergenerational boundary is a key issue in marital therapy with incest perpetrators and their spouses. Along with the necessary work on selfhood, interdependence, power/control and distance regulation, the partners usually require assistance with the skills of parenting (Burkett, 1991). This involves helping them recognize the appropriate developmental needs of their children, communicate effectively with each other and with the children regarding childrearing issues, and implement strategies for dealing with the personalities and circumstances unique to each child.

Solve relevant individual and family problems. Incest families are often multiproblem families; that is, there are likely to be a variety of situational and contextual variables influencing the behavior of family members. These range from diffuse social issues (such as poverty) to significant family system issues (such as unresolved conflicts with family of origin) to individual difficulties (such as chemical dependency). Though the therapist should be aware that highlighting other problems can be used by family members to avoid dealing with the incest, he must find a way to address these problems so that family members can recognize his concern and can trust that he will support their own efforts to deal with these difficulties.

THE STRUCTURE AND PROCESS OF MARITAL THERAPY

Each incestuous family is unique, and one of the strengths of an ecological approach to treatment is its flexibility. The timing and stance of marital therapy will depend upon a variety of factors. Has the nonoffending spouse taken sides for or against the perpetrator? Has the spouse concluded that she wants to, or should, seek a divorce? What is the meaning/function of the incest inside the family system? Do circumstances (such as incarceration) prevent the spouses from continuing to interact as sexual partners, companions, and parents? The answers to these and other questions will determine the role and timing of marital therapy in the overall treatment plan for each particular family. Nevertheless, our experience in treating these families has produced some general guidelines.

In almost every case, several sessions of conjoint therapy with the marital partners should be scheduled very early in treatment; in fact, we consider such meetings a significant part of the assessment process. Appraising the nature and condition of the marital relationship provides important insights into the interpersonal ecology of the family, including its positive resources (Gelinas, 1986). Further, such sessions enable the therapist to assist in stabilizing the marital unit, at least temporarily—an effort that is important for the children's sense of security. Even when the mother has sided with the victim and is alienated from her husband, unhelpful reactivity can be reduced by invoking the joint obligation of the spouses as parents. The therapist's efforts should be directed at role-modeling and eliciting a sense of *responsibility* that helps break up the power/control distortions embedded in the marital subsystem (Jenkins, 1990).

Following this initial stabilization effort, marital therapy typically should be deferred until somewhat later in the treatment process, although an occasional conjoint session for "checking in" or "troubleshooting" can be very useful—how much later depends upon a variety of factors, often determined primarily by the couple's living situation. Although it may appear contradictory to some, we are more likely to push for marital work sooner and more intensely when the offender is living outside the home in the hope that some continuing focus on the marriage will improve the stability of the family. If the partners have remained together, a longer period of individual work may help to offset the enmeshed dynamics of the marital relationship.

In our experience, therapy with the spouses tends to occur in two waves, focusing on different issues. Though their specific content is determined by the particular circumstances, the first issues tend to cluster around the dynamics of the perpetrator/victim interaction pattern, including reactions to the discovery of abuse. Anger, blame, hopelessness, betrayal, collapse, retribution, escape—any or all may be experienced by one or both spouses. Therapy focuses on issues of power/control as well as on the nature of the partners' commitment to the marriage.[1] Later in the treatment process, issues related to intimacy, trust, and shared sexual experience are emphasized—presuming that the partners mutually decide to maintain the marriage. Though raised previously in connection with the abuse, issues of parental cooperation also are highlighted in the later stages of marital therapy. Juxtaposing marital intimacy and parental competence provides an important arena for working on boundary management.

Throughout the treatment process, the therapist should convey to the spouses a sense of the open-ended quality of marital therapy. That is, the spouses should be encouraged to recognize that they may have additional marital issues in the future for which the therapist can be a resource. This is important for at least two reasons. First, the emphasis on the continuous availability of the therapist encourages both dependence and trust, which are central issues in the repair of the self-deficits that characterize victims and offenders. Second, the open-ended quality of therapy can assist the partners in recognizing that relationships are always in the process of change, requiring attention and energy to maintain. This also reinforces an important message: the issues in their marriage and family are *not* only about the abuse.

---

[1]We have found that spouses' reactions and the focus of treatment are largely the same even if neither of them is the incest perpetrator. Blaming of self or partner, denial, and feelings of hopelessness occur when the perpetrator is one of the children or a relative from one partner's family of origin. Virtually always, the dynamics of the perpetrator/victim interaction pattern are activated in the spouses, often because one or both have been victims of abuse themselves.

Marital therapy with incest perpetrators and their spouses, as well as with other child sex abusers or abuse victims and their partners, always requires a combination of individual and conjoint sessions. Addressing the dynamics of the perpetrator/victim interaction pattern along with the underlying intrapsychic issues of each partner requires considerable creativity and flexibility on the part of the therapist. Some individual issues can be addressed more directly with only one partner in the room. With or without both spouses present, the therapist should be prepared to create and resolve a variety of interpersonal triangles, as well as to be a "go-between" in the marital subsystem (Broderick, 1983; Zuk, 1981). This requires that the therapist have a strong sense of her own boundaries, as well as a clear and explicit policy for handling information between family members so that dysfunctional secrets are not reinforced.

Adjunctive sessions with either spouse's parents or siblings, even close friends or coworkers, can be very important contributors to effective individual and marital therapy. Used judiciously, such meetings can serve the purpose of support, confrontation, information-gathering, structural realignment, or insight and analysis of issues. In addition, first-hand contact with those who compose the interpersonal environment of the couple can provide the therapist with data useful in facilitating the family's "ecological fit" within a community context. Ongoing participation in perpetrator/victim interaction patterns tends to distort an individual's perception of feedback so that social isolation is increased.

The role of group therapy in the treatment of perpetrators and victims has been discussed briefly in Chapter 7.[2] Marital group therapy also has a place in the treatment of some couples involved in child sexual abuse (Dovenberg, 1985; Kroth, 1979; Mayer, 1983); however, the combination of self-deficit and power/control issues displayed in such groups can be daunting to even the most seasoned therapist. Therefore, group therapy with spouses is best placed into the late stages of treatment, when it can focus on intimacy and sexuality issues in ways that more closely resemble marital group therapy with nonincestuous couples.

Overall, marital therapy with incest offenders or with couples in incestuous families can be organized in a variety of ways and should proceed flexibly throughout the treatment process. The following schema summarizes the principles that can be used to shape such work:

- Initially include several conjoint sessions as part of the assessment process that focuses on the marriage.
- Plan to undertake a three-to-six-month sequence of conjoint marital sessions after things have settled down subsequent to the reve-

---

[2]We discuss the pros and cons of group treatment, as well as some group approaches, in our book *Child Sexual Abuse: An Ecological Approach to Treating Victims and Perpetrators.*

lation of abuse. Particularly if one of the spouses is the perpetrator and one or both have been victimized previously, a sequence of conjoint therapy should not begin until individual therapy with each spouse has gained some momentum in revealing the "true self" and maintaining adequate boundaries. The focus of this work should be on examining commitment to the relationship and reducing perpetrator/victim interaction patterns.

- Include at least an occasional conjoint marital session throughout treatment, either as a "check in" or to assist the partners in problem-solving upon request. Marital crisis sessions can be added if needed.
- A second sequence of conjoint marital sessions should be undertaken—with a focus on building intimacy, increasing sexual satisfaction, and improving parenting skills—when individual, family, and/or group therapy with family members have reached a point at which perpetrator/victim interaction patterns are minimal. At this point, family members often indicate that they take some pride in what they have accomplished and find some rewards in their relationships with each other. These sessions may be spaced close together at first and then scheduled at less frequent intervals.
- As other treatment ends, invite the spouses to utilize further marital therapy on an as-needed basis, in order to provide some security for each partner and to encourage them to view the marital relationship as an open-ended, ever-changing process.

Previously, we have detailed methods for addressing some of the intrapsychic dynamics that underlie distortions in the close relationships of victims and victims-turned-perpetrators. In the remainder of this chapter, we examine ways to improve marital interaction in the most important areas mentioned above.

CONFRONTING THE PERPETRATOR/ VICTIM INTERACTION PATTERN

Distortions in power/control that we have labeled the perpetrator/victim interaction pattern constitute a key dynamic in the marriage of an incest perpetrator, and often in the marriages of most members of an incestuous family. Unfortunately, the presence of this pattern signals the likelihood of significant resistance to therapeutic intervention into the marital system. Because the marriages of incest offenders (and most other child sex abusers) typically are highly differentiated according to gender, marital power and control also are separated along gender lines. This strict segregation in roles and modalities of expression creates a kind of stability for the marriage, even though there is an underlying brittleness and a resulting propensity for conflict, perhaps even violence, between the spouses (Boss, 1988; McGoldrick et al., 1989; Taylor, 1984). Some couples in incest families will acknowledge that they have "communication problems." Although this is probably true, their poor communication masks power/control issues that might destroy their fragile alliance if confronted too directly. Therefore, the communication difficulties are adaptive. Encouraging direct, open communication between the partners is best left until later in therapy — perhaps in connection with working on their sexual issues — when it can be very important in meeting the long-range goals of treatment.

Commitment to the Marriage

Finding out that her husband has been sexually abusing a child, particularly her own child, is understandably an unpleasant confrontation with reality for the nonoffending spouse. Because she may be a victim of childhood abuse or violence herself, the discovery might even be traumatic for her. Although reporting the abuse introduces an element of social control into the family that at first may appear helpful to the spouse, it can also precipitate considerable anxiety as she faces disloyalty on the part of a child, challenges to her own control issues by outside parties, and abandonment through potential loss of her partner. Therefore, it is not surprising that she either may resist accepting the actuality of the abuse or express uncertainty and ambivalence about her husband and her marriage. Relatively rarely does the nonoffending spouse demonstrate unequivocal relief at the revelation of abuse and absolute conviction regarding her future course. When this does occur immediately following disclosure of abuse, the helping professionals involved in intervention should be prepared for the possibility of her reversing directions at some point in an effort to remain loyal to her marriage.

Whatever may be the particular circumstances of her discovery of sexual abuse, the nonoffending spouse feels *victimized* in some way — by her husband for abusing, by her child for revealing the abuse, by outside agencies for interfering with the family's life. Even if she herself is not a victim of past abuse or trauma, the discovery of the current abuse and its aftermath is a wounding experience from which there is no escape without conflict and pain. Therefore, those who intervene should be prepared to deal with the aftermath of the crisis that has been engendered by uncovering the abuse. Follow-up therapy on an individual basis usually is necessary to manage the current crisis and any rekindled victimization issues of the past. This therapy should include emotional support and reassurance, an opportunity for telling her side of the story, assistance with maintaining her own boundaries and dealing with shame, mobilization of justified anger, provision of information, and help with practical everyday problems created by the disruption of family life (Haugaard & Reppucci, 1988; Horton et al., 1990; Sgroi, 1982; Tower, 1993).

The decision to seek a divorce immediately after the revelation of incest cannot necessarily be trusted. On the one hand, it may represent a full-blown victimization response, in which case there may be little energy or conviction behind it; therefore, ending the marriage is more likely to be an expression of what she believes she "ought" to do or what others are telling her to do. Alternately, the rapid decision to divorce may reflect a perpetrator-like reaction on the part of the nonoffending spouse; that is, she may use it to "get back" at her husband for the pain and humiliation he has caused her through the abuse and, perhaps, for other shortcomings in the marriage.[3] Counseling the spouse to delay her decision until further into treatment can be very useful, provided that the therapist also acts to construct a supportive environment for the fragile marriage and begins to deal with the perpetrator/victim dynamics triggered by the revelation of sexual abuse.

Avoiding the Rescuer Trap

Typically, both spouses have reorganized their identities around victimization experiences so thoroughly that they carry with them a propensity for replicating perpetrator/victim interactions patterns in just about any area of the marriage. The pattern has become familiar enough to provide a certain kind of security in coping with the contingencies of life. Intervention into a perpetrator/victim marital interaction pattern creates a triangle, with the therapist initially positioned to play Rescuer. The interpersonal dynamics of this situation are especially powerful yet subtle, for without a clear-cut, externally identified victim and perpetrator, both spouses are likely to play *both* roles interchangeably with each other—and with the therapist. The therapist's task is to construct a therapeutic triangle to rebalance the power/control distortions underlying the perpetrator/victim interaction pattern which, in turn, undergirds the entire incest family structure—no easy matter!

Because our therapeutic approach to the marriage is predicated upon the assumption that we are likely to be dealing with two individuals with incomplete self-structures, we expect expressions of "false selfhood" in close interpersonal encounters. This makes the utilization of conscious insight and the implementation of cooperative problem-solving noticeably

---

[3]As we have indicated previously, some wives in incestuous families will discharge their shame/rage by scapegoating the child who reports the abuse. This ranges from siding with her husband's denial to supporting the child's move to a foster home to more subtle forms of "punishing" behavior that may ensue after the husband has been removed from the household.

more difficult. Further, it throws into question the coherence and integrity of communication between the partners. On top of all this, the deeply embedded power/control distortions in the relationship create threats to the security of each individual and erode trust between them. Each is often hurt or made anxious by the other; however, they have few coping mechanisms other than to play out the familiar manipulative expressions of victimization or the countermanipulations of perpetration. Facing these complex dynamics, the therapist should avoid rescuing either spouse from the other; instead, he should work with both partners on power/control balances that reflect appropriate boundaries.[4] Specific techniques should be used interchangeably with each spouse, depending upon who is manifesting perpetrator-like or victim-like behaviors. This requires some delicate balancing, aided by the therapist's recognition that each partner is capable of both roles.

Principles for Intervention

Specific principles for therapy with couples involved in perpetrator/victim interaction patterns include the following:

Create an atmosphere of security and firm control where perpetrator/victim interaction cannot take place, even when conflict between the partners occurs. These couples inevitably will attempt to seduce the therapist into various transactions reflecting the perpetrator/victim/rescuer triangle, a dynamic inherent in all marital therapy, but particularly prominent in the marriages within incestuous families.

Accept both partners' views as meaningful and important, even though they may be very different. Do not side with the nonoffending spouse's view of marital issues just because her partner has been accused of, or admitted to, incestuous abuse. Give both spouses the benefit of therapeutic openness to their believability.

Just as in therapy with individuals who are abuse victims or perpetrators, *avoid rapid or simplistic interpretations of marital behavior patterns.* Working with incestuous dynamics may tempt the therapist to overinterpret or generalize certain transactional patterns, for example, believing that the perpetrator has "married his mother" or viewing the wife as "cold and rejecting" to her husband. Even when convinced these understand-

---

[4]An important exception to this is the immediate threat of violence on the part of either party, particularly the male. In this event, effective management requires sufficient control that the violence is averted, even if the potential perpetrator of the violence is overpowered in the process.

ings are accurate, the therapist should proceed cautiously, recognizing that either spouse may be shamed easily in front of the other.

Work with the partners together (as well as individually) to promote the capacity for appropriate responses to boundary challenges. A certain amount of boundary ambiguity is inevitable in close relationships (Boss, 1988); therefore, spouses need to learn that give and take can occur without going to the extremes of either capitulating helplessly to the demands of the partner or putting up artificial barriers for self-protection.

Continuously work with the partners to balance power/control in their relationship. Mutuality depends upon this balance. Each partner should be aided in assertiveness in the context of the relationship as well as in boundary-setting and maintenance. Couples trapped in perpetrator/victim interaction patterns often do not recognize that both power and control can be expressed by saying either "yes" or "no" to oneself and one's partner.

Do not push partners too soon or too directly on their goals for the marriage. In addition to the difficulties inherent in confronting the wants and needs of victims, partners in sexual abuse situations often are strikingly idealistic—even grandiose—in their marital expectations. Confronting these issues too soon or too bluntly can be very discouraging to both partners and may even deepen the wounds of shame for their failure to meet each other's needs. Most common in this regard is the nonoffending spouse who voices despair over her inability to satisfy her husband sexually, therefore "causing" the abuse. The tiny kernel of truth in this observation makes its premature introduction into therapy particularly hazardous.

Work carefully and continuously with the partners to help them make decisions and implement choices, ultimately including the decision about whether or not to stay married. We reiterate that clinicians working with incestuous families need to have considerable tolerance for ambivalence in order to intervene successfully in perpetrator/victim interaction patterns.

As in all aspects of therapy with incest families, *avoid replicating the perpetrator/victim interaction pattern in the institutional systems that relate to the partners.* The therapist may need to watch for and offset undue influences by outside professionals who may be pushing the spouses to divorce or to terminate parental rights. Even child custody issues arising in the context of divorce proceedings may be an occasion for those involved in intervention to unwittingly model perpetrator and/or victim behavior or to encourage the partners to view themselves within this frame of reference. While such a stance may appear to have some utility in the immediate situation, it ultimately is detrimental to a critical therapeutic objective and should be avoided.

TREATING DIFFERENT
DYADIC PATTERNS

We make the assumption that the presence of incest in a family practically guarantees perpetrator/victim dynamics in the meanings and behavior of *both* spouses. However, we repeat that this does *not* mean that the nonoffending spouse is morally responsible for the sexual abuse. A spouse may have some responsibility for stopping the abuse, if she knows about it—yet even this may be impossible. Nevertheless, couple dynamics in incestuous families virtually always contain embedded perpetrator/victim interaction patterns. Dealing therapeutically with these embedded patterns requires giving attention both to couple transactions and to individual personality structures. Briefly stated, the therapist's task is to create a context in which perpetrator/victim sequences are disrupted and in which power/control balances are modeled, elicited, and reinforced. Over time, partners are able to recognize and choose healthier transactions and the internalized template is weakened. We have identified four primary dyadic patterns among couples in incestuous families, based upon their response tendencies as either perpetrators or victims; these are detailed below.

IPp/V

The first dyadic pattern is that of the identified perpetrator (IP) who has adopted an overt *perpetrator* stance (p) and is married to a partner who has adopted an overt *victim* stance (V). This is a "classic" father-daughter incest scenario—an overpowering, domineering perpetrator married to a passive, often sexually repressed wife, who herself is likely to be a survivor of some sort of child abuse. This pattern is widely recognized in the treatment literature and fits a popular stereotype in the public mind, although we have encountered it no more frequently than two of the other patterns.[5] Encountering an obvious and well-practiced imbalance of power/control between the partners, the therapist must resist a strong pull toward the rescuer trap, which would only increase the perpetrator's opposition to intervention—perhaps escalating various forms of abusive behavior—and reinforce the spouse's passive helplessness. If the therapist confronts too directly a *victim*-partner on the need to stand up to her spouse and protect her children, it may reinforce her severe shame response for having failed the children—something she will experience as another victimization ex-

---

[5]This dyadic pattern of IPp/V stance also is found frequently in marriages in which women are victims of physical abuse by their husbands or lovers, that is, the "battered wife" syndrome.

perience, this time at the hands of the therapist. If the victim-partner is sufficiently immobilized by her victim role, she may be put in a significant bind with only two negative choices: She can attempt to align herself with her more powerful partner (and remain a victim of his perpetration), or she can leave the marriage (which, as a passive dependent personality, she will experience as a threat to her survival).

Under the pressure of outside intervention into the family system, this dyadic pattern sometimes shifts. The perpetrator claims to be the victim of the intervening professionals (including the therapist), and the nonoffending spouse assumes the overt role as a *perpetrator* — usually in an attempt to protect her *victim*-husband from the outsiders. A new dyadic pattern has been formed, although the relationship remains equally dysfunctional despite the gender shift in stances.

EXAMPLE

During a marital therapy session, Sharon, the nonoffending wife of an identified father-daughter incest perpetrator, Mike, complains that the daughter, Gina, has escalated her acting out behavior since her highly authoritarian father has been in jail. This complaint immediately follows up a criticism of her by Mike for not "laying down the law" with their daughter.

Sharon: [*Defensively*] That's easy for you to say — she's *afraid* of you. She knows you'll nail her if she doesn't toe the line; with me, she just smirks and does as she pleases. She treats me just like you do — like dirt!

Mike: [*Angrily*] Don't blame me for your shit! I rescued you from that hell hole you call your family. You couldn't even keep your paycheck away from your father — he drank that up just like he drank up everything else he could get his hands on. If it wasn't for me, you'd still be there shaking like a scared rabbit.

At this point, Sharon becomes quiet, her face expressing anger, but apparently unwilling to risk her husband's wrath by continuing. However, Mike now has momentum and tries to continue his tirade by listing additional faults of his wife while she sits silently looking at the floor.

Therapist: [*Ignoring the general conflict and refocusing on the original issue*] It's clear to me that the two of you agree on your respective parts in the drama that takes place with your daughter. You both agree that it is difficult for Sharon to stand up to Gina. Is that correct? [*Both parents nod in agreement, so she continues.*] You also agree that Mike scares Gina into behaving. Is that correct? [*Again, they nod.*] As I think about it, I'll bet you would agree on something else. . . . Let me run it by you and see if I'm correct. Can you agree that the way the two of you behave with each other is exactly the same as the way each of you behaves with Gina? Sharon, you can't stand up to Mike, and Mike, you scare Sharon into line? [*Sharon immediately nods in agreement, while Mike looks uncertain.*] Sharon, you seem to agree with my observation. Mike, you don't seem convinced. Let me ask another question. Sharon, if you were not afraid to stand up to Mike, what might you say to Mike about his part in Gina's disrespectful behavior toward you?

Sharon: [*Looking anxious*] Well, I guess I would tell him that he taught her to be disrespectful of me by treating me so disrespectfully . . . I wish he would stop it.

Therapist: Do you think that your asking him would have any effect?

Sharon: [*After a brief hesitation*] I don't really know. We're usually fighting when I tell him to stop it, and so we're not listening to each other.

Therapist: Sharon, do you think there is anything else you could tell Mike that might convince him of your sincerity about wanting to be treated differently by him?

Sharon: Nothing ever seems to help . . . It's awful to feel so alienated from him. We used to enjoy each other, but now we are either fighting or staying away from each other most of the time.

Therapist: [*Gently*] Perhaps you could take a risk and tell Mike just how painful it is for you to be so alienated from him . . . and how often you think about the distance between you . . . and that you miss not being close. . . . and how you would like it to be. [*The therapist glances at Mike, who is silently looking at Sharon.*] Why don't you try talking to him about those things right now. I'll be glad to coach you if you need it, maybe by asking some questions or something.

Here, the therapist is asking Sharon to "stand up" to her husband, that is, to give up her typical *victim* stance. However, instead of arguing back and reinitiating the escalating cycle of conflict, the wife is encouraged to share some of her real feelings and to "invite" her husband toward intimacy. This may trigger Mike's overpowering (abusive) behavior, although there still is a risk that he could begin to exploit her vulnerability — in which case, the therapist again would need to step in to interrupt the sequence. Subtly, the therapist is contradicting the wife's helplessness and encouraging her to present herself to her husband in terms of feelings and desires, but without weakness. Instead of demanding more respectful treatment, she is making a bid to touch the vulnerability inside the perpetrator's aggressive defenses. If successful, a small but potentially significant shift in couple interaction can begin, and the therapist can follow up with similar coaching of the husband to share what he currently is "missing" in the relationship with his wife. The therapist's challenge is to maintain a positive context around the exchange and to derail any hint of blame that may creep into the statements of either partner.

IPv/V

A second common marital pattern in incestuous families is that of an identified perpetrator (IP) interacting as a *victim* (v), married to a nonoffending spouse who is also interacting as a *victim* (V). Unlike the first pattern, in which power and control coexist in a complementary pattern, this couple reflects a symmetrical combination of underpowered and overcontrolled dynamics. Both partners' stances are oriented toward limiting the other's influence, yet both are without the inner resources to do much influencing. Control struggles rather than power struggles distinguish their conflict. Deprivation and desperation are nearly continuous experiences for both partners. Each brings substantial emotional needs to the marriage, but neither is equipped to provide much nurturance or support for the other. A pattern that is found often in affection-based incestuous families, the partners give the appearance of two children "playing house"; regardless of their ages, they seem too young to function as responsible adults in a marriage. In therapy, both partners seem to be waiting for the therapist to play Rescuer, that is, to "fix" things with little or no contribution from them. Simply engaging them sufficiently to do meaningful work in therapy can be daunting. The therapist may be seduced into overfunctioning, as a coach, educator, go-between, advocate — all these and more in a vain effort to overcome their passivity and helplessness. The partners' psychosocial deficits leave them without a clear sense of identity, making genuine mutuality between them impossible. In some sense, the challenge of marital therapy is to "grow them up and into the marriage." However, individual therapy may be a necessary prerequisite to successful marital treatment. Here, too, a notable trap exists for the unwary therapist. A therapeutic transference relationship is critical; yet too much emphasis on dependent attachment and too little on separation and individuation will leave untouched the partners' deep-seated fears of autonomy and independence.

Just as in the previous dyadic pattern, the therapist must avoid inadvertently shaming the partners, particularly by highlighting too directly their vulnerabilities in each other's presence. Such an intervention would be experienced as a "wound" to the self, an exercise of exploitive power by the therapist over which neither partner had any control, thereby deepening the internalized sense of victimization. In the course of therapy, both partners may appear to move through several "developmental stages." Verbal interaction between the spouses typically increases as they gain confidence and a sense of security. Marital therapy becomes easier, although the disappearing *victim* responses may be replaced by elements of perpetration. One common configuration among these couples emerging during therapy is a juxtaposition—sometimes obvious, sometimes subtle—of a "wounded self" description (victimization) and a "you are to blame" assertion (perpetration). This distorted power/control message is aimed most often at the spouse, sometimes at the victim, and with some frequency at the therapist.

The therapist should remember that the couple's control/control struggle ultimately is designed to protect each individual from further victimization. That is, it attempts to keep others out, though it succeeds primarily in preventing self-assertiveness and the development of personal identity. In the marital context, these control-oriented transactions also serve to keep both partners from maturing and becoming competent. It is as if each spouse were saying to the other—about almost everything: "If I can't do this, neither can you!" Further, the continuous control/control struggles resurrect the spouses' respective abandonment fears, for the ultimate form of passive control in any relationship is to leave.

These characteristics of each partner and of the relationship require that therapy proceed in a balanced fashion, so that neither partner outdistances the other too greatly in growth and change (to avoid triggering abandonment fears). If both spouses want the marriage to remain intact, the therapist should pay careful attention to pacing, both in overall treatment planning and in the course of each therapy session. For example, a nonoffending spouse might well be considered for at least occasional individual or group sessions if the perpetrating spouse is in regular individual and/or group therapy.

Similarly, therapeutic equidistance is important so that neither partner becomes unduly threatened by the therapist's relationship with the other. Couple therapy requires a special kind of "neutrality." Being both a marital therapist and an individual therapist for one of the partners seldom is a viable combination except under certain unusual circumstances. Certain techniques are helpful. For example, finding small ways to complement the clients as a *couple* or to positively connote *couple* behavior can be both reinforcing and reassuring. Or supporting and then challenging both partners in a reciprocal pattern can increase therapeutic leverage substantially. Metaphorically, it is as if the therapist were leaning first on one end of a balance scale and then quickly making a counterbalancing move on the other end just to be certain that motion is obtained without letting either end "hit bottom."

Some couples with the IPv/V pattern present a sort of "united front" of passive control against the influence of the therapist. They are highly unlikely to be doing this by design or even consciously; nevertheless, they appear to have an uncanny knack for minimizing the impact of therapy on their lives through mutual support of each other's resistant victim-like perceptions, communications, and behaviors. Activating the interpersonal processes of symmetrically control-oriented couples can be a substantial challenge in any kind of marital therapy. When these couples are part of incestuous families with a strong overlay of perpetrator/victim interaction patterns, the challenge can seem formidable. Taking advantage of inherent paradoxes in the relationship (for example, the "strength" of their shared helplessness) can be useful. We have found that "back-handed compliments" to the partners *as a couple* often are effective—"You're one of the most interesting couples I've ever worked with! Neither of you can find anything wrong with each other because each of you beats the other one to it by putting yourself down. It must be a relief to know you're so screwed up that your partner can't possibly criticize you! I'm not sure I can be of any help in working on your marriage because I have more faith in you than either of you has in yourself." Many times, however, the therapist's approach must be gradual and persistent.

EXAMPLE

Laura and Wayne, a couple in their mid-twenties with two small children, have entered marital therapy following a revelation that Wayne fondled Laura's two adolescent sisters on a number of occasions when he was drinking heavily at family gatherings. At one of the early sessions, the therapist begins with a gentle challenge:

Therapist: I'm surprised to hear that you two have spent the past few weekends at your parents' cabin, Laura, considering your concern about how difficult it is for Wayne to remain sober when he's around either of your families.

Laura: Yeah, I know that's true [*sighs*]. But it's so pretty up there at this time of year, and it really is the only social life we have. With both of us working such long hours all week we never see anyone. And it gives the kids a chance to play with their cousins while we have some fun, too.

Wayne: It would be boring to stay around home all weekend. The kids are always hanging on us when we stay in town, and we don't have decent babysitters close by, so it's just easier to go to the lake. Then the older kids can look out for the younger ones. You know how it goes.

Therapist: I understand that it can seem easier to take care of the kids when all of you are at the cabin. But I'm still concerned about the exposure to drinking all day long when you've struggled for such a long time with trying to get sober, Wayne.

Laura: [*Protesting*] I've tried to keep an eye on Wayne, and I don't think he's had anything to drink up there for weeks!

Therapist: [*Replying to Laura*] It appears you're now comfortable with Wayne going to the lake with your family and being exposed to drinking with your brothers and being around your sisters. What's different for you now from two months ago when you first began therapy and were so worried about this? I recall being impressed by your willingness — and yours, too, Wayne — to challenge the patterns that have been so destructive to your marriage, even if that meant dealing with alcohol abuse and with some difficult family issues.

Laura: [*Protesting again*] But Wayne's right! It's so hard to entertain the kids all weekend when we stay in the city. Besides, I visit with my mother and sisters while Wayne fishes with my father or my brothers, so people are around all the time.

Therapist: I see. Your weekdays are spent working and dealing with the needs of the children, and your weekends are spent with adults, but with all the men together and the women together, separate from each other. When do the two of you spend time together?

Both spouses are silent. After waiting for a long moment spent glancing back and forth between the partners, the therapist picks up two pens and small sheets of paper and hands them to each spouse.

Therapist: I would like each of you to write both of your names on your paper. . . . Good. Now, without looking at each other, I would like you to write down how old you feel when you are at the lake on weekends — that is, inside yourself personally, what age do you seem to be when you spending time at the cabin. . . . That's right. Next, I would like you to write down how old your partner seems to be when you are at the cabin — based on your observations of his or her behavior. . . . When you've finished with that, I would like each of you to write down how old you feel when you are at home during the week. . . . And now write how old your partner acts at home on the weekend. . . . Good. Now I would like each of you to decide if you are willing to share your answers with each other and with me. I don't want you to feel forced to do it if you don't want to.

With some hesitation and embarrassed glances at each other, both spouses agree to share their answers.

Therapist: Without giving an exact age, tell each other where you are the oldest — at home or at the cabin? [*Each partner indicates feeling older at home during the week.*] Now, where do you observe your partner acting younger — at home or at the cabin? [*Again, both agree that each acts younger at the cabin.*] Are either of you younger than 18 at the cabin? [*Both nod affirmatively.*] Are either of you younger than 18 at home during the week? [*Both shake their heads in negative reply.*] It appears that when you go to the lake, you return to being teenagers again, having fun and enjoying a social life. But when you're at home, you are forced to be grown-ups, working and taking care of your children. I wonder if that means that at the cabin you are both too young to be married. . . . You're old enough to date and have sex, but not old enough to be on your own and to be responsible for children who are dependent on you. I wonder if it's a way to return to the days before you became pregnant and decided to get married.

The spouses nod their heads slowly, and Laura appears noticeably sad.

Therapist: [*After a pause*] Perhaps we could explore together what it is that's so frightening about becoming your own family, separate and apart from any other family, but still connected to your families and to other people. I'd like you to turn and face each other. [*Laura and Wayne comply.*] That's right. Now talk to each other in any way you wish about what it is that is scary about being married and about being a family on your own.

Wayne: [*After a moment of silence*] I don't know quite how to say this . . . but when we go to the cabin, you seem happy. When we stay home, you're hassled and angry all the time—about everything—and we don't have any fun, and we just worry and fight, and then I can't stand it. . . . [*His voice trails off*].

The therapist steps in gently but firmly, sensing that Wayne may begin to blame Laura for something if permitted to continue:

Therapist: What you seem to be saying to Laura is that she isn't easy to be around when you stay home, but even more important, that you can't seem to find a way to help her feel better. Is that right?

Wayne: Well, yeah, sort of. . . . But you see—

Therapist: [*Interrupting*] Talk to Laura, Wayne, not to me.

Wayne: Well, you see, it's this way, Laura. When we're around home I get scared. You are so unhappy that you seem ready to just run away. When we're at the cabin you laugh, tease, flirt—we even make love once in a while, you know? You're different—more like you used to be before we got married.

Therapist: [*Addressing Laura*] I suspect you might want to respond to what Wayne just said, Laura, but I would like you to hold onto that and go back to my original question. Would you tell Wayne what's so frightening for you about becoming your own family, separate and apart from any other family, but still connected to others?

Laura: I don't know . . . This seems too hard to me. . . . Let's just agree to go to the lake less often, then things will be okay, won't they?

Wayne: [*Joining Laura*] All right, I can go for that—

Therapist: [*Interrupting again*] I want to go back to the original question,

Laura, because you agreed to talk with Wayne about it, and we still haven't heard your thoughts. Will you please tell Wayne why you are so frightened to become a family? He had the courage to tell you, and I believe you have the same kind of courage.

Laura: [*After a long pause*] All I do at home is work. And so do you, Wayne, doing chores and fixing things, because we never have any time. . . . You do that, and I do the kids and the meals and the house-work. And it's no fun. I get bored — it's lonely and boring doing the same things over and over and over again. So I get mad.

Therapist: [*Persisting*] And what's so *frightening* about being home, Laura?

Laura: Because it feels like there's nothing left in our marriage, and that I don't really want to be doing this — to be married to Wayne and . . .

Therapist: So you feel very frustrated and unhappy just like Wayne — and you feel hopeless, afraid that you may discover there is not enough there to stay married. Is that accurate?

Laura: Yes, I guess it is.

Therapist: Then perhaps each of you could tell me what it is at the cabin that helps your marriage be stronger and more interesting?

Wayne: [*After another long pause*] Well, when you put it that way, proba-bly nothing. Maybe it's a way of running away from our marriage — except, at least up there we sometimes have sex.

Laura: That's true. If we have a good day, I like having sex. That doesn't happen at home. . . . But then, he doesn't fool around with my sisters at home either.

Therapist: [*Pursuing a hypothesis*] But both of you agreed that you both are younger and "not married" when you're at the lake. I'm not con-doning what happened or trying to get Wayne off the hook, but I wonder if it doesn't explain some things that have gone on for both of you. Being at the cabin with your family, Laura, is like life before marriage. Plus, you're saying there's kind of an emphasis on fun — and even on sex. [*Both spouses nod and look thoughtful.*] Right now what's important is that you two agree that going to the cabin doesn't really help your marriage in the true sense of the word. In fact, the atmosphere of drinking and fun has led to some irresponsible things. Now you both recognize that it has been a kind of escape from your marriage. . . . I am tremendously impressed by your honesty with each other during these last few minutes. Together, you have recog-nized a pattern — an attempt to escape into the past in order to make your marriage more fun and stronger. Certainly, that is an indication that both of you have some investment in keeping this marriage going. But you have also agreed that going to the cabin hasn't really accomplished what either of you had hoped. In fact, you both might agree that it may have kept your marriage from growing and even created some threatening circumstances, is that right? [*The spouses look at each other and nod.*] In that case, it appears that we need to explore together what kinds of things you might do together—without other family members—to make your marriage stronger, and more fun. For example, I'm wondering if you could get either of your parents to take your kids for a week-end sometime soon so that the two of you could have some couple time together.

In this exchange, the therapist avoids directly challenging the couple's "united front" of resistance. A strong push toward individuation probably would be too threatening to the personal sense of security of each partner. Instead, the therapist takes advantage of the momentum of their pattern and works with it to encourage greater honesty in communication and to explore options for change. The partners are gently encouraged to name their fear—hopelessness leading to divorce (abandonment)—and then to work together to overcome it. The emphasis is on similarity of experience and mutual effort to deal with their issues. Compliments and challenges are addressed to each partner in turn in a balanced and evenhanded way. Some strategies will emerge for bridging their experiences, building upon their apparent "immaturity" rather than discrediting it. The therapist purposely decides not to address commitment issues too directly, for commitment to intimacy is an adult phenomenon, and neither has developed the capacity for it on any consistent basis. A likely possibility for homework assignments would be a series of "dates" with each other, carefully structured with the help of the therapist and premised upon mutuality of interest and effort and gradually addressing the issue of choice and commitment (creating the foundation for marital fidelity), which the partners bypassed when Laura's premarital pregnancy at age 17 led to a rather automatic decision to marry.

IPv/P

This third pattern seldom is discussed in the professional incest literature, perhaps because it appears to be "politically incorrect." Simply stated, the identified incest perpetrator (IP) has a *victim* (v) orientation (underpowered and overcontrolled), while the spouse is more *perpetrator*-like (P)—overpowered and undercontrolled. In therapy, the identified perpetrator is likely to be willing to acknowledge the sexual abuse and genuinely feels remorseful about it. Fear and shame are apparent in his demeanor. His spouse usually expresses anger, even righteous indignation, about the abuse. However, the anger has a quality suggesting pleasure as well as pain; that is, she appears to take some satisfaction in her spouse's misbehavior and resulting humiliation: "Now I have you where I want you" or "I'll never let you forget what you've done to me." Rather than anger for or about her child's victimization, the spouse in this dyadic pattern may be pleased to have a rationale for her anger at the perpetrator—perhaps at men in general—and at those who have intervened into the family's life. She may talk as if she is less upset at the nature of the abuse than at her husband's willingness to challenge *her* power over other family members. This may take the form of complete denial of any marital problems, minimizing of the incest's impact upon the victim (unless it serves her purpose to attack or shame the perpetrator), preoccupation with more peripheral issues such as how the revelation of abuse is affecting the family's status in the community, and the like. In the most blatant instances, the *perpetrator-stanced* spouse appears almost sadistic in her use of the abuse against the actual perpetrator—clearly, their roles have been reversed now that the incest has been revealed.

Spouses with this dyadic pattern often create triangles in which the children are pitted against the actual perpetrator, urged on by their mother, who thereby seeks to prevent them from acknowledging positive feelings and connection with their father (despite the fact that his orientation toward incestuous contact is likely to be affection-based). The mother may overtly fan the flames of anger against the perpetrator by all family members, including his family of origin—though she may also use the occasion to blame and attack them for being the "cause" of his unacceptable behavior. Anger at the perpetrator may be used as a test of loyalty to the spouse. Sometimes, one of the boys in the family may be recruited as a quasi-spouse, showered with affection and compliments in an effort to emphasize the disrepute of her husband, but also sought out for the nurturing and support he can provide that her spouse cannot.

By contrast, the actual incest perpetrator in this dyad usually seems compliant and even intimidated. He may agree readily that he is the "only problem" in the family. Often, he will quickly seek to make amends with the child(ren) he has victimized, actions based more upon his wish to relieve his own anxiety than on his genuine understanding of the abuse's impact upon the child. The therapist should be alert for pseudo-compliance on the part of the perpetrator, both in individual and in couple therapy. His *victim* stance is designed to control the influence of the therapist (in contrast to attempting to overpower her), just as he may spend an inordinate amount of time trying to deflect his wife's anger at him. As therapy gains momentum, this *victim*-like perpetrator may go through a stage at which he counters his wife's bullying by blaming *her* for the circumstances of the incestuous contact. Typically, this dyadic pattern is, in part, a manifestation of the husband's misguided attempts to resolve his considerable insecurities. In this endeavor, he chooses a "strong" wife whom he expects to "mother" him; instead, however, she becomes the personification of an evil parent, thereby confirming his feelings of victimization.

This dyadic pattern can be extremely difficult to restructure in marital therapy. The perpetrator protects himself by being "cooperative" but avoiding change; the nonoffending spouse protects herself by being angry and blaming, but also avoiding change. If the perpetrator opens up his overcontrolled exterior during couple sessions, he is exposed as a target for abuse by his wife. If the therapist succeeds in penetrating the overpowering exterior protection of the spouse, thereby gaining access to her victim-like interior, her husband is likely to become anxious and attempt to undo the progress. If the wife is exceptionally mean and abusive, the therapist will find it difficult to avoid confronting her—and thereby rescue the husband. The challenge is to facilitate the husband's own confrontation with his wife, helping him set limits with her regarding her behavior toward him, despite the fact that he has behaved in inappropriate and socially unacceptable ways. Rescuing him will only deepen the already existing dysfunctional pattern, further undermine his self-esteem, and increase the spouse's anger toward him. Instead, the husband needs to be empowered to stand up for himself appropriately, both with her and with their children. Only when he has gained a sufficient amount of dignity and self-respect will he be able to model for other family members an appropriate intolerance for any kind of abuse.

In addition, yielding to the temptation to join the wife's anger toward her husband will place the therapist in the trap of contributing to the dysfunctional interaction in the marriage. This is particularly dangerous if the therapist is seduced into believing that the perpetrator's apparent remorse and the spouse's apparent indignation are signs of successful treatment and indicators that the children will be safe from abuse in the future. The opposite may be true. Simply stated, the therapist's task is to help the perpetrator "grow up" and the spouse "reduce" her negative presence in the ecology of family life. Once again, the goal is a balanced system consisting of two adults who can take responsibility for themselves in age-appropriate ways, who can both challenge and support each other without perpetrating, and who can manage their partner's independence as well as dependence with affection, admiration, and support.

EXAMPLE

Steve and Sara have been married for seven years and have a 4-year-old daughter, Rachel. It is the second marriage for each partner. Sara's two children from her previous marriage live with them; Barry is 15 and Ruth is 12. In the course of mandatory family therapy resulting from Steve's incestuous activity with his stepdaughter, it has become clear to the therapist that the family has several dysfunctional coalitions. The marriage bond between Steve and Sara is tenuous. Instead, Sara and her two older children form a sort of family unit, who together perceive Steve as an "enemy." Rachel seems to be a kind of "orphan," without a clear connection to anyone, although her father plainly would like to recruit her to his "side" in the family conflicts. Attempts at marital therapy with the couple have been resisted by Sara, who tends to take on the role of cotherapist working to "fix" Steve. Feeling stuck after several such sessions, the therapist enlists the assistance of a consultation team. Somewhat curious, Sara and Steve agree to some meetings that include the team.

At the first consultation session, Sara seems anxious to use the team as an audience who will listen to her recite her litany of complaints against Steve.

Sara: I am still disgusted by what he did to my daughter. We are the talk of the neighborhood, and he just goes about his business as if nothing happened. I don't know how he can face people at work. They all know, and they work with him just like they did before, like nothing happened. I get to work, and all I want to do is hide my face. They ask me if he's getting better and I tell them that we are seeing you, but I don't think we're getting anywhere, and neither do they. Everyone thinks Steve should start going to a sexual addiction group and work on his hang-ups and—

Therapist: [*Interrupting*] I am sorry that life continues to be so difficult and embarrassing for you. It's probably good that you're talking with people rather than hiding in shame. Do you also talk to your friends about the various problems you and Steve have had in your marriage?

Sara: [*Sharply*] Certainly not! Why, when we talked about the marriage in the past few meetings, it sounded as if you were blaming me for Steve's behavior, when I didn't even know about it. Just because I'm not interested in oral sex with him doesn't give him the right to molest Ruth. The biggest problem is that I trusted him with the children when I shouldn't have!

Therapist: Are you saying that you sometimes have poor judgment when it comes to deciding who you can trust?

Sara: No! I don't have poor judgment—*Steve* has poor judgment. I know who to trust and who not to trust—that's not the problem. Steve has a hidden problem, and he managed to put one over on me before we got married. Since this all came out and I've talked to his family, they all agree that he's been putting things over on people since he was just a boy. Now he's been caught, and the whole world knows about it—and that's just what he deserves.

Steve: I wish Sara could be just a little bit understanding, like you have tried to be. I'm very willing to work on my problems, but I could use a little support, and Sara just wants to keep making me pay and pay for my behavior. When someone doesn't know about what happened, she's quick to tell them, and she enjoys humiliating me. I think it's hard on the children as well as on me. And I really am sorry for bringing all of this trouble on the family . . . and I know I've always been an embarrassment to my parents.

Therapist: Steve, what do you think you could do that would help Sara understand just how painful this has all been for you and just how hard you're trying to make things better?

Steve: Well, I was hoping you would have the answer to that. I guess I just need someone to convince her that I'm basically a good person and that I could be a good husband and a good father, if she only would give me half a chance. Sara doesn't seem to have the same understanding of this situation that you do . . .

At this point, the observing consultation team interrupts with a message via the telephone, suggesting to the therapist that Steve is attempting to have an affair with her, and she should make this known to the couple. Surprised and uncertain about this message, the therapist hangs up the phone, pauses for a moment, and then begins to ask Sara a question. Halfway through, the team again interrupts with a phone call to the therapist — stating even more emphatically that Steve's attempt to have an affair with the therapist is a key issue in the therapeutic impasse; it should be stated explicitly and clearly as an observation by the team.

Therapist: [*Tentatively*] The team has been reflecting seriously on the problems being discussed in this room . . . and they are convinced that Steve is trying to have an affair with me.

Sara: [*Shocked*] What?! They're saying that you and Steve are sleeping together?!

Therapist: [*With greater confidence as she begins to understand the strategy*] I said the team believes that Steve is *attempting* to have an affair with me, and they are wondering what, if anything, you will do about it.

Sara: I can't believe what they are saying! First Steve has an affair with the receptionist at the office — and now you. I knew there was something funny about this therapy —

Steve: [*Interrupting*] Hold on just a minute! I don't know what the hell they're talking about. I haven't done anything. I only said that I wished Sara could understand me the way you do.

Sara: That's exactly what you said when you had the affair with your receptionist! You said I didn't understand you and Claudia did. Now, here we go again — I can't believe it.

The phone rings again, and the team asks to speak with Sara, explaining that they are most interested in knowing what Sara believes is going to happen in their marriage from this point on. Sara hangs up the phone, but continues talking as if to the team.

Sara: It's true I didn't do a very good job of handling the situation when Steve got involved with Claudia—and so soon after we were married. But I just couldn't understand why he seemed to want so much time with me when I had two relatively small kids to take care of and a full-time job and a dying mother. And then he wanted sex—when I could hardly stay awake, let alone be romantic. Well, that's not going to happen again this time, I'll tell you that. We're either going to work out this marriage, or—I'm just not going to give up without a fight.

Capitalizing on Sara's own aggressive style, the consultation team has succeeded in making a shift in the structure of therapy. By taking a pushy, assertive role, the team paces the wife's *perpetrator* stance; by making an explicit observation about the husband's seductive *victim* behavior with the therapist, the team has warned everyone involved to be careful of the dangerous rescue triangle that may have been forming. Further, by framing the therapist and the wife as "rivals" for the husband, the team helps disrupt Sara's attempt to be the critical cotherapist working on her husband's problem. Finally, the team's intervention has taken the focus off Sara's diagnosis of Steve's "sexual addiction" and placed it back on problems in the marriage. For the first time in therapy, husband and wife may be able to work together on the marriage, and the therapist is more likely to maintain her role as an understanding "outsider."

IPp/P

A final dyadic pattern is that of the identified perpetrator (IP) with a *perpetrator* stance (p), married to a spouse who also behaves as a *perpetrator* (P). Since both partners are overpowered and undercontrolled, the stage is set within the family not only for sexual abuse, but often for marital violence as well. Both partners have adapted to their own childhood victimization experiences by dissociating from their pain, thereby losing their capacity for empathy with each other and with their children. Often, both partners deny that the incestuous contact occurred, or they contend that it was misinterpreted by the victim. They may develop complementary excuses or rationalizations, even if only one was involved in the actual abuse: "I used to watch videos with her in the family room, but she must have been dreaming when she said I touched her" may be followed by: "I think the kids must have gotten their hands on some porno movies, and that put ideas into their heads" from the spouse. This dyadic configuration underlies numerous instances of aggression-based incest, in which the partners' victimization experiences as children may have left them with the need to "get even." Other times, this dyad creates a pansexual family, and both parents are involved in incestuous contact motivated more by the need to exercise power than by anger per se. In such a case, one of the authors once was told by an offending parent, "I found out that my husband was having intercourse with our daughter, so I got him back by doing the same thing with our son. And I made sure he knew about it!"

Children of these parents often are neglected and/or physically as well as sexually abused, because the parents may be too focused on meeting their own needs to consider those of their children. Indeed, the parents' developmental deficits and defense mechanisms probably prevent them from forming any attachment at all with their children or with each other. In many instances in which only one spouse is involved in the incest, the nonoffending spouse knows about the sexual contact, but chooses to ignore it simply because she is preoccupied with her own problems. Sometimes, the spouse is even relieved that her partner's sexual interest has been directed at someone other than her. Whatever the particular elements demonstrated by partners in this dyadic pattern, the bottom line issue is the inability and disinterest of either adult in adequately parenting the children.

If family violence also is reported, the therapist working with this type of couple should not assume that only the husband is manifesting aggressive behavior. Although he may dominate physical encounters by his size or strength, his *perpetrator*-spouse actually may be initiating many such situations via verbal and physical attacks. Or she may devise less direct ways to perpetrate on him. One of the authors once worked with an incestuous family in which the nonoffending spouse retaliated for her husband's sexual infidelity and occasional physical aggression by lacing his breakfast cereal with gradually increasing amounts of rat poison containing arsenic. The *perpetrator/perpetrator* dyadic pattern underlies many domestic violence cases receiving dramatic media coverage in the United States. More often, however, the patterns of mutual perpetration by husband and wife occur subtly and indirectly in their everyday interaction within the abusive family.

Predictably, this dyadic pattern is extremely difficult to work with in marital therapy. Since both partners are well-defended and oriented toward perpetration, creating a positive alliance with either of them, particularly in the presence of the other, may seem impossible. When feasible, a male-female cotherapy team or a consultation team and one-way window can increase therapeutic leverage. If neither of these is available, a substantial amount of individual or group therapy for *each* partner is advisable prior to undertaking marital therapy. Marital therapy itself should include frequent individual sessions, both to solidify a working relationship with each spouse and to deal with certain intrapsychic issues too risky to expose directly in the presence of a partner oriented toward exploitation and abuse.

No matter how therapy is structured, the therapist must avoid the everpresent temptation to overpower the clients in response to their overt resistance and frequent attempts to perpetrate on him or her. This will only result in replicating the perpetrator/victim interaction pattern in therapy, which will render treatment ineffective and which can lead to victimization of the therapist. Although a firm display of control over the therapeutic process is essential, direct confrontation should be avoided in favor of more indirect strategies to facilitate change. Empathy, warmth, and support by the therapist are important, even when both partners present themselves as unlikable and resistant. Confrontation via positive reframing can be helpful in slipping past the defenses of a *perpetration*-oriented client of either gender. Similarly, taking a one-down position and appearing to submit to the client's need for dominance can be an effective way of pacing either partner to set the stage for a lead that can be followed by the client without losing face in the presence of the spouse. Overall, the challenge is to have an impact upon the marital system without unduly threatening either spouse or invoking the need for either or both partners to engage in power struggles that will immobilize the therapeutic process.

EXAMPLE

Rose and Leo have four children, two boys and two girls. Leo has been accused of sexually abusing both daughters and his younger son. The couple's oldest child, Willis, has been in a juvenile institution for some time for a variety of serious delinquent behaviors, including the rape of his 14-year-old girlfriend. Willis reports that his father never did anything sexual with him. After six months in the country workhouse, Leo currently is in a residential treatment program for sex offenders, where he will remain for at least a year, depending upon his "progress." The three younger children are living together in a foster home, and they are seeing a child therapist. The mother has not been involved in treatment prior to beginning the current marital therapy with male and female cotherapists.

Female Therapist: [*Beginning the session*] Whenever we meet, I get the feeling that no one really wants to be here. Leo, you've said this is a "waste of time," since you're getting all the therapy you need at the halfway house. Rose, you keep saying that you didn't do anything wrong, so you don't need treatment. And both of us [*pointing to herself and her cotherapist*] just seem to be putting in our time—like going to a meeting that we all think is a waste of time. Am I wrong about this, or do others feel the same?

Leo: [*Emphatically*] You're right about me. I'm in group or individual therapy every weekday at the house. I'm getting therapied out! I can't even think about things to talk about anymore.

Female Therapist: Rose, what about you?

Rose: You're right about me, too. Leo's getting what he needs, and all I want is to get my kids back. And you already said that you can't control that, so why are we here? I ain't got a clue!

Male Therapist: Well, you're right about me, too! Each time I've come into one of these sessions, I feel like I'm somewhere that I don't belong.

Female Therapist: Well, what should we do about this situation? Here we have four grown people who don't want to be here. I mean, I would like to be helpful to the two of you in figuring out what went wrong in your marriage that you've ended up in this awful situation, but I don't know . . . I mean, Leo, you've been to jail and now to residential treatment for molesting your kids — probably not exactly what you dreamed about doing when you were a kid yourself. And Rose, you're a mother without anyone to mother, and a wife without anyone to "wife" — at least for now. I'll bet that wasn't your childhood fantasy either!

Rose: It sure wasn't! But I didn't have anything to do with how we got into this mess. I didn't do anything, *he* just messed up everything.

Male Therapist: Is it safe to say, Rose, that your marriage is exactly the way you would like it to be, and your only problem now is how to get your children back? That seems to be what my partner here is saying, but I'm not sure I agree with her. I don't think that you're as naive as she seems to think. I think you know that your marriage has some big problems, but you haven't decided yet whether to trust us enough to work on it. And with good reason — hey, you hardly know us, so why in the world should you trust us yet? You're too careful for that.

Female Therapist: [*Looking at her cotherapist and speaking urgently*] I think you're wrong! If Rose believed she had a bad marriage, she would have been working on it by now. I'll bet Rose would say that she loves her marriage — always has, always will. My take on it is that she thinks this is no big deal, and things will be fine when Leo gets out of treatment.

Rose: [*Protesting*] Any possibility I can say where I'm at here?! You two think you have me all psyched out. Of course, my marriage isn't perfect, and Leo clearly isn't a big winner. Hell, he's been doing time — but what's to work on when he isn't living at home?

Female Therapist: Well, Rose, from my perspective you can work on just about anything in your marriage you want to, even though Leo is not living at home. My major concern is that if you don't work on your marriage, there won't be any marriage left by the time Leo comes home—it will have dried up like a grape into a raisin in the sun.

Male Therapist: Leo, what's your take on this conversation? My colleague is saying that Rose thinks the marriage is just fine, and Rose is saying she doesn't think it is. What do you think?

Leo: [*Sourly*] What marriage? How can you have a marriage when you hardly see each other? We've been apart for nearly eight months, my phone calls are monitored, my letters in or out are read by someone. How can you be married when people treat you like a two-year-old?

Male Therapist: Yeah, but that's only temporary. What about when you get out?

Female Therapist: [*Addressing the male therapist*] You know, I think you're missing something here, about how painful it is for Leo to be away from Rose. He's away from her day and night for months, having no influence on her day-to-day life, and you're asking him to threaten his marriage even more by talking about problems. No way!

Male Therapist: [*After a thoughtful pause*] Well, I can see your point about Leo being isolated and not having much influence on his wife. But not using these sessions to talk about some things certainly isn't helping his level of influence with her, is it?

Female Therapist: [*Still addressing her colleague*] That may be, but which is better—to open up stuff and work on some problems only to have them get worse, or to leave things as they are and try to pick up the pieces when it's all over? You can't really blame Leo for being tight-lipped. She has all this freedom and he has none. Why, he could be worried that she might find someone else to be with while he's away from home. So why try to fix things if she is going looking anyway?

Rose: [*Protesting loudly*] Who says I'm going to find someone else? I got no interest in finding someone else! Lady, don't you jump to conclusions without talking to me first!

Female Therapist: [*Apologetically*] You're right. I'm sorry for not checking that out with you. Sometimes I get rolling with my own thoughts and don't say things very well. Rose, are you saying that you've decided you want to stay married to Leo, even though he has been in jail for molesting the children, and probably can't come back home to live for a year or more?

Rose: [*After a pause*] Leo and I have been through a lot together. Why would I want to split up now?

Female Therapist: [*Turning to Leo*] That must be reassuring to you. You seem to have worried about that. It's been written all over your face at every session.

Male Therapist: [*Addressing his cotherapist and speaking sharply*] If you thought it was written all over his face every session, why didn't you say something before now? Leo can take it.

Female Therapist: Because it hasn't seemed that Leo wanted that from me, yet—from either of us. And I have tried to be sensitive to what Leo wants; he's had a pretty rough time for the past year or so. And he's been "therapied to death"—you heard what he said earlier. . . . Leo, would you like me to make any more comments about what I see when I look at you? I will only do it if you want me to.

Leo: [*Nodding*] I suppose it's okay. I wouldn't have been sure about Rose wanting to stay with me unless you said what you did, so I suppose it's okay.

Male Therapist: [*Interjecting*] Rose, I'm really impressed with how honest you've been with what you just told Leo and us. I wonder if you would like Leo to be as honest with you as you have been with him? Would you like him to tell you how he feels about staying married?

Rose: Sure. If I have to be honest so does he.

Male Therapist: Leo, are you willing to tell Rose whether or not you want to stay married to her? I would like you to think carefully about it . . . and answer only if you want to. If you're tempted to be dishonest in any way, then please don't answer.

Leo: [*Replying immediately*] Of course I want to stay married to Rose. Would I be here if I didn't? This ain't like going to a ball game, you know. [*Looking at the male therapist*] I don't know what you and your wife like to do when you see each other, but I don't particularly like the idea of coming to this office just to fight with my wife.

Female Therapist: I'm glad you were able to be honest with Rose about wanting to stay married to her. Now I think I understand why you two have been so careful about talking here at our sessions. You haven't wanted to do anything to jeopardize your relationship, like fighting about painful stuff. I'm sorry I was so slow in catching on about that. Thanks for telling me now.

Leo: So what can we talk about if we don't fight? Before all this happened, Rose and I were fighting all the time. In fact, sometimes I don't think we know *how* to talk without fighting.

In this sequence, the cotherapists are attempting to engage a difficult couple in the process of marital therapy. The partners have their own long history of distrust and conflict, along with the recent history of crisis and family disruption followed by separation. Yet, they give evidence of a commitment to the marriage. Together, the cotherapists literally enact the couple's ambivalence, focusing the power struggle between themselves rather than between the clients and the therapists. Further, each therapist adopts a position of alignment with the other-sex client, attempting to build an alliance through empathy. Gradually, the alliances become more viable as each client experiences a reduction in anxiety, with assistance from one of the therapists. A breakthrough occurs when each spouse is able to relieve the other's anxiety about rejection and abandonment. The therapists have opted to intervene directly into the couple's resistance rather than focusing on more threatening issues in the marriage. They have hypothesized, probably correctly, that accessing complicated issues and negative feelings at this delicate point in therapy might rupture the fragile ties holding together the marriage.

In summary, there are many variations on the four basic dyadic patterns we have outlined above; however, all will reflect elaborations on the behaviors we have described.[6] The marital therapist working with any of the four patterns is reminded that each spouse also brings certain resources to treatment and has some capacity to generate positive interpersonal transactions that do not depend upon the dysfunctional perpetrator/victim dynamics. Uncovering and utilizing these in therapy can be an important contributor to positive outcomes.

IMPROVING THE
SEXUAL RELATIONSHIP

As previously indicated, we take for granted that the sexual relationship between spouses in an incestuous family is highly *unsatisfactory* to one or both partners. We have found this to be true regardless of the frequency or type of sexual activity and level of sexual functioning. Therefore, dealing with their sexual relationship is likely to be a key element in successful therapy. However, even though the discovery of sexual abuse precipitates treatment, the couple's sex life is seldom a good place to begin marital therapy. Occasionally, the subject of sex may be an effective avenue into the underlying dynamics of their relationship; more often, it is not a useful path to take until progress has been made in other areas (in part this is because dealing with sex may keep the focus on the incest and prevent attention to other important but deep-seated issues).

Processing the crisis of incest discovery and confronting perpetrator/victim interaction patterns are the most important prerequisites to dealing with the partners' sexual relationship. Perpetrator/victim dynamics played a major role in creating their sexual difficulties in the first place and will continue to interfere with the development of a mutually rewarding and effective sex life. Such a relationship requires good boundaries, self-awareness, effective communication, positive feelings, and the ability to

---

[6]Elaboration of the intrapsychic characteristics of perpetrators and methods for confronting these in treatment can be found in our book *Child Sexual Abuse: An Ecological Approach to Treating Victims and Perpetrators.*

give and receive pleasure—all of which are antithetical to distortions in power/control between partners. Perpetrator/victim dynamics are easily discerned in the patterns of initiating sexual contact.

Issues in Sex Therapy with Incest Couples

A central focus of therapy with the couple should be the nature and meaning of sexuality in their marriage relationship. Based upon their respective families of origin, developmental histories, and past experiences with each other, each partner has created a set of sexual meanings, beliefs, and expectations which determine her or his behavior. These should be explored in detail in individual sessions with each partner before scheduling conjoint sessions to examine the fit, or lack of fit, between them. A detailed developmental sex history should be obtained from each partner early in the treatment process. In history-taking sessions, we promise confidentiality to each individual client, with two disclaimers: a reminder that we are required to report instances of sexual abuse and a prerogative we will assume for letting that individual know if we believe that having a "secret" is interfering with progress in therapy. For example, a husband who perpetrated against his son or stepson may not want his wife to know about his adolescent history of sexual contacts with other boys. Or a nonoffending wife may not wish to tell her husband that she, too, was sexually victimized by a relative or neighbor.

Some therapists have challenged this approach, pointing to the issue of role-modeling honesty in therapy in order to counteract the structure of family secrets that underlies the sexual abuse. This is a valid concern. Certainly, the therapist ought not to be modeling secretiveness to clients whose issues revolve around dishonesty and denial. However, there is an important, though subtle, difference. A key issue in incest families is *boundaries*, and boundaries both connect and separate individuals from each other. Mutuality requires both closeness and distance, both sharing and privacy. Therapists who stipulate they will not work with clients who do not share certain personal information with each other are actually modeling boundary violations. However, this does not mean that the therapist ought to foster secretiveness between the partners. Again, the challenge is one of balance. The focus of history-taking in therapy should always be primarily on the meaning of life experiences rather than on a factual chronology of events. Therefore, the therapist has an opportunity to explore each partner's experiences with a focus on their meaning *to the individual* as well as their meaning *for the relationship*. Most often, this results in the therapist and client working together to decide when and how, as well as what, to share with the partner.

Certainly, there may be some important pieces of factual information to be obtained from the sexual histories of the partners, that is, some data which could have consequences for the therapeutic work (as distinct from information useful for legal investigation). These could include such things as previous abuse that could be interfering with current sexual responsiveness, medications that could be affecting sexual function or interest, sexual fantasies that could signal same-sex erotic interest, details of contraceptive utilization that might create risk of pregnancy, and so on. Together, therapist and client can decide on the meaning and significance of such information and determine how it might be utilized in the treatment process.

Therapists working with couples in incest families should approach sexual issues in the same way that they approach sexual issues with other couples: *Assume nothing.* These partners may be having sex frequently or infrequently; they may have little variety or a great deal; they may be sexually responsive or dysfunctional. Some perpetrators of incestuous abuse have very unusual sexual preferences or fantasies; others may be strikingly ordinary. The therapist should avoid the temptation to develop hypotheses prematurely or to stretch too far the connections between the abuse and particular previous life experiences. Incestuous contact is seldom a simple substitute for lack of marital sex (although it may include this). Similarly, by no means all partners of offenders are sexually disinterested or dysfunctional. At the same time, the motivations for incestuous contact indeed may include complex and unusual expectations or fantasies on the part of either or both partners. Therefore, the therapist should be prepared for the occasional bizarre sexual history and should be able to listen and respond without undue reactivity. Just as in all sex therapy, the challenge is to be professionally tolerant without necessarily personally approving of the behavior described. Each couple relationship is unique and should be explored on its own merits.

Some couple issues are rooted directly in gender stereotypes. Each partner may believe that "Men always want sex" or that "Women who initiate sex are whores." Either partner may have very high expectations for sexual performance or for strong romantic emotions. Some of these expectations may be common to society, but they have been distorted to feed the motivation for incestuous contact. For example, a certain number of incest perpetrators stress the attractiveness of a slender, youthful child or adolescent in contrast to their dissatisfaction with a partner who has gained weight or become less physically attractive with age. Perpetrators' partners, too, may hold stereotypes that interfere with their sexual relationships ("He's never been romantic enough to turn me on") and may even facilitate the incestuous contact ("I knew that men need a lot of sex or they become even more difficult to deal with").

Some gender-linked expectations are more subtle. Perhaps both partners believe that men ought be in charge of families; therefore, various forms of abuse may be tolerated as a means to maintain male dominance.

Conversely, a husband may be indulged by his wife as a "little boy" in the family, or the husband may rationalize his sexual contact with a daughter based upon the failure of his wife to take care of him in some all-encompassing, maternally nurturing ways. Though these gender-differentiated views influence the overall relationship, they are most likely to have a significant impact upon the partners' orientation toward their sexual interaction. Therefore, they should be a prominent part of the sex-related therapy with the couple.

Accompanying the gender distortions indicated above may be a lack of accurate sex information. Once again, the perpetrator and his partner may reflect the general problem of society's failure to provide adequate sex education — not in itself a cause of sexual abuse, but a contributor to the distortions that set the stage for the incestuous contact to occur. A male whose sexual ignorance and anxiety lead him to think of himself as a poor lover who cannot satisfy his wife may turn to his children whose perceived sexual innocence is less threatening, just as an adolescent who is afraid to reveal his sexual naivete by dating may instead experiment sexually with a younger sibling. Nonoffending partners also may be maladaptive in their sexual ignorance, contributing to awkward, anxiety-laden encounters that eventually are dropped in lieu of the incestuous activities — some partners report being relieved when the perpetrators stop pressing them for sex.

Following closely from the distortions of gender stereotypes and sexual ignorance are communication problems between the partners. Direct communication is likely to be a problem throughout the relationship, but it may be particularly acute in the realm of sexuality. Many citizens of the United States and certain other technologized societies grow up without a comfortable and effective language system for couple sexual communication. In incestuous families, both general and sex-related communication is likely to be particularly inhibited and/or indirect, often characterized by triangulation.[7] In a sense, parent-child incest itself is a metaphor for the communication breakdown between the partners; the child somehow becomes part of the couple's sexual relationship, and the abuse sends a message regarding unresolved conflict. Of course, the power/control struggles characterizing the marriages in incestuous families usually are reflected in the sexual relationship. Sometimes, these struggles occur over a particular type of sexual behavior demanded or refused by one of the partners. For example, some perpetrators have noted that oral sex with a child was used to substitute for — and perhaps as punishment for — their partners' refusal or dislike of the activity. More often, however, power/control distortions will be revealed in the areas of sexual initiation, frequency, or meaning discrepancy.

---

[7]This is true even in erotic-based incest (the pansexual family), in which erotically tinged communication is everywhere but fails to be effective in solving actual sexual problems, such as sexual dissatisfaction in the marriage or appropriate parental guidance of the sexual socialization of their children.

When and how often sexual contact takes place between the partners is likely to be a recurrent, if not continuous, issue in the relationship. At times, the focus is on practical problems, such as differing work shifts, which interfere with sexual availability. Other times, the difficulty may be attached to conditions associated with sexual activity, such as refusal by one partner to engage in intercourse when he or she is tired at the end of a work day or the unwillingness of one individual to become sexually involved when the other has been drinking heavily. Natural biorhythms may affect partners' interests differently — presenting the widely recognized challenge of coordinating the sexual and social life of a "morning person" and a "night person" — and the couple lacks negotiation and problem-solving skills to deal with the dilemma.

Discrepancies in sexual meaning are among the most commonly reported issues between the partners and represent a major contributor to the sexual dissatisfaction experienced by the couple. One partner may be oriented toward the recreational or tension reduction aspects of sexual activity, while the other holds sexual contact to be a form of deep communication or the manifestation of a spiritual bond. Sometimes, sexual meaning discrepancies have direct behavioral consequences, affecting the willingness of a partner to engage in a particular activity. Sometimes, the partners' lack of congruence in meaning reflects religious or ethical beliefs, such as the refusal by one individual to employ mechanical methods of contraception so as not to block the natural expression of sex as procreation. Serious discrepancies in sexual meaning may make each sexual encounter a symbol of the gap between the partners, thereby becoming a source of growing alienation. The stage is set for decreasing sexual interest, increasing conflict, and perhaps also for a substitution of sexual partners.[8]

Sexual dysfunction (difficulties with arousal, erection, presence or timing of orgasm) may also surface during marital therapy with these couples. Some of these problems may occur secondary to the uncovering of the incest and result from the disruption of that crisis. More likely, the problems have been present for a significant period of time and may be, at least in part, the motivation — or at least the rationalization — for the incestuous contact. Some sexual dysfunctions arise out of "performance anxiety," that is, secondary to worrying about whether the sexual response itself will or will not occur on a particular occasion; thereafter, the worry becomes part of the vicious circle maintaining the dysfunction (Masters & Johnson, 1970; Kaplan, 1974). At times, the sexual dysfunction may result from situational factors, such as sleep deprivation, the pressure of a work deadline, or excessive alcohol intake by one or both partners.

However, in the cases in which sexual dysfunction is reported by these

[8]In treating both incestuous and nonincestuous child sexual abuse, we have concluded that creating shared sexual meanings is one component of the "grooming behaviors" engaged in by numerous perpetrators as part of the seduction of their victims.

couples, sexual response is likely to be inhibited or distorted by complex relationship factors and/or by deep-seated intrapsychic conflicts. In most instances, these will need to be addressed in therapy before the sexual relationship of the partners can be improved. For example, the wife of a perpetrator may be extremely aversive to intimate touch or erotic stimulation due to a past history of sexual abuse, and she may submit to sex with her husband only as a recapitulation of her victimization. In another case, a perpetrator who has molested his boys may reveal a history of conflicted homoerotic inclinations marked by anxiety, guilt, and lack of arousal in heterosexual situations, including his marriage. Sometimes, the complicated tangle of unresolved, sexualized dependency needs that frequently characterize incestuous family members may be so pervasive in the marital relationship that substantial individual therapy may be necessary before any kind of effective marital therapy can occur.

Family therapists often refer clients to specialized resources for sex therapy. While this can be perfectly appropriate in many cases, we believe it is best if the therapist working with the incestuous family can include the sexual/marital therapy in her own work. First, this simplifies the transference issues which are so prominent in incest family members, who are likely to be shame-based and resistant to developing close attachments. Further, avoiding a referral allows the sexual, marital, and family aspects of therapy to be better coordinated. Finally, handling the sexual issues in the context of family therapy permits the therapist to role-model and facilitate for the couple an integration of sexual, relational, and parenting roles without intermingling them in the inappropriate ways already so familiar to family members.[9]

Principles for Couple Sex Therapy

A few basic principles for approaching couple sexual issues can serve as guides for the family therapist. Research and clinical experience (Kaplan, 1974; LoPiccolo & LoPiccolo, 1978; Masters & Johnson, 1970; Schnarch, 1991) have shown that sexual problems differ in severity and ease of treatment based upon several factors. Although there are some exceptions, problems of sexual disinterest — or differing interest — are more difficult to treat than problems of arousal, which in turn are harder to remedy than problems with orgasm. Simply put, the earlier the sexual response pattern is interrupted, the more difficult the problem is likely to be to solve. Sexual desire problems are particularly complex (Kaplan, 1979; Schnarch, 1991). These problems range from significant differences in sexual interest levels

---

[9]If the family therapist is so unfamiliar or uncomfortable with a sex therapy focus, then referral is preferred over failing to deal with the sexual issues in a comprehensive and explicit way.

of the partners (in which no individual pathology need be implied) to reflections of psychiatric disorders (for example, depression) to substantial deviance from typical patterns of sexual interest: either hypoactivity (now often called "sexual aversion") to hyperactivity (currently labeled "sexual compulsivity" or "sexual addiction"). Similarly, sexual problems become more resistant to treatment as one moves from situational to relational to intrapsychic influences. Time can also affect the problem; the longer the problem has persisted, the more complex it is likely to be, if for no other reason than that its presence has had an ongoing effect on each partner and on the relationship.

Against this backdrop, the following are suggested as guidelines for approaching the sexual relationship of incest perpetrators and spouses:

Consider the simplest explanation and the most direct intervention first. Despite the possibility that complex intrapsychic and relational conflicts may be present, sexual problems should be approached using the time-tested rule of parsimony. More complex hypotheses and remedies can be added if the simpler ones are not successful (Sanderson & Maddock, 1989). This guideline is sometimes difficult for family therapists to implement, in that they are trained to recognize and confront the complexity of relationship systems; indeed, complexity is characteristic of incest families and couples. However, sometimes the flexibility necessary to address their issues effectively requires *simplification*.

Help partners take RESPONSIBILITY FOR SELF and be RESPONSIVE TO THE OTHER in their sexual interaction. Sexual socialization in Western technological societies, particularly in the United States, has produced problematic patterns of erotic interaction which can affect any couple. On the one hand, we have made females generally responsible for whether or not sex happens at all. They are required to be attractive and appealing in order to arouse male sexual interest; indeed, they may be credited with arousing even unwanted sexual desire by dressing or behaving in what is perceived as a provocative manner. Traditionally, we have acted as if males were not able to be responsible for their sexual arousal; in fact, a lack of sexual desire in a male is often attributed to his partner's "lack of attractiveness."[10] On the other hand, we have tended to make males solely responsible for the success of mutually chosen sexual encounters. Men are to be sexually experienced; women less so, or not at all. A woman's lack of responsiveness is often blamed on her partner's lack of skill as a lover. Taken together, these patterns create confusion and set the

---

[10]Further discussion of the "rape culture" that predominates in North America can be found in our book *Child Sexual Abuse: An Ecological Approach to Treating Victims and Perpetrators*.

stage for a diffusion of responsibility that contributes to sexual dysfunction and dissatisfaction.

In addition, the boundary difficulties and power/control distortions that characterize the perpetrator/victim interaction pattern make it difficult for spouses in an incestuous family to maintain the secure sense of self that is required in order to take appropriate responsibility for their individual sexual interests and preferences. These clients often characterize their erotic encounters as manifestations of victimization. Even those partners who initially report that their sexual relationship is satisfactory — some will even speak in glowing, ethereal terms — will almost always reveal eventually that anxiety, insecurity, and even resentment are everpresent in their sexual relationship.

Helping incest couples with this issue requires working on self-differentiation within the context of a relationship. No one has described this process more completely or eloquently than sex and marital therapist David Schnarch (1991). He recognizes that a close relationship like marriage is a "sexual crucible" in which are forged the individual identities of the partners. Building on the work of Murray Bowen and other family therapists, Schnarch describes a process of "self-validated intimacy" which combats the distortions of sexual socialization described above. Further, Schnarch's approach to sex therapy with couples focuses specifically upon helping the partners deal with the inevitable dialectical tensions (we call it the "complex ecology") that characterize an ongoing relationship. The boundaries required to tolerate and creatively resolve these tensions are typically not present in incest family marriages. According to Schnarch, "Troubled marriages face [an] inherent paradox: The path to other-validation is through self-validated intimacy. . . . Self-validated intimacy is the 'bottom line' in marriage, particularly troubled ones; without the ability to persevere when validation from the partner is not forthcoming, couples bog down" (p. 128). Couples in incest families, like those in other dysfunctional relationships, need considerable help discovering that intimacy is an individual internal experience which occurs from time to time in the process of relating rather than a relationship goal that implies a perpetual state of existence (Schnarch, 1991; Wynne & Wynne, 1986).

Give the couple permission to be sexual. In beginning the professional work that came to be known as "the new sex therapy" (Kaplan, 1974), William Masters and Virginia Johnson (1970) emphasized the importance of this principle. Utilizing appropriate professional authority, the therapist should convey to the partners that it is all right to be sexually active, to think about sex, to be interested in sex, to experience sexual feelings and fantasies. Clients can be helped to recognize that sex per se need not be associated with shame or guilt. Certainly this task is complex when the partners are dealing with their respective reactions to the incestuous behavior, activity for which feeling negative and guilty is an appropriate response. Nevertheless, the therapist must bear in mind that the sexual abuse results, in part, from the underlying dynamics of shame and guilt related to sexuality which characterize incest family members and are likely to be linked with childhood victimization experiences of one or both partners.

The therapist providing authoritative permission to be sexual in healthy ways is counteracting distorted societal messages and, very possibly, the earlier influences of the partners' families of origin. Curiosity about sex as a child was likely to be stifled or even punished. In a significant number of cases, perpetrators of child sexual abuse reveal that erotic contact with a child or adolescent carried them back to their own childhoods and seemed to be expressing some kind of unmet need to re-visit or explore sexuality from the perspective of being young again. Working on their sexual relationship in therapy can aid the partners in exploring sexuality in more appropriate and acceptable ways.

Provide sexual re-education for the partners. Therapists can provide partners (as well as other family members) with accurate information about sexual functioning in a positive and supportive atmosphere. They can help clients understand and appreciate their own bodies and their capacity for giving and receiving pleasure in age-appropriate ways. Some research evidence has suggested that sex offenders (including but not limited to child sex abusers) may have less sex education than the average individual, perhaps making them more particularly prone to believe sexual myths and misinformation acquired during their early years (Gebhard et al., 1965; Langevin, 1985; Malamuth & Donnerstein, 1985). The therapist can serve as a sort of tutor for the couple with regard to questions and concerns about sex, which does not imply that the therapist need be a "sex expert." Rather, books and other materials appropriate to the needs and abilities of the partners can be supplied from time to time, or the partners can be encouraged to embark on an educational program together through the use of carefully selected self-help books on sexuality (e.g., Barbach, 1976, 1982; McCarthy & McCarthy, 1984, 1989; Zilbergeld, 1992). Sometimes, women's groups and men's groups that include a focus on sex education can be useful as adjuncts to couple therapy.[11] Most important is that the sex education efforts in therapy be specific and individualized to the partners themselves. For most clients, abstract information about people in

[11]Today, most perpetrator treatment groups include a component of sex education, and most clients prove to be eager participants. Peer group interaction can be particularly useful in discussing and correcting myths and stereotypes commonly held by perpetrators. Outside resources can be utilized when appropriate, helping the therapist avoid the label of "sex expert," which can trigger resistance in the form of shame or competition by the perpetrators.

general is not useful—other than perhaps to reassure them about the commonality of certain behaviors, for example, oral-genital sexual activity. However, even information about general patterns of sexual behavior needs to be used carefully, since such knowledge can intimidate clients, violate their personal values, or even provide one partner with ammunition to use against the other.

Help the couple communicate about sexual/marital issues. An important element of couple marital/sexual therapy is increased self and partner awareness. Because of distortions in boundaries and responsibilities as well as in power/control, partners are likely to be unaware of their own sex-related feelings, likes, and dislikes. In addition, the lack of direct communication that characterizes incest families typically creates ignorance of each other's sexual feelings and preferences. However, this should not be done until sufficient progress has been made in resolving power/control issues, so that neither partner fears being vulnerable in self-revelation about sexual matters (building sufficient trust with the therapist is also important). Typically, individual sessions with each partner are useful to promote trust and self-disclosure as well as to allow self-exploration without fear of victimization. Discussion of personal feelings and attitudes, behavioral preferences, and particularly fantasies must be timed appropriately and handled sensitively, for such revelations can be very powerful for some individuals. When this aspect of therapy is positive, it can help to counteract earlier shaming, exploitive, anxiety-ridden experiences. Similarly, sharing thoughts and feelings about their sexual interaction can be a profoundly intimate experience for partners whose previous capacity for intimacy has been extremely limited. Most important, the partners have an opportunity to experience *mutuality,* which has been prevented by the presence of the perpetrator/victim interaction pattern.

We are convinced that this aspect of couple therapy is one of the most important parts of incest family treatment, which is why we advocate training in sex therapy for family therapists who regularly work with family sexual abuse. Referral at the point where these intimate transactions can occur potentially disrupts the therapist-client bond which is so important to successful therapy with victims and perpetrators—nevertheless, referral to a specially trained resource is far better than entirely neglecting sexual communication work.

Offer structured behavioral home assignments. Such assignments have been a hallmark of sex therapy since its origins with Masters and Johnson (as well as an important component of most forms of marital therapy). Some therapists (e.g., Annon, 1975; LoPiccolo & LoPiccolo, 1978; McCarthy & McCarthy, 1984) both conceptualize and structure assignments as behavior modification based upon principles of learning theory. Other therapists (e.g., de Shazer, 1982; Haley, 1973; Madanes, 1990) conceptualize and structure these tasks in a "strategic" manner, utilizing a variety of indirect and paradoxical techniques. Schnarch (1989, 1991) has made a useful distinction between "inherent" and "constructed" paradoxes, which reflects a uniquely ecological approach to behavioral assignments. In most instances, the tasks are assigned as "homework" for the couple to do on their own, although various "enactments" or behavioral "rehearsals" (not explicitly sexual) may occur during a therapy session. All of these structured experiences are designed in some way to reorient or retrain the partners in effective methods of sexual stimulation and response without undue pressure or anxiety, as well as to facilitate accurate communication.

Temporarily assume overall responsibility for the couple's sexual interaction. Doing so relieves the couple of having to worry about the nature and timing of sexual activities, freeing them to concentrate on improving their communication and to give themselves fully to the experience of giving and receiving physical pleasure (Maddock, 1975; Schnarch, 1991). While the exact timing and content of behavioral homework can vary from one case to another, it is important that the therapist remain "in charge" of the process, even acting as a "lightning rod" when tension and conflict develop between the partners. Much better that the clients be angry at the therapist who is "making" them do the homework than that they sabotage their sexual relationship with undue hostility toward each other.

This structuring by the therapist is perhaps most important when it comes to the timing and initiation of sexual activity by the partners. Here, the dichotomy of the "spontaneous" versus the "mechanical" is most evident; here also, the issue of differences in sexual interest is most likely to be highlighted. To confront these issues, the therapist can take charge of scheduling particular erotic activities on a prearranged basis or of assigning "spontaneous" initiation to either or both partners. We regularly utilize a weekly scheduling grid with couples at certain stages of sex therapy (see Figure 10.1 for an example). As therapy progresses, couples are encouraged to negotiate their own sexual homework schedule during a session. Eventually, couples are left to choose whether to continue a scheduling arrangement on a regular basis or to leave things more to chance through spontaneous initiation, hopefully, through better communication.

Direct therapeutic efforts at reducing anxiety and increasing pleasure in the couple's sexual interactions. Though there are many different conceptual frameworks, principles, and techniques of sex therapy, all efforts to help partners improve their sexual interaction should include:

Day	Time of Day	Location	Initiator	Activity
Sunday				
Monday				
Tuesday				
Wednesday				
Thursday				
Friday				
Saturday				
"Bonus"	Surprise			To Be Announced
"Bonus"	Surprise			To Be Announced

FIGURE 10.1   Sexual Intimacy Schedule

- improved security and comfort (anxiety reduction)
- more shared meaning regarding sexual expression
- greater capacity for focusing on sensory (physical) experiences of each partner
- increased flexibility in erotic behavior

Following these guidelines assures that the therapist can help the couple genuinely confront their sexual difficulties in a very concrete and specific way. Without this emphasis, the partners—and even the therapist—may be tempted to avoid the sexual area entirely due to awkwardness and tension or perhaps sabotage the effort with abstract generalizations and ineffective platitudes about "the importance of a good sex life."

A Summary of Sexual Dysfunctions

Sex therapy singles out erotic behavior for attention and direct intervention. Both sexual dysfunction and sexual dissatisfaction occur for a wide variety of reasons; they may be rooted in individual psychopathology or in severe relationship conflicts. However, they can also result simply from an individual's negative learning through past experience, from an escalating fear of failure, or from poor communication between the partners. Anxiety is probably the key factor in producing sexual dysfunction, unless the dysfunction is organically based. Anxiety interferes with the natural receipt of effective stimulation, the buildup of sexual tension, and the focusing of this tension into the pathways toward orgasmic release.

Drugs also affect both sexual functioning and sexual interest; they can inhibit either or both. Clients who report any sexual dysfunction or admit to chronic erotic disinterest should always be questioned about their alcohol and drug habits, including any regularly prescribed medications. Common medications, particularly mood-altering drugs and drugs associated with the treatment of cardiovascular diseases, can have a significant impact on various aspects of sexual functioning as well as on overall sexual desire.

Individuals who suffer from primary erectile failure are those who have never been able to achieve an erection with a sexual partner. The number of males with this problem is relatively small, and they are likely to require extensive individual therapy, since usually they have generalized social interaction problems. In many cases, this symptom is associated with either an organic disorder or a more extensive psychiatric disturbance.

Some males cannot achieve an erection in certain circumstances or on some occasions or with some partners. Some gain an erection during foreplay but lose it when they attempt intercourse. These are examples of secondary erectile dysfunction, the underlying cause of which is almost always relational or situational. Usually it is associated with anxiety related to the fear of failure in sexual performance. The treatment of this dysfunction attempts to remove pressure for performance, to reduce fear of failure, and to facilitate the client's relaxation and focusing on the experience of physical pleasure. Therapy sessions focus on exploring the client's feelings about himself and his body, examining his vulnerability to anxiety and threat, and uncovering unresolved interpersonal issues between the partners.

Like males with primary erectile dysfunction, some females with generalized sexual dysfunction may never have experienced pleasure from any source. Others may have responded sexually at some point but are unable to do so with their partners at the present time. Women who have never experienced sexual arousal from any source may require extensive individual therapy (occasionally, however, they may be suffering from some kind of organic impairment). Within the context of the incestuous family system, it is quite possible that the wife of the perpetrator herself may be a victim of sexual abuse, either incestuous or nonincestuous, which has produced a negative orientation toward all forms of sexual contact—a condition typically referred to as "sexual aversion."

However, difficulty with sexual arousal need not be a sign of underlying psychopathology; it may result simply from overwhelming amounts of negative sexual socialization. Regardless of its origins, treatment of generalized sexual dysfunction in women concentrates on helping them to fully appreciate the sensual and sexual aspects of their bodies, focus on genital pleasure, communicate their erotic likes and dislikes to their partners, and take responsibility for initiating the kinds of sexual contacts they find pleasurable and exciting.

Premature ejaculation is the most common of the male sexual dysfunctions. There is a tendency for most young males in contemporary technological cultures to be rapid ejaculators, due to the early sexual conditioning that burdens them with fear and guilt. Generally speaking, the definition of prematurity depends upon the expectations of both partners. If the female reaches orgasm in what seems to both partners to be a reasonable amount of time, then the male will be defined as premature if he cannot maintain an erection for this length of time without ejaculating. The most effective treatment for premature ejaculation is to increase the male's ability to perceive and appreciate his own erotic sensations, thereby providing him a greater amount of control over his own orgasm.

Some males are able to experience an erection in response to any kind of sexual stimulation; however, for a variety of reasons they may not be able to reach orgasm. Mild forms of delayed orgasm are much more common than generally recognized. This is particularly true of individuals who experience selective, or situational, ejaculatory delays. This sexual dysfunction usually reflects issues of anxiety and anger in some combination. Therapy focuses on clarifying and exploring the meaning and impact of these emotions, increasing the client's appreciation of sexual stimulation as pleasure rather than performance, and freeing him from what may be a compulsive need to exert conscious control over his orgasmic response.

The female who experiences orgasmic dysfunction usually is able to receive and appreciate some degree of sexual stimulation and to experience physical arousal. However, for a variety of reasons she may be unable to abandon herself to this pleasure and to achieve the necessary accumulation of tension to bring her "over the top" to orgasm. Females who have never experienced an orgasm in response to any kind of sexual stimulation are referred to as "preorgasmic," since virtually all such women can be taught to respond to some means of sexual stimulation culminating in orgasm.

A significant number of women experience occasional or situational difficulties attaining orgasm, varying with the means of stimulation, the partner, or contextual factors. Some of these difficulties represent just a normal variation in the ways in which sexual activity is fitted into the overall life experience of women in contemporary societies. When presented as a dysfunctional problem, therapy sessions deal with the anxiety an individual may feel when giving up self-control, or "letting go," in order to reach orgasm. Sometimes, therapy explores the woman's wish to withhold something from her partner due to her feelings of anger, hurt, or vulnerability. A third possible focus may be on direct communication to her partner concerning her preferences for physical stimulation, which may change from the early stages of arousal up to the point of orgasm. Both the woman and her partner may have been socialized to believe that such direct assertiveness in the realm of sex is not "feminine."

Vaginismus is an involuntary spasm of the muscles surrounding the vaginal entrance, sufficient to produce significant pain or even to prevent any kind of penetration from taking place. A number of women who seek treatment for vaginismus are sexually responsive and enjoy clitoral stimulation, even to orgasm. Others are sexually aversive and attempt to block all forms of stimulation. Though vaginismus sometimes results from childhood sexual abuse, other experiences—even severe guilt over sexual activity or fear of pregnancy—may also create sufficient anxiety about penetration to produce this problem. Clients who present this symptom should be referred to a physician to determine if the problem has any kind of organic cause (anatomical abnormalities or diseases may lead to painful intercourse, giving rise to the protective spasms). A combination of sex education, therapeutic focus on relevant issues, and behavioral assignments (for example, vaginal dilators used by the client herself) are typically helpful in cases of vaginismus.

In summary, numerous techniques have been developed to assist couples with sexual problems. However, they need to be timed appropriately and used sensitively to avoid producing secondary symptoms or increasing client resistance. In addition to the excellent systemic books by Schnarch (1991) and by Woody (1993), behavioral protocols for sex therapy can be found in a variety of resources (e.g., Annon, 1975; Heiman & LoPiccolo, 1988; Kaplan, 1974, 1979; Leiblum & Rosen, 1988; LoPiccolo & LoPiccolo, 1978; McCarthy & McCarthy, 1984).

STRENGTHENING THE
PARENTAL COALITION

The breakdown of the parental coalition in incestuous families usually is self-evident. Restructuring the parent-child relationships is a critical objective in therapy; however, the personalities and maturity levels of one or both parents are likely to be compromised sufficiently that competent parenting will require considerable effort on the part of all concerned. As we have seen, chronic abuse and neglect are common in the backgrounds of the spouses in an incestuous family. Either or both partners may be sufficiently preoccupied with their own family-of-origin issues that energy to parent the next generation adequately may be lacking.

We prefer not to defer work on parenting until late in the treatment process; instead, we introduce it during various stages of couple and family therapy, sometimes by design and other times as opportunities arise spontaneously. In part, this reflects our concern that the children begin to get the benefits of competent parenting at the earliest possible moment. More important, however, is our belief that acquiring effective parenting skills is a developmental process that should be linked to other aspects of self-development that are the focus of therapy for the partners, individually and together. In large measure, parenting is an expression of personality, and dealing with developmental issues of their own in suitable ways can result in the spouses' capacity to conduct transactions with their children in more age-appropriate and effective ways (Burkett, 1991). Engaging in parenting also provides the spouses with an opportunity to give and receive mutual support and to reinforce new learning about themselves by practicing appropriate, nonabusive nurturance of their children.

One distinct advantage of family sessions during incest treatment is the opportunity for parent-child interactions to occur with direct support and guidance from the therapist. Of course, this advantage is not present in the early stages of family work, when the therapist may spend more time disrupting and redirecting misguided attempts by the parents to overpower or overcontrol their children. Initially, the changes may be little more than an increase in awareness of the children's ideas, attitudes, and feelings as individuals. Gradually, the therapist can model empathy with the children and, later, can guide appropriate parental intervention either in the form of nurturing, limit-setting, or problem-solving. Parenting skills need to geared to the developmental stages of the children, an overwhelming task for adults who themselves have not resolved issues from their own developmental sequences.

EXAMPLE

The Gregory family is in therapy at the direction of the court, based on the 13-year-old son's inappropriate sexual contact with his 10-year-old sister. Individual therapy was discontinued because the boy, Carter, refused to talk at all with the therapist; he speaks very seldom during family sessions, almost always in anger. The family therapist has opted to continue the family therapy. The son is "included" in these sessions by talking to him respectfully even if he does not respond, as well as by talking about him (having observed that he listens intently) and, at times, even answering questions *for* him (a strategy that has begun to evoke short answers as he counters with his own point of view). The following discussion takes place at the beginning of the sixth session:

Therapist: I'm aware that Carter is looking angrier today. Has anyone asked him what's going on with him? [*All family members shake their heads or say "no."*]

Therapist: [*Addressing the boy*] Carter, by the look on your face and the way you've been moving around my office, I would say you appear quite angry today. Usually, you don't rummage around the office unless you want to provoke a reaction in someone. I would really appreciate it if you could simply acknowledge whether or not you're feeling angry.

Carter: Fuck you, cunt.

Therapist: Thank you for answering my question. You just confirmed for me that you are indeed angry today. [*Turning to the parents, who have remained silent*] Carter is being very clear about his feelings today. Is that how he usually lets people at home know he's angry these days?

Father: Oh, yes. *Everybody* knows when Carter is angry. He blasts someone just as he did with you, although it's not always the person he's really angry with.

Therapist: Is that your view as well, Mrs. Gregory?

Mother: Yes. I just hate it when he is so verbally violent like that.

Therapist: Yet I noticed that neither of you said anything to Carter when he was verbally abusive to me just now. On the one hand, I appreciate your recognition that I don't need to be taken care of. On the other hand, I wonder what message Carter gets when you don't respond to his sexualized verbal violence?

Father: [*Looking at his wife*] I never thought of it as *sexual*, did you?

Mother: Oh, yes! Always. In fact, you and I have talked about it exactly like that. It makes me furious when you forget these conversations. It's like they never happened—

Therapist: [*Interrupting*] The two of you may have some issues with regard to communicating about the children, and we can talk about that later. Right now, though, I want to get back to Carter. He's learning that he can get away with being verbally violent with people, particularly if it provokes a fight between his parents. And it's probably a fight that the two of you need to have, so we can make a plan to deal with it in our next session without the children. Right now, I'm thinking there is another fight that the two of you need to have — together, you need to fight with your son.

Carter: [*Just loud enough to be audible*] Go to hell, bitch.

Mother: [*Sharply*] Carter, what did you just say?

Carter: Nothing.

Mother: [*Insisting*] I don't believe you. I heard you say "Go to hell, bitch," and that's not acceptable. Further, what you said before was totally unacceptable, and I want you to apologize. [*Carter sits staring into space and says nothing.*] Carter, I said I insist you apologize to the Doctor!

Carter: [*Quietly, after a long pause*] All right, I apologize.

Father: [*Addressing the therapist*] What should we do in cases like this? I'm at a loss, so I just ignore it.

Therapist: I can appreciate your frustration about how best to handle Carter's verbal abusiveness, Mr. Gregory. As I recall, you were the perfect child in your family because your father would beat you if you weren't. So Carter is teaching you about your "dark side," the side of you that could never be expressed as a child. Carter seems to be doing it in a very raw, primitive form, not unlike very small children might do — for example, like the 4-year-old child who grabs a toy from another toddler and hits her with it — except that Carter does it with words. I think dealing with Carter requires three things: First, understand that he is doing what children in families often do for adults, and that is to find what the adults need to learn about and develop in themselves — and then push it right in the adults' faces. Second, once you recognize what he is doing, help him separate himself from the issues that really are yours. Third, teach him some more appropriate ways of expressing his feelings.

Father: I never thought about his behavior as helping me. . . . But if it's my dark side, does that mean it's his dark side too?

Therapist: In a sense. However, the way things are structured in this family right now, you seem to express only the light side, and Carter seems to express only the dark side. Both of you are missing important parts of yourselves. It's almost as if the two of you make up only one complete person, with both a dark side and a light side.

Father: [*Excitedly*] I think you're right! Maybe that's why Carter never says anything except when he's angry.

Therapist: One of the things you can do for your son is to take ownership of your own dark side. I wonder if you would be willing to ask your dark side to write a letter to you, telling you about itself—a letter we could talk about in an individual or couple session?

Father: [*After a pause*] Yes, I guess so. It could be interesting.

Therapist: Great! In the meantime, I wonder if the light side of you has anything to say to Carter about what just happened between him and me?

Father: [*Picking up the cue and addressing his son*] Carter, I am just understanding something I've never understood before—that I have hurt you by my own inability to accept myself. I'm very sorry I did that to you. I suspect what you said earlier comes from that somehow. But that doesn't excuse it. I know you apologized, and I appreciate that. The next time you are angry at her or at anyone, I want you to say "I'm angry at you about that," or "That makes me mad," or something like that. It is *not* all right for you to be verbally abusive, and we're not going to tolerate it any more. I also want to say that I believe your verbal abuse comes from some mistaken ideas about females, and that's what we are here to fix. I also want you to be aware of that fact. Are you?

Carter: [*Quietly, while staring at the floor*] I suppose so.

Father: Good! I will make a pledge to you that each time you are verbally abusive, I will remind you that it is unacceptable, and I will expect that an apology will be forthcoming.

Therapist: [*Turning to Mrs. Gregory*] What's your reaction to what has just occurred between your husband and your son?

Mother: Very good. I feel very good. I just hope he can follow through and not forget.

Therapist: It might be helpful if you would ask him how you might be able to be supportive of his efforts. Are you willing to do that?

Mother: [*Turning to her husband*] How can I be helpful to you? I really liked what you just did with Carter.

Father: Well, it would be great if you could compliment me when I do it. I think that would be very helpful.

Mother: But what about when you *don't* do it? If you. . . .

Therapist: [*Quickly blocking the negative interaction*] If I could interrupt, I think that relates to the fight I mentioned earlier that the two of you need to have in couple therapy. Perhaps after we excuse the children from this session, we could take a few minutes to make careful plans for that fight.

In this sequence, the therapist is working to help the family deal with boundary issues, alter meanings, and develop new coalitions. First, she helps the parents recognize the meaning of their son's abusive behavior within the context of family scripts, while still encouraging empathy for him. Second, she finds opportunities to strengthen the intergenerational boundary by building support for the parental coalition. Third, she empowers the parents to act appropriately in setting limits with Carter and enforcing personal responsibility for his behavior. Finally, she reinforces the intergenerational boundary from the other direction by building an appropriate boundary around the couple's marital issues.

Sometimes, the spouses require considerable assistance in working through issues in their own marriage that act to maintain the victim in a spousal role and which thereby prevent their functioning competently as parents.

EXAMPLE

Leonard sexually abused his now 16-year-old daughter, an only child, for several years from age 12 to age 15, at which time she ran away from home to live with her boyfriend, was picked up by the police, and revealed the incest. The parents' current attitude is: "It's in the past, so let's move on with life." Both the daughter and her mother, Millie, have been in individual therapy, and Leonard is currently in an outpatient sex offender treatment group. Leonard and Millie have recently begun marital therapy.

Therapist: Both of you are convinced that the sexual abuse is in the past, and that we should move on to other things that are more current. Am I reading you correctly?

Leonard: [*Quickly*] That's true. My wife and I have talked it over, and we feel finished with it.

Therapist: [*Nodding and turning to Millie*] So your husband has talked with you about how having sex with your daughter is connected to your marriage. And you're finished with all of those issues, too?

Millie: Yes, we've talked about it, and it's over.

Therapist: [*Persisting*] OK, so it's just me who needs to be clued in here. It would be beneficial to me in helping your whole family if I could understand how having sex with your daughter is connected with issues in your marriage. Could you two help me understand that?

Millie: We didn't really talk about it that way. Len told me that he did it, that he was sorry, and that he still loves me and wants us to go on. So we are.

Therapist: [*After a pause, the therapist assumes a puzzled expression and addresses Leonard*] Oh, then you *haven't* shared with your wife what you've come to understand about how the problems in your marriage are connected to your having sex with your daughter? Could you talk about that now, so that I can understand it too?

Leonard: [*Sounding irritated*] I don't know—it was just a mistake, that's all.

Therapist: [*Gently, but persistently*] I agree with you that it was a mistake, and I respect your awareness about that. But I'm concerned about a couple of things. First, if the two of you aren't aware of how the sexual abuse is connected to your marriage, then the marriage problems will still be there and will probably show up in some other way. Second, if the two of you don't understand the connection, then your daughter may find her way back into your marriage in some other way—which would be bad for her, bad for both of you, bad for your marriage. [*Leaning toward Leonard*] What's difficult about focusing on the meaning of how the incest hurt your marriage, as well as your daughter?

Leonard: It feels bad. It makes me feel dirty and inadequate—like I'm a no good who doesn't deserve to be alive.

Therapist: I see. If you look at the sexual abuse of your daughter, it means you become the lowest of the lowlifes, and it isn't worth being alive. Is that it? [*Leonard nods affirmatively, so the therapist continues*] Well, that's a tough one. I get the feeling that you would like to stay alive, so it creates quite a dilemma for you. . . . I wonder if you could find a way to think about the fact that you sexually abused your daughter without invoking the death penalty for yourself. Do you think that's a possibility?

Leonard: [*Quietly*] How could I . . . do that?

Therapist: Clearly, you've been suffering with this, and you feel badly about what you did. Otherwise, you wouldn't have found yourself guilty and sentenced yourself to death. But while incest is a serious matter, and even a criminal activity, it isn't punished by death. The court has already determined your guilt and pronounced its sentence. It seems to me that you're still rebelling against the law. I wonder if you could just give yourself permission to become a private citizen again and accept the court's decision about your guilt and appropriate sentence, and go on from there?

Leonard: What you're saying makes sense, but this was a really bad deal for both my daughter and my wife.

Therapist: I agree that it was a bad deal for everyone in your family. On the other hand, putting some energy into understanding what it was all about, and how it has affected you and your marriage, could maybe turn a bad deal into a learning opportunity. Does that make sense to you?

Leonard: [*Nodding*] Yes. So how *was* the abuse connected to my marriage?

Therapist: You're looking at me for an answer. How could your sexual abuse of your daughter possibly be connected with your marriage?

The answer to that question can be found inside each of you, certainly not inside of me. What are your ideas about that, either of you?

Millie: [*Following a moment of silence*] For a long time, I have thought that Len lost interest in me after our daughter was born. She became more important to him than I did, and that never seems to have changed. He always wanted to spend time with her, do things with her, be around her. It was okay if I went with them, but I clearly was a "third wheel." It was always plain to me that his energy was tied up with her.

Therapist: It sounds like you were feeling left out after your daughter was born. How did you deal with it?

Millie: I left him alone. He did his thing, and I did mine.

Therapist: So you made a decision to become even more distant from him than you already felt, in order to protect yourself from the hurt. What kept you from telling him then how hurt you were that he was neglecting you in favor of your daughter?

Millie: [*Tears coming into her eyes*] We never talked about stuff like that. I never saw that kind of openness in my family, and I never felt comfortable doing it in my marriage.

Therapist: This might be an opportunity to change all that. Despite your discomfort, could you tell your husband now how hurt you were when you lost him after your daughter was born?

After some maneuvering and gentle confronting, the therapist has begun to move the spouses from a denying, defensive stance toward potential cooperation. The stage has been set for understanding the connections between the distant past (family-of-origin issues, the early years of marriage and birth of their child) with the more recent past (the father's sexual abuse of his daughter) and the present (the partners' fears for their marriage). The therapist has made explicit his agenda to remove the daughter from her inappropriate role in the marriage, and the parents seem open to the possibility. The therapist's next step is likely to be helping the parents develop a plan for conveying to their daughter their understanding of how the abuse developed in their family, in order to clearly remove the burden of responsibility from her. This will set the stage for the couple to jointly assume the obligations of competent parenting.

In summary, assisting spouses in incestuous families to function effectively as parents requires a triple focus. First, *both* parents need to gain mastery over those aspects of development that were arrested by their own childhood experiences with inadequate and/or abusive parents, thereby fostering their own maturity and personal identity. Second, *both* parents need to use their evolving senses of selfhood and identity to make personal connections with their children in age-appropriate (nonexploitive) ways. Finally, *both* parents need to learn how to work together cooperatively so that the marital/parental coalition forms a solid foundation for the security of the children and the activities of the family. Attention is best given to these objectives on an intermittent basis throughout therapy. From the standpoint of the therapist, fostering parental competence requires a transference bond with *each* of the spouses. Further, the therapist must be prepared to weave into this bond of attachment a variety of strands from the marital relationship, the relationship of each adult to each child (including the victim), the relationships of the siblings, and even ties to the families of origin and to the community. In the end, the bonds must be both extensive enough and strong enough to anchor the family in its social context, endure the strains of intervention into the incest, repair damaged relationship trust among members, and guide the family as a unit through the future stresses of predictable and unpredictable crises in individual and family development.

SPECIAL ISSUES WITH THE
NONOFFENDING SPOUSE

We have dealt already with the most important issues facing the therapist working with the nonoffending spouse in the incestuous family — boundaries, meanings of the incest, perpetrator/victim interaction patterns, sexual-marital problems, and deficits in parenting. Without designating her as responsible for the incest, we have included her in the systemic transactions central to the family system, including the occurrence of the abuse itself. However, a few additional comments are in order insofar as the nonoffending spouse is in the position of being both a marital partner of a sex offender and a parent of a sexual abuse victim.

Nonoffending spouses vary greatly with regard to their knowledge of, and reactions to, the incestuous activity occurring in their families. Some spouses are completely oblivious to the abuse (whether due to their own issues or because of the care of the perpetrator to avoid discovery); some wonder about abuse, but take no steps to verify it; some know for certain but do not intervene; some find out and take immediate steps to intervene; some take steps to facilitate the abuse; some even participate in the sexual activity. Professionals involved in intervention should have no preconceptions regarding the role of the nonoffending spouse; in fact, her own description of her awareness may itself reflect distortions and defenses arising from her own developmental and boundary issues. As a general guideline for *therapy*, we consider nonoffending spouses equally responsible with perpetrators for the family dynamics that have set the stage for incest to occur — boundary difficulties, perpetrator/victim dynamics, dysfunctional coalition, and marital/sexual problems—and we hold them accountable as adults who are expected to put effort and energy into resolving these issues and caring for their children. In most instances, we consider unwillingness to be involved in family and marital therapy a negative sign reflecting the presence of unresolved issues of her own.

If the nonoffending spouse is the wife, as is most often the case, personal identity is likely to be a key issue in treatment. Since women's identities in many societies are tied to their roles as wives and mothers, a personal sense of self independent of marriage and family has been difficult for many to achieve. As a result, a woman capable of empathy with her abused child immediately may consider herself a total failure at the two things that primarily define her—being a "good" wife and a "good" mother. Helping these women recover from this wound to their sense of self is often the major component of therapy following the revelation of incest. The more *victim*-oriented the spouse, the more her capacity for empathy with pain may lead her to take onto herself the burden of the entire problem—perhaps even consciously or unconsciously absolving her perpetrating husband of any responsibility for his actions. At that point, the therapist may need to provide both support and reality testing; for example, how many people know what their husbands or wives are doing every moment of every day, even when they share the same house? Without direct observation or evidence or an assertive child who reveals the abuse, most spouses will be unlikely to suspect that incestuous activity is occurring within the family nor are most parents likely to reach such a conclusion immediately regardless of the symptoms that might be displayed by their children. Sometimes, nonoffending spouses are criticized, or even legally charged, for not protecting their children from incestuous abuse. Though evidence of collusion may be present in some instances, we believe it is a mistake for legal or social agencies to hold spouses or other family members responsible for what amounts to intuition or parapsychological abilities.

This issue extends into the treatment situation as well. Only under certain special circumstances should spouses be charged with "surveillance" of perpetrators, particularly for "supervising" the perpetrator's activities with the victim or other children. This can lead to problems. First, it removes the spouse from a coparenting role and identifies her as an agent of social control. This shift has the effect of creating even greater emotional distance between the spouses and further blurring the intergenerational boundary (the perpetrator becomes one of the "children"). In addition, it can sabotage one of the major objectives of treatment; when the spouse is responsible for controlling the perpetrator, he need not develop his own internal locus of control. The therapist should work with legal and social service agencies to identify realistic ways to make the spouses *mutually* responsible for their parenting—including protection from abuse.

The loyalty battle that may occur between the victim and one or both of her parents is another important consideration when working with non-offending spouses. Sometimes, it is made blatantly clear by legal authorities that termination of parental rights would facilitate a lighter sentence or might even result in dropping the charges altogether. More often, however, the expectations and pressures are subtle, both within the nonoffending spouse herself and from the social environment. A prominent but seldom spoken assumption seems to exist: It is better for the nonperpetrating adult to side with her children against her spouse in cases of child sexual abuse. Only recently have programs and therapists begun to express an open belief that in many case the best option is for the nonperpetrator to choose *both* her children *and* her spouse, in support of the efforts of the entire family to work its way through the incest crisis and emerge healthier as a result of the effort. In our experience, mothers who appear to "side with" their spouses are sometimes suspected of coperpetrating, even though this scenario is rare. Among other things, this conclusion fails to recognize the reality of the spouse's own issues and deficits. These individuals need time to deal with a variety of issues before they can make meaningful choices about their own lives and those of their children. At times their dependency may be mistaken for lack of motivation, or for an unwillingness or inability to attach to their children. While this is sometimes true, most mothers in incestuous families are bonded to their children to the degree their own psychosexual development will allow. Given some time and therapeutic effort, most can become adequate mothers to their children.

Of course, the numbers of sexual abuse survivors who marry men who will abuse their own or other children is both noteworthy and tragic. Their own histories naturally affect their responses to family members who reveal sexual abuse. Sometimes they have decided that their own abuse was "no big deal," and they may expect their children to reach the same conclusion and to put the incest rapidly into the past. This pressure may contribute to a dissociative response in the victim—and it may reflect the previous dissociative processes of the adult survivor. In other instances, nonoffending spouses have not moved beyond the pain of their own victimization; as a result, they overidentify with the victim's emotions and may create additional problems for the victim and perhaps all family members. Some nonoffending parents seem to need to stimulate their children's pain, until the victimization experience becomes the primary vehicle for their relationship.

In our experience, a mother's group or family and couple therapy are insufficient to resolve the issues of an incest mother who herself was sexually abused as a child *and who has formulated her primary identity around her victimization.* For such individuals, we recommend a specialized therapy group for adult survivors, preferably one that is characterized by an emphasis on self development and internal locus of control.[12] If such a group is not available, then individual therapy combining family-of-origin work with victim treatment principles can create an appropriate context for change. In working with nonoffending spouses, the most critical principle is to assume nothing until a thorough assessment has been completed as part of formal evaluation or as a beginning of treatment. This assessment should gather data regarding all of the intrapsychic and relationship issues outlined in this chapter in order to assure that the individual is provided with the necessary support and assistance for herself and the necessary help with her marriage and with her parenting that she can contribute meaningfully to the family's recovery from the dysfunction of incest.

CONCLUSION

This chapter has described the dynamics of marriage in the context of the incestuous family. With particular emphasis on the manifestations of the perpetrator/victim interaction pattern and the dysfunctional elements of the sexual relationship and the parental coalition, we have outlined some principles that should guide couple therapy. Again, we reiterate our conviction that marital therapy is a *necessity* for successful incest treatment, even if the partners decide to divorce as a result of exploring the relationship. Work on the marriage should be spread across the course of treatment, highlighting various issues as they become relevant and complementing family sessions as well as any individual or group treatment of family members. Repairing and strengthening the marital system, in the final analysis, may prove to be the best possible protection against recidivism and a contributor to better sexual health in the eventual marriages of the children.

---

[12]Such a group therapy model is described in our book *Child Sexual Abuse: An Ecological Approach to Treating Victims and Perpetrators.*

CHAPTER 11

The Social Ecology
of Incest Treatment

We learn from history that we do not learn from history.

— Georg Wilhelm Friedrich Hegel (1807)

*The world, as Hegel puts it, is "a unity of the given
and the constructed." It is difficult to determine what is
"given" and what are our "constructions." One way is to
compare the ways people in different times and places,
and even in the same time and place, experience the
world. All of us have been, or will be, surprised, even
incredulous . . . at how vast are the differences between
ways of experiencing.*

— R. D. Laing (1971)

F ROM AN ECOLOGICAL PERSPECTIVE, human behavior can be understood
only within a broader social context. We have noted already that a
family is both the primary ecosystem to individuals (particularly during
childhood) and a key subsystem of a society (a major arena for the implementation of cultural meanings and values, as well as the principal vehicle
for their transmission between the generations). As society's primary unit
of developmental transformation, the family plays a crucial role in the
evolution of sexuality across the life span of individuals. Further, the family's handling of sex-related matters mirrors the dynamics of sexuality in the
larger culture. Unfortunately, this means that the family system also may
be the place where the distortions and conflicts related to sexuality are
played out most vividly. Societal reaction to the revealed incidence of
child sexual abuse, particularly of incest, reflects the cultural context of
ambivalence that has shaped the character of sexuality throughout North
America and in other highly technologized societies. Predictably, there has

been a tendency toward extremes of response ranging from the contention by some that incest is a rare aberration to the fervent attempts by others to root out the "incest dynamics" they believe to exist in virtually all families. Further, dealing with the problem of incest and other forms of child sexual abuse is linked to broader sociopolitical issues involving gender and cultural diversity. Most of those who are sexually and/or physically abused — particularly on a repetitive basis — are females and children. Often both victims and perpetrators of abuse are members of socially stigmatized cultural groups as well.

Some attention has begun to be paid to the social conditions that underlie patterns of sexual and physical abuse within families. These include unequal social status of males and females, cultural attributions of "ownership" of women and children by adult males, elements of gender socialization that predispose males to be perpetrators and females to be victims in relation to sex, social sanctions for resolving conflicts with violence, manipulation of sexual imagery (including of children) through media advertising, social tolerance for poverty in a culture characterized by excessive material consumption (Lloyd, 1991; Maddock, 1986). Each of these factors has been associated with child sexual abuse in some studies. At the same time, no single social influence has been identified as a necessary or sufficient cause of such abuse — just as no single psychological characteristic seems to motivate or explain sexual perpetration. Therefore, an ecological framework emphasizing the complex transactions of intra-individual, familial, societal, cultural, and environmental factors must be the basis for understanding the etiology of child sexual abuse — as well as for preventing it (National Research Council, 1993).

Increased awareness of the social consequences of institutionalized sexism and growing concern for the welfare of children have combined to increase our sensitivity to the problems of child maltreatment, particularly within the context of family life. This increased sensitivity, along with other structural changes in society and the pervasive presence of the media, have contributed to an expanded definition of "victimization," particularly in relation to childrearing and to male-female interactions in close relationships. In turn, this has led to the development of numerous advocacy roles and organizations aiding women and children on an individual basis or promoting changes in social policy that improve the welfare of women and children. In the view of some commentators, the institutionalization of victimization has now reached such an extreme that the social context that surrounds the therapist treating incestuous families or their members is now "a nation of victims" (Sykes, 1992) characterized by a "child sexual abuse panic" (Kutchinsky, 1992b).[1]

---

[1]More general aspects of this issue are discussed in our book *Child Sexual Abuse: An Ecological Approach to Treating Victims and Perpetrators.*

AVOIDING THE MOST
COMMON "TRAPS"

Numerous pitfalls await the therapist dealing with incestuous families. Some of these have become painfully apparent over the past decade, as therapists are embroiled in social controversies surrounding the incest phenomenon. Well-meaning helping professionals have been threatened by angry family members, intimidated by attorneys, sued by accused perpetrators, fired from their jobs, boycotted in their communities, and publicly excoriated by the media. All of this is in addition to the more routine problems of treating abused children or offenders — client resistance, family upset, complicated record-keeping, lengthy report writing, unpleasant court appearances, and a variety of other pressures. Family-based incest treatment reflects all of these hazards and more. Further complicating the situation is the contemporary social context in which the family therapist must operate, for many of the controversies surrounding incest treatment are far from settled. At the same time, we believe that an ecologically oriented approach to incest treatment, initiated at the first intervention, can do much to reduce or eliminate many of the difficult and risky complications. Most important is to avoid the common "traps" into which the therapist treating incest is likely to fall. After a brief discussion of these, we will focus on the principles that should guide an ecologically balanced course of intervention and treatment in the contemporary social climate.

Trap 1: Lack of Access to the Family

We list this as a therapeutic trap despite the fact that gaining access to all members of an incestuous family may be — or may appear to be — beyond the control of the therapist. Depending upon her or his professional identity and work context, the therapist may be referred only part of the family; child victims and their mothers are the most typical combination. Even a professional who is clearly identified as a family therapist may not be expected to do therapy with the perpetrator, usually because he is in prison or in a structured offender treatment program. Previously, we have described and explained our bias toward early access to the entire family and have argued that the family therapist ought to be the key coordinator for treatment of all family members. Here, we want to reemphasize the importance of considering the entire incest family to be the primary client unit — although we acknowledge that the social service and legal systems may create barriers to family therapy. As we shall discuss later in this chapter, certain professionals in these systems may act to oppose or sabotage efforts at family treatment. As a result, a family therapist can find him- or herself in the awkward position of being held accountable for ensuring that family sexual abuse will not be repeated despite missing key ingredients for successfully resolving the underlying family dysfunction — *all* family members.

Trap 2: Rescue

We have emphasized repeatedly this most dangerous of pitfalls when intervening into the perpetrator/victim interaction pattern, that is, the illusion of saving one family member from another. The temptation to assume the mantle of powerful Rescuer should be rigorously avoided and should never be confused with the legitimate motivation to be helpful which rightfully undergirds the therapeutic endeavor. However, this helpfulness should encompass the entire family unit. Even if referred only an individual family member (such as a child victim), the therapist should remember that intervention almost certainly has created a *family* crisis, and that the incestuous behavior reflects disturbances in the family for which treatment can be helpful. We reiterate that the stance of the therapist should be one of equidistance from all members of the family affected by the incest and its revelation (which usually means everyone). The therapist attending to the social ecology of incest treatment will be continuously aware that each client is simultaneously an individual, a family member, and a citizen, and she must balance her interventions among these three.

Trap 3: Investigation

Regardless of the circumstances under which an incest case is referred, the therapist should avoid the temptation to become an "investigator" of illegal and socially undesirable behavior. This is particularly tempting at the time of initial assessment and history-taking. Ideally, the therapist should be able to work effectively with the family or family members around relevant issues without needing to know what "really" happened. In one sense, therapy with incestuous families is no different from therapy with families who have other problems. Seldom do therapists feel the need to probe for details of objective facts when clients report, "My parents fought with each other all weekend and took it out on me by being real strict" or "My wife is always interrupting me at the office to nag me about something." Naturally therapists gather information about the lives of their clients. However, the major focus is on the *meaning* of an experience to the client(s) and its impact on their lives. The narratives most useful to the therapist are not the same as those most useful to child protection agencies or legal professionals — nor will the stories told by clients necessarily be the same under various circumstances. Nevertheless, the verbal reports and written documents that may accompany an incestuous family in treatment can be used for *therapeutic* purposes. For example, pointing out the discrepancies in accounts of behavior among family members or using legal documents to challenge the denial of a perpetrator is legitimate when linked to the implementation of particular therapeutic hypotheses and strategies.

Trap 4: Role Confusion

Therapist, evaluator, and agent of social control are all necessary and important roles in the process of intervention into family sexual abuse. From our perspective, therapists should avoid having to function as agents of social control whenever possible. In some social agencies, particularly in rural settings, helping professionals doing child protection work sometimes are asked to do therapy with the abusive families they have investigated and reported. As sympathetic as we are to the problem of limited resources, we believe that this is a major mistake that should be avoided at all costs. Role confusion creates a blurring of boundaries that mirrors the boundary violations already occurring in the incestuous family, thereby compounding the very problem that intervention is intended to alleviate. Equally important is clarity about whether one is serving as an evaluator or as a therapist with members of an incestuous family. If asked to do therapy, one should not also conduct formal evaluations; conversely, if a therapist is hired or appointed to do an evaluation of an incest victim, perpetrator, or family, she should not be involved directly in therapy with members of the family. In the majority of child sexual abuse cases that achieved notariety for their controversial nature over the past decade, psychologists, social workers and other helping professionals were involved in both the evaluation of sexual abuse—on the basis of which legal action was taken—and in the treatment of at least some of those whom they had evaluated. Effective ecological treatment requires that these roles be kept separate.

Trap 5: Adversarial Assumptions

This trap is closely associated with that of rescuing. Various characteristics of intervention into incestuous family systems—the identified roles of victim and perpetrator within the family, the frequently conflictual nature of transactions among incestous family members, the court proceedings that often follow abuse reporting—may lead the therapist to mistakenly assume that some, perhaps all, family members see themselves as adversaries in the same sense as divorcing spouses who have drawn battle lines and recruited the children onto opposing sides. Though this can occur in some families, much more common is a display of the considerable ambivalence

that already characterizes these families, along with a variety of manifestations of family loyalty (see Chapter 4). Previously, we have discussed the
implications of these dynamics for therapy; here, we consider their impact
on the broader social ecology of intervention into incestuous abuse. From
this broad perspective, *the primary problem to be avoided is creating a
conflictual ecology of intervention that detracts from the benefits of therapy
for the family* and may also set the stage for various problematic sequelae,
such as disagreement among intervening professionals over the accuracy
of the abuse report, interagency squabbling over treatment plans, and
even lawsuits initiated by various family members against other family
members or against helping professionals. Assuming an adversarial stance
may lead to significant boundary distortion in the treatment ecosystem
which, in turn, can produce conflict rather than cooperation among treatment agencies and individuals. When this occurs, the social ecosystem has
become isomorphic to the negative dynamics of the incestuous family
system—typically it mirrors the perpetrator/victim interaction patterns—
and the broader system's ability to be helpful to the family members may
be severely compromised. As we suggested in Chapter 9, a consultation
team can be a useful addition to therapy when the agencies involved in
intervention begin to conflict in ways that hamper effective treatment.

Trap 6: Intergenerational Boundary Diffusion

This trap occurs most often among individuals or agencies whose stance
toward abuse intervention is strongly oriented toward victim advocacy (see
Chapter 1). However, any therapist can succumb to the temptation to let
her efforts to empower the victim of abuse escalate into a distortion of
power in the other direction. When this occurs, two problems may result.
The first is a kind of perpetrator/victim interaction sequence reversal.
Intentionally or unintentionally, the young victim may begin to abuse her
abuser, that is, to use the revelation of incest and subsequent intervention
to exploit the original perpetrator by meeting needs of her own at his
expense. Despite the noble-sounding language often employed by victims'
rights groups and/or attorneys, we are convinced that the majority of
lawsuits by adult survivors against their former abusers contain a strong
element of psychological revenge; the perpetrator is now the victim, and
vice versa. The second problem resulting from distortions in empowerment is its contribution to a continuing violation of intergenerational
boundaries. That is, the child now may be elevated into an adult role in
realms of family life other than the sexual activity. To some degree, this
may be unavoidable. The abuse victim who reports a member of her
family indeed does gain a necessary control over her own life and a certain
element of power over the life of the perpetrator. However, the family
therapist in particular ought to recognize the risks in this situation and

make efforts to creatively balance the power/control dynamics. Without such awareness, the therapist unwittingly may create problems not only for the perpetrator, but for the entire family including the child, who must overcome elements of grandiosity in order to ultimately heal from her victimization.

Trap 7: "Admitting" Requirements for Treatment

Numerous treatment programs require that the alleged perpetrator "admit" to the abuse before he can enter treatment, even if no legal action has been taken. In our view, this requirement satisfies various agents of social control at the expense of complicating therapy. Insistence on enforcing such a requirement can lead to several outcomes. One is to increase the resistance of the perpetrator, who may protest his innocence more loudly than before. Another is to mobilize the perpetrator's anger and rage, increasing the likelihood of more perpetrating behavior, leading to more external sanctions against him, and producing an escalating spiral of perpetrator/victim interaction now involving the professional community as well as family members. Still another common result is the fostering of "pseudo-compliance" on the part of the perpetrator, that is, his conscious or unconscious attempts to manipulate the therapist, thereby reinforcing an external locus of control which simply exacerbates his tendency toward perpetration.

Our willingness to work with accused incest perpetrators who have not admitted their guilt has had mixed consequences. On the positive side, it offers us easier access to the entire family for treatment; in addition, it has produced an extremely diverse group of abusive families to work with, from whom we have learned a great deal. On the negative side, this openness to begin therapy regardless of the legal status of the family has earned us a reputation among some social agencies as being "soft on offenders"; as a result, they do not refer to us. Thus far the most negative outcome has not occurred—we have not yet had to deal with an incest offender who duped us with his protests of innocence and then went on to reoffend. In fact, most offenders with whom we work eventually admit the incestuous behavior.

INTERFACING WITH
THE LEGAL SYSTEM

Throughout this book, we have emphasized role clarity for everyone concerned with intervention into incestuous family situations, particularly for the family therapist. Lack of clarity leads to boundary distortions, which already lie at the heart of the incestous family system. Firm, appropriate boundaries are both ethically responsible and practically useful in treatment. At the same time, we have described an approach to incest treatment that requires considerable creativity and flexibility on the part of the therapist—the capacity to move artfully within the social ecology of incest treatment in order to be able to make a connection, establish a position, and influence the myriad transformations among subsystems within an everchanging ecosystem. There is no single correct approach to incest treatment; in fact, the characteristics of particular incestuous families are such that even the most excellent prestructured treatment programs have a difficult time meeting the needs of every client.

Nowhere is the dialectic of firm boundaries and adaptive, flexible structures more important for the therapist than in relation to the legal system that is likely to be part of incest intervention. This is true for a variety of reasons. First, the complex circularity of ecosystemic theories and approaches to therapy do not mesh well with the causal-predictive theories and categorical approaches to decision-making of the legal system. Further, the legal system is power-oriented, and it is characterized by abundant boundary problems and perpetrator/victim interaction dynamics. In addition, the boundaries between the legal system and the mental health system have become particularly confusing. Finally, the broader society's preoccupation with victimization is largely legitimated through the legal system. Taken together, these factors have created a cultural context for incest intervention in which social control and treatment agendas are intertwined. This challenges the therapist to devise a clear set of treatment objectives and a treatment plan that takes account of the legal system's impact on some or all members of the incestuous family subsequent to reporting. The therapist must decide what role to play and what functions to serve within this broader context, despite conflicting pressures from various directions.

Managing Clashing Presuppositions

An inherent tension exists between legal and mental health professionals when dealing with human behavior that society deems both criminal and psychologically disturbed. For a variety of reasons (noted in Chapter 1), incestuous abuse brings this tension to the surface in especially powerful ways. Differing frames of reference lead, in turn, to differing agendas on how to proceed with intervention. Protection workers and criminal justice professionals are concerned primarily with punishment for illegal behavior and with what we have termed "management" of the client situation so that they can be guaranteed the abuse will not recur. Those with a therapeutic orientation are concerned primarily with assisting a family in crisis and with treating family members so that the psychological and relational dynamics which led to the abuse are altered. Inevitably, these perspectives and resulting agendas sometimes will clash. Therapists are challenged to avoid extremes when interfacing with the legal system around incestuous abuse. On the one hand, the therapist should not become an agent of the legal system, assuming the role of criminal investigator, legal advocate, or enforcer—no matter how much pressure is exerted by others. On the other hand, the therapist should avoid becoming adversarial with legal professionals, siding with the family members against those who may be regarded as "the enemy." Once again, a balance must be struck. Just as the therapist is challenged to remain equidistant from family members who are clients, so also should he or she remain equidistant from various agents of social control involved in the case. This form of ecological balancing is part of the "juggling" that is required to work effectively in treatment with incestuous families.

Dealing with Reporting Requirements

Most often, the family therapist works with incest families in which the abuse has already been uncovered, reported, and followed up by someone else. In these instances, the therapist's major concern is reporting either previously undisclosed abuse or recurring abuse by an already identified perpetrator. Occasionally, abuse is uncovered for the first time during family therapy in connection with some other identified problem, in which case the therapist is legally obligated to see that it is reported. Any of these situations creates a dilemma for the family therapist—even more than the therapist working with an individual client: how to fulfill mandated reporting requirements without unduly disrupting therapy or damaging her relationship with family members, particularly the perpetrator. Reporting the abuse can easily be interpreted by clients as "taking sides" or "betraying trust."

We have experimented with various ways of accomplishing this difficult task and have developed several principles that appear to be effective. First of all, the therapist should attempt to confirm any suspicion of abuse by building a consensus among family members—including the perpetrator—that in fact it has occurred. This should be done within the framework of a therapeutic assessment rather than as a legal investigation. If the recognition of abuse is shared among at least some family members and the perpetrator acknowledges it in some fashion, then the therapist can best support the family's own power and internal locus of control by facilitating them in filing a report themselves. If a single family member claims that abuse has taken place and/or if the alleged perpetrator vigorously denies its occurrence, then the therapist should report the allegation—*without stating any conclusions regarding its accuracy.* When necessary, we believe that the best approach for the therapist is to frame the situation as a reflection of the perpetrator/victim interaction pattern. Though the pattern itself is maladaptive, this approach fits the social ecology of the incestuous situation; therefore, it is familiar in some way to all family members. By "joining" the family pattern at this point, the therapist attempts to protect the connection with *all* family members, including the perpetrator. Further, this approach helps the therapist once again avoid the maladaptive Rescuer role into which he or she may be cast by various family members and others.

EXAMPLE

A family is referred for treatment after the stepfather, Andrew, has been convicted and imprisoned for child sexual abuse with preadolescent boys, including his 11-year-old stepson, Tim. Andrew has spent six months in a minimum security prison sex offender treatment program, and he now can obtain passes for family therapy and for weekend visits with his family. The children are claiming that molestation occurred on Andrew's last visit home.

Therapist: [*To Andrew*] Now that Tim has said that you masturbated him, and your two girls claim to have seen you do it, I'm stuck with having to file a report, even though you say it never happened. I feel really bad about having to do this, but I have no choice. My hands are tied; the law requires that I do this. But I don't want it to interfere with our work together, because I really want to be helpful to you and your family no matter what happened. But there's no way to avoid it; kids claiming abuse need to be protected. Of course, I'll indicate that you deny it took place.

In a carefully balanced way, the therapist is conveying empathy with the perpetrator while also modeling self-responsibility. He points to concerns about the therapeutic relationship while reinforcing the importance of intervention into abuse. The therapeutic concerns are emphasized even while the obligatory exercise of social control is occurring. In short, the therapist attempts to strike a pace/lead balance, speaking to both the perpetrator and the victim parts of the offender.

Within the family system some juggling also is required when the possibility of additional abuse is raised in the course of therapy. Unless there is evidence of retraumatization or imminent physical danger to a child (in which case drastic steps in management need to be taken, just as one might take them when an adult client is imminently suicidal), the therapist is well-advised to use one or more family therapy sessions, and perhaps some time with individual family members, to let the possibility of more abuse "cook out" of the family system in its own characteristic way. That is, the therapist can permit the family to experience another crisis in the form of discovering additional abuse or relapse on the part of the perpetrator. This time, however, the therapeutic context can aid family members in functioning more appropriately and effectively to handle the crisis. Boundary violations can be corrected, confused roles can be clarified, power/control dynamics can be rebalanced, and responsibility can be redirected. These changes can be an important remedy for the distorted transactional patterns that the family members brought with them into therapy, which may have been aggravated by various professional and legal agencies involved in intervention following the revelation of abuse. Again we remind the reader that the basic structure of intervention into the incestuous family system often tends to deepen the very patterns that therapy attempts to alter.

EXAMPLE

Therapist: [*To a 15-year-old incest victim*] So Linda, you're not sure you want to have any more visits from your dad, even if they're supervised, because you're upset that he seems to be doing some uncomfortable things with you again?

Daughter: Yes, he always pulls me up against him when he hugs me, like he's wanting to feel my breasts again.

Therapist: And I know it's still difficult for you to tell your father not to do something, because you don't want him to be any angrier with you than he is already — and that's hard, isn't it? [*Linda nods in agreement and begins to cry softly.*]

Therapist: [*To the father*] Howard, you're angry with her for accusing you again of doing something inappropriate when you can't figure out why she gets upset or how your attempts to be affectionate could be a problem?

Father: Yeah. She's the one who comes over to me for a hug, and I don't know what I'm supposed to do. Here I thought we were finally making some progress toward getting the family together again, and I've told everyone how sorry I am about what happened, and now this. . . . It's like we're starting all over again.

Therapist: [*Addressing the mother*] And, Gerrie, you're caught in the middle again, not knowing who to believe or what to do. [*The mother nods, begins to leak tears, and looks down to avoid eye contact as the therapist continues.*] On top of everything else, if any more sexual abuse occurs, it's supposed to be reported! Wow, it really *is* like things are back to where they were when you first were sent to see me. But this time, you've figured out some things, plus you've got me and others around to help out if necessary.

Father: [*Angrily*] This is ridiculous! [*Long pause following this **perpetrator-like outburst***] I seem to get in trouble no matter what I do — I can't win. [***Victim response emerges***]

Therapist: Maybe all of you can work together on this and do something different this time. Linda, when your father hugs you like he has, does it feel to you like he's abusing you just as he was before when you reported it?

Daughter: Not really, I just don't want him to do anything that would lead to anything like . . . you know . . . like before.

Therapist: So you need to know that he doesn't have the same things in his mind that he did before? How would you know that?

Daughter: I—I don't know.

Therapist: No, you can't really know for sure what's going on in his mind, can you? Just as he can't really know what's going on in your mind. Do you believe him when he says he's trying to do things the right way now?

Daughter: Yes.

Therapist: [*Addressing the father*] Did you know that your hugs were bothering your daughter?

Father: No—well, I knew something was wrong sometimes, but I thought it was just because we're both on edge about what's happened.

Therapist: But you heard her say now that it's bothering her. What could you do to be certain she wouldn't have to be at all worried?

Father: Well, I suppose I could just not hug her.

Therapist: But both of you agreed that she sometimes comes to you for a hug, perhaps for some reassurance that you won't be angry at her forever for reporting the abuse.

Father: Well, then, I guess I have to ask her what's okay.

Therapist: How about doing that right now, while everyone is here together? Perhaps everyone in the family should talk a bit about that. Gerrie, has your husband ever been affectionate or sexual with you in some way that you didn't particularly want, but were not able to be clear with him?

Mother: Yes, I guess so.

Therapist: All right, then, that's something the three of us can talk about in a marital session. Right now, let's figure out some ways that the entire family can be clear with each other about how to be affectionate.

Combined with an explicitly stated willingness on the part of the therapist to take action when she believes that reporting is necessary, this approach to the possibility of additional abuse within the family can facilitate a creative blending of therapeutic and social control agendas. The ecological balancing is further enhanced when the family therapist has a good working relationship with the child protection agency so that each trusts the other to use good sense in handling suspected incidents of reabuse (see below).

Distinguishing Evaluation and Therapy

Professionals involved in dealing with family sexual abuse always should make a rigorous distinction between the activities associated with evaluation and those associated with therapy. The burden of this distinction lies primarily with the therapist, since others may not recognize the differences in function or may wish to have the roles mixed to suit their own purposes. For example, an agency supervisor may know that the social workers responsible for child protection also have counseling skills that could be useful with families in crisis, thereby encouraging her to assign a staff member to carry out all of the functions necessary for dealing with a particular incest family. Or an attorney may advise her offender client to begin therapy prior to adjudication, with an eye toward requesting a formal evaluation for legal purposes at a later date. A therapist should avoid these dual roles, both for ethical and for practical reasons.

Formal evaluations of any kind are *not* a legitimate part of the therapeutic endeavor. Even when they are presumed to be written from a perspective favorable to a client, they often are not in the best interests of that client's *therapeutic* goals. Formal evaluations of individual clients or families that are to be used within the context of the legal system are *not* the same as psychological or family assessments conducted as an integral part of the therapy process. The former are constructed on the basis of the evaluator being "outside" the client system, minimizing the subjective elements of interaction with the clients. The latter are directed, in part, toward developing a relationship between the therapist and the client system in order to achieve the understanding and mutuality of effort necessary for effective treatment. Mixing these functions constitutes a dual relationship with the clients, an issue that is addressed as a potential ethical problem in the codes of conduct of most health professions (significantly, it is only beginning to be considered in the ethical codes of those in the legal professions).

It is always possible to have evaluations done by professionals outside the immediate treatment situation. Even in the smallest rural agency in which resources may be sparse, family members can be sent elsewhere for evaluation purposes. At the very least, staff at such agencies can agree to trade roles so that they are not put in the position of evaluating clients on their own therapy caseloads. We have resolutely refused to conduct formal evaluations with individuals or families with whom we work in therapy. When requested (or ordered) to provide such evaluations in connection with court actions involving our clients, we respond with carefully written *treatment summaries*, which may include recommendations for outside evaluation of the clients and of the effectiveness of our therapeutic efforts to date.

If we agree to serve as formal evaluators of individuals or to participate in the evaluation of an overall incest family situation, then we undertake an *ecosystemic analysis* that is designed to highlight the underlying structures and transactional patterns of the family (described in Chapters 3 and 4). Although we attempt to gain access to all family members, our approach is the same even if we are limited to only one individual. We consider the task to be one of examining the intrapsychic ecology of each family member as well as the social ecology of the family and its environment. On this basis we can (a) describe the events reported by various family members, (b) compare the data with that from other cases and research findings, and (c) draw conclusions about the functioning of the individual(s) and the family at the current time. While inferences can be drawn regarding what may have occurred in the past or what might be anticipated in the future, we typically leave these inferences to others in the legal system. We do not state whether or not incest in fact did occur in this particular family (an investigative task) or whether an individual will or will not reoffend (an act of prognostication for which a therapist is not equipped). Instead, we attempt to provide a very comprehensive picture of a complex ecology against the background of what is known about perpetrators, victims, and incestuous families. Ideally, this can provide assistance in drawing legal conclusions and in making judgments about a course of action to avoid abuse in the future. Verdicts of "innocent" or "guilty" belong to judge or jury, as do decisions regarding the safety of victims and the ajudication of perpetrators.

Writing Treatment Plans and Summaries

Therapists working with one or more members of an incestuous family should be prepared to develop specific treatment plans with revelant background, recognized diagnoses, and detailed treatment objectives (see Chapter 6). This is particularly important for the family therapist, whose role should include coordination of treatment efforts for various family members. Not only are such treatment plans a necessary part of responsible record-keeping, they also can be useful for inclusion in various documents or reports related to the legal disposition of the case. Naturally, clients need to be made aware of the various uses to which such plans can be put and to provide the necessary consent for such uses. Copies of client materials should be forwarded only if *each* client involved is convinced that such a step would be in his or her best interest. The therapist's primary loyalty must be to his client.

We recognize that the requirements of the legal system may limit the rights of minors or of offenders more than is typically the case among voluntary therapy clients. Nevertheless, we believe that the therapist should make every effort to protect clients' privacy within the limits of legal requirements and professional ethics. Again, the burden is on the therapist to recognize the objectives of treatment and to balance these against the circumstances of the larger social ecology, including the legal system. The therapist should be under no illusion that the release of certain records are for the client's good when, in fact, such release is required by the legal system. We have encountered numerous therapists who argue that "confronting offenders with the consequences of their misbehavior" is therapeutic. We agree in principle, but disagree with the process if it involves releasing case material against the wishes of a client. Clients whose materials are used by the legal or social service systems in ways beyond their control are victimized in this process. Such revictimization, even of a perpetrator, may be necessary; however, it should not be considered helpful to the therapeutic process. Alternately, what might be helpful is working with the client to develop a mutually acceptable report that still meets the requirements of the legal system.

Treatment summaries should contain a description of the treatment process and should reflect the therapist's understanding of the current status of the family (or family member) in the larger ecology of the treatment situation. Such summaries necessarily are written from the standpoint of the therapist as a *participant* in the treatment process, and such reports should not lay claim to undue objectivity. Certainly, the therapist need not assume the same perspective as the client, nor need the therapist reflect the internal experience of the family system. Nevertheless, she or he is attempting to represent that experience in some way to the outside world, and such a representation certainly should demonstrate considerable empathy with the client(s). At the same time, the therapist's report will reflect her self-interest; presumably, she wants the summary to cast a positive light on her treatment efforts. Here, too, a balance is required. A therapist should never write a treatment summary at the expense of a client; though resistance and failures on the part of the client(s) can be acknowledged, the therapist is an equal participant in the therapeutic ecosystem and must assume an equal share of responsibility for any shortcomings in the effectiveness of treatment. The therapist should avoid confusing ecosystemic analysis with prediction of behavior, although a risk assessment for danger to a child or relapse by a perpetrator can be legitimate in certain situations — as long as the therapist understands, and helps others understand, that an assessment is grounded in the present and cannot predict the future.

Responding to Subpoenas

Insofar as possible, the family therapist should avoid being placed into a position in the social ecology of incest treatment that will result in a summons to a legal deposition or court appearance. This reflects our very strong belief that a mental health professional *acting in the capacity of therapist* ought to have the same immunity from legal testimony as that afforded priests and attorneys — for essentially the same reasons. This is not simple self-indulgence. The role of the therapist vis-à-vis an individual client or family can turn a court appearance into an act of betrayal, even when the therapist's intention is to advocate. Further, the status of therapy as a form of moral discourse (see Chapter 2) sets the stage for significant conflict with the assumptions and procedures of the legal system. In reality, however, therapists currently working with incestuous families often have a high degree of exposure to legal mandates.

Given the therapist's position within the social ecology of incest intervention, we advise a vigorous attempt to avoid being deposed or summoned to the courtroom. Often, this can be accomplished by negotiating directly with clients or their attorneys regarding the balance of good to be served versus the potential for damage to the therapeutic relationship or to the clients. Whenever possible, this negotiation should be undertaken in a friendly and collaborative manner. Occasionally, however, the therapist may have to respond to heavy-handed legal tactics by asserting counterbalancing power, perhaps by pointing out to the attorney that he or she possesses information that could be damaging to more than one client or by noting that coerced testimony could lead to hostile responses which might negatively influence the attorney's case.

In situations in which the therapist is forced to provide information in a legal context against her or his wishes, a victim-like response similar to that used for mandatory reporting of abuse is the best attitude to adopt with the client(s) — even those on whose side the therapist may be required to appear. Regardless of the circumstances at the time of the required legal involvement, this orientation can be thought of as an investment in future therapy. That is, as much as possible the therapist preserves an equidistance between family members that will allow for greater behavioral flexibility in the future. Maintaining a kind of "neutrality" about the legal process will permit the therapist to embrace, critique, or reframe the results of any legal outcome in a way that can be useful to the clients in treatment.

The approach we have just described extends to the use of treatment records in building a court case. All narrative casenotes describing the therapeutic process should be considered "compromised" in the same way in which data gathered via hypnosis are often excluded from legal use. Not only is therapy a form of trance-like process in itself, the written records of therapeutic interaction reflect a substantial degree of subjectivity on the part of both client(s) and therapist, making their use as a basis for "findings of fact" extremely questionable. Casenotes are not an accurate account of what actually happened in therapy — depicting therapist-client interaction in the manner of a videotape recorder—any more than a client's report of experiences to a therapist is an objectively rendered account of actual life events. In our view, testimony from a therapist regarding incest treatment ought to be limited to more objective verifiable issues: presenting problem, formal diagnosis, dates and types of contact, and the like.

Preparing Children to be Witnessses

As previously described, serious questions again are being raised regarding the reliability of children's accounts of sexual abuse, with a particular focus on controversies over the nature of memory (Dent & Flin, 1992; Dziech & Schudson, 1991; Fincham et al., 1994a, 1994b; Gardner, 1992; Loftus & Ketcham, 1994; Myers, 1992; Ofshe & Watters, 1994; Schetky & Green, 1988). Despite these questions, children continue to be witnesses in incest cases. Although she may be consulted, the therapist typically does not decide whether or not a child testifies in court. That decision usually lies with an attorney or a judge, based upon certain legal criteria, which require that the child have (a) the capacity to observe events; (b) sufficient memory to recall events; (c) the ability to communicate; (d) the ability to distinguish fact from fantasy; and (e) an understanding of the difference between telling the truth and lying—along with an appreciation of the fact that it is wrong to lie (Myers, 1992). A therapist working with a young incest victim may be asked about the potential impact of testifying on the child's mental health. The therapist is expected to provide accurate information and to offer his professional judgment regarding the child. If the court deems the child a credible witness, the therapist should help the client manage this intrusive and threatening process. Assisting a child or adolescent with the court experience can be thought of as "simply another phase of treatment" (Everstine & Everstine, 1989, p. 172).

Certainly, the child's experience with the legal process can have a profound effect on therapy and on the eventual outcome of treatment. A criminal trial in connection with incest can be devastating for a child as well as for the relationships between family members. Because the victim's eyewitness account of the abuse is usually critical to successful prosecution of the perpetrator (indeed, it may be the only real evidence), the child may come under severe pressure from a defense attorney attempting to discredit her testimony (Goodman, 1984). Testifying in court can precipitate intense stress, thereby creating a secondary victimization experience for the child. In our experience, often the decision to separate the incest perpetrator and victim until the later stages of treatment is made for legal rather than therapeutic reasons. There is fear that the mere proximity of the perpetrating family member will cause the child to alter or recant her accusation, weakening the prosecution's case. Though this concern might be justified in a few cases, we believe that interaction in the context of therapy can reduce the likelihood of such changes; further, we believe that the risk is justified by the benefits of family therapy for all concerned.

While some psychological testing may be useful in judging the child's capacity and readiness for court testimony, the major criterion should be the therapist's assessment based upon ongoing work with the child. Here, too, the therapist's analysis should include the ecology of the incest situation and of the circumstances surrounding the revelation and intervention into the sexual abuse. Of primary importance is the child's current relationship with various members of her family and the potential impact of courtroom testimony on these relationships. A child with strong psychological ties to the accused perpetrator can suffer substantial difficulty, even trauma, if she perceives that her testimony results in his being sent to prison. Reassurance from outsiders can do little to lessen this pain. Even the angry victim is likely to experience some guilt in connection with her testimony against the alleged perpetrator. On the other hand, if the child's primary bond is with a nonoffending adult who is sympathetic and supportive, then the emotional impact is lessened considerably. Of course, some judgment will need to be made concerning the impact of the child's testimony on that adult. For example, successful prosecution that sends the perpetrator to jail and leaves the family in severe financial crisis may create such stress for the nonoffending spouse that the child's security is threatened, and the remaining parent may be unable to mask her anger about these consequences. Investigating family coalitions both before and after revelation of the incest can be extremely useful in evaluating a child's readiness for court testimony. In our view, the benefits of having the child participate in the legal process always must be balanced against the potential for long-range damage to the child and to her relationship to her family.

In addition, the therapist should weigh the nature, frequency, and severity of the child's current symptomatic behaviors. Stress indicators, such as nightmares, regressive behaviors (such as bed-wetting or soiling), depressive/suicidal ideation, self-injury, or patterns of acting out (such as fire-setting) raise questions about the child's ability to cope with the added pressures of testifying. Conversely, evaluating the child's functioning in other spheres of life, such as school and peer relationships, and the stability of support systems, such as friends and extended family members, can highlight resources that may help relieve the strains of participating in the legal process.

The child's ability to develop a positive bond with the therapist also is important. Will the child be able to utilize therapy as a resource to deal with the stress of testifying? Since the child inevitably will personalize the court process, an assessment of her capacity to express and manage her feelings about the sexual abuse can be an indicator of her ability to do the same with the trial. Evidence of resiliancy in coping with the incest and its disclosure suggest that the child can adequately manage elements of the legal process.

Cultural and ethnic factors also should be considered when assessing the potential role of a child in the legal process. Pressure may arise from a variety of sources in the extended family or the community. For example, an African-American child reporting incest may have the added burden of disclosing negative information not only about a family member, but about a male of her race whom her community is struggling to empower (and whom she has been raised to protect). An American-Indian adolescent may struggle with participating in a legal system dominated by those outside of her ethnic community. An Asian-American female may have been raised to honor cultural taboos against talking about sexual matters with males in a public setting. The social context can exert considerable pressure upon all family members involved in the prosecution of incest, and the resultant stresses on the child victim may be intense.

No single legal protocol exists for dealing with children, although courts across the country have attempted to make courtrooms and legal procedures more hospitable to children. Environmental alterations include the use of rooms with child-size furniture, various props to facilitate testimony, and one-way windows to permit more privacy for the child when testifying. Procedural changes such as closed courtrooms, televised interviews in judges' chambers, limitations on both direct and cross-examinations, and the creative use of videotapes to limit repetitive interviews are becoming more common (Dent & Flin, 1992; Schetky & Green, 1988). Perhaps more important than anything else in determining what the child will encounter in the legal prosecution of incest is the orientation of the judge trying the case. If a therapist has an ongoing role in assisting child victims during legal proceedings, she should make an effort to learn as much as possible about the local criminal justice personnel and procedures.

Sometimes, group approaches to preparation can be useful if there are sufficient numbers of children to justify the time and expense. An example is the "Court Prep Group," developed in Nashville, Tennessee, by the National Children's Advocacy Center (Dent & Flin, 1992). Two versions of the program are offered, one for preadolescent children and the other for teenagers. The first two sessions, held away from the court building, focus on developing comfort with others in the group, identifying feelings about the upcoming trial, and providing concrete information about court procedures through drawings and role-play. The next three sessions are held in the courthouse and include a tour of courtrooms, a game to help identify roles of key personnel, and a mock court role-play focusing on appropriate witness behavior. The final session reinforces what has been learned and provides closure on the group experience.

Therapists who work with only one child at a time can adequately prepare most clients even without a structured group experience like that described above. The same overall principles apply:

- Material should be geared to the age and developmental stage of the child.
- The legal proceedings should be described and explained so that the child will know what to expect.
- The child should be encouraged to talk about her feelings so that she can be reassured and given support (even negative feelings like anger or panic should be labeled and discussed).
- The child should visit the courthouse and meet as many of the trial's key personnel as possible so that she can become acquainted with the facilities and staff outside of the proceedings themselves.

The incest victim's ambivalence about testifying should always be kept in mind, even when it is not manifested directly in her words or behavior. Discussing the legal proceedings in the context of family therapy or in sessions involving selected family members can be extremely useful. However, if family members are split in their opinions of the child's revelation or they are angry at her for the disruption created by reporting the abuse, then the child will need help dealing with this discord. The therapist may need to help the child recognize that she can trust her own convictions and survive even if she is not believed by *any* other family members. However, the profound impact of this realization on the child should not be minimized; it will take time to work through. Sometimes, it is useful to work on preparing the child for court in the context of family sessions that include the alleged perpetrator. As contradictory as it might appear at first, working with the entire incestuous family on these issues takes advantage of the natural structures of ambivalence that already exist in the family system. We have had success at convincing perpetrator and victim that they do not have to "lose" each other simply because they were involved in activities that created this crisis. It is particularly useful to coach the perpetrator to reassure the young victim that permanent alienation and abandonment will not occur simply because she tells the court what she believes to be true. Although this approach does not work with every family, it is helpful in a surprisingly large number of instances.

Entire courses exist to train professionals in the etiquette of trial procedures and the strategies of courtroom testimony. This information and at least some of the techniques are applicable to children as well. For example, the child witness should know that she can ask for questions to be reworded and that she can say "I don't know" in response to questions for which she has no answer—despite the possibility of being pressured by an attorney. Typically, the child on the witness stand is frightened that she will do something wrong, so educating and encouraging her with ways to do it "right" can be very empowering to the child. At the same time, the therapist—and others concerned with the child's testimony—should be rigorous in their efforts to avoid "suggesting" information or answers that might influence the content of the testimony.

Again, we remind the reader of the diffuse intrapsychic and interpersonal boundaries of incest family members. An enduring problem to be faced in legal proceedings is the unconscious distortions of reality that the child has learned in her family of origin. On the witness stand, reconstructing her experiences within these distorted frameworks can make the child's account appear inconsistent or even untrue. This is particularly likely when a trial occurs prior to, or early in, the treatment process. At this stage, the child's reality is very much intertwined with that of other family members. Later in treatment, the child's sense of self may be stronger, and the delineation of boundaries that permits recognition of legitimate differences in experiences among family members is usually easier. At the same time, a child sexually abused by an older family member will continue to need recognition and support for the inevitable confusion in her feelings about activities that may have felt "good" even while being judged "bad" by others or that may have felt "bad" even while occurring with family members about whom she is supposed to feel "good." These are the inherent paradoxes of incest, and they are often the basis for the disturbing symptoms that can result.

Over and above the incestuous dynamics, the child testifying in court about incestuous activities will be violating a social taboo. Talking about sex in public, with strangers, can be extraordinarily stressful for children. Most North American children learn early in life that sex-related talk can be problematic in public—despite the proliferation of titillating topics on television talk shows and soap operas. If the victim has been told specifically not to talk about the incest, perhaps even threatened if she does so, she can find trial-related testimony enormously stressful. Again, working with the victim in the context of family therapy can be beneficial. Dealing with the incest in family sessions helps generate more open rules about communication. Thus the family works to counter its own previously imposed barriers to truth and openness, reducing the need for the therapist to counter these rules and freeing the victim to internalize greater comfort with openness.

Following a court appearance, any young member of an incest family is likely to need help processing the experience, particularly if testimony involved significant conflict or brought about substantial changes in the family system. No matter how well prepared the child is for the legal proceedings, the reality of testimony leading to conviction and imprisonment of the perpetrator and/or significant disruption to the family household (such as removal of other children from the home or termination of parental rights) will leave the victim feeling conflicted. Once again, *a major focus of therapy should be on the victim's loyalty to the family and her ambivalence about the results of intervention.* If the perpetrator is found guilty, it could mean prolonged separation and hardship coupled with feelings of relief that the abuse and its immediate aftermath are over. If the perpetrator is not convicted, the victim might fear retaliation or more abuse, along with relief that no one will go to jail. At this juncture, family therapy should focus on the delicate balance between strengthening family ties despite disruption and working to reduce the pathological aspects of family functioning.

Serving as an Expert Witness

Serving as an "expert" on a case most often is a voluntary undertaking by a professional not directly involved in the treatment process itself (Blau, 1984; Gardner, 1989; McClosky & Egeth, 1983; Melton, Petrila, Poythress, & Slobogin, 1987; Myers, 1992; Wynne et al., 1986). This individual may be hired by one of the sides in an adversarial situation or, less often, by the court itself to serve as a more neutral resource.[2] An expert can be useful when general information is sought about incestuous behavior, family dynamics, impact of abuse on victims, or the personalities of perpetrators. In addition, professionals may testify about the merits of diagnoses, treatment preferences, or other aspects of intervention into sexual abuse. Some experts are hired to examine the testing results or treatment records of clients or to conduct independent evaluations of a client's or family's status at a particular point in time. All of these are legitimate roles for professionals to assume if they are not already involved, and don't intend to be involved, in *treating* any clients in the case. By providing expert testimony, therapists are functioning as "scientists" rather than as "clinicians" (Barden, 1994).

Mental health professionals should make an effort to avoid engaging in a "battle of the experts," even though combat lines may be drawn by opposing attorneys. Experts should think of themselves primarily as courtroom educators or as advocates for a particular point of view on whatever phenomenon is in focus in the legal hearing, for example, the psychologi-

---

[2]Technically, the legal system can also designate as "expert witnesses" those professionals who are involved in the investigation, evaluation, or treatment of a particular child sexual abuse case. Such individuals may be invited or subpoenaed to appear in court in connection with the case, presumably utilizing their professional expertise in their testimony. For purposes of discussion in this chapter, we consider expert witnesses to be therapists and other mental health professionals who are *not* involved in a particular case, but agree to have a specific role in connection with legal proceedings. This distinction also reflects our strong opinion that the role of mental health professionals in the legal system, particularly as expert witnesses, ought to be modified.

cal consequences for the child of reporting incestuous abuse or the efficacy of a particular kind of treatment for offenders. The testifying expert should avoid drawing conclusions about the occurrence or non-occurrence of incest or about the guilt or innocence of a perpetrator; *drawing such conclusions is the responsibility of persons designated by the court.* However, some attorneys attempt to seduce or coerce such conclusions from expert witnesses, hoping to influence the judge or jury.

Similarly, therapists serving as expert witnesses should be extremely cautious about commentary on the work of other helping professionals, particularly about drawing conclusions regarding the "success" of their treatment. Our concern here is not with guild-like protectionism, but with appropriate modesty regarding the nature and results of therapy. The scientific research base for successful outcomes of therapy is mixed (Barkley, Guevremont, Anastopoulos, & Fletcher, 1992; Conte & Karasu, 1992; Lipsey & Wilson, 1993; Shadish, 1992; Shadish et al., 1993). Certainly, questions can be raised about the known extent or efficacy of certain treatment techniques. However, short of breaches of law, morality, or personal integrity, little that is done in the process of therapy can be scientifically proven to be "wrong" or "useless." Instead, there are differences in theoretical approach and in personal working style; differing criteria may be used to determine when a particular objective has been reached. Nevertheless, it is tempting for outside experts to retrospectively criticize certain actions of a therapist once an outcome is known. Hindsight is as much a part of therapy as it is of athletic events; in principle, anyone who is not personally involved in a given therapeutic situation (including untrained nonprofessionals) can find something to criticize or to suggest. Any experienced supervisor knows that reviewing tapes or records of therapy sessions provides endless opportunities for "what if" speculations and alternative scenarios that might have been more useful. Certainly, criticisms and concerns can be raised in the course of review and testimony by an expert witness. To be ethical, however, the professional should avoid drawing absolutistic conclusions on the basis of those criticisms and concerns. Such conclusions should be left to others who are appropriately designated in the legal system.

A variety of books have been written as guides for mental health professionals serving as expert witnesses in legal proceedings. Some of these (e.g., Blau, 1984; Brodsky, 1991; Veitch, 1993) contain practical, detailed advice on how to behave at depositions, in the courtroom, and in related situations: For example, make eye contact with the jury, don't volunteer information that is not requested, don't become angry when cross-examined by a hostile attorney, DO prepare carefully, and so on — many of them suggestions that can be helpful in the process of legal testimony in child sexual abuse cases. Other writings (e.g., Gardner, 1992; Myers, 1992) are directed more generally at providing information on the legal issues currently reflected in child abuse cases. For example, Myers (1992) analyzes the legal framework for interviewing children about sexual abuse, including a discussion of the current trend toward attacking the professional who did the interview as a primary defense against an allegation of abuse. In addition, these authors discuss the legal status of various scientific controversies related to child abuse, such as general incidence studies, the validity of various assessment instruments, the reliability of memory in adults and children, and the credibility of medical findings.

We strongly recommend that any therapist interested in serving as an expert witness on incest cases be thoroughly familiar with these materials as well as with the details of the cases themselves. Further, we concur with those who argue that mental health professionals ought to be more cautious and more modest in their interactions with the legal system. While we fully recognize the ethical responsibilities of mental health professionals and the necessary social implications of their roles, we repeat our conviction that *therapy must not be confused with social control*. We believe that therapists have become far too involved in legal proceedings in recent years (mostly around issues of child custody and child abuse), contributing to a misperception by the public and by legal professionals that therapists have the ability to decide whether or not a crime has been committed, to predict the future behavior of disturbed individuals, and to definitively cure individuals of socially harmful problems. Mental health professionals have had a role in setting the stage for the disillusionment and subsequent backlash. Despite the lure of financial gain from expert witness work, we believe that therapists' claims of expertise ought to become more circumspect.

Working with Penal Institutions

Therapists are most likely to interact with penal institutions in one of two ways. Sometimes, parole officers or other criminal justice personnel will contact therapists working with convicted offenders to obtain information or to discuss coordination of efforts. The therapist should exercise the utmost caution in disclosing any information or offering any opinions without discussing and obtaining consent from the client. At the same time, we applaud any efforts to coordinate treatment, and we urge the family therapist to creatively seek ways to work cooperatively with criminal justice staff. The other major form of interaction occurs when some kind of treatment takes place within the confines of a penal institution. Therapists may be employed as staff of a prison facility or hired as consultants to do evaluations or to conduct therapy groups. Many of these efforts have proven to be ineffective or even counterproductive in offender treatment.[3] As we have indicated, the biggest problem with prison-based therapy is that it reflects boundary diffusion and role confusion; further, with its compliance-based orientation, it replicates the perpetrator/victim interaction pattern already so familiar to offenders. In prison, the sex offender may be under even more pressure to perpetrate (at least in subtle ways) as a defense against being victimized by other inmates, guards, or even treatment staff.

In our experience, it is possible to structure treatment for many sex offenders, including incest perpetrators, in a way that takes advantage of the social control provided by the institutional context while developing a supportive therapeutic milieu via groups and one-to-one sessions.[4] A therapist can also undertake family therapy sessions at penal facilities or can secure passes for offenders to attend outpatient treatment (often accompanied by guards or parole officers). Occasionally, we have even secured a pass for an incarcerated female offender to travel to the men's prison for conjoint therapy with her spouse. These arrangements require good working relationships with criminal justice staff; under such circumstances, staff members can become supportive and useful in treatment efforts. However, boundaries and roles must be carefully clarified and maintained. Conducting family therapy while an offender is incarcerated sends a powerful message to clients that the welfare of family members and the value of the family unit are just as important as societal requirements for safety and justice. Further, the offender's prison experience typically includes elements of victimization that can be useful in treatment, potentially increasing the perpetrator's ability to identify with family members he has victimized. Of course, some aspects of the incarceration experience can also trigger rage, shame, and defensiveness; the family therapist must be prepared to control the conjoint sessions so that they do not work to the disadvantage of any family member (including the perpetrator).

INTERFACING WITH THE SOCIAL SERVICE SYSTEM

Throughout this book, we have noted the ecological complexity of family sexual abuse. The processes of intervention and treatment only in-

[3]One study in Minnesota (*Star Tribune*, 1991) found that sex offenders who received treatment while incarcerated had a higher recidivism rate than those not receiving treatment. Despite some obvious methodological problems with this nonacademic research effort, such results are disheartening. At the same time, some excellent prison-based treatment programs have been developed and evaluated over the past decade or longer, providing hope that some of the treatment techniques devised can be exported to other settings and adapted to the particular requirements of differing populations of offenders.

[4]A description of this approach can be found in our book *Child Sexual Abuse: An Ecological Approach to Treating Victims and Perpetrators*.

crease this complexity. Opportunities for boundary violations and role confusion proliferate, not to mention the tendency to isomorphically replicate the perpetrator/victim interaction pattern among helping professionals. We have described some of the difficulties therapists might encounter when interfacing with respreatatives of the legal system. Here we will discuss other problems that may arise in the attempt to coordinate therapy with other elements of intervention. One advantage of interacting with the legal system—the clear objectives and responsibilities of criminal justice personnel—is not necessarily present when interacting with social service workers, whose views and objectives may be considerably less apparent or more inconsistent.

Role Confusion

Sometimes, intervening into family sexual abuse appears to require "a cast of thousands." In reality, only a handful of professionals are likely to be involved in a given case; however, their own confusion about roles or procedures, plus problems in communication or delegation of responsibility, may produce uncertainty, duplication of effort, or repetition in steps taken to intervene into the abusive situation. Providing appropriate protection for victims, fulfilling certain legal mandates, and initiating treatment are all tasks to be undertaken by various social service personnel. Sometimes, an individual's disciplinary training or theoretical orientation may predispose her to mix social control and treatment agendas. At other times, agency administrators may assign multiple and conflicting tasks to a single staff person. Frequently, family members may attempt to solicit social service workers to undertake various functions outside the requirements of a given role. Clearly, social service professionals are required to do a great deal of "juggling" as the process of intervening into family sexual abuse gets underway.

Into this context the family therapist must enter and proceed to secure a place in the social ecology that permits both power and flexibility. Ideally, the therapist who works with the incestuous family ought to be considered the coordinator of treatment efforts. In practice, this role is often assumed by a child protection worker. This may appear logical to some; however, it is a maladaptive undertaking that creates confusion by mixing efforts at treatment and social control. In contrast, the family therapist can establish a position as advocate and resource for the *family*, without the aura of anxiety and suspicion that typically surrounds the protection worker in her role as surrogate parent.

Since role confusion is so typical of families in which sexual abuse has occurred, it should not be replicated in the family's treatment context, lest the family be influenced to maintain its maladaptive patterns of functioning. Further, confusion about roles and tasks in the environment is likely to lead to power struggles among helping professionals, further hampering treatment efforts by maintaining perpetrator/victim interaction patterns. Insofar as possible, both family members and participating professionals should be able to clearly identify the intentions and functions of each individual involved in the intervention process, including how these may change with the passing of time. This is no small undertaking and requires considerable energy for communication; however, it has great potential benefit for therapy.

A final observation: We believe that intervention into family sexual abuse tends to elicit extreme responses by the social service system. On the one hand, complaints frequently have been voiced in public forums about the *lack* of responsiveness of social service workers to many suspected cases of child sexual or physical abuse. On the other hand, there is evidence that the legal and social service systems sometimes may overcompensate by responding to certain cases with a barrage of activity involving a large number of personnel. Again, we advise balance; no worker should be involved with an incestuous family unless she or he has an active role with well-defined objectives.

Role Selection

In our experience, professionals working with incest families can develop mutual respect and appreciation for the requirements of each participant's role. Further, cooperative efforts can produce trust and a sense of support among those sharing a case. This eliminates competition among workers for the loyalty of family members, thereby reducing the polarization and triangulation that are so characteristic of perpetrator/victim systems. Establishing the family therapist as the coordinator of treatment sends a clear message to family members that their welfare as individuals and as a unit is of paramount importance. Further, it advertises the fact that the therapeutic work done by each individual has implications for all other family members. Finally, it aids in the all-important effort to separate therapeutic agendas from those of social control.

Also important is reaching agreement among those involved in intervention regarding who will play the role of the "heavy" at any given point in time. If at all possible, this role should be assigned by explicit agreement rather than having one particular person (such as the child protection worker) be cast automatically into that role by others or fall into it inadvertently while trying to do a competent job. Most incest treatment requires some sort of social pressure; however, the direction from which the pressure comes and its nature should vary from one situation to another and even from one period of time to another. In our experience, assigning the role of the social controller is best coordinated by the family therapist after assessing the meaning of the incestuous behavior in a particular family and examining the coalitions among family members (see Chapter 8).

Advocacy roles also should be agreed upon as explicitly as possible. Typically, a protection worker is viewed as a child advocate. Therapists working with individual family members usually are assumed to be advocates for the clients whom they are treating. However, an exception sometimes is made if the client is a perpetrator (Bera, 1990). Comfort with advocacy often differs according to the theoretical orientation and professional identity of various helping professionals.

The roles of school social workers, court personnel, foster parents, and the like are often unclear; therefore, they can be confusing to family members and even to others involved in intervention. A meeting of all those included in intervention and follow-up—with the family members present if at all possible—can be enormously beneficial in devising and implementing a viable treatment plan (see the discussion of team consultation in Chapter 9).

Coordination of Roles

Once selected or assigned, roles must be coordinated with an eye toward meeting the diverse objectives of social intervention (societal safety) and of treatment (effective individual and family functioning). A single professional such as the family therapist may serve formally as coordinator; however, productive cooperation requires self-conscious effort by everyone involved. First of all, each participant should be clear about what others expect in connection with his or her formal position and assigned role in a particular case. A spontaneous or planned change in role responsibility of one professional is likely to affect others, and a recalibration of the team's interventions is necessary. Those involved in incest treatment must make every effort to avoid stereotyping either family members or other professionals involved in the case. Expectations should be set by agreement rather than by default; anticipated difficulties should not be allowed to become self-fulfilling prophesies. In addition, the channels of communication and the limits of confidentiality need to be clear, and family members need to be informed of them. Some individuals may be privy to certain information to which others do not have access; this has to be understood and accepted. The misuse of communication, including secrets, is a fundamental characteristic of most incest families. Therefore, the modeling of openness and trust among professionals, balanced by respect for privacy, is an important contribution to family treatment.

Roles can and should vary somewhat over time. Not only is this necessary to meet the needs of the family (and perhaps the legal system), it also models the flexibility that the family members should learn. For example, although some sort of coercive pressure may have to remain in the background of treatment for some time, the person whose job it is to enforce certain requirements can change, for example, the monitoring efforts of a protective services staff member can be taken on by a school social worker, the frequent check-ins by an offender with a probation officer can be reduced and replaced by the regular check-ins with a group therapist, and so on.

All in all, the social service context of incest treatment can be a powerful force for positive change or an obstacle to effective therapy. Although the family therapist cannot control all of the variables in the intervention context, she can be assertive in bringing together various professionals for the purpose of better coordination. Further, she can be an advocate for the welfare of the incest family as a unit amidst the fluctuating, sometimes conflicting agendas of the social service system.

WORKING WITHIN MANAGED CARE SYSTEMS

The current focus on health care reform in the United States has created a climate of uncertainty and rapid change that challenges mental health professionals to examine both their methods and their results. Though the circumstances of the current transition are particular to the social and political context of the United States, the issues are by no means unique. All countries of the world confront the challenge of how to provide—and pay for—adequate health care services for their citizens. Health care delivery is truly one of the most prominent issues of human ecology. However, the strong emphasis on individualism and free enterprise in the United States, until recently, has permitted most social planners and policymakers to avoid dealing directly with issues that have faced other nations with more centralized social health systems. These countries have been forced to consider both short-term and long-term trends in health care delivery. Now, a combination of rapidly rising costs and the growing inaccessibility of health care to poor citizens has forced the United States to do the same.

A wide variety of issues in mental health care are highlighted when considering intervention and treatment services for family sexual abuse. The target is a multiproblem family in crisis whose members will probably require differing treatment and support services, usually on an involuntary basis; in addition, one or more of them may have been charged with a crime that is likely to have produced social and economic destabilization. In short, the uncovering of family sexual abuse typically produces a need for intensive, high-cost intervention and long-term follow-up—a discouraging combination for anyone having an economic stake in the situation. Thus, intervention into family sexual abuse might be thought of as confronting "a human ecological crisis."

In our view, the rationale for an ecological approach to incest treatment is clear. Intervention efforts must address simultaneously issues at the intrapsychic, familial, communal, and societal levels in order to effectively deal with the immediate problem and its potential long-term consequences for family members and for society. In countries with central government-based social health systems, the community's stake in comprehensive intervention into family sexual abuse is more readily recognized.[5] One way or another, the government will end up paying the bill, while in the United States an individual employer or insurance company can limit economic exposure by minimizing who is treated, under what circumstances, and for how long. For example, if an employed American father is convicted of incestuous abuse of his daughter, his insurance company may refuse to pay for his treatment because he has been charged with a crime or may limit any treatment coverage to a designated type of therapy or a specified amount of reimbursement. Further, the company may refuse coverage for "uninvolved" family members without a diagnoseable mental illness, thereby shifting liability for future problems (such as transmission of perpetrator/victim patterns that result in eventual offending behavior by one of the male siblings) to a different employer and insurance company. This may be smart business; however, it is bad social policy.

The emergence of more coordinated health care via health maintenance organizations (HMOs) and integrated service networks (ISNs) clearly has implications for family sexual abuse treatment efforts. There appears to be more support for broader ecological, family-oriented treatment methods among these organizations, just as there is in government-based programs. At the same time, the cost-containment efforts of managed health care require therapists to be more focused and more accountable for their work. In addition, dealing with involuntary clients at a time when large health care organizations are particularly wary of legal action that might be taken by dissatisfied or angry customers presents a continuing challenge.

Incestuous Families in a Managed Care Context

Careful coordination of treatment among various professionals is particularly important in the context of managed care. The intensive, crisis-oriented interventions following the uncovering of family sexual abuse can be an unwelcome intrusion into the busy schedules of mental health staff. The burdens of extra documentation or of interfacing with social service and legal personnel can create negative feelings about the case which spill

---

[5]This may explain why the principles and methods we are proposing in this book, until recently, have been received more positively by mental health professionals in Canada and in Western Europe than in the United States.

over into therapy sessions. Anxiety about treatment outcomes (including the possibility of complete decompensation by a traumatized victim or of recidivism by an offender) is likely to be high when the ambience of the organization is so highly focused upon demonstrated effectiveness within a framework of tight efficiency. Of course, these are potential issues for any professional dealing with family sexual abuse; however, the difficulties are likely to be intensified within the confines of a single managed care organization, such as an HMO. Thus, the risk of recreating the dysfunctional family patterns within the health care system is increased (Haley, 1975).

Members of incestuous families may have particular concerns about confidentiality when all or most of their treatment takes place under one roof, particularly if the organization is closely identified with an employer. This is especially true if the health care facility's staff had a role in uncovering and/or reporting the incest. Further, some family members may fear news of the abuse will get back to a primary health care provider within the system, further embarassing them or affecting the quality of services. Certainly, the offender and other family members will be anxious about the implications of any interaction between legal authorities and staff of the health care facility. Of course, the other side of the communication problems might also appear, for example, family members may be underresponsible in their own communications with their therapist and others because they presume that all of the health care providers within a given system are in continuous contact with one another. In view of these potential communication traps, collaborative planning and fully informed consent procedures with family members become especially significant.

Within the context of managed care, incest victims (particularly adult survivors), abuse perpetrators, and even entire families may become highly anxious and insecure about the extent and duration of treatment available to them. In many clinical settings today, therapy is seriously disrupted by uncertainty about reimbursement, by coerced switching of therapists due to staff turnover or changes in health coverage, or by drastic and abrupt termination of service following reviewers' decisions about lack of "medical necessity" for treatment. Since key elements of both victim and perpetrator therapy include relational stability, predictability of experience, and capacity for choice, these trends have created treatment complications. At least for the foreseeable future, sexually abusive families represent a considerable challenge for the managed health care industry.

At the same time, managed care facilities have certain potential advantages over independent mental health care practitioners. One is an increased possibility for coordination among professionals involved in intervention, including multimodal treatment options — individual, conjoint, and group therapies, offered simultaneously or sequentially — and even consultation team involvement. Another is better assurance of continuity and follow-up with family members, individually or together. Widely recognized difficulties with incest family treatment have included lack of follow-through on treatment by some family members, sudden disappearance of the family from therapy when coercive measures are removed, and refusal of contact by certain families or family members who are angered by intervention procedures at some point in the treatment process (see Chapter 12). The growing network of managed care facilities across the country increases the likelihood that individuals and families will remain in the same or affiliated health care plans and that records or other communications can travel more efficiently from one geographic area to another. Perhaps most important of all, networks of health care providers and underwriters may be encouraged to take more responsibility for comprehensive treatment of family sexual abuse and for its long-range effectiveness in order to reduce the staggering costs of child abuse and domestic violence to the national economy and to the employers who underwrite much of the cost of health care.

Brief Therapy on a Long-Term Basis

In the current managed care climate, increasing emphasis has been placed upon so-called "brief therapy." At the practical level, this term simply refers to accomplishing designated changes in the shortest possible time period, thereby cutting down on the cost of treatment. Further implied by the term when it is used within the context of managed care discussions is the notion that the outcomes of therapy can be observed and measured, thereby adding credibility to the effectiveness of some methods over others in utilization reviews (Poynter, 1994; Psychotherapy Finances, 1993; Woody, 1991). However, brief therapy also has a theoretical base, derived from several different historical sources. In part, the medical model of rapid symptom alleviation has been elaborated into crisis intervention, sex therapy, and medical hypnosis. Behavior modification techniques, rational-emotive therapy, and reality therapy also have made a contribution. However, the most prominent influences on contemporary brief therapy are to be found among clinicians associated directly or indirectly with family therapy, ranging from the communications analysis of Virginia Satir to the work of Gregory Bateson on the double-bind theory of schizophrenia to the indirect suggestions and metaphors in the hypnotherapy of Milton H. Erickson and the Neurolinguistic Programming tools of John Grinder and Richard Bandler (Bandler & Grinder, 1975, 1976; de Shazer, 1982; Haley, 1967, 1973, 1976; Satir, 1967; Sluzki & Ransom, 1976).

Today, the term "brief therapy" refers to a general cluster of methods sharing some common assumptions and principles. Such therapy is collaborative rather than hierarchical, focuses on solutions rather than problems, emphasizes meaning rather than truth, and utilizes constructive rather than analytic language (Epston, 1989; Friedman, 1993; M. White, 1986; White & Epston, 1990). Other than the earlier 10-session format of the Mental Research Institute's Brief Therapy Project (Bodin, 1981; Watzlawick, Weakland, & Fisch, 1974), this approach to treatment is not characterized by a single, specific time frame, although it may be advertised as "time-limited." In fact, its advocates tend to be open-ended, nondirective, even permissive in their problem-solving methods, creating an interesting juxtaposition of theory and practice in the context of managed mental health care.

In an elegant and provocative book, *The Complex Secret of Brief Psychotherapy*, James P. Gustafson (1986) summarizes the paradoxes inherent in the theory and practice of brief therapy:

> I ask this clinical theory of brief psychotherapy to help us in two broad ways. . . . First, the theory has to meet critiera of explanation for any scientific explanation. . . . Secondly, these scientific explanations have to meet the particular demands of clinicians in situations of brief psychotherapy. . . . The procedure of observation of clinicians is that they listen to stories. . . . The hypotheses used for explanation are less interesting as an ad hoc series, more interesting as they fit simply together. Parsimony is important in all of science. For clinicians it is probably essential. . . . Patients usually come demanding a change, being stuck or drifting in a direction that seems bad to them. They want movement in a different direction. . . . Of course, a practice aims to satisfy patients. This means they like the drift of their position after consultation better than their position before consultation. . . . The stories improve. (pp. 257–258)

Simply put, *brief therapy is briefer rather than longer and is characterized by a great deal of flexibility*: Gustafson adds, "[S]uch a method is always ready to start anew, to pose the problem differently, to propose different hypotheses" (p. 259). This view of brief therapy fits well within the ecological paradigm we have outlined in this book, and we believe it can be useful in the treatment of family sexual abuse, particularly for therapy undertaken within the context of managed care.

In ecological therapy, the key to successful treatment is to create a balanced, clearly boundaried context of power/control around the incestuous family so that relationships can be developed between therapist and family member(s) that will allow clients to practice the (non-sexualized) regulation of proximity and distance, in turn, producing interdependence without deprivation or exploitation. The central idea here is the creation of a positive emotional context, or "holding environment" (Catherall, 1992; Langs, 1976; Winnicott, 1965), in which the family as a system can safely alter its dysfunctional structures and family members as individuals can practice acting autonomously apart without evoking the perpetrator/victim interaction pattern.

Unfortunately, therapists dealing with sexual abuse (whether with victims, perpetrators, or entire families) often focus their efforts on only one side of the relational dialectic: attachment. Certainly, most members of incestuous families need help forming attachments. However, genuine intimacy is not possible without the differentiation that comes from separation. Therefore, an overemphasis upon closeness and support risks the creation of too much vulnerability which, in turn, diminishes internal locus of control, thereby perpetuating the skewed power/control balance. Working only with the power dynamic ("empowering" victims and "depowering" perpetrators) merely encourages them to exchange one role for another; now perpetrators begin to act like vulnerable victims, and victims begin to abuse power by perpetrating. The net result is to reduce both the effectiveness and the efficiency of therapy.

In applying the ecological model to a variety of client situations, we have evolved a number of principles and techniques for maximizing therapeutic benefits from fewer sessions. We have come to think of our work with certain clients — including those involved in incestuous abuse — as "brief therapy on a long-term basis." We make no claims for originality of this approach. It has elements in common with object relations analytic therapy, Rogerian therapy, interactional therapy, strategic therapy, feminist collaborative therapy, as well as with systemic, narrative, and solution-focused approaches.

Overall, this therapy can be characterized as collaborative, highly interactive, and constructivist in style; it is premised upon a strong transference relationship characterized by both closeness and distance and by conflicts over both power and control. At its heart, the development and maintenance of a relationship *is* the therapy. However, the transference bond is both created and disrupted on a planned basis by the recurrent actions of the therapist periodically unbalancing and then rebalancing various aspects of the relationship. For example, an adult survivor of sexual abuse initially is encouraged to trust the personal power of the therapist for her sense of security and later is challenged to make a decision to remain functional amidst crisis when the therapist acknowledges her own helplessness to change external circumstances — allowing the client's internal rage to be externalized into anger at the therapist's refusal to rescue her. Or a perpetrator who has formed the beginnings of attachment to the therapist may be confronted by the therapist's agitated worry that nothing he can say may be sufficient to convince the perpetrator to value himself enough to stay out of trouble. The course of therapy within an ecological framework roams freely among meanings, actions, and emotions. It requires that the therapist be sensitive, empathic, and honest in developing a relationship with clients whose capacity for relating intimately is likely to be extremely limited. At the same time, it requires that the therapist exert sufficient power/control to overcome resistance and to evoke dependent reactions in the client. Finally, the therapist needs to recognize, appreciate, and utilize the paradoxes that lie at the heart of all relationships. When the therapist is skillful enough to do this "ecological juggling" on an ongoing basis with a family, couple, or individual, then therapy can be done on a very efficient basis.[6]

Using this approach, therapy typically continues for a lengthy period of time, sometimes for years. However, the therapy usually is intermittent and involves a variety of treatment modalities scheduled on an irregular basis—family sessions, individual therapy, conjoint work (if appropriate), and some time spent in group therapy. Seldom do we conduct a formal termination interview. Even "graduation" from a group is not considered to be terminating the relationship between client and therapist. Instead, an occasional "check-up" session may be scheduled, or the therapist may propose a meeting with various family members at a distant time in the future. Even moving out of the city involves an arrangement for some continuing contact by letter or by phone. Gradually, clients come to view the therapist as a positive resource and to understand therapy as a *contributor* to their own problem-solving and decision-making abilities rather than as a substitute for these. We have discovered that the total number of therapy sessions (other than perhaps group therapy) is noticeably less than for other approaches to incest treatment. We believe that the results are much more positive for all concerned. In fact, we take it as a sign of success that so many of our clients return on a voluntary basis from time to time to deal with marital or family or individual issues. For example, a number of former spouses whose incest treatment eventuated in divorce have voluntarily returned for some marital therapy with *new* partners, and their greater awareness of issues and traps in relationships speaks to the success of previous work. Contributing to the ecological balance of clients' lives seems to us to reflect the heart of what therapy is at its best—and it still can be done within reasonable limits of time and money.

CONCLUSION

The social ecology has a significant impact upon the process of intervention into family sexual abuse. First, it determines to a significant degree whether any intervention will take place at all. In this respect, the climate of public opinion is currently divided between those who consider incest to be part and parcel of an epidemic of violence against women and

[6]More detailed descriptions of this therapeutic process with victims and perpetrators of sexual abuse can be found in our book *Child Sexual Abuse: An Ecological Approach to Treating Victims and Perpetrators*. Related principles and techniques also can be found in Dolan (1991), Gustafson (1986), and Johnson (1985).

children that must be stopped and those who believe that concern with child sexual abuse is highly exaggerated as a result of some combination of distorted psychic processes (false memory syndrome) and feminist anti-male political zeal (Armsworth, 1989). As we have indicated, our own view is that this diversity of opinion itself arises from a deep-seated ambivalence among Americans and others regarding gender and sexuality.

Second, the social context has an impact upon each specific intervention into family sexual abuse via the personal characteristics and actions of social service and legal personnel involved in the case and the organizations they represent. As we have indicated in this chapter, there is considerable opportunity for mishaps involving lack of coordination and replication of perpetrator/victim interaction dynamics among agencies and individuals. Amidst this complex ecology, the family therapist is challenged to maintain a close alliance with each family member and a clear set of objectives relevant to the good of the family system.

To improve the sociolegal process of handling family sexual abuse, we offer the following suggestions:

- At the broadest level, *a framework for understanding family sexuality and for distinguishing healthy from unhealthy patterns of family sexual interaction should be included in sex education courses and in all other efforts at child sexual abuse prevention* (see Chapter 3). Equipping both parents and children with such information will not only help to prevent abuse, but can facilitate reporting, investigation and treatment of abuse when it does occur.
- Scientific research, clinical work and public policy should all *distinguish more carefully between descriptive, explanatory, and evaluative accounts of incestuous behavior.* Political rhetoric and moral dogmatism about family sexual abuse can actually hinder creative efforts at intervention, leading both professionals and the public to look for simplistic solutions. The recent backlash against reporting among some parents and professionals should be taken seriously as an indicator of the complexity of intervention into the incestuous family (Fincham et al., 1994a, 1994b; Greenspon, 1993; Tavris, 1993a, 1993b; Wexler, 1990).
- In the course of intervention, *a balance should be struck between the welfare of the individual victim and that of the family system.* What is best is often difficult to determine amidst the competing and conflicting interests of the family members, helping professionals, and the legal system. Since the family is the incest victim's primary social context — albeit a somewhat dysfunctional one — its alteration or disintegration through divorce, foster placement, or generational alienation will substantially affect the victim's future. Naive or overzealous efforts to rescue the incest victim can set the

stage for a realignment of influences such that new patterns of perpetration/victimization can arise from the social system outside the family.

- As pointed out above, *the functions of evaluation and therapy should be strictly separated in working with the victim and her family.* Because these are two different experiential contexts with differing frameworks of reality construction, overlapping them can contribute to intrapsychic boundary diffusion in the victim and interpersonal boundary diffusion in the family, thus replicating the incestuous dynamics. Professionals intervening into family sexual abuse should carefully select and rigorously maintain their respective roles.

- *Standard protocols for interviewing children about sexual abuse should be used in incest assessment.* The increasing use of videotapes has helped reduce the number of times a child must recount incidents of abuse. Such videotapes should be made available for viewing by relevant persons who then can be asked to provide their interpretations of the data elicited. In legal proceedings, the professional interviewer should be questioned only about the specific contents and conduct of the interview itself. Interpretive opinions should be provided by professionals *other than* the individual who conducted the interview of the child.

- *Separation of family members should not be considered an automatic outcome of documented incestuous abuse.* Many perpetrators pose no further threat to the victim following discovery, although their influence on victims' possible recantation of abuse allegations needs to be assessed. Since severe family disruption itself can be a deterrent to reporting and seeking treatment, a careful analysis of the family's situation and resources, as well as the overall relationship between the perpetrator and victim, and between the perpetrator and other family members (particularly the spouse), should be conducted as swiftly as possible and should form the basis for decisions regarding social intervention and legal consequences.

- In the majority of incest cases, *legal proceedings should be handled in the context of family courts rather than criminal courts.* Closed hearings should be utilized, combining testimony by both victim and perpetrator with those of other family members, acquaintances, and various professionals as needed. Judgments should focus primarily upon mandatory treatment, probationary accountability, and restitutive measures rather than incarceration.

- As we have argued throughout this book, *the family system should be the centerpiece for incest treatment efforts.* Despite its dysfunctional aspects, the family should be viewed as a potential therapeutic resource—the primary ecosystem within which transformations among members' relationships will take place—rather than simply as an impediment to outside efforts at social control. Ideally, treatment of incestuous families should be coordinated by someone who is designated the *family's* therapist.

In the final chapter, we take up issues related to evaluating the impact of incest treatment efforts on individual family members and upon the family as a unit.

CHAPTER 12

The Evaluation of Incest Treatment

What we know about families is largely determined by how we know what we know.

— Robert E. Larzelere & David M. Klein (1986)

In 1991, the U. S. Department of Health and Human Services asked the National Academy of Sciences to convene a panel of experts to develop a research agenda on all forms of child maltreatment. The following summarizes the Panel's recommendations for research on interventions and treatment of child abuse and neglect (National Research Council, 1993, pp. 275–278):

- research on the operation of the child protection system, including an evaluation of the sequential stages by which children receive treatment following reports of maltreatment (*top priority*)
- controlled group outcome studies to develop criteria to assess the effects of treatment interventions for maltreated children
- well-designed outcome evaluations to assess whether intensive family preservation services reduce child maltreatment and foster the well-being of children in the long run
- studies of foster care that examine the conditions and circumstances under which foster care appears to be beneficial or detrimental to the child
- large-scale evaluation studies of treatments for perpetrators of sexual and physical abuse and neglect (familial as well as extrafamilial), with lengthy follow-up periods and control groups of untreated or less intensively treated offenders to compare different treatment modalities
- identification of effective interventions for neglectful families

Research in all of these areas, and more, is needed to guide interventions into family sexual abuse. However, child sexual abuse research, particularly therapy outcome research, is complex and problematic (e.g., Briere, 1988; Conte, 1990; Haugaard & Emery, 1989) and has been characterized as "a methodological quagmire" (Dempster & Roberts, 1991).

Still unanswered are many questions about the characteristics and family interaction patterns accompanying incestuous abuse. Few studies of family-based incest treatment have been reported, nor have the effects of intervention on family functioning been systematically examined (Daro, 1988; National Research Council, 1993; Finkelhor, 1984; Sgroi, 1988; Trepper & Barrett, 1986). Due to the lack of long-term follow-up and independent research, considerable uncertainty exists regarding the impact of intervention and therapeutic treatment on the *families* in which incest occurs. Anecdotal evidence to date suggests that current treatment efforts may neglect or even have a negative impact upon families as a unit (Finkelhor & Zellman, 1991; Gardner, 1992; Hutchinson, 1993). Missing from most sexual abuse treatment programs are organized criteria for evaluating family member interaction before and after treatment (Daro, 1988; Patton, 1991). Professionals dealing with child sexual abuse—psychological evaluators, treatment staff, legal and criminal justice personnel, and even social policymakers—have few agreed-upon standards for judging the effects of intervention. The major criterion, nonrecurrence of the abuse, may be only an artifact of the absence of the perpetrator from the home, the current age of a former victim, or the policing efforts of family members, social services, or parole officers. Therefore, objectively confirming program effectiveness or comparing several approaches to treating incestuous or nonincestuous sexual abuse is difficult. Meaningful evaluation requires outcome criteria and a method of pretreatment assessment that can be repeated in posttreatment follow-ups.

As we indicated in Chapter 1, ideas about treatment effectiveness themselves can be controversial (Friedrich, 1990; Trepper & Barrett, 1989; Wyatt & Powell, 1988), with some professionals emphasizing the successful separation of family members and incarceration of perpetrators, and others urging treatment that can enable the perpetrator to become a safe citizen and even an effective spouse and parent. Research to date has been limited, particularly with regard to outcomes for the incestuous family as a unit. Although demographic data on families (e.g., marital staus, number of children living in the household) are often collected in the context of assessment and/or follow-up, information on the characteristics of family *functioning* in relation to treatment is largely absent (Daro, 1988; Finkelhor, 1984; Friedrich, 1990; Truchsess, 1991).

Evaluating the impact of treatment on incestuous families has practical significance for clinical programs in a number of ways:

- providing methods and criteria by which families can be assessed prior to treatment, in order to differentiate "high risk" from "low risk" situations
- serving as a basis for setting treatment goals
- evaluating the effects of treatment according to standardized criteria
- facilitating comparisons between various treatment modalities (e.g., family therapy versus group therapy)

In addition, uniform standards for asssessing families can serve as a basis for designing policies to aid decisions such as removal of children from the home, sentencing guidelines for perpetrators, and selection of treatment options. Criteria of family functioning also can be used to evaluate various treatment efforts in order to make judgments about agency structure, funding priorities, and the like. Even far-reaching issues such as the relative merits of individual versus family treatment programs can be debated more fruitfully when empirical data are available to use as a basis for drawing conclusions.

THE CHALLENGES OF
CLINICAL EVALUATION

Previously we discussed goals and goal-setting procedures for therapy with incest families. Our approach to treatment implies certain success criteria related to ecological balancing, and our ecological perspective on family sexuality yields certain criteria for sexual health. In addition, each family has specific objectives of its own to be achieved in the context of treatment. Appropriate evaluation of treatment outcomes somehow must reflect all of these, in addition to meeting the explicit objective of societal intervention into incest families: *to stop the abuse.*

The literature on outcomes of family therapy in general (Andreozzi, 1985; Gurman & Kniskern, 1981; Gurman et al., 1986; Wamboldt, Wamboldt, & Gurman, 1985; Wynne, 1988b) shows that the majority of clients feel "helped" by treatment. Further, there is some evidence that family therapy may have effects above and beyond individual therapy, and it may be somewhat more efficient in producing changes (Andreozzi, 1985; Simmons & Doherty, 1995). Therapists themselves tend to believe that therapy is more successful when goals are clear and specific ("I would like to be able to have an orgasm during sexual intercourse" or "We would like our son to stop getting into trouble with teachers at school") rather than diffuse and general ("I'd like to be happier" or "We would like to have a better marriage") (e.g., Coleman, 1985; Guerney, Brock, & Coufal, 1986;

Haley, 1976; Watzlawick et al., 1974; Wolberg, 1980). In response to pressure from managed care interests, along with fear of client complaints to licensing boards and worry about malpractice suits, measures of client satisfaction with treatment are becoming more widespread.

Measuring client satisfaction and treatment success become considerably more complex when clients' participation in therapy is involuntary, particularly when the clients are entire families whose members are legally forced or socially coerced into treatment. This is the challenge facing those who attempt to conduct outcome studies of intervention into family sexual abuse. The challenge grows even more formidable when the criteria for successful outcome differ among the various stakeholders in the case. Clearly, an ecological approach to treatment requires ecologically oriented methods of evaluation. This raises challenges to traditional techniques of program evaluation. For example, should one reporter's view of the results of intervention—in cases of family sexual abuse, this is most often the nonoffending spouse who is also the caretaker of the child victim(s)—be taken as a valid measure of treatment effectiveness? And should changes in an MMPI profile—the relevance of which has been challenged in regard to incest perpetrators—be used to measure offender treatment success? These and similar issues have discouraged many clinicians, and even academic researchers, from undertaking comprehensive, carefully controlled studies of family sexual abuse and its treatment. However, some recent evidence suggests that the situation may be changing (Daro, 1988; Horton, 1992; Lockhart et al., 1989; Woody & Grinstead, 1992).

If intervention into family sexual abuse is to be comprehensively evaluated, then it is necessary to coordinate the evaluation process with the involvement of multiple family members in intervention and/or assessment and/or treatment efforts. Since therapy for various incest family members can be a lengthy process, a *minimum* of three to five years is necessary to conduct an effective family-oriented pre- and posttreatment evaluation study. Referrals of entire families for treatment may occur rather slowly, extending the time required to gather data from sufficient numbers of clients for meaningful analysis. Since relatively few agencies treat the entire incest family unit (Daro, 1988; Trepper & Barrett, 1989), many treatment programs are unable to provide entire families in which the offender is available to participate in the research. Sometimes, cooperation among a number of agencies or programs can facilitate the research effort.

Then there is the matter of client willingness to participate in the evaluation process. Programs that work with individuals actually involved in incest—usually the perpetrator *or* the victim—may have little or no contact with other family members. Therefore, therapists may work hard to recruit subjects, but important family members might refuse to participate. Some families may be reluctant to involve themselves in research, particularly when treatment is first beginning. Based upon our clinical and research experience as well as on discussions with others in the field, we have concluded that this difficulty is probably linked to two factors. One is the widely recognized resistance of incest families to involvement with "outsiders," even under the most favorable of circumstances, let alone following coercive social and legal intervention. A second factor is probably the recent cultural atmosphere regarding sexual abuse throughout North America and elsewhere. Controversies over "false accusations" and "false memory syndrome" have fueled family opposition to intervention and encouraged suspicion of the "helping" efforts of therapists.

Taken together, these factors have created substantial barriers to extensive, well-designed research and evaluation efforts. Further, the same societal atmosphere that affects family members has altered patterns of treatment. Intervention into family sexual abuse now tends to fall toward the extremes on a continuum; some suspected abuse is not investigated or is dealt with so nominally that treatment (particularly for the entire family) does not occur; other cases that can be clearly substantiated result in incarceration and/or residential treatment, making it less likely that such families will be seen on an outpatient basis. As a result, the census of incest families is down in many agencies, and therapy takes longer to implement. In short, effective treatment evaluation of sexually abusive families requires well-informed and motivated clinicians, careful coordination among professionals, and solid support from organizational administrators and other stakeholders.

AN EVALUATION PROTOCOL

One of the authors (JWM) has been engaged in a study of the effectiveness of treatment programs for family sexual abuse — part of a long-range research project on family sexual health that seeks to identify principles that facilitate *positive* expressions of intimacy and sexuality within families.[1] Like our treatment efforts, this research proceeds from the assumption that sexuality is a fundamental dimension of family experience that can contribute positively or negatively to the development and well-being of family members. Therefore, the study is concerned not only with the possible psychopathology of a perpetrator or the effects of sexual abuse on

[1]The research described in this chapter was conducted under the auspices of the Department of Family Social Science at the University of Minnesota — Twin Cities. In addition, several treatment agencies (both public and private) in the Twin Cities metropolitan area have collaborated on the project, recruiting families as research participants and filling out treatment assessment forms. Financial support for the research has come from a number of sources, notably the Family Sexual Abuse Project of the St. Paul Foundation (St. Paul), the Minnesota Agricultural Experiment Station, and the College of Human Ecology and the Graduate School at the University of Minnesota — Twin Cities.

a victim; we are also interested in disturbances in parent-child relationships, malfunctions among various family dyads (particularly the spouses),
family role performance difficulties, interactions of the family with the
community, and even the overall societal context that shapes family members' attitudes and behaviors related to sexuality, intimacy, and child socialization (Alexander, 1985; Bronfenbrenner, 1979; Garbarino, 1977; Gelles
& Straus, 1979; Trepper & Barrett, 1989).

An ecological approach to family sexual abuse suggests the following as
significant — though not necessarily exclusive — variables influencing the
occurrence of incest:

- highly differentiated gender role orientation
- gender and generational imbalances in family structure
- distance-regulation difficulties
- distortions in power and control
- communication deficits (both general and sexual)
- discrepancies in sexual meanings and attitudes, particularly between spouses
- social isolation and alienation of the family from the community

Therefore, we have concluded that these are important issues to investi-
gate as outcomes of treatment as well as to address in therapy.

Program Settings

Several public and private clinical treatment programs in the Twin
Cities metropolitan area have begun to implement a family evaluation
protocol as a regular part of their treatment of incest families (and other
clients involved in child sexual abuse situations). These programs represent a diversity of approaches to intervention, and their client populations
are ethnically and culturally diverse. Some offer primarily group treatment, while others emphasize individual and/or family therapy. The participating programs contribute staff time to the research effort by administering the research questionnaires within the context of their regular
clinical assessments. Initial interviews and follow-up data are obtained by
members of an outside research team.[2] In our experience, agency supervisors and administrative personnel have been largely supportive and helpful
in the evaluation effort.

[2]The research team is headed by one of the authors (JWM) and consists primarily of graduate
students at the University of Minnesota. Some staff members of cooperating clinical programs also participate in some of the research procedures. However, therapists are *not*
involved in research roles with subjects on their own caseload; that is, they gather data from
their own clients only to the extent that it is integral to clinical assessment and is considered
part of the case file.

Prior to beginning participation in the research effort, each of these treatment agencies gathered information in a rather typical fashion: using informal questionnaires and one or two individual assessment instruments to obtain data from the identified clients (usually only victims or perpetrators); meeting with available family members in an initial, abuse-focused interview; evaluating treatment outcome via a termination interview with individual clients. In addition to their regular intake interviews, participating therapists now administer a variety of questionnaires (described below) to all consenting family members and solicit their client families' involvement in (voluntary) family assessment interviews with researchers, both at the beginning and at the conclusion of treatment.

Evaluation Methods

Data have been collected via a combination of questionnaires and interview. Questionnaires are designed to be completed by all family members age 12 and older who participate in the treatment effort. The instruments that are part of the evaluation protocol are:

- *Family Adaptability and Cohesion Scales III (FACES III)* (Olson, Portner, & Lavee, 1985). A measure reflecting family processes in terms of "balanced" versus "extreme" and scoring on two widely recognized dimensions of family functioning.[3]
- *Bem Sex Role Inventory (BSRI)* (Bem, 1974). A questionnaire assessing the degree of behavioral sex typing internalized by individuals in a culture. Family members rate themselves in relation to idealized standards of "masculinity" and "femininity."
- *Primary Communication Inventory (PCI)* (Locke, Sabaugh, & Thomas, 1956). Not widely used in family research, but established as valid and reliable in the study of marital communication processes; adapted to examine gender-linked and generational communication patterns.
- *Index of Sexual Satisfaction (ISS)* (Hudson, 1982). A brief questionnaire about sexual interaction between spouses that yields an overall measure of satisfaction with the sexual relationship.
- *Power/Control Survey (P/C-S)* (Maddock, 1989). A new instru-

---

[3]A more recent version of this questionnaire (FACES IV) is being considered for use in future evaluation. An alternative is the *Family Assessment Device* (FAD) developed at McMaster University (Akister & Stevenson-Hinde, 1991; Epstein et al., 1983), which seems to provide a more richly textured set of measures on several relevant aspects of family functioning and discriminates "unhealthy" from "healthy" families as well as, or better than, FACES III.

ment that measures perceptions of spouses regarding the distribution of power and control in the marital relationship.
- *Sexual Meaning Scales* (*SMS*) (Maddock, 1988). A recently developed questionnaire providing information on aspects of meaning
that underlie subjects' attitudes toward sex; a semantic differential
consisting of 50 bipolar adjective scales (e.g., *close/distant*).

Along with filling out questionnaires, all participating family members — including younger children — are interviewed together by two interviewers.[4] A 25-question, semi-structured interview schedule has been devised to examine general family interaction patterns around gender and
erotic aspects of sexuality, sex-related attitudes, sexual communication,
and the like (see Table 12.1 at the end of this chapter). The interviews are
conducted informally, encouraging contributions from all members present and allowing individuals to elaborate in any direction that might be
important to them. The interview does *not* include any direct questions
about child sexual abuse, although some family members respond to general questions by talking about abuse.

In addition to the written measures filled out by family members, therapists in the participating clinics complete brief checklists focusing on perceptions of prognosis for pretreatment families and outcome for posttreatment families. Following the interviews, both interviewers fill out rating
scales identifying their impressions of family interactions around each of
the major issues addressed.

When the data gathered in the initial assessment are to be used as a
basis for evaluating program effectiveness, both therapists and clients can
recognize their potential contribution to the treatment effort itself. Over
several years, we have redesigned the questionnaire feedback materials
provided to therapists so that they can more readily understand the questionnaire results and incorporate them into ongoing work with family
members. This approach to evaluation research also has some practical
data management advantages. Considering the initial assessment and follow-up findings to be part of the clients' case records can simplify both
record-keeping and data-handling from the standpoint of privacy.

---

[4]We have made an effort to pay participating families a nominal amount for the time spent
in family interviews, since this is unrelated to any direct clinical assessment. The exact
amount is proportional to the number of members participating in the interview. Individuals
involved in the social interventions surrounding family sexual abuse often feel manipulated
in a variety of ways, and they become sensitive to the exploitive elements of these experiences. Even the symbolic gesture of nominal payment conveys a sense of respect for their
time, just as therapists and agencies expect to be compensated for time spent in providing
services. If all family members consent, interviews are audiotaped and transcribed to be used
for research purposes. Contents of the interview remain strictly confidential, unless special
arrangements are made upon request of the family (and the written consent of *all* family
members).

RESEARCH RESULTS

Though most family-oriented treatment programs for incestuous families report positive results and a low recidivism rate (e.g., Alexander, 1990; Anderson & Shafer, 1979; Bentovim & Van Elburg, 1987; Giarretto, 1976, 1978; Trepper & Barrett, 1989), well-controlled evaluations of family therapy for family sexual abuse are virtually nonexistent (Daro, 1988; National Research Council, 1993). Serious shortcomings characterize the little available research, including problems in experimental design, difficulties in quantifying complex phenomena in order to measure them, missing data from key family members, and unknown selection biases among samples of families in contact with different legal and social agencies (National Research Council, 1993; O'Donohue & Elliot, 1992; Ray et al., 1991). Most studies lack adequate comparison groups; when comparision groups are utilized, results may be confounded by unidentified cases of abuse in the nonclinical samples (Dempster & Roberts, 1991). Lack of clarity in concept definitions and differing theoretical frameworks also inhibit cross-study comparisons (Haugaard & Emery, 1989).

Information has not been systemically collected on the *baseline, non-abuse functioning* of families in which incest occurs, thereby limiting our knowledge of the risk and protective factors in its etiology. Similarly, the relative effects of abuse on victims in comparison to other family characteristics can be difficult to specify (Briere, 1988). A review of clinical literature (Friedrich, 1990) has found no single or essential family variable that explains the etiology or continuation of incest. Characteristics vary according to families treated, referral sources, and clinicians' treatment approaches and biases. All of these factors are substantial obstacles to systematically examining treatment efforts. Nevertheless, some common general themes do emerge, and these have formed the basis for our own evaluation efforts.

The Evaluation Process

The data-gathering process has proved manageable. However, some unanticipated difficulty has occurred in recruiting *post*treatment incest families—the category we originally expected to be easier due to the presumed benefits of treatment and better relationships with service agencies. Instead, we have found that numerous families are no longer in contact with their treatment programs. They have moved, "dropped out of sight," or, if contacted, often refuse to participate in follow-up research. Their continued alienation from the community and even from their "helpers" is apparent. This discovery has strengthened our commitment to fostering ecologically oriented, family-based treatment of incestuous abuse. It has taken approximately five years to design and implement an evaluation protocol for incest family treatment in a handful of programs. An important caveat: Since all participating families are being assessed at some point *after* incest has been reported, their characteristics and behaviors might well reflect the influences of social intervention as much as the effects of the incest itself—one of the inevitable limitations of clinical research in the area of child abuse. Preliminary analyses to date permit only a limited number of observations about a small number of families, simply to illustrate the kinds of data that result from this approach to research.

Multitrait, multimethod data-gathering procedures are important for understanding the characteristics and transactional patterns of complex systems such as families (Bryman, 1988; Gilgun, 1991a; Nye, 1988; Olson, 1977; Rank, 1988). Self-reports can provide information on how family members perceive their family functioning (the insider perspective), while observations of behavior are required to provide an outsider's perspective (Olson, 1976). Both insider and outsider perspectives are important for investigating incest. In addition, qualitative methods focusing on subjective personal meanings can be as important, or more important, than processes represented by numbers (Chodorow, 1993; Gilgun, Daly, & Handel, 1992; LaRossa & Reitzes, 1993). This study's use of information from multiple respondents, both inside and outside the family, permits valuable triangulation of data which can improve validity and reliability when measuring complex underlying variables like those derived from our theoretical model. Interactive research interviews with whole families themselves are an important methodological step in family research—advocated often, but utilized seldom. They allow more in-depth understanding of a family's interactive processes and provide access to the unique *meaning* of shared experiences for members of a particular family.

Questionnaire Results

FACES III. Cohesion and adaptability scores have demonstrated few differences between families before and after treatment. Families we have studied are more midrange and less extreme (unbalanced) than might be anticipated. Although incestuous families commonly are characterized by clinicians as "enmeshed," the families we have studied score moderately to extremely "disengaged" on this instrument. These findings might be interpreted as disproving clinical opinion; however, several alternative explanations are possible: (a) the reporting of incest and subsequent social intervention might create a reactive pattern of disengagement in incest family members whose emotional connections are rather fragile; (b) on self-report measures, family members' defensive denial may prevent them from recognizing the actual extent of their psychological enmeshment; (c) the FACES III cohesion scale may not measure the same phenomenon that clinicians refer to as "enmeshment."

BSRI. Both male and female scores suggest that posttreatment family members are less sex-typed than families prior to treatment. In our small sample, however, incest families do not show much greater sex role typing than a comparison group of nonincest families.

PCI. The PCI measures the perceptions of family members regarding general communication across gender and generational lines. First of all, overall communication is more effective in posttreatment than in pretreatment incest families. In addition, results tend to confirm the widely held clinical belief that incestuous families are characterized by cross-generational, within-gender alignments, which contribute to the parent-child role confusion accompanying family sexual abuse.

ISS. Given to spouses to assess satisfaction with their erotic interaction, thus far results on this measure have been mixed. Some pretreatment sexual satisfaction scores have approximated, or even exceeded, those of couples in a comparison group and among posttreatment couples. Perhaps this finding reflects the idealization and denial that seems to characterize a number of untreated incest families. Higher levels of sexual dissatisfaction post-treatment may also reflect the failure of therapy to address adequately certain problems in the marital relationship, a failure acknowledged by many treatment programs that focus on individual members rather than the family as a unit.

P/C-S. On this newly developed questionnaire, differences in scores suggest changes over the course of treatment. Couples in incestuous families are less balanced in power/control than a comparison group of nonincest couples. Husbands are perceived as more powerful in pretreatment incestuous families, with both power and control moving in the direction of wives in the posttreatment sample.

SMS. Discrepancies in sexual meaning are greater, as predicted, in pretreatment incestuous families than in either a comparison sample or post-treatment families. The instrument is still under development. Certain scale scores, or clusters of meaning, are currently being derived and validated, so that patterns of sexual meaning among family members can be detected more accurately.

As we continue to gather information from incestuous families—along with those involved in nonincestuous abuse, marital violence, and other sex-related problems—more elaborate data analyses will be possible. Family data are being organized in a variety of ways: individual family member scores, aggregate family scores, and sum of difference scores between family members. Data will be examined utilizing more complex statistical methods and modes of depiction permitted by computer simulation and analysis. Validity and reliability studies of the new instruments are continuing, and their results will be fitted to the theoretical model from which the variables were derived.

Interview Findings

The transcripts, notes, and ratings from family interviews have been examined informally to identify overall patterns and to gather impressionistic data. More thorough analyses are planned, using coding schemes and computerized methods of pattern detection tied to our ecological model (e.g., Leik, Roberts, Caron, Mangen, & Leik, 1990; McTavish & Pirro, 1984). Currently, we can compare only the narrative notes and impressionistic ratings of therapists and research interviewers. On average, incest families definitely are more difficult to interview than comparison families. Predictably, pretreatment families appear most chaotic. Conflicts between the perpetrator and the victim often predominate, and family members frequently take sides with one or the other. By contrast, posttreatment families sometimes emphasize the similarities and positive relationship of the perpetrator and victim—while expressing more marital alienation. Overall, pretreatment incestuous couples—those who are still together at the time this assessment occurs—have presented their marriages in a more positive light than than posttreatment couples. As one wife put it, "If I'm with someone I love and I'm married to him, it's sacred. . . . It should be a perfect union, with much eye contact and oneness like you might feel when meditating." Comparison couples seem more willing to reveal conflicts, particularly around gender issues. Perhaps this only indicates the greater constraints on the pretreatment families, whose recent contacts with social and legal agencies might motivate them toward more socially approved responses. However, families in incest treatment have appeared to the interviewers to be more traditional in structure, with the husband's domination accepted by both spouses. At the same time, interviews with both pre- and posttreatment incestuous families are sometimes characterized by subtle and not-so-subtle "male bashing," For example, one pretreatment mother stated, "[My daughter] feels I pay more attention to [my son] than the girls. I told her he's a boy—he needs that extra push." Somewhat surprisingly, very few instances of derogating females have been noted, even when the perpetrators are expressing anger. In most of the research interviews with families, both interviewers were female—thereby encouraging the subjects (who also were predominantly female) to align themselves with the researchers around the theme "you know how men are." Perhaps the families' response patterns would have differed in interviews with both genders.

The boundary difficulties of incestuous families are evident in many interviews. One pretreatment mother described her relationship with her young daughter as "more like a friendship," saying, "I'm not too good at being a parent." Another stated, "We're more like friends than mother and daughter." A posttreatment mother commented on her former relationship with the incest victim, "[My daughter] and I really have a bond. I was good at telling the bad things. I overdid it—told her my problems. We're trying to undo that—let her be a little girl."

As anticipated, signs of anxiety often become noticeable as the interview progresses toward more specific questions about sex—although no one is asked to report or describe their sexual behavior per se. A key question about the nature of sex-related communication in the family sometimes is a turning point in the interview. Family conversation either opens up or shuts down. Merely asking the question probably constitutes rule-breaking behavior in most families.

Methodological Issues

Structuring an evaluation protocol within the context of an existing treatment program and implementing the details of data-gathering can be difficult and time-consuming. Our conclusions and recommendations regarding the evaluation of incest family treatment include the following:

Treatment programs should solicit client participation in the evaluation process as a routine part of their own intake and assessment procedures. However, the actual data collection process and interviewing should be conducted by individuals *outside* the treatment process whose responsibility for evaluation is clearly designated. Several years of effort to secure subject families for evaluation research has taught us this important lesson. While such a combined approach may require greater initial effort (including extensive discussions with governing boards, administrators, and entire clinic staffs), it will build stronger support for the project, improve the recruitment process, and provide higher quality data than would be the case if the evaluation were left up to the therapists or conducted entirely by outsiders.

The most desirable location for interviewing family members is in their own home. Although interviews also can take place at the treatment agency, we have concluded that a fuller picture of the home environment enriches the sense of understanding reported by members of the research team. Spontaneous events such as visits from neighbors or disruptions from children or family pets provide valuable insights into the family's transactional patterns. Interviewers should make efforts to involve all family members as fully as possible, working to maintain a positive, open, and supportive atmosphere for the entire family while remaining psychologically equidistant from individual family members. At times this is difficult. Some interviews may be characterized by chaotic activity; others, by passivity or anxious inhibition; still others, by extremely uneven participation among family members.

Payment for interviews appears to be a significant incentive for family involvement in research. Undoubtedly, payment also plays a role in the self-selection of subjects. Families reported for incestuous abuse are often in financial crisis and can use extra income. Equally important may be the symbolic meaning of subject payment. Individuals involved in the social interventions surrounding family sexual abuse often feel manipulated in a variety of ways, and they are sensitive to the exploitive elements of these experiences. Payment conveys a sense of respect for family members' time, just as therapists and agencies expect to be compensated for time spent in providing services. Some families have indicated that payment is a major incentive, and they have discussed in the interview how the money might be spent. From the research standpoint, payment has helped broaden our study sample beyond the better-educated, intellectually curious subjects who often agree to be part of research studies.

Programs whose staff members have a sense of "ownership" of the evaluation data are more comfortable and cooperative with the data-gathering procedures and are likely to pass this along to their clients, improving response rates. The motivation of individual therapists to facilitate data collection — especially with family members other than their own individual clients — is minimal unless the researchers provide some kind of concrete feedback that is clinically useful. Working with sexually abusive families can be extremely stressful, and therapists are not anxious to add additional burdensome procedures, particularly if clients or family members react negatively. Over several years, we have redesigned feedback materials provided to therapists so that questionnaire results can be more readily understood and incorporated into ongoing work with family members. This approach to evaluation research also has some practical data handling advantages. Considering the initial assessment and follow-up findings to be part of the clients' case records can simplify both record keeping and data handling from the standpoint of privacy.

Researchers should directly address therapists' conscious and unconscious opposition to involving their "difficult" clients in such research. Even if program administrators and staff are interested in treatment evaluation, some resistance is likely to be present. Therapy with incest families requires some expert balancing to maintain rapport and momentum toward treatment objectives. Initially, evaluation may appear only to add something else to "juggle." Some therapists are able to acknowledge directly their resistance, expressing the concern that research procedures will create problems for clients or will mean extra time and energy for them when they are already feeling overworked. Some may be concerned that client involvement in research will increase the potential for legal complications. Certainly, the current social climate of litigation has produced understandable anxiety among therapists and agency personnel. More problematic to the research effort is a therapist's unconcious resistance, which can result in inadvertently sabotaging data collection, for example, by mixing up code numbers on questionnaire packets, forgetting to contact certain family members about an interview, or giving families incorrect information regarding consent procedures. Attention to detail and adequate back-up procedures are essential to successfully implementing evaluation research in clinical programs treating involuntary clients.

Complex evaluation procedures, such as extra steps to assure data privacy and to secure client consent, should be structured to contribute positively to the treatment process. Already complicated by mandatory reporting requirements and the involvement of social and legal agencies, therapy with incest families is a time- and labor-intensive process. Arranging for pretreatment and posttreatment data collection adds some procedural steps and requires additional organizational support, such as secretarial time and copying costs. However, data collection can be structured to contribute something positive to the effectivesness and efficiency of treatment. Certain procedures useful for evaluation also can be helpful in making and maintaining connections with family members as well as conveying concern about client welfare at the conclusion of treatment. Detailing procedures for privacy and consent at the onset of treatment can demonstrate respect for family boundaries and promote trust between family members and clinic staff. Discussion of questionnaire results can initiate constructive dialogue among family members. Whole family interviews for assessment purposes can provide valuable information on the family members' allegiances, communication processes, beliefs and attitudes which can be utilized in therapy. Completing written questionnaires and interviews after treatment can add to family members' sense of achievement in meeting goals and can enhance the bond between family members and therapist(s), increasing the likelihood that the family will view the treatment agency as a helpful resource in the event of any future difficulties.

Boundaries between therapy and research should be recognized and carefully maintained. The responsibilities of those involved should be delineated at each step. Certain precautions need to be observed, and the procedures necessary for ethical research have to be developed and used in appropriate ways. Clients must understand which aspects of their participation in a program are voluntary and which are not. They must be fully informed about any potential benefits and risks of participation in a research process. The special status of minors and of individuals involved in the legal system must be understood completely by all concerned.[5] In short, effective treatment evaluation of incestuous families requires well-informed and highly motivated clinicians, careful coordination among professionals, and solid support from organizational administrators and other stakeholders.

CONCLUSION

Though minimal to date, clinical research on family sexual abuse would appear to substantiate the belief that there are family as well as individual characteristics influencing the occurrence of incest. We also interpret our own and others' findings to indicate that incest families indeed are "out of balance" on a number of measures of internal family functioning—in addition to violating broader community mores. Based upon restricted sampling and other methodological limitations, few solid conclusions can yet be drawn regarding the distinguishing characteristics of families in which incest occurs. Nevertheless, we believe that we have demonstrated the value of an approach to studying whole families in a clinical context and of assessing the effects of social intervention on an abusive family system. Equally important, in our view, is the momentum gained for a longer term exploration of the dynamic processes of *ecological balancing* in the maintenance of healthy family sexuality, with the goal of preventing sexual abuse in the future.

---

[5]Those involved in treatment evaluation with incestuous families may wish to consider applying for a *Federal Exemption Certificate* from the U.S. Department of Health and Human Services. This certificate protects subjects in special categories and/or under special circumstances from disclosure of information obtained through the research and from the use of such information in a legal proceeding. However, both researchers and clinicians should be aware that use of such a certificate requires careful delineation of research data from case files. Further, research personnel could be placed into very complex and difficult ethical dilemmas if they become aware of unreported abuse in the course of gathering information from family members through questionnaires or interviews.

TABLE 12.1
Outline for a Semi-Structured Family Interview

Introductions by interviewer(s) and family members.

Summary of interview protocol, privacy, and consent procedures.

Ask family to give the interviewer a brief overview of the family . . . who is in the family (anyone not present?), who works where, who goes to school where, a bit of history.

1. What are the greatest differences between males and females in this family (e.g., behavior, attitudes, characteristics)?

2. Which sex is more respected by the family—females or males? Why do you say that?

3. Who sticks together more, the females or the males? Why do you say that?

4. How close are members of this family? Who is close to whom? (encourage elaboration)

5. How is affection expressed in the family? When two people like each other or are close, how do they show it?

6. If there is a disagreement between two or more family members, what happens? What is family conflict like in this family?

7. I would like you to describe characteristics of certain categories of relationships and tell me what these relationships are like in this family: (a) brothers and sisters, (b) mother and sons, (c) father and sons, (d) father and daughters, (e) mother and daughters, (f) grandchildren and grandparents.

8. Which family member is most likely to make choices based on the good of the entire family rather than on his or her own good?

9. Which family member is most likely to make choices based upon his or her own good rather than the good of the entire family?

10. How does your family *balance* between the overall good of the family as a unit and the needs and wishes of individual members?

11. Who has the most influence or makes most of the average, everyday decisions in this family?

12. Who has the most influence or makes most of the major decisions in this family—decisions that will affect the family for some time into the future?

13. Who is the most strong-willed person in the family? Who is the most easygoing member?

14. Who is best at keeping other family members from doing what they want? Why do you say that?

15. How would you describe the general attitude toward sex in this family? Is this attitude open and direct (that is, do people talk about it)? Or is it indirect? Why do you say that?

16. How is sex talked about in this family?

17. Suppose that the adults in the family were talking together about a sexual topic, and one of the younger children came into the room. What would happen?

18. Suppose that the children in the family were talking together about a sexual topic, and one of the adults came into the room. What would happen?

19. How is privacy maintained in this family?

20. Whose ideas and attitudes about sex are most similar? Explain how.

21. Whose ideas and attitudes about sex are most different? Explain how.

22. What are the connections you make between sex and religion, if any?

23. How do the rules about sexual behavior get set up in this family? Have there been any major disagreements about those rules? Explain.

24. (To children) What do you think is the most important influence on sex in the world today?

25. (To adults) In your opinion, what is the most important thing that has happened in our society during your lifetime to influence people's ideas and attitudes about sexuality?

26. (To adults) How do your family's ideas and attitudes about men and women compare to the ideas and attitudes in the families in which you grew up?

27. (To adults) How do your family's ideas and attitudes about sex compare to the ideas and attitudes in the families in which you grew up?

Conclude the interview by checking with family members about anything else that they think would be important to know in order to understand the family. In addition, give family members an opportunity to ask questions about the interview.

Epilogue

An ecological approach to therapy requires recognizing that change is a constant. Not only does the possibility of positive changes in individuals and families motivate therapeutic efforts, but the possibility of societal change also gives hope that incest can be prevented. During the 20-year period that we have been involved in incest treatment, a great many transformations have taken place in the United States and in other technologized societies. Some of these changes appear to have affected the incidence of incestuous abuse. As we observed at the beginning of this book, either more child sexual abuse is occurring or our recognition of it has been heightened—or perhaps a combination of the two. Certainly, societal awareness and response to family sexual abuse have been altered dramatically in that period. Unfortunately, many would argue that not all of the changes have been for the better and that an unnecessary social hysteria has been created over child sexual abuse. Although the social manifestations of victimization continue to be prominent in North American culture, we have noted a "backlash" of skepticism and disgruntlement over the attention being given to child sexual abuse, particularly about incest. As this book is being published, a furious debate rages over whether sexual abuse is a common family secret that finally has been uncovered to be confronted or a rare phenomenon artificially inflated by those looking for someone to blame for personal problems or for broader social ills.

Things appear to be at a critical juncture, and the stakes are high. If we are correct about the far-reaching implications of gender role changes in technologized societies and about the deep-seated ambivalence regarding eroticism that appears to characterize those societies, then the reasons for the extremism of the current debate are clear. The polarizations are already apparent—male versus female, child versus parent, "right-wing" versus "left-wing," lawyer versus therapist, agency versus agency. There is a very real danger that fears about abuse and violence could become confused with anxieties about sexuality and gender role changes, thereby creating pressure to suppress the legitimate aspects of sexuality in the name of safety and security. There is a very real danger that modern technologized societies, like various societies in previous historical periods, could come to think of sexual expression as inherently dangerous, thereby increasing the likelihood that it will be expressed in bizarre ways. More than most other phenomena, child sexual abuse, particularly within the family, conveys a message about the enormous complexity of sexuality in human experience and reminds humans of both its potential goodness and its capacity for harm.

This, then, is the social context within which the therapist attempts to contribute to the healing of individual psyches and family relationships that have been threatened or damaged by the tragedy of family sexual abuse. Throughout this book, we have argued that the major attention of therapists dealing with incest ought to be on assisting in the repair of fractured *families* as well as contributing to healing individuals *as family members*. In the current social climate, our advocacy for ecological balancing as a key therapeutic principle in the treatment of incest seems particularly timely. Like every juggler, the therapist must work skillfully within an atmosphere of uncertainty. Therapy, like juggling, is an art that depends upon the appropriate application of scientific principles. Certainly, the data provided by past, present, and future research studies will have an important role in determining society's outlook on the phenomenon of family sexual abuse. For example, research on memory eventually may make it possible to confirm the factual accuracy of reported abuse and of the circumstances under which it is likely to be recalled and reported. Similarly, family research might yield further insights into the configuration of relationships that may prevent incestuous behavior from occurring between certain family members.

However, nothing can replace the dedication and sensitivity that must lie at the heart of the therapeutic endeavor when incestuous families enter treatment. The compassionate therapist committed to helping troubled families as well as individual family members can be assured that some sort of good will come from her or his efforts. The therapist who can see the ecological wisdom in every family's unique structure, who has faith in the positive possibilities for change, and who is willing to persist in establishing and maintaining a relationship of trust with clients whose previous life experiences have left them anxious and untrusting will be able to envision positive outcomes despite frequent obstacles and occasional setbacks. We hope that this book can make a contribution to inspiring faith in the possibilities of clients' lives, trust in the therapist's own sense of personal and professional identity, and commitment to struggle, practice, and persevere in the face of ambiguity. We believe that the therapeutic objectives discussed in various chapters of this book and the efforts to balance distorted transactional processes among family members are worthy goals that can contribute to alleviating family sexual abuse. They can provide some assurance against recidivism and open up positive possibilities for *all* members of an incestuous family. In addition, we believe that these objectives, if taken seriously as principles to guide family life and the socialization of children, may someday end the threat of family sexual abuse and may instead promote the transmission of healthy family sexuality from one generation to the next.

References

Abel, G., Becker, J., Cunningham-Rathner, J., Mittleman, M., & Rouleau, J. L. (1988). Multiple paraphiliac diagnoses among sex offenders. *Bulletin of the American Academy of Psychiatry and the Law, 16*(2), 153–168.

Adams-Tucker, C. (1982). Proximate effects of sexual abuse in childhood: A report on 28 children. *American Journal of Psychiatry, 139*, 1252–1256.

Akister, J., & Stevenson-Hinde, J. (1991). Identifying families at risk: Exploring the potential of the McMaster Family Assessment Device. *Journal of Family Therapy, 13*, 411–421.

Alexander, P. C. (1985). A systems theory conceptualization of incest. *Family Process, 24*, 79–88.

Alexander, P. C. (1990). Interventions in incestuous families. In S. W. Henggeler & C. M. Borduin (Eds.), *Family therapy and beyond: A multisystemic approach to treating the behavior problems of children in adolescence*. Pacific Grove, CA: Brooks/Cole.

Allen, W. (1978). The search for applicable theories of black family life. *Journal of Marriage and the Family, 40*(1), 117–131.

American Psychiatric Association (1994). *Diagnostic and statistical manual of mental disorders* (4th ed.). Washington, DC: Author.

Andersen, T. (1990a). The reflecting team. In T. Andersen (Ed.), *The reflecting team: Dialogues and dialogues about the dialogues* (pp. 18–107). Kent, U.K.: Borgmann.

Andersen, T. (Ed.). (1990b). *The reflecting team: Dialogues and dialogues about the dialogues.* Kent, U.K: Borgmann.

Andersen, H., & Goolishian, H. (1988). Human systems as linguistic systems: Preliminary and evolving ideas about the implications for clinical theory. *Family Process, 27*, 371–393.

Anderson, L. M., & Shafer, G. (1979). The character-disordered family: A community treatment model for family sexual abuse. *American Journal of Orthopsychiatry, 49*, 436–445.

Andreozzi, L. L. (Ed.). (1985). *Integrating research and clinical practice.* Rockville, MD: Aspen.

Annon, J. S. (1975). *The behavioral treatment of sexual problems: Intensive therapy.* Honolulu: Enabling Systems.

Araji, S., & Finkelhor, D. (1986). Abusers: A review of the research. In D. Finkelhor (Ed.), *A sourcebook on child sexual abuse* (pp. 89–118). Beverly Hills, CA: Sage.

Armsworth, J. W. (1989). Therapy of incest survivors: Abuse or support? *Child Abuse and Neglect, 13*, 549–562.

Asen, K., George, E., Piper, R., & Stevens, A. (1989). A systems approach to child abuse: Management and treatment issues. *Child Abuse and Neglect, 13*, 45–47.

Auerswald, E. (1968). Interdisciplinary versus ecological approach. *Family Process, 7*, 202–215.

Auerswald, E. (1971). Families, change and the ecological perspective. *Family Process, 10*, 263–289.

Bagley, C., & King, K. (1990). *Child sexual abuse: The search for healing.* London: Tavistock/Routledge.

Bander, K., Fein, E., & Bishop, G. (1982). Child sex abuse treatment: Some barriers to program operation. *Child Abuse and Neglect, 6*, 185–191.

Bandler, R. (1978, March). *Basic patterns of communications and change.* Paper presented at Human Development Seminars, Minneapolis, MN.

Bandler, R., & Grinder, J. (1975). *The structure of magic* (Vol. 1). Palo Alto, CA: Science & Behavior Books.

Bandler, R., & Grinder, J. (1976). *The structure of magic* (Vol. 2). Palo Alto, CA: Science & Behavior Books.

Bandler, R., & Grinder, J. (1979). *Frogs into princes: Neuro-linguistic programming.* Moab, UT: Real People Press.

Bandura, A. (1969). *Principles of behavior modification.* New York: Holt, Rinehart & Winston.

Bank, S., & Kahn, M. (1982). *The sibling bond.* New York: Basic.

Barbach, L. (1982). *For each other: Sharing sexual intimacy.* New York: Doubleday.

Barbach, L. G. (1976). *For yourself: The fulfillment of female sexuality.* New York: Doubleday.

Barbaree, H. E., & Marshall, W. L. (1989). Erectile responses amongst heterosexual child molesters, father-daughter incest offenders, and matched nonoffenders: Five distinct age preference profiles. *Canadian Journal of Behavioral Science, 21,* 70-87.

Barden, R. C. (1994, June). *Avoiding malpractice lawsuits in the practice of psychotherapy.* Workshop presented in St. Paul, MN.

Barkley, R. A., Guevremont, D. C., Anastopoulos, A. D., & Fletcher, K. E. (1992). A comparison of three family therapy programs for treating family conflicts in adolescents with Attention-Deficit Hyperactivity Disorder. *Journal of Consulting and Clinical Psychology, 60*(3), 450-462.

Barnard, G. W., Fuller, A. K., Robbins, L., & Shaw, T. (1989). *The child molester: An integrated approach to evaluation and treatment.* New York: Brunner/Mazel.

Barrett, M. J., & Schwartz, R. (1993, March). *The systemic treatment of child sexual abuse, Part 2: Working with the perpetrator.* Paper presented at the 16th Annual Family Therapy Network Symposium, Washington, D.C.

Barrett, M. J., Sykes, C., & Byrnes, W. (1986). A systemic model for the treatment of intrafamily child sexual abuse. *Journal of Psychotherapy and the Family, 2*(2), 67-82.

Barrett, M. J., Trepper, T. S., & Fish, L. S. (1990). Feminist-informed family therapy for the treatment of intrafamily child sexual abuse. *Journal of Family Psychology, 4*(2), 151-165.

Barton, C., & Alexander, J. F. (1981). Functional family therapy. In A. S. Gurman & D. P. Kniskern (Eds.), *Handbook of Family Therapy* (pp. 403-443). New York: Brunner/Mazel.

Baseeches, M. (1980). Dialectical schemata: A framework for the empirical study of the development of dialectical thinking. *Human Development, 23,* 400-421.

Bass, E., & Davis, L. (1988). *The courage to heal: A guide for women survivors of child sexual abuse.* New York: Harper & Row.

Bass, E., & Thornton, L. (1983). *I never told anyone: Writings by women survivors of child sexual abuse.* New York: Harper & Row.

Bateson, G. (1972). *Steps to an ecology of mind.* Northvale, NJ: Jason Aronson.

Bateson, G. (1979). *Mind and nature: A necessary unity.* New York: Dutton.

Bateson, G., Jackson, D. D., Haley, J., & Weakland, J. H. (1956). Toward a theory of schizophrenia. *Behavioral Science, 1,* 251-264.

Beahrs, J. (1986). *Limits of scientific psychiatry: The role of uncertainty in mental health.* New York: Brunner/Mazel.

Beavers, W. R. (1976). A theoretical basis for family evaluation. In J. M. Lewis (Ed.), *No single thread: Psychological health in family systems* (pp. 46-82). New York: Brunner/Mazel.

Beavers, W. R., & Voeller, M. N. (1983). Family models: Comparing and contrasting the Olson circumplex model with the Beavers system model. *Family Process, 22,* 85-98.

Becvar, D. S., & Becvar, R. J. (1988). *Family therapy: A systemic integration.* Boston: Allyn & Bacon.

Beitchman, J. H., Zucker, K. J., Hood, J. E., DaCosta, A., & Ackman, A. (1991). A review of the short-term effects of child sexual abuse. *Child Abuse and Neglect, 15,* 537-556.

Beitchman, J. H., Zucker, K. J., Hood, J. E., DaCosta, A., Akman, D., & Cassavia, E. (1992). A review of the long-term effects of child sexual abuse. *Child Abuse and Neglect, 16*(1), 101-118.

Bem, S. L. (1974). The measurement of psychological androgyny. *Journal of Consulting and Clinical Psychology, 42*(2), 155-162.

Bentovim, A. (1991). Clinical work with families in which sexual abuse has occurred. In C. R.

Hollin & K. Howells (Eds.), *Clinical approaches to sex offenders and their victims* (pp. 179–208). Chichester, England: John Wiley.

Bentovim, A. (Ed.). (1992). *Trauma organized systems: Physical and sexual abuse in families.* New York: Karnac Books.

Bentovim, A., Boston, P., & Van Elburg, A. (1987). Child sexual abuse: Children and families referred to a treatment project and the effects of intervention. *British Medical Journal, 295,* 1453–1457.

Bentovim, A., Elton, A., Hildebrand, J., Tranter, M., & Vizard, E. (1988). *Sexual abuse in the family.* Bristol, England: John Wright.

Bera, W. (1990). The systemic/attributional model: Victim-sensitive offender therapy. In W. Bera, J. Hindman, L. Hutchens, D. McGuire, & J. M. Yokley (Eds.), *The use of victim-offender communication in the treatment of sexual abuse: Three intervention models* (pp. 45–76). Orwell, VT: The Safer Society Press.

Bera, W., Hindman, J., Hutchens, L., McGuire, D., & Yokley, J. M. (1990). *The use of victim-offender communication in the treatment of sexual abuse: Three intervention models.* Orwell, VT: The Safer Society Press.

Bergson, H. (1944). *Creative evolution.* New York: Modern Library.

Berliner, L. (1991, June). Effects of sexual abuse on children. *Violence Update, 1,* 1,8,10–11.

Bernard, J. (1972). *The future of marriage.* New York: Bantam.

Berne, E. (1964). *Games people play.* New York: Grove.

Berrick, J. D., & Gilbert, N. (1991). *With the best of intentions: The child sexual abuse prevention movement.* New York: Guilford.

Berstein, R. M., Brown, E. M., & Ferrier, M. J. (1984). A model for collaborative team processing in brief systemic family therapy. *Journal of Marital and Family Therapy, 10,* 151–156.

Beutler, I., Burr, W., Bahr, K., & Herrin, D. (1989). The family realm: Theoretical contributions for understanding its uniqueness. *Journal of Marriage and the Family, 51,* 805–816.

Blau, H. (1984). *The psychologist as expert witness.* New York: John Wiley.

Blick, L. C., & Berg, T. S. (1989). The Chesapeake Institute. In S. M. Sgroi (Ed.), *Vulnerable populations: Sexual abuse treatment for children, adult survivors, offenders, and persons with mental retardation* (pp. 285–309). Lexington, MA: Lexington.

Blick, L. C., & Porter, F. S. (1982). Group therapy with female adolescent incest victims. In S. M. Sgroi (Ed.), *Handbook of clinical interventions in child sexual abuse* (pp. 147–175). Lexington, MA: Lexington.

Blythe, B. (1988). Applying practice research methods in intensive family preservation services. In J. K. Whittaker, J. Kinney, E. Tracy, & C. Booth (Eds.), *Improving practice technology for work with high-risk families: Lessons from the Homebuilders Social Work Education Project.* Seattle, WA: Center for Social Welfare Research, School of Social Work, University of Washington.

Boat, B. W., & Everson, M. (1986). *Using anatomical dolls: Guidelines for interviewing young children in sexual abuse investigations.* Chapel Hill, N.C.: Dept. of Psychiatry, University of North Carolina.

Bodin, A. M. (1981). The interactional view: Family therapy approaches of the Mental Research Institute. In A. S. Gurman & D. P. Kniskern (Eds.), *Handbook of family therapy* (pp. 267–309). New York: Brunner/Mazel.

Bograd, M. (1984). Family systems approach to wife battering: A feminist critique. *American Journal of Orthopsychiatry, 54,* 558–568.

Bopp, M. J., & Weeks, G. R. (1984). Dialectical metatheory in family therapy. *Family Process, 23,* 49–61.

Boscolo, L., Checchin, G., Hoffman, L., & Penn, P. (1987). *Milan systemic family therapy: Conversations in theory and practice.* New York: Basic.

Boss, P. (1988). *Family stress management.* Newbury Park, CA: Sage.

Boss, P., & Thorne, D. (1989). Family sociology and family therapy: A feminist linkage. In M. McGoldrick, C. Anderson, & F. Walsh (Eds.), *Women in families: A framework for family therapy* (pp. 78–96). New York: Norton.

Boszormenyi-Nagy, I. (1985). Commentary: Transgenerational solidarity — therapy's mandate and ethics. *Family Process, 24,* 454–456.

Boszormenyi–Nagy, I. (1987). *Foundations of contextual therapy.* New York: Brunner/Mazel.

Bowen, M. (1978). *Family therapy in clinical practice.* New York: Jason Aronson.

Breunlin, D., & Schwartz, R. (1986). Sequences: Toward a common denominator of family therapy. *Family Process, 25,* 67–87.

Breunlin, D. C., Schwartz, R. C., & MacKune–Karrer, B. (1992). *Metaframeworks: Transcending the models of family therapy.* San Francisco: Jossey-Bass Publishers.

Briere, J. (1988). Controlling for family variables in abuse effects research: A critique of the "Partialling" approach. *Journal of Interpersonal Violence, 3,* 80–89.

Briere, J. (1992). *Child abuse trauma: Theory and treatment of the lasting effects.* Newbury Park, CA: Sage.

Briere, J., & Runtz, M. (1989). The trauma symptom checklist (TSC-33): Early data on a new scale. *Journal of Interpersonal Violence, 4*(2), 151–163.

British Psychological Society (1986). Report to the working group on the use of polygraph in criminal investigation and personnel screening. *Bulletin of the British Psychological Society, 39,* 81–93.

Broderick, C. B., & Schrader, S. S. (1981). The history of professional marriage and family therapy. In A. S. Gurman & D. P. Kniskern (Eds.), *Handbook of family therapy* (pp. 5–35). New York: Brunner/Mazel.

Broderick, C. F. (1983). *The therapeutic triangle.* Beverly Hills, CA: Sage.

Brodsky, S. L. (1991). *Testifying in court: Guidelines and maxims for the expert witness.* Washington, D.C.: American Psychological Association.

Bronfenbrenner, U. (1979). *The ecology of human development: Experiments by nature and design.* Cambridge, MA: Harvard University Press.

Bronfenbrenner, U. (1986). Ecology of the family as a context for development: Research perspectives. *Developmental Psychologist, 22,* 723–742.

Brown, P. (1991). *The hypnotic brain: Hypnotherapy and social communication.* New Haven: Yale University Press.

Browne, A., & Finkelhor, D. (1986). Impact of child sexual abuse: A review of the research. *Psychological Bulletin, 99*(1), 66–77.

Bryman, A. (1988). *Quantity and quality in social research.* London: Unwin Hyman.

Buber, M. (1958). *I and thou* (R. G. Smith, Trans.). (2nd ed.). New York: Charles Scribner's Sons.

Bubolz, M. M., & Sontag, M. S. (1993). Human ecology theory. In P. G. Boss, W. J. Doherty, R. LaRossa, W. R. Schumm, & S. Steinmetz (Eds.), *Sourcebook of family theories and methods: A contextual approach* (pp. 419–448). New York: Plenum.

Buckley, W. (1967). *Sociology and modern systems theory.* Englewood Cliffs, NJ: Prentice-Hall.

Bulkley, J. (1981). *Innovations in the prosecution of child sexual abuse cases.* Washington, D.C.: National Legal Resource Center for Child Advocacy in Protection, American Bar Association.

Bullough, V., & Bullough, B. (1977). *Sin, sickness and sanity: A history of sexual attitudes.* New York: New American Library.

Burgess, A., Hartman, C., & McCormick, A. (1987). Abused to abuser: Antecedents of socially deviant behaviors. *American Journal of Orthopsychiatry, 144,* 1431–1436.

Burgess, A. W., Holmstrom, L., & Sgroi, S. (1978). *Sexual assault of children and adolescents.* Lexington, MA: Lexington.

Burkett, L. P. (1991). Parenting behaviors of women who were sexually abused as children in their families of origin. *Family Process, 30,* 421–434.

Burr, W. R., Day, R. D., & Bahr, K. S. (1993). *Family science.* Pacific Grove, CA: Brooks/Cole.

Bursztajn, H., Feinbloom, R., Hamm, R. M., & Brodsky, A. (1981). *Medical choices, medical changes: How patients, families and physicians can cope with uncertainty.* New York: Delacourte.

Campbell, D., & Draper, R. (1985). *Applications of systemic family therapy: The Milan approach.* London: Grune & Stratton.

Campbell, T. (1992). Therapeutic relationships and iatrogenic outcomes: The blame in change maneuver in psychotherapy. *Psychotherapy, 29,* 474–480.

Caplan, P. J., & Hall-McCorquodale, I. (1985a). Mother blaming in major clinical journals. *American Journal of Orthopsychiatry, 55,* 345–353.

Caplan, P. J., & Hall-McCorquodale, I. (1985b). The scapegoating of mothers: A call for change. *American Journal of Orthopsychiatry, 55,* 610–613.

Carnes, P. (1983). *The sexual addiction.* Minneapolis, MN: CompCare.

Carter, B., Papp, P., Silverstein, O., & Walters, M. (1986). The Procrustean bed. *Family Process, 25,* 301–304.

Cartwright, D. (1959). *Studies in social power.* Ann Arbor: University of Michigan.

Catherall, D. R. (1992). Working with objective identification in couples. *Family Process, 31,* 355–367.

Cecchin, G. (1987). Hypothesizing, circularity and neutrality revisited: An invitation to curiosity. *Family Process, 26,* 405–413.

Ceci, S. (1991). Some overarching issues in the child suggestibility debate. In J. Doris (Ed.), *The suggestibility of children's recollections* (pp. 1–9). Washington, DC: American Psychological Association.

Ceci, S. J., & Bruck, M. (1993). The suggestibility of the child witness. *Psychological Bulletin, 113,* 403–439.

Ceci, S. J., & Bruck, M. (1994). How reliable are children's statements?...It depends. *Family Relations, 43,* 255–257.

Centre for Child and Adolescent Development (n.d.). *Sexual abuse treatment program: A family-based assessment and treatment program for sexually abused children and adolescents.* Edmonton, Alberta: Author.

Chapman, J., & Gates, M. (1978). *The victimization of women.* Beverly Hills, CA: Sage.

Charny, I. (1972). *Marital love and hate.* New York: Macmillan.

Charny, I. (1986). An existential/dialectical model for analyzing marital functioning and interaction. *Family Process, 25,* 571–585.

Charny, I. (1992). *Existential/dialectical marital therapy: Breaking the secret code of marriage.* New York: Brunner/Mazel.

Chodorow, N. (1978). *The reproduction of mothering: Psychoanalysis and the sociology of gender.* Berkeley, CA: University of California Press.

Chodorow, N. (1993). Perspectives on the use of case studies: All it takes is one. In P. A. Cavan, D. Field, D. Hansen, A. Skolnick, & G. E. Swanson (Eds.), *Family, self and society: Toward a new agenda in family research* (pp. 453–462). Hillsdale, NJ: Lawrence Erlbaum.

Chubb, H. (1990). Looking at systems as process. *Family Process, 29,* 169–175.

Cirillo, S., & DiBlasio, P. (1992). *Families that abuse: Diagnosis and therapy* (J. Neugroschel, Trans.). New York: Norton.

Coleman, S. B. (Ed.). (1985). *Failures in family therapy.* New York: Guilford.

Constantine, L. (1986). *Family paradigms: The practice of theory in family therapy.* New York: Guilford.

Constantine, L. (1988). *The geometry of family theory.* Paper presented at the Theory Construction and Research Methodology Workshop, National Council on Family Relations, Philadelphia, PA.

Constantine, L., & Martinson, F. M. (1981). *Children and sex.* Boston: Little, Brown.

Conte, J. (1985). The effects of sexual abuse on children: A critique and suggestions for future research. *Victimology: An International Journal, 10,* 110–130.

Conte, J. (1986). Sexual abuse and the family: A critical analysis. *Journal of Psychotherapy and the Family, 2,* 113–126.

Conte, J. (1988). The effects of sexual abuse on children: Results of a research project. In R. Prentky & V. Quinsey (Eds.), *Human sexual aggression: Current perspectives* (pp. 310–326). New York: New York Academy of Sciences.

Conte, J. (1990). The incest offender: An overview and introduction. In A. L. Horton, B. L. Johnson, L. M. Roundy, & D. Williams (Eds.), *The incest perpetrator* (pp. 19–28). Newbury Park, CA: Sage.

Conte, J. (1991). Child sexual abuse: Looking backward and forward. In M. Q. Patton (Ed.), *Family sexual abuse: Frontline research and evaluation* (pp. 3–22). Newbury Park, CA: Sage.

Conte, J., & Karasu, T. B. (1992). A review of treatment studies of minor depression 1980–1991. *American Journal of Psychotherapy, 46,* 58–74.

Conte, J., & Schuerman, J. R. (1987). Factors associated with an increased impact of child sexual abuse. *Child Abuse and Neglect, 11,* 201–213.

Conte, J., & Schuerman, J. (1988). The effects of sexual abuse on children: A multidimensional view. In G. Wyatt & G. Powell (Eds.), *Lasting effects of child sexual abuse* (pp. 157–170). Newbury Park, CA: Sage.

Conte, J. R., & Shore, D. A. (1982). *Social work and child sexual abuse.* New York: Haworth.

Corey, G., Corey, M., & Callahan, P. (1993). *Issues and ethics in the helping professions* (4th ed.). Belmont, CA: Brooks/Cole.

Cromwell, R. E., & Olson, D. H. (1975). *Power in families*. New York: John Wiley.

Cronen, V., Johnson, K., & Lannamann, J. (1982). Paradoxes, double binds, and reflexive loops: An alternative theoretical perspective. *Family Process, 21*, 91–112.

Crosbie-Burnett, M., & Lewis, E. A. (1993). Theoretical contributions from social- and cognitive-behavioral psychology. In P. G. Boss, W. J. Doherty, R. LaRossa, W. R. Schumm, & S. K. Steinmetz (Eds.), *Sourcebook of family theories and methods: A contextual approach*. New York: Plenum.

D'Emilio, J., & Freedman, E. B. (1988). *Intimate matters: A history of sexuality in America*. New York: Harper & Row.

Damon, L., & Waterman, J. (1986). Parallel group treatment of children and their mothers. In K. MacFarlane & J. Waterman (Eds.), *Sexual abuse of young children* (pp. 244–299). New York: Guilford.

Daro, D. (Ed.). (1988). *Confronting child abuse: Research for effective program design*. New York: Free Press.

Davis, L. V. (1991). Violence and families. *Social Work, 36*(5), 371–373.

Deacon, R., & Firebaugh, F. (1988). *Family resource management*. Boston: Allyn & Bacon.

Dell, P. (1985). Understanding Bateson and Maturana: Toward a biological foundation for the social sciences. *Journal of Marital and Family Therapy, 11*, 1–20.

Dell, P. (1986). In defense of "lineal causality". *Family Process, 25*, 513–529.

Dell, P. (1989). Violence and the systemic view: The problem of power. *Family Process, 28*, 1–14.

Dell, P. F. (1983). What is normal? From pathology to ethics. *Family Therapy Networker*, November/December, 29–31, 64.

Dell, P. F. (1984). Why family therapy should be both homeostatic and coherent: A Kuhian reply to Ariel, Carel, and Tyano. *Journal of Marital and Family Therapy, 10*, 351–356.

Dempster, H. L., & Roberts, J. (1991). Child sexual abuse research, A methodological quagmire. *Child Abuse and Neglect, 15*, 593–595.

Dent, H., & Flin, R. (Eds.). (1992). *Children as witnesses*. Chichester, England: John Wiley.

Denton, W. (1989). DSM-III-R and the family therapist: Ethical considerations. *Journal of Marital and Family Therapy, 15*, 367–377.

Denton, W. (1990). A family systems analysis of DSM-III-R. *Journal of Marital and Family Therapy, 16*, 113–125.

de Shazer, S. (1982). *Patterns of brief family therapy: An ecosystemic approach*. New York: Guilford.

de Shazer, S. (1983). Diagnosing equals researching plus doing therapy. In B. P. Keeney (Ed.), *Diagnosis and assessment in family therapy* (pp. 123–132). Rockville, MD: Aspen.

de Shazer, S. (1985). *Keys to solution in brief therapy*. New York: Norton.

deYoung, M. (1982). *Sexual victimization of children*. Jefferson, NC: McFarland.

deYoung, M. (1986). A conceptual model for judging the truth of a young child's allegation of sexual abuse. *American Journal of Orthopsychiatry, 56*, 550–558.

Dilworth-Anderson, P., Burton, L. M., & Johnson, L. B. (1993). Reframing theories for understanding race, ethnicity, and families. In P. G. Boss, W. J. Doherty, R. Larossa, W. R. Schumm, & S. Steinmetz (Eds.), *Sourcebook of family theories and methods: A contextual approach* (pp. 627–645). New York: Plenum.

Dinnerstein, D. (1976). *The mermaid and the minotaur: Sexual arrangements and human malaise*. New York: Harper & Row.

Doherty, W. (1986). Quanta, quarks, and families: Implications of quantum physics for family research. *Family Process, 25*, 249–263.

Doherty, W. J. (1995). *Soul-searching: Why psychotherapy must promote moral responsibility*. New York: Basic Books.

Doherty, W. J., & Boss, P. G. (1991). Values and ethics in family therapy. In A. Gurman & D. Kniskern (Eds.), *Handbook of family therapy* (pp. 606–637). New York: Brunner/Mazel.

Doherty, W. J., Boss, P. G., LaRossa, R., Schumm, W. R., & Steinmetz, S. K. (1993). Family theories and methods: A contextual approach. In P. G. Boss, W. J. Doherty, R. LaRossa, W. R. Schumm, & S. Steinmetz (Eds.), *Sourcebook of family theories and methods: A contextual approach* (pp. 3–30). New York: Plenum.

Dolan, Y. M. (1991). *Resolving sexual abuse: Solution-focused therapy and Ericksonian hypnosis for adult survivors.* New York: Norton.

Donovan, D. M., & McIntyre, D. (1990). *Healing the hurt child: Developmental-contextual approach.* New York: Norton.

Doris, J. (Ed.). (1991). *The suggestibility of children's recollections: Implications for eyewitness testimony.* Washington D.C.: American Psychological Association.

Dovenberg, D. C. (1985). *The family project: Multiple family/multiple therapist treatment of incest.* St. Paul, MN: Amherst H. Wilder Foundation, Wilder Child Guidance Clinic.

Doxiadis, S. A. (1989). Children, society and ethics. *Child Abuse and Neglect, 13,* 11–17.

Drane, J. (1982). Ethics and psychotherapy: A philosophical perspective. In M. Rosenbaum (Ed.), *Ethics and values in psychotherapy: A guidebook.* New York: Free Press.

Dziech, B. W., & Schudson, C. B. (1991). *On trial: America's courts and their treatment of sexually abused children* (2nd ed.). Boston: Beacon.

Edel, A. (1961). *Science and the structure of ethics.* Chicago: University of Chicago Press.

Edwards, B. (1979). *Drawing on the right side of the brain.* Los Angeles: J. P. Tarcher.

Ehrenberg, M., & Ehrenberg, O. (1988). *The ultimate circle: The sexual dynamics of family life.* New York: Simon & Schuster.

Epstein, E. S., & Loos, V. E. (1989). Some irreverent thoughts on the limits of family therapy: Towards a language-based explanation of human systems. *Journal of Family Psychology, 2,* 405–421.

Epstein, N. B., Baldwin, L., & Bishop, D. (1983). The McMaster Family Assessment Device. *Journal of Marital and Family Therapy, 9*(2), 213–228.

Epston, D. (1989). *Collected Papers.* Adelaide, South Australia: Dulwich Center.

Erickson, E. (1950). *Childhood and society.* New York: Norton.

Erikson, E. (1959). *Identity and the life cycle: Selected papers.* New York: International Universities Press.

Erikson, E. (1964). *Insight and responsibility.* New York: Norton.

Erikson, E. H. (1963). *Childhood and society* (2nd ed.). New York: Norton.

Erikson, E. H. (1968). *Identity: Youth and crisis.* New York: Norton.

Everstine, D. S., & Everstine, L. (1989). *Sexual trauma in children and adolescents: Dynamics and treatment.* New York: Brunner/Mazel.

Faller, K. C. (1981). *Social work with abused and neglected children: A manual of interdisciplinary practice.* New York: Free Press.

Faller, K. C. (1984). Is the child victim of sexual abuse telling the truth? *Child Abuse and Neglect, 8,* 473.

Falzer, P. (1984). The cybernetic metaphor: A critical examination of ecosystemic epistemology as a foundation of family therapy. *Family Process, 25,* 353–363.

Farrall, W. R., & Card, R. D. (1988). Advancements in physiological evaluation of assessment and treatment of the sexual aggressor. In R. Prentky & V. Quinsey (Eds.), *Human sexual aggression: Current perspectives* (pp. 261–273). New York: New York Academy of Sciences.

Farrell, W. (1986). *Why men are the way they are.* New York: Berkeley Books.

Feldman–Summers, S., & Pope, K. S. (1994). The experience of "forgetting" childhood abuse: A national survey of psychologists. *Journal of Consulting and Clinical Psychology, 62*(3), 636–639.

Festinger, L. (1957). *A theory of cognitive dissonance.* Evanston, IL: Row, Peterson.

Figley, C. (Ed.). (1985). *Trauma and its wake.* New York: Brunner/Mazel.

Fincham, F. D., Beach, S. R., Moore, T., & Diener, C. (1994a). Child sexual abuse: Finding common ground. *Family Relations, 43,* 264–266.

Fincham, F. D., Beach, S. R., Moore, T., & Diener, C. (1994b). The professional response to child sexual abuse: Whose interests are served? *Family Relations, 43,* 244–254.

Finkelhor, D. (1979). *Sexually victimized children.* New York: The Free Press.

Finkelhor, D. (1980). Sex among siblings: A survey report of its prevalence, variety, and effects. *Archives of Sexual Behavior, 9,* 171–194.

Finkelhor, D. (1984). *Child sexual abuse: New theory and research.* New York: Free Press.

Finkelhor, D. (Ed.). (1986). *A sourcebook on child sexual abuse.* Beverly Hills: Sage.

Finkelhor, D. (1988). The trauma of child sexual abuse: Two models. In G. Wyatt & G. Powell (Eds.), *Lasting effects of child sexual abuse* (pp. 61–84). Newbury Park: Sage.

Finkelhor, D. (1990). Early and long term effects of child sexual abuse: An update. *Professional Psychology: Research and Practice, 21,* 325–330.

Finkelhor, D., & Browne, A. (1985). The traumatic impact of child sexual abuse: A conceptualization. *American Journal of Orthopsychiatry, 55,* 530–541.

Finkelhor, D., Gelles, R. J., Hotaling, G. T., & Straus, M. A. (1983). *The dark side of families: Current family violence research.* Beverly Hills: Sage.

Finkelhor, D., Hotaling, G., Lewis, I. A., & Smith, C. (1990). Sexual abuse in a national survey of adult men and women: Prevalence, characteristics, and risk factors. *Child Abuse and Neglect, 14,* 19–28.

Finkelhor, D., & Korbin, J. (1988). Child abuse as an international issue. *Child Abuse & Neglect, 12*(1), 3–23.

Finkelhor, D., & Lewis, I. (1988). An epidemiologic approach to the study of child molestation. In R. Prentky & V. Quinsey (Eds.), *Human sexual aggression: Current perspectives* (pp. 64–78). New York: New York Academy of Sciences.

Finkelhor, D., & Zellman, G. L. (1991). Flexible reporting options for skilled child abuse professionals. *Child Abuse and Neglect, 15,* 335–341.

Fish, V. (1990). Introducing causality and power into family therapy theory: A correction to the systemic paradigm. *Journal of Marital and Family Therapy, 16,* 21–37.

Fish, V., & Faynick, C. (1989). Treatment of incest families with the father temporarily removed: A structural approach. *Journal of Strategic and Systemic Therapies, 8*(4), 53–63.

Fisher, L. (1977). On the classification of families: A progress report. *General Psychiatry, 34,* 424–433.

Fisher, S. (1989). *Social images of the self: The psychology of erotic sensations and illusions.* Hillsdale: Laurence Erlbaum Associates.

Flaherty, M. Y. (1991, June). *Couples treatment of adult female survivors of childhood sexual abuse.* Paper presented at the 10th World Congress for Sexology, Amsterdam, The Netherlands.

Ford, D. H., & Lerner, R. M. (1992). *Developmental systems theory: An integrative approach.* Newbury Park, CA: Sage.

Ford, F. R. (1983). Rules: The invisible family. *Family Process, 22,* 135–145.

Foucault, M. (1977). *The history of sexuality.* London: Allan Lane.

Fox, W. (1990). *Toward a transpersonal ecology: Developing new foundations for environmentalism.* Boston: Shambhala.

Freud, S. (1900). The interpretation of dreams. In J. Strachey (Ed. & Trans.), *The standard edition of the complete psychological works of Sigmund Freud,* IV–V. New York: Norton.

Freud, S. (1938). *The basic writings of Sigmund Freud* (A. A. Brill, Trans.). New York: Modern Library.

Friedman, S. (1988). A family systems approach to treatment. In L. E. Auerback Walker (Ed.), *Handbook on sexual abuse of children* (pp. 326–349). New York: Springer.

Friedman, S. (Ed.). (1993). *The new language of change: Constructive collaboration in psychotherapy.* New York: Guilford.

Friedrich, W. M., & Reams, R. A. (1987). Course of psychological symptoms in sexually abused young children. *Psychotherapy, 24,* 160–170.

Friedrich, W. N. (1990). *Psychotherapy of sexually abused children and their families.* New York: Norton.

Friedrich, W. N. (Ed.). (1991). *Casebook of sexual abuse treatment.* New York: Norton.

Friedrich, W. N., Grambsch, P., Damon, L., Hewitt, S. K., Koverola, C., Lang, R. A., Wolfe, V., & Broughton, D. (1992). Child sexual behavior inventory: Normative and clinical comparisons. *Psychological Assessment, 4,* 303–311.

Fromuth, M. E. (1986). The relationship of childhood sexual abuse with later psychological and sexual adjustment in a sample of college women. *Child Abuse & Neglect, 10,* 5–15.

Fulton, W. C. (1965). Why the need for a Sex Information and Education Council of the United States as a new, separate organization. *SIECUS Newsletter, 1,* 1–2.

Gagnon, J., & Simon, W. (1973). *Sexual conduct: The social sources of human sexuality.* Chicago: Aldine.

Garbarino, J. (1977). The human ecology of child maltreatment: A conceptual model for research. *Journal of Marriage and Family Therapy, 35,* 272–282.

Garbarino, J. (1992). *Children and families in the social environment* (2nd ed.). New York: Aldine De Gruyter.

Gardner, R. A. (1986). *Child custody litigation: A guide for parents and mental health professionals.* Cresskill, NJ: Creative Therapeutics.

Gardner, R. A. (1989). *Family evaluation in child custody mediation, arbitration, and litigation.* Cresskill, NJ: Creative Therapeutics.

Gardner, R. A. (1991). *Sex abuse hysteria: Salem witch trials revisited.* Creskill, NJ: Creative Therapeutics.

Gardner, R. A. (1992). *True and false accusations of child sex abuse.* Cresskill, NJ: Creative Therapeutics.

Gardner, R. S. (1987). *The parental alienation syndrome and the differentiation between fabricated and genuine child sex abuse.* Creskill, NJ: Creative Therapeutics.

Gazzaniga, M. (1985). *The social brain: Discovering the networks of the mind.* New York: Basic Books.

Gebhard, P., Gagnon, J., Pomeroy, W., & Christenson, C. (1965). *Sex offenders: An analysis of types.* New York: Harper and Row.

Gelinas, D. (1988). Family therapy: Characteristic family constellation and basic therapeutic stance. In S. M. Sgroi (Ed.), *Vulnerable populations: Evaluation and treatment of sexually abused children and adult survivors* (pp. 25–50). Lexington, MA: Lexington Books.

Gelinas, D. J. (1986). Unexpected resources in treating incest families. In M. A. Karpel (Ed.), *Family resources: The hidden partner in family therapy* (pp. 327–358). New York: Guilford.

Gelles, R. J. (1987). *Family Violence* (2nd ed.). London: Sage.

Gelles, R. J., & Cornell, C. P. (1985). *Intimate violence in families.* Beverly Hills, CA: Sage.

Gelles, R. J., & Loseke, D. R. (Eds.). (1993). *Current controversies on family violence.* Newbury Park: Sage.

Gelles, R. J., & Straus, M. A. (1979). Determinants of violence in the family: Toward a theoretical integration. In W. R. Burr, R. Hill, F. I. Nye, & I. L. Reiss (Eds.), *Contemporary theories about the family* (pp. 549–581). New York: Free Press.

Gendlin, E. (1962). *Experiencing and the creation of meaning.* New York: Free Press.

Gergen, K., & Davis, K. (1985). *The social construction of the person.* New York: Springer-Verlag.

Giarretto, H. (1976). The treatment of father-daughter incest: A psycho-social approach. *Children Today, 5,* 2–5.

Giarretto, H. (1982a). A comprehensive child sexual abuse treatment program. *Child Abuse and Neglect, 6,* 263–278.

Giarretto, H. (1982b). *Integrated treatment of child sexual abuse: A treatment and training manual.* Palo Alto, CA: Science & Behavior Books.

Giarretto, H., & Einfeld–Giarretto, A. (1990). Integrated treatment: The self–help factor. In A. Horton, B. L. Johnson, L. M. Roundy, & D. Williams (Eds.), *The incest perpetrator: A family member no one wants to treat* (pp. 219–226). Newbury Park, CA: Sage.

Giarretto, H. A. (1978). Humanistic treatment of father-daughter incest. *Journal of Humanistic Psychology, 18,* 59–76.

Gibbs, N. (1993, January 18). 'Til death do us part. *Time,* p. 37–45.

Gil, E. (1991). *The healing power of play.* New York: Guilford.

Gil, E., & Johnson, T. C. (1993). *Sexualized children: Assessment and treatment of sexualized children and children who molest.* Rockville, MD: Launch Press.

Gilgun, J. (1984). Does the mother always know? Alternatives to blaming mothers for child sexual abuse. *Responses to the Victimization of Women and Children, 7,* 2–4.

Gilgun, J. F. (1988). Self-centeredness and the adult male perpetrator of child sexual abuse. *Contemporary Family Therapy, 10,* 216–233.

Gilgun, J. F. (1990). Factors mediating the effects of childhood maltreatment. In M. Hunter (Ed.), *The sexually abused male, Vol. 1: Prevalence, impact, and treatment* (pp. 177–190). Lexington, MA: Lexington.

Gilgun, J. F. (1991a). Discovery-oriented, qualitative methods relevant to longitudinal research on child abuse and neglect. In R. H. Starr & B. A. Wolfe (Eds.), *The effects of child abuse and neglect: Issues in research* (pp. 144–163). New York: Guilford.

Gilgun, J. F. (1991b). Resilience and the intergenerational transmission of child sexual abuse. In M. Q. Patton (Ed.), *Family sexual abuse: Frontline research and evaluation* (pp. 93–105). Newbury Park, CA: Sage.

Gilgun, J. F., Daly, K., & Handel, G. (Eds.). (1992). *Qualitative methods in family research.* Newbury Park, CA: Sage.

Gilligan, C. (1983). *In a different voice: Psychological theory and development.* Cambridge, MA: Harvard University Press.

Glenn, M. (1984). *On diagnosis: A systemic approach.* New York: Brunner/Mazel.

Goldner, V. (1985). Feminism and family therapy. *Family Process, 24,* 31–47.

Goldner, V. (1988). Generation and gender: Normative and covert hierarchies. *Family Process, 27,* 17–31.

Goldner, V. (1991). Sex, power, and gender: A feminist systemic analysis of the politics of passion. *Journal of Feminist Family Theory, 3*(1/2), 63–83.

Gomes-Schwartz, G., Horowitz, J. M., & Cardarelli, A. P. (Eds.). (1990). *Child sexual abuse: The initial effects.* Newbury Park: Sage.

Gonsiorek, J. C., Bera, W. H., & LeTourneau, D. (1994). *Male sexual abuse: A trilogy of intervention strategies.* Thousand Oaks, CA: Sage.

Goodman, G., & Aman, C. (1990). Children's use of anatomically detailed dolls to recount an event. *Child Development, 61,* 1859–1871.

Goodman, G. S. (1984). Journal of Social Issues special issue: The Child Witness. *Journal of Social Issues, 40*(2), 1–193.

Goodman, G. S., & Bottoms, B. L. (Eds.). (1993). *Child victims, child witnesses: Understanding and Improving Testimony.* New York: Guilford.

Goodman, G. S., Rudy, L., Bottoms, B. L., & Aman, C. (1990). Children's concerns and memory: Issues of ecological validity in children's testimony. In R. Fivush & J. Hudson (Eds.), *Knowing and remembering in young children* (pp. 249–284). New York: Cambridge University Press.

Gordon, L. (1988). *Heroes of their own lives: The politics and history of family violence.* New York: Penguin.

Gottman, J. (1982). Temporal form: Toward a new language for describing relationships. *Journal of Marriage and the Family, 44,* 943–962.

Grauerholz, E., & Koralewski, M. A. (1991). *Sexual coercion: A sourcebook on its nature, causes, and prevention.* Lexington, MA: Lexington.

Gray, W. N., Duhl, F. D., & Rizzo, N. D. (1969). *General Systems Theory and psychiatry.* Boston: Little, Brown.

Gray-Little, B., & Burks, N. (1983). Power and satisfaction in marriage: A review and critique. *Psychological Bulletin, 93,* 513–538.

Green, L., & Hanson, J. (1989). Ethical dilemmas faced by family therapists. *Journal of Marital and Family Therapy, 15,* 139–158.

Greenspon, T. S. (1993, April 3). "False Memory" movement is backlash against survivors. *Minneapolis Star Tribune.*

Grinder, J., DeLozier, J., & Bandler, R. (1977). *Patterns of the hypnotic techniques of Milton H. Erickson, M.D.* Cupertino, CA: Meta Publications.

Grotevant, H. D., & Carlson, C. I. (1989). *Family assessment: A guide to methods and measures.* New York: Guilford.

Groth, A. N., Hobson, W. F., & Gary, T. S. (1982). The child molester: Clinical observations. *Journal of Social Work and Human Sexuality, 1*(1/2), 129–144.

Groth, A. N., & Birnbaum, J. (1979). *Men who rape: Sex in the family.* New York: Human Sciences.

Guerney, B., Brock, G., & Coufal, J. (1986). Integrating marital therapy and enrichment: The relationship enhancement approach. In N. S. Jacobson & A. S. Gurman (Eds.), *Clinical handbook of marital therapy* (pp. 151–172). New York: Guilford Press.

Guerney, D. P. (Ed.). (1977). *Relationship enhancement: Skill training programs for therapy, problem prevention and enrichment.* San Francisco: Jossey-Bass.

Gumper, L. L., & Sprenkle, D. H. (1981). Privileged communication in therapy: Special problems for the family and couples therapist. *Family Process, 20,* 11–23.

Gurman, A., & Kniskern, D. (1981). Family therapy outcome research: Knowns and unknowns. In A. Gurman & D. Kniskern (Eds.), *Handbook of family therapy* (pp. 742–775). New York: Brunner/Mazel.

Gurman, A. S., Kniskern, D. P., & Pinsof, W. M. (1986). Research on the process and outcome of marital and family therapy. In A. Garfield & A. Bergin (Eds.), *Handbook of psychotherapy and behavior change* (pp. 525-623). New York: John Wiley.

Gustafson, J. P. (1986). *The complex secret of brief psychotherapy*. New York: Norton.

Gutheil, T. A., & Avery, N. G. (1977). Multiple overt incest as family defense against loss. *Family Process, 16*(1), 105-116.

Hagons, K. B. (1991). *Pockets of craziness: Examining suspected incest*. Lexington, MA: Lexington.

Haley, J. (Ed.). (1967). *Advanced techniques of hypnosis and therapy: Selected papers of Milton H. Erickson, M. D.* New York: Grune & Stratton.

Haley, J. (1973). *Uncommon therapy: The psychiatric techniques of Milton H. Erickson, M.D.* New York: Norton.

Haley, J. (1975). Why a mental health clinic should avoid family therapy. *Journal of Marriage and Family Counseling, 1,* 1-13.

Haley, J. (1976). *Problem-solving therapy*. San Francisco: Jossey-Bass.

Haley, J. (1978). Ideas which handicap therapists. In M. Berger (Ed.), *Beyond the double bind* (pp. 65-82). New York: Brunner/Mazel.

Haley, J. (1984). Marriage or family therapy. *American Journal of Family Therapy, 12,* 3-14.

Hall, G. C. N. (1989). Self-reported hostility as a function of offense characteristics and response style in a sexual offender population. *Journal of Consulting and Clinical Psychiatry, 57,* 306-308.

Hare-Mustin, R. T. (1980). Family therapy may be dangerous to your health. *Professional Psychology, 11,* 935-938.

Hare-Mustin, R. T. (1986). The problem of gender in family therapy theory. *Family Process, 26,* 15-27.

Hargrove, E. (1989). *Foundation of environmental ethics*. Englewood Cliffs, NJ: Prentice-Hall.

Hartman, H. (1958). *Ego psychology and the problem of adaptation*. New York: International Universities Press.

Haugaard, J. J., & Emery, R. E. (1989). Methodological issues in child sexual abuse research. *Child Abuse and Neglect, 13,* 89-100.

Haugaard, J. J., & Reppucci, N. D. (1988). *Sexual abuse of children*. San Francisco: Jossey-Bass.

Heatherington, L. (1990). Family therapy, control, and controllingness. *Journal of Family Psychology, 4*(2), 132-150.

Hechler, D. (1988). *The battle and the backlash: The child sexual abuse war*. Lexington, MA: Lexington.

Hedges, L. E. (1994). *Remembering, repeating and working through childhood trauma: The psychodynamics of recovered memories, multiple personality, ritual abuse, incest, molestation and abduction*. Northvale, NJ: Jason Aronson.

Hegel, G. (1910/1807). *The phenomenology of the mind*. London: Swann Sonnenschein.

Heidegger, M. (1962). *Being and time*. New York: Harper & Row.

Heiman, J., & LoPiccolo, J. (1988). *Becoming orgasmic: A sexual and personal growth program for women* (2nd ed.). New York: Prentice-Hall.

Heiman, M. L. (1988). Untangling incestuous bonds: The treatment of sibling incest. In M. D. Kahn & K. G. Lewis (Eds.), *Siblings in therapy: Life span and clinical issues* (pp. 135-166). New York: Norton.

Henley-Walters, L., & Devall, E. (1989). *Use of an ecosystem perspective to conceptualize marital adjustment during the transition to parenthood*. Paper presented at the Theory Construction and Research Methodology Workshop, National Council on Family Relations, New Orleans, LA.

Herman, J. L. (1992). *Trauma and recovery: The aftermath of violence, from domestic abuse to political terror*. New York: Basic.

Herrin, D., & Wright, S. (1988). Precursors to a family ecology: Interrelated threads of ecological thought. *Family Science Review, 1,* 163-183.

Hildebran, D., & Pithers, W. D. (1989). Enhancing offender empathy for sexual-abuse victims. In R. D. Laws (Ed.), *Relapse prevention with sex offenders* (pp. 236-244). New York: Guilford.

Hindman, J. (1989). *Just before dawn: From the shadows of tradition to new reflections in trauma assessment and treatment for sexual victimization.* Ontario, OR: AlexAndria Associates.

Hite, S. (1987). *Women and love: A cultural revolution in progress.* New York: Knopf.

Hoffman, L. (1981). *Foundations of family therapy: A conceptual framework for systems change.* New York: Basic.

Hoke, S., Sykes, C., & Winn, M. (1989). Systemic/strategic interventions targeting denial in the incestuous family. *Journal of Strategic and Systemic Therapies, 8*(4), 44–51.

Hollin, C. R., & Howells, K. (Eds.). (1991). *Clinical approaches to sex offenders and their victims.* New York: John Wiley & Sons.

Horton, A. L. (1992). The transition from punishment to compulsory treatment for incest perpetrators: An emerging holistic model for family treatment. *Topics in Family Psychology and Counseling, 1*(2), 30–38.

Horton, A. L., Johnson, B. L., Roundy, L. M., & Williams, D. (Eds.). (1990). *The incest perpetrator: A family member no one wants to treat.* Newbury Park, CA: Sage.

Howitt, D. (1992). *Child abuse errors: When good intentions go wrong.* New Brunswick, NJ: Rutgers University Press.

Hudson, W. (1982). *The clinical measurement package: A field manual.* Homewood, IL: Dorsey.

Hunter, R. S., & Kilstrom, N. (1979). Breaking the cycle in abusive families. *American Journal of Psychiatry, 136,* 1320–1322.

Hutchinson, E. D. (1993). Mandatory reporting laws: Child-protective case finding gone awry? *Social Work, 38,* 56–63.

Imber-Black, E. (1986). The systemic consultant and human service–provider systems. In L. C. Wynne, S. H. McDaniel, & T. T. Weber (Eds.), *Systems consultation* (pp. 357–373). New York: Guilford.

Imber-Black, E. (Ed.). (1988). *Families and larger systems.* New York: Guilford.

Imber-Black, E. (1993). *Secrets in families and family therapy.* New York: Norton.

Imber-Black, E., Roberts, J., & Whiting, R. (1988). *Rituals in families and family therapy.* New York: Norton.

Ingersoll, S. L., & Patton, S. O. (1990). *Treating perpetrators of sexual abuse.* Lexington, MA: Lexington.

James, B. (1989). *Treating traumatized children: New insights and creative interventions.* Lexington, MA: Lexington.

James, B., & Nasjleti, M. (1983). *Treating sexually abused children and their families.* Palo Alto, CA: Consulting Psychologist Press.

James, K., & McIntyre, D. (1983). The reproduction of families: The social role of family therapy. *Journal of Marital and Family Therapy, 9,* 119–129.

Janoff-Bulman, R. (1992). *Shattered assumptions: Towards a new psychology of trauma.* New York: Free Press.

Janoff-Bulman, R., & Frieze, I. H. (1983). A theoretical perspective for understanding reactions to victimization. *Journal of Social Issues, 39,* 1–17.

Jenkins, A. (1990). *Invitations to responsibility: The therapeutic engagement of men who are violent and abusive.* Adelaide, South Australia: Dulwich Centre Publications.

Jenkins-Hall, K. D. (1989). Cognitive restructuring. In D. R. Laws (Ed.), *Relapse prevention with sex offenders* (pp. 207–215). New York: Guilford.

Johnson, S. M. (1985). *Characterological transformation: The hard work miracle.* New York: Norton.

Johnson, T. C. (1988). Child perpetrators—Children who molest other children: Preliminary findings. *Child Abuse and Neglect, 12,* 219–229.

Johnson, T. C., & Feldmuth, J. R. (1993). Sexual behaviors: A continuum. In E. Gil & T. C. Johnson (Eds.), *Sexualized children: Assessment and treatment of sexualized children and children who molest* (pp. 41–52). Rockville, MD: Launch Press.

Justice, B., & Justice, R. (1976). *The abusing family.* New York: Human Sciences Press.

Justice, B., & Justice, R. (1979). *The broken taboo: Sex in the family.* New York: Human Sciences.

Kaminer, W. (1994, January 23). Can someone be a victim and still be guilty? *San Francisco Examiner.*

Kantor, D. (1986). Genesis: How does a family begin? In S. Sugarman (Ed.), *The interface of individual and family therapy* (pp. 28–49). Rockville, MD: Aspen.

Kantor, D., & Lehr, W. (1975). *Inside the family*. San Francisco: Jossey-Bass.

Kaplan, H. S. (1974). *The new sex therapy*. New York: Brunner/Mazel.

Kaplan, H. S. (1979). *Disorders of desire and other new concepts and techniques in sex therapy*. New York: Brunner/Mazel.

Kaufman, G. (1980). *Shame: The power of caring*. Cambridge, MA: Schenkman Press.

Keeney, B. P. (1983). *Diagnosis and assessment in family therapy*. Rockville, MD: Aspen Publishing.

Keeney, B. P., & Ross, J. M. (1985). *Mind in therapy: Constructing systemic family therapies*. New York: Basic.

Keeney, B. P., & Sprenkle, D. (1982). Ecosystemic epistemology: Critical implications for the aesthetics and pragmatics of family therapy. *Family Process, 21*, 1–21.

Kegan, R. G. (1982). *The evolving self: Problem and process in human development*. Cambridge, MA: Harvard University Press.

Kendall-Tacket, K. A., Williams, L. M., & Finkelhor, D. (1993). Impact of sexual abuse on children: A review and synthesis of recent empirical studies. *Psychological Bulletin, 113*(1), 164–180.

Kerr, M. E. (1981). Family systems theory and therapy. In A. S. Gurman & D. P. Kniskern (Eds.), *Handbook of family therapy* (pp. 226–264). New York: Brunner/Mazel.

Kinsbourne, M. (1982). Hemispheric specialization and the growth of human understanding. *American Psychologist, 37*, 411–420.

Kinston, W., Loader, P., & Miller, L. (1987). Quantifying the clinical assessment of family health. *Journal of Marital and Family Therapy, 13*, 49–67.

Knight, C. J. (1985). Setting up a systemic therapy team in a local authority social services department area office: How to be one down and still invited to the ball. In D. Campbell & R. Draper (Eds.), *Applications of systemic family therapy: The Milan approach* (pp. 87–96). London: Grune & Stratton.

Knight, R. (1988). A taxonomic analysis of child molesters. In R. Prentky & V. Quinsey (Eds.), *Human sexual aggression: Current perspectives* (pp. 2–21). New York: New York Academy of Sciences.

Knight, R. A., & Prentky, R. A. (1990). Classifying sexual offenders: The development and corroboration of taxonomic models. In W. L. Marshall, D. R. Laws, & H. E. Barbaree (Eds.), *Handbook of sexual assault: Issues, theories and treatment of the offender* (pp. 23–51). New York: Plenum.

Knoetig, H. (1993). Human ecology: The exact science of interrelationships between Homo Sapiens and the outside world surrounding this living and thinking being. In S. D. Wright, T. Dietz, R. Borden, G. Young, & G. Guagnano (Eds.), *Human ecology: Crossing boundaries* (pp. 114–135). Fort Collins, CO: Society for Human Ecology.

Knopp, F. H. (1984). *Retraining adult sex offenders: Methods and models*. Syracuse, NY: Safer Society Press.

Knopp, F. H., & Stevenson, W. F. (1989). *Nationwide survey of juvenile and adult sex-offender treatment programs and models*. Orwell, VT: Safer Society Press.

Kohlberg, L. (1976). Moral stages and moralization: The cognitive-developmental approach. In T. Lickona (Ed.), *Moral development and behavior*. New York: Holt, Rhinehart and Winston.

Kohut, H. (1971). *The analysis of the self: A systematic approach to the psychoanalytic treatment of narcissistic personality disorders*. New York: International Universities Press.

Kohut, H. (1977). *The restoration of the self*. New York: International Universities Press.

Kolb, D. A. (1984). *Experiential learning: Experience as the source of learning and development*. Englewood-Cliffs, NJ: Prentice-Hall.

Kon, I. (1988). A sociocultural approach. In J. Geer & W. O'Donohue (Eds.), *Theories of sexuality* (pp. 257–286). New York: Plenum Press.

Kroth, J. (1979). *Child sexual abuse: Analysis of a family therapy approach*. Springfield, IL: Charles C. Thomas.

Kutchinsky, B. (1992a). Pornography and rape: Theory and practice? Evidence from crime data in four countries where pornography is easily available. *International Journal of Law and Psychiatry, 14*, 47–64.

Kutchinsky, B. (1992b). The child sexual abuse panic. *Nordisk Sexologi, 10*, 30–42.

Kutchinsky, B. (1994). Child sexual abuse: Prevalence, phenomenology, intervention, and prevention: An overview. *Nordisk Sexologi, 12*, 51–61.

Laing, R. D. (1971). *The politics of the family* (p. 89). New York: Pantheon.

Lally, C. F., & Maddock, J. W. (1994). Sexual meaning systems of engaged couples. *Family Relations, 43,* 53–60.

Laney, J. T. (1968). Norm and context in ethics: A reconsideration. *Soundings, 52,* 31–42.

Lang, R. A. (1991). Child sexual abusers who use pornography with children. In R. Langevin (Ed.), *Sex offenders and their victims* (pp. 53–75). Oakville, Ontario: Juniper Press.

Langevin, R. (1983). *Sexual strands: Understanding and treating sexual anomalies in men.* Hillsdale: Lawrence Erlbaum Associates.

Langevin, R. (Ed.). (1991). *Sex offenders and their victims.* Oakville, Ontario: Juniper Press.

Langs, R. (1976). *The bipersonal field.* New York: Jason Aronson.

Langs, R. (1978). *The listening process.* New York: Jason Aronson.

Lanier, J. (1970). *The evolution of Eve.* New York: Interbook.

Lankton, C. H. (1985). Elements of an Ericksonian approach. In S. Lankton (Ed.), *Ericksonian monographs* (pp. 61–75). New York: Brunner/Mazel.

Lankton, S. (1980). *Practical magic: A translation of basic Neuro-Linguistic Programming into clinical psychotherapy.* Cupertino, CA: Meta.

Lankton, S. R., & Lankton, C. H. (1986). *Enchantment and intervention in family therapy.* New York: Brunner/Mazel.

Lanyon, R. I. (1991). Theories of sex offending. In C. R. Hollin & K. Howells (Eds.), *Clinical approaches to sex offenders and their victims* (pp. 35–54). Chichester, England: John Wiley.

LaRossa, R., & Reitzes, D. C. (1993). Symbolic interactionism and family studies. In P. G. Boss, W. J. Doherty, R. LaRossa, W. R. Schumm, & S. Steinmetz (Eds.), *Sourcebook of family theories and methods: A contextual approach* (pp. 135–163). New York: Plenum.

Larsen, A., & Olson, D. H. (1990). Capturing the complexity of family systems: Integrating family theory, family scores, and family analysis. In T. W. Draper & A. C. Marcos (Eds.), *Family variables: Conceptualization, measurement, and use* (pp. 19–47). Newbury Park, CA: Sage.

Larson, N. R. (1980) *An analysis of the effectiveness of a state-sponsored program designed to teach intervention skills in the treatment of family sexual abuse.* Unpublished doctoral dissertation, School of Social Work, University of Minnesota.

Larzelere, R. E., & Klein, D. M. (1986). Methodology. In M. B. Sussman & S. K. Steinmetz (Eds.), *Handbook of marriage and the family* (p. 125). New York: Plenum.

Laws, D. R. (Ed.). (1989). *Relapse prevention with sex offenders.* New York: Guilford.

Leaman, K. M. (1980). Sexual abuse: The reactions of child and family. In K. MacFarlane, B. M. Jones, & L. L. Jenstrom (Eds.), *Sexual abuse of children: Selected readings (DHHS Publication No. OHDS 78-30161).* Washington, D. C.: U.S. Government Printing Office.

Lebow, J. (1986). Training family therapists as feminists. In M. Ault-Riche (Ed.), *Women and family therapy.* Rockville, MD: Aspen.

Lebow, J., Rasien, P., & Caust, B. (1982). Feminist and family systems therapy: Are they irreconcilable? *American Journal of Family Therapy, 10,* 3–12.

Lebow, J. L. (1984). On the value of integrating approaches to family therapy. *Journal of Marital and Family Therapy, 10,* 127–138.

Lederer, W. J., & Jackson, D. D. (1968). *The mirages of marriage.* New York: Norton.

Leiblum, S. R., & Rosen, R. C. (Eds.). (1988). *Sexual desire disorders.* New York: Guilford.

Leik, R., Roberts, C., Caron, W., Mangen, D., & Leik, S. (1990). Temporal mapping: A method for analyzing process. In T. Draper & A. Marcos (Eds.), *Family variables: Conceptualization, measurement and use.* Newbury Park, CA: Sage.

Lerner, M. J. (1980). *The belief in a just world: A fundamental delusion.* New York: Plenum.

Lerner, R. (1978). Nature, nurture, and dynamic interactionism. *Human Development, 21,* 1–20.

Levy, S. T. (1984). *Principles of interpretation.* Northvale, NJ: Jason Aronson.

Liddle, H. (1984). Towards a dialectical-contextual-coevolutionary translation of structural-strategic family therapy. *Journal of Strategic and Systemic Therapies, 3,* 66–79.

Liddle, H. A. (1991). Empirical values and the culture of family therapy. *Journal of Marital and Family Therapy, 17,* 327–348.

Lipsey, M. W., & Wilson, D. B. (1993). The efficacy of psychological, educational and behavioral treatment: Confirmations from meta-analysis. *American Psychologist, 48*(12), 1181–1209.

Lloyd, S. (1991). The darkside of courtship: Violence and sexual exploitation. *Family Relations, 40,* 14–20.

Locke, H. J., Sabaugh, G., & Thomas, M. M. (1956). Correlates of primary communication and empathy. In *Research Studies of the State College of Washington, 24*, pp. 116–124. State College of Washington.

Lockhart, L. L., Saunders, B. E., & Cleveland, P. (1989). Adult male sex offenders: An overview of treatment techniques. *Journal of Social Work and Human Sexuality, 7*(2), 1–32.

Loftus, E. (1991). Made in memory: Distortions of recollection after misleading information. In G. Bower (Ed.), *Psychology of learning and motivation* (pp. 187–215). New York: Academic Press.

Loftus, E., & Davies, G. (1984). Distortions in the memory of children. *Journal of Social Issues, 40*, 51–68.

Loftus, E., & Ketcham, K. (1994). *The myth of repressed memory: False memories and allegations of sexual abuse.* New York: St. Martin's.

Loftus, E. F. (1993). Psychologists in the eyewitness world. *American Psychologist, 48*, 550–552.

Long, S. (1986). Guidelines for treating young children. In K. MacFarlane & J. Waterman (Eds.), *Sexual abuse of young children* (pp. 220–243). New York: Guilford.

LoPiccolo, J., & LoPiccolo, L. (Eds.). (1978). *Handbook of sex therapy.* New York: Plenum.

Love, P. (1990). *The emotional incest syndrome.* New York: Bantam.

Lovelock, J. (1979). *Gaia: A new look at life on earth.* Oxford: Oxford University Press.

Luepnitz, D. A. (1988). *The family interpreted: Feminist theory in clinical practice.* New York: Basic.

Lundberg, S. (1990). Domestic violence: A psychodynamic approach and implications for treatment. *Psychotherapy, 27*, 243–248.

Lustig, N., Dressler, J. W., Spellman, S. W., & Murray, T. B. (1966). Incest: A family group survival pattern. *Archives of General Psychiatry, 14*, 31–39.

Lutz, S. E., & Medway, J. P. (1984). Contextual family therapy with the victims of incest. *Journal of Adolescence, 7*, 319–327.

MacFarlane, K., & Bulkley, J. (1982). Treating child sexual abuse: An overview of current program models. In J. R. Conte & D. A. Shore (Eds.), *Social work and child sexual abuse* (pp. 65–91). New York: Haworth Press.

MacFarlane, K., & Waterman, J. (1986). *Sexual abuse of young children.* New York: Guilford.

Madanes, C. (1981). *Strategic family therapy.* San Francisco: Jossey-Bass.

Madanes, C. (1984). *Behind the one-way mirror.* San Francisco: Jossey-Bass.

Madanes, C. (1990). *Sex, love, and violence: Strategies for transformation.* New York: Norton.

Maddock, J. W. (1973). Sex in adolescence: Its meaning and its future. *Adolescence, 8*, 325–342.

Maddock, J. W. (1975). Sexual health and health care. *Postgraduate Medicine, 58*, 52–58.

Maddock, J. W. (1986). The dialectics of victimization: The family's role in the problem and the solution. In M. H. Hicks & V. Sabbison (Eds.), *Victimization, families, and empowerment.* Beverly Hills, CA: Sage.

Maddock, J. W. (1988). Child reporting and testimony in incest cases: Comments on the construction and reconstruction of reality. *Behavioral Sciences and the Law, 6*(2), 201–220.

Maddock, J. W. (1989). *Power/Control Survey.* St. Paul, MN: Department of Family Social Science, University of Minnesota.

Maddock, J. W. (1993). Ecology, ethics, and responsibility in family therapy. *Family Relations, 42*, 116–123.

Maddock, J. W., & Larson, N. R. *Child sexual abuse: An ecological approach to treating victims and perpetrators.* New York: Norton. Manuscript in preparation.

Maddock, J. W., Larson, P. R., & Lally, C. F. (1991). An evaluation protocol for incest family functioning. In M. Q. Patton (Ed.), *Family sexual abuse: Frontline research and evaluation* (pp. 162–177). Newbury Park, CA: Sage.

Mahrer, A. R. (1985). *Psychotherapeutic change: An alternative approach to meaning and measurement.* New York: Norton.

Malamuth, N., & Donnerstein, E. (Eds.). (1984). *Pornography and sexual aggression.* New York: Academic Press.

Maletzky, B. M. (1991). *Treating the sexual offender.* Newbury Park, CA: Sage.

Mandell, J. G., & Damon, L. (1989). *Group treatment for sexually abused children.* New York: Guilford.

Marshall, W. L., & Barbaree, H. E. (1990). An integrated theory of the etiology of sexual offending. In W. L. Marshall, D. R. Laws, & H. E. Barbaree (Eds.), *Handbook of sexual assault: Issues, theories and treatment of the offender* (pp. 257–278). New York: Plenum.

Marshall, W. L., Laws, D. R., & Barbaree, H. E. (Eds.). (1990). *Handbook of sexual assault: Issues, theories and treatment of the offender.* New York: Plenum.

Mason, M. A. (1991). The McMartin case revisited: The conflict between social work and criminal justice. *Social Work, 36*(5), 391–395.

Masson, J. M. (1984). *The assault on truth: Freud's suppression of the seduction theory.* New York: Farrar, Straus & Giroux.

Masters, W., & Johnson, V. (1970). *Human sexual inadequacy.* Boston: Little, Brown.

Matthew, W. J. (1985). A cybernetic model of Ericksonian hypnotherapy: One hand draws the other. In S. R. Lankton (Ed.), *Elements and dimensions of an Ericksonian approach* (pp. 42–60). New York: Brunner/Mazel.

Matthews, J. K., Mathews, R., & Speltz, K. (1991). Female sexual offenders: A typology. In M. Q. Patton (Ed.), *Family sexual abuse: Frontline research and evaluation* (pp. 199–219). Newbury Park: Sage.

Matthews, J. K., Raymaker, J., & Speltz, K. (1991). Effects of reunification on sexually abusive families. In M. Q. Patton (Ed.), *Family sexual abuse: Frontline research and evaluation.* Newbury Park, CA: Sage.

Maturana, H. (1985). *The biology of cognition.* Paper presented at a conference on Gregory Bateson: The Pattern that Connects, College of St. Benedict, St. Joseph, MN.

Maturana, H., & Varela, F. (1980). *Autopoesis and cognition: The realization of the living.* Boston: Reidel.

Maturana, H. R., & Varela, F. J. (1987). *The tree of knowledge: The biological roots of human understanding.* Boston: New Science Library.

Mayer, A. (1983). *Incest: A treatment manual for therapy with victims, spouses, and offenders.* Holmes Beach, FL: Learning Publications.

Mayer, A. (1984). Do lie detectors lie? In J. J. Sullivan, J. L. Victor, & D. E. J. MacNamara (Eds.), *Annual editions: Criminal justice* (pp. 158–159). Guilford, CT: Duskin.

Mayer, A. (1988). *Sex offenders: Approaches to understanding and management.* Holmes Beach, FL: Learning Publications.

McCarthy, B., & McCarthy, E. (1984). *Sexual awareness: Enhancing sexual pleasure.* New York: Carroll & Graf.

McCarthy, B., & McCarthy, E. (1989). *Female sexual awareness: Achieving sexual fulfillment.* New York: Carroll & Graf.

McCarthy, B., & McCarthy, E. (1993). *Confronting the victim role: Healing from an abusive childhood.* New York: Carroll & Graf.

McCarthy, B. W. (1990). Treatment of incest families: A cognitive–behavioral model. *Journal of Sex Education and Therapy, 16*(2), 101–114.

McCarthy, I. C., & Byrne, N. O. (1988). Mis-taken love: Conversations on the problem of incest in an Irish context. *Family Process, 27,* 181–198.

McClosky, M., & Egeth, H. E. (1983). Eyewitness identification: What can a psychologist tell a jury? *American Psychologist, 38,* 550–563.

McGoldrick, M., Anderson, C. M., & Walsh, F. (Eds.). (1989). *Women in families: A framework for family therapy.* New York: Norton.

McGoldrick, M., Pearce, J. K., & Giordano, J. (Eds.). (1982). *Ethnicity and family therapy.* New York: Guilford.

McGovern, K. B. (1991). The assessment of sexual offenders. In B. M. Maletzky (Ed.), *Treating the sexual offender* (pp. 35–67). Newbury Park, CA: Sage.

McTavish, D. G., & Pirro, E. B. (1984, April). *Contextual content analysis.* Paper presented at the meeting of the Pacific Sociological Association, Seattle, WA.

Mead, G. H. (1934). *Mind, self and society.* Chicago: University of Chicago Press.

Meiselman, K. C. (1978). *Incest: A psychological study of causes and effects with treatment recommendations.* San Francisco: Jossey-Bass.

Melito, R. (1985). Adaptation in family systems: A developmental approach. *Family Process, 24,* 89–100.

Meloy, R. G. (1988). *The psychopathic mind: Origins, dynamics and treatment.* Northwale: Jason Aronson.

Melton, G. B., Petrila, J. D., Poythress, N. G., & Slobogin, C. (1987). *Psychological evaluation for the courts: A handbook for mental health professionals and lawyers.* New York: Guilford.

Meyer, A. (1984). Do lie detectors lie. In J. J. Sullivan, J. L. Victor, & D. E. J. MacNamara (Eds.), *Annual Editions: Criminal Justice 83/84* (pp. 158-159). Guildford, CT: Duskin.

Micklin, M., & Choldin, H. N. (Eds.). (1984). *Sociological human ecology: Contemporary issues and applications.* Boulder, CO: Westview.

Miller, S., Nunnally, E. W., & Wackman, D. B. (1975). *The Minnesota couples communication program: Instructor's manual.* Minneapolis, MN: Interpersonal Communication Programs.

Miller, S., Nunnally, E. W., & Wackman, D. B. (1976). A communication training program for couples. *Social Casework, 57,* 9-18.

Minuchin, S. (1974). *Families and family therapy.* Cambridge, MA: Harvard University Press.

Minuchin, S., & Fishman, H. C. (1981). *Family therapy techniques.* Cambridge, MA: Harvard University Press.

Montgomery, J., & Fewer, W. (1988). *Family systems and beyond.* New York: Human Sciences Press.

Mrazek, P. B., & Bentovim, A. (1981). Incest and the dysfunctional family system. In P. B. Mrazek & C. H. Kempe (Eds.), *Sexually abused children and their families.* New York: Pergamon.

Mrazek, P. B., & Kempe, C. H. (Eds.). (1981). *Sexually abused children and their families.* New York: Pergamon.

Murphy, W., & Peters, J. (1992). Profiling child sexual abusers: Legal considerations. *Criminal Justice and Behavior, 19*(1), 24-37.

Myer, M. H. (1985). A new look at mothers of incest victims. *Journal of Social Work and Human Sexuality, 3,* 47-58.

Myers, J. E. B. (1992). *Legal issues in child abuse and neglect.* Newbury Park, CA: Sage.

Myers, J. E. B. (Ed.). (1994). *The backlash: Child protection under fire.* Thousand Oaks, CA: Sage.

Naess, A. (1989). *Ecology, community and lifestyle: Outlines of an ecosphere* (D. Rothenberg, Trans.). Cambridge, England: Cambridge University Press.

National Research Council (1993). *Understanding child abuse and neglect.* Washington, D.C.: National Academy Press.

Nelson, K. (1985). *Making sense: The acquisition of shared meaning.* Orlando: Academic Press.

Nicholson, E. B. (1988). Child sexual abuse allegations in family court proceedings: A survey of legal issues. In E. B. Nicholson & J. Bulkley (Eds.), *Sexual abuse allegations in custody and visitation cases* (pp. 255-277). Washington, DC: American Bar Association.

Nye, F. I. (1988). Fifty years of family research, 1937-1987. *Journal of Marriage and the Family, 50,* 569-584.

O'Brien, M. (1989). *Characteristics of male adolescent sibling incest offenders.* Orwell, VT: Safer Society Press.

O'Connell, M. (1986). Reuniting incest offenders and their families. *Journal of Interpersonal Violence, 1*(3), 374-386.

O'Donohue, W. T., & Elliot, A. N. (1992). Treatment of the sexually abused child: A review. *Journal of Clinical Child Psychology, 21*(3), 218-228.

O'Hanlon, W. H. (1987). *Taproots: Underlying principles of Milton H. Erickson's therapy and hypnosis.* New York: Norton.

Odum, H. (1983). *Systems ecology: An introduction.* New York: John Wiley.

Ofshe, R., & Watters, E. (1994). *Making monsters: False memories, psychotherapy, and sexual hysteria.* New York: Charles Scribner's Sons.

Olson, D., McCubbin, H., Barnes, H., Larsen, A., Muxen, M., & Wilson, M. (1982). *Families: What makes them work.* Beverly Hills, CA: Sage.

Olson, D. H. (1976). Bridging research, theory, and application: The triple threat in science. In D. H. Olson (Ed.), *Treating relationships* (pp. 565-579). Lake Mills, IA: Graphic.

Olson, D. H. (1977). Insiders' and outsiders' views of relationships: Research strategies. In G. Levinger & H. Raush (Eds.), *Close relationships: Perspectives on the meaning of intimacy.* Amherst: Amherst University.

Olson, D. H., McCubbin, H. I., Barnes, H., Larsen, A., Muxen, M., & Wilson, M. (1985). *Family inventories: Inventories used in a national survey of families across the family life cycle* (Rev. ed.). St. Paul, MN: University of Minnesota.

Olson, D. H., Portner, J., & Lavee, Y. (1985). FACES III: *Family adaptability and cohesion evaluation scales.* St. Paul, MN: Department of Family Social Science, University of Minnesota Press.

Olson, D. H., Russell, C. S., & Sprenkle, D. H. (Eds.). (1989). *Circumplex model: Systemic assessment and treatment of families.* New York: Haworth Press.

Osborne, H. (1981). The contextual meaning of "meaning". *Dialectics and Humanism, 2,* 77–84.

Paolucci, B., Hall, O. A., & Axinn, N. (1977). *Family decision making: An ecosystems approach.* New York: John Wiley.

Papp, P. (1983). *The process of change.* New York: Guilford.

Patton, M. Q. (Ed.). (1991). *Family sexual abuse: Frontline research and evaluation.* Newbury Park, CA: Sage.

Pearce, J., & Friedman, S. (Eds.). (1980). *Family therapy: Combining psychodynamic and family systems approaches.* New York: Grune & Stratton.

Pearce, W. B., & Cronen, V. (1980). *Communication, action and meaning: The creation of social realities.* New York: Praeger.

Pence, A. (Ed.). (1988). *Ecological research with children and families.* New York: Teachers College Press.

Penn, P. (1982). Circular questioning. *Family Process, 21,* 267–280.

Peters, S. D. (1985, August). *Child sexual abuse and later psychological problems.* Paper presented at the annual meeting of the American Psychological Association, Los Angeles, CA.

Pezdek, K. (1994). Avoiding false claims of child sexual abuse. *Family Relations, 43,* 258–260.

Pfohl, S. (1984). The "discovery" of child abuse. In D. H. Kelly (Ed.), *Deviant behavior.* New York: St. Martin's.

Phelan, P. (1987). Incest: Socialization within a treatment program. *American Journal of Orthopsychiatry, 57(1),* 84–92.

Piaget, J. (1970). *Genetic epistemology* (E. Duckworth, Trans.). New York: Columbia University Press.

Plyer, A., Woolley, C. S., & Anderson, T. K. (1990). Current treatment providers. In A. L. J. Horton B. L., L. M. Roundy, & D. Williams (Eds.), *The incest perpetrator* (pp. 198–218). Newbury Park, CA: Sage.

Popper, K., & Eccles, J. (1977). *The self and its brain: An argument for interactionism.* Berlin: Springer.

Porter, F. S., Blick, L. C., & Sgroi, S. M. (1982). Treatment of the sexually abused child. In S. M. Sgroi (Ed.), *Handbook of clinical intervention in child sexual abuse* (pp. 109–145). Lexington, MA: Lexington.

Poster, M. (1978). *Critical theory of the family.* New York: Seabury.

Poynter, W. L. (1994). *The preferred provider's handbook.* New York: Brunner/Mazel.

Prentky, R. A., & Quinsey, V. L. (Eds.). (1988). *Human sexual aggression: Current perspectives.* New York: New York Academy of Sciences.

Prigogine, I. (1980). *From being to becoming: Time and complexity in the physical sciences.* San Francisco: Freeman.

Psychotherapy Finances (1993). *Managed care handbook.* Jupiter, FL: Ridgewood Financial Institute.

Quindlen, A. (1993, December 10). Victims or victimizers? People can fit both categories at once. *Minneapolis Star Tribune.*

Rabkin, R. (1986). A tower of babble: The sociology of body and mind. *Family Process, 25,* 153–163.

Raney, J. (Ed.). (1984). *Listening and interpreting: The challenge of the work of Robert Langs.* New York: Jason Aronson.

Rank, M. (1988, November). *The blending of quantitative and qualitative family research.* Paper presented at the Workshop on Theory Construction and Research Methodology, Annual conference of the National Council on Family Relations, Philadelphia, PA.

Ray, K. C., Jackson, J. L., & Twonsley, R. M. (1991). Family environments of victims of intrafamilial and extrafamilial child sexual abuse. *Journal of Family Violence, 6(4),* 365–374.

Realmuto, G. M., Jensen, J. B., & Wescoe, S. (1990). Specificity and sensitivity of sexually anatomically correct dolls in substantiating abuse: A pilot study. *Journal of the American Academy of Child and Adolescent Psychiatry, 29,* 743–746.

Reiss, D. (1981). *The family's construction of reality.* Cambridge, MA: Harvard University Press.

Reiss, I., & Reiss, H. (1990). *An end to shame: Shaping our next sexual revolution.* Buffalo, NY: Prometheus.

Renshaw, D. C. (1982). *Incest: Understanding and treatment.* Boston: Little, Brown.

Rest, J. R. (1986). *Moral development: A new phase of research.* New York: Prager.

Rettig, K. D. (1993). Problem solving and decision making as central processes of family life: An ecological framework for family relations and family resource management. *Marriage and Family Review, 18,* 187–222.

Ribordy, S. (1990). Treating intrafamilial child sexual abuse from a systemic perspective. *Journal of Psychotherapy and the Family, 6*(3–4), 71–88.

Rice, A. S., & Tucker, S. M. (1986). *Family life management.* New York: Macmillan.

Riegel, K. (1979). *Foundations of dialectical psychology.* New York: Academic Press.

Ritterman, M. (1983). *Hypnosis in family therapy.* New York: Brunner/Mazel.

Robins, M. (1991). *Assessing child maltreatment reports: The problem of false allegations.* New York: Haworth.

Robins, M. (1992, May). *Beyond validation interviews: An assessment approach to evaluating sexual abuse treatment.* Paper presented at The Third National Conference on Allegations of Child Sexual Abuse, Portland, OR.

Rogers, C. R. (1961). *On becoming a person.* Boston: Houghton Mifflin.

Rosenfeld, A. A. (1979). Incidence of history of incest among 18 female psychiatric patients. *American Journal of Psychiatry, 136*(6), 791–795.

Rossi, A. (1977). A biosocial perspective on parenting. *Daedalus, 106,* 1–31.

Rossi, A. (1985). Gender and parenthood. In A. S. Rossi (Ed.), *Gender and the life course* (pp. 161–191). Hawthorne, NY: Aldine.

Rush, F. (1977). The Freudian cover-up. *Chrysalis, 1,* 31–45.

Rush, F. (1980). *The best kept secret.* New York: Prentice-Hall.

Russell, D. E. H. (1983). The incidence and prevalence of intrafamilial and extrafamilial abuse of female children. *Child Abuse and Neglect, 7,* 133–146.

Russell, D. E. H. (1986). *The secret trauma: Incest in the lives of girls and women.* New York: Basic.

Ryan, G. (1989). Victim to victimizer: Rethinking victim treatment. *Journal of Interpersonal Violence, 4*(3), 325–341.

Ryan, R. (1986). Problems, errors and opportunities in the treatment of father-daughter incest. *Journal of Interpersonal Violence, 1*(1), 113–124.

Rychlak, J. (1976). The multiple meanings of dialectic. In J. Rychlak (Ed.), *Dialectic: Humanistic rationale for behavior and development* (pp. 1–17). Basel: Karger.

Saba, G. W., Karrer, B. M., & Hardy, K. V. (Eds.). (1989). *Minorities and family therapy.* New York: Haworth.

Salter, A. C. (1988). *Treating child sex offenders and victims.* Beverly Hills: Sage.

Sander, F. M. (1979). *Individual and family therapy: Toward an integration.* New York: Jason Aronson.

Sanderson, M. O., & Maddock, J. W. (1989). Guidelines of assessment and treatment of sexual dysfunction. *Obstetrics and Gynecology, 73,* 130–134.

Sandler, J. (1960). *On the concept of the superego.* New York: International Universities Press.

Satir, V. (1967). *Conjoint family therapy: A guide to theory and technique* (Revised ed.). Palo Alto, CA: Science and Behavior Books.

Scanzoni, J., Polonko, K., Teachman, J., & Thompson, L. (1989). *The sexual bond: Rethinking families and close relationships.* Newbury Park, CA: Sage.

Scharff, D. E., & Scharff, J. S. (1987). *Object relations family therapy.* Northvale, NJ: Jason Aronson.

Scheinberg, M. (1992). Navigating treatment impasses at the disclosure of incest: Combining ideas from feminism and social construction. *Family Process, 31,* 201–216.

Schetky, D. H., & Green, A. H. (Eds.). (1988). *Child sexual abuse: A handbook for health care and legal professionals.* New York: Brunner/Mazel.

Schnarch, D. M. (1989). Use of inherent paradox in post-modern sexual-marital therapy. In L. N. Ascher (Ed.), *Therapeutic paradox* (pp. 219–254). New York: Guilford.

Schnarch, D. M. (1991). *Constructing the sexual crucible: An integration of sexual and marital therapy.* New York: Norton.

Schoenewolf, G. (1989). *Sexual animosity between men and women.* Northvale, NJ: Jason Aronson.

Selvini-Palazzoli, M., Boscolo, A., Cecchin, G., & Prata, G. (1980). Hypothesizing-circularity-neutrality: Three guidelines for the conductor of the session. *Family Process, 19,* 3–12.

Selvini-Palazzoli, M., Cecchin, G., Prata, G., & Boscolo, L. (1978). *Paradox and counter-paradox: A new model in the therapy of the family in schizophrenic transaction.* New York: Jason Aronson.

Sgroi, S. (Ed.). (1988). *Vulnerable populations: Evaluation and treatment of sexually abused children and adult survivors.* Lexington, MA: Lexington.

Sgroi, S. (1989). *Vulnerable populations: Sexual abuse treatment for children, adult survivors; offenders, and persons with mental retardation.* Lexington, MA: Lexington.

Sgroi, S. M. (1982). *Handbook of clinical intervention in child abuse.* Toronto: Lexington.

Shadish, W. R. (1992). Do family and marital psychotherapies change what people do? A meta-analysis of behavioral outcomes. In T. D. Cook, H. Cooper, D. S. Cordray, H. Hartmann, L. V. Hedges, R. J. Light, T. A. Louis, & F. Mosteller (Eds.), *Meta-analysis for exploration: A casebook* (pp. 129–208). New York: Russell Sage Foundation.

Shadish, W. R., Montgomery, L. M., Wilson, P., Wilson, M. R., Bright, I., & Okwumabua, T. (1993). Effects of family and marital psychotherapies: A meta analysis. *Journal of Consulting and Clinical Psychology, 61*(6), 992–1002.

Shapiro, S., & Dominiak, G. M. (1992). *Sexual trauma and psychopathology: Clinical intervention with adult survivors.* New York: Lexington.

Sheinberg, M. (1992). Navigating treatment impasses at the disclosure of incest: Combining ideas from feminism and social constructionism. *Family Process, 31,* 201–216.

Shields, C. G. (1986). Critiquing the new epistemologies: Toward minimum requirements for a scientific theory of family therapy. *Journal of Marital and Family Therapy, 12,* 359–372.

Sholevar, G. P. (1975). A family therapist looks at the problem of incest. *The Bulletin of the American Academy of Psychiatry and Law, 3*(1), 25–31.

Siegal, N. (1991). *Knowing children: Experiments in conversation and cognition.* London: Lawrence Erlbaum.

Siegel, D. J. (1992, February). Using the memories of childhood trauma in the treatment of adults. Paper presented at the American College of Psychiatrists Annual Conference, San Francisco, CA.

Silver, R. L., & Wortman, C. B. (1980). Coping with undesirable life events. In J. Garber & M. E. P. Seligman (Eds.), *Human helplessness* (pp. 279–340). New York: Academic Press.

Simmons, D. S., & Doherty, W. J. (1995). Defining who we are and what we do: Clinical practice patterns of marriage and family therapists in Minnesota. *Journal of Marital and Family Therapy, 21*(1), 3–16.

Sjoegren, L. H. (1994, June 5). *Child sexual abuse—The common idea of high prevalence and some consequences of such a misconception.* Paper presented at The Second Congress of the European Federation of Sexology, Copenhagen, Denmark.

Skinner, B. F. (1953). *Science and human behavior.* New York: Macmillan.

Slipp, S. (1984). *Object relations: A dynamic bridge between individual and family treatment.* New York: Jason Aronson.

Sluzki, C., & Ransom, D. (Eds.). (1976). *Double bind: The foundation of the communicational approach to the family.* New York: Grune & Stratton.

Sluzki, C. E. (1983). Process, structure and world views: Toward an integrated view of systemic models in family therapy. *Family Process, 22*(December), 469–476.

Smith, H., & Israel, E. (1987). Sibling incest: A study of the dynamics of 25 cases. *Child Abuse and Neglect, 11,* 101–108.

Smith, R. (1991). Ethical issues in marital and family therapy: Who is the client? *The Family Psychologist, 7,* 16.

Sommers-Flanagan, R., & Walters, H. A. (1987). The incest offender, power, and victimization: Scales on the same dragon. *Journal of Family Violence, 2*(2), 163–175.

Spiegel, J. (1971). *Transactions: The interplay between individual, family, and society.* New York: Science House.

Spiegel, J. (1982). An ecological model of ethnic families. In M. McGoldrick, J. K. Pearce, & J. Giordano (Eds.), *Ethnicity and family therapy* (pp. 31–51). New York: Guilford.

Spoentgen, P. A. (1992). *Goal setting in family therapy with intrafamilial sexual abuse families.* Unpublished doctoral dissertation, Department of Family Social Science, University of Minnesota.

Sprey, J. (1988). Current theorizing on the family: An appraisal. *Journal of Marriage and the Family, 50,* 875–890.

Stanton, M. D. (1981). Strategic approaches to family therapy. In A. S. Gurman & D. P. Kniskern (Eds.), *Handbook of family therapy* (pp. 361–402). New York: Brunner/Mazel.

Stanton, M. D. (1984). Fusion, compression, diversion, and the workings of paradox: A theory of therapeutic/systemic change. *Family Process, 23,* 135–167.

Star Tribune (1991, November 10–12). Free to Rape, Series: Repeat offenders, lenient sentences, and what to do with rapists. *Star Tribune.*

Starr, R. H., & Wolfe, D. A. (E.). (1991). *The effects of child abuse and neglect: Issues and research.* New York: Guilford.

Steinem, G. (1992). *Revolution from within* (pp. 80–81). Boston: Little, Brown.

Steiner, B. (1973). *The rescue triangle.* Unpublished manuscript.

Stierlin, H. (1969). *Conflict and reconciliation.* New York: Science House.

Stierlin, H. (1987). Coevolution and coindividuation. In H. Stierlin, F. B. Simon, & G. Schmidt (Eds.), *Familiar realities* (pp. 99–108). New York: Brunner/Mazel.

Stock, W. (1985). The influence of gender on power dynamics in relationships. In D. Goldberg (Ed.), *Contemporary marriage* (pp. 62–99). Homewood, IL: Dorsey.

Stokols, D. (1992). Establishing and maintaining healthy environments: Toward a social ecology of health promotion. *American Psychologist, 47,* 6–22.

Stoller, R. J. (1975). *Perversion: The erotic form of hatred.* New York: Pantheon.

Straus, M. A. (1980). Sexual inequality and wife beating. In M. A. Straus & G. T. Hotaling (Eds.), *The social causes of husband-wife violence* (pp. 211–234). Minneapolis, MN: University of Minnesota Press.

Straus, M. A., Gelles, R. J., & Steinmetz, S. K. (1981). *Behind closed doors: Violence in the American family.* Newbury Park, CA: Sage.

Sugarman, S. (Ed.). (1986). *The interface of individual and family therapy.* Rockville, MD: Aspen.

Summit, R. (1983). The child sexual abuse accommodation syndrome. *Child Abuse and Neglect, 7,* 177–193.

Sykes, C. J. (1992). *A nation of victims: The decay of the American character.* New York: St. Martin's.

Szasz, T. S. (1961). *The myth of mental illness.* New York: Harper & Row.

Tafoya, T. (1994, Spring). Epistemology of Native healing and family psychology. *The Family Psychologist,* 28–31.

Taggart, M. (1982). Linear versus systemic values: Implications for family therapy. In L. L'Abate (Ed.), *Ethics, values, legalities and family therapy* (pp. 23–39). Rockville, MD: Aspen.

Taggart, M. (1985). The feminist critique in epistemological perspective: Questions of context in family therapy. *Journal of Marital and Family Therapy, 11,* 113–126.

Tavris, C. (1993a, February 16). An abuse of memory? Established methods for digging out sexual trauma are questioned. *Star Tribune,* p. 1, Variety Section.

Tavris, C. (1993b, January 3). Beware the incest-survivor machine. *The New York Times Book Review, 7,* 16–17.

Taylor, R. L. (1984). Marital therapy in the treatment of incest. *Social Casework, 65*(4), 195.

Teilhard de Chardin, P. (1965). *The phenomenon of man* (B. Wall, Trans.). New York: Harper & Row.

Teilhard de Chardin, P. (1966). *Man's place in nature* (R. Hague, Trans.). New York: Harper & Row.

Terr, L. C. (1990). *Too scared to cry.* New York: Basic.

Thoennes, N., & Tjaden, P. G. (1990). The extent, nature, and validity of sexual abuse allegations in custody/visitation disputes. *Child Abuse & Neglect, 14,* 151–163.

Thomas, D. L., & Wilcox, J. E. (1987). The rise of family theory: A historical and critical analysis. In M. B. Sussman & S. K. Steinmetz (Eds.), *Handbook of Marriage and the Family* (pp. 81–102). New York: Plenum.

Thomas, E. (1994, August 29). Day and night. He lived two lives: An inside look at O. J. Simpson's world. *Newsweek,* p. 43-49.

Thorman, G. (1983). *Incestuous families.* Springfield, IL: Charles C. Thomas.

Thorne, B., & Henley, N. (1975). *Language and sex: Difference and dominance.* Rowley, MA: Newbury House.

Thorne, B., & Yalom, M. (Eds.). (1982). *Rethinking the family: Some feminist questions.* New York: Longman.

Tierney, K., & Corwin, D. (1983). Exploring interfamilial child sexual abuse: A systems approach. In D. Finkelhor, R. J. Gelles, G. Hotaling, & M. A. Straus (Eds.), *The dark side of families* (pp. 102-116). Beverly Hills, CA: Sage.

Tillich, P. (1951). *Systematic theology.* Chicago: University of Chicago Press.

Tillich, P. (1963). *Morality and beyond.* New York: Harper & Row.

Tomm, K. (1984a). One perspective on the Milan Systemic approach: Part I. Overview of development, theory and practice. *Journal of Marital and Family Therapy, 10,* 113-125.

Tomm, K. (1984b). One perspective on the Milan Systemic approach: Part II. Description of session format, interviewing style and interventions. *Journal of Marital and Family Therapy, 10,* 253-271.

Tomm, K. (1985). Circular interviewing: A multifaceted clinical tool. In D. Campbell & R. Draper (Eds.), *Applications of systemic family therapy: The Milan approach* (pp. 33-46). London: Grune & Stratton.

Tomm, K. (1986). On incorporating the therapist in a scientific theory of family therapy. *Journal of Marital and Family Therapy, 12,* 373-378.

Tomm, K. (1987a). Interventive interviewing: Part I. Strategizing as a fourth guideline for the therapist. *Family Process, 26,* 3-13.

Tomm, K. (1987b). Interventive interviewing: Part II. Reflexive questioning as a means to enable self-healing. *Family Process, 27,* 167-183.

Tower, C. C. (1993). *Understanding abuse and neglect* (2nd ed.). Boston: Allyn & Bacon.

Trepper, T., & Barrett, M. J. (Eds.). (1986). *Treating incest: A multiple systems perspective.* New York: Haworth.

Trepper, T. S. (1986). The apology session. *Journal of Psychotherapy and the Family, 2,* 93-101.

Trepper, T. S., & Barrett, M. J. (1989). *Systemic treatment of incest: A therapeutic handbook.* New York: Brunner/Mazel.

Truchsess, J. E. (1991). *Family sexual abuse: Correlations between sexual abuse interventions and victim and family status.* Unpublished doctoral dissertation, Department of Family Social Science, University of Minnesota.

Vander Mey, B. (1988). The sexual victimization of male children: A review of previous research. *Child Abuse & Neglect, 12*(1), 61-72.

Vander Mey, B. J., & Neff, R. L. (1982). Adult-child incest: A review of research and treatment. *Adolescence, 17*(68), 717-736.

Vasington, M. C. (1989). Sexual offenders as victims: Implications for treatment and the therapeutic relationship. In S. M. Sgroi (Ed.), *Vulnerable populations: Sexual abuse treatment for children, adult survivors, offenders, and persons with mental retardation* (pp. 329-350). Lexington, MA: Lexington.

Veitch, T. H. (1993). *The consultant's guide to litigation services: How to be an expert witness.* New York: John Wiley.

Vizard, E., & Tranter, M. (1988). Helping young children to describe experiences of sexual abuse-general issues. In A. Bentovim, A. Elton, J. Hildebrand, M. Tranter, & E. Vizard (Eds.), *Child sexual abuse within the family* (pp. 84-104). Bristol, England: John Wright.

Wakefield, H., & Underwager, R. (1988). *The real world of child interrogations.* Springfield, IL: Charles C. Thomas.

Walker, C. E., Bonner, B. L., & Kaufman, K. L. (1988). *The physically and sexually abused child: Evaluation and treatment.* New York: Pergamon.

Walker, L. (1989). Psychology and violence against women. *American Psychologist, 44,* 695-702.

Walker, L. E. A. (1988). *Handbook on sexual abuse of children: Assessment and treatment issues.* New York: Springer.

Walsh, F., & Olson, D. H. (1989). Utility of the circumplex model with severely dysfunctional family systems. In D. H. Olson, C. Russell, & D. Sprenkle (Eds.), *Circumplex model: Systemic assessment and treatment of families* (pp. 51-78). New York: Haworth Press.

Walters, D. (1975). *Physical and sexual abuse of children: Causes and treatment.* Bloomington, IN: Indiana University Press.

Wamboldt, F. S., Wamboldt, M. Z., & Gurman, A. S. (1985). Marital and family therapy research: Meaning for the clinician. In L. L. Andreozzi (Ed.), *Integrating research and clinical practice* (pp. 10–26). Rockville, MD: Aspen.

Wasserman, J., & Kappel, S. (1985). *Adolescent sex offenders in Vermont.* Burlington, VT: Vermont Department of Health.

Waterman, J. (1986). Overview of treatment issues. In K. MacFarlane & J. Waterman (Eds.), *Sexual abuse of young children* (pp. 197–203). New York: Guilford.

Wattenberg, E. (1985). In a different light: A feminist perspective on the role of mothers in father-daughter incest. *Child Welfare, 64,* 203–211.

Watzlawick, P. (1966). A structured family interview. *Family Process, 5,* 256–271.

Watzlawick, P., Beavin, J., & Jackson, D. (1967a). *Pragmatics of human communication.* New York: Norton.

Watzlawick, P., Beavin, J. H., & Jackson, D. D. (1967b). Toward a theory of schizophrenia. *Behavioral Science, 1,* 251–264.

Watzlawick, P., Weakland, J., & Fisch, R. (1974). *Change: Principles of problem formation and problem resolution.* New York: Norton.

Weeks, G. R. (1986). Individual—system dialectic. *American Journal of Family Therapy, 14,* 5–12.

Weeks, G. R., & L'Abate, L. (1982). *Paradoxical psychotherapy: Theory and practice with individuals, couples, and families.* New York: Brunner/Mazel.

Weinberg, G. (1975). *An introduction to general systems thinking.* New York: John Wiley.

Weinberg, S. K. (1955). *Incest behavior.* New York: Citadel.

Welwood, J. (1985). The holographic paradigm and the structure of experience. In K. Wilber (Ed.), *The holographic paradigm and other paradoxes* (pp. 127–135). Boston: New Science Library.

Wendorf, D., & Wendorf, R. (1985). A systemic view of family therapy ethics. *Family Process, 24,* 443–460.

Wexler, R. (1990). *Wounded innocents: The real victims of the war against child abuse.* New York: Guilford.

Whitaker, C. (1976). The hindrance of theory in clinical work. In P. J. Guerin (Ed.), *Family therapy: Theory and practice* (pp. 154–164). New York: Gardner.

Whitaker, C. (1986). Becoming a psychotherapist. In S. Sugarman (Ed.), *The interface of individual and family therapy* (pp. 113–116). Rockville, MD: Aspen.

Whitchurch, G. G., & Constantine, L. L. (1993). Systems theory. In P. G. Boss, W. J. Doherty, R. LaRossa, W. R. Schumm, & S. Steinmetz (Eds.), *Sourcebook of family theories and methods: A contextual approach* (pp. 325–352). New York: Plenum.

White, M. (1986). Negative explanation, restraint, and double description: A template for family therapy. *Family Process, 25,* 169–184.

White, M., & Epston, D. (1990). *Narrative means to therapeutic ends.* New York: Norton.

White, S. (1986). Interviewing young sexual abuse victims with anatomically correct dolls. *Child Abuse and Neglect, 10,* 519–529.

White, W. L. (1986). *Incest in the organizational family.* Bloomington, IL: Lighthouse Training Institute.

Whitehead, A. N. (1929). *Process and reality.* New York: Macmillan.

Wiehe, V. R. (1990). *Sibling abuse: Hidden physical, emotional, and sexual trauma.* Lexington, MA: Lexington.

Winnicott, D. W. (1965). *The maturational processes and the facilitating environment.* London: Hogarth.

Wolberg, L. R. (1980). *Handbook of short-term psychotherapy.* New York: Thieme-Stratton.

Wolman, B. B. (1960). *Contemporary theories and systems in psychology.* New York: Harper & Row.

Woody, J. D. (1993). *Treating sexual distress: Integrative systems theory.* Newbury Park, CA: Sage.

Woody, J. D., & Grinstead, N. (1992). Compulsory treatment for families: Issues of compliance. *Topics in Family Psychology and Counseling, 1*(2), 39–50.

Woody, R. H. (1991). *Quality care in mental health: Assuring the best clinical services.* San Francisco: Jossey-Bass.

World Health Organization (1975). *Education and treatment in human sexuality: The training of health professionals* (No. 572). Geneva, Switzerland: World Health Organization.

Wright, S. (1991). Family effects of offender removal from the home. In M. Q. Patton (Ed.), *Family sexual abuse: Frontline research and evaluation* (pp. 135–146). Newbury Park, CA: Sage.

Wright, S. C., & Herrin, D. A. (1988). Family ecology: An approach to the interdisciplinary complexity of the study of family phenomena. *Family Science Review, 1*(4), 253–281.

Wyatt, G. E. (1985). The sexual abuse of Afro-American and White American women in childhood. *Child Abuse and Neglect, 9,* 507–519.

Wyatt, G. E., & Peters, S. D. (1986). Issues in the definition of child sexual abuse in prevalence research. *Child Abuse & Neglect, 10,* 231–240.

Wyatt, G. E., & Powell, G. J. (1988). *Lasting effects of child sexual abuse.* Newbury Park, CA: Sage.

Wynne, L. (1988a). An epigenetic model of family processes. In C. Falicov (Ed.), *Family transitions: Continuity and change over the life cycle.* New York: Guilford.

Wynne, L. C. (Ed.). (1988b). *The state of the art in family therapy research: Controversies and recommendations.* New York: Family Process Press.

Wynne, L. C., McDaniel, S. H., & Weber, T. T. (Eds.). (1986). *Systems consultation: A new perspective for family therapy.* New York: Guilford.

Wynne, L. C., Shields, C. G., & Sirkin, M. I. (1992). Illness, family theory, and family therapy: I. Conceptual issues. *Family Process, 31,* 3–18.

Wynne, L. C., & Wynne, A. R. (1986). The quest for intimacy. *Journal of Marital and Family Therapy, 12*(4), 383–394.

Yapko, M. D. (1994). *Suggestions of abuse: True and false memories of child sexual trauma.* New York: Simon & Schuster.

Zaragoza, M. S., Graham, J. R., Hall, G. C., Hirschman, R., & Ben-Porath, Y. S. (Eds.). (1995). *Memory and testimony in the child witness.* Thousand Oaks, CA: Sage.

Zilbergeld, B. (1992). *The new male sexuality.* New York: Bantam.

Zuk, G. H. (1981). *Family therapy: A triadic-based approach* (Rev. ed.). New York: Behavioral Publications.

Index